INTERNATIONAL JOURNAL OF
PSYCHOANALYTIC PSYCHOTHERAPY

International Journal of Psychoanalytic Psychotherapy

Edited by ROBERT LANGS, M.D.
and the Editorial Board

Volume Five
1976

JASON ARONSON • NEW YORK

JOURNAL POLICY

All manuscripts should be submitted in triplicate and typewritten double-spaced throughout on white bond paper. For headings, footnotes, and references, follow the style used in this Journal (see the *Chicago Manual of Style*). The title page of each article must contain the author's full name and address, academic affiliation, date of submission, and a 150-word summary of the article's contents. Charts and tables must be on separate pages, keyed to the manuscript. Footnotes should be listed separately at the end of the article.

Submit all manuscripts to Robert J. Langs, M.D., 70 Glen Cove Road, Roslyn Heights, N.Y. 11577.

ISBN: 0-87668-279-4

Library of Congress Catalog Number: 76-1920

typeset by Frank Kotkov — Nestor Latronico — Jeanne Lombardi
New York, N.Y.

Manufactured in the United States of America

First Paper Prize

The Editorial Board of the *International Journal of Psychoanalytic Psychotherapy* announces a annual competition for the best first paper submitted to the *Journal* each year. All first papers deemed suitable for publication will be specially identified, and that paper judged best by the Editorial Board will receive a cash prize of $100 and full acknowledgment of the award at the time of publication. There are no qualifications for eligibility, except that the manuscript be an original, previously unpublished paper pertinent to the purview of this journal and that it be the first published paper by the author.

ROBERT J. LANGS, M.D.
for the Editorial Board

TABLE OF CONTENTS

INTERNATIONAL JOURNAL OF PSYCHOANALYTIC PSYCHOTHERAPY

Volume 5, 1976

PSYCHOANALYTIC AND PSYCHOTHERAPEUTIC STUDIES OF SEVERE PATHOLOGICAL STATES

TRANSITIONAL PHENOMENA

Ego Functioning During Paranoid Regression

M. Gerard Fromm, Ph.D.

Austen Riggs Center
Stockbridge, Massachusetts

This paper is based on the psychotherapeutic work with a paranoid schizophrenic man during a period of acute psychotic regression lasting approximately two weeks. The author reviews what seemed to be the precipitating factors in the decompensation, then elaborates descriptively and speculatively on two major aspects of ego functioning during the regression, namely, the experiences of fragmentation and of dedifferentiation. The role that seemed to evolve for the therapist is also discussed as it relates to the aforementioned aspects of ego functioning. Finally, a tentative hypothesis is developed concerning pretense as one possible genetic factor in these ego disturbances.

INTRODUCTION

With much hesitation and over a period of weeks, the patient, Mr. C., a man in his late twenties, whom I had been seeing in intensive psychotherapy in a hospital milieu for nearly a year, began to speak of his anxiety about beginning to feel close to a woman whom he knew. Since this developing relationship seemed to me from both current and past data to be, among other things, Mr. C.'s way of warding off some anxiety in the transference situation, I responded to his association to a former therapist by inquiring as to whether some of the concerns about closeness were being experienced with me. The patient reacted quickly, "No, thank God. I'm not at all inclined to feel close to you. If I felt close to you that would mean that I was weak and that would mean that I was a homosexual." A week later, following his being rejected in a sexual advance by this woman, Mr. C. almost immediately became acutely and psychotically paranoid. This period of regression lasted about two weeks, during which the patient displayed the usual paranoid symptomatology (persecutory, somatic, and grandiose delusions, auditory hallucinations, intense suspiciousness and anger, and a flooding of ideas of reference), as well as the concerns about closeness, weakness, and homosexuality, which had so preoccupied him all along. In addition, he manifested the structural qualities of fragmentation and dedifferentiation, which shall constitute a major focus of this paper.

As the patient's ego functioning, always precarious during the year that I had known him, became devastated by the overwhelming anxiety experienced at this time, a particular kind of relationship developed within therapy, a relationship which differed markedly for both parties and which seemed to fit the needs of the patient during an obvious psychological crisis. As at least a partial consequence of the therapeutic relationship, this frightening (for all concerned), but nonetheless fascinating, regressive state was navigated with no significant use of medication (infrequent doses of a minor tranquilizer) and in an open and voluntary hospital setting. At its end the patient termed it "a Laingian experience," "hectic but instructive," leading to "greater confidence." This sanguine, even romantic, view of what at the time seemed to be a truly terrifying regressive experience, perplexed me and led me to suspect a resurgence of the brittle denial always so heavily relied on by this patient, instead of the greater integration of which he spoke. Subsequent data are, however, moot on this point, and my focus here will not be on long-term gains or deficits; rather I want to concentrate my attention on the patient's ego functioning during the regression because of the psychotherapeutic insights it offers, as well as the clinical data it adds to a broadly psychoanalytic view of cognitive and affective processes. Specifically, I would like to elucidate further two aspects of the patient's ego functioning during this time and the kinds of activity with which I responded to him, activity which seemed related to the specific areas of deficit the patient was experiencing and useful in the sense of calming him and assisting him toward recovering these temporarily lost capacities. Before doing this, I shall comment on what I feel were significant factors precipitating the regression, and then, finally, I wish to speculate briefly on one possible genetic root of the particular ego disturbances this patient displayed.

DYNAMIC FACTORS PRECIPITATING REGRESSION

Mr. C. was admitted following a brief hospitalization in his home city, with a history of several acute paranoid episodes over the previous years. Treatment prior to his admission consisted of brief hospitalizations, the use of phenothiazines, sporadic psychotherapeutic contacts with a local psychiatrist, and home care. Each psychotic episode seemed triggered by a disappointment or rejection in a heterosexual relationship and was marked by confusion, agitation, and the belief that people, including family members, were referring to him as a homosexual or making homosexual advances toward him (despite the fact that the patient had had several heterosexual experiences and no homosexual ones). The patient also experienced suicidal ideation and demonstrated considerable bizarre and erratically violent behavior. He was referred to this hospital for long-term intensive psychotherapy following a psychotic episode that began when the consulting psychiatrist was away on vacation, that again required hospitalization and phenothiazines, and that was marked by the patient's utter terror about his delusional belief that a sex change operation was to be performed on him.

As I have mentioned, the immediately precipitating factors in the patient's several regressive periods seemed to be rejection or disappointment in a relationship with a woman. (Indeed, the patient's difficulties became overt in early childhood around the loss of a maid who had looked after him since birth.) As this sequence of events became identified and elaborated in the therapy, it became clear that each such failure overwhelmed this patient with feelings of weakness, humiliation, jealousy, and incompletion. There followed then a crumbling of a narrow and rigidly conceived sense of identity, particularly, that of himself as a man, though this crumbling was punctuated by exaggerated efforts at restitution. At one point in his life, the patient "wanted to dress like a man, wear a tie and have short hair, so that I could feel like a man." In the end, there was exquisite vulnerability to people in general, and that deep sense of inferiority which Sullivan (1956) stresses as being basic to paranoid development. In the weeks prior to this patient's regression, he elaborated on this theme. He spoke of his struggles to prove wrong his father's prediction that he would never achieve success in a job. In relation to a past psychotic episode, he said, "I felt so weak. I felt I didn't have anything and I had to go crazy to defend against it." He also spoke poignantly and somewhat plaintively, after having ruined the motor of his car by driving without oil, of the fact that no one ever told him about having to get oil changes.

These embarrassing blunders, which for this patient deepened a crippling sense of inexperience and naivete, seem to me to be not infrequent in paranoid patients, perhaps because the overwhelming need to present a facade of competence steers the patient away from all areas of insecurity. Learning begins in a state of lack, and the truly paranoid patient seems unable to tolerate his own awareness of this feeling, much less its exposure to others. It is significant then that this patient, though he was determined to become a musician, steadfastly refused to take lessons from anyone, and that, particularly during the regressive episode, he became enraged by any response from other people that smacked of sympathy. Obviously, such a person would have extreme difficulty in defining himself temporarily as a patient, and indeed much of Mr. C.'s first year of psychotherapy revolved around this issue. It is noteworthy then that his major regression occurred in the month following a decidedly greater involvement in the therapeutic process. In contrast to his feeling "under therapy," he felt then that he could "take things in today. I feel open to taking things in. It's like a high. It's something that occurs sometimes, not very often. If it goes on too long, I get scared."

It is also noteworthy that the patient's feelings of being "under therapy" (that is, of being overwhelmed by or submitting to a powerful and perhaps dangerous adversary—a major resistance and transferential element in the therapy to that point) shifted to something more collaborative with me following the kind of heterosexual loss that eventually triggered the regressive episode to be described. After this earlier loss, the patient reacted with near-manic efforts to ward off his anxiety; my clear recommendation against this manic flight from treatment and my working with the patient and his father to clarify what the latter would or would not support for the patient led to Mr. C.'s renewed and deeper involvement in the therapy. In contrast to the usual murky and deceptive ways in which these two people dealt with each other, father and son seemed relieved at their openness with each other and at the clarity of my recommendation. In the hours, the patient was then able to own and reflect on the depressive and aggressive feelings toward women that formerly had been strenuously denied, as well as to demonstrate a new degree of flexibility in his daily behavior; in addition he seemed considerably more attached to me.

From historical and clinical (including psychological testing) data, the following dynamic elements seemed to me of great significance at this preregressed point: (1) the early frustration of dependency needs (via his mother's psychological unavailability, his maid's dismissal, his siblings' cruelty, etc.) leading to (2) intense pregenital aggression (described in the psychological test report as the "ravenous and destructive" aspects of his personality). (3) The intensity of this aggression and the infantile ego's crucial reliance on projective operations created severe distortions of reality in early life (Kernberg, 1967). (4) The child then attempted to cope with maternal loss by an incorporative identification with mother (experienced as a kind of fusion with her) and by turning to his father for nurture. (5) Consequently, there developed the need to defend against homosexual wishes toward father and sadistic aggressive impulses toward the merged image of frustrating parent by compensatory efforts toward heterosexual potency, efforts motivated by the wish to, on the one hand, outdo father and short-circuit the pain-ridden need for him and, on the other hand, rob a woman sexually and aggressively of love denied at an oral level. Heimann (1955 a,b) has usefully discussed paranoid states and the early stages of the Oedipus complex, placing particular emphasis on the " 'polymorphous' stage of instinctual development which is interpolated between the oral and the anal organizations." In this stage, "pregenital and genital impulses, heterosexual and homosexual aims coexist, and furthermore libidinal wishes are fused and confused with cruel urges of an archaic and most savage nature" (Heimann, 1955 b, p. 258). (During periods of acute emotional arousal, Mr. C.'s mouth seemed to literally form itself into an involuntary snarl.) Heimann continues:

> In my view it is this admixture of cruel aims in his love impulses characteristic of the early infantile Oedipus complex which leads to guilt and horror for the incestuous wishes, be they of a heterosexual or of a homosexual kind. This polymorphous state of the instinctual urges constitute a serious difficulty for the early infantile ego, underlying as it does the fluid condition of the ego, its need to achieve integration and unification, and the alternation that occurs between coherence and incoherence . . . advance in integration at this stage leads to the poignant conflict of ambivalence with guilt and despair for the hatred experienced against the loved objects, and for directing cruel impulses toward them . . . in response to this conflict of ambivalence there are forward, constructive movements representing the drive to make reparation, as well as regressive techniques, such as denying the conflict by taking flight from unity, splitting the emotions and doubling the objects, so that two separate relations arise: love is then felt to be directed toward a good object and hatred toward its bad double . . . instead of feeling guilt for hating the loved object the infantile ego oscillates between the delusion of bliss from the one and the delusion of persecution from the other object. [p. 258]

It is my hypothesis that a major precipitating factor in the therapy itself leading to Mr. C.'s paranoid regression was his correctly perceiving my countertransference problems in response to his efforts to integrate libidinal and aggressive urges toward one person, while I remained unaware of them. In part, my reactions to his new heterosexual relationship were disappointment and frustration. I felt concerned that he would be severely hurt by this woman, whom he spoke of marrying after their first week's association. I also felt that this relationship indeed doubled the objects, in a way that would once again render the therapeutic relationship (as well as the relationship with the woman) sterile and one-dimensional. I would once again be seen as the controlling, persecutory outsider, at precisely the point in treatment when the hours were beginning to contain a far greater emotional texture and richness.

It is my impression now that the patient perceived these reactions of mine far more clearly than I (in contrast to the clarity between us during and following the earlier loss of a girlfriend), and that he then characteristically contaminated his accurate perceptions via projective processes. Thus, my disappointment implied retaliatory castration: my wish that he not leave me for her might be interpreted as homosexual interest in him. The major point I wish to make here, following Searles' (1972) lucid discussion of delusional transference, is that, since the reality of my reactions was not available to me, the psychotic transference distortions of the patient could not be analyzed and effectively processed by him against the reality of his perceptions of me. Thus, there was no effective check on the tremendously anxiety-arousing delusional transference, and regressive behavior pervading his entire life situation ensued.

In retrospect, I believe that the unavailability of my disappointment to me reflected the unawareness of my relief at the patient's defensive withdrawal from treatment via a woman. This relief was based on the mutual anxiety aroused by the commingled nature of his libidinal longings and primitive aggressive impulses. Furthermore, his efforts to make me aware of this most significant block in me (replicating, I believe, the dynamic situation between child and parent, and between child-parent images) led mainly to responses on my part, which, though unconsciously intended as clarifying kinds of inquiries, unconsciously kept the patient at arm's length and undermined still more his sense of some intuitively grasped reality. Indeed, the kind of transference-directed question with which this paper was begun unwittingly but rather cruelly encouraged the patient toward focusing on material which, at that point, was unhealthily charged with ambivalence for me.

The breakdown, then, of ego functions during the regression can thus be seen as a frightened response to the suggestion of the therapist, as a compliant response relocating the problem within the patient and as a defensive response opposing the continued frustration by the therapist. It may also be considered an adaptive effort to enlarge, albeit in an unmodulated, caricatured, and bizarre way, the field of awareness between two people. Rather ironically, the role then assigned to me, following my unconscious injury to his reality testing, clearly included the patient's frantic reliance on my perceptions of reality. Thus, he forced me, by the sheer absurdity yet intensity of his psychotic productions, to examine more carefully and noncomplacently the minutiae of our interactions, particularly their countertransferential elements, and to work toward establishing minimal but secure areas of consensus between us.

FRAGMENTATION

Here I refer to the patient's subjective experience of rapidly shifting states of feeling. With regard to affect, cognitive functioning, and bodily sensations, Mr. C. experienced sharply contrasting, sometimes opposite conditions during this regression. He reported his body feeling hot, then suddenly cold; feelings of affection, rage, and sadness, among others, were experienced with intensity and fullness, yet fleetingly. He oscillated between states of terror and humorous detachment, losing then regaining, a sense of perspective on his anxiety. Correspondingly, his thought processes ranged between extremes of incoherence and lucidity. The spectrum of feeling was enormously broad over the two-week span, and even within one session. Besides the feelings already mentioned, the patient spoke of guilt, jealousy, trust, mistrust, superiority, appreciation, urgency, and others. Frequently there seemed to be an association between or among certain feelings. By the latter I mean that one feeling seemed connected inseparably to another or was called forth immediately by another. A further explanation would be that both sides of ambivalences surfaced at once, and the awareness of one side led almost immediately to the other side and then back again. For example, no sooner had the patient expressed gratitude for something that I had given him (a moment's concern about his cough) before he expressed in a trembling tone the fear that perhaps someone had given him venereal disease.

What I am describing as the experience of fragmentation seems to occur as well at a cognitive-perceptual level, or, perhaps more accurately, the patient turns from the experience of internal affective chaos to his powers of cognition and perception in an attempt to process the experience. Thus added to the list of shifting feeling states are those of clarity versus confusion, security in relation to hypothesis-forming versus anxiety in relation to questioning, reality-connectedness versus being-without-moorings. This patient's constant question, "What's happening to me?" bears on this cognitive experience. In essence, this patient's delusional thinking, particularly his ideas of reference, seemed to demonstrate his attempt to both gain distance on the internal experience by believing it to exist outside of himself, and solve, that is, make sense of, the internal experience by semiscientific cognitive procedures.

Two particular aspects of the patient's functioning during this state of fragmentation interested me because of their rarity prior to the regression, their frequency during the regression, and their conceivably positive significance for the patient's growth. First, his moments of clarity; these were rather startling and genuine, lucidly and emotionally delivered. Generally, they were not accompanied by anxiety, but rather seemed like the eye of a storm, quite calmly given but surrounded temporally with confusion and agitation. Some examples: "My problem is I could never take a 'no' from anybody." "Maybe I always felt like I was trying to get my mother's love and never really got it." "Suicide would be a solution to the indirectness of life." "I blame you for everything; I'm always angry at you, and I really don't need to be" (though in specific instances, as I have already mentioned, the patient's anger at me was quite appropriate). The fate of these sudden elements of self-awareness in terms of their serviceability to the patient over time remains, however, unclear to me.

Second, this patient's expression of positive feelings toward me during this time was also striking. Although the range and intensity of his affect in general was greater during the psychotic episode than it had been previously, perhaps for the first time in the treatment this other side of the patient's affect life was expressed, and quite movingly. The patient spoke of trusting me, of gratitude, consideration, affection, and a wish to give something to me, though he felt he had nothing to give. To be sure he also brandished his fists, mocked me, and accused me of engaging in a homosexual seduction, but issues related to antagonism, contempt, influence, and submission had been in the work all along. What seemed quite new was the patient's hunger to love and to be loved and his feeling that he utterly lacked anything that might allow this to happen.

The paranoid patient in a state of acute regression seems to me to feel literally enslaved by his feelings and interprets reality accordingly; for example, this patient at one point felt that the girl whom he had liked was "casting a spell" on him and reacted with the terror and rage that one might anticipate given the reality of such an assumption. What he in fact was referring to was his affection and sexual attraction toward this woman and in effect was saying that the sway of his own feelings toward her, which indeed she had a hand in stirring, obliterated his sense of his own volitional self. Similarly, this patient's belief in "mind control" seemed related to his anxiety about his own susceptibility to the influence of others, by way of his feelings in response to them; my hypothesis in the previous session is that the regression itself dramatically demonstrates this point. Though this highly condensed and oversimplified way of thinking if allowed to stay out of the realm of its relationship to affect can lead to the detached delusional systematizing common to paranoid patients (Tausk, 1919), my experience with this patient suggests that this need not occur if interpretations (or better, elaborations) are made by the therapist aimed at helping the patient realize the connection between his concept of his experience and his own anxiety-arousing feeling states.

The experience of fragmentation, then, seems to have functional significance in both warding off a malignantly paranoid synthesis and bringing into the field of awareness various dissociated cognitive and affective possibilities, such that a new and perhaps better adaptation is also conceivable. Nevertheless, the patient's experience of the fragmented condition itself is characterized, I believe, by several more general and potentially dangerous feeling states. First, there is the experience of ever-gathering momentum, as one moves from one feeling to another, one thought to another, one event to another. Mr. C. at times was unable to sit in my office nor was he easily able to sleep in his room. Momentum as it builds verges on panic, the patient's and those around him, and here it seems to me there is a critical juncture in the therapeutic work with such a patient. The therapist must be able to accept the anxious communications of the patient, to hold them within himself, and then to respond in such a way as to return them, divested of their inordinate anxiety. This ability on the part of the therapist—to contain something and not recoil from it—has been seen (Bion, 1962; Palmer, 1973) as central to the patient's developing capacity for personal differentiation, for self-esteem, and for thought. I agree with this viewpoint and here wish to emphasize the extent to which the paranoid patient during an acute regression is extremely sensitive to and easily introjects aspects of his environment (hence Mr. C.'s concern with both influence and contagion). Another paranoid schizophrenic patient of mine repeatedly made clear to me that he believed that through some strange surgical procedure a different person had been placed inside of him. Indeed, one tragic benefit of a hardened paranoid integration is that it renders the patient almost impervious to those around him, a state of being seemingly and perhaps logically preferred to that of permeability.

This touches on a second general experience of the fragmented condition, the feeling of discontinuity. One is not the same from moment to moment, and at times the shifts are so radical that one questions whether or not one is the same human being from moment to moment. "The center cannot hold" (Yeats, 1920), and thus there is aroused a basic threat to one's sense of oneself as a whole, identifiable, and continuous person. Searles (1961) has elaborated on the fear of ego loss as being at the core of paranoid schizophrenic pathology, as has Guntrip (1969) more from the angle of schizoid withdrawal. Mr. C. made clear his feeling that "something terrible is happening to me and something good at the same time—I don't know who I am or what I'm supposed to do." Further, his sense of a lost continuity across differing life situations is illustrated by his asking me at the end of a session, "Do I have to go by *that* clock?" as if the time on my clock bore no relation to that on any other clock, and one step more generally, as if in the face of his own psychotic perplexity, events could be nothing but arbitrary. To be sure, the patient's question is a clear expression of his intense neediness as well as an effort to clarify what my feelings toward him might be, whether he can or cannot remain with me, whether our connection is itself an arbitrary one. Nevertheless, I want to highlight the degree to which such consuming anxieties can fragment one's feeling of existing in reliable spatial and temporal dimensions, even as they offer to the therapist further opportunities to cope with the transference-countertransference crisis.

This very frightening feeling of discontinuity, with the immense strain it places on what is already a precarious identity formation, at best leads or perhaps is synonymous with feelings of identity diffusion (Erikson, 1959). With Mr. C. two possibilities for resolving this particular tension were striking. One had to do with adopting a view of himself as "homosexual." The patient hesitantly described this anxiety as "a certain kind of tension with men, that I'm below them, not acceptable to them, not on their level." Whatever else might have dynamically contributed to the fear about homosexuality (in the previous section, I have outlined the homosexual configuration in the early oedipal relationships), I would suggest that the feeling of ego weakness itself is of paramount importance, the feeling that one has not been able to hold ground against events, that one's ability to perceive, process, and respond appropriately to external reality has become disturbed, and consequently that one's sense of self has been substantially eroded. The patient almost literally equated "weakness" with "homosexuality," much the way his family did. Despite, however, the cruel criticisms inflicted on most deviant behavior by this patient's cultural background, homosexuality with its clear connectedness to others must have seemed far preferable to the feeling of basic ego weakness resulting from fragmentation.

Drawing on some of Winnicott's formulations, Guntrip (1969) has suggested that it is the "female element" in all of us, "the individual's capacity for experiencing a sense of 'being' (as opposed to 'doing' which is seen as masculine) [1] that is left primarily dissociated, left unrealized at the start of development" (p. 255). He suggests that the deeply schizoid patient, struggling with basic ego weakness, "cannot get at his capacity to feel real because at the start of life no one evoked it. His mother gave him so little genuine relationship that he actually came to feel unreal" (p. 255). Further, he states,

> The female element is best exemplified in the maternal feeling that evokes and fosters an experience of "being" in the infant as a starting point of all personality growth; the capacity to feel with, and then to feel for, the capacity to feel oneself as "in relationship," the basic permanent experience of ego relatedness of which the sense of "being" is the core and without which the psyche loses all sense of its own reality as an ego. [p. 254]

These formulations, far too briefly treated here, bear on both the following section on the subject of dedifferentiation as well as on the possible frequency with which concerns about homosexuality—meaning basically the experience of insecure or weakened "being" in the maternal, and potentially later the therapeutic, relationship—prevail in paranoid patients.

The alternative to viewing himself as homosexual seemed to be for Mr. C. to identify with his therapist. He explicitly expressed during this period the wish to learn from me as a model in dealing with frustration; he clearly relied on my perceptions and apperceptions of what he reported going on around him. He even wished to join the therapy staff of the hospital in order to work with me as a colleague and wondered how he might apply for such a position. Searles (1959) makes the same point about the fragmented patient:

> Further, such a patient tends naturally and healthily to identify wholeheartedly with the therapist as a refuge from the fragmentation which over-

whelms him, as a means of finding in symbiotic relatedness to the mother-therapist a sufficient island of wholeness for him now to turn, to put it in an oversimplified way, and integrate the dissociated components of his personality one by one until such time as he has enough ego of his own to endure the resolution of this symbiosis. [p. 308]

This inclination toward identification with me, however, was not without fears of loss of self, of personal autonomy, and of family attachments. Mr. C. was concerned that he might have to relinquish his religious preference and affiliate himself with mine. Further, he became anxious that I was a homosexual trying to draw him into a liason. Indeed, he felt that "people look at having a therapist as homosexual," adding, "Everybody's having sex here, and I'm talking to you."

These fears and accusations usually came during brief phone conversations initiated by the patient when he became acutely anxious (throughout the patient's psychotic episode, I accepted his phone calls). He used these occasions to "check in" with me regarding the range of delusional ideas occurring to him in his living environment, to process these ideas through my reality testing, and to bring into our relationship, via his projections onto me, central dynamic concerns regarding homosexuality, submission, individuation, object constancy, etc. His need to spurn his relationship with me reflected his fear of a dangerous longing for contact—dangerous because, from his point of view, I would surely reject, scorn, or enslave him, as evidenced perhaps by the countertransference block he clearly sensed; dangerous also because of the long-established readiness for rage which freighted this patient's libidinal wishes.

It seems to me that the projective and introjective processes so prevalent during a paranoid exacerbation, besides ridding the patient's image of himself of noxious attributes, also provide the therapist with an opportunity to try on for size, as it were, those same disowned attributes. I would suggest that this usually follows the patient's unconscious perception of a basic split between patient and therapist along some transference-countertransference dimension and that this represents an effort to regressively re-fuse self and object. It also, however, creates the possibility of a new integration in the therapist with which the patient can usefully identify. Despite his periodically severe mistrust, Mr. C. clearly demonstrated this thrust toward temporary identification with me, and I believe that this phase should be accepted as adaptive, indeed necessary, for the acutely fragmented patient.

Finally, I would like to comment briefly on the therapist's reactions to the fragmented patient. I have already suggested that elements of continuity and control over mounting anxiety are aspects of the therapist's functioning that are important to the patient; yet they are easily lost in the face of one's necessarily fragmented reactions to fragmented communications. During the height of such a condition, one feels (or at least I felt) frightened, bewildered, overwhelmed, tugged, pushed, and buffeted in one direction and then another, and basically frustrated in one's efforts to comprehend even the surface meaning of what is being said. The patient's sense of identity is devastated during an acute regression; projection and delusional transference abound. In very basic ways, the therapist is misidentified by the patient or else identified accurately, perhaps painfully, then distorted grotesquely. All of this places enormous strain on the therapist's professional and even personal identity. One consequence then is the wish to gain distance, to withdraw from the whirlpool of communications that exert such power. And it is of course true that a reasoned overview is an indispensable complement to one's emotional responsiveness. The serious danger here, however, is the potential for actual abandonment of the patient, as well as for failure to attend to the patient's fantasies of abandonment. The therapist must struggle to identify the wish to withdraw, the feelings underlying that wish, the ways in which the patient stimulates those feelings, and the dynamic meaning of the patient's action in doing so. Withdrawal itself tends either to escalate the patient's panic or to defensively enclose him further. The therapist's efforts here are toward the wholeness of his person (for example, my need to make available to myself and then, in some form, to the therapy the conflicted feelings both highlighted and stimulated by the patient's renewed romantic involvement) so that the patient can reclaim himself as a whole person (for example, by recognizing his anxiety-arousing longings toward me).

DEDIFFERENTIATION

This second aspect of the acutely regressed, paranoid patient's ego functioning can be defined as the severe impairment of the cognitive ability to make certain important discriminations or, in other words, the loss of the capacity for differentiated psychological functioning. This term, first used in the psychological literature by Hartmann (1939), was later developed by Searles (1961) as it relates to paranoid schizophrenia. He suggests several crucial distinctions that are blurred in paranoid functioning: that between inner experience and outer experience (otherwise termed the loss of ego boundaries [Federn, 1952]), between fact and fantasy, between past and present, and between feeling, thought, and action. Further, he adds to this list the patient's confusion about what is significant and what is insignificant, what is intendedly communicative and what is not, what is metaphorical and what is concrete. It seems to me that the well-documented overinclusiveness of schizophrenic thinking (Cameron, 1946), as well as its fluidity, arbitrariness, and associative looseness, can also be subsumed under the heading of dedifferentiated ego functioning, insofar as these all involve a failure of some kind of defining boundary or categorizing function. (Searles [1961] seems to classify dedifferentiation phenomena under the general heading of fragmented ego functioning; I find it more helpful to think of these phenomena as interrelated but conceptually distinct, the former referring to a reversal of differentiated psychological functioning, the latter referring to a reversal of integrated psychological functioning. I am also inclined toward thinking of dedifferentiation as a drastic diminution of a certain kind of *cognitive activity*, while thinking of fragmentation more as an *experience* and largely at an *affective* level. The relationship between these two sets of phenomena is an interesting one and worth further exploration.)

Mr. C.'s statement equating the feeling of "closeness" toward another person with the more personally applied feeling of "weakness" with finally the identity element of "homosexual" would be, I believe, an example of dedifferentiation. Another series of interactions exemplifies this phenomenon further. The patient was speaking to me soberly and somewhat fearfully about another patient who had recently died in a car accident and began to suspect some sort of foul play. He had noticed that another therapist had looked at him recently and thought that the therapist, who happened to be the consultant to the patient community group and also a Vietnam veteran, wanted him to join the army and "be shot and killed in Vietnam." "He wants me dead." He noted that the patient who had recently died was also Jewish, then disclaimed any responsibility for that person's death. He observed that he thought I looked upset, as though in mourning, and asked me why I was in mourning. I told him that I did not feel that I was in mourning. He responded by saying that perhaps he felt like mourning, mourning for somebody who had died, perhaps for a part of himself that had died, the part of himself that "laughed, joked, and played my horn." (Mr. C. played several musical instruments, self-taught on all of them.) At this point the patient was near tears, talked of feeling used by people, and then suddenly became concerned that he was responsible for a temporary power failure in the hospital, that perhaps he had that kind of power or maybe that people were trying to make him think so.

This sequence illustrates, I believe, a number of aspects of paranoid functioning, not the least of which is the underlying role of feelings of loss (the mourning) and the associated vulnerability (the persecutory delusion) and sense of weakness (the power failure). Of particular interest here are the examples of dedifferentiation phenomena: the inability to discriminate (1) accidental events from intended ones (the car accident and the power failure), (2) fantasy from fact (the persecutory fantasy in response to the other therapist's look versus the probable reality of that therapist's feelings), (3) inner experience from outer experience (his feeling mournful versus his thought that I felt mournful), (4) contiguity (or perhaps wish) from actual causality (his reaction to the power failure and the car accident), and even (5) one person from another (his feeling that because of the Jewishness shared with the dead patient that he also was marked for death, the place of which he would then have in common with his persecutor, the Vietnam war veteran).

One final example of this phenomenon would be the loss of the capacity to differentiate between what is actual and what is potential, illustrated by the patient's near-violent rage that the woman toward whom he was attracted had slept with another man. When I asked him what evidence he had for this supposition, he wound down a bit and said that actually he didn't believe that she had in fact done this, but rather he was "jealous of the fact that she's free to have sex with others if she wants to and doesn't have to have sex with me." I suggested that he was feeling possessive, and he agreed rather calmly; thus something that had originally been taken as an event came to be seen as in relation to a feeling — and a possible event.

An aspect of dedifferentiated functioning related to the concept of ego boundaries was evident in the patient's use of language in the series of sessions immediately preceding the grossly psychotic period. At this time I noted that the patient seemed to be talking so much around whatever his point was that it was impossible to follow him. His sentences were endless, full of dangling phrases and clauses and words whose meanings could not be inferred clearly from the context. Indeed, the purpose of the words seemed to be quite the opposite of communication; that is, as Sullivan (1946) has pointed out, this seemed an example of the use of language for the purpose of maintaining security by obfuscating meaning rather than clarifying it. To put it another way, this intensely ambivalent patient thwarted his wish to connect communicatively with someone by using the means of communication itself to gain distance and perhaps then a feeling of personal boundary. A way of viewing the patient's belief in "mind control," differing slightly from the view presented in the section of this paper on fragmentation is that, in the interpersonal situation at least, there exists such anxiety during a period of regression that gross conceptual condensation takes place; the patient then is simply unable to sustain a kind of open contact long enough to elaborate in language what he might at some level feel or mean. Toward the end of the period of regression, this patient seemingly willfully turned to this mode of ambivalent and evasive communication, leading me to feel teased and actively mystified, in an effort, I believe, to reinforce, resubstantiate, or perhaps even practice with the notion of himself as a separate person from me.

That this language barrier, as it were, served the function (among others) of strengthening ego boundaries is suggested by another contrasting aspect of the patient's use of language at that time. Prior to the regression, I noted that words of mine occasionally and rather immediately entered into the patient's speech in ways that were not in any way appropriate to the contextual sense. Thus they seemed foreign, even more so because the patient's facial expression indicated as much confusion in hearing himself speak these words as I felt in hearing them. These words had something of the disconnected quality that the patient reported about certain of his thoughts, particularly like the hostile epithets that intruded on his consciousness and obsessed him without his being aware of any affective counterpart. Another regressed paranoid patient of mine at one point felt that a boyfriend's thoughts had, literally as if they were physical objects, entered into her mind, and she struggled with how she would get them out. Here then are two examples of the permeability of ego boundaries by words, such that the secure distinction between inner and outer is lost.

The dynamic bases for these ego dysfunctions begin to emerge from the material presented so far in this section. The "foreign" words intruding into Mr. C.'s speech were mine. The vulgar or otherwise offensive epithets occurred to him while speaking with an elderly, unmarried, and rather venerated nurse; thus they took on an outrageous, even blasphemous, quality. Similarly, his willfully evasive style of communication contained a clearly sadistic element toward me. In the earlier vignette, he sees himself as one with both the murderer and the murdered. Essentially, the patient's regression to dedifferentiated functioning seems to me to represent lifelong wishes to merge with the important other, to take in that person, and to be nourished and protected in that union, in the context, however, of the intense aggression born of early frustration. Thus the sustaining object may be annihilated in the incorporative process and, by projective processes, annihilating. (The psychological test data on Mr. C. noted the prominence of oral-aggressive impulses as well as overwhelming concerns for his own safety.) The power failure then represents his fear that his neediness would deplete me, that his rage would destroy me, that his craziness would immobilize me (though, in a more convoluted way, it might also represent a partial loss of his own omnipotence in denying his troubles). This dynamic picture creates an acute danger situation, seriously eroding of higher level ego functions. Moreover, the very projective and introjective mechanisms that so undermine a separate sense of self and a reliable appraisal of reality also allow one to maintain the fantasy of being rid of hateful murderous feelings and of being in union with that which is good—further reinforcing a reversal of psychological differentiation. During an acute regression, such as Mr. C.'s, a regression from relatively intact functioning, these ego deficits themselves generate enormous anxiety, pervading the entire life situation.

The therapist of the severely dedifferentiated patient faces something of a dilemma in selecting material for response and even in deciding where within a range of complex tasks to intervene. This dilemma can be stated as follows:

if the therapist addresses the dynamic issues in an exploratory and interpretive fashion, he must also deal somehow with the patient's devastated observing ego and with his need to project; if the therapist addresses the ego deficits themselves in an effort to reduce anxiety and hault the regressive process, he must deal somehow with the patient's delusional transference. Obviously some integration of these tasks is required, accenting one pole more than the other, depending on the patient's state, the environmental tolerance for disturbed behavior, the reasonable probability that the therapist's activity during a psychological crisis will not lead to an unanalyzable impasse later, etc.

My effort with Mr. C., during these two weeks, was quite frequently toward supplementing his own impaired ego functioning with mine, toward assisting him in screening, processing, and testing reality. During evening or weekend phone conversations and in the hours themselves, he would present me with the various preoccupying events of his day and with the array of delusional ideas that had occurred to him; he seemed then to wait for, at times even ask for, my reactions. At one point he began the session by saying to me, "Something very paranoid is going on around here. Tell me about it." This could be heard as rather classically paranoid (as if the patient had said, "Something very *strange* is going on around here. You're in on it. Now tell me about it."), or it could be heard as something closer to the neurotic person's occasional complaint about "paranoid" feelings in various social situations, referring to the feelings of insecurity and anxiety, and perhaps the need to actively call into play reality-testing operations. In this latter sense, it could be hypothesized that Mr. C.'s statement referred to an awareness at some level of his distorting his experiences and his turning then to me to help him clarify them. My efforts at doing so seemed indeed useful to this patient. As he was beginning to recompensate, he asked early in one session if I heard a telephone ringing. I said that I didn't, and he smiled and said with pleasure and some relief that neither did he. A moment or two later he seemed to feel the same way about our agreeing on the color of a lamp in my office.

Given what was a definite impairment of reality-testing ability on Mr. C.'s part and what I took to be his wish that I assist him with those particular ego functions, I consciously oriented my interventions toward what seemed like the patient's distortions of reality. Sometimes, I simply stated my contrasting impressions of events, and sometimes I elaborated a distinction that the patient seemed not to be making. For purposes of exposition, the following would be examples of the kinds of statements aimed at dedifferentiated functioning: "Yes, I think that that is so," or "No, I don't believe that that is so"; "Your view differs from mine; perhaps we can notice how that difference arises"; "Could that be a distortion of what is actually happening?"; "I don't view the situation that way, I view it this way"; "Yes, I am feeling that," or "No, I don't believe that I'm feeling that"; "I believe you may feel (or think) that, but I am not sure that that is actually happening"; "If you mean by that, this (etc.), then yes, I agree; but if you mean that (etc.), then I don't agree"; "This (etc.) is different from that (etc.); I do want this, I don't want that." This last kind of statement occurred in connection with the patient's concern that my suggestion that he consider taking some tranquilizing medication during this period meant that I wanted him to kill himself.

Obviously, statements about distortion could lead to argument with the patient, and indeed, Mr. C. often would want to debate with me or became furious that I had challenged his perceptions directly (although he kept asking for my views). My delivery of such statements, however, and my response to debate was generally quite dispassionate, and argument never got started. I consciously phrased my interventions with Mr. C. in such a way as to make clear what was opinion on my part and what I took to be relatively factual, concentrating on the latter. I felt and conveyed very little investment in what I had to say to the patient, which seemed to render my statements more acceptable to him. Indeed, it makes little sense to speak of an investment in facts; investments, as the patient knew clearly at some level are for beliefs, some of which deny facts. Most of my interventions during this period were brief, stated in a way that I hoped would be comprehensible to the patient, and declarative.

In retrospect, I realized that I asked very few questions—some exceptions being inquiries like, "What is your evidence for that?" or "What are you (not somebody else) feeling?" aimed at dedifferentiated functioning. Nor did I emphasize interpretations, especially about the transference, although I remained aware of communications the patient was making to and about me while speaking of somebody else. Searles (1959) makes the well-taken point that this kind of interpreting to the transference with the dedifferentiated patient contributes to the problem, in that it blurs the distinction between people (the therapist and the subject of the patient's communication) and thus shrinks the dedifferentiated patient's already constricted areas of discrete experience. With Mr. C. I often felt that interpretations in general were counterproductive, that within the delusional persecutory transference interpretations were usually viewed with suspicion as being bad food, to be rejected and perhaps attacked. In addition, interpretations as inferences were the same currency that the patient was caught up with so urgently and so uselessly (in ideas of reference). Better I thought to observe rather than infer and to be a model for that more basic reality-connected process.

This is not to say that I believe transference psychosis precludes the "mutative interpretation" (Strachey, 1934); rather, my general experience suggests to me that such interpretation can be critical in forestalling a severe regression and that one strongly operant factor in such an interpretation is the reinforcement of the differentiation between past and present objects. I do

wish to highlight, however, the vicissitudes of reliance on interpretation with
a patient in such an acutely regressive ego state that he is convinced of the
absolute sameness between the therapist and the original frustrating/per-
secuting object. Moreover, I would suggest that the premature interpretation
of projective processes (for example, had I interpreted the patient's murderous views of me regarding medication as reflecting his rage at me) not only attacks the defense too directly but also nullifies the patient's views of the therapist, their potential relevance to the transference-countertransference problem, and their potential value to the curative-integrative processes in the therapist.

These dangers, to some extent, inhere in the more straightforward, reality-
oriented approach that I have been describing. There is also with the latter
approach the added danger of vitiating the patient's actual experience of the
moment and undermining his belief in a knowable reality. My flat statement,
after a moment's reflection, that I did not feel in mourning might have had
such effects; the patient, however, had the strength to bridge the gap between his experience of me and mine, namely, to consider the possibility that
he had accurately identified a feeling state but misidentified its locus in himself. Thus, the patient made the crucial distinction without interpretive assistance on my part; rather than my putting something back into him (with the
attendant potential for paranoid fantasy that such activity implies), the patient was able to reclaim it himself. The patient cannot bridge the gap, however, if the therapist's reading of his own experience is inauthentic or otherwise in error. It has been my hypothesis that this latter kind of transference-
countertransference situation contributed toward the patient's regression,
and it seemed to me that the patient during the regression repeatedly tested
my own crucial access to the uncomfortable feelings he stimulated in me.
Such testing, I believe, must occur before the regression can end and before
any mutual formulation of the critical dynamic variables, and their broader
life significance, can be made.

The therapist's effort to maintain his own ability to discriminate his actual
experience from the patient's constructions of his experience and to utilize
this ability in the work with a regressed patient can indeed be augmented by
inquiry and a degree of tentative interpretation that is closely tied to the reconstruction of specific events between the patient and others. Heimann
(1955b) recommends an approach to the persecutory delusion which minutely and exclusively examines its data base in reality. Searles (1972) captures beautifully the elusive tactfulness with the essential tactic:

> Since the possesses so very precarious a sense of reality, and since this tends
> to be destroyed so quickly when vigorously challenged by me, collaborative
> relatedness between us occurs best, I long ago learned, when I rela-

tively strongly confirm that she is perceiving such-and-such, while not pretending that I am at one with her in that perception, and meanwhile putting before her, in a non-coercive way, bits of my own mode of experiencing the situation. [p. 27]

In realizing all that I did not say to Mr. C., I come upon the subject of silence and what I think is its great value in allowing the patient some respite from his own frenzied need to process all of his experience, putting himself in a continuous state of overstimulation. How often nursing reports use the phase "winding up" to describe the imminently decompensating patient and how often paranoid patients themselves resort to isolation as a means of controlling burgeoning anxiety. It seems to me important that a person in such a state be able to isolate himself, as it were, with somebody and that the silent, relatively controlled therapist can indeed be that person.

The acutely regressed paranoid patient is obviously struggling with a massive assault to his reality-testing operations. In addition, the ego problems of fragmentation and dedifferentiation, themselves solutions to problems (of massively dissociated rage, of impulses toward merger, of the potential for hardened paranoid synthesis, etc.), lead the patient toward a kind of relationship with the therapist, a hoped-for interpersonal solution, that itself can perpetuate the problems. To be less elliptical, the fragmented patient moves toward a kind of identification with the therapist to reinstate a lost feeling of personal continuity. The dedifferentiated patient moves toward an employment of the therapist in the capacity of reality tester to regain a lost command over experience processing. Both solutions depend on a temporary unity with the therapist — a temporary symbiotic (Searles, 1959) relationship to him — which itself can pose a major threat to ego boundaries, to a shaky identity formation, and to a shaky grasp on one's autonomy. Thus, at critical junctures during Mr. C.'s regression, his reality and his efficacy as an individual needed explicit confirmation.

Three examples are prominent. First, the fact that medication was clearly and repeatedly stated as being available to him but not compulsory (he frequently and angrily ranted that he would not be forced into taking medication) had its own deeply relaxing effect, because it verified the reality of his choice and of his boundaries vis-a-vis the fantasied intrusive, destructive staff. Similarly, his being confronted by other patients with their emotional reactions to his depriving his former girlfriend (also a patient) of the roses sent to her by her mother on her birthday led to his sleeping all night for the first time in a week and to his cleary greater ability to fantasize the next day. Finally, one interchange with me I found particularly dramatic.

Mr. C. came to one therapy hour in an absolute rage about the things "going on behind my back," and I found myself anxious that he might physically assault me, more so than I had been in previous agitated sessions during this time. When I acknowledged that he indeed seemed very angry, he pounded on the chair, then brandished his fists at me, and shouted, "Yes, you're god-dam right I'm angry. I'm angry at you. I'm angry, angry, and I'm not afraid to show my anger with my fists because I'm not afraid of being hit back, and how come you're sitting there so calmly? How come? How come?" At that I called him by name and emphasized that he definitely had the capacity to make me anxious, if that's what he was asking. His reaction was immediate. He sat back, relaxed visibly, and began to talk about feelings of loss. "This is the worst situation I've ever been in in my life—I've lost four or five girls here recently, and I'm really feeling shot down about it—maybe something good will come along."

I wish to make two points regarding this sequence of events. First, the re-gressed paranoid patient's very tenuous view of himself as a person, with a separate reality and with an ability to affect his world (Mr. C.'s belief in his causing the power failure at the hospital nicely condenses the feelings of lost capacity and compensatory magical potency), is accentuated by the impulses toward merger with the therapist and toward reliance on the therapist's ego functioning. Second, this occasionally leads in the therapy to situations where the therapist's actual affective responses serve to reduce anxiety by restoring to the patient a feeling of his own efficacy and individuality.

Finally, this patient's regression highlighted a particular means of com-munication, that is, the telephone, and led me to realize its relationship to boundary issues and thus to dedifferentiation. In using the phone to speak with me, as the patient did frequently during this time, especially when I was at home, the patient essentially was able to construct a boundary of physical space between the two of us. This seemed temporarily to facilitate the expres-sion of his very intense feelings toward me, perhaps because there was no pos-sibility of his immediately acting on them. A parallel might be the accessibil-ity of primary process in dreams partly because the motor apparatus is disen-gaged in sleep. Second, however, the telephone (and the fact that for that limited period of time I was generally available), besides constructing a boun-dary between two people and between feeling and action, also served to over-come a boundary, that is, the boundary of time between us. Indeed, separa-tion was undone in a matter of seconds, and since to some extent I was not be-ing seen as a distinct person by this patient but rather, as I have been suggest-ing, as an extension of his own ego, the immediate access gained by phone al-lowed for the modulation of anxiety by facilitating my assumption of that role. To concretize drastically, the oscillation between primary and secondary processes, between more primitive impulses, feelings, fantasies, and higher level, reality-integrating ego operations, normally occurring intrapsychically, preconsciously, and almost instantaneously, could be approximated by this patient with someone in his external field via the telephone.

PRETENSE

In the previous two sections I have tried to develop two aspects of paranoid functioning during regression that bear on the patient's grasp of what is real, whether it be internal or external reality, and what is not. Tentatively, I would like to suggest from this patient's history that one of the genetic factors in such a disturbance is a longstanding and systematic reliance on pretense on the parts of both child and parents, primarily as a means of avoiding areas of painful confrontation, and perhaps secondarily of implementing various tactics related to a conflict of wills.

Mr. C. was born to parents who, for reasons of their age, their current life interests, their marital troubles, and their own particular psychological development, experienced the new child with strongly mixed feelings, feelings further exacerbated by the infant's accumulating difficulties. As a baby, Mr. C. was allergic to milk; later, and indeed throughout childhood, intense power struggles occurred in the areas of feeding and of toilet training. Finally, upon the departure of the maid, whom he liked and imitated, Mr. C.'s behavior erupted into extreme willfulness and demandingness, leading his parents to despair in their efforts at disciplining him and, less consciously, to withdraw from the child's rage, grief, and anxiety about loss. His siblings tended to tease him rather cruelly, and he subsequently spent much time alone in his room immersed in fantasies, some of which would then get dramatized with family members.

Some examples of his fantasy life and its dramatization would be appropriate here. As a young child, Mr. C. would "pretend" to be a military commander or a great artist and insist vehemently that he be called only by his new name. There was a similar dogged insistence on certain idiosyncratic mealtime rituals and a rather frenzied edge to his wildly imaginative tales about the evil characters that inhabited his house. Repeatedly there were instances where adults would "play along with" him in his usually grandiose fantasy life, marveling, even delighting in his "unlimited front," but feeling puzzled, helpless, and uneasy in response to the driven quality in his behavior.

There is obviously the strong suggestion in this data that Mr. C., during a particular phase of childhood, struggled vigorously to deny and expel the negative self-images stimulated by his experience, to restore magically a primary feeling of self-esteem based on omnipotence, and to control by demand the sources of nurturance experienced as only precariously available. This data also highlights the child's conflicts centering around aggression—his wishes to express his internal state freely, his opposing efforts to keep order, and his intense fear of retaliation—in a context of insecure boundary formation (these "evil characters" were felt to be actually within his house). Indeed, the patient's more obvious developmental difficulties—about eating, toilet training, and the dismissal of the maid—contain enormous potential for damage to the child's sense of separateness and bodily integrity. What I mainly wish to note here, however, is the parental cooperation with the child's magical solutions. Further, I would suggest that this cooperation reinforces the genuine, defensively-motivated blurring on a child's part of what is "pretend" and what is actual, and that without the child's acquiring this critical distinction, the capacity for healthy, growth-facilitating play is severely compromised. As Erikson (1961) puts it, "The play age relies on the existence of the basic family in one of its exemplary forms, which must gradually delineate where play ends and irreversible purpose begins . . . " (p. 156).

Similarly, I believe that the patient's parents' failure to set limits on their child facilitated further the blurring of the distinction between actual and fantasied. As Singer (1970) writes: "To be sure, the setting of limits brings in its wake what Sullivan (1953) called the 'shrinking to life size,' but the avoidance of setting limits inevitably results in lack of definition, in diminution of the sense of reality, and subsequent terror" (p. 159). Mr. C.'s parents, for example, eventually gave up their efforts to have their son go to bed at a reasonable hour. Further, they never managed to get him to confront and test out his many childhood fears, particularly fears in the areas of physical activity and of making trips away from home. Indeed, Mr. C. made it clear as a child that he would not be "sent away" (to camp, for example), that preconscious fantasy of expulsion determining, or so it seemed, much of his own behavior as well as that of his parents. Yet his siblings never got particularly hurt while involved in sports and always returned from camp. Similarly, he knew that he had never learned the skills he claimed nor had he ever seen a child with those skills. Again that basic question, "What's happening to me?" seems appropriately asked in circumstances like these. What was happening I would suggest was this: that his parents' permissiveness, if it can be called that, served at once to confirm the validity of the patient's deepest fear, that is, that his parents indeed were immobilized by the negative part of their ambivalence toward him (as he himself was filled with commingled aggressive-libidinal impulses toward them), while at the same time it undermined the reliability of the information-gathering and -processing methods that would lead him to that conclusion.

The evidence, at least the surface evidence, suggests indulgence and acquiescence, never overt rage or rejection; however, that his parents would repeatedly avoid his fear of being sent away implies a certain grave danger in the topic, as it also implies the child's continued clinging to infantile omnipotence. Indeed an issue of conflicting wills so consistently unmet must generate in each party an underlying resentment that might seriously threaten defenses against deeper hostility and, at the very least, create a family atmosphere quite the opposite of what Erikson (1961) calls "the good will" that "ensues from a mutual limitation of wills" (p. 155). Mr. C.'s history suggests that it was this perception of an emotional reality, and its subsequently magnified and convoluted processing by the infantile ego, which no one could face, preferring instead to keep this awareness in the realm of imagination, childishness, and therefore disbelief. Yet certain critical events throughout childhood lent considerable if only circumstantial confirmation to this more intuitively grasped idea, events (such as his parents' losing a favorite stuffed animal) that though from one angle appeared accidental from another conveyed parental frustration and their longing for relief.

In reporting this historical data as bearing on the patient's ability to perceive and process reality, I certainly do not mean to minimize the importance of the earliest mother-child interactions on subsequent schizophrenic pathology. I do mean, however, to suggest a pattern of interaction that perpetuates earlier deficits. Nowhere in the patient's history is this manipulation of the surface reality more clearly demonstrated than during his early adult years, when aspects of both his living and working circumstances were arranged for him, monitored, and sustained by family members, without Mr. C.'s being clearly aware of any of these facts. This effort to produce a particular feeling (of confidence, independence, etc.) in the patient via manipulation, an implanting of a feeling, as it were, was inevitably self-defeating. Eventually the patient sensed the pretense, tested it in one way or another, and began to deeply mistrust not only his caretakers but also the actual feeling that was supposed to benefit him. Like foreign and unintegratable organs, it was as if such feelings were then expelled from his system and replaced by their opposites (dependency, inadequacy, anger — all of which carried the security of familiarity and of somehow being his and only his; if not something he wanted for himself, at least something that no one else wanted for him), as well as by the further assurance that something between parent and child could not be confronted openly.

At this point my earlier hypothesis regarding the onset of the regression can be broadened as follows: that the core pretense structured into the relationship between parent and child, a pretense seriously damaging to the child's ego functioning, was partially replicated with regressive consequences in the therapeutic relationship. To restate it simply, the patient's valid perception of countertransference impediments in me, a perception accurately sensed but anxiously and projectively distorted, was met by me with conscious puzzlement and inquiry; such inquiry, however, unconsciously functioned to suggest to the patient that his ways of knowing the world were unreliable, even as their tone confirmed my retreat from him. Moreover, these countertransference impediments in content replicated, to a degree, the parental ambivalence in response to the commingled aggressive-libidinal energies directed toward them. Finally, this transference-countertransference problem crystallized around an issue of acting out, unlimited in any way in the treatment.

Within such traumatic replication, however, there is also the potential for an important reworking of basic issues. Indeed, an effort toward serious psychotherapeutic work during regression thrusts upon the therapist the requirement of reexamining the transference-countertransference dimension of the relationship and of reintegrating partially dissociated feelings toward the patient. Moreover, the acutely regressed patient demands increased contact with the therapist, makes his psychic life increasingly available to the latter, requires and actively tests the latter's psychological availability and integration in relation to him. Further, the patient's assigning the role of auxiliary ego to the therapist is one mechanism of this restitutive process. This is not for the purpose of acquiring false reassurance about the unreality of his problematical feelings and fantasies; reassurance would only replicate further the parental manipulation of surface reality. Rather, the patient's examination of and reliance on the ego functioning of the therapist recognizes implicitly the locus of the countertransference problem and at the same time the critical need to depend on the therapist's efforts toward his own integration. Presuming relatively successful integrative work on the therapist's part, his temporary role of auxiliary ego involves neither heavy-handed imposition of his views of reality onto the patient nor underhanded persuasion. Instead, it involves primarily the simple observation of a distinction between two people's subjective views of their experience, and subsequently, by minute degrees, the analysis of that gap toward some basic synthesis. Inevitably, therapist and patient are led to the issues underlying the earlier pathological pretense between them.

Erikson, in his paper "Play, Vision, and Deception" (1972), writes that

any "true" vision, that is, one that awakens some universal sense of *reality* at any particular time in history, will be found to be in reasonable accord with the *factual*, that is, the facts as then known, and the techniques then mastered, and with the *actual* in the sense of a heightened and productive interplay among the members of a community. [p. 33]

But collusion with "pseudorealities' means "a kind of dirty interplay which sooner or later undermines such playfulness as is necessary for vitality" (p. 47). I am hypothesizing here that Mr. C.'s earliest efforts to recognize emotional reality in the familial setting (and his later efforts to recognize reality in the therapeutic relationship) rarely came to be "in reasonable accord" with what was presented to him as fact by the relevant others. To some extent, even the techniques by which one corroborates an intuitive perception came to be employed in the service of pretense. Nor did the patient's efforts actualize anything between self and object; rather than "heightened and productive interplay," there occurred only greater psychological withdrawal. In consequence, a "pseudoreality" was structured which seriously undermined vitality by rendering extremely anxiety-arousing the cognitive and effective processes of play. Without such psychological "leeway" (Erikson, 1972, p. 11), it seems to me that higher-level integration and differentiation is compromised, if not totally aborted.

CONCLUSION

I will now briefly reiterate the main points of this paper.

1. Paranoid psychotic regression, when it occurs in a psychotherapeutic context, is an integral part of that therapy—in terms of precipitating factors, the material that emerges during it, and the role relationships that evolve between patient and therapist.

2. In such acute paranoid regression, an underlying transference-countertransference problem may be a potent preceipitating factor, and the ordinary means of rational discourse may be being used to unconsciously structure a pretense which skirts that problem.

3. The partial fusion of aggressive and libidinal urges and of objects as well, characteristic of what Heimann (1955 a, b) refers to as the polymorphous phase of development, may have important dynamic significance with regard to paranoid states.

4. The ego states of fragmentation and dedifferentiation contribute enormously to the anxiety of the regressed paranoid patient and must be considered in one's therapeutic approach.

5. The therapist must work toward (a) control over his own potentially burgeoning anxiety, (b) continuity in his approach to the patient, and (c) clear examination of his own experience, including his own affective states; within this last effort, he must discover and partially at least resolve the countertransference problem.

6. Powerful but experientially fleeting, feeling states are central to the fragmented patient's distorted conceptions of his interpersonal life; the therapist can be very helpful in elaborating this connection with the patient, in a way which divests these feelings of their inordinate anxiety.

7. To the degree that the dedifferentiated patient retains enough observing ego to recognize his loss of reality-testing ability, he may then rely on the therapist to help him make certain crucial distinctions. This effort must begin with the therapist's and patient's recognition of differing views of their subjective experience; this may then proceed to a very gradual analysis of that difference, an analysis securely anchored in the details of each person's observations.

8. The patient in a fragmented or dedifferentiated condition moves toward either identification with the therapist or an employment of the thera-

pist as an auxiliary ego; these role relationships seem temporarily adaptive to the patient's emergence from regression.

9. The indicated role relationships, however, contain the potential for the severe anxiety attendant upon the patient's impulse toward a regressive re-fusion of self and object; thus, at crucial junctures, the therapist will have the opportunity of confirming the patient's individuality and efficacy, even as a kind of temporary, healthy, symbioticlike relationship is taking place.

NOTES

1. The parenthetical statement is mine.
2. Erikson's (1972) idea of a "countervision" based on "pseudospeciation" might be discussed with refer-ence to Mr. C. in terms of the complex of attitudes and feelings regarding homosexuality.

REFERENCES

Bion, W. R. (1962). A theory of thinking. *International Journal of Psycho-Analysis* 43:306-310.

Cameron, N. S. (1946). Experimental analysis of schizophrenic thinking. *Language and Thought in Schizo-phrenia*, ed. J. S. Kasanin. Berkeley: Univ. of California Press, pp. 50-64.

Erikson, E. H. (1959). Identity and the life cycle. *Psychological Issues* 1:Monograph 1.

_____(1961). The roots of virtue. *The Humanist Frame*, ed. Julian Huxley. New York: Harper, pp. 147-165.

_____(1972). Play, vision, and deception. Presented in 1972 as the Godkin Lectures at Harvard University; represented at the Austin Riggs Center.

Federn, P. (1952). *Ego Psychology and the Psychoses*. New York: Basic Books.

Freud, S. (1911). Psycho-analytic notes on an autobiographical account of a case of paranoia (dementia para-noides). *Standard Edition* 12:3-82, London: Hogarth, 1958.

Guntrip, H. (1969). *Schizoid Phenomena, Object Relations, and the Self*. New York: International Universities Press.

Hartmann, H. (1939). *Ego Psychology and the Problem of Adaptation*. New York: International Universities Press, 1958.

Heimann, P. (1955 a). A contribution to the re-evaluation of the Oedipus complex: the early stages. *New Direc-tions in Psycho-Analysis*, ed. M. Klein, P. Heimann, and R. E. Money-Kyrle. New York: Basic Books, pp. 23-38.

_____(1955). A combination of defense mechanisms in paranoid states. *New Directions in Psycho-Analysis*, ed. M. Klein, P. Heimann, and R. E. Money-Kyrle. New York: Basic Books, pp. 240-265.

Kernberg, O. (1967). Borderline personality organization. *Journal of the American Psychoanalytic Association* 15:641-685.

Palmer, B. (1973). Thinking about thought. *Human Relations* 26(1):127-141.

Searles, H. (1959). Integration and differentiation in schizophrenia. *Collected Papers on Schizophrenia and Related Subjects*. New York: International Universities Press, 1965.

_____(1961). The source of anxiety in paranoid schizophrenia. *Collected Papers on Schizophrenia and Re-lated Subjects*. New York: International Universities Press, 1965.

_____(1972). The function of the patient's realistic perceptions of the analyst in delusional transference. *British Journal of Medical Psychology* 45: 1-18.

Singer, E. (1970). *Key Concepts in Psychotherapy*. New York: Basic Books.

Strachey, J. (1934). The nature of the therapeutic action of psycho-analysis. *International Journal of Psycho-Analysis* 15:127-159.

Sullivan, H. S. (1946). The language of schizophrenia. *Language and Thought in Schizophrenia*, ed. J. S. Kasanin. Berkeley: Univ. of California Press, pp. 4-16.

_____(1953). *The Interpersonal Theory of Psychiatry*. New York: Norton.

_____(1956). *Clinical Studies in Psychiatry*. New York: Norton.

Tausk, V. (1919). On the origin of the "influencing machine" in schizophrenia. *Psycho-Analytic Quarterly* 2 (1933): 519-556.

Yeats, W. B. (1920). The second coming. *Selected Poems and Two Plays of William Butler Yeats*, ed. M. L. Rosenthal. New York: Macmillan, 1962.

M. GERARD FROMM, PH.D.

DR. FROMM is currently a staff psychologist at the Austen Riggs Center in Stockbridge, Massachusetts, and consulting clinical psychologist to a number of educational institutions in Berkshire County. Formerly, he was associated with St. Elizabeths Hospital in Washington, D.C.

Psychoanalytic Contributions to the Relationship Between Dreams and Psychosis— a Critical Survey

John Frosch, M.D.

Director, Department of Psychiatry
Brookdale Hospital Medical Center
Brooklyn, N.Y.

The author surveys psychoanalytic contributions to the relationship between dreams and psychosis as well as adding some of his own observations. He uses as his frame of reference questions relating to the similarities between dreams and psychosis, whether there are psychotic dreams and whether dreams may presage psychosis. There seemed to be some general consensus that the answers to these questions were positive, depending upon the frames of reference used, i.e., whether one referred to the topographical or structural model of the mind, the level of ego cathexis, the function of the ego vis-a-vis reality, etc. Most contributors felt that a dream taken out of context from the overall clinical situation would be difficult to evaluate as either presaging or representing a psychosis despite the fact that many dreams may appear which are suggestive.

INTRODUCTION

Among others, Freud frequently drew analogies between dreams and psychosis. In the *Interpretation of Dreams* (1900), he reviewed some of the literature on this subject, conveying the impression that there were distinct similarities between the two phenomena. He said, "When we speak of the relation of dreams to mental disorders, we may have three things in mind: (1) etiological and clinical connections, as when a dream represents a psychotic state, or introduces it, or is left over from it; (2) modifications to which dream life is subject in cases of mental disease; and (3) intrinsic connections between the structure of dreams and psychoses, analogies pointing to their being essentially akin" (p. 88). It is the last concept to which he repeatedly returned, and to which I would first like to address myself.

SIMILARITIES BETWEEN DREAMS AND PSYCHOSIS

Freud essentially emphasized the analogy between the dream world to the waking life of the psychotic. He discussed this analogy in relation to consciousness and the role of the "censor," and referred to the role of censorship as the guardian of health as well as to the fact that, in the process of dreaming, external action is eliminated. Psychosis eventuates during the awakened state while the "gateway to the power of movement stands open," weakening censorship with a "pathological intensification of unconscious excitation." It is apparent that he made little distinction between the processes in psychoses and those in dream states, but at this stage he left open the question of the nature of the factors which enter into the relaxation of the censorship during the waking state and that of the increase in the drives which may overpower the censor.

As he refined the topographical hypothesis, Freud found it necessary to differentiate between these two aspects of the problem. It is at times difficult to keep one's bearings in Freud's discussion of this subject. This may be due to more than the inadequacies of the topographical hypothesis. The fact is that the analogy between dreams and psychosis is more apparent in some uses of the concept of the unconscious than in others. The analogy is clearer when the term "unconscious" is used in a descriptive rather than in a dynamic or systemic sense, as Freud (1917) himself realized in his discussion of differences between dreams and psychosis. In a brilliant tour de force, he applied the topographical hypothesis to the phenomenon of regression in both these states.

He summarized the differences between these two phenomena by saying, "In dreams, the withdrawal of cathexis (libido or interest) affects all systems equally.[2] *In the transference neuroses, the Pcs cathexis is withdrawn;*[3] *in schizophrenia, the cathexis of the Ucs;*[4] *in amentia, that of the Cs*" (p. 235).[5]

Of course, this is only a model and Freud himself had to qualify it to account for various clinical phenomena, such as hallucinations in schizophrenia, whose preferred explanation would appear inconsistent with a strict application of the model. In dreaming, the discharge through motility is not available and regressive perceptual modes are necessary. Freud could not simply say that hallucinations in schizophrenia, as in dreams, exist because of regression to more primitive modes of perception. It would be well to realize that Freud was concerned with the central and basic features which differentiate dreams from schizophrenia; hallucinatory experiences are not among the primary disturbances in schizophrenia. In order to account for the occurrence of hallucinations in schizophrenia, he had to postulate that they constituted an attempt to reestablish contact with the object. He had done the same with the use of language in schizophrenia. There are many other inconsistencies which Freud had to account for when he used the topographical hypothesis as a frame of reference. Subsequent theories required the reexamination of many of the phenomena seen in psychosis.

Varying views exist about the relationship between dreams and psychosis, although most agree that there is a close similarity in their structures. Federn (1952), still seeing an analogy between the two, postulated that in both the dream state and schizophrenia there is a lowering of ego cathexis. Lewin (1950, 1952, 1954) is another who saw a close relationship between dreams and psychosis. In his discussion of mania and sleep (1950), he interpreted some of the classic symptoms of mania, such as elation and flight of ideas and hyperactivity, as if they were dream elements. Summarily, he likened the benign stupors to blank dreams. At one point, he said, "Mania thus could be a kind of sleep even if it is not a deep stupor. So considered, a typical elation or mania is seen to resemble the dream of a small child with its playful fantasy wish fulfillments" (p. 85). However, he added,

It should be stated that in the elations, the fantasies, words, and deeds are used mainly for denial and that they resemble the denying secondary elaborations that come after the distortion of the latent dream thoughts. The content of the elations is a direct denial of a fact, is believed unreservedly and gladly and so resembles the believed dreams of the child rather than the playfully held fantasy.

Although Katan (1960) sees many superficial similarities between dreams and psychosis, he feels that basically they are different, both as to structure and the dynamic factors which enter into their production. As to the latter point, Freud (1933) said,

The state of sleep involves a turning-away from the real external world, and there we have the necessary condition for the development of a psychosis. The most careful study of the severe psychosis will not reveal to us a single feature that is more characteristic of those pathological conditions. In psychosis, however, the turning away from reality is brought about in two kinds of ways; whether by the unconscious repressed becoming excessively strong so that it overwhelms the conscious which is attached to reality, or because reality has become so intolerably distressing that the threatened ego throws itself into the arms of the unconscious instinctual forces in a desperate revolt. The harmless dream psychosis [sic] is a result of a withdrawal from the external world which is consciously willed and only temporary, and it disappears when relations to the external world are resumed. [p. 16]

Katan (1960) points to the fact that the underlying cause of the dream is different from that of psychosis:

> In the dream the ego has to keep its level of cathexis as low as possible; it is governed by the principle of economy in order to sleep. The withdrawn cathexis can easily be reversed; the psychosis occurs in waking life. The regression does not result from the pressure of the principle of economy. Danger arises from conflicts which force the ego to regress. [p. 347]

Furthermore, he feels that the wish-fulfilling tendency which is so characteristic of the dream is completely lacking in psychosis. What is essential to the delusional system is that the psychotic, in his attempt at restitution, copes with a conflict that calls for the breaking off of the ties with reality, and that this conflict is now mastered by unrealistic means; dangerous urges (the id) are projected so that what we see here is not wish fulfillment but attempts to master a danger by unrealistic means.

According to Katan, dreams facilitate the attempts of the ego to avoid reality in order to fulfill its function of keeping cathexis as low as possible:

> The dream ego does not want to return to objective reality; in contradistinction to the dream-ego's aim, the ego of the psychotic would like to return to reality but is unable to do so. The psychotic lives in a subjective, completely unrealistic world. Thus the dream ego does not want to return, the psychotic ego cannot return to normal reality. [p. 347]

[Although Katan does not say so explicitly, this is because the reality is dangerous and is responsible for the break and withdrawal to begin with.]

It is our view that wish-fulfilling tendencies are not lacking in psychosis. We would say that the wishful thinking expressed in so many psychotics is utilized in the service of constructing a (subjective) reality, but one which is different from the reality from which the psychotic has taken flight. When the patient of Freud (1894) imagines her lover as having returned, this may have been preceded by a withdrawal from a painful reality. Then the forces which operate to push for reality contact exert themselves and she creates a wish-fulfilling hallucination by means of what we may view as an hysterical mechanism.

Katan does feel that in what he calls the prepsychotic phase [sic] and in the dream the egos are in certain respects similar:

> The ego in the prepsychotic phase, and the ego in the dream, each have to ward off id instincts. The dream in fact should therefore be comparable only to the pre-psychotic phase. This conclusion would remove the dream completely from the sphere of psychosis proper. The difference between the

dream and the pre-psychotic phase would then be mainly that the ego in the dream wants to stay away from reality as much as possible, whereas the pre-psychotic ego puts up desperate efforts to maintain its contact with reality. [p. 347]

In discussing similarities and differences between dreams and psychoses it might be of some interest to take note of the more recent psychophysiological findings. By and large, biochemical and polygraph studies of psychotic states and dream states have pointed in the direction of the two as not being the same condition (Hartman, 1967). Kety (1959), for instance, demonstrated that oxygen consumption was decreased during sleep but not in the schizophrenic state, although during the dream state oxygen consumption was somewhat higher than in the rest of the sleep state. There have been some indications that serotonin metabolism is involved in dream states and that impairments of this metabolism also exist in psychotic conditions.

The consensus of these contributions indicates that although there are many apparent superficial similarities between dreams and psychosis, they do differ in some basic respects; certainly insofar as the factors are concerned which play a role in their production. The spectrum of viewpoints depends upon the frames of reference used, i.e., the topographical model of the mind, the level of ego cathexis, the function of the ego vis-à-vis reality, etc. Psychophysiological studies emphasize the difference between the two phenomena.

PSYCHOTIC DREAMS (DREAMS INDICATIVE OF PSYCHOSIS)

We would like to turn to the other question raised by Freud, namely, whether there is anything specific about the dream of the psychotic. Are there such dreams as can be called psychotic? Is the content of the dream significant? Is, for instance, the presence in dreams of flagrant and manifest oedipal, homosexual, or more primitive material, such as cannibalistic manifestations, at the beginning or early in treatment, to be viewed with alarm as reflecting psychosis or possibly a developing psychosis? Is the affective quality of the dream, i.e., undue anxiety or a nightmarish quality, of significance? All of these questions have been answered positively by some contributors.

In directing himself to this question, Freud (1922) discussed two patients, one of whom had fully developed delusions of jealousy, while the other was paranoid, but not clinically overtly so. The delusions the first patient had were transitory and were depreciated by him. Freud seemed rather surprised that the dreams of this overtly paranoid patient were relatively free of delusions. They revealed the underlying homosexual impulses, he says, "with no more than the usual degree of disguise. Since I had had little experience with the dreams of paranoiacs, it seemed plausible at the time to suppose that it was true in general that paranoia does not penetrate into dreams" (p. 227).

On the other hand, he noted that the second patient, who was clinically not classifiable as psychotic or grossly delusional, produced a great number of persecutory dreams which Freud regarded either as forerunners of or substitutes for the delusional ideas. He, on one occasion, produced a dream which Freud characterized as a transference dream in which he reflected an overt attitude of playing down his delusion.

Freud discussed the question of whether or not psychosis can penetrate into dreams by maintaining that this is not really the true question. The fact is that the dreamwork can be applied to preconscious ideas which may contain obsessional, hysterical, or paranoid material, and, when we undo the dreamwork, we may find delusional elements or other fantasies. We cannot speak of unconscious material in the id as being hysterical, obsessional, or paranoiac. However, Freud says a pathological idea which exists in the preconscious can be transformed into a dream, like anything else which exists in the preconscious. In both cases, the dream took up the material that was at the time forced into the background in waking life. In the paranoid patient who was not overtly psychotic, the delusional material which was pushed away from consciousness into the preconscious, and depreciated, was worked over into the dream. Both Van Ophiujsen (1920) and Arlow (1949) reported patients in whom paranoid trends of a persecutory nature could be established through an understanding of the latent dream content. One may therefore say according to this viewpoint that the latent content of the dream and the latent wish may be more closely identified with the nature of the psychosis than the manifest form of the dream.

More recent studies related to the question whether there are dreams which may reflect psychotic phenomena dealt in the main with manifest form and content. Kant (1940, 1942) did not feel that there was anything to differentiate them from others. Douglas Noble (1951) also felt that there were no dreams specifically characteristic of schizophrenia; although he did feel that they tended to be simple, frank statements, with little elaboration of basic problems, they were often primitive in nature. He found that as the patient improved the dreams became more complicated and were associated with more affect. He also felt that dreams during the improvement period could shed light on some of the problems with which the patient was struggling during the overt psychosis.

Richardson and Moore (1963) submitted manifest dreams of schizophrenic and nonschizophrenic patients to a panel of analysts, who were asked to differentiate the schizophrenic from the nonschizophrenic dreams. The degree of correlation did not appear too good, and the criteria used by the panel seemed as valid for one type of dream as the other. Nevertheless, with some degree of correction, the authors felt that there was a significant difference in accuracy of prediction for the nonschizophrenic. They found that the presence of unusual, strange, uncanny, and bizarre qualities was more common for the schizophrenic than for the nonschizophrenic dream. They postulated that neutralized energy which is not available to the schizophrenic in the awakened state is available to him in sleep and can be used to effect distortion, etc. —in other words, to do the dreamwork. On the other hand, secondary revision, which is more clearly aligned to the waking state, is impaired in the schizophrenic. It is ordinarily secondary elaboration (secondary process) which gives an element of coherence to the dream, and, when this is not carried through satisfactorily, we obtain the bizarre and uncanny quality about the dreams reported by schizophrenics.

Katan (1960) seems to feel that during sleep the psychotic is more normal than when he is awake and is in the same state of mind as any other person. He has to withdraw cathexis in order to sleep and thereby lessens the involvement with reality and conflictual situations. Whereas he does feel that the latent content of the dream and the content of psychotic symptoms may be the same and that we have no way of determining from the *manifest* content whether it belongs to a dream or to a psychosis, it is his definitive opinion that the structure, cause, and function of dreams and psychosis are totally different.

Langs (1966) compared the manifest content of three clinical groups— severe hysterical character disorder, paranoid schizophrenic reaction, and psychotic depressive reaction. He felt that there were significant differences in the dreams of such patients which were consonant with the clinical pictures.

The manifest dreams of severe hysterics are characterized by themes of illness and injury, voyeurism, sexuality, uses of the mouth, and direct references to the body. Their dreams reflect a view of the environment as both traumatic and helpful and others are either injured or in positive roles. Interaction between the patient and others is prominent. The overall dream tends to be lengthy, detailed, and unambiguous. The paranoid schizophrenics' dreams reflect a proneness to conflict with others and a view of the environment and others as traumatizing and overwhelming. The dreams center around the patient herself and are the furthest from daily reality. The psychotic depressives' dreams are brief and barren. They center on family members and appear to reflect an extensive decathexis of external objects and reality and a pervasive utilization of defensive denial.

Insofar as the findings of the schizophrenic patients were concerned, they appeared to be at variance with those of Richardson and Moore.

Rochlin (Mack, 1969) questioned whether there was any such thing as a "psychotic dream," i.e., anything within the dream itself that indicated a psychosis. On the other hand, he felt we could obtain important clues if we were to look to the other indications of regression occurring in the dream. Ernest Hartmann (1967) asserted that the consensus of most reports is that manifest dream content does not provide one of the more useful diagnostic tests for schizophrenia, depression, or any other mental illness. Dream recall seems to be reduced in severe depression, so much so that Hartmann suggests disappearance of dream recall as indicative of impending suicide.

The impact of mental illness on the patterning of dream time has been of interest to the psychophysiologists. According to Hartmann various studies of dream time in schizophrenics have not shown any significant reaction. Studies of depressed patients did reveal decreased dream time, although in delusional periods such time was increased. Hartmann found that dream time was higher in depressed than in manic states. During a study of a paranoid patient, Hartmann found an increase in dream time with the breakthrough of his grossly psychotic picture. But this finding was not consistent. The latency period, from the time a patient fell asleep to the time he began dreaming, was shorter in depressed patients. Also, in schizophrenics, the separation between D (REM-rapid eye movement) sleep and S (non-REM) sleep was not so sharp. In general, Hartmann concluded that psychic pain and stress were significant factors in affecting dreamtime and that the latter may be elevated with stress.

The relationship between nightmares and psychosis has been of recurrent interest. To what extent are such dreams reflective of psychosis and may they be indicators of impending psychosis? Mack (1965, 1969a, 1969b, 1969c, 1970) sees analogies between the manifest features of nightmares in childhood and certain acute psychoses in adults. Manifestations such as terror of overwhelming intensity, perception of external danger, violence, the use of projection and distortion mechanisms, the state of helplessness and vulnerability of the ego — all seem to be shared by the two conditions. He regards the nightmare as an encapsulated or delineated state, intermediate between normal dreaming and acute psychosis. Mack feels that a history of repeated nightmares in childhood (which he refers to as "micro-psychoses") may be found in individuals who subsequently develop acute paranoid psychoses. In both, he suggests that what we may be dealing with is the ego's struggle to integrate an overwhelming experience. The ego is overwhelmed and reality testing may be lost for the child experiencing a severe nightmare in a way that can be quite similar to what occurs in an acute paranoid psychosis. For the child, whether his nightmare will furnish the anlage of later acute psychoses depends on the fate of his childhood conflicts, how the parents deal with early anxiety situations, how the ego defenses develop during adolescence and the further development that occurs during young adult life. The implication of nightmares for later psychosis has also been discussed by Sperling (1958), who described a type of nightmare associated with hypermotility, psychoticlike behavior with delusions and hallucinations, and retrograde amnesias. She viewed these as psychotic episodes during nighttime whose recurrence had prognostic significance for later psychosis.

Fisher (1970) studied voluntary subjects who gave a history of nightmares. True nightmares occur during stage IV and like most pathological manifestations of sleep occur during non-REM sleep. According to Fisher, the deeper the sleep the more intense the nightmare. Discussing the relationship between nightmare and psychosis, this author pointed to the close resemblance between the nightmare and an acute psychotic episode with respect to its outward manifestations and the intensity of the panic associated with it. He viewed these as psychoticlike ego disturbances, more like a brief and reversible psychotic attack than a dream. He was, however, not certain of the significance of such phenomena for future psychotic development. He described one patient with stage IV nightmares who also had "day-mares" that closely resembled in feeling certain of his nightmares. Fisher felt that if such "day-mares" increased in intensity they would be difficult to distinguish from a psychotic state. Most of Fisher's subjects were borderline and showed evidence of underlying paranoia.

It is interesting to note that, in a recent report by Lairy (1967), the suggestion was made that nightmares had a discharge function which protected the individual against the appearance of severe disturbance in the awakened state. These studies showed that nightmares did not occur during the dream period but during S (non-REM) time. If a psychotic patient is awakened during such a period he is found to be extremely disturbed and he displays the worst features of his psychosis at this time. This is not the case if he is awakened during the usual dreamtime. This phenomenon may be related to the condition of *schlaftrunkenheit* (sleepdrunkenness) which takes place in episodic disorders such as bruxism, somnambulism, etc. when the patient is forcibly aroused during deep S (non-REM) sleep. In several of our patients whom we considered psychotic characters, the appearance of nightmarelike dreams was a common occurrence. The manifest dream content was generally of violence, including murder and rape, or fire. Although not followed by psychotic states, the reporting of dreams was often accompanied by a sense of realness and persistent states of agitation, anxiety, tension, and depression, sometimes lasting for days.

In our own studies about the relationship of dreams to psychosis, we direced ourselves to the question of the nature of the conflict or danger which the patient was struggling with and to what extent this could be reflected in the content and form of the latent and manifest dream. In addition, we were concerned with the context in which the dream was occurring, i.e., whether the patient was in treatment, the stage in treatment, the state of the awakened ego following such dreams — that is could such dreams be distinguished from reality—etc. In earlier communications (Frosch 1964; 1967a,b,c; 1970) we tried to establish frames of reference which may be used to differentiate between neurosis and psychosis. One of these was the nature of the conflict or danger uniquely associated with psychosis in contrast to that of neurosis. In the psychotic, there is a threat to psychic survival which is represented by a fear of disintegration and dissolution of self. Much of the symptomatology of the psychotic may be understood either in the abandonment of the patient to psychic death represented by such dissolution or by a struggle to maintain contact with the object (reality) by the formation of symptoms. The neurotic is concerned with instinctual conflicts at a higher level of psychic development. His ego structure and functions are sufficiently developed to cope with the dangers deriving from the conflict, whether they center around separation, castration, superego punishment, or anything else that is crucial.

With this as a frame of reference in trying to evaluate whether the dream is that of a psychotic, we must assume that, just as the symptomatology of the psychotic during the awakened state reflects his attempts to deal with certain urges and conflicts, the dream of the psychotic may equally in one form or another reflect such attempts. It appears to us that the crucial issue is the nature of the danger (problem) which the psychotic is trying to resolve both in his awakened and dream states. If, as we have proposed, in psychosis the basic danger lies in the threat to survival and the fear of dissolution of self, it is clear that the motivational factor in dreams of the nonpsychotic may under ordinary circumstances be different from those of the psychotic. It appears to us that the dangers present in the psychotic will influence his dreams both as to form and content. If a terrifying dream is concerned with the fear of breakthrough of instinctual drives, whether they are aggressive or libidinal, we will be less concerned than if this terrifying dream reflects a fear of ego disintegration and dissolution—a fear which characterizes the psychotic.

We had an opportunity to examine the fear of ego disintegration in patients who had been receiving shock treatment (EST) and who had already seemingly recovered from the psychosis which had indicated the need for such treatment (Frosch, 1948). We proposed that the assault of EST in some patients produced ego-disintegrative reactions which brought in their wake marked anxiety. In some such patients dreams during this period were tremendously frightening and had a nightmarelike quality, reflecting the fear of disintegration. One patient awoke from such dreams terribly frightened, shouting that he did not know who he was. On another occasion he awoke from a dream which had a nightmarish quality, shouting, "Something has happened to me. I have never been this way before." This was followed by an exceedingly agitated psychotic state during which fears of body disintegration were among the many anxieties expressed.

The opportunity to analyze a patient who had recently completed a series of EST was also described in that communication. She presented herself as depressed and suicidal, for which she was given EST. She had many obsessional thoughts, images, and impulses of an aggressive and hostile nature. As EST progressed, she became increasingly agitated, restless, and anxious; at this point, treatment was discontinued. Sonn afterward, she was referred for therapy and entered analysis. During the early stage of analysis her dreams contained latent content of deep hostilities toward both parents and incestuous wishes for her father, all of which were relatively poorly disguised. All of these dreams had a frightening quality and she was in a constant state of apprehension. Her fear was of not being able to stay together, of falling apart. Her feeling of disintegration was expressed not so much in the manifest content of the dreams as in the affect accompanying the associations to the dream and in her reactions to the dream as a whole. As treatment progressed and she achieved more ego integration, these reactions subsided.

Another frame of reference which was found of some significance as an indication of psychosis was the reaction of the patient to the dream. We are inclined to believe that the inability to distinguish a dream from reality is a more important frame of reference than the dream content as such. Freud (1907) made the difficulty of differentiating dream from reality the basis of this study of Jensen's *Gradiva*. He indicated that the inability to differentiate dream from reality created a delusional system in the waking state. Whether Harold the Dreamer was therefore realy psychotic was a question to which Freud did not direct himself. In connection with this he says,

> if a belief in the reality of the dream-images persists unusually long, so that one cannot tear oneself out of the dream, this is not a mistaken judgment provoked by the vividness of the dream images, but is a psychical act on its own; It is an assurance, relating to the content of the dream, that something in it is really as one has dreamt it; and it is right to have faith in this assurance. [p. 57]

It is interesting to note that it is this very element which he subsequently states that accounts for the fixity of delusions (Freud, 1937).

Leveton, (1961) utilizes the term "night residue" to designate those aspects of the dream which "persist in some form into the waking state. . . ." One of the manifestations is the failure to separate dream from waking thought so that sleep and waking—in the extreme form—are indistinguishable. This lends to the dream a marked feeling of reality and at times an inability to distinguish the dream as dream. Rochlin (Mack, 1969) believes that in the case of the person who is becoming psychotic the nighly regression that occurs in the dream cannot be shrugged off during the daytime with such self-assurance as "it is only a dream." Rather, the regression runs from the dream of the night into the day.

Mack (1969a,b,c) as well as others have called attention to the state of confusion, disorganization, and inability to distinguish internal from external perceptions seen in the dreamer who awakens from a nightmare. This resembles the state described above as sleepdrunkenness. He describes the case of a woman who

> several days before hospitalization had a dream in which an enormous man without a face and wearing a pointed hat and brown cape was trying to destory her. She woke up screaming in terror, but the image persisted in the corner of the room for many minutes. Her husband had to comfort her and to take her to the spot where she hallucinated the man before the image receded.

Mack is of the opinion that this element, the capacity to distinguish dreams from reality, facilitates the maintenance of sanity. He feels that the confusion may operate in two directions. The patient may be unsure as to whether a dream has actually taken place or he may have difficulty establishing the fact that an actual traumatic situation has not been a dream.

In our own experiences with borderline and psychotic patients, they not infrequently have dreams which take on a strikingly real and vivid quality, invading their daily lives to such an extent that it is difficult for them to say what is real and what is a dream. In a previous communication (1967b) I referred to a patient who showed a marked tendency to regression. Very frequently, after a night's dreaming, there was a carryover of both the ego state of sleep and the contents of the dream. Throughout the day, events and situations from the dream continued to have a vivid quality barely differentiated from reality. On one such occasion, she said, "My body feels awake, but my mind is still fuzzy-wooly, like it's still with my dream" (p. 611).

One of my borderline patients agitatedly reported a dream in which her mother was lying on top of her, having intercourse with her. What troubled her was that the sensation was so vivid that she was not sure that it had not happened and kept wavering about the reality of the experience. Another acutely psychotic patient came into the hospital in a panic, thinking that he had murdered his brother-in-law. It turned out that he had had a dream of choking his brother-in-law to death. The feeling in his hand was so real that he began to wonder whether he had really committed the deed and rushed into the hospital in a panic. During a psychotic state, one patient had a dream of being a prostitute. She was quite agitated and disturbed by the implication that she was dissolute. In contrast, as she was recovering from this state, she dreamed that she was having an affair with a person who clearly represented me. She did not feel too upset by this, saying, "After all, it's only a dream."

In the patients we alluded to above, the vividness of the dreams contributed to ego states which contained many of the ingredients of nightmares. Although such individuals were able to recognize these as being dreams, the anxiety, the apprehension, the feeling tone, the terror, etc. seemed to persist. It appears from the foregoing that there is no consensus as to whether the manifest dream was of itself a meaningful guide to the presence of psychosis. Viewpoints ranged from those who felt that it was the latent content that was most tale-telling to those who seemed to feel that there might be features about the manifest form and content which could be of significance, indicating the presence of psychosis. On the other hand, it is felt by some investigators that the patient's attitude toward the dream, difficulties in differentiating dream from reality, and the persistence of dreamlike states invading the waking life may offer clues to the possibly psychotic nature of a dream.

DREAMS PRESAGING PSYCHOSIS

This issue touches upon the question raised by Freud, whether dreams may presage or usher in psychosis or even continue into it. After reviewing the literature (1900), he decided that this was the case and that there are certain dreams which represent the first outbreak of a delusion. He quoted Sancte de Sanctis to the effect that psychosis may come to life at a single blow with the appearance of the operative dream which brings the delusional material to light, or it may develop slowly in a series of further dreams which may still have to overcome a certain amount of doubt. The probability is, as Freud indicated, that in the dream the patient is already struggling with the material which essentially comes into the psychosis.

Some time before the onset of his second illness, Schreber[7] dreamed that his previous illness had returned; he also wondered before he awoke or was in a half-waking state, what it would be like to be copulated with as a woman. Freud (1911) discusses this dream as a reactivation of Schreber's homosexual wishes about Flechsig and the wish to see Flechsig again. However, one may very well raise the question whether this is not a variant of an examination dream, namely, that it may reflect an awareness of the oncoming illness and its underlying conflict and a reassurance that Schreber would equally recover from this illness and master the conflict as he did his previous one. To some extent Katan (1960) reflects this thought when he says,

every initial dream which is emphasized by the patient as the starting point of his psychosis still contains the wish to be able to prevent the outbreak of a psychosis. . . . Upon awakening, the patient may discover that his ego is no longer able to manage the situation by reality means. The wish in the dream was the last barricade which the ego could erect against the oncoming psychosis. [p. 349]

The subject of dreams presaging psychosis was also dealt with by many investigators, some attaching significance to the form of a dream, others to a specific type of content, still others to the merging of the dream with the ensuing psychotic state, and still others to the psychic processes which made this phenomenon possible.

Form and Structure of the Dream

Many of the writers reported dreams in patients reflecting the ego's inability to cope with a threatening danger, a loss of control, a sense of helplessness to cope with a danger or deal with a situation effectively. Focus in some instances was placed on the ego disintegration in the face of such situations, which was projected in the awakened state into world disintegration delusions. Several reports stressed the relationship of such dreams to frightening aspects of the transference.

Atkins (Mack, 1969) advanced the view that there were certain dreams in which the form and structure of the content could be particularly useful in reflecting the dreamer's ego attitudes, defensive capacities, and abilities to establish object relations. He thought that a psychosis may be anticipated by certain dreams which can in their manifest content reflect the ego's response to danger. In his opinion, there are at least two general classes of dreams associated with psychotic potential or development—those that reflect the threat or actuality of regressive disorganization and those with defensive delusional restitutional elements. He nevertheless felt that a series of dreams could be more indicative of the ego state of the patient than a single dream.

A patient reported by Savitt (Frosch, 1967b) had four dreams preceding a psychotic break during analysis. The fourth of these was as follows: "I am driving a Volkswagen. It has baby carriage wheels. I am running low on gas and flip the stick which regulates the emergency supply of gasoline. In the dream it fails. It was following this dream that the psychotic episode took place." [p. 614]

Bartemeier (1950) presented the case of a mother who awoke in terror from a dream in which she was helpless to prevent the drowning of her daughter. She developed a psychoticlike state resembling a psychotic episode she had had six years previously. Bartemeier felt that both the dream and the acute reaction were indications of an abrupt change in the transference and that this was a repetition in miniature of the previous psychosis, which had occurred after a love object had left for military service.

Richardson (Mack, 1969) reported a patient who developed a transient psychotic reaction which followed a dream related to the development of the transference neurosis. Richardson's patient may or may not have had a real psychotic episode. It was, in any event, related to passive homosexual fantasies about the analyst. He was trying to defend himself against these fantasies by projecting them upon his wife. He then had the dream which reflected this struggle in the latent content. Such content consisted of his absorption with his wife's presumed infidelity and masturbatory fantasies about her employer who was a doctor. These turned out to be defenses against the patient's passive feminine masturbatory fantasies about his analyst. Following the dream, he suffered from a period of agitation, associated with the conviction that his wife was unfaithful to him. As a result, he wanted to divorce her. The episode lasted about twenty-four hours. Richardson does not demonstrate what in the dream could have presaged this transient psychotic break.

Dreams which reflect ego disintegration and fragmentation have been considered by many as prodromal of an impending psychosis. On the other hand, they may represent the ego's reaction to instinctual drives directed against the outside and the self. In this case, we are dealing with a much higher level of psychic development and the basic psychotic fear of loss of self is not the area of conflict (Frosch, 1967b,c). The author's own experience has been that such dreams encountered during analysis do not necessarily presage a psychotic break; more significance may be given to such dreams when they occur outside the therapeutic setting.

At the beginning of her illness, a psychotic patient expressed some end-of-the-world ideas as well as delusions of persecution. In the course of her illness, these recurred in florid form, and as she improved eventually disappeared. Sometime afterward, following a whole series of disturbing events with a beginning resurgence of anxiety, withdrawal, and agitated behavior, she reported the following dream:

> There is a beautiful tree with lovely golden leaves. [The patient as well as her mother had blonde hair.] The bark begins to peel off this tree and the tree begins to rot inside and gradually the earth begins to seep up into the tree, the branches, and the leaves. The leaves turn brown and the tree begins to pulsate and throb and it turns into the beating of waves and water and the waves have sharp spikes.

It was immediately after this that the patient had a recurrence of her psychosis in which world destruction delusions were prominent. One more comment about ego disintegration or world destruction dreams is in order. I am inclined to believe that such dreams should be evaluated within the framework of the existing psychic state. For instance, they may occur in connection with physical illness, fevers, and many other similar conditions.

Content of Dream

Although the form and content of dreams are clearly related (i.e., ego disintegration reflects itself in content), there was also the feeling on the part of some investigators that repetitive terrifying dreams reflecting relatively undisguised forbidden impulses were of significance in presaging a psychosis. In a patient reported by Bartemeier a dream was followed by psychosis. This was a young woman who dreamed that her girlfriend had been murdered and that she and her mother had been dismembering the corpse and packing the parts into a trunk to conceal the crime. When the patient awoke, she became ill, fearful of noises, depressed, agitated, spoke of suicide, and was hospitalized with a picture of agitated depression. The hatred which filled this girl had been aroused by an act of preference her mother had displayed for a friend of hers. This had reactivated a childhood situation of jealousy toward a younger sister. Bartemeier feels that dreams which are followed by acute reactions during psychoanalytic therapy indicate momentous events in the transference relationship.

We have also called attention heretofore (pp. 45-47) to the views of some investigators not only to the analogy between nightmares and psychosis but to the fact that such dreams occur with increasing frequency in impending psychosis. Mack (1969b) called attention to the phenomenon of the continuation of dreams into the daytime as particularly characteristic of the nightmare. The difference comes down to the capacity to reestablish reality testing.

Interesting to note is a report by Bradlow (1971), who reported a series of patients who had been initially or finally diagnosed as psychotic or borderline characters. In many of these, the theme of murder was present in the first reported dream of analysis. He felt that this manifestation had particular significance in portending eventual psychotic breaks in the course of treatment.

Merging of Dream into Psychosis

Many instances have been reported in which a dream not only ushers in a psychosis but is incorporated into the ensuing psychosis and the delusional system. Freud (1900) early dealt with this question when he said, "In these instances the dreams are represented as the etiology of the disorder, but we should be doing equal justice to the facts if we said that the mental disorder made its first appearance in dream life, that it first broke through in a dream." The carrying over of dream contents as well as dream states into consciousness is characteristically seen in children (Lewin 1950, p. 96). Ordinarily, this is eventually outgrown and ". . .night thought; except pathologically or sporadically, does not enter into waking formation". A number of investigators (Schur, 1970; Brenner, 1951; Esman, 1962) describe hallucinations in children during the awakened state which were ushered in by an attack of pavor nocturnus merging into the hallucinatory condition. Whether the latter could be viewed as psychotic was questioned by some of these authors. As was indicated (p. 54), particularly characteristic of nightmares was the continuation of such dreams into the daytime.

Fisher and Dement (1961) reported a patient who had a nightmarish dream which repeated over a period of many weeks and was later incorporated into the content of the delusions that developed in his psychotic period. The repetitive dream was to the effect that he was placed into a mental hospital by his wife and mother because they were afraid he was going to become violent. In this dream, he is in a room by himself, feels as if he is suffocating, with the walls closing in on him, and someone is speaking to him in a very mean voice; he is reminded of a scoutmaster who once tried to seduce him. The doctor keeps saying over and over again that he is crazy and accuses him of following in his mother's footsteps. Within a short time after the dream the full-blown psychotic symptomatology appeared. This psychosis contained much of the manifest content of the dream. He thought his wife or mother had got in touch with Dr. Fisher or were behind him looking at him. He felt that they were spying on him and sending information about him to Dr. Fisher. A big "showdown" was coming, after which he would be sent to a mental hospital. There is no record of what the dreams were like during the psychosis and whether the repetitive dream continued during this period. It is also not entirely clear whether the quality of the dreams changed, i.e., whether the dreams that the patient had before and those he had after his acute outburst were markedly different. According to the writers, the dreams did suggest a more primitive and clearer expression of instinctual drives during increasing pressure (p. 89).

I have referred to a patient who dreamed she was a prostitute—a dream which disturbed her very much (p. 50). Subsequently, during a brief period of remission, there was a flare up of psychotic behavior during which she actually became a prostitute for a period of two weeks. However, this behavior was clearly related to a delusion in which she felt she was being tested to determine whether she was homosexual. She believed that the men with whom she was having intercourse were women in disguise. The penises were not real—on occasion she attempted to tear them off. During the period of hospitalization she displayed reactions to both overt and latent homosexual preoccupations against which she was defending herself .

An interesting manifestation of behavior related to dreams was provided by Sterba (1946), who reported acting-out behavior in patients which preceded the narration of a dream of the night before. Clear examples demonstrated that this acting out was closely related to the dream content.

The close connection between the acting out and the dream gives the impression that the acting out functions like an association to the dream. . . . Actually, the acting out as well as the dream which it precedes are both the expression of the same unconscious instinctual dynamism which succeeds in breaking through the repressing forces of the ego, particularly when the defenses are loosened up through the analytic work. [p. 179]

It becomes clear that on occasion dreams may not only usher in a psychosis but may even become part of a delusion in a patient's psychotic behavior. In Fisher and Dement's patient, the dream reflected a conflict already quite pressing, namely, the unconscious passive homosexual feelings toward the experimenter. It is interesting to note that in both Fisher and Dement's patient, as well as in mine, it was the manifest content that was incorporated into the psychosis. This would suggest that just as the manifest content of a dream is a distortion of latent conflict, so are the delusions and psychosis compromise operations which manage to preserve the psyche by means of distortion. It is clear that both the dreams as well as the psychotic manifestations were struggling with the same unconscious conflict. The question therefore may well be asked whether they both represent in the one case the resultant of dreamwork and in the other something we may perhaps designate as "psychosis work."

Freud (1907) alluded to this when he said,

a delusion very often arises in connection with a dream, and, after what we have learned about the nature of dreams, there is no need to see a fresh riddle in this fact. Dreams and delusions arise from the same source—from what is repressed. Dreams are, as one might say, the physiological delusions of normal people. Before what is repressed has become strong enough to break through into waking life as a delusion, it may easily have achieved a first success, under the more favorable conditions of the state of sleep, in the form of a dream with persisting effects. [p. 62]

Psychic Processes Facilitating Merging of Dream with Psychosis

As indicated in the previous section, in dreams merging with an ensuing psychosis we find continuing attempts on the part of the ego in trying to deal with unresolved conflicts from sleep into the awakened state. Such attempts may represent further elaboration of the dream. Freud (1900), as indicated, had already suggested this when he pointed out that in the dream the patient is already struggling with the material which essentially carries into the psychosis. However, it is essential to establish what makes it possible for such a dream to break into the awakened state in the form of a psychosis. It is clear that specific ego defects or states facilitate this process.

Lewin (1950) described a series of patients in whom undisguised forbidden wishes broke through into their dreams. He went on to say:

> These patients were menaced by insight that came to them in dreams, and they sought escape from instinct and anxiety in alcoholic stupor or hypomania. The older, natural sleep had become unreliable, because of the weakness of the censorship; the stupor and the hypomania were the new equivalents of sleep, where the censorship, ego defense, and the wish to sleep prevailed, in the case of stupor because of the complete absence of consciousness, in the hypomania because of the alertness and possibility of acting out a denial. [p. 100]

Several authors tend to account for the alteration of ego states which facilitate the breakthrough of the dream in the psychosis by the increase in instinctual pressures which make for a weakening of ego function, especially if to begin with there is an ego defect in neutralization. As indicated earlier, Hartmann (1967) found an increase in dreamtime in a paranoid patient with the breakthrough of his psychotic picture. Fisher and Dement (1961, 1963), proposing the idea that a dream may represent the safety valve for partial discharge of instinctual drives, observed an increase in dreaming time just before the outbreak of a full-blown psychosis in a patient being treated for narcolepsy by means of psychotherapy.[8] On the assumption that the dream acts as a safety valve for partial discharge of instinctual drives, they maintain that when an increase in such instinctual drives occurs, there should ensue both qualitative and quantitative alterations in dreaming. Qualitatively, there may appear more open expressions of instinctual gratification as against more disguised forms of them. There is clinical evidence that dreamtime represents a rough quantitative measure of the pressure of instinctual drives toward discharge. It is difficult to evaluate this in practice, where we concentrate upon the remembering and reporting of dreams.

It is their observation that psychotics find it difficult to maintain control over upsurging instinctual drives, especially in the presence of the ego defect in neutralization. One therefore wonders whether there is a relationship between increase of dream time and the emergence of delusions and hallucinations. The opportunity arose of studying a case relevant to this problem. Their narcoleptic patient developed a paranoid state; concomitantly, they observed an increase in dreaming time which rose to the point at which a breakthrough into the waking ego life of the patient took place, with the development of delusions and hallucinations.

There is evidence to support the view that increasingly uncontrollable instinctual dream pressures pushing into the awakened state and resulting in psychosis comes from another source. As Leveton (1961) pointed out, ". . . as waking repression failed to separate dream from waking thought, there was no residue at all, as night and day, sleep and waking were indistinguishable." It is as though the important process of secondary elaboration, which generally distorts the latent dream wish, fails to operate both in the sleep state and in the awakened state or takes on a psychotic form in the awakened state.

Of course, this observation raises many questions. Is it purely a matter of the quantitative increase in the drive or are there certain qualitative defects in the ego which will ultimately permit the breakthrough into waking life? Sleep deprivation seems to be an essential factor in promoting ego defects. It is apparent that various ego defects permit the breakthrough to take place during the waking state. A dream goes on into the awakened state simply as the continuation of a process in an attempt to deal with an incompatible wish under increasing instinctual pressure and reality and eventuates in psychosis by virtue of severe ego defects.

Under certain circumstances the differentiation between sleeping and waking may be lost by virtue of such ego defects. I refer to the general dedifferentiation in the process of psychotic development, bringing in its wake severe disturbances in certain ego functions concerned with reality e.g., the ego's relationship with reality, the feelings of reality, and the capacity to test reality (Frosch, 1964). The dedifferentiation between S sleep alluded to by Hartmann (1967) in some schizophrenics may find its analogy in the *schlaftrunkenheit*, which we see in some cases where the state of sleep and the state of wakefulness merge. The confusion between dream and reality is a logical counterpart of this lack of differentiation, with the consequences that the dream flows into the waking states. In psychosis, because of the disturbances in the ego, especially with regard to reality, the dream may be accepted as reality.

As one of the "night residues" Leveton (1961) describes the merging of the manifest dream into reality and becoming the content of the psychosis. This reflects the ego's difficulty in maintaining repression—a frequent difficulty with psychosis. It was his feeling that in such instances, in order to handle through dreaming what repression has failed to control, namely, the breakthrough of an unacceptable wish, there is a subsequent breakthrough into the awakened state and the ego must use other defenses which in some instances may result in psychosis. In such instances, disturbed sleep and disturbing dreams are the reflection rather than the cause of the eventual development of a psychosis. He reports the case of a patient who complained of increasing tension and fears of going to sleep because of a recurring terrifying dream. The patient became more and more agitated in the morning, finally becoming acutely psychotic, with a delusional content the same as his reported dream. The patient said, "Then all of a sudden one night I just lose all track of time and I can't tell night from day, because the dream just goes on all the time. I can't wake up at all. Sleeping or waking, it's all the same to me."

Pursuing the trend of thought in the preceding section, a number of investigators felt that in the psychosis following a dream there is a continuing attempt by a severely impaired ego to deal with reactivated unresolved childhood memories. Katan (1960) felt that dreams ushering in psychosis have a special function, and that, in a sense, the delusions amount to associations to the dream and represent a working over of childhood memories which would ordinarily have come to the fore in simple associations to the dream. It is in this way that from Schreber's delusions Katan attempts to reconstruct childhood situations.

Martin (1958) also seems to agree with Katan. He described an agoraphobic patient who in the fourth year of analysis had a resurgence of symptoms during which she became terrified, confused, and afraid to drive a car. She also began to express suicidal ideas as well as suspicions of the analyst. At this point, a long dream in which she felt she was going crazy contained the overt content of the therapist's making sexual advances to her to which she was very receptive. Martin considered this dream an attempt to fend off the impending psychosis by gratification of her wish to get and to give what she had never experienced in her earliest infancy. This failed and she was hospitalized with a full-blown paranoid psychosis. It became clear in the subsequent analysis that the psychosis fulfilled her infantile need; Martin considered the psychotic episode an acting out of the fantasy of her narcissistic striving through symbiotic union with the mother — a psychotic resolution. A similar viewpoint was represented by one of the disputants in a well-known discussion about the Wolf Man's psychosis following a dream during his analysis with Mack Brunswick (1928). It may be remembered that for a whole period before he came to Brunswick he had had numerous somatic preoccupations with a paranoid flavoring. At one point in the analysis, Brunswick began to undermine his grandiosity, whereupon, following a dream, a full-blown paranoid psychosis broke out. He talked wildly, seemed cut off from reality, and threatened to shoot both Freud and Brunswick. The essential feature of the dream which underlined the persecutory trend was the gleaming eyes of the wolves. "Their eyes gleam, and it is evident that they want to rush at the patient, his wife and the other woman. The patient is terrified fearing that they will succeed in breaking through the wall" (p. 460). "The shining eyes of the wolves now remind the patient that for some time following the dream of four years he could not bear to be looked at fixedly. He would fly into a temper and cry 'why do you stare at me like that?' An observant glance would recall the dream to him with all its nightmare quality" (p. 461).

Brunswick repeatedly referred to this as a persecutory dream. "Of course the dream derives its chief significance from its persecutory content. . . . With the destruction of the patient's ideas of grandeur his full persecution mania made its appearance" (p. 461). Yet, it is not too clear why a psychosis developed following this dream and whether the dream per se could be viewed as one presaging psychosis. In a critique of Brunswick's understanding of what transpired during this analysis, Harnik (1930) expressed the view that the gleaming eyes of the wolves were significantly related to a childhood re- action. He felt that the outbreak of the psychosis following the dream could be related to a regressive reactivation of earlier oral features which repre- sented a fixation point necessary for the element of projection to take place. He made the point that the aversion of the Wolf Man to being looked at and the current anxiety about his nose had essentially the same meaning. He felt that the development of the psychosis following the dream constituted a nega- tive reaction to a correct interpretation; as a matter of fact, he observed such negative responses lasting a short time to every correct interpretation. But why this was a psychotic reaction was not explained by Harnik, although he did postulate that the oral ambivalence of the Wolf Man which played an im- portant role in the paranoid mechanism was reactivated in the analysis.

In rebuttal, Brunswick (1930) asserted that the anxiety of being stared at represented a projection of the Wolf Man's own observation of the primal scene. Such projection led to his ideas of reference. Brunswick took issue with Harnik by denying that the psychotic reaction was a transient negative reac- tion to a positive interpretation. She felt that the mounting passivity activated by the primal-scene material eventuated in the patient's fear of being stared at, which reached such proportions as to seek a way out in paranoid path- ways. In response to this, Harnik (1931) continued to insist upon the reacti- vated pregenital oral factors as the specific determinations of the developing paranoia. He related the whole paranoid illness to the orality of the Wolf Man, which to him was the crucial feature in the latter's character structure.

In all of this discussion, the question which I have raised is not really an- swered. That question was what in the dream itself, either in the manifest or latent content, could have presaged the outbreak of a full-blown psychosis? It was clear that the megalomania protected the Wolf Man against many fears and was obviously a cloak for his passive homosexuality. For him to accept this was apparently unbearable, but it is not clear why this should result in a psychotic break, unless one is to assume that all of this was taking place in a person who was borderline (Blum, 1974; Wolberg, 1973), or, as we believe, a psychotic character (Frosch, 1967), in whom manifestations of severe ego defects in the area described were already present and played a role in the continuing inability to deal with an ongoing childhood problem.

As one reviewed the various contributions to the subject of whether there are dreams which presage psychosis, there was some suggestive evidence that this was the case. It was generally felt that in such instances the psyche was struggling with a conflict under the impact of ever-increasing instinctual pres- sure. The psyche, in fact, tries to deal with this ongoingly, at a time and in an ego-state phase-related manner, i.e., during sleep and in the awakened state. Where the instinctual pressures related to the conflict are too great, this struggle will continue into the awakened state; and where there are ego defects which will prevent repression, or there are existing difficulties in the ego's position vis-a-vis reality, breakthrough into the awakened state may eventuate in psychosis and even merge into the psychosis. Such dreams may assume a terrifying, nightmarish, and ego-disintegrative aspect with undisguised instinctual qualities. On the other hand, at a recent panel (Mack, 1969), the consensus was that it would be difficult in the course of analysis to tell whether a dream could presage the outbreak of a psychosis without taking many other factors into consideration. It is, for instance, necessary to understand what was occurring during the analysis at the time. Knowledge of the state of the transference or the course of events in the patient's life could be of help. Previous knowledge and evidence of ego defects suggesting difficulties in relating to reality would be of help in evaluating a dream as presaging psychosis.

CONCLUSIONS

Freud originally formulated the following questions concerning the relationship between dreams and psychosis: (1) What are the etiological and clinical connections between dreams and psychosis? Can, for instance, a dream presage or usher in a psychosis? (2) Are there identifiable psychotic dreams? What are the dreams of the psychotic like? (3) What analogies are there between the structure of dreams and of psychosis? The psychoanalytic contributions to these questions varied, with a degree of consensus in some areas, providing there was a redefinition of the frames of reference used. For instance, there appeared to be similarities and differences between dream and psychosis, the spectrum of viewpoint depending upon the frame of reference used, i.e., the topographic model of the mind, the level of ego cathexis, the function of the ego vis-à-vis reality, etc. Psychophysiological studies emphasized the difference between the two phenomena.

The consensus of many subsequent contributions was that it is difficult in the course of analysis to identify dreams as either presaging or representing psychosis without taking many other factors into consideration. It was suggested that the repetitive occurrence of nightmares in childhood and the consistent pattern of nightmares during analysis are indications of ego weakening, which may have psychotic implications. It was felt by some that dreams reflecting ego disintegration and dreams reflecting loss of ego control occurring at certain periods in the analysis could be of some significance. It should be emphasized that, whether the dream occurs during analysis or during other forms of exploratory psychotherapy, or the same dream occurs spontaneously in a nontreatment setting, is not without import, since the latter should be viewed as more malignant and significant of psychotic implication. It is generally agreed that a patient's attitude toward dreams, reflected in difficulties in differentiating dreams from reality and in the persistence of dreamlike states invading waking life, is most significant and generally reflects already-existing severe ego defects vis-à-vis reality. There appeared to be general agreement that the psychosis which follows a dream represents the ongoing work of a defective ego trying to deal with a dangerous threat deriving frequently from childhood. However, most recent contributors feel that a dream taken out of the context of the overall clinical situation cannot of itself be seen as either presaging or representing a psychosis during analysis despite the fact that many dreams may appear which are suggestive of this state.

NOTES

1. Are there identifiable dreams indicative of psychosis?
2. This, of course, is not true, as Freud himself later recognized.
3. Withdrawal from thoughts or ideas about objects to the Ucs object representations or things.
4. Freud referred to the nonhallucinatory aspects of the disease, where there is withdrawal from the thing or object representation. This results among other things in the kind of indifferent relation to the environment so common in schizophrenia, in which human relations are impaired, yet the environment remains in some way as part of a perceptual experience. A person's name or the name of an object remains without too much meaning, dissociated from the person or object; so it (namely the name), i.e., the word, may be linked to anything and everything.
5. Implied here is a break with and denial of reality. There is a loss of reality testing, a function of the conscious. Wish fulfillment plays the main role in replacing reality. What he also meant here, I think, is that the system Pcpt, insofar as it relates to external sensory stimuli, is decathected.
6. It should be noted that in these reports no distinction is made between night terrors and nightmares. The former occur during S sleep and seem to have a different form and structure and are viewed as having a closer relationship to psychosis than do nightmares.
7. Dr. Daniel Paul Schreber, who published his *Memories of a Neurotic* in 1903.
8. The author pointed out on a previous occasion (1967a) that this view was questioned by I. R. Feinberg, who asserted that it had been subsequently established that the medication the patient had received induced the increased dreamtime (personal communication).

REFERENCES

Arlow, J. (1949). Anal sensations and feelings of persecution. *Psychoanalytic Quarterly* 18:79-84.

Bartemeier, L. H. (1950). Illness following dreams. *International Journal of Psycho-Analysis* 31,1:8-11.

Bradlow, P. A. (1971). Frontiers of psychiatry. *Roche Reports* 1,1:6.

Brenner, C. (1951). A case of childhood hallucinosis. *Psychoanalytic Study of the Child* 6:235-243.

Brunswick, R. M. (1928). A supplement to Freud's "History of an Infantile Neurosis." *International Journal of Psycho-Analysis* 9,4:439-476.

Brunswick, R. M. (1930) . Rebuttal. *International Zeitschrift fur psychoanalyse.* 16: 1, 128.

Esman, A. H. (1962). Visual hallucinosis in young children. *Psychoanalytic Study of the Child.* 17:334-343.

Federn, P. (1952). *Ego Psychology and the Psychoses,*: ed. E. Weiss. New York Basic Books.

Fisher, C., and Dement, W. (1961). Dreaming and psychosis: observations on the dream sleep cycle during the course of an acute paranoid psychosis. *Bulletin of the Philadelphia Association for Psychoanalysis* 11: 130.

_____(1963). Studies on the psychopathology of sleep and dreams. *American Journal of Psychiatry* 119:1160.

Fisher, C., Byrne, W., Edwards, A., and Kahn, E. (1970). A psychophysiological study of nightmares. *Journal of the American Psychoanalytic Association* 18:4.

Freud, S. (1894). *The Neuropsychosis of Defense. Standard Edition.* Vol. 3, London: Hogarth, 1962.

_____(1900). The Interpretation of Dreams. *Ibid.* 4: 88-92 (1959).

_____(1907). Delusions and dreams in Jensen's Gradiva. *Ibid.* 9:3-114 (1959).

_____(1911). *Psychoanalytic Notes upon an Autobiographical Account of a Case of Paranoia (Dementia Paranoides). Ibid.* Vol. 12 (1958).

_____(1917). A metapsychological supplement to the theory of dreams. *Ibid.* 14:222-235 (1957).

_____(1922). *Some Neurotic Mechanisms in Jealousy, Paranoia and Homosexuality. Ibid.* Vol. 18 (1955).

_____(1933). *Revision of the Theory of Dreams in New Introductory Lectures on Psychosis. Ibid.* Vol. 22 (1964).

_____(1937). *Construction in Analysis. Ibid.* Vol. 23 (1964).

_____(1938). An outline of psychoanalysis. *Ibid.* pp. 144-207.

Frosch, J. and Impastato, D. (1948). The effects of shock treatment on the ego. *Psychoanalytic Quarterly* 17:2

Frosch, J. (1964). The psychotic character-clinical psychiatric considerations. *Psychiatric Quarterly* 38:81-96.

_____(1967a). Severe regressive states during analysis: *introduction. Journal of the American Psychoanalytic Association* 15,3:491-507.

_____(1967b). Severe regressive states during analysis: *summary. Journal of the American Psychoanalytic Association* 15,3:606-625.

_____(1967c). Delusional fixity, sense of conviction and the psychotic conflict. *International Journal of Psycho-Analysis* 48: 475-495.

_____(1970). Psychoanalytic considerations of the psychotic character. *Journal of the American Psychoanalytic Association* 18,1:24-50.

Harnick, J. (1930). Kritisches uber Mack Brunswick's nachtrag zum Freud's geschichte, einer infantile neurose. *International Zeitschrift fur Psychoanalyse.* 16,1:123-127.

Hartmann, E. (1967). *The Biology of Dreaming.* Springfield, Ill.: Thomas.

Kant, O. (1940). Differential diagnosis of schizophrenia in the light of the concept of personality stratification. *American Journal of Psychiatry* 97:1342-357.

_____(1942). Dreams of schizophrenic patients. *J. Nerv. Ment. Dis.* 95:335-347.

Katan, M. (1960). Dreams and psychosis: Their relationship to hallucinatory processes. *International Journal of Psycho-Analysis* 41: 341-351.

Kety, S. (1959). Biochemical theories of schizophrenia. *Science* 29, 3362-3363:1-12.

Lairy, C. (1967). Nocturnal terror, nightmares as protective devices, Report in *Medical Tribune.*

Langs, R. J. (1966). Manifest dreams from three clinical groups. *Archives of General Psychiatry* 14:634-643.

Leveton, A. F. (1961). The night residue. *International Journal of Psycho-Analysis* 42: 506-516.

Lewin, B. (1950). *The Psychoanalysis of Elation.* New York: Horton.

_____(1952). Phobic symptoms and dream interpretation. *Psychoanalytic Quarterly* 21:295-322.

_____(1954). Sleep, narcissistic neurosis, and the analytic situation. *Psychoanalytic Quarterly* 23:487-510.

Mack, J. (1965). Nightmares, conflict, and ego development in childhood. *International Journal of Psycho-Analysis* 46: 403-428.

_____(1969a). Dreams and psychosis. Panel Report. *Journal of American Psychoanalysis* 17,1:206.

_____(1969b). Nightmares and acute psychoses: A study of their relationship. (Unpublished manuscript)

_____(1969c). Disordered ego function in the dreaming of acute schizophrenic patients. (Unpublished manuscript)

_____(1970). Nightmare and Human Conflict. Boston: Little, Brown.

Martin, P. (1958). A psychotic episode following a dream. *Psychoanalytic Quarterly* 563-567.

Noble, D. (1951). A study of dreaming in schizophrenia and allied states. *American Journal of Psychiatry* 107: 612-616.

Richardson, G. B., and Moore, R. A. (1963). On the manifest dream in schizophrenia. *Journal of the American Psychoanalytic Association* 11: 281-302.

Schur, H. (1971). Hallucinations in children. *The Unconscious Today: Essays in Honor of Max Schur,* ed. M. Kanzer. New York: International Universities Press.

Sperling, M. (1958). Pavor nocturnus. *Journal of American Psychoanalytic Association* 6: 79-94.

Sterba, R. F. (1946). Dreams and acting out. *Psychoanalytic Quarterly* 15:175-179.

Van Ophuipsen, J. H. W. (1920). On the origin of the feeling of persecution. *International Journal of Psycho-Analysis* 1: 231-234.

The Mirror Transference in the Psychoanalytic Psychotherapy of Alcoholism: A Case Report

James Gustafson, M.D.

Assistant Professor of Psychiatry
University of Wisconsin Medical School

The development of a mirror transference in the successful outpatient psychoanalytic psychotherapy of an alcoholic patient is described in this paper. Important features of the case were a very severe initial period of resistance, a dramatic shift from a climate of bitterness and rancor to one of quiet and satisfaction that coincided with the establishment of the mirroring relationship, then recall of important genetic material, and, finally, a period of many gains in the patient's contemporary relationships.

Very few interpretations were given. The psychotherapy was chiefly an attempt to provide the object relationship that would be therapeutic, an archaic relationship of the grandiose self and the mirroring self-object. The theoretical work of Balint and Kohut was applied to this problem (with the alcoholic patient) and proved extremely helpful in predicting the major turning points in the psychotherapy and in guiding the strategy of the therapist. The principal difficulty not fully predicted was the extent and depth of the resistance to a positive transference; once this resistance was overcome, the psychotherapy proceeded in a way similar to that generally described by Kohut with regard to patients who became involved in a mirror transference.

INTRODUCTION

There are probably a great variety of separate personality constellations and psychopathologies for which alcoholism serves as the common solution (Devito et al., 1970; Yorke, 1970). Since the broad category of alcoholic patients is generally considered resistant to successful psychoanalytic psychotherapeutic treatment, it becomes important to identify those types that are treatable and by what means. One such type is the patient whose alcoholism represents primarily an expression of a narcissistic personality disorder (Kohut, 1971).

Kohut devotes only a few paragraphs to alcoholism and addiction in his monograph, enough to outline the subject, but there have been no case studies in depth reported from this perspective. Balint (1968) describes a similar level of pathology, which he terms "the level of the basic fault," also briefly in relation to the special defensive solutions of alcoholism and addiction. However, to the best of my knowledge, there have been no in-depth case studies of the treatment of an alcoholic patient from this point of view either. Kohut and Balint have recommended strategies of treatment for the narcissistic personality disorder (the basic fault), and reported considerable success based on these strategies, but we do not know to what extent they can be successfully applied to those narcissistic patients whose defensive solutions include addiction to alcohol.

The present case report describes such a successful application of the ideas of Kohut and Balint to the psychotherapy of a very self-destructive alcoholic patient whose core disturbance proved to be that of a narcissistic personality disorder (or a disturbance at the level of the basic fault). How common such patients are within the general class of alcoholics remains to be discovered. Hence how broadly applicable the management of this case may prove to be cannot be known at this time. The general plan of this paper is as follows. I will begin with a brief summary of previous psychoanalytic work on the nature of the relationship between the analyst or therapist and the alcoholic patient. Next, I will delineate the views of Kohut and Balint in considerable detail, insofar as they also apply to this relationship between analyst or therapist and alcoholic patient. Finally, I will present and discuss what I took to be the decisive events in my treatment case.

The descriptions of what the alcoholic patient seeks from the therapist have been quite consistent, from Knight (1937) to Chafetz (1959) to Silber (1974). What each writer details is an individual with massive passive-dependent wishes, a need to control the need-fulfilling object, and rage when this is thwarted. Many other motivations are also described, including homosexual gratifications, relief from punitive introjects, and so forth. Yet the patient's wish for a passive-dependent relationship remains a typical finding, and the recommended therapeutic relationship attempts to meet this need constructively. Knight (1937) argues for the necessity of supplying substitutes for alcohol, both literally in the form of other liquids and in the form of a kindly attitude; yet the therapist must also limit these offers: "Too much frustration will spoil the necessary tender relationship between physician and patient, and too much gratification will lead to experiments in drinking (which by now he feels he has under perfect control)." Chafetz (1959) recommends a similar therapeutic relationship, and the therapist's chief consideration again turns upon the limits to gratification: "While the therapist must be an active, continually supporting substitute for alcohol, he cannot help being aware of the insatiable demands of alcoholic patients." Silber (1974) starts from a similar assessment of the patient's impossible wishes and rage at these being thwarted. Silber suggests a method that will gratify the magical wishes, and yet assist the patient with his difficulty with limits. The method is to focus, very early in the treatment, on the patient's anxiety over his rage at important, but secondary, persons in his current environment. The primary relationships, with parent or mate or therapist, are not to be interpreted in this way. "Since this was all initiated early in the therapy, a magical element was introduced: the therapist had a special knowledge about what was going on in the patient's mind, and was thus elevated into the role of a magical, omnipotent figure." Thus, the gratification has a different emphasis from that described by Knight and Chafetz: the therapist provides special understanding rather than literal nurturance.

This difference is a critical one for Balint (1969). The latter thinks that there are many patients who can be treated in a therapeutic relationship which provides the right climate of understanding; he calls this "regression aimed at recognition." Silber's strategy would seem to be suitable for these patients. Others demand a "regression aimed at [literal] gratification." For these patients, it seems that one must manage the gratification as best one can, as suggested by Knight and Chafetz.

Balint's views about how to manage such a "benign regression" (aimed at recognition) and how to recognize patients who require this kind of therapeutic relationship are not easy to summarize, having been developed over several decades and many papers. Balint devoted a small book, *The Basic Fault*, (1968) to summarizing his views. We may only outline his major points here and refer the reader to the book for further understanding.

We should emphasize first that the alcoholic patient, in Balint's view, is only one special type of the general category of patients who suffer from narcissistic disorders, but a type that dramatically illustrates the general problem, because of clear and rapid shifts between adult and primitive relationships. The alcoholic, according to Balint, forms shaky object relationships, and is easily thrown off his balance when there is a clash of interest with the love object. The alcoholic withdraws into solitary narcissism, which makes him feel the center of every attention, but forsaken and miserable. "The first effect of intoxication is invariably the establishment of a feeling that everything is now well between them and their environment," that is, a state of "harmony" is reestablished, the yearning for which Balint feels is the most important cause for alcoholism (p. 55). Interestingly enough, Bateson (1971), approaching the subject from an entirely different theoretical tradition, came to a nearly parallel formulation in the terms of generaly systems theory.

The critical implication for treatment is that this state of "harmony" can be generated in the psychotherapeutic relationship, relieving the patient from the need to seek it through alcohol. The conditions are these: "the absolute demand that one partner—the analyst—must be 'in tune' with the other—the patient—all the time, the absence of conflict, the relative unimportance of the customary forms of interpretation" (p. 58). If there is to be a "benign (therapeutic) regression," given these conditions, it has five primary characteristics, according to Balint: (1) a mutually trusting, unsuspecting relationship is formed without much difficulty, in which the patient feels at peace; (2) the patient has the sense of a "new beginning" in which he discovers new freedom to behave as a child in relation to the analyst, and which in turn allows him freedom in adult relationships; (3) the regression is for the sake of recognition of his internal problems rather than for (4) demands, expectations, and other "needs"; (5) there is an absence of hysterical symptomatology or genital-orgastic elements in the regressed transference.

Kohut (1971) has described very similar regressive relationships which support the therapeutic effort. The vocabulary developed by Kohut is different from that of Balint, but I think the range of phenomena described by each is essentially the same or overlapping in most aspects. Balint's writing is the more poetic and evocative, whereas Kohut's terminology is helpful in defining more precisely some crucial aspects of the therapeutic process. [1] Again, as with Balint, Kohut treats alcoholism as a special type of narcissistic disorder, the special characteristics of which he has given some attention to. In summary, Kohut thinks that the ego of the addict (alcoholic) lacks certain functions that would allow him to soothe himself, insulate himself against overstimulation and supply himself with tension-reducing gratification. For these purposes he requires an archaic object relationship in which these functions are provided by the external object. In a regressive archaic relationship in which the boundaries between self and other are blurred, and the analyst becomes a "self-object," these aforementioned ego functions of the analyst are put in the service of the patient, who has lacked them. Thus, Kohut gives a more precise description of what functions are shared in the "harmony" or "harmonious mix-up" of the patient-analyst relationship. Kohut also describes several important variations on the connection between the more adult relationships of the patient and the archaic self-object relationship: namely, the possibility of either a "horizontal" or "vertical" splitting of these ego states. In "horizontal" splitting, the archaic object relationship is repressed; in "vertical" splitting, these relationships are acted out side by side with the more adult ones, but in different situations, at different times, and with different persons. The use of alcoholic intoxication in order to achieve a state of "harmony" with archaic objects would be an instance of "vertical splitting," the patient alternating between modest, sober adult states and intoxicated grandiose states of involvement in archaic object relationships. This structural formulation fits with Balint's clinical descriptions of the rapid alteration from adult to primitive object relationships.

Furthermore, Kohut describes two important variations of the archaic object relationship, which is mobilized in the transference: namely, the idealizing transference arises from the revival of the idealized parent imago, with which the patient tries to maintain a continuous union. Silber's description of the therapeutic relationship with his group of alcoholic patients is consistent with this paradigm. [2] However, there is another important variation of the archaic relationship which is quite distinct metapsychologically and which requires an entirely different therapeutic strategy: this is the mirror transference, which depends on the mobilization of the grandiose self (as opposed to the idealized parent imago, a self-object). The analyst's function in this relationship is to be an extension of the grandiose self: in the most primitive form, the merger transference, the analyst is experienced as an extension of the grandiose self over which the patient expects unquestioned dominance; a less primitive form, the alter ego transference, involves the analyst as either the same as or very much like the patient; the mirror transference in the narrower sense requires the analyst to mirror the patient's exhibitionistic display and thus to confirm it.

Balint also describes two variations on the archaic narcissistic relationship, for which he has coined two unusual names, ocnophilia and philobatism.

> The ocnophil's reaction to the emergence of objects is to cling to them, to introject them, since he feels lost and insecure without them; apparently he chooses to *over-cathect his object relationships*. The other type, the philobat, *over-cathects his own ego functions*, and develops skills in this way, in order to be able to maintain himself alone with very little, or even no, help from his objects. . . . In the philobatic world the objectless expanses retain the original primary cathexis and are experienced as safe and friendly, while the objects are felt as treacherous hazards. [p. 68]

These formulations are clearly parallel to those of Kohut, ocnophilia to the idealizing transference, philobatism to the mirror transference. However, in the latter pair of formulations, the emphasis falls differently: both philobatism and the mirror transference involve "overcathexis" of aspects of the self; but in philobatism the description emphasizes the pleasure in objectless expanses, whereas in the mirror transference the emphasis is upon the devoted attachment of an attentive object to the grandiose self. In my own clinical practice, I have found that these two characteristics commonly are shared by the same patients, namely, a pleasure in objectless expanses and a pleasure in mirroring the wanderings of the self through such spaces. Both aspects confirm the grandiose self. Both characteristics are found together in Ernest Jones's description of the God complex (1951).

Finally, Kohut augments Balint's descriptions with a precise formulation of the stages in the analysis of narcissistic patients. The first stage is that of resistance to the mirror or idealizing transference: in the case of the mirror transference, the patient fears isolation or rejection if the extent of his narcissistic aims were known; or he may fear the pain of giving up some aspects of these aims in entering the relationship. Kohut thinks that these early resistances are easily overcome if the therapist is simply empathic with the presentations of the patient. The second stage is that of the mirror (or idealizing) transference itself: the heart of the treatment here is the revelation of the grandiose fantasies of the patient. There are many more complexities of this second phase, to which Kohut has devoted several long chapters ("The Therapeutic Process in the Mirror Transference"; "Some Reactions of the Analyst to the Mirror Transferences") in his monograph (1971), which may only be summarized here. Two important factors in therapeutic change are these: the mirroring of the grandiose self helps to keep it mobilized in the therapeutic relationship, despite the fact that its infantile aims are frustrated. "Under the pressure of the renewed frustrations the patient tries to avoid the pain (1) by recreating the pre-transference equilibrium through the establishment of a vertical split and/or of a (horizontal) repression barrier; or (b) through regressive evasion" (p. 198). These two undesirable escape routes are blocked by transference interpretations and genetic reconstructions which assist the cooperative ego: "In view of the fact that all regressive roads are blocked while the infantile wish for mirroring is kept alive without being gratified in its infantile form, the psyche is forced to create new structures which transform and elaborate the infantile need along aim-inhibited and realistic lines" (p. 199).

Having reviewed the work of Kohut, Balint, and others, we may turn to considering the alcoholic patient whom I saw in outpatient psychotherapy for approximately one year. The work divided very clearly into two phases, the first a phase of severe resistance, during which I saw the patient twice a week for six months, and the second phase, in which a mirror transference was established, during which I saw the patient three times a week for six months.

CASE MATERIAL

The patient, Mr. A, forty-two years of age, married for twenty years, with no children, had been a heavy drinker since the age of sixteen when he left home. Briefly the major events that emerged in his history were as follows: His mother had a stroke when he was three, leaving her with a severe aphasia, but nevertheless she remained the parent who took daily care of the patient. She and the patient fell to yelling and fighting continually with each other. The patient felt continually misunderstood by his mother, whose use of lan-

guage was restricted to short phrases, and who, thus, probably *did* continually misunderstand the intentions of the child or failed to convey her understanding. In a personal communication, Dr. Kohut has suggested that the
language impairment accounts for only one aspect of the disturbance in the
relationship between this patient and his aphasic mother: "I would assume
that without a broader disturbance in empathy (perhaps as a consequence of
emotional dulling due to an organic defect in the basal ganglia) the language
disturbance would not have been (equally) traumatic." A sister, three years
older, and his father left him at the mercy of his mother. The father continually worked, including evenings and weekends, at his office, and rarely took
the boy anywhere. When he did appear, it was to lecture the boy and berate
him for his halting replies: "Come out with it, why do you take so long to say
things?" He slept in his father's bed until age twelve, and again when he returned from the army at age nineteen.

Eight years prior to starting psychotherapy, he had a myocardial infarction
and subsequent open heart surgery on the coronary vessels. He was *abstinent*
for the next three years. Four years prior to therapy, he fell in love with a
beautiful, narcissistic woman, with whom he had a tumultuous affair. Their
relationship, at first ecstatic and very gratifying sexually, became more and
more revengeful, that is, like his relationship with his mother. The surgical
bypass of occluded coronary vessels, two years prior to therapy, shut down a
few weeks later in the midst of more retribution between the patient and his
mistress. The patient's father died about this time as well. The angina became so severe that he was operated on again one and a half years prior to
therapy, and a Weinberg procedure was performed.

Thus, there was strong evidence for a sudden, traumatic disturbance in the
mother's capacity to mirror the intentions and capacities of the three-year-
old child. According to Kohut, such a complete and sudden shift in the
mother's involvement in the child is a typical history for patients who will develop a mirror transference in the psychotherapy (pp. 253-254).

At the time of therapy Mr. A was taking over a hundred nitroglycerin
tablets per week for angina. He had been involved in several automobile accidents while drunk, nearly costing him his life. He was drunk more days than
not. He had broken off the relationship with his mistress, but thought of little
else but her. He had seen one psychiatrist while in his twenties for a few visits.
He came for psychotherapy, he said, because he was destroying his life. He
had always been considered "no good" and felt compelled to "fuck up." He
was referred by a physician friend.

The first six months we met twice a week. The themes were consistent: (1)
on the one hand, how bitterly disappointed he had been by his cardiac surgeon, his mistress, an encounter group leader, his wife, and so on; all had
used him to make themselves look good, and with no consideration for his

needs; (2) his own remarkable power of recuperation and his power to "fuck up" whatever was going well.

An example of our hours together in this period went, briefly, like this: I (therapist) was right in the last hour about his pride. He delighted in being able to see into customers, selling them articles they didn't want, or in keeping his mistress under his thumb. He didn't want to let anyone "help" him; he would do the opposite of what doctors told him. (A brief episode of angina at this point.) He hated his surgeon, and envied him his confidence; he resented the doctor's view of the failed operation and regarded it as a great technical failure for the doctor! (The patient's failure to get better not appearing to matter.) Yet he made the "fastest recovery ever seen." He thought of running in the Boston Marathon. He could drink because his body "can take anything." The next hour was missed; he got drunk and ended up in the state hospital. He said, on returning, that he felt "defenseless" after the last hour, markedly exposed to criticism from me. During the drunk, he had pulled a coup, which he reported with an air of triumph: walking into a bar without money, he claimed that he had to have a loan or the lady cab driver outside would beat him up. His audience roared with laughter and gave him money.

My responses to these accounts were intended to be empathic, to reflect accurately that I understood the pleasure and anxiety of his performances and his anger and anxiety over being used by the surgeon or others. For many months, however, this seemed to make little difference, save that he did keep coming regularly. The pattern, exemplified by this last hour, was one of narcissistic display, or rage at those who used him, followed by drunkenness. The anxiety, reported in this last hour as his feeling "defenseless," seemed to be based on the fear of alienating me by his displays or his rage and causing me to retaliate. This anxiety, which was frequently manifested in the hours as angina, seemed to be relieved temporarily by the drunkenness, in which he seemed to be able to mobilize his grandiose self with some sense of triumph, as in the example in which he compelled others to appreciate his wit and provide for him. This would be a very clear example of vertical splitting (Kohut, 1971), through which the patient keeps the intense archaic object relationship separate from the therapeutic relationship. Of course, as Kohut has emphasized, this is not only motivated by the anxiety of alienating the therapist by the manifestations of the grandiose self, but also by the secondary gains of continuing a pleasureful acting out. Such secondary gain may contribute importantly to lengthening this phase of resistance to establishing the mirror transference, which lasted six months, rather than yielding easily to the empathy of the therapist, as would be typical of most narcissistic patients described by Kohut.

This pattern of the first several months was interrupted by an automobile accident, in which the patient nearly lost his life, but escaped serious physical

harm. The patient had lost control of his car while drunk. He was very frightened by this, and he resolved to stop drinking for several months, until New
Year's, which he managed to do. I then began to hear, regularly, bitter and
detailed criticism of the mistress and the surgeon. The theme was their devotion to their own selfish aims, with utter disregard for the patient himself. He
became very incapacitated by angina during this phase, feeling empty and as
if he were "locked in a vise." The transference implications of his position
seemed to be that a close relationship with me would also be a hell of being
used by me and entailing bitter and vicious attacks and counterattacks. This
became quite clear when he told me that he had decided to quit psychotherapy. He said that he had decided to be responsible for himself, and that he
was tired of being a "case" for doctors. I urged him to continue, inasmuch as
we were getting to the point of intensity where I might be useful to him. In the
next hour, he poured out a wealth of material about how he was treated by
the surgeon and how helpless and enraged he felt. He then made his own
transference interpretation about confusing me with the other doctor (the
surgeon). In retrospect, it has seemed to me that my countertransference during this period had resulted in my treating him somewhat distantly as a
"case." The intensity of his rage and his displays led to a subtle withdrawal,
which was hidden from me by my idea that I was being consistently and stra-
tegically empathic concerning his situation. In fact, I was being empathic
from a considerable and cool distance. This, according to Kohut, is a typical
countertransference reaction:

> The most common dangers to which the analyst is exposed vis-a-vis the
> twinship and merger are boredom, lack of emotional involvement with the
> patient and precarious maintenance of attention (including such second-
> ary reactions as overt anger, exhortations, and forced interpretations of re-
> sistances, as well as other forms of the rationalized acting out of tensions
> and impatience). [1971, p. 273]

After this crisis, subtle signs of a new climate in the therapy began to appear with increasing frequency over the next two months. These would take
the form of a quiet, peaceful smiling after he had recounted certain kinds of
incidents: for instance, how he had talked to his wife at length and she had
listened ("I talk. She listens."). My own capacity to respond with more
warmth also was recovered in this period. For instance, when I reflected to
him how it must feel to be confined in the narrow space of his house by the
angina, he also seemed to relax and smile with appreciation. These were har-
bingers of the mirror transference that was to become clear after about two
months of oscillation between incidents like these and further descriptions of
bitterness with his mistress. Both of these incidents show the patient's appreciation for warm and accurate mirroring of the patient's self and his predica-

ment. A more decided change in tone occurred during a very quiet hour which the patient began by saying that he didn't have much to say and didn't know what he had accomplished. I commented on the smile which followed this statement, to which he replied, smiling again, that he could spend his time as well drinking coffee. He then said that he had come to the conclusion that his bitter brooding was some kind of avoidance of looking to the future. I agreed that his blaming of others or of himself did seem to leave him in the same place. In the next hour, he continued, wondering thoughtfully, "How do I get out of all this blaming?" He said that he continually swung between blaming others and then blaming himself: "When I blame myself I can keep the same thing going because there is nothing to do about it and I'm still not responsible." "But then pride enters in—if I begin to take responsibility—then I'd have to admit I was wrong before." He then began to laugh aloud, for the first time since I had known him, and said: "There's no humiliation in this—People I'm close to *know* I've been wrong about a few things!" I then reflected to him in the same spirit, "Then it wouldn't exactly be a new idea for your friends to think, 'A (the patient's name) surely is wrong about this or that.' " He continued to laugh heartily, which was a dramatic change for a man who had been little but grimly serious for the first six months of our work. I then said, "But it would be a new kind of relationship with them to be open about your shortcomings?" to which he replied that he had induced so much tension and hatred in himself by the previous way he related with them.

These several sessions had the quality of a "new beginning" as described by Balint: the emergence of new behavior and energy in the context of an unsuspecting, trustful relationship. The next session he reported he had been drinking again, but the tone with which he reported it was altogether different: while drinking at home, he had listened to records of Barbra Streisand, his adolescent love, with satisfaction. In the subsequent sessions, a quiet, slow, but moving conversation took the place of bitter, rapid accusation. He said he was relieved not to feel so full of hate. He was relieved not to be hurried. His father had always impatiently said, "Get to the point." Now he felt I could wait for him to express himself as he needed to. I probably had begun to appreciate his need for this unhurried relationship in the month previous and probably did slow down the pace of my own interventions, letting him finish his thoughts without interruption, and so forth. It did seem to me that this slow tempo and quiet was more important than the content of what I said to him in providing the right conditions for his "new beginning." Why is this the case? In the first place, we have the patient's direct statement that hurried interruption reminds him of his relationship with his father, and is thus tantamount to inducing a negative transference. In the second place, we know from his history that his mother continually yelled at him from the time that he was three years old, when she had had a stroke and had become aphasic.

Perhaps prior to this traumatic disruption, he had had a peaceful, unhurried, satisfying relationship with his mother. We do not know, but his acute sensitivity to the nonverbal qualities of the climate provided in my office would be consistent with this hypothesis: that is, when I left him in peace to express himself slowly and carefully, I was being like his mother in the first years; when I inadvertently conveyed to him that he should move along or when I jumped in with my thoughts, I was reminding him of the traumatic years that followed with both mother and father. According to Balint, this nonverbal or preverbal sensitivity is one of the central qualities of these patients who are capable of a new beginning, once the sensitivity is appreciated and adjusted to by the analyst. Generally, with these patients, when one does not yet appreciate the specific requirements of the necessary "climate," one does well to provide an environment with as few irritants as possible. The classical analytic setting usually is suitable: "the quiet, well-tempered room, a comfortable couch, unexciting environment, the analyst not interrupting the patient unnecessarily, the patient being given full opportunity to speak his mind, and so on. On the whole, this kind of satisfaction might be described also as looking-after, or even as a kind of psychological nursing" (1968, p. 186).

This patient seemed to have great difficulty soothing and calming himself: that is, he tended to become overstimulated, tense and bitter, and contentious, as he continually demonstrated in the first six months of treatment. As Balint would say, when I became "attuned" to this and began to respond to his occasional smiling, his pauses, his need for a very slow unfolding, I helped him to calm himself. It does seem clear in reviewing my notes, and the occasions for them, that I made many fewer responses to the exciting, irritating aspects of his presentation and more responses to his smiling and pleasure and thoughtfulness as the case went on. Thus I mirrored the patient's capacity to soothe and insulate himself against overstimulation, which seemed to have the effect that he could then do this better for himself when he was away from me and on his own.

What then was the nature of this mirroring relationship which helped the patient to calm himself? How did the mirroring help him to provide this for himself? The reader will perhaps remember Kohut's formulation: the alcoholic lacks these ego functions, that would allow him to soothe himself, insulate himself against overstimulation, and supply himself with tension-reducing gratification. In a regressive archaic relationship in which the boundaries between self and other are blurred, and the therapist becomes a "self-object," these aforementioned ego functions of the therapist are put in the service of the patient who lacks them. Kohut's formulations about the alcoholic or addict are made in one of his chapters on the idealizing transference, as if all alcoholic or addictive patients would require an idealizing transference to be able to control their internal tension. In fact, as I am demonstrating here,

Kohut's formulation is easily modified: the patient has the ego functions to soothe himself, etc., but is unable to use them until they are mirrored or confirmed in the context of an archaic relationship with the therapist in which the boundaries between patient and therapist are blurred. The patient's situation is like that of a young child who has acquired the capacity to soothe himself, through thumb-sucking, holding onto a favorite blanket, or some other use of a transitional object. However, this child often needs the mother's support for these self-comforting activities, which is given by the mother's confirming smile or pat on the head or even a reminder to go get the blanket. Or the child may need to come away from the exciting situation that is making him too tense, so that he may administer his self-calming help to himself. In these ways, the mother gives invaluable aid to the child's capacity to calm himself and is thus part of his system for doing this. She has to be quite in tune with his level of tension and also with his capacity to do something helpful for himself. In this sense of intimate rapport and confirmation of the child's capacities, there is a blurring of the boundaries between child and mother, who together constitute one tension-reducing system. This is the way in which the mirror transference with the alcoholic patient revives an archaic relationship and functions as such to help the patient calm himself and thus have less need for alcohol to help him perform these functions.

What was unmistakable was that a rather dramatic change in the climate of the therapeutic relationship, from one of hurried bitterness to unhurried calm, took place at the same time as many manifestations of the mirror transference appeared. I have explained how the mirror transference would accomplish this calming effect; now I would give the further evidence that such a mirror transference was established at this point in our relationship. Several hours after the "new beginning" I have described, in which the patient had felt he could leave off blaming and had begun to laugh so heartily, he asked if he could come three times a week, and I agreed after some discussion. Within the same hour that this request was made, the patient compared himself with Stewart Alsop, the columnist who had died of cancer; however bleak his situation, he had gotten something out of the treatment, which was a new interest in reading newspapers. This sense of common fate, and thus a common bond, with Stewart Alsop, seemed to have enabled him to take an interest in Alsop's field. Quiet references to this fantasy relationship with Alsop continued through several hours after the "new beginning." This sense of alter ego or twinship relations of a grandiose nature continued to be observable in dream and fantasy material, and I will return to it later. These materials would suggest the "alter ego" version of the mirror transference was present, but generally I felt that his expectations from me were for mirroring in the strict sense rather than for my being just like him. That is, he began to tell me directly how much he wished to be approved of and admired, how he had felt impelled to swim across the lake alone, to walk the parapets of a ten-story hotel, to be admired in the bar, and so forth. Yet these solo honors never had satisfied him and he had ended up damaging himself. He often wept in telling me about these exploits, and seemed very grateful that I understood how his wish to be admired had driven him. Kohut comments on this charac-teristic phase of treatment as follows: "Hand in hand with the increasing ac-ceptance of his archaic narcissism, and with the increasing dominance of his ego over it, the patient will grasp the inefficacy of the former narcissistic dis-play in the split-off sector" (1971, p. 185). As is evident from Kohut's ac-counts, it is not uncommon for a patient to show some evidence for an alter-ego transference, but yet to move into a mirror transference in the stricter sense (Kohut, p. 250).

I have devoted considerable detail to the first six months of the treatment and the overcoming of the severe resistance to the mirror transference rela-tionship, since, in this aspect, the case of this alcoholic patient differs so clear-ly from the majority of cases of narcissistic personality described by Kohut. Such resistance is also unusual for those patients described by Balint as capa-ble of a new beginning. In summary, my findings concerning this period were as follows: (1) Contrary to the typical case of narcissistic personality, the "ap-propriately attentive, but unobtrusive and noninterfering behavior of the analyst" did not suffice to remove the initial resistance to the regression into a mirror transference (Kohut, p. 29). (2) "Vertical splitting" of the grandiose states of mind (experienced while intoxicated) from the sober analytic rela-tionships was the initial form of the resistance. (3) The next form of the resis-tance (after a nearly catastrophic auto accident persuaded the patient to quit drinking and blocked his expression of the grandiosity in the drinking) was a bitter, tense several months in which the patient seemed to be saying that any close relationship would be a hell of mutual recriminations. This was partial-ly relieved by a transference interpretation, made essentially by the patient, about how he had confused me with the surgeon who had hurt and used him. (4) A countertransference problem, that had kept me at a rather cool and detached distance was overcome after the transference interpretation had been made. (5) I gradually became attuned to the patient's need for a very slow and quiet unfolding of his thoughts without interruption and for mirror-ing of his smile and "small" pleasures. This resulted in the patient's increasing capacity to calm himself and thus change the bitter, contentious climate of the treatment. Balint's formulation about the preverbal needs of the patient and Kohut's formulation concerning the need for an archaic relationship to provide the basis for the exercise of tension-reducing functions were found to be applicable to the events of this phase. (6) A "new beginning" of a relative-ly unsuspecting, trustful relationship in which the patient felt it no longer necessary to restrict himself to blaming others or himself relieved the patient of the "viselike" constriction that had held him for the previous several months. (7) This new climate of unhurried calm in the treatment coincided with the clear establishment of a mirror transference relationship, in which the patient brought forward directly his wish to be thought well of and the perilous exploits he had performed in order to be admired previously.

A very recent contribution by Anna Ornstein provides a theoretical bridge for connecting these findings (1-7). She suggests that the *characterological* defenses often block the emergence of the therapeutic narcissistic transferences:

> One obvious difference between optimal infantile conditions and the narcissistic transferences is the presence of character features in the patient that may resist the perception of the analyst's empathy. The analyst's empathy and the patient's increased ability to perceive it are the conditions that constitute the *sine qua non* for the establishment of relatively stable narcissistic equilibria in the transference. [pp. 238-239]

In her case illustration, she shows how a patient's masochistic-paranoid character defenses distorted the perception of the analyst: the latter was believed to be only interested in the patient when she felt bad; feeling good was believed to lead to loss of interest and desertion by the analyst, as it had with her mother. The analyst's real interest and warmth could not be perceived, and, hence, a mirror transference could not be established, until this masochistic merger transference was worked through.

This hypothesis would also explain the long period of resistance to the mirror transference in the present case we are discussing. As the patient himself stated, closeness for him meant a hell of mutual recriminations, such as he had had with his mother following her stroke, and such as he had repeated later with his mistress. However, this intense masochistic-paranoid merger with the mother was all he had to hold onto, as long as his father remained unavailable to him. The earlier archaic mirroring object relationship that was later mobilized was both disavowed and repressed (vertical and horizontal splitting). As Ornstein suggests, the character defenses (merger) act as " 'fortifications' of the primary modes of defense—disavowal and repression" (p. 234). Thus, our patient would hold onto the masochistic-paranoid merger with me, perceive my interest in masochistic and paranoid terms, look elsewhere for empathy (vertical splitting), and gradually involve me in the masochistic-paranoid relationship, for which distance and coolness would be one countertransference reaction (1-4). The transference interpretation (3) allowed the patient to begin to hear my interest as genuine, in contradistinction to that of the mistress and the surgeon. My overcoming my countertransference reaction, appreciating his need for a very slow and quiet unfolding and mirroring (4-7) provided him with the new beginning of the narcissistic equilibrium that he needed. Both aspects, I think, were crucial: overcoming the "viselike" masochistic-paranoid merger, and offering "the appropriately attentive, but unobtrusive and noninterfering behavior of the analyst."

The next major shift in the treatment that needs explanation occurred about three to four months after this clear establishment of the mirror transference and consisted of the patient's cessation of all drinking and a reduction in his need for nitroglycerin (for angina) by one-third. I cannot explain this second major change as clearly as the first. In general, what I could observe is that the lesser need for alcohol and nitroglycerin signified a major reduction in his state of bodily tension and that this reduction in tension followed revelations to me of the intense need he had had for a close relationship with his father. He had needed to be rescued by the father from the terrible burden of being left alone with his aphasic mother. Being left alone with her had filled him with tension, rage, and guilt. The recall of these very painful memories, in the safe, buffering context of the mirror transference relationship, seemed to result in a general reduction of bodily tension.

I will describe only two incidents from the long series of hours in which painful memories were recalled, to give the reader some sense of this period. In the first incident, the patient told me about how he had gone to the bar on Saint Patrick's Day in a green vest, green tie, and green shirt, with a figurine leprechaun. He was having a good time, as he said, talking with his leprechaun, when he accidentally dropped it and it broke. He ended up hurling the remains of the leprechaun at a wall. When he got to this point in his narrative, he began sobbing and then later said that the only other time he had felt this way was when his father died. When I asked him in the next hour about the leprechaun and what it had meant to him, he told me that it reminded him of the song he had always loved and which he had listened to before he had gone to the bar that day. The song was "Danny Boy," which he went on to explain was a song about a father saying good-bye to his son, sending him to war. When I asked the patient what the father says to the son, he replied that the father says, "I love you so much," and then the patient began to sob again and shake. In these two hours, the patient clearly brought forward the intensity of his need to be loved, and began to grieve over the loss of his father or the loss of the father that he had imagined for himself, that was represented by the leprechaun.

The second incident, several months later and just prior to his report of having ceased drinking and having reduced his need for nitroglycerin, began with an hour in which the patient reported himself in a rage with me, feeling an urge to break up my office. In the next hour, he reported the following dream: "My dad and a lawyer are sitting at the kitchen table. I am filling a black bag—with trash . . . hangers are sticking out—I am falling off a curb with the weight of it. My father stands by (doing nothing) — It's the same be-wilderment." His associations were that the black bag represented all his dif-ficulties, for which his father offered no help, that the father had even resisted his seeing a psychiatrist early in his twenties because the father was afraid of being criticized. I did not interpret or explore the connection between his rage at me in the previous hour and the dream which would seem to explain the transference (from father to me). In retrospect, this seems like an over-sight, but in any case I did not make transference interpretations concerning the patient's rage at me, in the last few months of treatment. Instead, I said that I appreciated from the dream how intensely bereft he must have felt and how this explained more clearly than before his anger at his father. Whether or not it was an error, the effect of not interpreting this aspect of the transfer-ence was twofold: (1) the patient began to experience his anger at other peo-ple in his present life who had let him down, and he began to defend himself quite appropriately in relation to these people; (2) within a month, he had decided he had gotten what he had needed from me and was ready to termi-nate. An agreed-upon termination followed after yet another month. I will return to this last phase, but, in regard to the second major shift in the treat-ment, that of the reduction of bodily tension and cessation of the need for al-cohol and reduction of the need for nitroglycerin, my main point is that this was preceded by the intense emergence of memories and affects concerning the patient's father. The patient seemed able to tolerate these painful memo-ries because of the stability of his mirror transference relationship with me. Kohut explains this phase of treatment as follows:

The transference, however, functions here as a specific therapeutic buffer. In the mirror transference in the narrower sense the patient is able to mobi-lize his grandiose fantasies and exhibitionism on the basis of the hope that the therapist's empathic participation and emotional response will not al-low the narcissistic tensions to reach excessively painful or dangerous levels. [Kohut, p. 191]

Some of my explanation then is that the tension that had been generated by the need to repress these memories and affects was reduced. In addition, he became able to discharge narcissistic tensions more directly in his current re-lationships. Why was this the case? I do not think my answer is complete, but, in part, he overcame his intense shame and embarrassment over his intense need to be loved by his father and to be more adequately taken care of by him by presenting these needs to me, with their genetic antecedents and affects, and having them confirmed and appreciated. He subsequently began to act as if he had accepted these needs himself and was thus able to reduce his own tension over them appropriately. When he began to be able to do this for himself, he no longer needed alcohol and had much less need for nitroglycer-in. In other words, as the intensely charged unconscious narcissistic aspirations (to be loved and taken care of) were brought into awareness and into contact with the central reality ego, they became progressively more neutralized and capable of being channeled into daily, realistic pursuits, thus enabling the patient to reduce his own tension. (Kohut; 1971, p. 187 and p. 248)

In a personal communication, Dr. Kohut suggested that the shift of the transference, in this case from the mother to the father, represents a typical event in the successful treatment of narcissistic personality disorders. The child turns

> from a frustrating self-object to the other self-object; . . . narcissistic psychopathology occurs only when both attempts to gain the response of the two self-objects fail; . . . in treatment the cure seems to hinge on the re-establishment of empathic contact with the less damaging of the two early self-objects, i.e., often with the father. This movement is in general from mirroring toward idealization. In your case—a more rare sequence—it seems to go from maternal to paternal mirroring.

This perspective explains the first and second phases of treatment and the shift from one to the other most clearly and simply. The first, as previously discussed, consisted of a very frustrating pathological merger with the mother self-object, while the relationship with the paternal self-object was disavowed (vertical splitting) and repressed (horizontal splitting). The second phase was entirely concerned with material concerning the patient's father, his intense wish to be loved, protected, and faithfully mirrored by his father, as represented in the story of Danny Boy and reexperienced in the transference, and the terrible disappointments that had interfered with his getting this from his father, as represented in the dream of the black bag that his father left him with. When these disappointments were to some extent worked through within the protection of the paternal mirroring transference, the patient, in the third phase of treatment, turned back again to the material concerning his mother and was able to reduce his guilt about her and stop injuring himself.

The third and last major event of the treatment, for which we had advanced a preliminary interpretation, was the patient's decision that he had gotten what he needed from the treatment and was ready to terminate. In the last several months of treatment, the patient took a much more active role in relation to the external circumstances of his life and felt free to assert his own wishes where they might conflict with those of other people (which he had not been able to do previously): free not to talk about his problems with other people when he felt this was inappropriate; free to disagree with the police (regarding an alleged traffic violation); free to criticize an official of the Motor Vehicle Division who wanted him to "confess" his alcoholism; free to differ with his priest. He successfully took over the defense of a legal matter in which his lawyer had been dallying. These new capabilities reflect an area of progressive neutralization of narcissistic aims. As Kohut states, "the (new) structures built up in response to the claims of the grandiose self appear in general to deal less with the curbing of the narcissistic demands but with the *channeling and modification of their expression*. (Kohut, p. 187) Thus, the patient made fewer empty grandiose claims, but rather argued in the service of realistic demands. My role in these matters was usually to notice his anxiety as he brought up the issue and to comment on it, and he would proceed to analyze his fear that his demands were not legitimate, etc.

What had prevented him from defending himself previously was most clearly revealed in a series of dreams. I will first summarize the manifest content of these several dreams, which concerned injury to his mother (or his mistress). In the first of this series, he imagined himself locked up in a prison, while watched by his mother. In the second he found himself digging out an area under the floor which revealed a big slab with his mother on it covered by a white sheet. A large white horse then jumped through the opening that had been dug. In the third dream, he brought his mother to me on a hospital bed, and I said I had a colleague directly above who could heal her speech problem. In a fourth, he dreamed that the woman with whom he had had the bitter affair had been dismembered by a gang of teen-agers. He found her in a black bag and reported this to the police. He emerged from this last dream with a great sense of relief that he had not actually committed the crime, even though he might have wanted to. After the discussion of this last dream in the series, he said that he felt free of the pervasive guilt that had prevented him from defending himself and that he now felt he could lead his life without injuring himself or allowing himself to be injured by others. Indeed his conviction about this has been borne out by one year's follow-up in which he has been remarkably free of the self-destructive incidents that had been daily or weekly occurrences.

His associations to these dreams usually took the form of recalling very disturbing memories about his relation to his mother: a bewildered, "profound" feeling about not understanding what he was doing with her; being an unwanted child, continually told that his birth had caused his mother's stroke; being left all alone in the house with his mother, and then having his father refuse to take him for a walk because he had wanted to take along a doll; and finally, the enormous relief of getting the distinction clear between having wanted to hurt her (and also his mistress and also his father) and not actually having done it. In these dreams and a number which followed, there were frequent references to a fatherly figure (a copilot in one dream) who did not leave him alone with his terrible burden.

The manifest content of these dreams suggested various ways in which he could be exculpated: he was a pure white horse leaping free from his mother's bed; I could arrange for God (the colleague directly above) to heal his mother's stroke; some teen-agers had mutilated the woman and he had only come upon her on the road. The latent content concerned his memories and feelings of bewilderment, terror, and guilt over being left alone with her and left with the (felt) responsibility for her condition. Finally, he seemed to emerge with a sense that he no longer had to carry these feelings alone, that a fatherly figure was with him, and that this father appreciated the distinction between his criminal feelings and actual crimes. There are probably several ways of explaining how these several factors relieved him of his self-destructive pattern. First, one could argue that the manifest content represented denials of his criminal intent, and that these defenses were not challenged by the therapist and thus remain part of his defensive structure. Second, the recall of bewildering states of mind in relation to his mother and the sharing of these with the psychotherapist helped to give them some shape and this dispelled some of their terror. This calming relationship with the therapist helped him to distinguish his wishes and fantasies of destructive intent toward his mother from the reality that he had actually not committed the crimes. This help is like that given a very frightened child who wakes from a terrible dream, whose dream is then not minimized but rather appreciated by the parent; yet the child is reassured that the dreadful acts have not been committed. The patient was thus helped to integrate regressive states of mind in which fantasy about his mother and reality had not been distinguished, but which had been split off from the central reality ego, because his father had not made himself available to help the boy with them. As these regressive states were understood, the patient felt a great deal more confidence in being able to use his aggression constructively, confident that he could distinguish real wrongs from those he might imagine. Of course, mirroring of his capacity to make these judgments remained crucial, and became the essential working-through process of the last two months of treatment. Thus, he became able to dispute a traffic violation (he had not just imagined he was driving properly) and so forth, as I have described.

Clearly, the analytic work was not completed. The patient left treatment with a powerful unanalyzed transference of a very special relationship with me. Within the year following our termination he returned twice for a few sessions to discuss difficulties concerning not being appreciated by a teacher (he had returned to college part-time), and later, concerning the death of another cardiac patient whom he had felt was his "twin," and, indeed, I expect I may see him again. In sum, he still tends to form mirror transference relationships outside of psychotherapy, which can get him in some difficulty. However, he has remained free of drinking problems and other self-destructive activities and has been much more able to defend his interests in disputes with other people.

In summary, the principal difficulty in this case was the prolonged resistance to the establishment of a positive transference, which finally after six months took the form of a mirror transference as described by Kohut. The largest part of this paper has been devoted to describing the work of Balint and Kohut concerning the treatment of the narcissistic personality and then to demonstrating how this work could be applied to these problems of severe resistance in this case of an alcoholic patient who was successfully treated in twelve months of outpatient treatment (2-3 visits per week). Once this positive transference was established, the patient brought forward intense, disturbing memories that permitted him to be relieved, in turn, of severe bodily tension and regressive states in which fantasy and reality were poorly distinguished and had led to considerable guilt. As the bodily tension was reduced, he no longer needed alcohol and reduced his nitroglycerin usage by one-third. As his regressive states were controlled and guilt was reduced, he ceased the pattern of injuring himself or allowing himself to be injured by others. The mirror transference was a necessary precondition for the recall of these disturbing memories and states of mind, for some working through of the rediscovered grandiose aims, and their adaptation to realistic ends. Thus, the principal contribution of this paper lies in describing how the work of Balint and Kohut offered a new way of working with a very difficult and resistant alcoholic patient. The principal question for the future is to what extent mirror and idealizing positive transference relationships can be mobilized with other alcoholic patients and so facilitate progress in one of the most difficult areas of psychoanalytic psychotherapy.[3]

NOTES

1. Since my primary task is to discuss the application of Balint's and Kohut's ideas to the problems of alcoholism, I will limit here what could be a lengthy paper comparing their points of similarity and difference. Certainly a case could be made for the importance of certain differences, but I think that the therapeutic implications of each of their views are the same or complementary.

2. Kohut argues that the active encouragement of an idealizing transference (such as recommended by Silber) may be a necessary emergency measure to keep the patient in treatment. A similar active technique to that recommended by Silber with alcoholic patients was that employed by Aichhorn with juvenile delinquents (see Kohut, 1971, p. 162).

3. I would like to acknowledge my debt to Harold Sampson, Ph.D., and Joseph Weiss, M.D., who first introduced me to psychoanalytic psychotherapy that would emphasize understanding the object relationship that the patient requires in order to bring forward new themes and capabilities. In the terms of Weiss (1971), the mirror transference would be a special case of the "conditions of safety" required by the patient for the emergence of new themes or for a "new beginning" (Balint, 1968).

REFERENCES

Balint, M. (1968). *The Basic Fault, Therapeutic Aspects of Regression*. London: Tavistock.

Bateson, G. (1971). The cybernetics of "self": a theory of alcoholism. *Psychiatry* 34:1-18.

Chafetz, M. (1959). Practical and theoretical considerations in the psychotherapy of alcoholism. *Quarterly Journal of Studies on Alcohol* 20:281-291.

Devito, R. A., Flaherty, L. A., and Mozdzierz, G. J. (1970). Toward a psychodynamic theory of alcoholism. *Diseases of the Nervous System*, 31: 43-49.

Jones, E. (1951). The God complex, the belief that one is God, and the resulting character traits. *Essays in Applied Psychoanalysis*. London: Hogarth and Institute of Psychoanalysis.

Knight, R. P. (1937). The psychodynamics of chronic alcoholism. *Journal of Nervous and Mental Disorders* 86: 538-548.

Kohut, H. (1971). *The Analysis of the Self*. New York: International Universities Press.

Ornstein, A (1974). The dread to repeat and the new beginning: A contribution to the psychoanalysis of the narcissistic personality disorders. *Annual of Psychoanalysis* 2: 231-248.

Silber, A. (1974). Rationale for the technique of psychotherapy with alcoholics. *International Journal of Psychoanalytic Psychotherapy* 3:28-47.

Weiss, J. (1971). The emergence of new themes in psychoanalysis: A contribution to the psychoanalytical theory of therapy. *International Journal of Psychoanalysis* 52:459-468.

Yorke, C. (1970). A critical review of some psychoanalytic literature on drug addiction. *British Journal of Medical Psychology* 43:141-159.

JAMES GUSTAFSON, M.D.

DR. GUSTAFSON is Assistant Professor of Psychiatry at the University of Wisconsin, where he teaches and supervises in the areas of group relations and therapy and psychoanalytic psychotherapy. Dr. Gustafson was trained at Harvard Medical School (M.D., 1967) and Mt. Zion Hospital and Medical Center, San Francisco (Residency, 1968-1971). He is also, presently, Chairman, North Central Group Relations Center (A.K. Rice Institute).

Psychotherapeutic Schema Based on the Paranoid Process

W. W. Meissner, S.J., M.D.

*Boston Psychoanalytic Institute
and the Massachusetts Mental Health Center*

A psychotherapeutic schema is proposed based on the analysis of the paranoid process. The paranoid process involves a paranoid construction of the patient's view of reality and his environment, particularly the social environment. The paranoid construction sustains and makes sense out of the patient's projective system. These projective elements reflect and are derived from the introjects—the internalized objects around which the patient's inner world and his experience of himself are organized. The schema aims at focusing the therapy on these introjects as central to the psychopathology. The following steps of the schema are outlined and discussed: establishing the therapeutic alliance, defining the projective system, testing reality, clarification of the introjects, derivation of the introjects, motivation of the introjects, mourning of infantile attachments, emergence of transference dependence, transference resolution, and termination.

INTRODUCTION

The present paper is an attempt to apply some of the aspects of the paranoid process (Meissner, 1974, 1976) to a schema of psychotherapy. The basic schema derives from the previous analysis of aspects of the paranoid process, insofar as the schema is organized around the basic principle that the externalized elements of the paranoid process—specifically the paranoid construction, with its inherent and contributing projections—must be traced back to the underlying organization of introjects from which they derive and on which they depend. The organization and supportive forces contributing to the maintenance and shaping of the introjects can then be effectively worked through. In this broader sense, then, the schema being suggested here can be envisioned in terms of the conversion of paranoid (projective) manifestations into depressive (introjective) issues, and the subsequent working through and resolution of the latter.

88 International Journal of Psychoanalytic Psychotherapy

Although the clinical and theoretical basis for the approach outlined here is spelled out in detail elsewhere (Meissner, 1976), a word about the derivation of the notion of the paranoid process from previous concepts may be useful. The basic concepts of introjection (narcissistic identification) and projection were advanced by Freud, but were extensively elaborated by Melanie Klein and her followers (Segal, 1964). The understanding of introjection and its relation to projection, and to the building up of the self, with its correlative structures, comes not so much from Klein, as from the work of Hartmann (1939) on internalization, Anna Freud (1936) on identification with the aggressor, Rapaport (1967) on structure, Jacobson (1964) on self-object relations, and Modell (1968) on the relation to reality. The concept of introjection employed here falls closely in line with the formulations of Schafer (1968), with, however, greater emphasis on the structural aspects of introjects than Shafer's more explicitly representational account.

The psychotherapeutic schema, which reflects the dynamics of the paranoid process, is not limited in its application to paranoid forms of psychopathology, just as the paranoid process itself is not limited to the forms of paranoid psychopathology, but rather introduces a wide spectrum of clinical conditions (Schwartz, 1963; Shapiro, 1965). Instead, it is more generally applicable as an organizing and guiding schema for the therapeutic approach to a wide spectrum of diagnoses which can be treated in a more insight-oriented and interpretive form of psychotherapy. Such psychotherapy is typically based on and utilizes psychoanalytic principles to direct its efforts.

The patterns of dynamic organization to which the schema addresses itself can be seen with greater or lesser clarity and impact in various forms of psychopathology. Perhaps the clearest and most striking expression of these dynamics can be found in more primitive forms of pathology, including schizophrenia, the manic depressive psychoses, and the psychotic depressions. In these more primitive forms of psychopathology, the organization of the paranoid construction and the projective orientations included in it can reach delusional proportions and are driven by powerful underlying needs and dependencies. Such powerful needs may serve in these forms of pathology to maintain the paranoid construction and projective elements with a rigidity and resistance that create considerable therapeutic difficulties (Polatin, 1975).

While the projective elements may dominate the clinical picture, we need to remind ourselves of their derivation from underlying introjects. The paranoid construction serves ultimately to sustain the introjective alignment.

By way of contrast, the forms of borderline pathology function at higher levels of ego capacity and personality organization, but the rapid and often fragile oscillation between projective and introjective alignments gives such patients an often chaotic and rapidly vacillating quality (Kernberg, 1969). In

such cases the paranoid manifestations serve as important defensive alignments against the underlying depressive core which centers around the introjective configuration.

It is important to realize, however, that not only does the interplay of projective and introjective mechanisms have a decisive role to play in the less organized forms of psychic impairment, but that even in the more elaborate
and more highly integrated forms of personality organization such mechanisms play significant roles in the determination of psychopathology. Thus
the elements of the paranoid (projective) construction and the derivation
from underlying introjects play important functions in the organization of the
character disorders, including the narcissistic personality disorders (Kohut,
1971) and the schizoid personality (Guntrip, 1969). Kohut (1971), for
example, has pointed to the archaic narcissistic configurations of the grandiose self and the idealized parental imago which reflect the operation of introjective and projective mechanisms at quite primitive levels in the differentiation of primary narcissism. Similarly, schizoid withdrawal can be seen in
terms of an immersion in severely pathogenic introjects, or, in Guntrip's
(1969) terms, leading

to the creation of an object-world that enables the ego to be both withdrawn yet not "in the womb," the Kleinian world of "internal objects,"
dream and fantasy, a world of object-relationships which is also withdrawn
"inside" out of the external world. This, par excellence, is the world of psychoneurotic and psychotic experience. [p. 82]

A very clear manifestation of the function of introjects can be found in the
forms of neurotic depression, as well as in the more severe and incapacitating
psychotic depressions (Jacobson, 1971). Moreover, the same configurations
can be identified even in relatively well-organized and well-functioning personalities, such as those with the more neurotic disorders, and the hysteric or
obsessive-compulsive or phobic manifestations. Consequently, the mechanisms with which we are dealing in this psychotherapeutic schema are not
limited to one or another form of psychopathology, but rather cut across all
forms of personality organization and reflect the operation of basic mechanisms which play themselves out in human development and in the shaping of
psychopathological manifestations (Meissner, 1976).

A few words can be addressed to the overall nature of the schema itself. It
does not provide a paradigm of psychotherapy, nor does it offer a basis on
which technical conclusions or directives can be made. Rather it offers a more
or less natural progression within which the therapist's thinking and orientation to the therapeutic process can be placed, based on an understanding of
the mechanisms and dynamics of the paranoid process. Consequently, it

should be stressed that the schema is in no sense univocal or prescriptive. Rather it must apply in idiosyncratic fashion to each particular patient and to the unique therapeutic problems presented by each.

In fact, the schema must be individualized, that is, adapted to each patient and his particular needs and difficulties. The aspects of the schema which come into play will vary in intensity and focus and in level of therapeutic difficulty from patient to patient, so that the therapist cannot dictate the course of therapy in terms of such an overriding schema. Thus the schema can provide no more than a general orientation and a guide to the relevant therapeutic issues; even so it offers a logic of the progression and organization of the levels of pathogenic structure and the manner in which they play themselves out in the therapeutic process. It emphasizes the questions of priority of issues with the implication that an important aspect of the therapy is the working through of prior issues and prior levels of function and organization before subsequent issues can be meaningfully and advantageously approached in the therapy.

Consequently, there may be a shifting back and forth among the aspects of the schema until successive issues are adequately defined, clarified, and worked through to the point where their progressive resolution allows for therapeutic movement and a more meaningful approach and working through of subsequent issues. It can also be pointed out that the psychotherapeutic schema as it is suggested here provides a frame of reference not only for more intensive and long-term approaches to the patient's difficulties, but also serves as a framework for conceptualizing and focusing the levels of difficulty involved in briefer and more short-term forms of psychotherapeutic intervention. In either case, the schema provides a logical framework within which the therapist can organize and integrate his own conceptual formulation of the therapeutic issues and the technical approach he may wish to adopt with any given patient.

THERAPEUTIC SCHEMA

Establishing the Therapeutic Alliance

The therapeutic alliance is a major part of any meaningful therapy, and it provides the more or less realistic basis on which the therapeutic work proceeds (Zetzel, 1970). The therapeutic alliance takes place between the working ego of the therapist and that part of the patient's ego which is relatively unembroiled in conflictual tensions, is capable of self-observation, and can join the therapist in the work of the therapy. It is this observant ego, which in fact enters the therapeutic contract and makes it, together with the therapist, a viable and vital reality (Greenson, 1967).

The point here is that the therapeutic alliance as essential must be established and sustained. It does not simply happen, but must be watched for, taken into account, worked at, and, at repeated and important junctures during the therapy, reinforced by the activity of the therapist. The more primitive, the deeper the level of the patient's pathology, the more difficulty there is in establishing and maintaining the alliance and the more central it is to conducting the therapy. This is particularly the case with those patients in whom the developmental defect or deviation lies at an early level of developmental experience, in which the issues of trust and autonomy have not been adequately worked through (Zetzel, 1971).

In most neurotic patients, the therapeutic alliance happens in one or other degree. However, by and large if the therapy makes effective inroads on a patient's neurosis, the therapeutic alliance is often threatened and disrupted, so that the further development of the therapy requires that it be sustained and reinforced or, if need be, repaired. In other more primitive patients, the work on the alliance may form the central core of the therapy. This is very frequently the case with borderline and psychotic patients, in whom the therapeutic alliance remains fragile over extended periods of time and requires continual reinforcement and frequent repairs in the face of disruptions and formations of antitherapeutic misalliances. Nonetheless, the alliance is essential for therapy with all patients (Langs, 1974).

The question then arises as to how the alliance is established. It is difficult to be specific about this question since so much of our knowledge about the alliance is as yet quite simple and undeveloped. The basic issues, insofar as we are able to define them at this point, center around trust and autonomy. The alliance is stabilized to the degree that the patient can develop a meaningful trust in the therapist and to the extent that the former is increasingly able to sustain a sense of autonomy within the therapeutic relationship.

The therapist's contribution to this development is not altogether clear. The most important elements generally have to do with empathic responsiveness on the part of the therapist to the idiosyncratic needs, anxieties, and inner tensions felt by the patient, such that the therapist responds to the patient in terms of the latter's own individuality, rather than in terms of the therapist's own needs or in terms of some preexisting therapeutic stereotype.

Thus important elements that might be focused on in this regard are the therapist's patient and attentive listening to the patient's productions. This involves a sort of active presence within the therapeutic situation and within the therapeutic relationship. You will notice here that I am not talking specifically about activity, although in some cases, because of the patient's difficulties in relating to an object in a relatively unstructured context, activity on the part of the therapist may be desirable. Active presence, however, is something different, more in the line of presenting the patient with a consistent and available and "present" object.

In addition, the therapist contributes through his empathic understanding of what the patient experiences and feels, what Schafer (1959) has referred to aptly as "generative empathy." The therapist's being attuned to the patient's feelings in this way gives the latter a feeling of communication and response and that he is being effectively understood, thus contributing important meaningful dimensions to the experience of the relationship. The therapist's attitude is thus one of respectful unintrusiveness. It is difficult to operationalize such a concept in behavioral terms, since the unintrusiveness cannot be spelled out in terms of specific behaviors. It has to do rather with a very central attitude on the part of the therapist which allows him to present himself within the therapeutic context with an attitude of openness and availability, without forcing himself on the patient's attention or invading the latter's inner world. It should be noted that both elements of the description are extremely important in that the therapist's response to the patient must be both respectful of the latter's individuality and the central core of his fragile identity, as well as unintrusive, in that the therapist does not violate the slender threads of the patient's fragile autonomy.

In this vein, it is useful to recall Winnicott's (1963) notion of "holding" and its importance in psychotherapy. He commented:

> You will see that the analyst is *holding* the patient, and this often takes the form of conveying in words at the appropriate moment something that shows that the analyst knows and understands the deepest anxiety that is being experienced, or that is waiting to be experienced. [p. 240]

The "holding function" is all the more important in more primitive forms of psychopathology, but it plays a central role—explicitly or implicitly—in all psychotherapeutic interactions. Masud Khan (1972) makes this explicit.

> The two distinct styles of my relating to the patient I can differentiate as:
> 1. Listening to what the patient verbally communicates, in the patently classical situation as it has evolved, and deciphering its *meaning* in terms of structural conflicts (ego, id, and superego) and through its transferential interpersonal expression in the here and now of the analytic situation.
> 2. Through a psychic, affective, and environmental *holding* of the person of the patient in the clinical situation, I facilitate certain experiences that I cannot anticipate or program, any more than the patient can. When these actualize, they are surprising, both for the patient and for me, and release quite unexpected new processes in the patient. [p. 99]

In addition to such empathic responsiveness, there are certain technical procedures by which the therapist can contribute to the shaping of the therapeutic alliance. Such things would include a definition of a therapeutic situation and the setting of the therapeutic contract in the very beginning of treatment (Langs, 1973). Second, it may be important not only in the beginning of therapy, but from time to time during critical points during the therapeutic process, that the respective roles of doctor and patient be clarified and specified. Another important dimension is the therapist's attention to the often implicit and minimally expressed distortions on the patient's part of the therapeutic alliance itself (Langs, 1974). This may express itself in terms of the fear of judgment or criticism from the therapist, as the patient's sense of helplessness or impotent dependence on the therapeutic situation, or finally even in a regarding of the therapeutic situation as a more or less confessional one in which the recitation of sins and defects is to be responded to by the therapist's curing absolution. In my own experience it is also not infrequent, for example, that students will respond to the therapeutic situation as though it were a school arrangement in which a certain standard of performance is expected and in which an evaluation or criticism is to be delivered by the therapist.

Another variant of alliance distortion is found in the narcissistic alliance [1] (Corwin, 1972), in which the patient enters treatment and submits to the process with the (often unconscious) intent of gaining something from the therapist which will enable him to attain a narcissistically invested and usually unrealistic objective. This usually represents some form of narcissistic wish fulfillment and may embrace omnipotent, grandiose, or magical fantasies. It impedes the establishing of any more realistic or meaningful therapeutic alliance.

In all of this, it is important to remember that actions speak louder than words. The therapist must maintain a certain therapeutic consistency between what he utters and the behaviors that express his attitudes and feelings in contrary ways. His task is to constantly work at building the patient's trust and to constantly encourage and foster the latter's autonomy. Consequently, it is of major importance that the therapist do his best to engender trust in the patient by the way in which he deals with him, by the way in which he manages his contacts with the patient whether in or out of the therapeutic situation. Particularly with patients who cling to a helpless and infantile position in many of their behaviors, it is a constant temptation for the therapist to step into a parenting role and thus find himself unwittingly in the position of undermining his patient's trust and autonomy. The disparity between verbal formulations and specific actions is a rich field for the examination of the countertransference attitudes that may often be unconscious in the therapist.

But the therapist must constantly remind himself that this consistency is of the utmost importance in the establishing and maintaining of the therapeutic alliance, and that he must do nothing to further undermine the patient's sense of trust, autonomy, and self-esteem. This becomes particularly difficult at points in which the therapist begins to work on the patient's resistances. The therapeutic task is, in effect, to analyze the resistances so that the therapeutic work can progress, but the risk is that, in contributing to the dissolution of resistances, the therapist may undermine the patient's fragile sense of self-esteem and autonomy. Consequently, the therapist's skillful interpretations of the patient's resistances must be accompanied by attention to alliance factors. This same caution applies to other therapeutic interventions as well. Confrontations, whether routine or heroic, are effective only to the extent that they serve to establish or reinforce, or occur in a context of a working alliance (Corwin, 1972; Buie and Adler, 1972; Adler and Buie, 1972).

In fact, the patient is constantly confronted with the question whether he can enter the therapeutic relationship and process without the loss of the minimal sense of self-esteem and fragile autonomy that he already possesses. Where the therapeutic alliance enjoys a certain solidity and stability, the task of entry is vastly simplified. But where the alliance is fragile or contaminated by elements of misalliance, the task can often be extremely difficult and tentative. In any case, establishing and sustaining and continually reinforcing the alliance must be a constant therapeutic preoccupation, since such alliance is the essential requirement for assuring the patient's capacity to do therapeutic work and to progress in the course of therapy.

Defining the Projective System

The theoretical frame of reference for developing this schema is that of the paranoid process, as indicated. This process sees the patient's experience—both cognitive and affective—as structured around three important constituents, namely, his introjections, the correlative projections, and the paranoid construction (Meissner, 1976). It is in terms of these three aspects that the patient organizes his experience, not only of himself, but of the ambient world in which he moves and breathes.

The basic organization of the paranoid process takes its point of departure from the structuring of the patient's inner world in terms of introjects, that is, internalized object relations derived from his developmental experience. It is on the basis of such organization that the patient derives and externalizes certain aspects of his own self-organization in the form of projections, in terms of which he orders his experience of external objects and relates to them. To sustain this tissue of projections, the patient in parallel organizes his cognitive view of the world in such a way as to incorporate and sustain the projections and to give them an integral sense of meaning.

The entire process is in the service of confirming, reinforcing, sustaining, and validating the prior introjective constellation, around which the patient organizes and sustains his sense of self. At this level of working within the therapeutic schema, we are beginning to tune in on the elements of the patient's projective system. Our tactic in general will be to identify the elements of the paranoid construction, and thus elicit and define within them the projective aspects, enabling us to shift back to an inner frame of reference and deal with the organization of the introjects as a central issue of the therapeutic endeavor.

In our first approach to the projective system, the task is primarily one of listening to the patient's account of his experience of himself and the world in which he lives. Equivalently, this is a descriptive account of his paranoid construction. It is within that construction that we will be able to identify the projective elements. This aspect is essentially passive. There is no need to confront or refute the elements of the projective system. Our primary objective is to learn about that system, to find out what is in it, and to become as familiar with it as we reasonably can.

The patient tells about his projective system and its correlative paranoid construction from the very first. There is little in his demeanor, verbalizations, and expressed opinions that does not provide us with data about his view of the world and himself. The student who tells us how anxious he becomes when he feels he might be called on in class, how he stutters and becomes confused in conversation with his professors, and how he becomes anxious and impotent when intimately involved with a date is telling us something about his image of himself and his perspective on the world around him. We are not surprised to learn that he was the baby of the family, anxiously and obsessively hovered over by an insecure mother, that he always felt he was a messy kid who would never grow up. Consistent with this is his persistent enuresis until about age fifteen. These details blend into a picture of a helpless child-victim lost in a hostile and threatening world of powerful grown-ups. Consequently, his reaction to the therapist as threatening, intrusive, and powerfully controlling seems perfectly consistent.

Such a patient may present the world of his experience as fact, that is as simply the way things are. A relatively attractive and very intelligent young professional woman stoutly maintained that she was worthless and inadequate because she did not have the sort of physical attributes that men found attractive. No amount of questioning or contrary evidence would dent her conviction. She was plainly displaying her construction of the social environment in such a way as to reinforce her own feelings of inadequacy and her perception of herself as unlovable and lacking as a woman. Quite consistently she saw the therapist as devaluing her in the same way; he was, after all, a man like any other man!

The critical elements in these organizations have to do with the patient's projections. Projections, specifically, have to do with the modification of object relations (Meissner, 1971). In the cases cited, relationships were contaminated by the patients' convictions, based on projection, that significant others were critical, demeaning, out to do them harm, put them in their place, and the like. In each case, these projective elements related to significant introjective components derived from parental imagos.

There are certain defining techniques which can facilitate this descriptive account. First, it is important to get as much detail as possible. The detail should be explicit and concrete. We want to know as much as possible in terms of concrete events, actions on the part of various individuals, expressions of affect, and particularly the patient's own perceptions and feelings. Second, it is useful to be able to elicit as many parallel accounts as possible, both those which deal with an interpersonal frame of reference and those which may come from historical levels of the patient's experience. Again, the orientation toward details is important, since it is often in the eliciting of such details that the patterns of the patient's behavior and attitudes begin to emerge. Particularly helpful, of course, is the eliciting of historical accounts which suggest that similar patterns have taken place earlier in the patient's experience, the earlier the better.

It should be noted that, at this level of the schema, we are not dealing solely with the elements of the paranoid construction, but that the patient may introduce direct expressions from the level of the introjects. He may tell us in a variety of direct and indirect ways how he sees himself, how he feels about himself, how he thinks others may regard him and react to him. This is particularly the case in focusing on the patient's feelings. Here, in eliciting the details of feeling, often the hidden affects of depression, fear, shame, inadequacy, weakness, and vulnerability may become more manifest as direct expressions of the pathogenic sense of self.

A more important aspect of this stage of defining the projective system is the focus on the therapeutic relationship. The therapist needs to remind himself that that system operates in all spheres of the patient's experience, particularly those which are affectively important and in which the patient has some stake or investment. Thus the projective system can be presumed to operate within the therapeutic relationship and as the therapy progresses will be manifest most dramatically within the transference neurosis. Usually this is the most vivid and most dramatic manifestation of the patient's projective system and thus becomes the primary vehicle for the therapist's not only recognizing and defining the system but beginning to deal with it.

Several points can be made. The most important vehicle for the expression of these elements is the patient's affect. Affective channels of communication carry the weightiest information load. Second, the therapist may get signals from his subject's affect—sadness, bitterness, regret, anger, fear, etc.—but the therapist's own affective response to the patient may also provide important signals for identifying projective content. Thus the physician's feelings of boredom, irritation, incompetence, inadequacy, etc.—even hatred (Winnicott, 1947)—can provide important signals for the reading of the patient's stance. And, third, it is important to remember in this realm of the counter-transference-transference interaction that the patient not only distorts his perception and representation of the therapist, but frequently even works to elicit responses from the latter which will serve to confirm his distortions and misrepresentations.

Testing Reality

The phase of reality testing, following on the definition of the projective system, marks the first stage of the therapeutic approach to the projective system. It would seem obvious that the elements of the patient's projective system need to be tested against the hard stuff of reality, but the question is how this is to be accomplished. Our basic tactic here is to shift the focus of the therapy from the projective system back to the underlying introjective constellation from which it derives. The testing of the projective system does not usually best take place by challenging or confronting the system as a whole, or even explicit elements within it. This is not to say that any of the varieties of confrontation may not find their appropriate place (Corwin, 1972), but in this context they run the risk of playing into the projective system. Rather, the undermining of the projective system, which carries within it so many of the residues of the patient's pathology, is undertaken by following the tactic established in the previous step of defining the projective system. That is to say, the system is tested against reality by the process of detailed accounting. As the patient fills out the details of the picture, he is in effect confronting himself with more and more of the specifics or concrete elements of the reality. This tactic is obviously initiated in the stage of defining the projective system and carries over into the first stage of the testing of its reality.

There are, nonetheless, some important specific techniques which have as their intent the calling into question of elements of the projective system and the creating of some sense of distance between the projective elements as such and what can be seen to be emerging as a reality perspective. The first important technique involves the tagging of feelings. That is, when the patient expresses some content in terms of feeling, it is useful for the therapist to simply tag the content as one of feeling. Thus, when the patient says, "I don't feel that I could ever do anything right," it is useful for the therapist to tag not the specific content of the statement but the feeling quality of it: "That seems to be how you feel."

The tagging of feelings as feelings may need to take place over a long period of time and embrace many concrete circumstances and details of the pa-

tient's affective experience. The tagging technique, however, has an intention
and a direction. The intention is that it seeks to establish the distinction between feelings (and their intimate connection with fantasies) and reality.
Thus this technique forms an important aspect of the reality-testing phase of
the schema. The direction of tagging is toward a gradual amplification of the
awareness of the patient's feelings, as forming a coherent and consistent pattern of his experience of himself, and a gradual establishing of the connection
of the pattern of organization of feelings to specific fantasies. Again, the feelings tend to relate more directly to introjective elements, so that the direction
of the tagging approach is one which seeks to establish not only the fantasy
proportions of the patient's perception of reality around him, but also the
fantasy proportions of his perception and appreciation of himself as a human
being.

The second important aspect of testing the reality of the patient's perspective has to do with defining the specific areas within which his knowledge is
lacking. The patient will frequently offer interpretations, explanations, conclusions, hypotheses, attitudes, etc., as though they were accepted fact. Frequently enough, these expressions tend to imply the patient's inadequacy or
defectiveness or are otherwise deleterious. The therapist's approach to such
formulations cannot be by way of challenging the evidence or trying to refute
the patient. Such an approach would only meet with staunch resistance and a
rigidifying of his position. Rather, the therapist can tactfully point out the
areas within which the patient's knowledge is uncertain. Thus if the patient
offers the opinion that people at work do not like him, the therapist's approach, following the schema, would be to elicit further details on the situation at work, particularly those which might suggest that indeed other people
at work do not like the patient. When the latter fails to provide such details,
as is usually the case, the therapist can point out that the patient feels unwanted (tagging), but that he really doesn't know whether people at work
want him there or not.

It is important to note that the therapist's position is neither pro nor con.
He is neither saying that people in the patient's work setting want to get rid of
him, nor is he saying that they don't want to do so. He is merely saying that
the patient really doesn't know; carrying it a step further, where the patient
does not have real knowledge, the therapist's tendency is to fill in the blanks,
to fill the empty spaces with something that comes from someplace else. The
someplace else, of course, is the patient's own head, and by inference the
therapist is carrying the therapeutic process a step further, making the point
that what fills in the blanks in the patient's experience of his reality comes out
of his own head, namely, out of the constellation of introjections which form
the substance of his inner world.

I can remember this process vividly in a young man in his mid-twenties who came seeking help because of the total paralysis his life was in. He had had a paranoid schizophrenic episode about two years before, followed by a profound clinging depression. His life was paralyzed by fear. Everywhere he went he met hostility; people stared at him, laughed at him, thought he was a sniveling weakling with no backbone or guts — a worthless creep. He could not shop at his local grocery because the clerk had given him a funny look, presumably thinking that he was a worthless degenerate. He fulminated against the capitalist system, social values, corporations, the American government, etc., etc., because he felt victimized and impotent in his dealings with them. His posture was one of impotent rage.

It was hardly difficult to discern the dimensions of this paranoid construction and the introjective configuration from which they derived. It was only after repeated and prolonged testing of many of these situations that he was able to grasp the projective nature of his reactions and to turn his concern to an internal frame of reference. As this shift evolved, his capacity to tolerate social situations gradually increased to the point of holding a steady job and having a sexual relationship.

As this patient strikingly dramatized, the drift in this process is toward a progressively clearer and more discrete delineation of the realm of the patient's fantasy life — both in its external and internal referents — which had functioned by and large at an unconscious level. The further clarification of these introjectively derived fantasy systems and their role in early object relations, as well as in any current transference relation, helps to specify the introjective configuration and progressively delineate it from reality. Further steps of the schema elaborate these aspects.

It should be noted that the present schema does not represent a conflict-focused approach. Rather, it is concerned with the critical pattern of introjections which underlie and give rise to intrapsychic conflicts. The severely phobic and paranoid young man just discussed was severely conflicted, but the origin of his conflicts lay in the pathogenic introjects derived from highly ambivalent and narcissistically disturbed relationships with his parents. We should not overlook that one classic organization of introjects forms the superego.

Thus the testing of the reality of the projective system, or rather its testing against reality, is an extremely important juncture in the therapeutic progression. As the elements of the projective system come increasingly under detailed examination, their stability and utility for the patient become diminished and important therapeutic elements become mobilized. As the therapeutic process engages with the projective system more and more meaningfully, that system is increasingly undermined and the patient's needs to defend and maintain it are mobilized often to an intense degree. The therapist has to deal not only with the systems as such, but has to deal in important ways with the defensive responses which the patient throws up as the system is put under increasing pressure. It must be remembered that the projective system is not simply there as a matter of chance. It is an intensely invested cognitive, effective, and defensive organization whose purpose is essentially the preservation of the patient's sense of self as well as his narcissistic needs, which become focused on the issues of preservation of the introjects as core elements around which the patient's sense of self is organized. Consequently, the defensive titer in the face of the gradual undermining of the projective system can become quite intense.

As the projective system is gradually modified, however, there is a progressive affective shift, so that the underlying (usually repressed) affects which motivate the system and against which it operates as a defense become increasingly available to the patient. Usually the affects which are thus mobilized are depressive or have to do with the patient's underlying affects of guilt and shame. Both in the working through of the patient's defenses and in the tolerating of the painful underlying affect, the importance of the therapeutic alliance remains a major consideration. These operations become possible only to the extent that the therapeutic alliance remains firm and intact and allows the patient sufficient room and distance within the therapeutic relationship to engage with the therapist with a sense of alliance and supportive assistance from the latter.

Nonetheless, the therapist needs to be mindful that in the face of such intolerable depressive affects, the patient may regress to a more projective defense, and may reinvest the projective system or modify it to one which is more readily sustainable in the face of therapeutic pressures. It should also be noted that the undermining of the projective system and the emergence of painful depressive affects carries the therapeutic process on to its next stage, insofar as the depressive affects are intimately tied up with and dynamically related to the organization of the underlying introjects. It is these depressive affects which tend to bring the introjects into sharp relief and make them increasingly available for therapeutic intervention.

The Clarification of the Introjects

Recalling for a moment the organization of the paranoid process, it becomes immediately obvious that the undermining of the projective system and the paranoid construction calls into question, and shifts the focus from, the projective system as such to the introjects from which the critical projections derive. The projective system, including the paranoid construction, consequently can be seen explicitly in terms of its defensive function in both avoiding the impact of the pathogenic introjects and at the same time in sustaining them.

Consequently, the undermining of elements of the projective system leads to an unveiling of the introjects. The focus shifts from the external world to an internal one, and the patient begins to give us an account of that internal world. Usually the content is depressive, in the sense that the patient sees himself in terms of overwhelming weakness, inadequacy, helplessness, inferiority, defectiveness, worthlessness, and vulnerability. Just as the therapist exposed the projective system through a detailed process of definition, here too the process of definition, now focused on the inner world, the world of the patient's introjects, becomes the focal part of the therapeutic process.

The therapist thus seeks to know the details, concrete and specific, of his inadequacy, of his helplessness, inferiority, etc. Again, the reality of these elements must be tested, moving toward the vital insight that just as the elements of the patient's projective system had more to do with fantasy than reality, so the elements of the patient's introjective system have more to do with fantasies about himself and what he is than with the reality. Here again, the presumption is that the patient does not know his own reality, so that the conclusions, attitudes, and feelings that he generates about himself are based on an unknown quantity.

The primary ground on which the introjective organization is manifested is of course the therapeutic relationship. Within that relationship, the patient tends to play himself off against the therapist in a variety of ways. Most typically within the therapeutic relationship the patient will see himself as weak and inferior, while he sees the therapist as powerful, strong, and competent. He may also see himself prominently as the therapist's victim, that is, as subject to the therapist's evaluation, criticism, and control.

Thus far, we have been addressing ourselves to only one half of the economy of introjects. Frequently enough patients will be easily in touch with the inferior and inadequate or the helpless and victimized aspect of their introjects, but we know from experience that there is more to it. If there is a part of the introjective economy which relates to the fantasy of the patient's weakness, we also know that there is a parallel part which stands at the opposite extreme and bespeaks the patient's destructive power. If there is a part which expresses his worthlessness, we know that there is also a part that holds out for his specialness and entitlement.

What comes into perspective in this context is the inherent polarity of the introjects, which relates to the splitting of introjective elements on both sides of the middle ground of reality (Kernberg, 1966). In relation to important objects, this works in two ways. If the self is seen as inferior, the object is seen as superior; conversely, if the self is seen as superior, the object is seen as inferior. Correspondingly, if the self is seen as helpless victim, the object is seen as powerful aggressor; on the other hand, if the self is seen as powerful and destructive, the object is seen as victimized and helpless.

Thus the polar aspects of the introjects tend to focus on one or other side of the self-object differentiation and often shift back and forth. This vacillating of the introjective elements is like an emotional seesaw. If my end is up, yours is down; if your end is up, mine must be down. Latent in this introjective polarization and the implicit seesawing are all the dynamics of narcissism and particularly envy. A similar patterning can be played out in terms of the aggressive determinants which can be specified in terms of identification with the aggressor and identification with the victim.

What is critical to this phase of the therapeutic process is that both aspects of the polarity be seen as deriving from the patient's own introjects. Thus the vacillation between the self as superior and special on the one hand and as inferior and worthless on the other is an intrinsic vacillation, both aspects of which derive from the patient's introjective organization. Hence if one polarity of the introjective economy escapes repression and is available to the patient's awareness. the therapist knows that the opposite polarity is lurking somewhere under the surface. And sooner or later it will show its hand. Thus the young man, whose life was a continual paroxysm of persecutory anxieties and fears, saw himself in one dimension as weak, impotent, helpless, and victimized. But only reluctantly did he unveil the opposite polarity of the introjective configuration: his sense of cold, ruthless superiority, his contempt for those around him, his profuse fantasies of humiliating, killing, or reducing to rubble most of the people who crossed his path.

It is important to note that the organization and the dynamics of the introjects are based on the patient's inherent narcissism, and that the introjects tend to function in terms of the dictates of that narcissism. Thus as the correlative and polarized aspects of the introjects become more and more clearly defined, it becomes apparent that they operate very much in all-or-nothing fashion. If the therapist is seen as superior and competent and intelligent, the patient tends to see himself as totally inferior and abject, without any competence or worth at all. When the therapist comes to hear this unmitigated logic of extremes—the logic of all-or-nothing, black or white, either/or—he knows that he is closing in on introjective territory.

A further important point is that the polarized aspects of the introjects are locked together in a reciprocal defensive organization. This understanding provides a critical insight into the patient's depressive dynamics. It makes no sense to cling with the intensity one often experiences to a perception of oneself as inferior, inadequate, helpless, vulnerable, and victimized. That intense clinging, which resists therapeutic intervention so stoutly, becomes understandable only in terms of the opposite polarity which says that the patient is special, entitled, exceptional, etc. The critical point is that where one is allowed to see one aspect of the introjects, their polar opposite is irrevocably and unquestionably present and operative. The therapist must understand

and the patient must come to see that the polarized opposites are irrevocably linked together, they feed off each other, they are bound together by the iron clasps of reciprocal defense and they cannot be separated. Consequently, the patient is in the position of accepting and integrating the whole package or of rejecting it and surrendering it as a whole.

Parallel to this process of definition of these elements of the introjective economy, there is another important dimension of their clarification which we have already touched on. As the introjects are more clearly defined, the process of testing can go on apace. Thus, for example, the patient's feelings of weakness, inadequacy, and helplessness can be repeatedly tagged as feeling elements, and the gradual understanding developed that such elements relate to a fantasy which reflects the organization of the underlying introjects. The fact is that the patient knows only the fantasy, or that he has accepted the fantasy as a part of his real self for so long that he no longer knows what the substance of his real self is like. It should be pointed out once again in this regard that the primary testing ground for distinguishing between these introjective fantasy elements and the reality of the patient's self lies in the therapeutic relationship, most specifically and directly and powerfully in the distinction between transference neurosis and the therapeutic alliance.

The Derivation of Introjects

The work of clarification of the pathogenic introjects, including the gradual delineation of the component elements themselves, involves identifying particularly their polarized aggressive and narcissistic dimensions. It entails the emerging awareness of their reciprocal defensive involvement and the manner in which they form an integral whole within the subject's experience of himself, as well as progressive differentiation between elements of fantasy and reality. All these factors contribute to the gradual delineation and undermining of the embeddedness and investment in the introjects. However, this rarely provides a sufficient ground for effective therapeutic intervention in dealing with them. An extremely important procedure in determining the organization of the introjects, and a logical and necessary next step, lies in exploring and establishing their derivation.

It must be remembered in this context that the introjects themselves are equivalently internalized object relationships, so that the exploration of their derivation has to do with establishing and clarifying those specific ties to past and/or present objects in the patient's experience. The manner in which one elicits this sort of information and brings it to bear as a potential source of meaningful insight to the patient is a matter of technique. With some patients adequate exploration of this area of their experience can be done fairly actively, but this is not often the case. More frequently the acquiring of this information must be done in more indirect and subtle ways, and requires a considerable degree of self-discipline and patience on the part of the therapist.

Little by little the picture of the patient's past relationships, particularly with parental figures, emerges and more clearly takes shape. There are of course many pitfalls, as any experienced therapist knows. It often takes a considerable amount of time and amplification of areas of the patient's experience before reliable information about past experiences becomes available. Consequently, one cannot take the early reminiscences and the first or even second rendition of the patient's past experience as having unquestionable validity. The picture which the patient paints in the first rough sketching of his past will be progressively filled in, resketched, refined, and recast as the therapy progresses. It should also be remembered that in none of this recounting can one simply think in terms of recapturing a past reality. Rather, what is in question is the recapturing of the patient's experience, which may be overladened and permeated with elements of fantasy, wish, desire, and defense.

The task at this level of the therapeutic schema is to retrace the patient's experience to establish the links between the present organization and structure of the introjects and the patient's past experience of object relationships. The critical objects in this context are, of course, the parents, though not exclusively. Other important figures may enter in, depending on the peculiarities of the patient's life experience. Often siblings play a vital role, and frequently other relatives such as aunts or uncles, or even nonfamily figures, may play a significant part.

One finds in time that the previously described polarized aspects of the introjects are derived from the elements of ambivalent relationships to the significant objects of the patient's experience. To simply take the primary polarities organized around the dynamics of aggression and narcissism, the relative aspects of these dimensions can usually be related to specific objects in the patient's experience. Thus in terms of aggression, the victim-introject derives from the patient's relationship with and attachment to a victimized object. In the typical form of sadomasochistic relationship between parents, this "identification with the victim" more frequently takes place with the mother, for both male and female children. The father, however, may not be excluded from this internalization. Frequently enough when the opportunity presents itself to examine the patterns of family interplay, particularly interaction between the parents, one finds that there are also aspects of the relationship in which the father alternately functions as a victim.

The aggressive aspects, the "identification with the aggressor," correspondingly relates to the attachment to and dependence on a relatively aggressive object, and here the father tends to be the primary figure. Here again, however, one frequently runs into aggressive, hostile, and destructive elements within the mother's character which form the basis for the child's emerging identification with the aggressor. Similarly, if we turn to the narcissistic elements of the introjective polarity, again we find that the content of the introject derives from the narcissistic elements involved in the relationships with the same significant objects. Thus the child may introject the depressive and devalued aspects of the parental object, but at the same time internalizes the parallel elements in the parents' own introjective alignment of aspects of narcissistic grandiosity, specialness, and entitlement.

The progression at this stage takes its point of departure from the prior clarification of the introjects within the patient. The question which is posed at this juncture is, "Where in the patient's experience have these elements been displayed within the relations with objects with whom he has been significantly involved?" Thus the introjective accumulation within the patient can be seen to represent a re-creation within himself of elements derived from these important objects, so that the introjects come to represent a form of dependent, narcissistically motivated clinging to the infantile past, and they can be thus understood as serving to preserve the level of infantile fantasy and involvement with these objects.

This derivation of the introjective configuration was dramatically demonstrated in a young housewife who came into treatment for her chronic depression and dissatisfaction with life. Behind the feelings of worthlessness and inadequacy she felt, not only as wife and mother, but also as a human being, there emerged the correlative feelings of specialness, entitlement, and the feeling that she was different from other people, set aside by the fates to suffer and to go unrecognized and unrewarded for her extraordinary merits. Important determinants of these feelings, as might be expected, were her intense penis envy, directed particularly at a much older brother who had been a brilliant student, concert pianist, and the apple of her mother's eye. Even more critically, however, stood the figure of her mother, a woman who saw herself as mistreated by the fates, who held herself apart as being different and superior to other human beings, who reveled masochistically in her victimization and suffering, and who jealously reviled the world for its failure to pay her her due and to acknowledge her superiority. The introjective configuration in my patient was derived directly and dramatically from the mother. Mother and daughter had formed a special magical bond, a union of narcissistic glorification through suffering, solidified by the constant expectation that true worth and superiority would have their day. The bond was motivated by the intense and continually frustrated yearning of this young woman for closeness, acknowledgment, and acceptance from a narcissistic mother whose own pathology allowed her to acknowledge little merit in her daughter, yet alone in herself.

At times the parallels between the organization of the patient's introjects and the source objects are striking enough, but often they are more obscure. Introjection is after all a dynamic process. The product of the introjective internalization is compounded not only of elements derived from the object but also of dynamic determinants from the patient's subjective inner world. Together these elements interact to constitute a realm of internalized object relations which remains essentially transitional (Modell, 1968; Meissner, 1971).

Here it must be reemphasized that one of the most critical and most vital and forceful areas, wherein the pattern of relating to significant objects manifests itself, is within the therapeutic relationship. A patient's increasing dependence on and involvement with the therapist give rise to regressive pressures which activate infantile projections, serve as the basis on which infantile distortions of the therapeutic relationship are organized, and represent the core elements in the organization of the transference neurosis. This same patient, in the elaboration of the transference, saw me as a powerful and all-knowing wizard who would finally bring about a magical change in her life which would bring her the acknowledgment and admiration that she so desperately sought.

The exploration of the derivation of the introjects serves an additional and important purpose. It serves to clarify the patient's understanding that the pattern of his experience of himself and. by derivation, of the world around him — and particularly his relationships with other important figures in his environment — are dependent on a pattern of experiencing and responding that derives from his own infantile past. Consequently, the disparity between that past and his own present experience underlines the essential insight into the fantasy quality of the experience generated around the introjects and clarifies the distinction between elements of that experience and the real world of the patient's present life and activity. It is in the transference neurosis, of course, that this understanding and realization are borne in upon the patient with particular force, since it is in that critical relationship that he can see most clearly and most vividly that the patterns of infantile relating play themselves out in inappropriate and unrealistic ways.

The Motivation of the Introjects

The progressive clarification and exploration of the derivation of the introjects leads to the next logical question, namely, what is the patient's motivation for retaining these introjects and in fact clinging to them with such dire necessity? This is a critical juncture in the therapeutic progression and often gives rise to the stiffest and most vigorous resistance. Up until this point in the therapeutic process, the focus has been primarily on the clarification of the elements involved in the patient's pathology and an attempt to understand their organization along a number of important parameters. At this juncture, however, we begin to tap the patient's motivation for the neurosis or other psychopathology.

This becomes a very difficult piece of work and is often the level at which many therapies stagger. It is at this juncture that one begins to approach not merely what is involved in the patient's pathology, but his own inner reasons for clinging to it. I say "clinging" because it is my experience that one rarely finds a patient who is eager to surrender his neurosis. Rather, the patient *clings* to his introjects, defends them in a variety of ways, and fights off the therapist's attempts to make any inroads on them. The question then which naturally arises is, "Why are these introjects so intensely invested and so important to the patient?" The answer lies in the inherent narcissistic dynamics of the introjects themselves. It must be remembered that the latter provide the essential core in many of these patients around which the experience of his inner world and sense of himself, as an individuated and in some degree coherent entity, are organized. It is this threat to the patient's organization of his sense of self that creates the often rigid and intense barriers to therapeutic intervention.

What emerges from this reflection is that the introjection represents an adherence to the now internalized infantile objects of the patient's experience, and serves to prolong the infantile dependence on and attachment to those objects. Thus the most important parameter of this dependence is that of narcissism. The introjection preserves the patient's sense of infantile narcissism and is bound up in and expresses itself in the often repressed or split off feelings of omnipotence, superiority, and specialness. The dynamics of the paranoid process operate in such a way that these patients, often in hidden and subtle and difficult-to-elicit ways, see themselves as exceptional, in the sense in which Freud (1916) described the "exceptions." It can be said that the working through of this level of the patient's narcissism is absolutely essential to the success of the therapy. It should also be noted that this stage of the therapeutic work summons up all of the difficulties of working with pathological narcissism that have been matters of such current concern and controversy.

Besides the preservation of the patient's infantile narcissism, yet closely involved with it, the introjects and the clinging to them also preserves the patient's sense of attachment to infantile objects. This clinging to infantile objects tends to prompt a rehearsal of the elements of the patient's past experience with those objects. One frequently finds in such patients an unsatisfied and frustrated yearning for acceptance, love, closeness, and caring on the part of objects which have consequently been introjected. The introjection thus serves as a sort of defensive repossession of the object which cannot be achieved in reality. At the same time, it serves as an important defense against the underlying sense of rage, disappointment, and disillusionment in the relationship with these same objects.

The paradox in this infantile involvement and its derivatives is that they serve to preserve and sustain the objects at the cost of the subject. This is true not only of the external aspects of the relationship with objects, but also of the patient's inner world, since the internalization of these pathogenic introjects serves as a source of quasi-distortion and impairment within his own organization of himself and inhibits or distorts his capacity to achieve any real sense of autonomous self-identity. The cost, for example, to the depressed young housewife described above, was monumental in terms of her chronic dissatisfaction, depression, and sense of tormented worthlessness and envy. She was willing to pay this exorbitant price to gain a golden fleece — a sense of specialness, superiority, moral hauteur, and entitlement. The idealized and aggrandized image of her mother was preserved at considerable neurotic impairment and unhappiness.

But the dynamics operate also to preserve objects within the realm of the patient's external experience. For example, one frequently finds in relationship to the family involvements of such patients that there are hidden loyalties which operate in such a way as to reinforce and sustain the patient's introjective alignment, while at the same time they serve to protect the relationships within the family and the individuals involved in them. Often in this context family myths will arise which represent forms of adherence to a family projective system, usually organized in such a way as to preserve the introjective alignment of all the family members and to maintain a delicate balance in the narcissistic equilibrium. Frequently, then, the introjective alignment within the patient actually serves as a vehicle for the preservation of elements of threatened parental narcissism. This same young woman's adherence to the narcissistically embedded code of specialness and superiority through suffering was from this perspective calculated to reinforce and sustain the mother's highly vulnerable and fragile narcissism.

The Mourning of Infantile Attachments

The prior work of articulation of the introjects has led to a clarification of the elements involved in them and an examination of their derivation and motivation. This has involved focusing on the intrinsic relatedness and unity of the introjective polarities, the understanding that these polarities derive from each other and are locked together in mutual and reciprocal defensive interaction, and that they thus serve to reinforce each other and in consequence form an inseparable unity which is welded together in such a way that the patient is forced to a radical choice: he must either take both sides of the polarity together and work with them, or he must surrender both. He cannot have one without the other.

This radical choice is quite dramatic in depressive patients who come complaining of their depression and are relatively willing to surrender the devalued, diminished, and depleted polarity of their introjective alignment, but are quite unwilling to surrender the specialness and entitlement and exceptional dimensions of the opposite polarity. It remains, however, that they cannot surrender the one without surrendering the other. In addition, the work of articulation has brought into increasing focus the fantasy aspect of the introjects and their disparity from the elements of the real world of the patient's experience of himself and his environment.

The issue generated by these progressive insights is inevitably that of the surrender of the introjects. This requires some form of confrontation or working through of the infantile dependence and the narcissistic investment in the introjects. Not infrequently, as the narcissistic defenses are diminished, one begins to meet the intense rage and envy against the significant objects, which frequently has a highly oral character. This rage and envy often plays itself out in the relationship to the therapist and becomes a significant phase of the therapeutic work. It is another manifestation of the narcissistic dynamics, which divides the world into haves and have-nots, and divides the distribution of goods in terms of either/or or all-or-nothing. Thus the patient's envy of the therapist and what he has—whether that be in terms of worldly goods, social position, intelligence, or even a penis—must be worked through in terms of the underlying narcissistic dynamics.

This working through sets in motion an important mourning process in which the attachment to the infantile objects is gradually given up and the loss of those objects accepted and integrated. As the mourning process works its way through and the potency and influence of the introjects increasingly diminishes, one begins to experience with such patients a gradual and increasing emergence of autonomous ego capacities.

The Emergence of Transference Dependence

As the underlying determinants of the introjective economy become increasingly apparent and the mourning process of the immature and largely narcissistic attachments takes place, the patient's infantile dependence on past objects begins to be modified and gradually begins to wane. As that dependence wanes, however, the therapeutic dependence may begin to wax in important and problematic ways. In other words, the patient is often unwilling to surrender and resign infantile attachments, but rather seeks to replace them and substitute for them by a dependency relationship with the therapist.

The motivational basis for this process needs to be explored, clarified, and focused in the same terms as the patient's by-this-time explicit and recognizable narcissistic needs. Dependence on the therapeutic situation and on the therapist thus needs resolution on its own terms, and quite independently of the working through of infantile attachments to past significant object relationships. Dependence on the therapist can be seen in the same terms of emotional vacillation as the previously explored attachments. This is again a form of the emotional "seesaw." Most typically, this aspect of the emerging therapeutic dependence calls to mind the inferior, weak, vulnerable, and victimized aspect of the organization of the introjects—equivalently the victim-introject.

Again, the therapist must remind himself that the more powerful, superior, special, and entitled dimension of the introjective economy remains latent in this condition. These residual elements of the introjective dynamics will express themselves in terms of the patient's feelings of inadequacy, difficulty in dealing with periods of interruption of the therapy or absence of the therapist, apprehensions over the apparent therapeutic progression, the looming possibility of termination of the therapy, thus being faced with doing without the therapist, and so forth. All of these issues must be worked through in terms of the therapeutic relationship and must be seen specifically in terms of the resolution of the residual aspects of the patient's introjective dynamics—particularly the narcissistic dynamics.

As the pressure of these dependency needs increases, drawing the patient progressively into replacement of the objects of infantile dependence with the object of therapeutic dependence, there may be a defensive shift in the direction of a denial of such dependence and a retreat to a position of artifactual autonomy and self-sufficiency. This may take the form of a more or less narcissistic self-sufficiency, which defends against the pressure of dependency needs by a precipitous feeling of not needing the therapist or even of belittling or devaluing therapist and therapy. This may lead in the direction of the activation of the more powerful, superior and even grandiose aspects of the introjective economy—leaving the more inferior and inadequate and needy dimensions of the victim-introject more or less out of the picture.

Underlying this pressure toward narcissistic withdrawal and self-sufficiency or pseudoautonomy, there may be operating residual defenses against the patient's sense of narcissistic affront with accompanying feelings of rage and envy concerning the therapist. This may be accompanied again by the patient's anxiety and guilt over such rageful and envious feelings, along with a longing for love and caring and acceptance on the part of the therapist. It is not difficult to see that these motivations are restimulations of infantile concerns and serve as important defensive maneuvers against the working-through of immature attachments and dependencies.

Transference Resolution

What we have described thus far is a clarification and illumination of the introjective dynamics and the underlying motivation, particularly narcissistic, which support and drive them. The dynamics underlying the introjects are then shifted specifically into the transference relationship where the issues of dependency are worked through again on a different level with a hopefully therapeutic resolution. It is precisely this task which is undertaken in the present step of the therapeutic schema. When the patient's dependence on the therapist has become sufficiently intense, the next important step involves working through and surrendering that infantile dependence within the therapeutic relationship. Thus the mourning process, having to do with the surrendering of infantile attachments to past significant object relationships, is now extended and reworked within the therapeutic relationship in regard to the infantile attachment to the therapist. The patient must be helped to work through a variety of regressive infantile pressures which operate to keep him in a position of dependency and serve to satisfy underlying narcissistic needs. As these elements are gradually worked through, there begins to be established within the therapeutic relationship an increasing degree of autonomy and an increasing area for the exercise and expression of the patient's sense of initiative and industry. Finally, there is the clearer and more decisive emergence of the patient's own sense of identity.

The resolution of the transference dependency requires the reactivation and extension of the mourning process, which deals specifically with the loss of the transference object. As this mourning process takes place, the therapist is gradually surrendered along with the patient's sense of reliance and dependence on him. The therapeutic relationship particularly in regard to its transference elements is gradually replaced with a more real relationship based on the more mature and autonomous aspects of the patient's developing personality. Thus the mourning of the transference object is made possible by the gradual enlargement of the therapeutic alliance, which takes place through the increasing absorption, reworking, and reintegrating of the infantile aspects of the therapeutic relationship, most acutely and intensely the elements of the transference neurosis, into the therapeutic alliance.

Termination

The working through of the mourning process over the loss of the transference object and the resolution of the transference elements sets the stage for the final achievement of the therapeutic process, namely, the termination. As the infantile underpinnings and motivations for the organization of the introjects are gradually eroded, the potentiality becomes available for the introjection of aspects of the therapist and elements of the therapeutic alliance which offer the possibility of a more reasonable, realistic, and adaptive organization of the patient's functioning sense of self.

These emerging introjections, derived from the therapeutic relationship and most particularly influenced by aspects of the therapeutic alliance, are considerably less susceptible to regressive drive influences and drive distortions. They are correspondingly less involved in defensive needs for protection and sustaining of the patient's sense of narcissistic investment. Increasingly, the patient's capacity for modeling himself on the more realistic and adaptive aspects of the therapist opens the way for emerging identifications which enhance the autonomy and structural capacity to resist drive derivatives in the patient's ego. The termination work continues and enhances the critical internalizations which form the basis of inner structural changes, specifically changes in the ego and superego, which serve as the basis for longer-lasting and adaptive therapeutic change. Thus there is a shift from defensive to adaptive concerns, a refocusing of the patient's interest and investment from the past to the present and future, and, in general, an unleashing of developmental potential which leads in the direction of increasing personality growth which is more reasonable, more stable, more adaptive and mature.

CONCLUDING COMMENT

The foregoing schema sets forth a logic of the therapeutic progression based on the paranoid process. It does not solve the dilemmas of psychotherapy, nor does it substitute for the hard knocks of therapeutic experience and the guidance of good supervision. It does provide a frame of reference for the logical progression of the therapeutic process which has proven helpful in the writer's own experience and useful in the experience of others. Patients offer an infinite variety of problems and difficulties which challenge any approach to the understanding of therapy. I would hope that the above schema, compressed and condensed through it is, may provide a helpful orientation — possibly a guide for the perplexed — since even such a simple frame of reference may help in the dark thickets of psychotherapy where we are all often perplexed and frequently frustrated.

NOTE

1. The notion of narcissistic alliance has been proposed by Dr. Robert Mehlman.

REFERENCES

Adler, G., and Buie, Jr., D. H. (1972). The misuses of confrontation with borderline patients. *International Journal of Psychoanalytic Psychotherapy* 1(3):109-120.
Buie, Jr., D. H., and Adler, G. (1972). The uses of confrontation with borderline patients. *International Journal of Psychoanalytic Psychotherapy* 1(3):90-108.

Corwin, H. (1972). The scope of therapeutic confrontation from routine to heroic. *International Journal of Psychoanalytic Psychotherapy* 1(3): 68-89.

Freud, A. (1936). *The Ego and the Mechanisms of Defense*. Rev. ed. New York: International Universities Press, 1966.

Freud, S. (1916). Some character-types met within psycho-analytic work. *Standard Edition* 14:309-333. London: Hogarth, 1957.

Greenson, R. R. (1967). *The Technique and Practice of Psychoanalysis. Vol. 1*. New York: International Universities Press.

Guntrip, H. (1969). *Schizoid Phenomena, Object Relations and the Self*. New York: International Universities Press.

Hartmann, H. (1939). *Ego Psychology and the Problem of Adaptation*. New York: International Universities Press, 1958.

Jacobson, E. (1964). *The Self and the Object World*. New York: International Universities Press.

———(1971). *Depression: Comparative Studies of Normal, Neurotic, and Psychotic Conditions*. New York: International Universities Press.

Kernberg, O. (1966). Structural derivatives of object relationships. *International Journal of Psycho-Analysis* 47:236-253.

———(1967). Borderline personality organization. *Journal of the American Psychoanalytic Association* 15: 641-685.

Kohut, H. (1971). *The Analysis of the Self*. New York: International Universities Press.

Langs, R. J. (1973). *The Technique of Psychoanalytic Psychotherapy. Vol. 1*. New York: Aronson.

———(1974). *The Technique of Psychoanalytic Psychotherapy. Vol. 2*. New York: Aronson.

Masud R. Khan, M. (1972). The finding and becoming of self. *International Journal of Psychoanalytic Psychotherapy* 1:97-111.

Meissner, S. J., W. W. (1971). Notes on identification. II. Clarification of related concepts. *Psychoanalytic Quarterly* 40:277-302.

———(1974). Correlative aspects of introjective and projective mechanisms. *American Journal of Psychiatry* 131:176-180.

———(1976). *The Paranoid Process*. New York: Aronson.

Modell, A. (1968). *Object Love and Reality*. New York: International Universities Press.

Polatin, P. (1975). Psychotic disorders: Paranoid states. *Comprehensive Textbook of Psychiatry II*, eds. A. M. Freedman, H. I. Kaplan, and B. J. Sadock. Baltimore: Williams and Wilkins, pp. 992-1002.

Rapaport, D. (1967). *The Collected Papers of David Rapaport*, ed. M. Gill. New York: Basic Books.

Schafer, R. (1959). Generative empathy in the treatment situation. *Psychoanalytic Quarterly* 28:342-373.

———(1968). *Aspects of Internalization*. New York: International Universities Press.

Schwartz, D. A. (1963). A review of the "paranoid" concept. *Archives of General Psychiatry* 8:349-361.

Segal, H. (1964). *Introduction to the Work of Melanie Klein*. London:Heinemann.

Shapiro, D. (1965). *Neurotic Styles*. New York:Basic Books.

Winnicott, D. W. (1947). Hate in the countertransference. *Collected Papers:Through Pediatrics to Psycho-Analysis*. New York: Basic Books, 1958.

———(1963). Psychiatric disorder in terms of infantile maturational processes. *The Maturational Process and the Facilitating Environment*. New York: International Universities Press, 1965.

Zetzel, E. R. (1970). *The Capacity for Emotional Growth*. New York: International Universities Press.

———(1971). A developmental approach to the borderline patient. *American Journal of Psychiatry* 127:867-871.

W. W. MEISSNER, S.J., M.D.

DR. MEISSNER is currently associate clinical professor of psychiatry at Harvard Medical School in Boston as well as staff psychiatrist, Massachusetts Mental Health Center, Boston and Cambridge City Hospital. He also serves as chairman of faculty, Boston Psychoanalytic Society and Institute.

Victim, Victimizer: Interaction in the Psychotherapy of Borderline Patients

Theodore Nadelson, M.D.

Associate Psychiatrist
Beth Israel Hospital, Boston

Assistant Professor of Psychiatry
Harvard Medical School, Boston

Borderline and narcissistic patients suffuse relationships with intense pregenital aggression to which the therapist, despite his level of training or self-understanding, is not totally immune. Aggression is considered an energetic expression of the narcissistic defense against vulnerability. The therapist is subject to a continuing siege of projections and projective identifications. Vigilance against repetitive sadomasochistic interactions is a necessary and often wearying extension of therapeutic concern. Most necessary, too, is the willingness to make second efforts at understanding the patient's vulnerability. Such understanding comes from attentiveness to countertransference feelings.

INTRODUCTION

Borderline patients and a subgroup, narcissistic personalities, have a number of characteristics in common. They are frequently angry and anxious and defend with splitting, denial, projective identification, and omnipotence (Kernberg, 1975).

The impact of such a patient's aggression on the therapy and the therapist[1] is the focus of this paper. Although there are some major differences between the two character typologies, they have similar defenses and share the tendency to extremes of pregenital rage; so that for the purpose of this paper, reference to the more general category of borderline conditions will be understood to subsume narcissistic character conditions as well.

It has been suggested that the narcissistic defenses of such patients invariably engender a sense of helplessness (Adler, 1972), frustration, anger, shame, and depression (Little, 1966; Maltsberger and Buie, 1974; Money-Kyrle, 1956). Other patients, with different diagnoses, may engender such feelings in therapists. The view presented, however, is that the therapist's most important focus is on the form and meaning of the primitive aggression and that access to the understanding of the rage within the patient obtains from the sensitivity of the therapist to his own feeling states (Heiman, 1950, 1960; Little, 1951; Maltsberger and Buie, 1974; Winnicott, 1949). The patient, because of the nature of early object relations and "bad," i.e., hostile, introjects, influences the relationship in the direction of a rapid shift from victim to victimizer interactions. The patient's unconscious omnipotence and control, transferred to the therapist and alternately retrieved, is both elusive and destructive. The difficulty for the therapist is that constant vigilance is both wearying but necessary because the patient's mode of interaction suffuses the relationship as a totality and not just in discrete interactions. In a context in which there is conscious expectation of relief, the continued repetition of familiar, demeaning and frustrating sadomasochistic exchanges can be devastating; for in the patient's psychology, if the therapist cannot make changes occur, no one can.

Modell (1975) notes that reasonably well-integrated therapists experience more or less similar reactions to such attacks and this phenomenon is more a reflection of the patient's problems than of the specific nature of the therapist's past. Such "usual," "normal," or "objective" countertransference feelings represent the therapist's essentially human response to the patient's attack, control, and nullification. There is, I believe, always a potential susceptibility on the part of all therapists for such interactions with borderline or narcissistic patients, although some therapists may be more repetitively susceptible. The literature on this subject supports this contention (Adler, 1972; Chase and Hire, 1966; Fliess, 1953; Kernberg, 1965, 1968, 1975; Kohut, 1966, 1971; Little, 1951, 1966; Money-Kyrle, 1956; Winnicott, 1949, 1960).

Would the "ideal" therapist not experience such reactions to the patients' infantile rage and contempt, or not be susceptible to reciprocal victim become victimizer interactions? The experience of this writer (and those cited in the paragraph above) is that such an ideal is more a hypothetical construct than a reality. It seems better to speak of the "good enough therapist" (to modify a phrase of Winnicott's) ; mindful of the probability of the presence of his own emotional responses and the possibility that such responses might be interjected into the therapy.

The therapist's analysis or psychotherapy may tend to increase awareness of pregenital issues but does not confer absolute immunity against their presence while working with borderline patients. Little (1951) comments: "The ever quoted remedy for countertransference, more analysis of the analyst, is at best incomplete, for some tendency to develop unconscious infantile countertransference is bound to remain." The present paper contains three clinical vignettes which characterize one therapist's struggle with the issue. It is assumed that other therapists have similar experiences although there are undoubtedly differences in degree and form of reaction. It is hoped that they can serve as a "forewarning and rearming" (Winnicott, 1949) regarding the necessary strain, sometimes overwhelming, in treating borderline patients. The therapist's wish to help and repair is an autonomous function and also partly dictated by narcissistic needs. Yet all those who perform therapy, in order to do it, must possess this impulse. The difficulty and confusion, partially charted in this paper, comes from the wish to help, and consequent anger at not understanding, not being understood, and being rejected or negated. Concern for the patient is manifested when in the midst of such feelings the therapist can step back and make the good "second effort."

AGGRESSION AND SPLITTING: DEFENSES OF THE PATHOLOGICAL EGO STRUCTURE

Kernberg (1966, 1967, 1975) and Kohut (1966, 1971) have recently illuminated the complex etiology of borderline conditions. Attention here will be on understanding aggression, primarily its defensive aspect, as it appears in the therapy and affects the therapist's internal state and responses. It is recognized that such a view does not encompass the totality of aggression. The emphasis on aggression as defense and on the defensive aspect of splitting (and subsidiary defenses) has been found to be more helpful than a nonspecific approach which locates the difficulty with such patients in their "extreme aggressiveness," "poor impulse control," or "weak ego." A better-articulated "structural analysis" finds "highly specific defensive operations" beneath the aggressive surface activity (Kernberg, 1966, 1975). There is therapeutic importance in perceiving the defensive aspect of the patient's aggression while reacting to attack. Such a mental operation both helps to delay the therapist's own human response and also may bring him closer to the essential issue of the patient's narcissistic vulnerability.

Aggression as Defense; Projection as Defense Against Aggressive Introjects

Severe early frustration is a usual finding in patients with borderline conditions, and although constitutional issues may be a factor, they still remain as conjecture. The form of aggression, moreover, repeatedly directed toward the therapist, is seen as a specific reflection of such early deprivation (Kernberg, 1965; Little, 1966).

My view of the borderline and narcissistic characters emphasizes, primarily, their narcissistic vulnerability, arising from inability to synthesize or metabolize good and bad introjects. They thus have never arrived at a sense of self; they have no "right to a life" (Modell, 1965). Such a patient suffers from a continuing conviction of being unwanted and unloved, of being unredeemable, damned, and guilty. This unsupportable feeling state is dealt with largely by splitting (to be discussed below) and projection of aggressive part objects. However, and this is an additional emphasis here, aggression, which suffuses the relationship with others, is in itself *the energetic expression or assertion of self-preservation against the threat of psychic annihilation*. It is defense, rather than drive, as Rochlin (1973) points out. Such patients often assert that, when they feel angry, they experience more of a sense of being "alive" and in contact with the world—although such feelings are always transient. The difficulty for the borderline patient is that there is no way of achieving permanent distance from aggression. The defense itself reminds them of their "badness," just as splitting (which defends against being overwhelmed by aggressive introjects), in itself, perpetuates difficulty in modulating emotional dispositions (Kernberg, 1975).

Early frustration by parental figures is emphasized as an etiological factor here. Such patients report the feeling of having been teased or "toyed with" without regard to their individual emotions. Such feelings are often projected onto the therapist who is seen as using the patient for his own ends. It may be true that, in such early parent-child interactions, the parents may excessively project their own needs onto their children, never ceding to them their own individuality. (As therapy proceeds, this issue often becomes a foremost concern for borderline patients with regard to their own offspring.)

In summary, emphasis has been given to the defensive rather than drive aspects of aggression. Aggressive past objects are split off from libidinal counterparts and projected; aggression itself is used as an assertive expression of self-defense. Early frustration by parental figures is viewed as the primary etiological factor. The role of intense aggressive drive or constitutional lack of anxiety tolerance (Kernberg, 1975) is less emphasized because it seems to have less therapeutic importance. Often it is the case that the therapist, when attacked, may feel that the patient is simply an angry, demanding person. The understanding of the projective and defensive aspect of the patient's rage may allow for increased tolerance and empathy with the patient's vulnerability.

Splitting

The early mother-child relationship engenders a crisis in terms of a number of conceptually separable, but interrelated factors: (1) self-object differentiation (Kernberg, 1967, 1975; Little, 1966; Zetzel, 1971); (2) internalization of ego identity (Zetzel, 1971) or "integration of self and object images built up under libidinal drive derivatives with their corresponding self and object images built up under aggressive drive derivatives" (Kernberg, 1975); and (3) the capacity to master loss and narcissistic injury (Zetzel, 1971).

Stable one-to-one relationships, given basic self-object differentiation, depend on internalization of ego identity. The basic borderline defense against identity diffusion is splitting; a normal part of the development in which opposite and contradictory impulses (good versus bad internal objects or positive and negative introjections) are built up separately (Kernberg, 1967, 1975). The mechanism was mentioned by Freud (1911) as an early factor in the development of paranoia and later more fully defined (1940). Kernberg's (1975, pp. 30-34) exposition of the early sources of ego weakness articulates the complexity of the splitting defense and the subsidiary defenses of projection, projective identification, denial, omnipotence, and reciprocal devaluation. Such a process is seen as a means of allaying primitive anxiety during the first year of life, before the normal integrative capacity of the ego develops higher levels of defense. In the borderline condition, however, splitting remains the active process, protecting the ego from conflict by separating the introjections of libidinal and aggressive impulses. Contradictory attitudes toward objects alternate with great intensity; the separation minimizes "the diffusion of anxiety within the ego but is detrimental ultimately to a stable ego identity." Splitting maintains the borderline and narcissistic characters as a specific personality organization rather than a fluctuating state between psychosis and neurosis.

Transference, Projective Identification, Projective Counteridentification, and Countertransference

The patient projects upon the therapist a sense of uselessness, lack of worth, greed, or hostility (Kernberg, 1968). When the therapist feels drained and frustrated, he is experiencing the intense distrust of the patient manifested by a primitive form of projection: projective identification (Kernberg, 1968, 1975; Klein, 1945; Money-Kyrle, 1956; Segal, 1967). Projective identification is a continuing factor in the relationships of borderline characters who identify and "empathize fearfully" with the person on whom they have projected their own aggressive part object (Kernberg, 1975). Projective identification differs from projection in that it represents a weakening of ego boundaries particularly with regard to specific aggressive part objects. As a result identification occurs with the person on whom the aggressive part objects have been projected. (In projection the mechanism leads to rejection of, not empathy with, the other person.) The therapist, on whom the patient has projected strong oral-aggressive feelings, is experienced in the transference as a hostile, attacking person. The patient empathizes with this aggressive drive (Malin and Grotstein, 1966) and tries to control the therapist in a sadistic way to overpower him in the struggle. The patient may be aware of his hostility but feels it to be self-preservative (Kernberg, 1968). Also, borderline patients rarely state positive feelings toward the therapist, the more usual expressions are of negation or disappointment. Often underlying this frequent maneuver is the patient's feeling that any closeness would mean that the therapist would come within range of the patient's destructiveness (Malin and Grotstein, 1966). The therapist's reaction of anger is similar to the patient's feeling state in kind, but rarely in intensity. Depending on the degree to which it is manifested, it can be viewed as a "natural" or "objective" countertransference (Winnicott, 1949). (I am not speaking here of extremes of reactivity, or explosions of rage or rejection which mimic the patient's intense pregenital rage.) The failure of the therapist in realizing the defensive aspect of the aggression and its origin in split and projected introjects represents a self-preservative response to attack and also the difficulty the therapist has in recognizing his own narcissistic vulnerability. When projective defenses are employed (whether projection or projective identification) the *patient* experiences the qualities or emotions as *within* the therapist. The *therapist* may only be aware of the patient's attempt to attribute feelings to him: he is aware of the projection *onto* him. Often the therapist remains unaware of the effect of the patient's aggressiveness on his own feeling states; he remains unaware of the patient's projected feelings *within* him. This has been termed projective counteridentification; it is the therapist's response to projective identification. "The [therapist feels or] behaves as if he had really and concretely acquired characteristics of the patient by assimilating the aspects projected onto him" (Grinberg, 1962). I believe that this is, in varying degrees, the essence of "usual" countertransference feelings experienced with borderline patients. A related feeling of disinterest or loss of empathic attention often occurs when the therapist is "dehumanized" or treated as if he were not present (Kohut, 1966).

It is as if all patients with borderline conditions engender a countertransference anger which represents the emergence of the aggressive part of the patient from within the therapist (Kernberg, 1968; Maltsberger and Buie, 1972; Money-Kyrle, 1956). The therapist's response sometimes, however, is to disengage for a prolonged period from the patient, to treat him also as if he were not present. This is viewed as a form of *folie à deux*, a response of the therapist to the patient's identifying with him. Such counteridentifications continually interfere with empathy by interrupting necessary "transient trial identifications" (Fliess, 1953). The process of therapy has, as an important ingredient, this "trial acting with smallest quantities of cathexis" in order to contain and examine the thought of the patient. This produces similar small quantities of affective processes in the therapist as he experiences another's feelings (ibid.).

The usual attitude in therapy, then, also places the therapist in the most vulnerable position for narcissistic injury. The attitude of attentive listening focussed on the patient; emotional reactivity to the patient, and necessary identification with him sometimes clouds both apperception of his own feeling states and his objectivity. The therapeutic situation itself may lull him into a "stuck" counteridentification (Reich, 1951). Further, since he intends, primarily, to help the patient, such intent leaves him open to the latter's aggression and often does not allow him to perceive that he may be angry as well, when his own sense of separateness is under attack.

The pivotal issue in treatment, given the therapist's more or less stable narcissistic equilibrium, experience, and skill, resides in understanding the issue of the projected and defensive aggression as it appears in treatment between the two principals. Such exploration requires the therapist's willingness to realize that strong, angry feelings may be present, coexistent with a reparative impulse which may obscure them (Money-Kyrle, 1956). The therapist may experience a sense of unrest, disinterest, or discord with the patient. He may feel that he does not understand, simultaneously with a feeling of wishing to just "let the issue go." Such feelings are signals that the empathic bond has been broken, that the therapist does not understand and has become more fixed in counteridentification or projective counteridentification. It is necessary for the therapist to react to his own discomfort not by more distancing, but by self-examination. Clarity, however, often forms up slowly and the good "second effort" is of more help than the immediate assumption and interpretation. In other words, the therapist may have to experience discomfort.

The therapist must feel good about himself and separated from the patient to continue helpful dialogue (Leibovich, 1973). Often it is necessary to realize, repeatedly, that he is subject to emotional forces which at times are too difficult for immediate mastery, that he wishes to help as best he can, that the patient is defending against a sense of vulnerability (rather than being, simply, an aggressive, hostile person), and that he also defends for the same reason. Given enough time, they may be able to understand and respect each other as individuals. In the meantime, he is under "strain" (Winnicott, 1960), and his recognition of the strain and its meaning gives him access to the center of the patient's fragility.

SADOMASOCHISTIC RECIPROCITY

Case 1

A thirty-year-old nurse, in treatment for five years, angrily and contemptuously accused me of ineffectiveness, banality, and lack of interest, incisively enumerating my failures. I asked what more she wished and raised the question as to what was really troubling her. The patient was totally rejecting of such inquiry; it was "more of the same pat psychiatric formula." I was aware

of a personal sense of physical discomfort, experienced with the patient previously. I thought, "I have not really helped; I am repetitious; there is nothing more I can think of to say—I am like this frequently—all of the time—
with her and with others."

I then asked quietly if we should discuss interrupting treatment at this
time; she had for a long time said it was no help and that we should stop.

The patient cried out in a terrified way, "Please don't shout at me."

At the moment when I suggested the discussion of interruption of treatment I felt that it might be best for the patient; she could be relieved of her
hostility toward me and terminating might also be perceived as freedom to
leave a relationship in which she felt trapped and angry. Also, at a preconscious level, *I* felt trapped, defeated, and depressed. I was not aware, totally,
of the reason for my physical discomfort until the patient ended her lacerating criticism and openly expressed the sense of helplessness, fear, and self-
negation that she had projected onto me.

Not only is the tendency to counteridentification most important, but so is
the receptivity and susceptibility of the therapist to take it on, often repetitively. It was this phenomenon which immobilized me from the appropriate
clarification regarding the patient's affect; I reacted to her feeling state
within me. After, when I saw this cycle, and realized it had happened before,
I could offer an appropriate clarification directed toward her underlying self-
negation. I could only do this after I appreciated that *I was placing back
within her the self-negation and helplessness* which she had thrust on me. The
elusive, but important, issue presented by Malin and Grotstein (1966) is that
identification is always a part of the more primitive process of projective identification. *For patients with borderline characters, projective identification
represents an important means of achieving object relationships.* My initial
agreement with her projection (by indicating that I might be of no further
help) was largely unconscious and was a form of projective counteridentification; an assimilation of her projections onto and into me. Also unconscious
was a wish to *rid myself* of the patient, in order not to experience negative
and/or sadistic feelings and to be free of the necessary and wearying self-ana-
lytic vigilance. There was then, an associated anger concomitant with the reflex to extrude the patient from within (or to be outside of the patient). At
such a moment, the "I-thou" relationship, at least temporarily, ended. When
I was subsequently free to scrutinize the affectual oscillations of both of us,
and to help her to examine her projection, dialogue was reestablished and our
relationship had far less reciprocal negation. I also was aware of my own general impulses and sensitivity to the stress such patients impose on me. This
episode started a new, positive phase of treatment with more of a sense of alliance. Attention was then directed toward her sense of lack of value and to her

Interaction in the Psychotherapy of Borderline Patients   123

anticipation of ridicule, which made for cycles of rejection of others, and terror of loneliness which forced her into subservient positions.

Case 2

A young lawyer, in treatment for five years, complained persistently of his hopelessness with regard to real change. He (and his wife) were still virgins after a two-year marriage. He contemplated suicide often and engaged in self-destructive behaviors. Despite this he did well at work and received several promotions. He often resented the fact that others saw only his good functioning and were concerned only about his continued productiveness. That complaint and his sense of his own destructiveness (linked to the death, in his youth, of an ailing father) were constant and central.

After many years, he complained of my lateness (of a few minutes), compensated by an extension (often an overextension) of time at the end. The regularity of my lateness was at first denied by me, but eventually was undeniable as I realized that despite a conscious effort I still was, often, late. Sometimes he confronted me with the fact. At one point I told the patient that I would try not to be late again.

The patient was in the midst of a stress at work. An important legal case had come up at a time when I missed an appointment. The patient, prior to this, had been continually self-destructive, with minor automobile accidents, falls, and wandering on the streets in dangerous areas. My attempts to set limits were met by indifference. My own anger was not totally known to me then. After missing the appointment, despite renewed resolution to be on time, I was late again. The patient, sadly, yet angrily, confronted me with my lateness and with my possible anger.

I realized, only after my final lateness, that I had been continually reacting to the patient's negation of me and indifference to my own impulse to help. My occasional overextension of time at the end of the hour was an attempt to both undo my reciprocal anger toward him as well as from an impulse to help. A stalemate in treatment had ensued, which I felt in terms of its repetitive, boring quality. Yet I did not have free enough excursion of feeling and thought to understand it. Immediately after I recovered from the surprise of my own countertransference action I was better able to perceive the total process in which I had been a participant, alternately as victim and victimizer. I felt suddenly more relaxed; my anger had been placed back into the patient; or rather his rage was back where it belonged. My own narcissistically engendered hostility was reduced and replaced more by concern. I did not feel throttled or confined and the patient and I discussed what had happened. I indicated my culpability, saying simply that I was at fault, and told him that I had not been attentive to my own feelings and my lateness was the result. We could speak of our frustration with the direction and slowness of treatment. We both acknowledged a temporary stalemate. The patient spoke of his sense of distance from me (and others) and consequent emptiness. He seemed relieved and eager to talk. (I felt suddenly relaxed and engaged with him.) He indicated that "closeness" threatened total rejection from me because I would then perceive his "meanness" or badness and reject him ultimately. I felt that it was necessary not to burden the patient with agonizing self-confession and revelation of intrapsychic issues. My simple (oversimplified) explanation of "inattention because of frustration" or annoyance was enough. I was aware very strongly of my own narcissistic needs to be in charge, all-knowing and all-curing, and their personal origins. I also sensed that too much confession on my part would bring the oscillation back to the position where I would again be the patient's victim. My feeling of comfort, similar to the patient's, occured when the tone was one of dialogue between separate individuals. Subsequent to that episode the patient made frequent references to feeling "close" with me, and continued treatment despite ensuing discomfort. It was easier, subsequently, to avoid distancing and destructive behaviors. I felt, since then, that my repeated lateness took place partly as an unconscious attempt to break through a bind, to stir things up, to make a change. In analyzing that impulse, it seemed clear that there was hostile intent: a wish for me to do to the patient what he had done to me, to treat with indifference. In addition to this sadistic intent, however, I felt there was also a wish to put therapy on a new footing in order to help the patient.

Although such an end was accomplished, it was difficult to assess the residual effect of such an act on the totality of the therapy. I believe that the patient continued in treatment partly because of the continued concern I manifested toward him even after the episode. My sense is that a greater degree of vigilance regarding my feeling state might have avoided the episode and allowed a more contained, reasoned approach to the same end.

Case 3

A twenty-six-year-old single, black administrative assistant started psychotherapy mostly at the request of her employer. She had finished college despite a general steady state of resolute depression punctuated by three suicide attempts requiring hospitalization.

Her father had left the home before she was three and her mother remarried a merchant seaman who was at sea for months; then would return home to drink and play seemingly endless card games. Her mother, an upright, churchgoing woman (who raised the patient with dogmatic moral restrictions) was powerless to make any changes. The patient fought openly with him; when he died, after a long illness (he had a demyelinating disease), she did not go to his funeral.

She often indicated disgust with everybody, "regardless of race, creed, or color." She claimed that her universal contempt absolved her of bigotry; yet her most lacerating anger was directed at black people. She shared this prejudice with her mother who was open in her dislike for dark skin.

I was overtly spared her total negation, but often I was aware of my discomfort as she sat silently, or repetitively stated that nothing had changed — and nothing would. Medication for depression seemed to help lift her mood for a short period, then she lapsed again into her steady state. She came to every hour, however, and on occasion we would explore her past. In between hours she indicated that she barely functioned; on two occasions she made suicidal gestures. Sometimes she talked in detail, with some emotion, about her childhood, but afterward would indicate, more or less, that all that was said did not matter. I shifted from such explorations to feeling that my role was just to "be there," so that she could talk to "someone," and then would try again. I also supplied analgesics for headache and premenstrual cramps. I often defined the task for myself as a "holding action," especially when she became more depressed after we had discussed her feelings of desperation. After doing this for a while, I began to feel a loss of empathy and interest, and I was aware of the feeling of wanting her to go away, sometimes wishing that she *would* suicide.

During one therapeutic hour, after listening to her contempt directed again toward the people at work and her neighbors, I felt my own anger toward her more strongly. After years of listening, nothing had changed, and she was going to continue telling me that there was no hope. On this occasion I realized what I thought was the nature of the combined attack and defense in the treatment. I was her victim, to be dragged down in helplessness and frustration in a situation that mimicked her own life. Her defense was not to respond to any extension of help from me. I realized that through most of her life, her family and friends were exposed to the manuever. She lived without hope because the inevitable disappointment was too much to bear. I felt great compassion, during subsequent hours, feeling my empathy restored and during one hour I experienced a kinesthetic sense of holding her, like a baby. Immediately after, I felt the object writhe, trying to get away. I then said, "What happens if someone tries to hold you, support you, comfort you?" She started to say "I've got—" and I finished the sentence "—to get away." She looked fixedly at me, tearfully. We started for the first time to talk about her absolute emptiness and hopelessness.

As the treatment went on, references to her emptiness became easier. We both frequently referred to her worthlessness as a precipitant of suicide attempts. She remained sad, but more functional and increased, very slowly, some social contacts. She resumed going to school. She seemed more "in treatment." As a result we both looked forward to seeing each other as therapy continued.

In this case the sadomasochistic interaction was more subtle; and also was, fortunately, more contained, perhaps because I was attacked with less intensity. Of greatest general importance, however, is the way in which a therapist can become potentially stuck in a "supportive" role, feeling that he is doing his best for the patient who cannot "tolerate" psychodynamic explorations (Maltzberger and Buie, 1972). In this case the therapist, for a while (longer than he would like to admit), was identified with the patient, experiencing her frustration, feeling demeaned as only a dispenser of analgesics, sharing her hopelessness. Both principals were simultaneously victim and victimizer in a dull repetition of the patient's past. The therapy and therapist, then, again presented to her what she expected, no hope, no way out. The therapist's awareness of his own feeling state and the *necessity of attending to it* pulled him out of this collusion with the patient's punitive, primitive superego and allowed empathy and hope to enter the treatment situation. It was then that helpful treatment began.

CONCLUSION

Aggression is presented as the pivotal issue to be confronted by the therapist in treatment of borderline conditions. It is viewed as a portion of the narcissistic defense against psychological negation and annihilation. The aggression is often so intense and pervasive that in most interactions with borderline people, a usual human impulse is to counterattack as a similar, reciprocal defense against the onslaught. Although the therapist may be generally aware of the patient's feelings of vulnerability, the oral aggression leveled at him leads to feelings of negation and, often, anger. He usually reacts inwardly, but may often act out his countertransference anger in subtle or gross ways, either compensating for his own anger by submitting to the patient's, or by direct expression. Although such events are regrettable, the therapist, at his best, is vigilant and aware both of his own anger and of the potential that such feelings may escape his attention. Denial of such feelings (or the significance of consequent actions) presents the therapist with the most difficulty. It distorts psychotherapy in the direction of perpetuation of overt and covert sadomasochistic interactions while simultaneously eroding the therapist's self-esteem.

Three vignettes were presented. In the first two examples, the therapist became an active part of victim into victimizer reciprocity unwittingly, and dealt with it at first by denial and only later, in acknowledging the fact to himself, brought the essential issue to bear for the patient. In the third example, the feelings of aggression were more contained, and, as the therapist sat with the patient, he gained a sense of the overall nature of the patient's interaction with the world by analyzing the countertransference feelings as a *means of access* to the patient's unconscious. Once understood and assimilated, such feelings were elucidated to the patient. Although it is frightening, in a fog, to become suddenly aware of a warning beacon, the alternative is usually worse.

Concern, Vigilance, and the Therapist's Vulnerability

Vigilance toward one's own countertransference feeling is an extension of concern regarding the patient. The therapist's acknowledgment, understanding, and acceptance of his own vulnerability will allow him to be empathic rather than distancing when encountering the patient's defense against such feelings.

Acknowledgement or confession alone of uncomfortable or depressing feelings accompanying hostile impulses or countertransference acting out does not confer absolution or relief for the therapist. What helps the therapist is working through the crisis engendered by such recognition. The use of countertransference must be tempered by rational process, however. There must be more cues to the patient's underlying affectual state than the therapist's impulse to reveal his own feeling state. Such feelings and urges to reveal the truth are best inspected within the therapist for a time; they should be allowed to "mature" slowly.

Supervision is of aid, certainly, in furthering understanding, but continued self-analysis and expectation of such crises is part of the "therapist's burden." That particular kind of crisis is what the reader may have discerned to be the starting point for this paper. I am most clearly aware that the most important frontier in the performance of therapy exists within the therapist.

NOTE

1. "Therapist" is used throughout the rest of this paper to designate the person providing treatment of any sort, including psychoanalytic treatment. The focus of this paper is on the shifts of feeling in a therapeutic setting and it is assumed to be relevant for any treatment mode.

REFERENCES

Adler, G. (1972). Helplessness in the helpers. *British Journal of Medical Psychology* 22:454-461.
Chase, L., and Hire, W. (1966). Countertransference in the analysis of borderlines. Read at the Boston Psychoanalytic Society and Institute, March 23, 1966 (mimeo).
Fliess, R. (1953). Countertransference and counteridentification. *Journal of the American Psychoanalytic Association* 1:268-284.

Freud, S. (1911). Psycho-analytic notes on an autobiographical account of a case of paranoia. *Standard Edition* 12:3-84. London: Hogarth Press, 1961.

_____ (1940). Splitting of the ego in the process of defense. *Standard Edition* 23:271-278. London: Hogarth Press, 1961.

Grinberg, L. (1962). On a specific aspect of countertransference due to the patient's projective identification. *International Journal of Psycho-Analysis* 43:436-440.

Heiman, P. (1950). On countertransference. *International Journal of Psycho-Analysis* 31:81-84.

_____ (1960). Countertransference. *British Journal of Medical Psychology* 33:9-12.

Kernberg, O. (1965). Notes on countertransference. *Journal of the American Psychoanalytic Association* 13: 38-56.

_____ (1966). Structural derivatives of object relationships. *International Journal of Psycho-Analysis* 47:236-252.

_____ (1967). Borderline personality organization. *Journal of the American Psychoanalytic Association* 15: 641-685.

_____ (1968). The treatment of patients with borderline personality organization. *International Journal of Psycho-Analysis* 49:600-619.

_____ (1975). *Borderline Conditions and Pathological Narcissism*. New York: Aronson.

Klein, M. (1946). Notes on some schizoid mechanisms. *Developments in Psychoanalysis*, ed. J. Riviere. London: Hogarth Press, 1952.

Kohut, H. (1966). Forms and transformations of narcissism. *Journal of the American Psychoanalytic Association* 14:243-272.

_____ (1971). *The Analysis of the Self*. New York: International Universities Press.

Leibovitch, M. (1973). An aspect of the psychotherapy of borderline patients. *What Is Psychotherapy?* Proceedings of the Ninth International Congress of Psychotherapy, Oslo. Reprinted in *Psychotherapy and Psychosomatics* 25:365-369.

Little, M. (1951). Countertransference and the patient's response to it. *International Journal of Psycho-Analysis* 32: 32-40.

_____ (1966). Transference in borderline states. *International Journal of Psycho-Analysis* 47:476-485.

Malin, A., and Grotstein, J. (1966). Projective identification in the therapeutic process. *International Journal of Psycho-Analysis* 47:26-31.

Maltsberger, J., and Buie, D. (1974). Countertransference hate in the treatment of suicidal patients. *Archives of General Psychiatry* 30:625-633.

Modell, A. (1965). On having the right to a life. *International Journal of Psycho-Analysis* 46:323-331.

_____ (1975). A narcissistic defense against affects and the illusion of self-sufficiency. *International Journal of Psycho-Analysis* 56:275-282.

Money-Kyrle, R. (1956). Normal countertransference and some of its deviations. *International Journal of Psycho-Analysis* 37:360-366.

Nadelson, T., and Nadelson, C. (1973). Reflex and reflection: Defining psychotherapy in supervision. *What Is Psychotherapy?* Proceedings of the Ninth International Congress of Psychotherapy, Oslo. Reprinted in *Psychotherapy and Psychosomatics* 25: 207-216.

Reich, A. (1951). On countertransference. *International Journal of Psycho-Analysis* 32:25-31.

Rochlin, G. (1973). *Man's Aggression*. Boston: Gambit.

Segal, H. (1967). Melanie Klein's technique. *Psychoanalytic Forum* 2:199-211.

Winnicott, D. (1949). Hate in the countertransference. *International Journal of Psycho-Analysis* 30:69-75.

_____ (1960). Countertransference. *British Journal of Medical Psychology* 33:17-21.

Zetzel, E. (1971). A developmental approach to the borderline patient. *American Journal of Psychiatry* 127: 7, 867-871.

THEODORE NADELSON, M.D.

DR. NADELSON is assistant professor of psychiatry at Harvard Medical School and associate in psychiatry at Beth Israel Hospital in Boston. He is head of the Consultation-Liaison Service at that institution. He has published papers on dynamics of doctor-patient relations as well as on psychoanalytic topics.

The Self as a Transitional Object: Its Relationship to Narcissism and Homosexuality

Joseph M. Natterson, M.D.

Clinical Professor
Department of Psychiatry
University of Southern California

Men with significant narcissistic and homosexual trends can show a tendency to experience a part of the self as a transitional object. Specifically, these men regard themselves as dolls. Excerpts from three psychoanalytic cases are offered to demonstrate this clinical finding. It is believed that this occurrence represents a significant arrest in the development of the self. The recognition, interpretation, and reduction of this transitional phenomenon constitutes a significant therapeutic experience in the analyses of these men.

THE HYPOTHESIS

In recent years I have come to recognize that certain male patients who have significant problems with narcissism and homosexuality show a surprising tendency. Putting it simply, it is a tendency to regard the self as one's own transitional object. This may be considered a fixation, a partial but very significant arrest in the development of the self, the ego, and one's identity. This occurs as a result of acute and chronic trauma at an early age, and it becomes a focus of regression from the difficulties which occur at later stages of development.

The relationship between narcissism and homosexuality is familiar, but it is not fully understood. A fixation at the level of the transitional object, making a significant part of the self such an object, provides some further understanding of the relationship between homosexuality and the object. The transitional object is extremely important in the early pregenital period, but transitional phenomena can persist until much later. This early occurrence of such phenomena is closely connected with intense narcissism, and the phenomena have a high order of relevance to autoerotism, fusion, symbiosis, separation anxiety — all profoundly connected with narcissism.

The transitional object is the mother—in transition. This means that if one becomes his own transitional object, he will experience a profound reinforcement of his sense of femininity, due to a fixation derived from the period of deepest identification with the mother. This likening to the mother causes the boy to feel feminine from virtually the dawn of consciousness, and it contributes sizably to a crucial confusion of sexual identity as genital issues and conflicts emerge later on during oedipal, latency, pubertal, and adolescent phases. There is, in the face of these stresses for the predisposed boy, as described, an irresistible temptation to find succor and relief in his fantasy that he is his own transitional object. The narcissistic and homosexual consequences become the exorbitant price he pays for this psychosexually primitive mode of relieving anxiety. This psychological phenomenon has subtle and varied manifestations, yet it can also appear with stark simplicity and directness. Material from three analytic cases will be presented in this paper.

CASE I

A thirty-year-old bachelor entered analysis because of depression, feelings of emptiness, intermittent homosexuality (cruising and pickup variety), no intimate relationships with men or women, multiple work failures due to inability to maintain an interest in work and paralyzing anxiety when he attempted to be effective, and an exaggerated concern with appearance and health. The diagnosis of narcissistic personality was quickly established. He will be called Bill.

Bill was the firstborn of two sons to Jewish parents. The father had grown and slaughtered chickens when Bill was a youngster. But he later had expanded his business to become a very successful real estate investor. Bill's mother almost died during the boy's complicated delivery. He was a sensitive, shy, petulant child. He was fearful of physical and psychological contact, and he was complaining and irritable. He recalled various incidents of being embarrassed over his clothing, e.g., a shirt, a bathing suit, etc. He regarded his mother as beautiful, but he experienced her as an incompetent cook, cleaner, and homemaker. He felt his father was uninterested in or critical of him. He did not remember feeling that his father felt proud of him. Rather he recalled the father's scorn of him for being overweight and a poor athlete. Also his father always seemed to have an exceptional interest in his own clothes—only the most tasteful and expensive. Bill shared this taste. He was very sophisticated in the areas of fabric and fashion; yet he did not own a single suit or other set of "dress-up" clothes. His brother was born when Bill was three years old. Bill always felt mildly fraternal but mostly resentful of his younger sibling. The resentment always centered on the brother's greater closeness to the father. The two (father and brother) shared interests and confidences, and the brother entered the father's mammoth corporation.

Bill instead was unable to find himself. After lackluster school years, he took an advanced business degree. This he did under the father's pressure, but he could not be effective in business. He absorbed enormous amounts of knowledge and skill in various art forms and had the ambition to become a great theatrical set designer. He had excellent contacts and made good starts in set design jobs, but he lost interest and became ineffectual whenever the threat of success became imminent.

Bill also had a dismal record in psychotherapy and analysis. He began therapy at age twenty with a male psychologist because of depression, etc. At some point the therapist seduced Bill (or vice versa) and a sexual relationship ensued which continued until Bill left with angry feelings of being exploited. He felt this sex with an older man upon whom he was dependent was very important in intensifying an already significant underlying homosexual trend. Bill subsequently had abortive stints with two male psychoanalysts and then five years of analysis, five times per week, also with a male analyst. Bill left this last analysis in a stalemate. He felt let down, suicidal, and a complete failure. At this point he was referred to me. I spoke with his most recent analyst, who had counterpart feelings of disappointment, regarding Bill as a "borderline personality" who was intrinsically incapable of significant change.

Bill began his analysis by falling instantly in love with me — in a sexual and romantic way. This was particularly intriguing because the only good report Bill made about his preceding analysis was that he had been only minimally homosexual for six months before coming to see me. So here was Bill employing every device short of direct physical assault to establish a physical sexual relationship with me while simultaneously discharging his fury at his first therapist, who "caused" his homosexuality, and at his father and his recent analyst who disdained him because (as Bill saw it) he did not meet their narcissistic expectations of him.

This split transference situation was quickly recognized, and was interpreted to Bill. As the understanding was achieved, his sexual passion for me diminished, and it became possible for him to experience toward me his negative father feelings. It was both interesting and predictable that as the negative transference became intense, Bill would engage in compulsive homosexual cruising, lose interest in his work, which he had by now resumed, and become depressed. It was quite clear that his splitting mechanisms were very crucial to his maladaptive life.

His incomplete ego identity and his warped sense of self were accountable for this. But why? As time passed, and events in Bill's life and analysis unfolded, a possible partial answer was developed. In the following passages it will be described how Bill had never given up his transitional object and that he himself was his own transitional object. Another way to state this is that he was never able to sublimate and diffuse transitional phenomena in a normal way.

In the preceding, Bill's split was illustrated from one vantage point, i.e., his inability to integrate positive and negative attitudes toward the analyst. If one attitude became intensely conscious, the other became submerged, and then handled in some neurotic way, either inhibitory or acting out. Other lines of cleavage could also be discerned. If a woman became sexually attractive, she became intellectually or aesthetically impoverished. This is a typical example of the powerful ambivalence and the associated splitting in Bill. In all situations, *some part of Bill's self was elsewhere*; thus he could not become engaged, committed, and fulfilled in love or work. In the course of our endeavors I concluded that the absent part of the self was the part that had become Bill's transitional object. Thus his ego identity always was sufficiently incomplete to prevent success. This crucially unavailable self was his companion, his comforter with whom he spent his long, lonely, but also cozy, vigils in his house, in front of a warming fire. Perhaps Bill held himself (his little doll or blanket) in loco parentis.

After one year of analysis, while Bill was in a state of mildly positive, but still split, transference to me, the father demanded an interview with me. Bill refused and his enormous hostility to his father increased. That same night Bill felt loving toward an older heterosexual male friend who was a powerful executive in Bill's field. Also that night an older man suffered a heart attack in a restaurant at which Bill was dining with his friend. And earlier that same day Richard Nixon resigned the Presidency. Bill had always felt hatred and contempt for Nixon. During that evening Bill thought longingly of a reigning beauty, an actress, an intellectual. He knew her socially but was terrified of her. She symbolized blonde, symmetrical, glorious, hard-soft American beauty. Bill was just beginning to recognize his identification with her.

During the night he had two dreams. In the first dream he was swathed in rich cashmere and there was abundant, delicious food; he had a good feeling of emotional warmth. In the second dream I was there, with several of my patients. Then we were in a Jewish Center which was like a nursery school owned and run by analysts. There was an important executive who was like the president of the national psychoanalytic association. Bill performed a feat of great strength and skill by cutting through the center of a large piece of wood. The executive and I were unimpressed. Then the wife of the executive psychoanalyst was there, simultaneous with the disappearance of her husband. She looked pretty and young. She in turn was looking for another woman who was a Jewish yenta. I was clearly less important than the executive, so I also disappeared.

In his associations to *center* and *cut*, he thought of center cut = cunt. He had abundant associations to fabrics, art objects, textures, tastes in his life, relating these to a deficiency of milk from mother and semen from father. He had a feeling that I was not giving him enough, nor was he giving enough to me. He feared his dependency upon me. He yearned but feared giving himself totally to me.

Then his thoughts turned to having a vagina into which I might insert my penis, while he inserted his penis into a woman's vagina. The beautiful blonde whom he yearned for led him, in his fantasy, by a beautiful pink satin ribbon through his nose (as she would lead a bull with a metal ring). He felt he could accept the fantasy of having a vagina. Thus a greater conscious awareness and acceptance of his feminine wishes indicated a reduction of castration anxiety and an increased feeling of his masculinity. Now he felt like a naked mannequin—stripped before me. A mannequin seemed to him the same as a Barbie doll.

At this point I told him that he had been his own security blanket, his own comforting doll. I said that one part of himself had this important attitude toward another part. I said that this provided an illusory sense of comfort and security whenever he faced any pain or stress in life. For example, I told him, Nixon's political demise and Bill's heightened conflict with his father had stimulated murderous impulses toward me and that he escaped from these by becoming a very little child who swathed himself in cashmere and bathed his interior with warm food. (The gist of this interpretation was that he had been his own transitional object, always turning back to self-love, self-dependency, and consequent emotional isolation at any time of stress, as in this moment of intense oedipal hostility to his father.)

Bill sobbed in response and expressed despair that at his core he was a factory doll (cutting the wood). "I am crying for myself." He felt awful as he recognized the feeling that at his center all that existed was a lifeless factory doll.

As he left the session Bill also reported that on the days when he did not see me he cruised and had furtive homosexual encounters.

In the following session, two days later, Bill brought two more dreams:

1. He was in Paris, first at the Hotel Athenée, then in the Hotel Raphael. He was trying to find his way to gay bars. He succeeded by going through labyrinthine passages from one bar to another. The logistics of this travel were boring and tedious.

2. He was in a large house of the kind one sees outside London, but it was in an affluent area of Los Angeles. It was Italianate, with beautiful round cut glass windows. It was a shell. The beautiful blonde woman whom he yearned for had purchased it. Bill was impressed and *envious*. Remodeling had begun but questions remained. The interior was being modernized. Bill suggested a partition to separate a rear lanai area from the front (my thought—elimina-

tion of cloacal fantasy?). Someone like his mother indicated that Bill's was a bad idea.

In the morning prior to this session Bill masturbated to a fantasy of having coitus with a girl while a man simultaneously put his penis into Bill's anus. Then it changed to two fellows doing this to him. He had orgasm at this point. He was more aware of his penis; he was having painful sensations and feared cancer of the penis, although he had consulted an oncologist who assured him he was well. He went to dinner and then cruised after the last session. He had been extremely moved by the interpretation of himself as his own transitional object and of its relation to his narcissism, and he cruised to diminish and blur the strong emotions. He felt anger to me for *"taking away my identity as a 'fag.'"* I indicated that he was becoming more aware of his penis, his maleness. Bill agreed, adding that his penis seemed larger than it used to. During this discussion he tended to have one or both hands on his penis. He expressed chagrin at having been alive so long and having done so little. Then he had a vivid fantasy of his penis being cut off and he (or it) ending up being shit out by his mother. There then was a fantasy of feathers, bones, and offal emerging from his rent abdomen. Also white birds, cranes, and storks flew out, symbolizing the loss of innocence and purity. "Now I feel my cock is shrinking and is becoming a cunt."

Bill's associations to the separation in the house dream led to thoughts of the guillotine, of Genet. He then recalled reading something about how heterosexuality equaled rejection by the mother. As the hour drew to a close he apologized for playing with his penis in my presence, but said that he was becoming more secure with me.

It appeared that, as he reacted to the interpretations of the first hour, Bill unconsciously moved up the psychosexual ladder: he acknowledged the bitter loneliness of homosexuality in the first dream, and in the second he attempted to reconstruct himself and achieve a more mature concept of his sexual identity—but his mother disapproved. There was an eruption of acute castration dread almost immediately after Bill began to feel more like a man and less like a doll (a "fag"). As usual, it was not clear whether the prime castrator was the chicken butcher of a father, or the resentful mother who almost died in giving birth to Bill. After the idea was achieved that part of Bill's self was his transitional object, some other aspects of his psychology could be better understood. In his dreams for example, fabrics, textures, and small objects (like dolls) were very frequent. To regard this as just an expression of his decorator tastes would be simplistic and tautological. The important question is why were these interests so intense in him and in many men with strong homosexual trends?

The answer may again be that a part of the self has become the transitional object. And the dreams, fantasies, and aesthetic preferences may be the clues which enable the therapist to detect the transitional phenomenon. Inevitably the question arises as to what the nature of this part of the self is. The simplest answer is mother. Although correct, this answer is also incomplete. Winnicott (1953) indicated the complexity of transitional phenomena. Busch, et al. (1973), reinforce Winnicott's emphasis; for example, they differentiate between primary and secondary transitional objects which occur at different epochs of childhood and probably have different psychological meanings (pp. 194-195). From a drastically different standpoint, viz., the study of adult and mostly schizophrenic patients, Searles (1960) discusses extensively the issue of identification with inanimate objects which become inanimate self-representations. While Searles's case material does not converge with mine, it is possible that at a deeper level a similarity exists in that there is a sequence wherein an inanimate object becomes the mother who in turn becomes a part of the self.

Winnicott (1953), in his classic discussion of transitional objects and transitional phenomena, makes the following statement about the fate of the transitional object:

> Its fate is to be gradually allowed to be decathected, so that in the course of years it becomes not so much forgotten as relegated to limbo. *By this I mean that in health, the transitional object does not "go inside" nor does the feeling about it necessarily undergo repression.* It is not forgotten and it is not mourned. It loses meaning, and this is because the transitional phenomena have become diffused, have become spread out over the whole intermediate territory between "inner psychic reality" and the external world as perceived by two persons in common, that is to say, over the whole cultural field. [p. 91, italics added]

Here Winnicott does appear to anticipate that an abnormal fate of "going inside" can befall the transitional object and can become a significant part of the individual's self-system. This is the issue in my cases.

Winnicott also indicates that "The transitional object may, because of anal erotic organization, stand for feces" (p. 93). This might help explain Bill's frequent fantasy: "I am a large piece of shit located up in your colon." This fantasy was also in the material presented wherein Bill is shit out by his mother. Another point of conjunction of the doll and feces was that Bill repeatedly stated that his infatuation with the blonde beauty whom he could never touch involved the following: she was his antithesis; she was the beautiful, clean doll and he was dirty, rotten, shit. Within her was concealed shit, and his wish to be her was to transform himself from shit. But although his exterior was transformed, his interior remained a foul, hard mass.

CASE 2

In another case, Vic, a thirty-five-year-old man, married, and the father of several children, showed traits suggesting that he also experienced himself as his own transitional object. Vic had lived a life of almost unbelievable trauma and privation, including loss of his father through divorce in his first year; an almost fatal illness in the same year; an unstable, alternatingly seductive and rejecting mother; multiple hostile-to-brutal stepfathers and other figures; the loss of a loving grandfather around age seven; and finally the suicide of his natural father when Vic was in late adolescence, just as he was beginning to reestablish a relationship with him.

Vic had extended psychotherapy and then several years of analysis, both with men. He emerged from both experiences with feelings of being betrayed and misunderstood and not helped. He came to see me as a measure of desperation, since he was about to terminate his promising career as a possible first step toward suicide. Vic showed both narcissistic and latent homosexual characteristics. In the course of his analysis it was possible to observe transitional phenomena in Vic's emotional life from which he was able to achieve some satisfaction. Some of these were direct, such as absorption in his car and his clothing. Others were more sublimated, as in his intellectual interests. It was striking that the latter were much more inhibited than the former. Bill, on the other hand, also displayed direct and sublimated transitional phenomena, but unlike Vic was able to derive almost no pleasure from any of the experiences.

In addition, there seemed to be a hint of a fetishistic flavor to Vic's interest in his clothing, automobile, etc. Furthermore, fantasies of being a doll, specifically a windup doll, were present. Elements of bitterness were contained in this fantasy because it implied that Vic had no identity or independence. On the other hand, there was also a very significant comfort in the fantasy. Initially Vic could not divulge the fantasy. He did reveal it later in an intense and dependent positive transference when I was making repeated interpretations to the effect that he was constantly seeking to receive toys from me, toys which quickly became boring and required new ones to keep him pacified. I pointed out that my interpretations were his toys, but that he was like a very young and very disturbed child in that these interpretation toys quickly lost their meaning for him. It was following this that Vic, in an act of propitiation, symbolically gave me a "toy" by revealing that he regarded himself as a doll. He told me that in addition to the humiliated feeling that as a doll he was at the mercy and pleasure of others, he also derived a very substantial sense of soothing and comfort from this feeling of being like a doll. I pointed out that he seemed to be having very intense and needy feelings toward me, that he was fearful about my ability to meet these needs and that he therefore turned to a part of himself, as he might in childhood have turned to a doll, for the comfort and security he yearned for. This to me exemplified the transitional phenomenon as it occurred in Vic. Here again was a situation in which one part of the self regards another part as a transitional object. A variation of the doll fantasy occurred in the "transference" when Vic had a fantasy of being the puppet Pinocchio. He is swallowed by me and emerges as a real living boy. During the loneliest period of Vic's childhood, he had an imaginary companion who helped relieve his feelings of isolation. Vic knew the companion was imaginary, not real.

CASE 3

A third male analysand was Dave. He was in his early thirties. He was an only child. His father had been ill with a life-threatening disease since Dave's birth. Thus, the shadow of death had hung over Dave throughout his life, and it was therefore not surprising that Dave feared "growing up" and getting older. And it was also no surprise that Dave's unconscious conflicts were centered around this father-son relationship and the corollary issue of sexual identity. Of necessity, Dave's mother undertook many of the roles which in normal circumstances would have been the father's. Thus, secondarily, there developed a heightened and ambivalent sense of dependency upon women (mother), roughly equivalent to the frightened distance from men (father). There were intense erotized sadomasochistic fantasies during the latter part of latency and early adolescence. For example, Dave identified with Nazi SS troopers even though he was Jewish. And from time to time he would hurl himself painfully to the floor. He experienced sexual excitement with both the sadistic fantasies and the masochistic acts. During adolescence Dave was plagued with severe compulsive rituals, primarily of a cleansing kind, stimulated by reaction to parental anal function and with the obsessional fear of father's death as a consequence of nonperformance of the rituals. As he grew older, Dave's obsessive-compulsive symptoms diffused into character traits involving obsessional inhibition of affect and activity, marked ambivalence in intimate relationships, impairment of libidinal satisfaction, and periodic eruptions of rage.

In the analytic relationship, Dave related like a little boy who had found a strong father. He complained a great deal about his own appearance, e.g., how a hair stylist had done a poor job on his hair, a shoe salesman had persuaded him to purchase an unattractive or flawed pair of boots, and similar complaints. When asked about this, he revealed that he was seeking compliments from me about his good looks. From such discussions he would associate to a picture of himself as a cute and lovable teddy bear. And he reported that women almost invariably found him to be cuddly like a teddy bear.

So here is another self-attitude of being like a doll. However, this self-image was distinctly fetishistic since it obviously enhanced the erotic aspect of Dave's contacts with women. As this fantasy became clearer to Dave, a concomitant experience of frank sexual feelings developed toward me. First these appeared in dreams wherein I became like a woman, and Dave seduced me. Later, the more frightening passive homosexual fantasies arose. In these, Dave would be in the recumbent position and would be seduced in a rough, rapelike way by me.

DISCUSSION

Bill, Vic, and Dave had sizable problems with narcissism. All were caught up in significant feminine identification and each man clearly experienced self-attitudes of being a doll. Ambivalent emotions accompanied the doll fantasy, including — on the positive side — definite feelings of comfort and relief from anxiety. The importance of dolls in the course of feminine psychosexual development is presented in fascinating detail by Kestenberg (1975, pp. 101-154). For instance, she shows how a little girl may project onto a doll an aspect of her femininity until she is ready to make this a part of her sexual identity. It seems possible that some similar process of projection and reintrojection of feminine attitudes may have occurred in the childhood development of my cases.

There is evidence in these men that regarding oneself as a doll is a transitional phenomenon as defined by Winnicott (1953) and that a part of the self is thus a transitional object.

A number of interesting papers have appeared in recent years which discuss clinical events which constitute transitional phenomena. Tolpin (1972) suggests that, contrary to Winnicott's opinions, transitional objects do indeed "go inside" in normal development and become psychic organizers.

However, there are instances where the internalization is disturbed and incomplete. For instance, Volkan (1973) cites an adult narcissistic case who had transitional fantasies. Volkan states, "I suggest that my patient's blankets . . . were those pet soothing fantasies that had not been effectively internalized" (pp. 362-363). As described by Volkan, these fantasies were quite varied in their content.

Kafka (1969) reported a case of a self-mutilating woman who used her own body as a transitional object. The acts of self-mutilation had significant comforting and soothing elements in them (p. 209).

Benson and Pryor (1973, pp. 470-471) reported the case of a boy who had an imaginary companion from outer space named Ronzar, who originally functioned as a transitional object. Later, due to external interventions, Ronzar lost his position in the transitional zone as a "self-object" (these authors are here employing Kohut's [1971] concept and terminology).

My cases have some similarity to all the others; yet they are different enough to merit separate presentation. The distinctive transitional phenomenon of Bill, Vic, and Dave is that each clearly and consciously viewed himself as a doll. This was a comforting, but severely regressive, event. The conscious explication of this defensive self-regard as a transitional phenomenon enabled each of these analysands to undertake a new and very productive phase of working through. Each analysand experienced a definite step forward in the development of his self and his ego identity when he became fully conscious of his neurotic use of the self as a transitional object.

This indicates a complex set of adjustments. In order to understand the changes which occurred within the analytic situation, it is necessary to examine some developmental circumstances which were recalled or reconstructed during the analyses. In all three cases there was an inability to move out of symbiotic bondage to the mother. However, the basis for this fixation differed in each case. Bill's mother was narcissistic and apparently quite clumsy and ineffectual in her mothering. Vic's mother was more fluent in her mothering, but she was inconstant, unstable, and actually absent for extended periods. Dave, on the other hand, had a devoted and effective mother who seems to have had some difficulty permitting her son enough existential space during his childhood. The poverty of mothering correlates positively with the severity of disturbance in regard to narcissism and sexual identity. Bill was the most deeply disturbed, Vic was intermediate, and Dave was the least damaged.

In each case a serious problem in the relationship to the father existed. Bill's father was in search of a narcissistic extension of himself, and when Bill disappointed the father in this respect, the latter became critical and rejecting. This was complicated enormously by the birth of a younger brother at the onset of the oedipal phase. The father turned to the newborn son, while Bill turned away from the necessary oedipal struggle with his father and retreated in search of the pregenital mother.

Vic lost his natural father during infancy, and he endeavored to find a father surrogate in his grandfather and stepfathers. All failed him, so he also was forced to turn back to his marginal mother for identification. In Dave's case the father and mother were competent and loving. However, the father's grave illness interdicted normal father-son give-and-take, imposing the necessity of regressive identification with the supervening mother.

The common factor of insufficient fathering (for whatever reason) is noteworthy and of course suggests a possible paradigm for the condition reported here.

The developmental issues cited above were reflected in the transference events of the analyses of Bill, Vic, and Dave. Sometimes the transference reactions preceded and helped in the recovery of important memories. At other times a memory was already quite well established, and the occurrence of the corresponding transference attitude helped verify the relevance of the memory to the neurotic problem.

Each of these three men began his analysis viewing the analyst as a rescuer, a source of comfort and strength. These feelings were particularly blatant in Bill and Vic. In retrospect it would appear possible that the analyst was experienced as the transitional object in this early phase as one aspect of the constellation of transference attitudes. In the instances of Bill and Vic, this phenomenon, occurring at the very beginning of the analysis, might be seen as an emergency move to deal with the acute failure of the self-transitional object as a defense. Somewhat later in the analyses, these men were able to achieve more autonomy. This was evident in the ability to express hostile feelings to the analyst and to reveal the use of the self as a transitional object. Thus in the analyses, the emergence of the use of a part of the self as a transitional object was a step toward individuation, following as it did the initial clinging to the analyst.

In each case the understanding of the use of the self as a transitional object became possible when the pregenital-dependent transference became firmly established and the analysand thus felt safe enough to reveal and then relinquish this self-doll fantasy. Feelings of helplessness, emptiness, and grandiosity diminished. Self-esteem increased. And improvement in the spheres of work and intimacy occurred. Thus the pregenital fixation had become diminished, and progress in psychosexual and ego development could be resumed.

In this paper I have sought to demonstrate that men with narcissistic and homosexual problems can use a part of the self as a transitional object. In the presentation of the clinical material and the discussion I have tried to show how this phenomenon may be detected and understood. My purpose has been to add to the resources available to the psychotherapist in treating patients with problems involving narcissism and homosexuality.

REFERENCES

Benson, M., and Pryor, D. (1973). When friends fall out. Developmental interference with the function of some imaginary companions. *Journal of the American Psychoanalytic Association* 21:457-473.

Busch, F., Nagera, H., McKnight, J., and Pezzarossi, G. (1973). Primary transitional objects. *Journal of the American Academy of Child Psychiatry* 12:193-214.

Kafka, J. (1969). The body as transitional object: a psychoanalytic study of a self-mutilating patient. *British Journal of Medical Psychology* 42:207-212.

Kestenberg, J. (1975). *Children and Parents: Psychoanalytic Studies in Development.* New York: Aronson.

Kohut, H. (1971). *The Analysis of the Self.* New York: International Universities Press.

Searles, H. (1960). The nonhuman environment. *Normal Development and in Schizophrenia.* New York: International Universities Press.

Tolpin, M. (1972). On the beginning of a cohesive self; an application of the concept of transmuting internalization to the study of the transitional object and signal anxiety. *Psychoanalytic Study of the Child* 26:316-353.

Volkan, V. (1973). Transitional fantasies in the analysis of a narcissistic personality. *Journal of the American Psychoanalytic Association* 21:351-376.

Winnicott, D. (1953). Transitional objects and transitional phenomena. A study of the first not-me possession. *International Journal of Psycho-Analysis* 34:89-97.

JOSEPH M. NATTERSON, M.D.

DR. NATTERSON teaches at the University of Southern California and the Southern California Psychoanalytic Institute, where he is a training analyst. He is in the private practice of psychiatry and psychoanalysis. His publications deal with the psychology of fatal illness, technical issues in psychotherapy and psychoanalysis, and other topics. He is now completing a book on dreams.

Transitional Phenomena and Therapeutic Symbiosis

Harold F. Searles, M.D.

Georgetown University Medical School

This paper suggests that the analyst (or therapist) can best understand transitional-object phenomena as being tributary to, or consisting in various different facets of, the—for him in his work with patients—more comprehensive realm of therapeutic symbiosis. The author highlights data concerning objects or phenomena which are transitional for both patient and analyst concomitantly. He suggests that the patient's symptoms have become, early in the phase of therapeutic symbiosis, transitional objects for both patient and analyst simultaneously. As with the patient's symptoms, so with his transference images of the analyst: it is suggested that, in order for any effective transference analysis to occur with any patient, whether neurotic, borderline, or psychotic, the analyst must have come to accept at least a transitional-object degree—if not more deeply symbiotic degree—of relatedness with the particular transference image which is holding sway presently in the analysis.

INTRODUCTION

In 1958 I postulated that symbiotic relatedness constitutes a necessary phase in psychoanalysis or psychotherapy with either neurotic or psychotic patients, and introduced the term "therapeutic symbiosis" for this mode of patient-analyst relatedness (Searles, 1959a). In my monograph concerning the non-human environment (1960) I emphasized that, in normal ego development, the infant is subjectively undifferentiated from his nonhuman environment as well as from his human one. I also suggested that throughout subsequent life we all struggle against deep urges to yield up our identities as individual human beings and to regress to subjective oneness with our nonhuman environment, as a means of escaping from various conflicts inherent in our living as human individuals. In 1966-1967 I suggested, "It may well be that the pre-

dominance of personality functioning, even in healthy adult persons, is subjectively undifferentiated, at an unconscious level at least, from the great inanimate realm of the environment . . ." and stated that "the very fact of one's
preoccupation with the uniqueness of one's own identity is likely to be serving
as a defense against one's unconscious fear of recognizing that human existence is lived largely at a symbiotic level of relatedness."

In the above-mentioned monograph and in various subsequent writings, I
have described instances of the patient's transference to the analyst as being
something other than human—as being, for example, the pet dog from the
patient's childhood, or a tree, or an inanimate object, or whatever. In 1961 I
wrote concerning schizophrenic patients that

> each of these patients—and, I think, this is true to a lesser degree of the
> neurotic patient also—needs in the course of the therapy to project upon
> the therapist the subjectively unfeeling, nonhuman, and even inanimate as-
> pects of himself, and thus to see his therapist, in the transference, as the
> representative of the parents who were, to the child's view, incapable of hu-
> man feeling, as has been the patient himself in his own [repressed] view
> [of himself]. Only by thus reexternalizing his pathogenic introjects can the
> patient make contact with his own feeling-capacities and come to know, be-
> yond any further doubt, that he is a human being. This aspect of the trans-
> ference, this aspect of the healthy reworking of very early ego-differentia-
> tion, cannot be accomplished unless the therapist is able to be self-accept-
> ing while spending hour after hour without finding in himself any particu-
> lar feeling whatever towards the patient. He must be sufficiently sure of his
> own humanness to endure for long periods the role, in the patient's trans-
> ference experience, of an inanimate object, or of some other percept which
> has not yet become differentiated as a sentient human being.

In 1973, paraphrasing comments from some of my earlier papers, I said of
the patient—either psychotic or nonpsychotic—that "the individuation which
he undergoes more successfully this time, in the context of the transference relationship, is in a real sense mutual, in that the analyst too, having participated with the patient in the therapeutic symbiosis, emerges with a renewed
individuality which has been enriched and deepened by this experience"
(1973a). In one or more of my earlier papers, I had described the phase of
therapeutic symbiosis as involving not only the patient's, but also the analyst's, enhanced ego integration of previously repressed, subjectively nonhuman identity components, such that a deepened sense of humanness evolves in
analyst as well as in patient.

In the previously mentioned monograph (1960), in discussing the role of
the nonhuman environment in the development of object relations, I devoted

a number of pages to excerpts from, and comments about, the work of Winnicott (1953) and Stevenson (1954) concerning the role of transitional objects in the life of the infant and young child. These comments included the following:

> I believe . . . that this work by Winnicott and Stevenson provides a valuable frame of reference for the further investigation of various manifestations of schizophrenia. In my own experience I have seen, for instance, that some schizophrenic patients show "objectless" behavior [referring here to Stevenson's having found children in a residential-nursery setting whom she called "objectless"—that is, devoid of any transitional-object attachments]; some are strikingly destructive of all inanimate objects which come within their reach; and others cherish certain inanimate objects for long periods of time. Each of two of my [chronically schizophrenic adult] patients who manifested at first a particularly conspicuous noncherishing of inanimate possessions came to show an intense cherishing of such objects as therapy progressed. . . .
>
> It is evident that the above-described "transitional objects" are transitional in two respects. First, although the teddy bear (for example) is not objectively a part of the infant's body, it is not experienced by him as coming, either, from the outside world—as are the later toys. In the same way, it still stands in a close affective relationship to mother. Thus this security-engendering object helps the infant through the transition period leading up to the recognition that there *is* an outside world. Secondly, and by the same token, the teddy bear represents a transition step in the child's becoming aware of his own aliveness, for here we see that an inanimate object is experienced as being a part of the infant's body, to a degree at least approximating that of his own thumb, before the next phase is reached when inanimate objects (toys, blankets, and so on) are experienced as coming from, or "belonging to" the outside world rather than being a part of his own alive self. [1960, pp. 69-70]

Since Winnicott's pioneering work concerning transitional objects and transitional phenomena appeared in 1951, the wealth of related findings has attested, and continues to attest, to the seminal nature of his discoveries in this regard. For me however, the psychoanalyst or psychotherapist can best understand transitional-object phenomena as being tributary to, or consisting in various different facets of, the—for him in his work with patients—more comprehensive realm of therapeutic symbiosis. He comes in fact to discover how pervasive, at largely unconscious levels of ego functioning, is symbiotic relatedness not only with one's fellow human beings but also with the totality of the "outside" world, including the vastly preponderant nonhuman realm of that world. Concomitantly he becomes progressively less amazed to discover, as many of the writers since Winnicott have discovered, that this or that particular additional increment, too, of the objectively nonhuman environment is being experienced by the patient as a "transitional object"—as existing, that is, in the transitional realm between no-longer-fully-inner, and not-yet-fully-outer, reality.

Thus I find many of the writings concerning transitional objects to be too particularistic, too phenomenological. I believe that a number of these writers are still unconsciously staving off, while gingerly approaching, the degree of recognition of the pervasiveness of symbiotic phenomena, involving nonhuman as well as objectively human realms of existence, which my long-term work with chronically schizophrenic adults compelled me, against tenacious unconscious resistance on my part, to see.

In this paper I shall dwell particularly upon data concerning objects or phenomena which are *transitional*—if one must use that word; the word *symbiotic* is more appropriate to the patient-therapist context—for both patient and therapist concomitantly. By seeing the development of the phase of therapeutic symbiosis as one in which the patient's symptoms have become—if you will—transitional objects for both the patient and the therapist simultaneously, I hope to contribute to our increasing understanding of the nature of the therapeutic process in psychoanalysis.

As I write this paper I am conscious once again of my debt, acknowledged more than once before, to Harry Stack Sullivan (1947), whose lectures and writings helped to drive home to me the indispensability of our keeping in view, in our attempting to understand seemingly exclusively intrapersonal phenomena, the interpersonal frame of reference. That frame of reference does not provide, by itself, an adequate conceptual framework; but to the extent that the analyst is ever-mindful of it, he rarely indeed would equate himself, even in working with the most ill patients, with a visitor strolling through a zoo. My own writings have stressed repeatedly the increments of reality in even the most delusionally distorted of my patient's transference-perceptions of me. A paper in 1972 (presented over some eight years previously as a lecture in several different educational settings), describing nearly seven years of intensive psychotherapy with a chronically schizophrenic woman, gives some hint of the extent to which I believe the analyst's own unconscious processes are involved in such matters as transitional-object phenomena, or subjectively nonhuman experiences, in the context of psychotherapy:

> Two weeks later I had occasion to see, still more clearly, that in back of the patient's rages stood *terror*. During this particular hour she told me, "There is a vapor over people sometimes." She added that there is sometimes a "vapor" over me as well as over other people. It is difficult to de-

scribe her tone when speaking of this, but it clearly conveyed terror and weirdness . . .

As the work with her went on, Millie became more and more able to tell me when she was experiencing me with a "vapor" over my head. There were times when she let me know that, instead of seeing my face, she was seeing a death's-head. On one occasion I got the *feeling*, from the way she was looking at me, that my face was comprised of hooded cobras. I hope that I am conveying some idea of how extremely uncomfortable this was for me. But I want particularly to emphasize my belief that my ability to en-dure such nonhuman transference roles—to endure such projections of her own subjectively nonhuman components upon me—greatly helped her to become sure that she was a human being. From another standpoint, I had to become sure—on my *own* part—that my humanness would assert itself over such subjectively nonhuman components of myself. From this point of view, we see how in successful therapy the patient eventually confirms, at a deeper level, the therapist's own humanness. [1972b]

THE ANALYST'S RELATIONSHIP TO THE
PATIENT'S SYMPTOMS

Instances in Which the Analyst Feels That the
Patient's Symptoms Are Being Inflicted upon Him
(the Analyst)

As a third-year medical student I chose a one-month elective in psychiatry, and it happened that each of the two patients assigned to me for psychothera-py during that month was suffering from depression. Toward the end of the month, my roommate commented that he had not seen me smile during the whole month. I had been largely unaware of how greatly the work with these two depressed patients had been depressing me.

In later years I became aware of how commonplace is the difficulty, in the training of psychiatric residents and of analytic candidates, of the doctor's un-consciously overidentifying with his patient.

But I have seen, too, that all too often the analytic candidate (for ex-ample) is given by various of his teachers, and by his readings in the psycho-analytic literature, to assume that any intensely felt, conscious sense of one-ness with the patient is a countertransference (in the classical sense of the term) -intrusion into his attempted maintenance of a neutrally hovering at-titude toward the patient. My own opinion having long since departed from such a classically psychoanalytic view, in this regard, is indicated by the fol-lowing comments, concerning the sense of identity as a perceptual organ, in a paper published in 1966-1967:

During the past two years I have had occasion to do single interviews for teaching and consultative purposes with a relatively large number of hospitalized patients. In this work I have encountered the well-known problem of how best to cope with massive amounts of data which need quickly to be assimilated; what criterion, what point of orientation, to employ in order to find coherence and meaning in all that transpires. I have found that the most reliable data are gained in these necessarily brief contacts from my noticing—and, increasingly, sharing such information with the patient—the vicissitudes in my own sense of identity during the session. It is thus, I have found, that I can best discern what are the patient's most centrally important transference-distortions in his reactions to me, and what are the aspects of his own identity which he is repressing and projecting upon me . . .

I cannot claim to have achieved an unbroken sense of inner harmony in this regard (if such equanimity were possible for anyone to maintain, and I am confident that such a state is more a cruel and analytically stultifying illusion, essentially autistic in nature, than a desirable goal). For example, I wrote five years later that

On numerous occasions, for example at the Sheppard and Enoch Pratt Hospital in Baltimore, I have had teaching interviews during the course of the day with two or three schizophrenic patients, each of whom tended powerfully to deny unconsciously the presence of the crazy, sadistic introjects within him, to attribute these instead to me—to, quite literally, experience them as residing within me—and to leave at the end of the interview with its having been formidably established, in not only his mind but in the minds of the onlooking staff and in my own mind, that he is the human being deserving of compassionate rescue from the inhuman, unfeeling monster of schizophrenia personified by myself. Then, at the end of the day, during the hour and a half of high speed and hazardous rush-hour beltway driving to my office in Washington to see training analysands in the evening, I would feel one or more of those patients as disturbingly present within myself. [1971]

It would be simple to say that I was overidentifying with the patients in these particular instances; most of my return trips from that hospital involved no such degree of inner turmoil. But part of the difficulty in the overall field of the psychotherapy of schizophrenic patients consists in *under*identification on the therapist's part with the patient. Relatively few psychiatric residents, for example, develop sufficient ability to identify with schizophrenic patients so as to become much interested in this aspect of psychiatric practice. Part of the difficulty, in this regard, is that there is an all-too-prevalent tendency, among psychiatric colleagues, to regard as crazy any therapist who experiences such identification phenomena as those I have just described. Most psychiatric residents tend to be afraid to report analogous treatment experiences to their supervisors, for example.

Several years ago, for the first time in more than fifty years of remembered experiences, I had the sense of a sudden, entirely unexpected explosion somewhere in my torso. I could not locate it more precisely than that; it did not feel, for example, located specifically in my cardiac region. This was more than a mere fantasy; there was enough of a feeling of bodily participation in the mental imagery so that I found the experience distinctly disturbing, and even frightening, although not to the point of panic. This experience recurred on some half-dozen occasions, at seemingly random times and in seemingly random circumstances, over the next few months. At this writing I still rank these experiences as being among the most upsetting ones of a predominantly psychological causation that I have ever had.

With the very first of these experiences, as well as with the subsequent ones, I almost immediately felt sure that what I was experiencing had its predominant causation—however multiple might be its determinants from other sources—in my relationship with one or another of my patients. Although I myself have had an explosive temper throughout my life, this particular experience was so foreign to me that I felt sure that it represented (among, as I say, whatever additional meanings it had) a reaction to some otherwise-undetected component of my relationship with one of my patients. Had this happened some years earlier, I would have assumed, equally promptly, that here was one more evidence of my craziness, and that I really must get back for more analysis.

The task of ascertaining which one among my patients was involved in this experience was not easy, for I was seeing more than one in whom there was the symptom of poorly controlled (because largely repressed), explosive, murderous rage, and more than one whose youth had been characterized by a notable preoccupation with the contriving and setting off of explosives. A chronically schizophrenic woman whom I long have treated had expressed more than once the delusion that we are living in a bomb, and on other occasions had experienced herself as being, essentially, a bomb filled with a radioactive material. Incidentally, she has spoken more recently, many times, of persons' being "exploded," and of her own having been "exploded."

The detective work required great patience, and went on while many other analytic detective works were simultaneously in process and were holding, nearly all the time, the major foci of my interest. It was actually not until some few years later that one of my patients came to express, over the course of many months, previously repressed transference feelings and attitudes toward me which dovetailed so precisely with these now long-past experiences within me that I felt thoroughly convinced that she had been the one most involved in them. If space here permitted me to quote many of her detailed comments in this regard, I am confident that the reader would share, to a considerable extent, my feeling of conviction about the centrality of her role in this matter. Parenthetically, at no point have I ever confided to her the feeling experiences which I have described; had any one of these delayed-time-bomb experiences occurred during one of my actual sessions with her, in all probability I would have reported them to her as being data of obvious relevance for her analysis.

Another example of my experience of certain thoughts and feelings referable to a patient's unconscious (or, in the following instance, perhaps preconscious) contents, comes from my work with a male patient in analysis several years ago. This man at the beginning of his analysis was so maddened, at times, by his own thoughts that, while lying on the couch and trying to report what he experienced to be going on in his head, he would suddenly feel driven to desperation and begin beating his head fiercely with his fists. I of course not uncommonly felt maddened also in trying to fulfill my function as analyst; the interaction between this man and me reminded me often of a paper I had published entitled "The Effort to Drive the Other Person Crazy . . ." (1959).

In the course of my work with him, sometime after his own head beatings largely had ceased, I began to experience within myself a phenomenon I could not remember having experienced before in relation to anyone. The "example" of it which I shall report here will be several in actuality, derived from my notes made during the sessions over a number of months.

My earliest note in this regard was made in a session during which he was reporting his thoughts concerning four different situations, in recent weeks, about which he had felt unaccountable anxiety. He described his having come to realize that some particular aspect seemed central to all four situations. As he put it, "That was a common — [momentary pause] well, something common to the four of them." My notes describe, with regard to that pause: "Here is one of the many times in the past several sessions when I think of the obviously missing word, and on some of such occasions the word has come to be present in my mind with somewhat disturbing force — sort of pulsating or reverberating, with almost explosive force. In this particular instance the word is *element*."

In a session nearly two months later, he was speaking of his wife's childhood, saying, "It seems as though her mother really doted on Alice when Alice was a baby, and then after that just — [momentary pause] had nothing to do with her for the rest of her life." Of the pause, my notes record: "Here the word *dropped* comes to my mind, and I have a fantasy of its echoing in my mind all the rest of my life, with me helpless to stop it from doing so."

A couple of weeks later, my notes include the comment, "The expression 'window-dressing' is still reverberating sporadically in my mind from one of his manipulative omissions about *20* minutes previously."

A few days later, in describing a running battle which one of his sons, a high school student, was having with his French teacher, and after mentioning some of the teacher's complaints, he expostulated, "But *he* [the teacher] is a — [momentary pause] Why does he *subject* himself to that?" Concerning the pause, I wrote in my notes, "Here the phrase 'bitch on wheels' starts repeating in my mind." Later on in the same session, speaking again of his wife's background, he was saying, "So that's what she got from her mother. That's her — [momentary pause] That's what she brought with her when she left her mother's home for good." Of the pause, my notes mention that "here the word *legacy* repeats a few times, vividly, in my mind."

During the following week, while recounting some of the experiences a colleague had had during a visit to Alaska, he commented, "Alaska *does* seem —." My notes mention, "Then he veers off into other content, such that the word *primitive* starts booming slowly in my mind, for several moments (causing no more than mild discomfort in me)."

In summary, as regards my work with this particular man, it seems to me that, upon such occasions as I have detailed in a few examples here, I was experiencing within myself the symptom of being inflicted with maddeningly obsessive thoughts and feelings, a symptom which earlier had used to so madden the patient as to impel him to beat his head with his fists, and a symptom which he was now, for a time, successfully projecting into me (as being, from other data which need not be included here, a mother figure in the transference). Significantly, as I mentioned above, his own head beatings during the sessions largely had ceased at the time I began having these experiences — experiences unprecedented, in my memory, in relation to anyone.

Instances in Which the Analyst Fears That He
Personally Is Inflicting the Patient's Symptoms
upon the Latter

These are instances in which the analyst is being reproached, whether explicitly or implicitly, as being to blame for the patient's symptoms, and in which the analyst is experiencing anxiety, guilt, and remorse in this regard. Since such transference situations, with illustrative clinical details, have been reported many times in my previous writings, I shall limit myself here to a presentation of a few of my previously published summarizing comments about this topic.

In my paper entitled "Phases of Patient-Therapist Interaction in the Psychotherapy of Chronic Schizophrenia" (1961), in one of the passages descriptive of the phase of ambivalent symbiosis, I stated that

> At its fullest intensity, this phase is experienced by him [i.e., the therapist] as a threat to his whole psychological existence. He becomes deeply troubled lest this relationship is finally bringing to light a basically and ineradicably malignant orientation towards his fellow human beings. He feels equivalent to the illness which is afflicting the patient; he is unable to distinguish between that illness and himself. This is not sheer imagination on his part, for the patient is meanwhile persistently expressing, in manifold ways, a conviction that the therapist constitutes, indeed, the affliction which threatens to destroy him and with which he, the patient, is locked in a life-and-death struggle. In my theoretical view, the therapist is now experiencing the fullest intensity of the patient's transference to him as the Bad Mother. [1965, p. 533]

In a paper entitled, "Feelings of Guilt in the Psychoanalyst", I suggested that

> our most troublesome guilt reactions are a function of our having regressed, in our relationship with the patient, under the impact of, and as a defense against, the helplessly ambivalent feelings that our work with him tends to inspire in us, to a defensively symbiotic relationship with him, in which our view of ourself and the world is an omnipotent view. In this state of subjective omnipotence, we are totally responsible for all that transpires in the analysis, for there is no world outside us; there is no real, flesh-and-blood other person. Hence all our erotic and angry responses to the patient are felt by us as crazy, for we fail to see their interpersonal origin; these are felt instead as being exclusively crazy and frightening upwellings from within us, threatening irreparably to damage or destroy the patient, who seems so insubstantial and fragile. Since we do not experience any clear and firm ego-boundaries between ourself and the patient, his acts are, in their guilt-producing capacity, our own acts; we feel as guilty, about his sexual or aggressive or whatnot kinds of acting out, as though we ourself had committed and were committing those acts. [1966]

In a paper concerning my long-continued work (18 years at that writing) with a chronically schizophrenic woman, I reported that

> The most difficult aspect of the work . . . is the enduring of a quite terrible feeling of unrelatedness between us . . . Moments of feeling related to her, of seeing where her delusionally expressed views are linked up with my own view of my reality, have aroused . . . in me a deeply guilty sense of being totally responsible for her plight. This subjective-omnipotence-based sense of guilt seems clearly a sample of that against which she herself has

been defended, unconsciously, over the years, by reason of her psychotic mechanisms such as projection and introjection, dedifferentiation, splitting, and denial. [1972a]

The contributions from Kleinian analysts, while describing little or nothing of the *analyst's* feeling experiences which are my main topic of discussion at the moment, contain some vivid examples of the kind of *patient* behavior which tends to give rise to such feelings in the analyst as I have been detailing. For example, in the following excerpts from Rosenfeld's (1962) paper, "The Superego and the Ego-Ideal," I find what he says concerning persecutory anxieties in the patient to be particularly relevant:

> I am following Klein's work on the early superego (1933). In her view the earliest beginnings of the superego contain mainly idealized and persecutory aspects of the breast . . . [In describing his work with a woman from whose analysis his paper mainly derives, a woman who had had a particularly traumatic weaning experience, he says that] The analysis of the weaning situation and the superego built around this experience . . . brought the early persecutory superego right into the analysis with convincing dynamic force. The analyst was experienced again and again as a sadistic, critical superego figure who took pleasure in destructively criticizing everything the patient was doing or saying, or who took everything out of the patient, enriching himself and leaving the patient empty and destroyed. At the height of the persecution the patient would often threaten to kill herself.

At this juncture I wish to emphasize that, although I have just quoted material having to do with persecutory anxieties, I would not want the reader to infer that, either in this portion of the paper concerned with the analyst's relationship to the patient's symptoms, or in the larger subject of the paper as a whole, I am concerned exclusively or even predominantly with schizophrenic patients, for that is not the case. Each of the points concerning psychodynamics which I offer in this paper is something which, so my experience has indicated to me, is valid for any patient, to a varying but nonetheless significant degree, at one or another phase of his or her psychoanalysis or psychotherapy.

Instances in Which the Analyst Has Come to Feel That
the Patient's Symptoms "Couldn't Be Happening to a
Nicer Guy"

In my experience with patients of whatever diagnostic category, I find that a phase of the work develops during which I no longer feel helplessly inflicted with the patient's symptoms; nor anguished at my inability to rescue him from them; nor deeply concerned and guilty lest I be somehow the primary cause of his symptoms, and even personally equivalent to his symptoms, his illness. Now, instead, when he anguishedly or reproachfully or furiously reports his symptoms for the nth time, I experience a freedom from these long-accustomed forms of personal suffering, and I think to myself, as I listen to him, "It (whatever tenacious symptom of which he is complaining at the moment—whether a headache, or suicidal urges, or various forms of marital— family anguish, or whatnot) couldn't be happening to a nicer guy." The feeling is one which involves, obviously, irony, and a sense of vindictive, sadistic gratification derived from a degree of my identifying with the symptom which is affecting him in the manner of which he is complaining.

In my paper in 1961 entitled, "Phases of Patient-Therapist Interaction in the Psychotherapy of Chronic Schizophrenia," in my discussion of the phase of resolution of the therapeutic symbiosis, I described the therapist's experiencing his newly won sense of individuation from the patient in terms somewhat analogous to those I am using here. But in that earlier paper I was discussing, in particular, treatment situations in which the therapist has come to terms with his erstwhile feelings of concern lest the patient suicide or remain chronically psychotic for the remainder of the latter's life. At that time I did not yet see as clearly as I have come to in more recent years that it is an inherent part of the psychoanalytic process, in one's work with a patient of whatever diagnostic category, that one develop, among one's other feelings toward the patient, the kind of hard-won and only ostensible callousness which I am describing here.

From a theoretical point of view, I have come to believe that when the analyst has developed this "It-couldn't-be-happening-to-a-nicer-guy" internal reaction to the patient's symptoms, one could say (to employ Winnicott's term) that the patient's symptoms have become "transitional objects" for the analyst as well as for the patient himself. In the theoretical terminology more congenial to me, I would say that the phase of therapeutic symbiosis is now relatively near, with the unhealthy pseudoindividuality crystallized in the patient's symptomatology soon to be relinquished by both participants in the analytic situation.

A few years ago, as I was becoming aware of the apparently general relevance of the analyst's development of the kind of feeling orientation which I am discussing in this section of this paper, I made the following notes concerning

a session with Mrs. Jones* recently. . . . In essence, I had just come to feel a change in myself, from the state of feeling which I had obtained almost from the beginning of the work with her, predominantly a guilty, anxious, intimidated feeling of trying to *provide* her with enough supplies to relieve her dissatisfaction, her anxiety, her fury—always with a feeling that I *owed* her much more than I was giving her. Such feelings have become interlarded, increasingly, with resentment and rage at her for browbeating me, but with no *direct* expression of this rage visualizable in the work with her, because of the likelihood that the treatment-relationship would be severed, or that I would lose face in my own eyes—lose stature—through having essentially a temper tantrum.

All this has evolved such that as she continues to report or express such symptoms as sexual frigidity, or anxiety, or intense dissatisfaction, or fury, I have come more and more to find myself feeling a vindicative satisfaction, a grim relish, above all a calm kind of neutrality, in hearing about it—a kind of calm balance between my urges to try, once again, to bring her relief, and my sadistic gratification at the evidence that her symptoms are wreaking upon her a savagery which I am not free to wreak more directly. Most of all, I feel a sense of conviction that all this change in me is *necessary* and useful in her analysis, for it enables me to achieve a useful overall analytic neutrality toward her, such that, for example, I no longer intervene in her many silences of a few minutes in length—silences into which I used anxiously and guiltily to intrude with attemptedly relieving interpretations or other comments.

Somewhat to my surprise, all this seems to be working relatively well. For example, she becomes verbal again each time after one of her silences, reporting the fantasy in which she had found herself immersed during it. I get the distinct impression that the more schizoid aspect of her, which is formidable, finds more comfortable the kind of analytic neutrality I have achieved, whereas her more hysterical aspects previously had been very provocative of my doing much interacting with her.

The theoretical view that the patient's symptoms have come to have the meaning of transitional objects for the analyst (as well as their having come to have such a meaning for the patient) is supported by a number of familiar clinical phenomena and relatively well-established theoretical concepts, not all of which I can encompass here in any attempt to "prove" my hypothesis conclusively.

First, there is the subjective experience of the analyst that the patient's symptoms are enabling him vicariously, as it were, to be having a significant effect upon the patient, whereas he had come, long since, to feel helpless to have any more direct effect, and above all any symptom-relieving effect, upon the patient. He feels now, in other words, clearly partially identified with the

*A pseudonym, as is each of the patient's names included in this paper.

patient's symptoms, and I think it a clinical experience familiar enough to us all to find that the patient's symptoms develop not only such sadomasochistic transference meanings as I have been implying, but come to represent, also, the bond of mother-infant dependency between patient and analyst. I surmise that many analysts, nowadays, are receptive to the idea that just as a patient's illness can come to be seen to be a kind of security blanket for the patient (personifying both the early mother and his own rudimentary ego), so the patient's illness can invest the analyst, in the course of the transference evolution, with the sense of a security blanket for him also. The result is that the eventual resolution of the patient's symptoms gives cause for feelings of loss, as well as of rejoicing, on the part of analyst as well as patient, just as the mutual individuation which develops from a healthy mother-infant symbiosis, in normal development, gives mother as well as infant occasion for feelings of loss as well as of personal fulfillment.

My hypothesis concerning the patient's symptoms as transitional objects for both analyst and patient is buttressed also by the familiar clinical finding that each of the patient's symptoms can become discerned, over the course of the analysis, as referable to some pathogenic introject or introjects, undigested and distorted internal-object representations of part aspects of mother and other persons significantly involved in the child's earliest years. These introjects need to become reprojected upon the analyst, in the course of the transference evolution, in order for them to become resolved into increasingly healthy ego on the part of the patient.

From among the whole range of symptomatology, it is the category of psychosomatic symptoms which most commonly and readily acquaint the analyst with what I believe to be a general truism—namely, that the long-manifested symptom comes to have a meaning, as the transference neurosis or psychosis becomes established, of an introjective representation of the analyst (who is being unconsciously reacted to here by the patient as personifying some part aspect of mother, or father, or whomever). Thus, for example, when the patient complains of "my sore asshole"—or of his excruciating headache, or bellyache, or whatever—the analyst soon finds reason to surmise that this is an unconscious transference reference to himself, but that the patient is not yet able to experience the contempt and rage toward him, as well as the very body image degree of dependent symbiosis with him, which is crystallized in the symptom in question.

In my monograph in 1960, I stated that

. . . For the deepest levels of therapeutic interaction to be reached, both patient and therapist must experience a temporary breaching of the ego boundaries which demarcate each participant from the other. In this state there occurs . . . a temporary introjection, by the therapist, of the patient's pathogenic conflicts; the therapist thus deals with these at an intrapsychic, unconscious as well as conscious level, bringing to bear upon them the capacities of his own relatively strong ego. Then, similarly by introjection, the patient benefits from this intrapsychic therapeutic work which has been accomplished in the therapist. . . . [pp. 421-422]

I acknowledged that "John L. Cameron, a colleague on the Chestnut Lodge staff, has helped me to see this." On this point I always have felt, subsequently, that I had been less than candid. To put it more simply and honestly, he taught me this, as a teacher does with a pupil. The remainder of that paragraph, not quoted above, is so far as I know my original contribution.

Incidentally, as regards any of these excerpts from my previous writings, I undoubtedly would phrase them somewhat differently, and to my present way of thinking, more adequately now; but I cannot devote these pages to doing so.

In a paper in 1959, I mentioned that

Coleman (1956) and Coleman and Nelson (1957) have described a psychotherapeutic technique, which the former has employed with borderline patients, termed "externalization of the toxic introject." This technique consists in the therapist's deliberate impersonation of—conscious and calculated assumption of the role of—a traumatic parent, or other figure from the patient's early years, the long standing introjection of whom comprised a "toxic introject," the core of the borderline schizophrenic illness. The authors' psychodynamic formulations are of much interest. . . .

The great difference between Coleman and myself, however, is that in my experience the therapist does not express, in such situations, affects which are merely a kind of play-acting, deliberately assumed and employed as a technical maneuver indicated at the moment. Rather, in my experience [with frankly schizophrenic patients], the affects are genuine, spontaneous, and at times almost overwhelmingly intense. . . . [1959c]

Marie Coleman Nelson, et al., in their volume entitled *Roles and Paradigms in Psychotherapy* (1968), report upon the further development of their technique of externalization of the toxic introject and related techniques for the treatment of patients in general, but with particular emphasis upon the treatment of borderline individuals. In a subsequent review of this book, a highly favorable review in the main, I took issue with Ms. Nelson's opinion that "genuineness as a therapeutic quality *per se* has no intrinsic merit, is often lost upon the patient and may even be felt as artificiality." I commented that

I, for one, cannot believe that the therapist or analyst can set aside his *real* feelings and still function effectively with the patient. But the authors are highly aware of the crucial significance of this question, and one finishes the volume with a sense of admiration of them for dealing recurrently, candidly and in thoughtful detail with this question in various contexts. . . . [1968-1969]

In any event, irrespective of this particularly controversial facet of the matter, the technique detailed by Ms. Nelson and her colleagues, of "externalization of the toxic introject," is relevant to this present subtopic of my paper, namely, the analyst's "It-couldn't-be-happening-to-a-nicer-guy" response to the symptom-ridden patient.

Another brief example from my own clinical work concerns a man whom I analyzed for a few years, who on the one hand seemed endlessly reproachful of me for not freeing him from the symptoms which had brought him into analysis, often demanding that I give him relief from them, but who on the other hand clearly derived enormous grandiose satisfaction from the abundant evidence that I seemed incapable of having any effect upon him whatsoever. In the course of time, anguished efforts to help him through carefully formulated interpretations which he derisively rejected as futile, and largely suppressed feelings of hurt and rage at him for his tenaciously maintained resistance in the analysis, I came to a relatively stable orientation of feeling, when he would once again anguishedly demand relief from his symptoms, that these couldn't be happening to a nicer guy.

Since I long since had come to feel unable to have even a successfully aggressive impact upon him, let alone an effectively psychoanalytic participation with him in any more conventional sense, it gave me a kind of vicarious sadistic pleasure that, even though he had demonstrated, over and over, that I personally was incapable of drawing blood from him, at least his symptoms were capable of doing so. In the sadomasochistic transference relationship which had come into being in the treatment situation—so typical of those which I am describing in this section of the paper—"his" symptoms of which he was complaining could be regarded as either transitional objects in terms of his masochism toward me or transitional objects in terms of my sadism toward him. Kafka's (1969) comments concerning sadism and masochism, to be quoted in my review of the literature toward the end of this paper, will be seen to be relevant to my work with this man.

For myriad reasons which would take me too far afield it was not yet timely for me to report to him this feeling orientation I found had developed in me. But there was solid evidence that it was accurately attuned to the etiology of his own illness. His own marriage was being rendered neurotically miserable partly because of his inability to achieve this kind of feeling (among others, of course), toward his wife who suffered from chronic alcoholism. It was clear to me the patient was helping to perpetuate her alcoholism, through his acting out in the marriage of unconscious death wishes toward her as a mother figure.

For example, in one session he described what he had found himself feeling, during the previous evening, while his wife was drinking once again. "I have this terrible feeling that Clara is slowly being destroyed—not by me, so much as by herself; but I feel helpless to do anything about it." I found it notable that he showed, in this session, no awareness whatever of any vengeful satisfaction in the thought that his wife was drinking herself to death—notable in particular because he had spent the previous day's session, as so frequently before, in expressing resentment, bitterness, and contempt about her perceivedly selfish, inconsiderate, demanding (and so on) behavior, punctuating that flow of predominant hatred and contempt with a few moments of crocodile-tears kind of "pity," as he had called it, for her, whom he termed, in a most unconvincing way, "pathetic." In the current day's session, then, he went on, regarding her, "We're just on separate planets," a statement expressive not only of his conscious despair about his marriage but also of his unconscious need to disclaim any responsibility for his wife's neurotic illness.

The analysis came to reveal much data to the effect that this patient's "It-couldn't-be-happening-to-a-nicer-guy" feelings were so deeply repressed primarily because the circumstances of his childhood had left him convinced, at an unconscious level, that he himself had been responsible for the prolonged physical illnesses, and eventual deaths, of both his mother and an older sister. Until he came into analysis, just as he had never grieved at all fully over their deaths, neither had he been able to become conscious of how much contempt, hatred, and death wishes he had had toward each of them. In the evolution of the transference, I was much of the time in the position of a parental figure from whom he consciously and anguishedly sought rescue from his symptoms, but at the same time a mother or older sister whom he unconciously had written off, hatefully and scornfully, as being as good as dead. To the extent that, in my own private feeling orientation toward him, I could experience such sadistic feelings, contempt, and death wishes as he had been repressing, I became able to help him gain access not only to comparable feelings in himself, but also to the feelings of love and unworked-through grief which had been repressed along with those negative feelings.

The kind of patient-analyst relatedness I have described in the clinical example just mentioned, in which the patient's symptoms may be discerned to be transitional objects for analyst as well as patient, can be seen to be on a continuum, as regards individuation and symbiosis. The more predominant interaction is the symbiotic one, as mentioned earlier, respecting the phase of ambivalent symbiosis in the treatment of the chronically schizophrenic patient. Here the analyst becomes unable to maintain a clear differentiation between the patient's illness and the analyst's self to such a degree that he feels on occasion fully and directly — not merely partially and vicariously — responsible for the patient's illness, by reason of his subjective experience that he personally *is* that illness. As I described this latter phenomenon, more predominantly symbiotic transference relatedness, in a more recent paper concerning schizophrenia, "the analyst . . . may come to experience himself, as I have done more than once, as being indistinguishable from the terribly malevolent affliction from which the patient is suffering" (1973b).

Now I must step back a bit from this specific topic, to comment more generally about the topic of the analyst's emotional neutrality, as related on the one hand to the need for him to be emotionally involved, to a degree, in the analytic relationship with the patient, and on the other hand to the need for him not to be overly so involved — overidentified with the patient.

A year ago today, so it happens, I made this note:

> It occurred to me today [as I found myself thinking of all my current patients collectively], while driving over to my office, how important it is for an analyst not to try to beat each of his patients at the latter's own game. My feeling is that one of my greatest difficulties in doing psychoanalysis is that I do get very much involved in just that — trying to out-passive-aggressive Jenkins, out-tough and out-humor Bradley, out-granite Weiss, out-insult Clara, and so on. It is folly for an analyst to fight with the patient's choice of weapons, for the patient has spent a lifetime in becoming adept with these.

On the other hand, the following comments which I made in a recent paper concerning psychoanalytic therapy with schizophrenic patients are, in my experience, to a significant degree valid for one's psychoanalytic work with neurotic patients also. In discussing many analysts' attempts to maintain, from the beginning of their work with such a patient, a demeanor of evenly hovering, benevolent neutrality, I suggested that

> That . . . classically analytic position is indistinguishable from the omnipotent parental transference-position which the schizophrenic patient tends so powerfully to lure, and demand, the analyst to occupy, while making life hell for him to the degree that he attempts to acquiesce to this tantalizing transference-demand.
> . . . the emotions which schizophrenic patients foster in the analyst are so intense, and conflictual or disco-ordinate, that it is quite untenable for one to attempt to carve out such a position for oneself at the beginning; this

can only become established much later, after many stormy interactions, in proportion as the patient's ego-functioning becomes predominantly normal-neurotic in nature. Further, any such early attempt involves . . . an offensive condescension on the part of the analyst, who is being so presumptuous as to imply that nothing within the patient, either now or within the future of their work together, can ever seriously discommode the analyst. . . . The patient can only become increasingly determined to be taken seriously by the analyst, and make intensified, and surely eventually successful, efforts in that direction. As for the analyst, his attempt to maintain a dispassionate stance surely is serving as a defense against the activation, within himself, of reality-nuclei for the patient's various and disco-ordinate transferences to him — transferences which need to become perceived by both participants, and their reality-nuclei basis in the analyst (as well as in the patient) perceived by both participants, in order for the transference-psychosis to become manageably evident and to evolve into a transference-neurosis of anything like the usual analytically-explorable proportions. [1973b]

Of some relevance for psychoanalytic work with neurotic patients is the following observation, also from the same paper.

The passively-aggressive, sadistic gratifications afforded the chronically schizophrenic patient, in response to the anguished efforts of the analyst and others to bring him relief, are limitless. A typical dilemma for the analyst is how to achieve ways of functioning, during the session, which will make it possible for his own personal suffering to become less than that of the patient; in my own experience, the treatment cannot proceed usefully for either patient or analyst so long as the patient's schizophrenia is inflicting, evidently, more of conscious suffering upon the analyst than upon the patient. [p. 5]

Any such patient derives enormous sadistic gratification from watching detachedly while the well-intentioned analyst endeavors, valiantly but with intensifying despair and anguish and repressed infantile-omnipotence-based murderous rage, to rescue the patient from the grip of the schizophrenia which seemingly — and of course in various regards really — is causing the patient such intolerable suffering. [1973b]

I regard it as inescapable, and inherently necessary, to the psychoanalytic treatment process that the patient's transference responses and attitudes will become focused upon, and will mobilize to a degree, corresponding components of the analyst's actual personality. Both in terms of his coming to experience feelings, then, such as the patient as a child had found in the particular parent relevant to the current transference phenomenon, and in terms of the analyst's inevitably becoming at times involved in some identifying (whether unconsciously or consciously) with the patient as an aggressor, the analyst feels involved in a degree of struggle with the patient as to which one of them is going to succeed in imposing the symptoms in question upon, or into, the other participant.

Rosenfeld's (1952a, 1952b) writings contain, as I mentioned, excellent examples of this situation as regards the processes at work in the *patient*. But to comprehend more fully and deeply these patient-analyst phenomena, we need to see that the analyst's feelings are by no means so consistently and fully detached from what is transpiring as Rosenfeld's clinical portrayals would suggest.

I have found many times that, in my work with patients whose marital-family situations were severely and chronically disturbed, my own domestic scene has become disturbed perceptibly. Whereupon it was felt to be at issue usually in a treatment atmosphere of long-maintained and nearly intolerable suspense, not merely upon whom—patient or analyst—the *individual* psychopathology would be inflicted permanently, but whose *family*—patient's or analyst's—might be destroyed by a family-engulfing kind of psychopathology.

I hope it is clear that I do not recommend the analyst actually actually attempting to bring about the destruction of the patient and/or the latter's whole family, in order to preserve himself and his family relatively intact. What I am trying to describe is an aspect of one's work with particularly difficult patients, and a corresponding aspect of one's work with any patient during the more particularly stressful crises in that work, whereby both the patient and to a significant degree the analyst also are involved in a struggle as to whose will be the psychopathology in question. I suggest that some degree of this kind of really mutual struggle is inherent not only in the analyst's becoming able to develop and maintain a *predominantly* neutral emotional orientation toward the patient and the latter's symptoms but necessary also to both participants' coming to accept the symptoms as "belonging" functionally to both of them—as being equivalent to transitional objects for both of them—prior to the development of a stratum of more directly and unimpededly therapeutic symbiosis in the transference relationship.

For example, I remember a time in my work over several years with a woman whose recurrently psychotic mother had threatened repeatedly to burn down the family home with the whole family in it when the patient's mother identification in this particular regard had been ragingly at issue in the analysis for many months. (I say "ragingly" even though, while the patient indeed raged much of the time, I said little or nothing, in session after session; the struggle between us was predominantly subterranean.) One of the turning points in the work occurred when my feelings had finally become sufficiently firmly integrated that I told her grimly, "If one of us is going to go home and burn down our own family home, it's not going to be me." No discernible harm resulted from my having expressed to her my hard-won determination on this score; still I think one could make a good case that it is superfluous to say such a thing to the patient. The main thing is to achieve the necessary bedrock feeling of determination which such words bespeak, and in my clinical experience, in marked contrast to that which Rosenfeld reports, such a feeling is not merely to be assumed as a given on the part of the well-analyzed and experienced psychoanalyst, but is something which develops in him, over and over, in relatedness with one individual patient after another.

In my view, the deepening spiral of the patient's coming to experience the increasingly intense fullness of the transference neurosis (or psychosis) is a function not only of the *patient's* becoming gradually able to withstand the intensity of such experienced feelings but also of increasing strength in the patient-analyst relationship, which involves the *analyst's* becoming (predominantly through finding that the patient and he have been able to deal successfully with increasingly intense transference phenomena) progressively able to endure his own being the object of such intense transference responses on the patient's part. His "enduring" such experiences is, for me at least, often just that in feeling tone: far from finding myself immersed predominantly in an emotionally neutral apartness, I have to learn to be at home with various inner emotional reactions to the patient for which my early readings in the classical psychoanalytic literature and my traditional training had ill equipped me.

Many years ago, in working with one or another chronically schizophrenic patient, I used to feel on occasion (and came to confide so to the patient, usefully), during some of the most stressful of the sessions with him (or her), that the *only* appropriate response to the way he was behaving at the moment would be for me to beat the hell out of him. To include the erotic realm in this discussion, in the instance of my work with one hebephrenic man, as I reported in a recent paper, "It required some years before I realized, sitting in one of the silences which still predominated during our sessions, that it had now become conceivable for me to be tangibly related to him without my having to either fuck him or kill him" (1974).

I had many stormy sessions with this man, whose history was marked by murderous violence and innumerable sadomasochistic homosexual conquests. It is only in more recent years, during which I have subjected myself to relatively little work with patients of this degree of illness, that I have become able to indulge myself in the luxury of doubting whether increments of raw emotion are *ever* needed, by any patient, from the therapist or analyst. Theoretically, at least (although I still do not believe this can obtain in the actual clinical work with hebephrenic patients, for example), the analyst's functioning consistently in a self-possessed "neutral" demeanor should provide him an effective outlet, in sublimated form, for all the sadism, vengefulness, sexual lust, tenderness, and so on, which he finds engendered in him in response to the patient's transference reactions and attitudes toward him.

In this same spirit, it has occurred to me, as regards my long-continued work with a chronically schizophrenic woman, that whereas I used to feel immobilized at times when it felt to me that the only appropriate response to her infuriating behavior would be for me to beat the hell out of her (as her mother used to do frequently during the patient's childhood, but as was barred, of course, to me), I have become more interested in the technical problem of *how* to beat the hell out of her in a sublimated and psychoanalytically effective fashion. Of such sublimations, I surmise, is the analyst's "neutral position" comprised—not, as I say, comprised early and permanently back in the years of his psychoanalytic training, but comprised anew, in a far more dynamic fashion, with each patient in turn, largely as a function of the transference evolution in each instance.

Two years ago I made the following note:

This idea has occurred to me several times, in sessions with one or another patient, for perhaps a year or two now: the worst thing I can do to the patient (Connolly, for example) is to analyze him successfully. This serves as a beautiful avenue or context for the sublimation of my hatred toward him, because analytic progress brings with it, for him, the experience of feelings of loss, grief, deflation of grandiosity, and so on. This idea is amply supported by data from past years (in the work with Connolly, for instance) which indicate that the analysis, to the extent that it has been successful, indeed has opened him up to the awareness of suffering of various forms—anxiety, disappointment, jealousy, and so forth.

Significantly, a note I made only four days later, concerning that day's (Tuesday's) session with Connolly, mentions that

On Sunday I was looking forward with pleasure to the hour with him on the following day—a pleasureful sense of interest in the work with him, of companionship with him—for the very first time in all our work together. There have been many times in the past when I've looked forward to the next hour with him in a spirit of vindictive determination, but never before in this manner.

Connolly, with whom I worked altogether for more than six years, early had proved to be a highly sadomasochistic, remarkably murderous-hate-engendering person with paranoid psychodynamics of a borderline schizophrenic degree of severity. It is apparent that my above-quoted notes indicate that only now had my previously relatively raw, unintegrated feelings of murderous rage and hatred toward him become sublimated into a *relatively* neutral analytic orientation. In subsequent months of his analysis, he came to express feelings of heartfelt gratitude to me for the help I had given him; he expressed at the same time feelings that this help had been also in the nature of an affliction, for I had helped him to come to experience many emotions against which his former autistic grandiosity had shielded him effectively— such emotions as loneliness, anxiety, grief, and gratitude. While expressing gratitude to me, in short, he was also providing strong confirmation of my previously noted realization that the worst thing I could do to him was to successfully analyze him.

Instances in Which the Analyst Reacts to the Patient's Symptoms as Being His —the Analyst's—Allies

When I was working in a V.A. out-patient clinic many years ago before beginning my psychoanalytic training, I made an interpretation to a belligerent young man, who thereupon was obviously hard put to keep from hitting me. I dreaded the next week's session with him, for he had left so very angry that I feared that next time he indeed would physically attack me. To my great relief—and clearly to his, also—when he did appear for the following week's session, he had a large bandage on his right hand. It turned out that he somehow had cut his hand, quite severely, with an ax. This piece of undoubted acting out on his part proved at least temporarily to be an ally of the treatment process, an ally of both his and mine; I still believe that, had this fisticuffs-precluding accident not happened, our work together would have been destroyed by his previously barely suppressed rage at me.

In one of my supervised cases during my analytic training a few years later, the patient was a borderline young woman whose impulsivity, involving erotic as well as aggressive impulses, I found to place, frequently, a barely tolerable strain upon my ability to continue in the relatively classical analytic position I was struggling to maintain. I could not help feeling relief, as well as concern, when the intensity of the transference relatedness would be decompressed, for a few sessions, by reason of her having just acted out, once again, her poorly integrated sexual and aggressive impulses. I typically was able to report to the supervisor that "We've been making pretty good headway even though she has been continuing to act out"; I doubt that I was as free then (partly because of the analytic-training context) as I have since become to experience that analytic progress is being made not so much despite, but because of, continued acting out on the patient's part. I do not mean to suggest that acting out inherently is a good thing; yet as the years go on I find less and less cause to wonder at the analyst's temporarily reacting to this symptom on the patient's part, like others among the patient's symptoms, as serving as an ally to each of them during otherwise intolerably intense times in the course of the analysis of the transference.

Six months ago I made a note, in this same vein, concerning

> my current work with Mrs. Lombardi. . . . I feel a kind of co-worker, or ally, feeling toward her acting-out symptoms (drinking, overeating, and shopping sprees) which help to stave off psychosis — very much as I felt with Bryant [the above-mentioned supervised case]. It is to be emphasized that my comrade-in-arms feeling toward such symptoms is a furtive, guilty one; I feel that if only the caliber of my analytic work were what it should be, my work wouldn't need any such allies.

Instances in Which the Patient's Symptoms Are Experienced as Transitional Objects by Both Patient and Analyst

For the past eleven years, in lecture material concerning psychoanalytically oriented intensive psychotherapy with schizophrenic patients, I have included comments, relevant here, concerning the therapist's participation in the resolution of pathogenic introjects in the patient. I have emphasized the importance of the discovery, by both patient and therapist, that these introjects in the patient have both a root in which might be called his inner reality — that is, a link to repressed components of his own identity — and an external root, traceable to unconsciously denied perceptions, on his part, of the therapist (perceptions much distorted and exaggerated, of course, by transference factors, but with nuclei of reality in them as regards the actual personality functioning of the therapist) :

> Over the long course of the therapy, the patient needs to become able to discover a sample of everything [that is, of every conceivable kind, and combination, of feelings and attitudes] in the therapist, and in himself also. During the phase of therapeutic symbiosis, the patient comes to see in the therapist all the figures from his [the patient's] own past, and these percepts become now so free from anxiety that the patient can [partly by identification with the therapist who can accept within himself the reality nuclei for his being so perceived] discover them in himself, too, with a freedom which enables him now to experience them as really acceptable components of his own self. Thus they need no longer be defensively either projected or introjected.
>
> With one schizophrenic woman in particular, I learned this lesson: whenever any murderous feeling, for example, arose during a session, it

was important that each of us become able to acknowledge murderous feelings in ourself and in the other, and likewise with envy, or adoration, or contentment, and so on, over the whole range of feelings [referring here to many months, collectively, in the overall treatment]. So very often she saw, for instance, murderousness in me, and was able to discover the projectional element in her perception only after I had become able to recognize, and acknowledge in one way or another, that there was and is, indeed, murderous feeling in me. Comparably, many times she would experience as being exclusively a feeling attribute of herself [i.e., she would now be manifesting introjection, rather than projection] something which had a counterpart in me also, and I found that her ego boundaries could become healthily established only in this setting of a free intercommunication of emotion over the whole gamut of feeling. This identity grows out of such variety of mother-child symbiosis, or in the treatment-situation therapeutic symbiosis, as this is not a defensive identity but an identity emerging out of the reality of both participants' own feelings.

I have already mentioned, earlier in this paper, how difficult it is for the therapist to endure various "nonhuman" transference roles toward the patient. This is true particularly when his conscious sense of his own identity is such as to require him to keep repressed, as being indeed horrifyingly nonhuman, those components of his (unconscious) identity which form the reality nuclei of the patient's particular transference response to him.

Over many years I have learned during supervisory sessions or while listening to colleagues' case presentations, that the most effective therapists of chronically schizophrenic patients are persons who have unusually free access to their own sadistic identity components, who do not easily or frequently become inhibited by guilty fears that their patient's perceptions of them, at times when the negative transference is in full sway, as being diabolically nonhuman, are overwhelmingly and unanalyzably accurate perceptions. It seems to me that the chronically psychotic patient can be helped back to the world of reality only by a therapist who is able relatively comfortably to participate with him in a transference relatedness in which the patient is experiencing a kind of half-reality, a sort of twilight or purgatory state — the greatest degree of experienced reality that he can yet tolerate, in actuality, because of his enormous unconscious ambivalence as to whether to become more fully reality-oriented or to return to his erstwhile more fully psychotic state. In the latter the therapist is perceived by him as being a diabolically sadistic, nonhuman creature who is playing tantalizing, tormenting games with his (the patient's) yet-unfirmly-established sense of reality.

Parenthetically, the transference atmosphere to which I am referring here is one in which not only is the patient reacting to the therapist as being a transitional object, but also the therapist is not frightened off by indications that, to a subtle but detectable degree, the reverse is true also: patient and therapist are functioning as transitional objects for one another. In other words, then, for the therapist to become able to foster this so-necessary transitional-object atmosphere in the sessions, he must gain unusually free access to his own sadism — as well as to his own feelings of symbiotic dependency toward the patient as being a preindividuation mother figure to him.

In my work, extending now for more than twenty-two years, with a severely ego-fragmented woman (work of which some aspects were described in a recent paper [1972a]), it has seemed to me that, of all the etiologic factors in her childhood, none was more conducive to later schizophrenia than the experience, on her part, of finding that those figures upon whom she had to depend for her development of reality relatedness had an investment (presumably a largely unconscious investment) in playing games with her not-yet-well-established, and therefore highly vulnerable, sense of reality. The analysis of her corresponding transference-reactions to me has required me to become somewhat accustomed to, and to find in myself reality nuclei bases for, her perceiving me as correspondingly shockingly sadistic and nonhuman in this regard. She has thrived to the extent that I can participate in such sessions in a game-playing kind of spirit, really enjoying the seeming violence that is being done to any conventional concepts of reality.

Marie Nelson, writing of the therapist's deliberately functioning in an ambiguous manner, as one of the frequently employed techniques of what she terms paradigmatic psychotherapy (a treatment approach which she and her colleagues have utilized much with borderline — as well as other — patients), says that

> the atmosphere most conducive to the treatment of the borderline patient . . . is one in which the patient remains slightly mystified concerning the motivations underlying the analyst's *overdetermined* interventions, somewhat intrigued by the analytic process. . . . [1962]
>
> An outstanding characteristic of the paradigmatic intervention is its selective avoidance of direct interpretation of the problem centrally in focus at any given time. This avoidance may be manifested, for example, in the analyst's pursuit of some theme other than the one consciously selected by the patient, by diversions such as word play, puns, jokes or nursery rhymes, by deliberate attention to subordinate notions and phrases and by oblique, multiply-determined comments on the patient's productions. . . . The conventional therapeutic situation, wherein the content of the presenting problem constitutes the figure and the associative material the ground, is reversed; the peripheral material is encouraged to occupy the foreground of attention and the presenting problem is relegated — in the *conscious* interchange, that is — to a peripheral position. [1968, p. 37]

There have been times, in my teaching interviews with borderline patients such as are many of those of whom Coleman writes, when I have had the delightful experience of the patient and myself as being two subjectively diabolical sadists fully enjoying ourselves and one another in childlike playfulness which clearly was doing both of us a great deal of good. Such experiences are a far cry from, and represent a kind of resolution of, one's experiences with more deeply ill patients wherein one has horrifying fears lest one be equivalent to the schizophrenia with which the patient is afflicted. Modell says of borderline patients that

The relationships established by these people are of a primitive order, not unlike the relationship of a child to a blanket or teddy bear. These inanimate objects are recognized as something outside the self, yet they owe their lives, so to speak, to processes arising within the individual. Their objects are not perceived in accordance with their "true" or "realistic" qualities. I have borrowed Winnicott's concept of the transitional object, which he applied to the child's relation to these inanimate objects (Winnicott, 1951), and have applied this designation to the borderline patient's relation to his human objects. . . . The relationship of the borderline patient to his physician is analogous to that of a child to a blanket or teddy bear. [1963]

In a similar vein, he says that

A defective sense of identity in borderline and psychotic individuals is, I believe, a major element in the creation of the qualitatively different transference relationship that occurs in these patients (see also Zetzel, 1956, 1965). It is not true, as Freud once believed, that the psychotic remains inaccessible to the psychoanalytic method because he is incapable of forming a transference. For we now know that psychotic people do in fact form a transference relationship of the most intense sort, a transference corresponding to the mode of the transitional object relationship—the person of the analyst becomes a created environment. [1968, pp. 45-46]

My concept of the therapeutic symbiosis is fully consonant with Modell's view that the borderline or psychotic patient forms a transitional-object form of transference relationship with the analyst. But, as I have indicated in my several papers about the therapeutic symbiosis, it can equally well be seen that the analyst manifests, in that phase of the work, a transitional-object relatedness with the patient—and, in fact, a considerably deeper degree of symbiotic relatedness than that. Moreover, as I have reported in various of these earlier papers (1965, 1973a), I regard the phase of therapeutic symbiosis as being present—though less prominently—in the analysis of the neurotic individual also, particularly as regards the areas of autism which are to be found in any such individual. Where Modell says in the above-quoted passage, concerning psychotic people, that the person of the analyst becomes a created environment, I have indicated in a recent paper on therapeutic symbiosis that this is true in the reverse direction also. Writing of the resolution of autism in patients — whether schizophrenic, borderline, or neurotic — I reported that

> In my experience, for the resolution of the patient's autism to occur, the analyst must do more than function as a more reliable maternally protective shield for the patient than the latter's biological mother had been during his infancy and early childhood, in the manner that Khan (1963, 1964) has described. First the analyst must have become increasingly free in his acceptance of the *patient's* functioning as *his* — the analyst's — maternally protective shield. In my own way of conceptualizing it: to the extent that the analyst can become able comfortably and freely to immerse himself in the autistic patient as comprising his (the analyst's) world, the patient can then utilize him as a model for identification as regards the acceptance of such very primitive dependency needs, and can come increasingly to exchange his erstwhile autistic world for the world comprised of, and personified by, the analyst. [1973a]

It seems to me probable that, in order for any effective transference analysis to occur with any patient, whether neurotic, borderline, or psychotic, the analyst must have come to accept at *least* a transitional-object degree of relatedness with the particular transference image, or percept, which is presently holding sway in the analysis. I myself characteristically feel a much clearer and more tangible correspondence than that, with components of my own identity as I customarily know it in daily life. It seems to me particularly unworkable to relate to a psychotic patient as though his transference reactions to me were "purely" transference, and his projection-distorted perceptions of me were "pure" projections; he needs some acknowledgment, no matter how implicit, from me that his perceptions of me are not purely and completely crazy. But even a neurotic patient must be receiving, from his analyst, some kind of implicit acknowledgment that the patient's transference responses are not as "purely" — essentially, that is, delusionally — transference as classical analytic authors (such as Modell, where he states flatly concerning borderline patients, as quoted above, that "Their objects are not perceived in accordance with their 'true' or 'realistic' qualities") portray.

Under the impact of particularly intense transference responses from the patient, on occasion I find that something occurs in me whereby I disavow any reality nucleus for the patient's particular transference perception of me,

whereby in other words I temporarily flee from the erstwhile degree of symbiotic relatedness with him in which his symptom — in this particular instance,
his symptom of murderous paranoid hate — has been serving as something like
a transitional object for myself as well as for him. Now, instead, I find immunity from such relatedness by regarding him as being the bearer of all the
psychopathology in the situation — as being, in short, crazy. The following
notes were made during a Friday session several years along in a woman's
analysis:

Two days ago . . . I had been feeling relatively free of any animosity toward her, and therefore was much jolted to find that, on her arrival, she
was filled with murderous rage at me because of some minor litter she had
seen in the corridor outside my door. . . .

In that session two days ago, as many times before over the years, I was
conscious mainly of the remarkably intense hate which is the atmosphere in
which her analysis takes place, or proceeds — murderous hate, mutual murderous hate. Innumerable times, I have had fantasies that she would come
here and, in cold-blooded paranoid hate, shoot me. Lately I have not been
feeling frightened of her, but have felt — two days ago — what a strain it is to
experience, sustainedly, this extremely intense hate.

There are more positive aspects, too, and as a matter of fact on Sunday,
for the first time, I found myself looking forward with comfortable pleasure
to the session with her on the following day.

Yesterday she was being her usual schizy self in reaction to the death,
earlier that day, of her elderly aunt.

Today she was a few minutes late in arriving, and meanwhile I found
myself feeling very angry at her — feeling the violent, murderous hate — and
then when the door from the corridor opened with (an usual) infuriating
violence, I felt even more violently murderous rage at her.

Then, as if by a conscious decision which emerged out of my being unable to tolerate, or unwilling to tolerate, that degree of violent, murderous,
sustained hate toward her, I decided to regard her as schizophrenic (as yesterday's session had served once again to highlight her to be), and said to
her, "Hello, Bernice," in a very conventionally friendly tone as she walked
in. She was looking pale, extremely tense, schizy (as she very frequently
does).

I found this a striking example of how one's view of the patient as being
schizophrenic serves as an unconscious defense against one's intolerably intense *personal* feelings toward her.

There is a definite balance in this regard which a skillful analyst must
achieve. During the past few days in my work with the fantasy-immersed
Mr. Marshall, I have come to feel that I take my patients' symptoms too

personally. The steady analysis-of-the-transference focus does foster one's taking the patient's symptoms personally, in a sense.

All this is a very complex and most important question.

It seems to me that any symptom on the patient's part which proves, over a long course of time in the analysis, highly resistant to further analysis is apt to have developed an unrecognized transitional-object function for the analyst as well as for the patient. The problem is not that the symptom has *developed* this function, but rather that both participants have had to keep under *repression* this mode of relatedness with it. This transitional-object mode of their relatedness with the symptom in question has proved to be not a preliminary to the necessary degree of therapeutic symbiosis between them, but rather to have become an unconscious defense, for both of them, against a more free, constructively therapeutic symbiosis. In such an instance — and, in my experience, such instances are very common, indeed, in psychoanalytic work — the tenacious symptom in question, unconsciously related to by each participant as being a transitional object for himself or herself, can be seen to be in the nature of an autistic, essentially paranoid, defense against the development of therapeutic symbiosis.

A common example of such a treatment-resistant symptom is a patient's obsessive preoccupation, throughout seemingly endless analytic sessions, with the unsatisfactory qualities in his or her spouse. Notes I made some seven months ago concern such a situation:

> In yesterday's session, Mr. Robinson spent the session in a way highly typical of him — vituperating about his wife, Edna, as being so insensitive, unhelpful, selfish, sitting on her ass and not helping sufficiently in the care of their young sons, almost never showing any sexual interest in him, and so on.
>
> As in many dozens, if not hundreds, of sessions previously, I felt much exasperation and futility at his massive resistance to becoming aware of the very clear displacement of his unconscious transference feelings toward me onto Edna; and the almost equally clear parallels, for a very long time now, between hiw own ways of functioning during the session and the way the unhelpful, selfish Edna functions at home. [For years, it had become increasingly clear to me that he typically treated me, unconsciously or preconsciously, in ways remarkably like the ways he found so offensive in Edna's treatment of him; and increasingly clear, likewise, that Edna was oftentimes an only slightly displaced transference image of me. But many dozens of interpretations, over the years, about various aspects of this, as well as of its totality, had proved completely unavailing.]

What was very evident to me in the session yesterday (a not entirely new discovery, but clearer than before) was the extent to which the "Edna" of whom he talks in the session—devoting most of his analytic time to such talk, year after year—needs to be seen as having parallels in both himself and in me [as was accomplished successfully in my work with the schizophrenic woman mentioned at the beginning of this subsection of the paper]. What was a new idea to me, during the session yesterday, was that the "Edna" he talks of during the session is an unconscious defense against the symbiotic linkage between himself and me. The "Edna," that is, is the area of symbiosis between us.

In the last-quoted sentence, where I wrote of "the area of symbiosis between us," I was referring to that area of our relatedness wherein he was unconsciously in symbiosis with me, and wherein I was, as I was only now becoming aware, symbiotic with him. I recall its becoming vividly clear to me, during this particular session, that for all practical purposes as regards his functioning during the analytic sessions, this "Edna" of whom he spoke was only *seemingly* a third real person, and needed to be seen, for analytic purposes, as predominantly an *unconscious construct*, comprised largely through displacements and projections on his part—and on my own part. One of the clues that "Edna" had come to play a significant role in my own unconscious functioning is that many times, over the years, I had found myself making some comment which served to bring him back to the subject of "Edna," at times when he was functioning relatively freely and being able to do without "her" for the moment.

At this juncture in this paper, it seems to me accurate to hypothesize that, as with any tenaciously treatment-resistant symptoms in general, so with persistent transference-images which the patient maintains in his response to the analyst: in order for these to become resolved, they must go through a phase of functioning as transitional objects for both patient and analyst, and of being acknowledged, no matter how implicitly, by both participants as having developed this status in the relationship between the two of them.

The following detailed material is from my work with a thirty-five-year-old divorced woman, Mrs. Pauline Bryant, whom I analyzed for a number of years. During the past few years she has been able to live alone outside the sanitarium. As her analysis went on, her experiencing of auditory hallucinations, which she had begun having some few years prior to entering analysis, proved to be an analytic theme of paramount value for her ego differentiation and integration.

Early in our work, whenever she "heard voices," she evidently experienced these as emanating from some weirdly nonhuman source; she spoke of them, with a psychotically-threatened demeanor, as being "electric voices." In that early phase of the analysis, more often than not she reacted to me also as being something other than human, as being, very often indeed, either inhumanly unfeeling or a frighteningly crazy sex fiend.

As the analysis progressed, she became able gradually to work collaboratively with me during the sessions in this as well as in other regards, reporting to me during the sessions whenever she had just heard the voices. Gradually these were taking on, evidently, more and more human characteristics, as I helped her to become able to identify with these previously unconscious and projected components of herself. Concomitantly and equally much, I helped her to see them as being, at the same time, unconscious transference perceptions of components of myself, perceptions which did not fit with her conscious images of me, and which therefore were being displaced onto these hallucinatory experiences.

In the chronologically arranged excerpts given below, one readily can see instances in which the voices say to her things—helpful, explanatory, sympathetic, or confirmatory things—which, at an unconscious or preconscious level, she is wishing I would say to her. Increasingly, the voices can be seen as referable to either her own conscious identity, or to her consciously perceived image of me. The voices become more and more simply human in quality, and at times difficult or impossible for her to distinguish from her "own" thoughts and feelings.

Friday, June 2, 1969. She reported having heard, in a store where she was shopping on Wednesday, "so many voices—I thought [tone of helplessness], "Hafta talk to my doctor and tell them—" At this point I interjected, "Tell *them?*" She agreed that this is the way she had said it. She then "corrected" this slip of the tongue, "—talk to my *doctor* and tell him to tell them to go away—well, maybe when I talk to my doctor I think it *is* them—connected to so many doctors—aren't ya, Dr. Searles?—connected to so many doctors?" While saying these last few phrases, in a very intimate, teasing tone, she was leaning over toward me. This was the most intimate few moments we'd had in years, in terms of physical proximity and atmosphere of intimacy. [As regards this paper, her slip of the tongue, in which she said "tell them" instead of "tell him" seemed to me a strong clue that she was equating me, unconsciously, with the voices.]

As the sessions went on, much data emerged which indicated that the voices were unconsciously equivalent, also, to the subjectively unwanted-by-other-people parts of herself. For example, it was clear to me, from her description of her weekly attendance, yesterday, at a Baptist church-group meeting, that she had felt much more isolated, unwanted, and lonely there than she had been aware of feeling.

Some minutes later she said, decisively, "I just don't want those voices." I suggested, "You are surer of that than you are of what you *do* want," to which she responded promptly, "I'd like life to be a *little* easier than it is—I think people are shown too hard a time—I heard the voices say, 'It's true; things *don't* have to be so difficult' [strongly confirmatory tone quoted; then after a few seconds of silence]—I heard the voices say, 'People don't have to be so nasty' [companionable, consoling tone quoted]. I don't know what they're referring to—It's something I don't understand—voices in the air that I'm—that come my way—the voices say, 'You know why this occurred?—Something happened to you.' " [helpfully-explanatory tone quoted]

In this session she went on to report some new and important material about the initial onset of her overt psychosis, several years previously. Also, she proved to be more than usually accepting of my suggestion to her that she is more lonely than she had been realizing.

Friday, December 8, 1969. In the middle of a (usual weekly) two-hour session (I have had two-hour sessions with a number of patients over the years), during which we had been arguing (as not infrequently had happened in the course of her analysis) a great deal, I made my usual brief trip to the men's room across the corridor. She reported, as I returned and sat down again, "I just heard voices say, 'Dr. Searles has realized that you've had enough of his fussing around with you.' You open the door and let the voices in," she said, laughing warmly. I asked, "It's as though they come in at the same time I do?" She nodded, explaining, "When you opened the door to the hallway"—on, she later made clear, my way back into the office.

Friday, January 12, 1970. When, on coming from the corridor into the waiting room where she was sitting waiting for her session, I opened the door, she whirled and looked at me in a psychotically fearful way. Then five minutes along in the session, after talk about other matters, she explained, "When you opened the door, it seemed like you let some voices in, and they said, 'Don't worry so much; you're a very sweet woman.' "

Then after about an hour and a half of this same two-hour session, within a few seconds after my return from the men's room, she reported hearing the voices say, "Why do you refuse to learn? Do you think your father doesn't know you're nervous with him and Eddie [her brother]?" Here, the tone quoted was one of such warmth, intimacy, and liveliness that I burst into laughter. The tone was entirely that of a family member. I told her that I thought of her mother (who had died about ten years previously). She replied, "Well, she thought I was a very sweet person by nature," in a confirmatory tone, and went on, "Yeah; but this voice didn't sound like her voice—I just heard the voices say, 'Guess what's gonna happen with you and Bill [her brother-in-law]?" Again the tone had the same heartwarmingly intimate, family-member quality. I suggested, "Pauline, one of the ways I think is that if you can ever find someone to share your life as warmly and intimately as the voices do, you won't need the voices." She laughed warmly on hearing this. (It had been most rare for her to be so receptive to any interpretation wherein I cast the voices in so benign a light. One of the, to me, interesting features of this excerpt is that it gives some glimpse of the intense ambivalence so characteristic of her — at one point psychotically threatened, at another point overwhelmingly warmly intimate.)

Friday, March 30, 1970. Toward the end of the first half of a two-hour session, she was saying, "I worry about those voices," in a tone clearly conveying that she unconsciously was concerned about their welfare. Within at most two minutes later, she was telling of having seen recent TV newscasts of interviews with some of the wives of men who were trapped in a disabled submarine. Her "I worry about the voices" had been said, I thought now in retrospect, *very* much the way a submariner's wife might worry about her husband. At the time I first heard it, she had sounded more like a worried mother speaking about her children.

She went on to speak of various deceased parental-family members who had died during the spring months (such as this). "I feel they went through a winter that wasn't good for them," she said.

A bit later, I suggested, "Your tone in saying that you worry about those voices was that you worry that they may be dying." At this, she immediately made a disgusted, annoyed, rejecting wave of her hands at me, and plunged down on the couch pillow [having been sitting up on the couch, as she usually did]. All this she did with such warmth and intimacy that I laughed happily.

At a later point in this session when she was appearing more fearful again, she was saying about the voices, while glancing rapidly around at the floorboards in the office, "*I* think it has something to do with a radio or something like that—or caused with a battery, something electrical. *I* don't know; I'm just guessing—I heard the voices say, 'It has something to do with money.' "

Friday, May 25, 1970. In expressing fond memories of her mother, she said, "She was a nice woman—she always worked hard—I always thought she worked too hard and I wanted to help her—I used to say my mother was very close, my best friend. I always loved her so; we always wanted to be close together—[few seconds' silence] I heard the voices say, 'She loved you, too.' " [quoted tone is one of gentle assurance]

Tuesday, June 5, 1970. After having reported that she had just heard the voices again (their content being usual enough), she said, "Oh, the voices, Dr. Searles, I hate 'em!", plunging her head down on the couch pillow from her previously sitting position. This was said with no more than moderately hateful intensity. The striking thing, to me, was the " 'em"—so close to " 'em," so close, then, to the meaning, "Dr. Searles, I hate 'em!" [That is, I felt that the displacement of her unconscious hatred of me, onto the voices, was here unusually transparent.]

Several minutes later in the session, she confirmed my impression that she had felt frightened on seeing my pen [with which I had written the date]. "Sometimes I don't feel that my mind is my own." After a few seconds of silence I said, in a manner intended to encourage her to elaborate further, "Sometimes you don't feel that your mind is your own?" She agreed, adding only, "Sometimes I wonder." [I would assume that she was unsure whether her mind were being controlled by my pen — a kind of paranoid experiencing which would be fully in accord with that which had been so predominant in the early years of our work.]

Tuesday, July 17, 1970. During the first several minutes of the session, she reported, several different times, having just heard the voices, and quoted what they had said to her. On most of these occasions, in my private opinion, the voices had said things to her which she very likely might have wished I would say, but which are not typical of me — more the kind of things which a friend, or a person involved in doing supportive psychotherapy, would say. I had been remaining silent throughout. After seven minutes of this, she said after a minute or so of silence, "You haven't any comment to make about what I've said, have you?", to which I made no reply. [I regard this vignette of relevance here because of the evidence, in it, of her experiencing me, in terms of "interpersonal" cathexis, as being on a par with the hallucinatory voices. It was much as if she had said, "The *voices* have been making comments, several times, about what I've been saying. *You* haven't any comment to make about what I've said, have you?"]

Tuesday, July 31, 1970. At the beginning of the session, she said she had been quite pleased yesterday at not hearing the voices. But then today, after sitting downstairs in the lobby of this building for a time, when she had gotten up to walk to the elevator to come up to her session, "I heard the voices say, 'It's not because you're bad, I guarantee ya' — " Her facial expression while she recounted this was complex — mainly, I would say, tortured, helpless. I commented, "Those voices really tease you cruelly, don't they?" I was planning here, assuming (as I fully assumed) that she would agree to suggest to her next the possibility that there was an aspect of her *self* fully as cruelly tantalizing as this [as aspect of herself of which I personally felt the impact innumerable times over the years].

But she promptly retorted, with conviction, "What about your *self?*" I replied, "Are you referring to what I said on Friday about — [having in mind the following incident: She had asked me what the little slabs in my new mobile were made of, and I had said petrified wood, and then had added, teasingly, "Did you notice that I avoided looking directly at you when I said, petrified wood?" Thereupon she had looked — naturally enough — very hurt, very cruelly teased by me, and I felt I had been very mean, very cruel to her. Parenthetically, I generally felt that my own sadism was in evidence much less often than hers, during the sessions; but hers was still largely unconscious.]

She interrupted me vigorously by saying, decisively, "I'm referring to right now." It was said with considerable antagonism, although I did not feel, this time, that the retort was fully deserved.

Later in the session, after commenting about something, she said in an unusually spontaneous, good-naturedly teasing way, "As my analyst, what d'ya say?—I think that's a good joke, don't you?", with amused laughter which I shared. [She regarded this as a joke for the reason that, in her opinion, an analyst is by definition someone who never responds when asked to do so.] "Couldn't help saying what came to mind," she added with a half-sarcastic, but half-serious, note of apology; it was apparent that to permit herself even this bit of conscious teasing of me caused her to feel rather guilty.

After a brief silence, she reported, "The voices just say, 'If ya had any sense, ya'd leave Virginia.' " [She was living in suburban Virginia.] I suggested, "They talk as though that's what *they* would do if *they* were in your position?" She replied, less rejectingly than usual of such comments from me, "Maybe they wanta travel; I don't know—If I go somewhere ya think they're gonna come along, Dr. Searles?" I said nothing.

Shortly thereafter, she said, "I just heard the voices—and I was getting along *so well* yesterday—." I interrupted, suggesting, "It's as though you're hardly the same *person* ya' were yesterday," with which she agreed promptly and emphatically, "*Yeah, yeah.*" I found it impressive, indeed, that she was able so fully to accept this comment.

Later in the session she was saying, with an impressively healthy, spontaneous rapidity and fluidity of feeling, "I was thinking of the [ornamental] rocks I saw in Camalier and Buckley [one of the local stores she frequented], and I was thinking, 'My doctor doesn't have any,' and I heard the voices say, 'He doesn't want any'—I think that's funny," and indeed she sounded genuinely amused.

Friday, September 7, 1970. She described a bus ride yesterday during which another passenger commented, of a talkative young man a few seats away, that "he has a need to talk." I suggested to her, "Perhaps, too, those voices have a need to talk" [thinking of them as being, in this regard, a projection of an unconscious aspect of herself]. She replied promptly and spontaneously, with an amused laugh, "Maybe so—I wish they'd go away from *me*, though."

Friday, November 23, 1970. About fifteen minutes before the end of this two-hour session, she said that she had just heard the voices for the first time in the session. "I heard the voices say, 'You're getting older, you know; but aren't we all?' [tone quoted is gentle and friendly] Now, *that's* the way *I* very *often talk* isn't it?" I replied, "Yes—but it didn't sound like your voice?" She responded, "No [but] it's the way I very often talk."

Thursday, January 2, 1971. She was speaking of the Peanuts comic strip [which I had not read in many years], and said, "I was trying to think of the dog's name and I heard the voices say, 'Snoopy.' " I asked, "*Is* that the dog's name?" She replied, "Snoopy, yeah." She had said all this in a relatively comfortable-sounding tone, indicating the voices to be as comfortably companionable with her as I had ever known her to indicate.

Friday, January 11, 1971. After we had been discussing the Library of Congress, on the basis of our each having been there on various occasions, there was a silence of perhaps half a minute, and she then reported, "I heard the voices; but they were very far away. I don't know if I really heard them or if it was in my mind. They said, 'Do you know why he *really* went there?'—I don't think I really heard the voices; I think it was in my mind."

Friday, Janaury 18, 1971. She described how complex her life became repeatedly, just at times when she was feeling most secure. She said this with exasperation but also with amused laughter. She then asked, in a half-teasing, half-serious way, "How'm I doing, Dr. Searles?—*You're* my psyche." I replied, in a manner neither challengingly questioning nor fully confirmatory, "I'm your psyche," and she agreed. I did not reply to her question as such. A few minutes later, after other back-and-forth conversation between us, she reported, "I heard the voices say, 'You *are* a nice lady.' [reassuring tone quoted]

Tuesday, Janaury 29, 1971. About fifteen minutes along in this session she said that she had just "heard the voices say, 'It's true—people should be more considerate.' Now, I don't know if it's actually a voice or in my mind—it's close to my feeling about it."

Tuesday, February 12, 1971. She said that today she was starting to get on a bus, when she heard a (real) woman and a man talking to one another "and somehow through that I heard some voices," and because of this, "I decided not to get on that bus." She had waited for the next bus, got on that one, and did not hear voices. "Somehow I felt that if I had got on that other bus I would have heard voices—I heard, just now, 'It's true; there's something about you that looks very worried.' " Later in the session she mentioned that, upon having heard those voices at the bus stop, "The first thought I had was, 'Why should I go on that bus to hear voices?—and it's crowded!—so I didn't go." [I include this item partially to indicate that the hallucinations were still influencing her daily-life behavior, although far less constrictingly than used to be the case years before, when she had led a severely cramped life, afraid to venture into, for example, certain stores where she had heard them terrifyingly loud and "thick and fast" when she had dared last to go in there.]

Friday, February 15, 1971. This was a chilly, overcast day, with combined snow and sleet predicted. About fifty minutes along in her two-hour session this morning, she reported, "It seemed to me that a voice has been trying to come through and I get very nervous with it. I didn't actually hear it; it's very distant." I commented, "You're not aware, I gather from what you say, of feeling at times distant from me, or that I seem at times distant from you." After a few moments of thought she responded, with a warmly amused laugh, "I don't know about *distance* — you know I don't like to compare" [she smiled in an empathic way in making this aside; she was alluding here to the major area of dissension between us in earlier years: my talking in comparative terms often — not excessively so by any usual standards, in actuality — and her having only relatively recently become largely free of her long-held conviction that this was frightening craziness on my part] "but I feel you're like the weather — you're about the same temperature toward me as the weather — cold." [I found very impressive the degree of ego differentiation involved in her being able to liken to the weather my feeling attitude toward her. For years I had endeavored, in vain, to help her to come to know that she was experiencing as purely weather phenomena — she talked endlessly of the weather in those years — phenomena which basically had to do with the complex and changeable emotional climate of the relationship between us. For years, in short, she had projected onto the weather many of her unconscious feelings, and had displaced onto it many unconscious transference perceptions of me.]

Then a few moments of silence ensued, and she said, "I was thinking it's nice to know that the voices have stopped, and I heard, 'You've won' " [simply said], and she laughed with amusement which I shared.

Tuesday, February 26, 1971. This was our first session in a week, for I had been out of town. [This I assume to be significant for what occurred during my absence.] She said that on Friday she had had to spend two and a half hours in a beauty parlor, having repeatedly to wait for the different steps to proceed, and had heard voices while there. "I was really *very* frightened [with unmistakable seriousness]. I never heard them so loud — kept telling me, '*Leave! — leave!* — ya don't like it here — leave — why don'tcha leave *Virginia?*' " She had stayed, obviously, nonetheless, but said, "I'm very hesitant about going back there. I like the way they fix my hair; but I *didn't* like those voices — Seems to me I was *detained* there especially to hear the voices; I can't help feeling that — And it does seem a shame; the work was really very well done — matter of fact, better than ever before." But because of the voices, she reemphasized, "It made me *very* nervous — I have this frightened feeling that it may return." [I include this material to show that on occasion still, such as during an unusually long separation between us, she experienced the hallucinatory voices with frightening intensity. She was still not ready for any interpretation from me that the voices had been, in part, projected expressions of her unconscious and intense wishes that I, as a hated and unwanted transference figure — and of course in any case I would not employ such technical terminology — would leave the city permanently and never return; and also, in part, displaced unconscious perceptions of me as trying to send her into exile.]

Much later in the session she returned to the incident at the beauty parlor. 'Other people get provoked, too; it's just too long to wait—I heard the voices say, 'It's true; things don't hafta be so hard for you." I suggested, calmly, Sounds as though that's said in a very sympathetic way." She responded assertively but unangrily, "Very matter-of-fact, I'd say. Not unsympathetic; but not so sympathetic."

Friday, March 1, 1971. She mentioned that she hadn't heard any voices yesterday or today, until she reported hearing them briefly, a time or two, relatively early in this two-hour session. Then much later in it, after we had been discussing some of the ways she had felt very early in her illness, there was a pause of a few seconds, and she then said, "I just heard, 'That's true; you've had plenty of problems' [tone mild, somewhat offhand, not actively sympathetic]—but not very loud, almost like it was *my* mind." Her tone in saying "almost like it was *my* mind" was one of pretty much accepting that it probably *was* her mind; there was not note of surprise, nor of any anxiety, in her voice.

Tuesday, July 2, 1971. Upon coming into the office, and before sitting down on the couch, she said, "I just heard the voices say, 'You're a very nice woman.' I was going to tell you I felt so good because I didn't hear the voices weekend or yesterday—so, this [tone of mild exasperation] is what I get."

I found this interesting because, in the same process, the voices had behaved in a tantalizing way toward her and she had behaved in a tantalizing way toward me. That is, I felt, ironically, as she was telling me all this, how close I had come to hearing her make a gratified and gratifying, rather than a complaining, report about the days since the last session. The ironic aspect of my feeling had to do with my seeing clearly her largely unconscious investment in tantalizing me.

THE FUNCTIONING OF AN APPURTENANCE IN THE ANALYTIC SITUATION AS A TRANSITIONAL OBJECT FOR BOTH ANALYST AND PATIENT

I shall give but a few examples from a wide range of appurtenances which, in my experience, have come to function as transitional objects for both analyst and patient at sometime during the course of their work together.

I. A Tape Recorder

Mrs. Joan Douglas, a much more deeply ill woman whose history and course in psychotherapy I reported in some detail previously (1972a), has been working with me for nearly twenty-two years, four hours per week, at the present time. For the first eleven years I met with her at Chestnut Lodge, and since then she has come by taxi to my office several miles away in Washington. Although she has improved in a number of important regards over this tremendous span of time, she has continued to manifest an extremely severe degree of ego fragmentation and unrelatedness, experiencing herself and perceiving me, more often than not, for example, as comprised of multiple and unrelated persons or fragments of persons.

Ten years ago I began taping our sessions, openly and with her knowledge, and have taped all of them for the past 9½ years on 7-inch reels, all of which I have kept on file. Occasional playbacks of these tapes, privately, have confirmed my conviction that they are of immense research value as regards the psychodynamics, and psychoanalytic therapy, of schizophrenic patients.

With only a dozen or so exceptions I have used the same recorder, throughout, for taping all these sessions, and this recorder long ago acquired enormous personal feeling value for me. Among other meanings for me, it is a link to her, a link to Chestnut Lodge, a link to my cherished collection of tapes; and it is symbolic, too, of the scientific life and the academic life, for one who feels all too burdened, these days, with workaday clinical responsibilities.

When I began taping the sessions I started augmenting this form of data collection by noting down briefly, during the hours, facts concerning some of the nonverbal processes which the recorder could not register—such as, for example, whether she nodded in agreement or shook her head in disagreement in response to a comment of mine.

Between one and two years ago I began, very tentatively at first, to try to dispense with this note taking and to make, instead, comments to the nearby microphone on my desk which led to the recorder over on the other side. I did this partly in an attempt to make the situation a bit less artificially encumbered by data collecting, and also because it seemed less of a bother for me to do.

Throughout all the foregoing years I had had a persistent difficulty which consisted in my pulling my punches with her, fearing her apparent fragility and vulnerability, while she rode roughshod over me, doing unfettered violence to my own sense of reality. Similarly with my beginning, in a gingerly way, to make brief asides to the tape recorder, I was concerned lest she be jarred and offended, even though one of my most frequent experiences with her, over the years, had been for me to sit helplessly by while she was immersed in a vigorously lively dialogue with one or another projected internal image—of, more often than not, some mother-figure giantess—during which she was vocalizing, in different voices, both sides of the dialogue.

Moreover, anything resembling play therapy has always come to me with great difficulty. Bit by bit over several months, however, I dispensed more and more with my note taking, and became able to utilize the tape recorder with some relative versatility in my relationship with Mrs. Douglas. For example when I was feeling particularly furious at her and determined to hurt her in retaliation for what she had been doing to me, I would deliberately talk, in a coldly clinical, lecturing fashion to the tape recorder, about her diagnosis of chronic schizophrenia. And when I was feeling particularly warmly fond of her, and sensed that she was suddenly being frightened away by this response from me, I would turn, with a barely perceptible change of tone or volume, and talk in an intimately companionable way with my recorder, with which she could identify in proportion as she became able to do so.

In a previous paper (1973a) I mentioned that

In my work with [a hebephrenic] man, as well as with another patient earlier and many subsequently, I have seen that ambivalently symbiotic relatedness often comes to have, at first weirdly, a quality of *group* relatedness, with jealousy a most important and difficult complicating factor.

This had been true, for some years, of my work with Mrs. Douglas prior to my starting to talk with my tape recorder. Now it became commonplace for a quality of group interaction to be present in the room while she was talking with some projected mother image up toward the ceiling, and I was talking simultaneously with my tape recorder.

As for her own responses to the tape recorder directly, she seems to this day convinced that there are people in it who have been shrunken and placed there. On occasion, at her request, I have played it back for a couple of minutes or so during a session, and although she has come regularly to confirm that my voice from it does indeed sound like my voice, she is firmly convinced that her voice from it is not hers. She is aware of my attachment to the recorder; I was once baffled at her referring to it as "your daughter," in all seriousness, until I remembered that, in both her marital family and in her parental family, the daughter was the apple of the father's eye.

I am convinced that my way of utilizing the presence of the recorder promoted, in this atmosphere of group relatedness, her increasing ego integration. In a session on April 3, 1974, for example, in which I was weaving many comments to the tape recorder into the interaction between her and me, she said with an amused laugh, of some person who had just occurred to her, "She can come and join our group therapy." A few minutes later she, who seldom had mentioned realistically any of her fellow patients at Chestnut Lodge, and who rarely indeed had spoken of the group of them in her cottage as a whole, said in regard to the question of whether one has to eat to stay alive, "The group we have at the Lodge now is disputing that. They say, 'You *do not*; you *do not eat ever* in your whole life.' Millie and Betty [two of the other patients in her cottage] believe you *have* to eat."

In the July 17, 1974, session she referred to herself as "this group," and clearly confirmed, when I inquired, that she was experiencing herself as being a group. This was merely one of many indications that a change was taking place, from her more customary sense of her own identity as discontinuous and unrelated over the course of time, shifting unpredictably from one day to the next or even from one moment to the next, to a sense of identity which, while still multiple, involved a sense of a group of "selves" simultaneously existing in group relatedness with one another. Similarly, a careful study of this session shows her being able to be more collaborative with me, more related realistically with me, in a setting of my repeatedly interspersing brief asides to the tape recorder into moments of unrelatedness between us. To me it seems clear that this "group" relatedness involving us threatens her less with devouring or being devoured than does my erstwhile attempt to focus my attention single-mindedly upon her.

In the preparation of this present paper, I came upon Ekstein's (1965) paper entitled "Puppet Play of a Psychotic Adolescent Girl in the Psychotherapeutic Process." His paper, in which he portrays the puppet as functioning as a transitional object for the girl, is one which I find in many details reminiscent for me of my work with Mrs. Douglas, work during which the tape recorder served as a transitional object for me and, increasingly, for her, as she is progressively able to let herself be the object of various responses which I have diverted temporarily to the recorder, until such time as she is able, through identification with that quasi-person, to endure and enjoy being comparably related to, directly, by me in the transference situation.

The Analyst's Notes

A borderline-paranoid woman, who had been in analysis for a number of years, commented after I had quoted something back to her from the notes I had been taking during the session, ". . . as you read from your notes . . ." To myself, as the session went on, I privately noted the following thoughts:

She did not especially emphasize the word *your*; but I was struck that there could well be an underlying confusion in her mind as to whether my notes are *mine* or *hers*, since what I quote — and have obviously noted — are statements *she* has made. Thus it seems to me the notes *could* be reacted to unconsciously by *each* of us as being in the uncertain realm that is neither clearly "me" nor clearly "not me."

Some six months after the foregoing incident, during a session in which she was expressing newly derepressed murderousness of the kind which I had perceived in her for years, but which only recently had become possible to interpret with any success, I made the following notes:

One thing that interests me about the above [referring here to many verbatim notes, setting down her reporting of this newly-derepressed material]
is that it provides confirmation of my *many* threatened fantasies [which I
had experienced for years]—still present at times—lest she shoot me, or
destroy me by lawsuit. Ever since the last session—on Saturday—I recall
having had the fantasy of her refusing to use the couch, my suddenly quit-
ting with her, her vowing to destroy me—implying, by legal means—and
my hastily renting a safety-deposit box big enough to hold the notes at least
from the first couple of years of her analysis, and my putting them there—
or—I also recall fantasying—secreting them in one of the boxes labeled "JD
Tapes". My fantasy was that she broke into the storeroom, determined to
get her notes—I'm struck by my calling them here "her" notes, rather than
mine, which to me indicates symbiosis between us, and my unconscious
anxiety at the prospect of loss of this symbiosis, anxiety defended against by
paranoid fantasies and feelings on the part of myself as well as of the patient—and she overlooked this portion of her notes, because they were in
the box so labeled. . . . One of the valuable aspects of this material is that
the notes are so likely (in psychoanalytic work in general) to be, as I feel
reasonably sure they are here, a transitional object for both analyst and patient. . . . I do not trust her sufficiently to tell her my fantasy since the Saturday session—not even *nearly* enough to do so.

The Couch

A woman who characteristically reacted much to even brief absences on my
part had been saying, for several sessions, that when she came here and saw
me, she remembered that I was going to be away on Saturday of next week.
Then, at the beginning of the week in question, she revised this:

It's when I come in and sit on the couch that it occurs to me that you
won't be here on Saturday; it's not when I look at you, but when I sit on the
couch. . . . This couch has more—something—more substance. It's more
real to me than you are; it really is. . . . This couch is even more than you
—it has something more—it's because I lie on it and touch it and I do
things to it, and I can't touch you, I can't do things to you—This couch
stays here and it's nice and certain. . . . It's no wonder people get attached
to their furniture, their belongings—That's why the couch is more important than you are—

Later in the same session I set down some of my own thoughts as follows:

I sense that the time will shortly come—though it is not yet here—when
it will become a moot issue whether the couch is *hers* or *mine* (i.e., when

the couch will have the function of a transitional object for each of us). In this session I referred to it [in speaking to her] as "my couch," without feeling that she is of a mind to make any great issue of it; but it is noteworthy that she doesn't refer to it as "your couch," but "the couch" or "this couch."

About three weeks later, the day before I would be away again for a day, she got up at the end of the session and, while tidying up the two small rugs I have over the foot of the couch, said in a warmly possessive tone, which I felt sure was expressive of feelings displaced from me, "If *this* were *my* couch, I'd have one large—instead of two small." I replied, "I'll see you Friday," to which she replied, with warm fondness, "Don't forget," and I replied in the same tone, "I won't forget."

As for the meaning of the couch to me in terms of my relationships with my various patients, I find it easy to believe that it comes often to function as a transitional object; for one reason, I feel toward it, while tidying it up, so much of the fondness, tender feeling, contempt, fury, or whatever, which I have toward the just-departed patient whom the couch represents, fleetingly, to me. Parenthetically, as regards my feelings toward one patient after another in sequence in the course of the day's work, in the relatively infrequent instances when I tend to confuse one patient with his predecessor, the image I have of the just-departed patient evidently is serving me momentarily as a transitional object toward the establishment, or reestablishment, of my relationship with the newly arrived patient. At the same time it is shielding me from the fullness of my loss-and-relief feelings at the departure of the one who has just left.

Psychotropic Drugs

Thus far, despite many recurrent conflicts, I have never prescribed psychotropic drugs for my patients, and shall only touch here upon this vast and complex subject.

Following my presentation of a paper on another subject a year ago, during the discussion period the question came up as to whether the treatment of chronically schizophrenic patients can be speeded up with the aid of one or another mechanical contrivance—such as, I gathered, the use of bottle feeding as reported by Duhl (1951). I told the audience that if they indeed were referring to such mechanical contrivances, I reacted against such techniques as being expressive, in my opinion, of unconscious contempt on the therapist's part toward the patient, and as putting unhelpful distance, emotionally, between the two. I mentioned to them, in a spirit of not knowing whether it were relevant to that discussion, my experience with the tape recorder in my work with Mrs. Douglas. I suggested that maybe the tape recorder functions as a transitional object for me, noting that just as she long had been talking with her hallucinated, and delusionally distorted, mother image (for example) during the sessions, I had come, more recently, to talk more and more with my tape recorder, such that there was an at least four-"person" conversation going on during the sessions.

At this juncture, Jerry Morrow (1973) contributed the valuable thought, "You have made clear, perhaps, what is the essential difference: *if* the mechanical contrivance, whatever it is, is being employed by the therapist as a transitional object of the latter, and as being the only way he knows of reaching the patient, then it is useful, rather than its being expressive of any alienating scorn on the therapist's part."

It occurred to me subsequently that the point Morrow made may be applicable, also, to the therapist's (or analyst's) utilization of a psychotropic drug in the treatment of one or another of his patients: if the drug is of sufficient affective meaning for the therapist to have the function for him (and, presumably, for the patient also during some phase of the work) of a transitional object, then such drug therapy need not necessarily represent the kind of subjectively nonhuman intrusion into the psychotherapeutic or psychoanalytic relationship which I have tended to regard it as being.

Of interest in this connection is Berman's (1972) paper, "The Role of Amphetamine in a Case of Hysteria," in which he describes the symbolic meaning of this drug to the patient, and the role it played in her symptom complex as revealed in the course of her analysis. His summary includes the statement that "As an emergency narcissistic supply to relieve her feelings of separation anxiety, it served as a transitional object."

Review of Literature

Taken with the items already mentioned, I can include here only a sampling of the literature concerning transitional objects and closely related phenomena, not only because of limitations of space, but also because I cannot claim to have read the greater part of it. I shall not even touch here upon another section of literature which is of hardly less relevance to the present paper, namely, that having to do with the psychodynamics of the therapeutic process in psychoanalysis. Some of my previous writings (1965) have dealt with that subject.

Much of what I have written here has implications concerning disturbances in the body image — for example, the transference meaning of the psychosomatic symptom as being an introjective representation of the analyst, or Mrs. Douglas' speaking of herself as "this group." In this connection, Greenacre's writings concerning fetishism — a phenomenon analogous with transitional phenomena — are of much value. In the following passages from her article

(1953) "Certain Relationships Between Fetishism and Faulty Development of the Body Image," note in particular those which mention instability in the formation of the body image:

> Fetishism is the result of a rather definite combination of genetic influences, in disturbances of pregenitality. These consist of (1) disturbances in the early months of life, producing instability in the formation of the body image, with uncertainty as to outline, and fluctuations in the subjective sense of size; and (2) complementary disturbances in the phallic phase, which produce an exaggeration of the castration complex. The genital area of the body image is under any circumstances less certain in the early months of life than other parts of the body except the face. Under normal developmental conditions, the genital area of the body image becomes consolidated during the phallic phase, due to the increase in the spontaneous endogenous sensations arising then. Under the disturbed conditions of pregenitality described, the overly strong castration anxiety is combined with body disintegration anxiety from the early phase, and depletes rather than reinforces the genital outlines of the body. These conditions also contribute to increase bisexuality and contribute to a corresponding split in the ego.
>
> Due to the marked pathology of the first month, there is a persistence of the unusually strong primary identification (which in many cases has played a part also in confusing the genital part of the body image). This persistent tendency to primary identification, especially through vision, again influences what happens with attempts at intercourse. Then the sight of the penislessness of the partner brings into focus the underlying feminine identification and makes genital performance impossible unless special support is offered.
>
> The support is attained through the use of the fetish; which is tangible, visible, generally inanimate, unchanging in size, also not readily destroyed. It offsets the effect of the identification with the partner, and "pegs" the genital functioning by furnishing this external and material symbol of the phallus to be reintrojected and reaffirm the genital integrity of the fetishist.
>
> Thus, while the fetish is precipitated in the situation of the need to preserve the idea of the mother's phallus and so deny anatomical differences between the sexes, it *functions* by reinstating, through visual, olfactory and actual introjection, the phallus of the individual.

Greenacre's work as sampled above made me think also, for instance, of my experience with the recorder in the work with Mrs. Douglas. Another paper, the stimulating originality of which can only be hinted at in the following brief excerpts from it, is "Significance of the Body Image in Schizophrenic Thinking," by Torsten Herner (1965). Herner's paper is an outgrowth of his psychotherapeutic work — in much isolation from his colleagues, since no others in that Swedish hospital were engaged in such work with chronically schizophrenic patients. He says,

> Because of my nearly complete isolation, I felt committed to an especially intense, intellectual working through of the material. Most of it came from the countertransference, which constitutes the "royal road" to an understanding of schizophrenic phenomena. . . .
>
> On the most primitive level, the body which constitutes the "world" is not, *nota bene*, the body as usually perceived but a very strange body *image*. Of all the bizarre ideas encountered in my therapeutic work with the schizophrenic woman I have already referred to, this one was the most startling; it overwhelmed me. Ever since then, however, this particular idea has been the point of departure in all my attempts to understand not only schizophrenic thinking, but all sorts of primitive thinking. Apparently, the nucleus of the problem of the ego is to be found in the stage where "world" is represented by the body.

By way of summary, he states that "The split body image observed in schizophrenic patients is the introjected, disorganized, interpersonal relationships perceived by the infant to whom the family is the world."

In the following excerpts from a paper by Martin Wangh (1962), "The 'Evocation of a Proxy,' " relevance to the present paper can be seen if we think, in retrospect, of Mr. Robinson's "Edna," or of Mrs. Bryant's auditory hallucinations, as being psychodynamically equivalent to what Wangh calls a proxy: "A 'proxy' shall be defined as a person other than oneself who is used to experience feelings, exercise functions, and execute actions in one's own stead." In his conclusion, he states,

> I have hypothesized that in the cases cited, the inclination to resort to it [i.e., the evocation of a proxy] is genetically tied to a persistence of symbiotic needs and to the failure in the proper development of a sense of identity.
>
> I have postulated that the insufficient dissolution of the early symbiotic tie to the mother produces weak spots in the development of the sense of identity, of the sense of reality, and of the ability to control impulses by offering fixation points in a period when such reliance upon another individual for the exercise of these functions is quite the normal order. . . .
>
> Separation from any object that has prevalently served as a narcissistic extension of the self, that has functioned more like a transitional object and less like a true object, becomes, under these circumstances, a particularly grave threat to the integrity of the self. The "evocation of a proxy" utilizes such symbiotic and transitional foundations for defensive purposes. An-

other person is mobilized to function as an "alter ego." Selected superego qualities, ego functions, and id manifestations are evoked in and assigned to a partner. The anxiety aroused in the proxy stirs him—instead of one-self—to actions, emotions, judgments, and controls. . . .

I have tried to demonstrate at least two ways in which these patients un-consciously attempt to involve the analyst in the transference in the proxy-creating process. The wish may be to make him represent the previous nar-cissistic extension object which needs to be protected against the attack of an incited outsider, or the wish may be that the analyst himself becomes the attacking or seducing proxy.

Some of Modell's work has already been cited. His paper (1970), "The Transitional Object and the Creative Act," also is relevant here:

. . . In this essay I restrict my attention to the very specific characteristics of paleolithic art that suggest a correspondence to Winnicott's concept of the transitional object.

Not infrequently the paleolithic artists made use of the natural geologic formation of the walls, floor, and ceiling of the cave itself. . . .

I view the transitional object as a watershed concept, a great psychologic-al divide: on one side there is a sense of connectedness of the subject to the object, a sense of connectedness that supports a denial of separation; while on the other side there is an acknowledgment of that which is outside the self; the transitional object is a thing in the environment and not entirely self-created. Therefore I would interpret the paleolithic artist's use of the actual formation of the cave walls and ceilings themselves as a concretiza-tion of the interpenetration of the inner and the actual environment, that is, the art work itself is a tangible expression of the psychology of the crea-tive process.

What is created is not an entirely new environment but a *transformation* of that which already exists. This suggests that an essential element of crea-tivity is an *acceptance* of that which is outside the self. . . .

We have suggested that the environment itself may be equated with this, the child's first love object. . . . If we understand the transitional object concept as a great psychologic divide with a progressive and a regressive side, we can discern an analogy in creative processes between primitive and more mature modes of loving. Mature love requires an acceptance of the nonself. We believe that true creativity, whether in art or science, also re-quires the acceptance of a prior tradition which stands for the nonself, that is transformed by the creative act. . . .

I have employed the analogy of the transitional object to describe the creative illusion of transference in certain borderline and schizophrenic people (1968). In these people the element of illusory connectedness between self and object is retained to the point where the analyst's separateness, that is, his uniqueness, cannot be fully acknowledged. . . . culture, which is the creative transformation of the environment, bears the imprint of the psychological equation, mother = environment. [Modell explains that "mother" here stands for all protective parental objects.]

This interesting paper fits in beautifully, at many points, with my monograph concerning the nonhuman environment published ten years previously and which he evidently had not read.

Volkan has contributed a number of papers which are highly relevant to, for example, what I have reported here of Mr. Robinson's "Edna" and of Mrs. Bryant's hallucinatory voices. I find Volkan's work brilliant, but showing the limitation characteristic of classical psychoanalytic writings, in that the phenomena described as taking place in the analytic session are spoken of as if they were predominantly autistic phenomena on the patient's part, with little or no feeling involvement in them on the part of the analyst. I see subtle indications, which I shall not detail fully here, that he is moving into a more comprehensive view than this—a welcome development which, I feel sure, will strengthen greatly his already impressively creative contributions.

In his paper (1972), "The Linking Objects of Pathological Mourners," he reports that

A study of adults involved in pathological response to the death of a loved/hated person discloses the use of controllable symbolic objects to perpetuate the link with the dead individual. Although resembling in some respects fetishes, transitional objects, and inherited items that are simply valued and put to appropriate use by a mourner, they are sufficiently specific in their function of maintaining psychophysical balance in the face of loss to be differentiated as unique entities. An externalization process is suggested by which linking objects provide a focal point in which the self-representation of the mourner merges with that of the dead person, and in which the painful work of mourning an ambivalent object relationship can be accommodated. . . . The linking object belongs both to the deceased and to the patient himself, as if the representations of the two meet and merge in an externalized way. The ambivalence which had characterized the relationship with the dead one is invested in the process of distancing the object in a representation of psychic distancing, but at the same time keeping it available. . . .

In adult life, linking objects mark a blurring of psychic boundaries between the patient and the one he mourns, as if representations of the two persons, or parts of them, merge externally through their use. . . .

The linking object provides a means whereby object relationships with the deceased can be maintained externally. The ambivalence of the wish to annihilate the deceased and the wish to keep him alive is condensed in it, so that the painful work of mourning has an external reference and thus is not resolved.

Volkan's paper (1973), "Transitional Fantasies in the Analysis of a Narcissistic Personality," (which is, incidentally, a beautiful paper concerning narcissism) is relevant, similarly, to the productions of the same two patients of mine mentioned above. He reports, of the man upon whose analysis his paper focuses, that

> His reality testing in intimate relationships was so blurred . . . by his protection of the belief that he had precedence over all others, that one must ask what kept him from exhibiting generalized psychotic manifestations. The answer seems to lie in his use of specific fantasies in a way that suggested my term, transitional fantasies. He employed them as intangible representations of transitional objects, regarding them as though they had lives of their own and behaving as though he were addicted to them, although they were at the same time subject to his absolute control, whereby he could maintain the illusion that he had similar control over the real environment. . . . At the start of the fourth year of analysis I came to understand his specific fantasies and visual images as transitional objects. . . . Fantasies and other images slowly lost their magic. He became capable of remorse and sorrow and spoke of suicide. . . . He began to use me as a transitional object more than his own productions. He then came to see me as another human being and became curious about me as a person. . . .
>   Perhaps more important than his verbal acknowledgment of the fact that he had used fantasies as transitional objects was his working through his addiction to them; this occurred in the third year of analysis when, in transference, his use of me as a transitional object became obvious.

It is noteworthy that, in the context of the last quote, Volkan does report a bit of his own feelings in that phase of the work: "I felt somewhat fused with him, just as he fused me with external objects." This is a tentative bit of the kind of reporting of the analyst's feeling involvement which I have detailed in my papers on therapeutic symbiosis. I would assume that, in the earlier quote, where he reports that "Fantasies and other images slowly lost their magic," that these fantasies, long reported by the patient, had now lost their magic for the analyst as well as for the patient and that, in retrospect, they could be seen to have been serving as transitional objects not only for the patient, but also for the analyst — as in the present paper I hypothesize to be the case in the instance of any long-manifested symptom in the transference relationship. Similarly in the instance of the previously mentioned paper by Ekstein (1965), concerning the puppet play of a psychotic adolescent girl, the wealth of verbatim taped material which he presents, from his sessions with her, includes data which indicate to me that the puppet served as a transitional object not only for her—as Ekstein suggests in his theoretical formulations in the paper—but, on occasion, for him also.

Volkan and Kavanaugh, in their paper (1973), "The Cat People," report that

> Two female borderline patients became intensely preoccupied with their pet cats when their analysis focused on their working through the severance of the symbiotic tie to the mother/analyst. For their psychotic parts their cats *became*, as pre-symbolic transitional objects, the me, not-me, and the link between the two. A third patient, a schizophrenic unable to differentiate between self and object representation, in her involvement with her cats *became* her cats.

Where these authors see the patient to be relating to the pet cat, or to the analyst, as being a transitional object for the patient, in my concepts concerning therapeutic symbiosis I find—as mentioned previously—that in this phase of the analysis *both* analyst and patient relate to one another as what might be termed transitional objects for one another. Likewise, although they explain that "we will in this paper use the terms transitional object relatedness and symbiotic relatedness interchangeably" (usage which the present paper indicates to be acceptable enough to me), it has to be kept in mind, in reading their paper, that the authors do not portray the analyst as *participating in* that relatedness to any significant degree.

Marjorie McDonald's paper (1970), "Transitional Tunes and Musical Development," applies the psychoanalytic understanding of transitional phenomena to a study of the Suzuki method of violin teaching and introduces, in so doing, the term "transitional tune." She explains that

> It is Suzuki's goal to teach children as young as three years of age to play the violin and to do so in a manner which resembles as closely as possible the way children have learned language. Recognizing the importance of the parent in this process, Suzuki begins by teaching the parent, who plays a small-size violin such as the child will later use. As the parent plays and enjoys the instrument, the child spontaneously wants to join the activity. He then attends both private and group lessons with his parent and soon is participating himself, enjoying the violin as a new toy. As he has learned language from his parents, so he learns the violin, at first from them, and later

from his teacher and from group play sessions where he is exposed to older and more advanced pupils. The emphasis is always upon having fun through playing music.

McDonald presents the hypothesis that

some children, who have experienced music from birth onward as an integral part of the loving motherly and fatherly caretaking environment, might make use of music in a very particular way. My hypothesis is that these children find in music their own special "transitional phenomenon." Some may even select from a musical repertory a special "transitional tune," just as another child selects from among his toys a special transitional toy.

In her summary she mentions that

In his original article on transitional phenomena Winnicott (1953) included sounds and tunes among the wide range of normal transitional experiences.

Confirmation for the concept of a transitional tune comes from direct observation of young children, from biographical and autobiographical accounts of the early lives of musicians, and from music itself, in the form of lullabies and cradle songs. . . .

Finally, I have proposed a developmental line for music, in which the "transitional tune" stage occupies an early and probably an important position. The success of Suzuki's method of teaching the violin to young children seems to be based on its close adherence to and support of this natural developmental line for music.

Paul C. Horton in his paper (1973), "The Mystical Experience as a Suicide Preventive," describes depressed patients' utilization of mystical states as being, essentially, transitional phenomena which protected them against suicide —a finding which seems to me closely comparable with Volkan's observation (1973), as mentioned above, that his patient's utilization of transitional fantasies served as an unconscious defense against frank psychosis.

Three suicidal adolescents suffering from schizophrenic reactions developed the ability to conjure up a mystical consciousness. Directly experiencing this "oceanic" state (or just its memory) provided the patients with a reliably soothing safeguard against their overwhelming loneliness and possible suicide. Recognition by the psychiatrist of the mystical state as a transitional phenomenon points the way to the most effective therapeutic stance. . . .

Winnicott said of the transitional object: "Its fate is to be gradually allowed to be decathected, so that in the course of years it becomes not so much forgotten as relegated to limbo" (1953). The same is true, one can hope, for the mystical experience insofar as it serves as a suicide preventive rather than as part of a healthy religio-philosophical life-style. The therapist can best facilitate this decathexis by himself becoming a transitional object, thereby providing a reliably soothing, nurturant, reality-oriented relationship.

Horton's recommendation that the therapist become a transitional object for such a patient is reminiscent to me of Volkan's (1973) finding, in the third year of his analysis of his narcissistic patient that, as the patient's working through of his addiction to his transitional fantasies proceeded, "his use of me as a transitional object became obvious."

Horton's views concerning psychotherapy with these patients have some similarity to my concepts concerning therapeutic symbiosis; however, when he indicates that it is well that the patient's mystical experiences be "shared" with the psychiatrist, he is using the term "shared" quite differently from my use of it in discussing therapeutic symbiosis. He clearly is recommending that the psychiatrist facilitate the patient's *telling him of* the latter's mystical experiences, whereas I would assume that in the therapeutic-symbiosis phase of one's work with such a patient, one would literally share, to a degree, in mystically felt symbiotic relatedness with the patient at times during the sessions. Further, where Horton, like Modell and Volkan, describes the patient as reacting to the therapist as being a transitional object, I suggest, as mentioned before, that there are times in the work when patient and analyst rc` :e in terms of being transitional objects for one another.

Kafka's paper (1969), "The Body as Transitional Object: A Psychoanalytic Study of a Self-Mutilating Patient," is not only highly relevant to this present paper in general, but in particular gives a richer portrayal of tne analyst's feeling participation in the phenomena under analytic investigation than is the case with the other writings I have been citing here. I had the pleasure of discussing Kafka's developing ideas with him during several years, and in the following passages I can give only relatively meager samples from a fascinatingly many-sided paper. Kafka says,

A point to be developed concerns the notion that the patient's own body can be treated by her as a transitional object and that this can be related to the history of self-injury. . . . My experiencing an unusual degree of erotic and sadistic fantasies found its place in the analysis as representing some repressed aspects of father's, but predominantly of mother's relationship with the patient. To be singled out for further description and theoretical con-

sideration will be one of the many examples in the analysis, when echoing
her own experience of her body, I experienced her as not quite living matter. . . . In the course of the analysis she described how, when she slowly
and deliberately cut herself (for instance, with a razor-blade or with a
broken light-bulb smuggled under her bed-covers while gazing lovingly at
her "favourite nurse" who was "specialing" her) she would not feel it, but "I
always stopped as soon as I did feel it" and she managed to convey the exquisite border experience of sharply "becoming alive" at that moment.
This sharp sensation was then followed by the flow of the blood which she
succeeded in describing as being like a voluptuous bath, a sensation of pleasant warmth which, as it spread over the hills and valleys of her body,
moulded its contour and sculpted its form. Blood was described by the patient as a transitional object. In a sense, as long as one has blood, one carried within oneself this potential security blanket capable of giving warmth
and comforting envelopment.

What he says above, about the patient's experience that "the flow of the
blood . . . spread over the hills and valleys of her body, moulded its contour
and sculpted its form" is reminiscent to me of Modell's (1970) concepts concerning paleolithic art as transitional object. Kafka goes on,

   In the countertransference I experienced this patient frequently as a not
   quite living, not quite animate object; in other words, as a transitional one.

The following passage indicates a feeling on his part analogous to, although not identical with, that which I have described here on the analyst's
part, in regard to the patient's symptom, that "it couldn't be happening to a
nicer guy":

   My experience in the face of her self-mutilations was not always "don't do
   that . . . don't hurt yourself . . . I won't let you hurt yourself." My experience was perhaps more in line with what Winnicott (1949) has called "hate
   in the counter-transference" or at least my subjective feelings could have
   been verbalized in some such fashion as "go ahead, slice yourself to rib-
   bons; let's find out if you're alive or not."

Kafka asserts that

   On the descriptive level we are on rather firm ground in applying the
   transitional object concept to the situation. This patient certainly *did* treat
   parts of the surface of her body as though she were not dealing with quite
   living skin and there is much evidence to support the notion that she was
   much preoccupied with the, for her, very much *unfinished business* of establishing her body scheme.

I have mentioned earlier in this paper the role of ambiguity in psychoanalytic technique, and Kafka makes some interesting comments concerning the developmental significance of ambiguity:

> I have come to think of benevolent parental communication of tolerance of ambiguity—the ambiguity, for instance, of pain through, but hunger for, contact—as related to the offspring's individuation without alienation. The dynamic semi-permeable membrane, which helps to define the individual, yet permits two-way passage from and to the social environment, is gradually formed by sequences of parental communications or meta-communications appropriate to the age of the offspring . . . to the effect that ambiguities and contradictions are tolerable. . . . This . . . tolerance of ambiguity, permits the gradual formation of a membrane which is ego syntonic to the extent to which it was not prematurely and externally imposed but individually established through much active exploratory crossing and recrossing of the culturally poorly or ambiguously defined border territory.

He closes with some comments about sadism and masochism:

> While sadism and masochism are generally considered two sides of the same coin, it remains a fact that one or the other side of the coin often dominates a particular clinical picture. The study of how one's own body can be a "not-me" object may illuminate the general question of the sadistic or masochistic preference. In a sense the cutter's choice is a transitional one between the sadistic and masochistic object, his *own not-me* skin. It is his skin—which, however, he experiences as *not* his own. In analysis the ebb and flow of sadomasochistic transference and countertransference may be conceptualized as a factor contributing to the re-formation of a more integrated, more bodily-ego-syntonic membrane, and thus contribute to the eventual elimination of the symptom.

Busch and McKnight's paper (1973), "Parental Attitudes and the Development of the Primary Transitional Object," seems to stand largely alone in the literature in its focus upon the role of parental attitudes in the development, or nondevelopment, of transitional-object behavior on the part of the child. I am reminded here, of the rarity with which the analyst's feeling participation in the exploration of the adult patient's transitional-object experience is reported in the literature. These authors report upon their study of forty children from twenty-three different families, an investigation of the qualities of the child's relationship to the primary transitional object. Their investigation included extensive interviews with the mothers. They report that

Research on the primary transitional object has ignored the subtle inter-actions that occur between parents and children in the development and use of the primary transitional object. While conscious expectations of whether the child will develop a primary transitional object do not seem to be an important factor, unconscious motivations seem to determine if par-ents serve as either facilitators or disturbers of the child's relationship to the primary transitional object. The ways in which parental attitudes may af-fect the development of the primary transitional object, and the conse-quences of this are described. . . .

Given our agreement with Tolpin (1971) that the primary transitional object as a soother aids greatly in the separation-individuation process, we would see [arbitrary] restrictions of the primary transitional object as a dis-ruptive factor in a critical developmental process. [But] There are other times when the primary transitional object may serve other than adaptive purposes, and the sensitive mother may well attempt to interfere with this process.

In 1974, when the original draft of this paper had been completed, Khan's book of collected papers, entitled *The Privacy of the Self*, was published and, having read only a few of his papers before, I now had occasion to become more fully acquainted with his work. His book is eminently worthy of perusal by anyone interested in matters allied to the subject of my present paper. A few quotes from his book will serve to indicate how closely related, while far from fully congruent, are some of his views and my own.

In one of the papers which his volume includes, "On Symbiotic Omnipo-tence" (1969), there are passages suggestive of my concept of patient and analyst as becoming, in the early phase of therapeutic symbiosis, transitional objects for one another. Khan states that

I can express this equation of relationship only by the statement that the "self" of the child functions as a "transitional object" between the child's ego and the mother. It is treated as special, idealized and, at one remove, psychically by both parties. [1974, p. 86] . . .

Only the transference relation let my patients and me see that they were trying to *actualize* a relationship with another person where symbiotic omnipotence would be the exclusive vehicle of relatedness, where both the patient and the object would emphasize [empathize?] into a relatedness where the *special self*—object of both the patient's ego and instinctual cathexes as well as the other person—is endorsed. The situation would be of two persons (egos) devoted to the maintenance of *this special self.* [1974, p. 89]

But from Khan's writings, in contrast to mine, one gets little or no portrayal of the analyst's dependency (whether symbiotic dependency or postindividuation, object-related dependency) upon the patient, beyond that evoked purely as an adaptation to the patient's transference.

In another paper, "Regression and Integration in the Analytic Setting" (1960), Khan writes, concerning a psychotic patient who manifested manic and depressive states in the course of her over object for Mrs. X. Her whole relation was to *it*" (1974, p. 147). I find this to be an example of my concept of the symptom as a transitional object for the patient.

Khan, in addition to being one of our foremost psychoanalytic clinicians and theoreticians in his own right, is almost certainly the foremost living authority on Winnicott's work and thought. Winnicott's final book, *Therapeutic Consultations in Child Psychiatry* (1971) reported his employing an exchange of drawings, which he called the Squiggle Game, as the basis of his technique in these consultations. Khan describes beautifully the theoretical rationale of this technique:

> The essence of the therapeutic space that Winnicott establishes with the child for the Squiggle Game is that it is a transitional space, in which both Winnicott and the child are separate and private to each other, and yet through playing on the surface of the paper, find both a relating and a communication. Winnicott makes a very specific distinction between *relating* and *object-relationship* in this context. It is because there is only relating without the sophistication of an object-relationship that he can find his access with the child to the child's reverie. [1974, p. 265]

That passage is highly relevant to this paper's section on appurtenances, concerning the functioning of one or another kind, in the analytic situation, as a transitional object for both analyst and patient.

SUMMARY

The analyst (or therapist) can best understand transitional-object phenomena as being tributary to, or as consisting in various different facets of the —for him in his work with patients—more comprehensive realm of therapeutic symbiosis. Nonetheless, the transitional-object (or -phenomena) concept proves a useful theoretical instrument, a kind of scalpel or microscope lens, in achieving a relatively differentiated sample of the more global theoretical concept of therapeutic symbiosis.

In discussing various different kinds of relationship between the analyst and the patient's symptoms (depending upon the phase of the treatment), I presented clinical examples in which the analyst felt that the patient's symptoms were being inflicted upon him (the analyst) ; in which the analyst feared that he personally was inflicting the patient's symptoms upon the latter; in which he came to feel that the patient's symptoms "couldn't be happening to a nicer guy"; in which he reacted to the patient's symptoms as being his—the analyst's—allies; and instances in which the patient's symptoms were experienced as transitional objects by both patient and analyst.

I also gave examples of, or hypotheses concerning, the functioning in the analytic situation of an appurtenance—a tape recorder, the analyst's notes, the couch, a psychotropic drug—as a transitional object for both analyst and patient.

I dwelt particularly upon data concerning objects or phenomena which are transitional for both patient and analyst concomitantly. I suggested that the patient's symptoms have become, with the development of the early phase of therapeutic symbiosis, transitional objects for both patient and analyst simultaneously. As with the patient's symptoms, so with his transference images of the analyst: it was suggested that, in order for any effective transference analysis to occur with any patient, whether neurotic, borderline, or psychotic, the analyst must have come to accept at *least* a transitional-object degree—if not more deeply symbiotic degree—of relatedness with the particular transference image or percept which holds sway at that time in the analysis.

Finally, I reviewed some of the relevant literature, including my previous writings concerning the nonhuman environment and concerning therapeutic symbiosis.

REFERENCES

Berman, L. E. A. (1972). The role of amphetamine in a case of hysteria. *Journal of the American Psychoanalytic Association* 20:325-340.

Busch, F., and McKnight, J. (1973). Parental attitudes and the development of the primary transitional object. *Child Psychiatry and Human Development* 4:12-20.

Coleman, M. L. (1956). Externalization of the toxic introject. *Psychoanalytic Review* 43:235-242.

_____, and Nelson, B. (1957). Paradigmatic psychotherapy in borderline treatment. *Psychoanalysis* 5:28-44.

Duhl, L. J. (1951). The effect of baby bottle feedings on a schizophrenic patient. *Bulletin of the Menninger Clinic* 15:21-25.

Ekstein, R. (1965). Puppet play of a psychotic adolescent girl in the psychotherapeutic process. *Psychoanalytic Study of the Child* 20:441-480.

Greenacre, P. (1953). Certain relationships between fetishism and faulty development of the body image. *Psychoanalytic Study of the Child* 8:79-98.

Herner, T. (1965). Significance of the body image in schizophrenic thinking. *American Journal of Psychotherapy* 19:455-466.

Horton, P. C. (1973). The mystical experience as a suicide preventive. *American Journal of Psychiatry* 130:294-296.

Kafka, J. S. (1969). The body as transitional object: A psychoanalytic study of a self-multilating patient. *British Journal of Medical Psychology* 42:207-212.

Khan, M. M. R. (1960). Regression and integration in the analytic setting. *International Journal of Psycho-Analysis* 41:130-146 (reprinted on pp. 136-167 in his 1974 volume cited below).

_____ (1963). The concept of cumulative trauma. *Psychoanalytic Study of the Child* 18:286-306.

_____(1964). Ego distortion, cumulative trauma, and the role of reconstruction in the analytic situation. *International Journal of Psycho-Analysis* 45:272-278.

_____(1969). On symbiotic omnipotence. *Psychoanalytic Forum.* Vol. 3 (reprinted on pp. 82-92 in his 1974 volume cited below).

_____(1974). *The Privacy of the Self—Papers on Psychoanalytic Theory and Technique.* New York: International Universities Press.

Klein, M. (1933). The early development of conscience in the child. *Contributions to Psycho-Analysis*, 1921-45. London: Hogarth, 1948.

McDonald, M. (1970). Transitional tunes and musical development. *Psychoanalytic Study of the Child* 25:503-520.

Modell, A. H. (1963). Primitive object relationships and the predisposition to schizophrenia. *International Journal of Psycho-Analysis* 44:282-292.

_____(1968). *Object Love and Reality—An Introduction to a Psychoanalytic Theory of Object Relations.* New York: International Universities Press.

_____(1970). The transitional object and the creative act. *Psychoanalytic Quarterly* 39:240-250.

Morrow, J. F. (1973). Personal communication.

Nelson, M. C. (1962). Effect of paradigmatic techniques on the psychic economy of borderline patients. *Psychiatry* 25:119-134.

_____, ed. (1968). *Roles and Paradigms in Psychotherapy.* New York: Grune & Stratton.

Rosenfeld, H. A. (1952a). Notes on the psycho-analysis of the superego conflict in an acute schizophrenic patient. *International Journal of Psycho-Analysis* 33: 111-131. Reprinted on pp. 66-103 in *Psychotic States—A Psychoanalytical Approach.* New York: International Universities Press, 1965.

_____(1952b). Transference-phenomena and transference-analysis in an acute catatonic schizophrenic patient. *International Journal of Psycho-Analysis* 33:457-464. Reprinted on pp. 104-116 in *Ibid.* New York: International Universities Press, 1965.

_____(1962). The superego and the ego-ideal. *International Journal of Psycho-Analysis* 43:258-263. Reprinted on pp. 144-154 in *Ibid.* New York: International Universities Press, 1965.

_____(1965). *Psychotic States—A Psychoanalytical Approach.* New York: International Universities Press.

Searles, H. F. (1959a). Integration and differentiation in schizophrenia. *Journal of Nervous and Mental Diseases* 129: 542-550; also reprinted on pp. 304-316 of *Collected Papers* (see below). This paper was first read at the annual meeting of the American Psychoanalytic Association in 1958.

_____(1959b. The effort to drive the other person crazy—an element in the aetiology and psychotherapy of schizophrenia. *British Journal of Medical Psychology* 32:1-18. Reprinted on pp. 254-283 in *C.P.*

_____(1959c). Integration and differentiation in schizophrenia: an over-all view. *British Journal of Medical Psychology* 32-261-281. Reprinted on pp. 317-348 in *C.P.*

_____(1960). *The Nonhuman Environment in Normal Development and in Schizophrenia.* New York: International Universities Press.

_____(1961). Phases of patient-therapist interaction in the psychotherapy of chronic schizophrenia. *British Journal of Medical Psychology* 34:169-193. Reprinted on pp. 521-559 in *C.P.*

_____(1965). *Collected Papers on Schizophrenia and Related Subjects.* London: Hogarth and New York: International Universities Press.

_____(1966). Feelings of guilt in the psychoanalyst. *Psychiatry* 29: 319-323.

_____(1966-1967). Concerning the development of an identity. *Psychoanalytic Review* 53: 507-530.

_____(1968-1969). Review of *Roles and Paradigms in Psychotherapy* by M. C. Nelson, et al. (see above). *Psychology Review* 55:697-700.

_____(1971). Pathologic symbiosis and autism. *In the Name of Life—Essays in Honor of Erich Fromm*, ed. B. Landis and E. S. Tauber, pp. 69-83. New York: Holt.

_____(1972a). The function of the patient's realistic perceptions of the analyst in delusional transference. *British Journal of Medical Psychology* 45: 1-18.

_____(1972b). Intensive psychotherapy of chronic schizophrenia. *International Journal of Psychoanalytic Psychotherapy*, 1: 30-51.

Psychoanalysis. Vol. I, pp. 247-262. New York: Quadrangle.

_____(1973b). Psychoanalytic therapy with schizophrenic patients in a private-practice context. Read as part of a panel discussion, "Treatment of Early Developmental and Psychotic Problems and Countertransference Issues," Ninth Annual Conference of the Postdoctoral Program in Psychotherapy, Adelphi Univ. Institute of Advanced Psychological Studies, Garden City, N.Y., May 24, 1973. This paper will be a chapter in *Techniques in Psychoanalytic Psychotherapy*, ed. G. D. Goldman and D. S. Milman. Springfield, Ill.: Thomas, 1975.

_____(1974). The development of mature hope in the patient-therapist relationship. Read as part of a panel discussion, "The Role of Hope in Psychotherapy," Ninth Annual Symposium on Psychotherapy, Department of Psychiatry of Tufts Univ. School of Medicine, Boston, April 26, 1974.

Stevenson, O. (1954). The first treasured possession: a study of the part played by specially loved objects and toys in the lives of certain children. *Psychoanalytic Study of the Child* 9:199-217.

Sullivan, H. S. (1947). *Conceptions of Modern Psychiatry*. Washington, D.C.: William Alanson White Foundation. New ed., New York: Norton, 1953.

Tolpin, M. (1971). On the beginnings of a cohesive self. *Psychoanalytic Study of the Child* 26:316-352.

Volkan, V. D. (1972). The linking objects of pathological mourners. *Archives of General Psychiatry* 27:215-221.

_____(1973). Transitional fantasies in the analysis of a narcissistic personality. *Journal of the American Psychoanalytic Association* 21:351-376.

_____, and Kavanaugh, J. G. (1973). The cat people. Read at the meeting of the American Psychoanalytic Association, New York, Dec. 15.

Wangh, M. (1962). The "evocation of a proxy." *Psychoanalytic Study of the Child* 17:451-469.

Winnicott, D. W. (1947). Hate in the counter-transference. *International Journal of Psycho-Analysis*, 30:69-74. Reprinted in *D.W. Winnicott—Collected Papers*, pp. 194-203. New York:Basic Books, 1958.

_____(1971), *Therapeutic Consultations in Child Psychiatry*. New York: Basic Books.

_____(1953). Transitional objects and transitional phenomena—a study of the first *not-me* possession. *D. W. Winnicott—Collected Papers*, pp. 229-242. New York: Basic Books, 1958. First published in *International Journal of Psycho-Analysis* 34: 89-97, 1953.

_____(1971). *Therapeutic Consultations in Child Psychiatry*. New York: Basic Books.

Zetzel, E. (1956). Current concepts of transference. *International Journal of Psycho-Analysis* 37: 369-376.

_____(1965). The theory of therapy in relation to a developmental model of the psychic apparatus. *International Journal of Psycho-Analysis* 46: 39-52.

HAROLD F. SEARLES, M.D.

DR. SEARLES is Clinical Professor of Psychiatry at Georgetown University School of Medicine, Supervising and Training Analyst in the Washington Psychoanalytic Institute, and Consultant in Psychiatry at the National Institute of Mental Health. He was President of the Washington Psychoanalytic Society from 1969 to 1971.

Object Choice and
Actual Bisexuality

A. Limentani, M.D.

Fellow Royal College of Psychiatrists

Actual bisexuality is to be distinguished from homosexuality in a latent state and from conscious bisexual fantasies. Contemporary social changes have caused an increased demand for help by those men and women capable of engaging in protracted heterosexual and homosexual relations. Among such people narcissistic and borderline states are common.

Clinical material is presented in some detail. The author suggests that the condition is associated with a tendency to be caught up between the anaclitic and narcissistic types of object choice. The concurrent involvement with a male and female love object against a background of pseudogenitality creates the illusory appearance of two objects being involved, covering up the fact that there is splitting of the original love object together with severe preoedipal disturbance.

INTRODUCTION

Psychoanalysis has thrown much light on the factors which enable some people to retain their homosexuality in a latent state, while others can successfully satisfy the needs of the male and female parts of their personality without being compelled to act out their id experiences in a fully fledged perversion. The capacity of certain individuals to engage in sexual activities with members of both sexes continues to present a challenge to our theoretical understanding of human sexuality and of the perversion as such. In general, theoretical and clinical discussions tend to concentrate our attention on the homosexual aspect of the dichotomy, neglecting Freud's reminder that even heterosexuality requires justification.

In this paper, I shall not enter into a detailed review or reexamination of the intricate psychopathology of the homosexual syndrome. However, it is relevant to state that I regard that syndrome as part of those defensive movements directed at lessening anxiety or at creating barriers against the eruption of unbearable unconscious conflicts, and that quite often their aim is to ensure survival. In this context defense is understood to be directed not only at protecting the ego against anxiety aroused by instinctual drives, the superego, or external dangers, but also and preferably at including all the techniques used by the ego to dominate control and channel forces which might lead to neurosis or psychosis. In those bisexual cases where homosexuality is predominant, the heterosexuality may well assume a defensive role, which does not become apparent until one outlet is suddenly unavailable.

Psychoanalysts are only too familiar with the difficulties of analyzing patients who are tormented by the presence of conscious bisexual fantasies and impulses that are often enough almost ineradicable. A comparison with actual bisexuality must be maintained throughout. Masud Khan in his paper, "Ego Orgasm in Bisexual Love" (1974), has also drawn attention to the danger of confusing bisexual love, unaccompanied by physical contact, with latent homosexual love. Khan's thesis rests on the dissociation between the male and female elements in the personality of a given person, which, if unresolved, leads to a lack of affective surrender in the heterosexual situation. The dissociated affectivity is acted out in an ego-promiscuous fleeting attachment with objects of the same sex. However, although Khan's conclusions are indirectly relevant to this discussion, it will be readily seen that there is an enormous difference between an intense brief encounter between two men or two women without any physical contact and the man who has intercourse with his male lover shortly after he has had a satisfying experience with his wife.

We do not know how common actual bisexuality is, but we should not be misled by its prevalence in certain circles, since it is quite clear that those who practice it, because it is fashionable, regard it as an ego-dystonic experience. In such cases we are perhaps correct in assuming that a lenient group superego is all that is required to break down shaky defensive barriers. We must, nevertheless, recognize that bisexuality is on the increase generally and as therapists we see more cases than at any other time in the past. It is said to occur in situations of stress, particularly in prisons. Such explanations may amount to rationalizations and should not be accepted too readily. In males, psychopathic disturbances or borderline states are prevalent. In females of predominantly heterosexual disposition, an immature personality will combine with an unresolved and profound ambivalent attachment to the mother. Few bisexual individuals present as having no commitments whatsoever to either sex. Just as it is a serious mistake for the diagnostician to dismiss such cases as being the result of contingency, it is an even worse mistake to try and eradicate either of the possible sexual outlets without having established the possible risk of a severe psychotic illness or even suicide. Psychoanalytic literature contains few references to this subject. Weissman (1962) wrote on the structural considerations in overt male bisexuality, but his interesting paper suffers from a scarcity of material on which his conclusions are based. Furthermore, some of his cases seem to feature almost exclusively that type of bisexual man who is passive in his sexual exploits. We know of course that all homosexuality is basically passive, but it is also true that sexual practices range from passive to active, in accordance with a variety of defensive maneuvers. Weissman's thesis may be restated as follows: if the overt homosexuality is derived from preoedipal identification with the mother and object relations are at a narcissistic level, then the overt bisexuality is basically a homosexual perversion. Strong archaic superego and ego-ideal demands lead to the establishment of overt pseudoheterosexuality. To explain this, Weissman puts forward an ingenious suggestion: the homosexual achieves the state through the utilization of a fetish, i.e., the woman's body as equated to the phallus. An alternative type of psychopathology occurs when bisexuality is oedipal in origin; Weissman suggests that the superego demands a regressive object choice along with the heterosexual object choice. The acting out of the homosexual component is said to be part of the repetition of the entire oedipal conflict. On the other hand, we could say that the homosexual's ideal image could be restored by supplying a phallus to the woman and then being able to enjoy his lovemaking within a pseuudoheterosexual position. But I think the real problem with this explanation is our knowledge that the fetish is often used to ward off the homosexual acting out which arises from excessive castration anxiety. Gillespie (1964) writing more or less on the lines suggested by Weissman has emphasized that pseudohomosexuality and pseudoheterosexuality occur in response to religious, moral, social, or parental attitudes, but we may ask what kind of extraordinary or multiple splitting processes would be required to take place in the subject and the object to allow for bisexual conditions to exist in order to stem the flow of a psychosis.

There seems to be no end to the complications which arise from any attempt to bring sense and order to a study of the perversions. Treatment is also made all the more difficult because the actively bisexual patient belongs almost invariably to the borderline group, displaying a marked tendency to act out, with a concurrent outstanding dispersal of transference manifestations. The patient in the early stages appears quite satisfied to defend against his heterosexuality with his homosexuality and vice versa. The analyst at first feels nowhere except as a reflection of the patient who is caught up in an impossible choice. In a second stage, the analyst is able to mobilize the patient's feelings in one or other direction; the location of the transference is clearer but nonetheless nebulous insofar as there is utter dependence, quickly alternating with movements to break away from it. In many cases the early appearance of narcissistic transference creates further problems in the understanding and general handling of the situation. Worse things are still to come when the patient establishes a dependent relationship or makes a narcissistic choice of a love object outside the transference. The importance of recognizing the fluctuation between the narcissistic object choice and defenses, and the object choice of the attachment type, is a familiar concept to those analysts who have worked extensively with borderline and predominantly narcissistic patients. Eisnitz (1974) has underlined the danger of mistakes in the handling of this delicate area which can cause a repetition of a trauma suffered by the patient in his developing years.

I was able to observe all of this during the supervision of the analysis of a bisexual male who had come for help because his homosexual interest was threatening his marriage. His wife had recently become pregnant and he had been very active in promoting her abortion because his dependence on her was clearly endangered by the appearance of a prospective rival. His male partners were expected to submit to his aggressive demands and, as might have been expected, similar behavior soon made its appearance in the transference. In the course of time such an attempt was seen to be part of a subtle maneuver to cover up deep dependence and attachment to the analyst.

A subsequent review of some cases of bisexuality which had come under my observation during the last few years showed a striking similarity in terms of their psychopathology, transference manifestations, and above all the attempt to retrace the development of their object relations, leading to some degree of separation between the analytic and the narcissistic object choice.

The cases to be described are a random sample, the choice being confined to patients who were capable of having sexual contact with both sexes during one period of their lives, which period could spread over months or years. A further factor in the choice was my direct acquaintance with the patients' partners in some instances supported by reliable reports from colleagues who had also become involved with them.

CLINICAL MATERIAL

Mr. A. was a married man aged forty-four whose family insisted he should have some treatment because it was thought that his homosexual attachments to young boys represented a threat to the safety of his children. He was sent at the age of seven to public school where he was in the care of older brothers who ignored him. He was reduced to an abject state of depression and emotional isolation, disturbed only by much teasing and bullying. A schoolmaster who seduced him was later imprisoned. Mr. A. married a very young, inexperienced, and helpless woman. During the initial phase of the marriage he made her utterly dependent on him, fulfilling all the functions of both parents for her. He obviously needed her to carry his own dependence because when she matured and later told him of having an affair he became promiscuous with both sexes. His bisexuality came into the open as a result of a dangerous bit of acting out when he seduced the son of his father-in-law's business associate. Until then his dual life had been a well-kept secret, but by that time Mr. A. and his wife were going their separate ways. She was very active socially, and a very efficient mother, while he was driving himself compulsively as a company director, with his own secret hideout where he entertained large numbers of male and female adolescents of dubious character. He entered analysis as a seriously distraught man who was warding off his deep depression by whatever means at whatever cost, but he broke it off after a year because basically he was too dependent on the analyst and could not tolerate his inability to control him. However brief, the analysis revealed (1) a lack of a good-enough maternal experience in infancy; (2) his passion for boys was of the classical narcissistic type; (3) he loved his father-in-law as the man who protected him, which indeed the elder did at the time of the social scandal; (4) his pseudoheterosexuality was notable for its complete indifference and was probably only a vehicle for creating dependency in women as a relief from his profound feeling of dependence upon and attachment to them. He remained in a curious way attached to and dependent on his wife, who in turn remained loyal to him.

Mrs. S. was thirty-two when first seen during a serious depressive illness which had been precipitated by an unhappy affair with a woman a great deal older than herself, who eventually could not tolerate her demanding behavior. During the long association her whole life had orbited around her partner. She had been married for twelve years and had three children. She met her husband as a teenager when they were both traveling on a bus, each carrying a copy of the Bible. She had been very jealous in her late childhood because her mother had two more boys and her father had ignored her throughout. Strong religious influences and uncertainty about her feminity had played an important role in the severe inhibition in her heterosexual development. Improvement was gradual and, when she began to enjoy her sexual life with her husband, I felt my initial optimism to be justified.

Unhappily there had been some omissions in her psychotherapy which were revealed when it was resumed two years later. Seeing her again in a deep depression made me aware that when I had previously terminated her treatment she had been in a manic state. She was now profoundly dependent on me and had been since we had parted. Acute separation anxiety was indeed a very serious complication. Mrs. S. was again frigid and for the first time she revealed that her husband was not only an obsessive-compulsive character to some extent, which I knew, but also was a sexual pervert. Sexual relations at infrequent intervals would extend over several hours with endless preliminaries in the course of which she was required to wear certain articles of clothing, etc. She would also have to parade naked and allow herself to be observed at length. In the course of the next few years I was in no doubt about the early origins of her disturbance. In her childhood she had shared a bed with an aged grandmother and later a maid. This was hardly due to lack of accommodation or social or financial stress. Her depression recurred at intervals, associated with intense homosexual feelings which were carefully evaluated in the transference but at the same time were acted out in a variety of ways at work. As various aspects of the preoedipal attachment to the mother were investigated the depression would begin to lift. Heterosexual feelings would follow and with them the manic defense would appear as a clear response to guilty feelings. Her husband was helped into treatment, and later a daughter whose clinging attachment she could not bear was also taken on for psychotherapy. This situation required meetings with a psychiatric social worker and a reasonably sympathetic relationship was established. Slowly the attachment to me was loosened and her treatment was brought to a close, but not before some momentous crises accompanied by suicidal threats. On one particularly dramatic occasion, conscious murderous impulses toward her husband led to an acute confusional state, requiring a few days, hospital treatment, followed by a quick recovery and much insight.

The diagnosis in such a case is a matter of interest, since the possibility of a manic depressive illness had to be considered. The total lack of any response to antidepressant drugs, on the other hand, and the symptomatology pointed more to a narcissistic disorder. It would also seem that this patient had chosen her partner on a narcissistic basis. This was shown quite clearly in the perverse activity when she was gratified through her identification with him in his admiring and looking at her body. The attachment to the older woman, fully relived for long stretches of time in the transference, amounted to a split in the object choice. This created endless complications in the treatment situation, which cannot be discussed on this occasion.

Mr. C. was a twenty-four-year-old social worker, married, with a child aged two. He had been actively bisexual for two years. When he was first seen his suitability for psychotherapy was in doubt because he claimed never to have been happier since he had gone to live with a twenty-six-year-old man while still seeing his wife. His father had died when he was six. He claimed his mother tried to press feminine things on him throughout his childhood. There had been only some casual sexual play with boys when still at school. As soon as he became engaged he suddenly experienced an intense urge to have intercourse with men. He caught gonorrhea and passed it on to his fiancee, who reacted by putting intense pressure on him to get married. His promiscuous activities with men began during the sixth month of his wife's pregnancy. After seeing his wife for a few hours each week and having fully satisfying sexual relations with her he would quickly return to his friend and have anal intercourse with him. This acting out was at first claimed by him to be related to his need to reinforce his feelings of masculine supremacy. But it was more than that since heterosexual experiences for him amounted to a total emotional surrender (A. Freud, 1952) which threatened his very existence. In his very complex way of relating, this man projected his femininity upon the wife and was exasperated by her mishandling of her own femininity. He bitterly complained that his wife would not do things for him half as well as his older male partner did. In his relationship to the latter it was clear that there was a reenacting of a profound attachment to the mother.

In the early stages of treatment an inadequacy in the handling of the psychotherapeutic relationship caused Mr. C. to act out by bringing his wife to the session. I saw no reason nor could I find a good excuse for not seeing her. She turned out to be a very charming, feminine, slightly overweight young woman who confirmed everything he had said. She quickly admitted to her feeling of having been starved of love by her mother and expected her husband to compensate her. In this joint interview they mirrored each other to perfection, except that she readily confessed that lesbians horrified and repulsed her while she had no objection to male homosexuality. In another interview they both fought bitterly for my attention. He eventually came out with the statement that he often felt he could strangle her. She seemed to be not at all disturbed by this and had little conscious awareness of the danger she was in. Next day he reported that after this very tense interview, he had gone home to his friend, who comforted him and allowed him to lie in his arms while he masturbated himself to sleep. It was also as a result of this interview that I concluded that he had come for help because he urgently needed to remove himself from an impossible heterosexual involvement, but had not the strength to do so. After the final break with his wife had occurred, Mr. C. felt relief and remarked, "I no longer see a reflection of myself in her. I have taken my feminity back into myself and I have gone back to X who is much more like the mother I need." In the same momentary mood of insight he added, "I suppose like so many other homosexual relationships we shall end up as brothers or perhaps I shall marry again."

This patient's psychotherapy is still in progress and at the time of writing I can only say that his profound identification with the first love object is a continuous threat to his integration. His very real and dangerous impulse to murder his female partner is related to his seeing in her a reflection of his passive feminine self. What I find very puzzling in this case is the fact that such a man, who is so completely homosexual in his orientation, should be at all capable of having such satisfying sexual experience with a woman. If it is true that the female body is the fetish, I would be inclined to regard such fetish as a transitional object which would also account for his inability to break away from it.

The case histories which have been described so far concern individuals who display a predominantly homosexual orientation. Severely disturbed patients with poor heterosexual adjustment are always at risk to act out the underlying homosexual impulses while undergoing psychotherapy. Khan (1964) has shown that psychoanalysis is no guarantee that such acting out will not occur and, in the case he then described at length, the patient was able to make full use of it in furthering the growth and expansion of her personality and femininity. Something of a similar nature occurred during the treatment of a young girl in circumstances which again indicated an attempt to separate the two classical object choices.

Miss D. was nineteen years old when she was referred for psychotherapy while a patient in a mental hospital where she had spent the previous three years. When I first met her she presented as a charming and highly intelligent person who could have been either a boy or a girl. Her behavior disorder had become more acute after an abortion at sixteen. She was utterly confused not only about her sexual identity but also of other people as shown by her Rorschach test. She is now in the eighth year of her psychotherapy which on her initiative has frequently been interrupted. There have been innumerable crises with severe depressive phases, suicidal attempts, abortions, and promiscuity. Progression and regression have occurred in rapid alternation, as we could expect in a case of severe narcissistic disorder associated with a borderline state. The most dangerous complication was her gradual addiction to soft drugs escalating to hard drugs. Her paranoid anxieties were maximal during this phase but well controlled by the addiction. Close contact was maintained throughout this period. However, with the removal of the addiction her homosexuality emerged in full, together with an exacerbation of the paranoid anxieties within the maternal transference. She broke off treatment once more and when she returned some months later she reported that she had had a fairly prolonged lesbian relationship which had left her with a general feeling of disillusionment. Her interest in men had not altered during this phase, and on the whole she had felt "liberated" and was now more able to enjoy her heterosexual pursuits. However, her more constant male partners had invariably been violent but gifted and capable of engaging in a sado-masochistic relationship. They were in fact indistinguishable from the patient in their existential approach to life and other personality characteristics. They simply could not understand the reasons when Miss D. broke away from them, quite suddenly, as if she could no longer bear to see her own reflection in a mirror. In the transference there had been extreme dependence with much ambivalence. The lesbian episode was understood as being related to a splitting off of the libidinal, sexual aspect of the transference but was also seen as the supreme testing out of her fear of being swallowed up or merged with a mother figure.

The end of the road is not in sight, but Miss D. is emerging very feminine, though still struggling with her entry into womanhood. Her latest partner does not reflect her habitual narcissistic object choice. She is also attempting to establish a new sense of individuation by not keeping her appointments and by turning up when she is not expected.

This was an unusual case where the split transference turned out to be almost an advantage because there were less opportunities for misinterpretation and mistakes. By bringing her partners, and by requesting on occasions that they should be present at her sessions, Miss D. also made sure that nothing was missed.

As a corollary to this account I should add that I have observed acting out of homosexual impulses and similar attempts to split the transference in a number of cases of transvestism, notably that of a transvestite whose fear of homosexuality had greatly interfered with his heterosexual adjustment.

DISCUSSION

The patients described had certain features in common which could not be outlined in any detail. Even taking into account the one-sided perspective of their early upbringing, there was fair evidence of deficiencies in parental handling; and at times the parents' behavior suggested a severe degree of personality disturbance. Some of the mothers seem to have been quite unable to promote a smooth passage from the early stages of closeness and intimacy to separation and final individuation. Typical was the case of Miss D., who had been involved in a symbiotic relationship with her mother, who needed prolonged psychotherapy and support in order to facilitate her daughter's own treatment and development. All the patients were highly intelligent but had been precocious, and without distinction exhibited evidence suggestive of an exquisite awareness of early bodily experiences. Bisexuality, however, is by no means confined to the intellectually better endowed. A survey of patients, including others not presented in this paper, points to the occurrence of unbearable separation anxiety, each subject developing his or her own individual way of dealing with it, ranging from denial to transvestism. Splitting processes figured prominently and no one could doubt the capacity of these patients to dissociate the male and female parts of their personality, linked with projective identification and profound disturbance in interpersonal relationships.

If the heterosexuality is viewed separately, the only fair conclusion to be reached is that it has a definite "pseudo" quality to it. In one case, that of Mr. C., the patient reported an ecstatic quality to his sexual experience with his wife, easily traced to a projection of his femininity to her which left him empty and drained. Again, a careful investigation of the homosexuality taken in isolation would reveal little which is not likely to occur in this syndrome with all the variations of its underlying psychopathology. Quite frequently an overall factor which has been stressed by Masud Khan (1964) is that, as these patients tend to split off their bodily and feeling experiences, the aim of the homosexuality is to mend the split. If we viewed the total situation of these patients' lives and personal relations, and if we had the opportunity of observing their partners from close quarters over a long period, a different picture might emerge. As already indicated, my observations suggest that in the majority of cases of manifest bisexuality the subjects are caught up between the two types of object choices available to them—the attachment and the narcissistic; in some extreme cases they almost set one up against the other.

Writing on the classical theory of object choice, Laplanche and Pontalis (1967) have stated that the two types are purely ideal and liable to alternate or combine. They also remark that it is doubtful whether an antithesis even with ideal types is tenable, a view which I find quite acceptable. Eisnitz, in the paper to which I have already referred, suggests that, in the narcissistic object choice, the cathexis is directed at self-representation and in the attachment type is directed at object representation—a fair account of the situation, as is often seen in clinical practice. However, he goes on to say "whereas at any one time either the narcissistic or the attachment elements may predominate, attempts to separate them completely either in therapy or in theory are artificial."

In my opinion, this is precisely what happens in the bisexual who is trying to achieve the impossible: the separation of his original two types of object choice. Prodigal expenditure of libido in self or object through such dissociation accounts not only for the frantic rushing to and from one unreal person to another, but also for much unhappiness and a sense of loss and incompleteness in each relationship and in the self. In the therapeutic situation, havoc is caused in the transference and as I have already hinted this results in enormous difficulty in locating the latter. There are of course few other instances where we can observe with such clarity the use made of narcissistic defenses against regressions within the attachment situation when it becomes too threatening, and we also know only too well how valuable such defenses can be in coping with separation anxiety. As it happens, in the transference of bisexual patients we are confronted by the challenging situation that they have a ready-made potential displacement by the very nature of their complaint. In the countertransference the analyst is soon caught up in the problem of not knowing quite what is best for his patient: to be heterosexual, homosexual, or both. Even when the impact of the transference is successful in drawing some of the fire away from the patient's turmoil in his external life, for long periods we operate within a triangular situation. The illusion that we are dealing with two objects can be perpetuated if we do not realize that we are only dealing with one (the original) object. In this writer's opinion, this means that all those instances of protracted and recurrent bisexual behavior, including the acting out of homosexual impulses in the course of psychotherapy, cannot be understood as being the result of unresolved oedipal conflicts. It is conceded that on first examination these people will impress the therapist as wishing to keep both the male and female partners, i.e., father and mother; or that they are unable to give up either of them, thus creating the appearance of being in the throes of an unbearable oedipal conflict. Careful investigation will show that there is little depth to it. We should also note that their impressive heterosexual exploits on close scrutiny also turn out to be suggestive of pseudogenitality rather than mature genitality. The occurrence of similar psychopathology in men and women and the predominance of preoedipal areas of disturbance in the majority of the cases which I was able to observe at length would support the view which I have just put forward. However, this does not mean that the father plays no part. On the contrary, the bisexual's psychic life is dominated by an intense longing for a "good" father who will rescue him or her from an impossible predicament. The male often believes that he has found such an ideal object in the masculine partner, only to discover that it was illusory, or that the mate compulsively uses him in some way. In my judgment the establishment of a good, but not idealized, father-transference relationship was essential to progress and development in the cases included in this report—patients whose real fathers were absent or remote figures. (Mr. A.'s father was ineffectual and disinterested; Mrs. S. complained that her father had ignored her throughout her life; Mr. C.'s father had died when he was six; and Miss D. saw her father as a distant, cruel figure.) In understanding the role of the absent father, I have found Andre Green's remarks in his paper, "The Analyst, Symbolization and Absence in the Analytic Setting" (1975), very helpful. He writes, "there is no such couple formed by mother and baby without the father. For the child is the figure of the union between mother and father. . . . It is true that the father is absent from this relationship [of the mother and child]. But to say that he is absent means that he is neither present nor non-existent but that he has a potential presence" p. 13). There is indeed little hope of success in treating a bisexual patient unless this potential presence is fully understood and made more real.

CONCLUDING REMARKS

Bisexuality is a complex state of mind associated with a multiplicity of etiological factors. Analysts who have had the opportunity of observing a large number of cases agree that those who are so affected have been exposed to direct influences in their environment which have resulted in the formation of an imperfect superego. Investigation of most of such cases will usually show that either a parent, a teacher, or a person in a similar position of authority has actually encouraged or condoned the insurgence or establishment of feelings for, and sexual acts with, persons of both sexes. I would, however, consider this to be only an additional or aggravating factor and arguably responsible for the prevalent attitude of bisexuals in asserting that their behavior is well within normality. In the cases included in this report the condition was seen to be related to severe narcissistic disorders of character and personality often in the setting of a borderline state. The etiology would principally be that encountered in these conditions. I would underline here the frequency of an ineffectual or absent father as being of considerable importance. But cold, remote, or possibly mentally disturbed mothers are not uncommon. In my own experience the mothers of bisexuals who have come to my attention were not seductive mothers, as we often meet in the case of homosexuals. A constitutional intolerance, frustration, and limited impulse control are other common features.

Having suggested that actual bisexuality is in general associated with narcissistic and/or borderline states, the issue of treatment becomes relevant. The contrasting views of analysts with regard to the choice of psychoanalysis and other forms of psychotherapy for such conditions is well known. Kernberg (1970) has stated his position very clearly when, in discussing prognostic considerations, he suggests "that narcissistic personalities, in spite of the fact that their defensive organization is, broadly speaking, similar to that of the borderline personality, benefit very little from expressive, psychoanalytically oriented treatment approaches geared to that category of patients, and that psychoanalysis is the treatment of choice for narcissistic personalities." It might be appropriate to speculate about the possible outcome in three of the cited cases had there been opportunity to offer them psychoanalysis. It would be fair to assume that in the case of Miss D. the homosexual acting out might have been averted, but on the other hand it is highly questionable whether any of these patients would have been able to tolerate the rigors of the full psychoanalytic process, a situation also recognized by Kernberg. It is even possible that my patients would not be considered suitable for any form of analytic psychotherapy; yet in my opinion once the treatment is undertaken there must be an all-out effort to trace the early development of object choice, and this can only be done by making full use of the transference. This is contrary to the view expounded in the already cited article by Kernberg, who writes "In patients with narcissistic personalities and overt borderline states . . . psychoanalysis is contraindicated. These patients cannot tolerate the severe regression and reactivation of very early pathogenic conflicts in the transference without psychotic decompensation; a supportive treatment approach seems best for this group." Returning to the subject in a later paper Kernberg (1974) reiterates his belief that those narcissistic personalities who function on an overt borderline level are prone to the development of a transference psychosis. This and the insufficient integration for a more effective social functioning creates a contraindication for analysis and even for the modified psychoanalytic procedures recommended by Kernberg for most patients with borderline personality organization.

In this paper I have tried to show that in addition to employing a number of other instrumental parameters these patients can be approached through the transference in its positive and negative aspects; I hope this will stimulate further discussions as to the numerous issues involved not only in connection with the treatment of bisexuals but also of narcissistic and borderline states. The treatment of bisexuality should not be undertaken lightly and not before there is a full assessment of the patient's motivation for a change and the therapist's willingness to contain a difficult situation over a long period with little to show in the way of apparent improvement. The advantage of working in close contact with the staff of an institution, with the availability of medical, auxiliary, and other administrative support, should not be underestimated, especially when the patients' partners may also need help. Perhaps the answer in dealing with some of the more complex and challenging cases which come our way is flexibility.

REFERENCES

Eisnitz, A. J. (1974). On the metapsychology of narcissistic pathology. *Journal of the American Psychoanalytic Association* 22:279-291.

Freud, A. (1952). A connection between the states of negativism and of emotional surrender. *International Journal of Psycho-Analysis* 33:265.

Gillespie, W. H. (1964). Symposium on homosexuality. *International Journal of Psycho-Analysis* 45:203-209.

Green, A. (1975). The analyst, symbolization and absence in the analytic setting. *International Journal of Psycho-Analysis* 56: 1-22.

Kernberg, O. F. (1974). Contrasting viewpoints regarding the nature and psychoanalytic treatment of narcissistic personalities: A preliminary communication. *Journal of the American Psychoanalytic Association* 22: 255-267.

_____ (1970). Factors in the psychoanalytic treatment of narcissistic personalities. *Journal of the American Psychoanalytic Association* 18: 15-85.

Khan, M. M. R. (1964). The role of infantile sexuality and precocious object relations in female homosexuality. *The Pathology and Treatment of Sexual Deviation*. New York: Oxford Univ. Press.

Weissman, P. (1962) Structural consideration in overt male bisexuality. *International Journal of Psycho-Analysis* 43:159-168.

A. LIMENTANI, M.D.

DR. LIMENTANI is a training psychoanalyst and president of the British Psycho-Analytical Society. He is a fellow of the Royal College of Psychiatrists and for many years has been associated with the work of the Portman Clinic, London, in treating severe cases of sexual disorder and delinquency with analytical psychotherapy.

Transvestism: A Disorder of The Sense of Self

Lionel Ovesey, M.D.

Clinical Professor of Psychiatry
and

Ethel Person, M.D.

Clinical Assistant Professor of Psychiatry
at

The Psychoanalytic Clinic for
Training and Research
Department of Psychiatry
College of Physicians and Surgeons
Columbia University

Transvestism is not simply a sexual disorder, but is best understood as primarily a disorder of the sense of self. A descriptive background of transvestism is provided through a review of developmental history, clinical course, personality structure, and family history. The predominant transvestic fantasies and their modes of enactment are described. The disorder of the sense of self that gives rise to transvestic behavior is identified as a split in the ego into incompatible male and female gender identities. The split is attributed to an early identification with the mother as a defense against unresolved separation anxiety engendered during the separation-individuation phase of infantile development. The effect of this split upon the sense of reality, object relations, and adaptation to stress in transvestism are examined from a psychodynamic point of view.

INTRODUCTION

Transvestism is traditionally defined as heterosexual cross-dressing in which the clothing is used fetishistically for sexual arousal. It is usually classified by psychoanalysts as a sexual perversion, even though clinically the sexual component is far outweighed by nonsexual phenomena. We believe it may be more aptly described as primarily a disorder of the sense of self manifested by certain symptomatic distortions of both gender identity and sexuality, rather than broadly as a sexual disorder (Ovesey and Person, 1973).

In most of the psychoanalytic literature on transvestism, the transvestite appears as a man who struggles with the wish to don female attire, or who may actually do so in the tortured privacy of his bedroom. This picture accurately reflects the presentation of those transvestites who seek psychoanalysis, but the picture is skewed, because there are many more transvestites, rarely seen by analysts, who manifest more widespread symptomatic behavior. Thus, transvestic phenomena exist on a gradient and range from the simple, unenacted fantasy of wearing female clothes to the dramatization of floridly elaborated transvestic fantasies with extensive involvement in an actual transvestic society. Some transvestites act out their fantasies to the extent of living fulltime as awomen, and, of these, a small number ultimately seek a transsexual resolution through sex reassignment (Person and Ovesey, 1974a, 1974b). Transvestites intimately involved in the transvestic society (or network) may occasionally seek psychiatric consultation for depression but very few enter into psychoanalytic treatment.

This paper presents an explication of our point of view that transvestism is best understood as a disorder of the sense of self. We will focus on those patients rarely seen in the analyst's office, namely the network transvestites, who not only have transvestic fantasies but are compelled to act them out. These patients demonstrate an urgent need to objectify internal fantasies in the external world. Understanding both the fantasies and the urgency to action sharply illuminates the disturbed sense of self and is crucial to the conceptualization of transvestism. We will first provide essential background by describing some developmental and clinical features common to transvestites in general. Next, we will describe the predominant transvestic fantasies and catalogue the modes in which they are acted out. We will then turn our attention to the sense of self and attempt to explain in psychodynamic terms the intrapsychic disorder which gives rise to the transvestite behavior we have described.

The paper is based on the psychiatric study of twenty network transvestites (ten of whom were seen for ten or more sessions; the other ten from one to five sessions), analytically oriented ongoing psychotherapy with two other transvestites, and observations made during a series of visits to transvestic sorority meetings and drag balls. It is supplemented by a study of a representative portion of the very extensive transvestic literature, both pornographic and nonpornographic.

DEVELOPMENTAL HISTORY AND CLINICAL COURSE

Transvestites are never effeminate in boyhood, but are appropriately masculine. They engage in boyish pursuits and neither play with girls or become mother's helpers. They fantasize about being girls, particularly when cross-dressed, but invariably value their assertiveness and maleness. In this respect, they are unlike transsexuals and effeminate homosexuals (Person and Ovesey 1974a, 1974b).

Cross-dressing typically begins in childhood or early adolescence. It can start nonsexually to promote a sense of well-being, in which case it may become secondarily sexualized, or it can be sexual from the beginning. The initial experience may involve partial or total cross-dressing; should it be the former, it often progresses to totality. When sexualized, the favored article of clothing becomes erotic in itself and may habitually be used as a fetish, first in masturbation, later in intercourse. Even when cross-dressing is sexualized there is a tendency in some transvestites for the sexuality to drop away. although cross-dressing continues as an antidote to anxiety. Cross-dressing, while intermittent in the beginning, in some transvestites is escalating, progressive and may become continuous. Many transvestites at all times carry photographs of themselves as women; others may continually wear hidden female garments, such as ladies' underpants, when dressed outwardly as males.

Transvestites are invariably preferential heterosexuals, although sometimes there is a history of occasional homosexual encounters. Frequently, they express a preference for the subordinate role in sexual intercourse, that is, with the woman on top. Fetishistic arousal can be intense, but interpersonal sexuality is almost always attenuated. It is unusual for a transvestite to report sexual experiences with more than three women, and often the experiences are limited to one or two.

PERSONALITY

The personality is organized on an obsessive-paranoid axis with attenuation of both tender affectivity and sexuality. Transvestites are hyperaggressive and hypercompetitive and engage in endless struggles for power with other men. For this reason, transvestites preferentially seek self-employment in order to avoid conflicts with authority. There is a frequent history of job rotation which on scrutiny reflects the pervasive power struggle. Tender affectivity, to the extent that it exists, is invested mainly in the marital partner. Relationships with children, while often dutiful or distantly loving, are seldom warm and affectionate. The relationship with the wife is essentially dependent in nature. As such, its success is determined by the personality of the wife and her capacity to tolerate both cross-dressing and minimal sexuality. The tolerance apparently is not too great, since the incidence of divorce is high.

Mental life is characterized not only by irritability and preoccupation with power struggles but also by bouts of depression. These are either empty or angry, and occur under stress whenever dependency or masculinity are threatened. They are countered most frequently by cross-dressing, and in many instances by resort to alcohol. The latter is as prevalent among transvestites as are drugs among drag queens (narcissistic, aggressive, effeminate cross-dressing homosexuals). Suicide attempts are common, as we would expect in a patient population so prone to depression.

FAMILY HISTORY

The mother, as remembered, is usually warm and affectionate, less often dominating and overbearing. In both instances, however, maternal care appears erratic, due either to ineptness or to misfortunes which overwhelm the mother. In consequence, the child is not consistently deprived, but, rather, maternal gratification is repeatedly interrupted. In our opinion, this is the most prominent feature of the mother-son relationship in transvestism. In contrast, Stoller (1968, 1970) states that the most prominent feature is the mother's need to feminize her little boy. According to Stoller, this need is expressed primarily through cross-dressing the boy as a girl. Stoller concludes that the transvestite is partly the creation of his mother's unconscious wish and not just the product of his own defenses.

Our clinical experience has been different from Stoller's. In our unselected sample of twenty-two consecutive transvestic patients, we elicited only two histories of maternal induction into cross-dressing, one punitive and one nonpunitive. In the predominant pattern, the child spontaneously cross-dressed, the activity most often remained surreptitious, and it was not reinforced by the mother or a mother surrogate. We believe the transvestic defense is usually the patient's own invention. It is intimately related to the process of self-object differentiation, and only sometimes "primed" by explicit parental directives, but not created by them. Even so, we recognize that we are dealing with retrospective data. In some instances reported in the literature there is pictorial evidence of family conspiratorial cross-dressing, and, obviously, we cannot quarrel with such data. The question is how widespread such practices are in the histories of transvestites and to what extent they lead to transvestic behavior.

Another striking feature in the family histories is the high incidence of fathers perceived either as verbally abusive or physically violent. The majority of the fathers reported by our subjects fell into this category. In the minority of cases, the father was either absent altogether or perceived as aloof and self-contained.

TRANSVESTIC FANTASIES AND THEIR ENACTMENT

The key transvestic fantasy is so simple and devoid of structure that one hesitates to call it a fantasy. For example, a patient reports that he goes to sleep thinking of himself in a blue dress. If the patient is asked what happened after he put on the dress, his reply is, "Nothing." In fact, the act of putting on the dress is the central action, the point of the fantasy. Thus, the fantasy of dressing is per se the height of excitement, not a prelude to further action. Although the enactment of the fantasy, that is, actually dressing, may be accompanied by erection, masturbation, or sexual intercourse, this association is variable and its frequency tends to diminish over the years as the transvestism, itself, continues. Nonetheless, it is this variable association between dressing and eroticism which has led to the classification of transvestism as a sexual disorder.

In some transvestites, there are consciously elaborated fantasies. Others have a stereotypic or impoverished fantasy life and produce few dreams. With the latter, one can only surmise the underlying fantasies from their transvestic enactments or from the patient's preoccupation with certain pornographic stories. Enactment assumes a myriad forms. Elaborations of the key transvestic fantasy with the more common modes of enactment follow.

The "Closet" Transvestite

Certain transvestites, though pursuing transvestism in isolation from other persons, spend a great deal of time reading pornography. By doing so, interior fantasies are to some degree objectified in reality by sharing an intimate fantasy life with anonymous others.

Transvestic Pen Pals

Some transvestites desire contact with other transvestites but not in the flesh. This aversion to meeting other transvestites is usually rationalized on the basis of reality fears, for example, fear of exposure with consequent damage to professional reputation or disclosure to family. We believe, however, there is a more pertinent psychological reason. These transvestites have the need to objectify the reality of their fantasies, but dread too complete a validation which might threaten to engulf their everyday male identities. Such persons happen upon the solution of exchanging tapes or letters with other transvestites.

There are numerous instances of such pen pal relationships, extended over years with a mutual sense of intimacy, in which the participants never meet. Some transvestites carry on multiple correspondences, sometimes in the hundreds. Frequently, they do not know one another's true identity but write to anonymous others known only by female pseudonyms at a post office box number. Contact is made through the classified section of transvestic periodicals. These correspondences are more successful insofar as the correspondents share certain fantasy preoccupations. Some pairs engage in collaborative writing of pornography, each composing alternate sections of a transvestic story or novel.

Vicarious Transvestites

Some transvestites, who for the most part are no longer actively engaged in cross-dressing themselves, achieve vicarious satisfaction by tutoring novices, serving as male escorts for dressed transvestites, or "rescuing" operated transsexual transvestites by finding jobs or offering money. A few transvestites have formalized these activities into moneymaking propositions by setting up businesses which cater to the needs of the transvestite network.

Cross-Dressing

Cross-dressing in solitude, usually in front of a mirror, is the simplest and commonest enactment of the unadorned transvestic fantasy. As already mentioned, many transvestites habitually wear some female undergarment or carry pictures of themselves dressed as women. These are mini-symbols for cross-dressing and enhance the illusion of being a woman even while dressed as a man.

Passing

Not only does the transvestite wish to don female clothes, but he also wishes to fool other people into thinking he is a woman. In consequence, transvestites derive great pleasure from the bravado and danger which accompany successful forays into "straight" society while disguised as women. Thus, they may shop, ask a policeman for directions, or go to a restaurant. Stories of successful deceptions are endlessly recounted and passed along the transvestic network.

Initiation Fantasies

Jucovy (in press) intuitively recognized the importance of initiation fantasies on the basis of his analytic experience with one transvestite patient. Initiation fantasies permeate the collective fantasy life of transvestites as revealed through letters in the personal columns of sex magazines, transvestite pornography, and the social organization of transvestite sororities. In order to verify the widespread existence of such fantasies, one need only glance through the personal column of any sex magazine or newspaper. Many letters from transvestites invite the acquaintance of a woman or another transvestite for purposes of instruction in the art of dress. For example: "Novice wishes to meet T.V.s, T.S.s, interested females to dress me, make me up, sincere, go out together," "wish help of someone to turn me into complete woman." This theme of initiation may also be masochistically elaborated, for example:

"Servant in silks: teach me, dress me, make me up, scold me, but don't hurt me. My wife has tried but no person could satisfy this need to be totally FE-MALE. Liberate me."

The central theme in transvestic literature is female impersonation and its causes (Person, in press; Beigel and Feldman, 1963). The comments on transvestite pornography which follow are based on two sources: an article by Beigel and Feldman (1963) which analyzes ninety-three works of transvestite publications. Our own studies parallel those of Beigel and Feldman. As will become clear, the themes which appear in the pornography are often acted out in the lives of individual transvestites.

In the literature, initiation into cross-dressing is usually forced upon the hero by either a dominant, big-breasted, corseted, booted "phallic" woman, often perceived as glamorous as well as dominant, who "enslaves" him, or by a kindly, protective woman who does so in order to save his life, for example, by disguising him and thereby concealing him from members of the Mafia who wish to kill him. In both instances he is taught about femininity by the initia-tor. In the stories, it is only rarely that the man had any desire to cross-dress prior to his initiation. Once he cross-dresses, the assumption is that he con-tinues to live as a woman, or at least pursues a double life. The story often ends with the hero enjoying a sexual relationship with one or the other of the two women, either the dominant woman who enslaved him or the protective woman who saved him.

The Lesbian Connection

Transvestites often use pornography featuring female homosexuality for genital arousal. This preoccupation was first noted by Fenichel (1953). On the rare occasions in the pornography when the hero is castrated by a woman surgeon, he becomes a "lesbian" lover of that same woman. This pornograph-ic theme also has its counterpart in reality, wherein some operated transvestic transsexuals remain on intimate sexual terms with their wives. In another realization of the lesbian fantasy, a transvestite, who otherwise despises homo-sexuality (between males), will have sex with another transvestite while both are dressed as women.

The Community of Women

Sometimes, in the pornography, the conclusion of the story is not sexual at all; rather, the point of cross-dressing seems to be the permission it accords the transvestite to live in easy intimacy (nonsexual) with women, for ex-ample, in a dormitory or women's barracks, while his true sex remains un-known. This fantasy is reflected in reality through participation in organized transvestite social groups and activities.

Transvestite Sororities

The penultimate culmination of transvestic acting out occurs at the sorority meetings and parties, drag balls, Mardi Gras festivals, and transvestic vacation spas. Sororities of transvestites, some on a national scale with chapters in different cities, have existed in this country for at least fifteen years. At such gatherings, the transvestite enters into his dreamworld made tangible, a world in which gender differences are blurred and only the female gender is in evidence. By and large, the parties and meetings are tame affairs despite the lurid appearance. Transvestites take the opportunity to dress, to exchange information on makeup and clothes. Many bring their wives. Talk varies from specifically transvestite concerns to mundane exchanges about quite masculine topics, i.e., fixing the roof, work problems, automobiles, etc. Some groups flounder over charges of homosexuality, but in the main overt behavior is clearly asexual.

Collusion with Wives

Some transvestites avoid disclosing their transvestic activities to their wives. Still others are determined to bring about full disclosure and to live at least part-time with their wives as two women living together. Here, again, we see the transvestite's need to objectify his inner reality by insisting on its validation in the real external world. Many marriages break up over this issue; some few apparently thrive. (We would warn here that any global speculation about the wife's willingness or need to participate is unjustified; we have found the motivation to be variable.) The need for wifely validation and support is sufficiently widespread so that the issue is treated extensively in the transvestic press, which includes advice on disclosure to wives (above all, she must be reassured that the cross-dressing has no homosexual connotations), advice to wives on how to respond, and accounts of successful unions with full disclosure. One publication is co-written by husband and wife.

Female Physicality

Transvestites may develop transsexual impulses as a regressive phenomenon under stress (Person and Ovesey, 1974a, 1974b). As previously stated, a few may become full-blown transsexuals and go on to surgical sex reassignment. A much larger number, however, who have no intention of becoming transsexuals, use female hormones and settle for the possession of breasts. An unhappy side effect of such medication, of course, is a concomitant decrease in sexual desire. The trick, therefore, is to take hormones to develop breasts, and then reduce the medication to a level sufficient to maintain them, but still permit potency. Such patients refer to themselves as "breast fetishists." Transvestites may also have pregnancy fantasies. These are rare on a conscious level, but appear in dream life.

Sexual Discharge

Transvestites use clothing fetishistically. Cross-dressing, therefore, may be accompanied by sexual discharge, either through masturbation or intercourse, and may be a prerequisite for discharge to take place.

Sadomasochism

The fantasy or enactment of submission to a dominant woman while crossdressed may be masochistically elaborated in the form of bondage, whipping, or discipline.

Enactment with Prostitutes

Some transvestites attempt to enact elaborately scripted fantasies with the assistance of prostitutes.

There is a characteristic ebb and flow in transvestite fantasies in which periods of acting out alternate with periods of renunciation. For example:

Mr. X spends a year collecting a large assortment of female attire and dressing every lunch hour in his office. At the end of the year he throws out all his female clothes and resolves never to dress again. Some months later he is again irresistibly drawn to collecting female clothes.

Renunciation of the perverse activity while a patient is in treatment may lull some therapists into the mistaken belief that they have achieved a "cure." One of our patients was written up by a former therapist as an example of a "cure" by a particular method on grounds that he had given up perverse behavior, this despite the fact that he maintained his contacts with other transvestites. His renunciation was attributed to a particular insight which emerged during therapy. Unfortunately the renunciation was short-lived after the termination of treatment. In retrospect, it seems less convincing that insight had anything to do with the patient's renunciation of perverse activity; rather, the cycle of perverse behavior and renunciation has continued unabated.

In some patients, the cyclic nature of the acting out does not change with time, but remains more or less the same; in others, although the transvestic activity is punctuated by renunciation, the involvement is progressive.

THE SENSE OF SELF

In the full-blown syndrome the transvestite often expresses the feeling that he has two personalities, male and female. The female personality may be perceived as "fighting" with the male personality and crowding it out. Even in less fully developed cases in which the transvestite subjectively feels his personality as more continuous, he experiences different ego states depending on whether or not he is cross-dressed. As a woman, the transvestite feels greater ease, but the differences are more comprehensive than involving simple differences in anxiety levels. For example, one transvestite described different appetites for food depending on how he was dressed; as a man he relished hamburgers for lunch, while as a woman he intensely disliked hamburgers. Differences in modes of assertiveness are paramount. Money (1974) highlights the split in personality or the dual identifications by entitling a paper "Two Names, Two Wardrobes, Two Personalities."

Transvestism has been viewed in several related yet subtly disparate ways by a number of observers. Dual or multiple identifications have been stressed by some (Arlow, 1954; Fenichel, 1953; Segal, 1965); alternatively, transvestism has been viewed by others as a defense in which the perversion represents a reparative condensation of self and object (maternal), either for purposes of security (Segal, 1965; Ovesey and Person, 1973; Person and Ovesey, 1974b) or to alleviate castration anxiety through an identification with a phallic female (Bak, 1968). These explanations are not mutually incompatible, but the focus varies slightly. The variations are predicated on differences in psychodynamic interpretations, while attempting to explain the same observations. In order to align these variant views, one must return to the Freudian concept of splitting the ego in the service of defense. Freud (1940) formulated this concept to account for the existence side by side in the ego of two contradictory attitudes, one fitting in with the reality, the other with the wish to deny the reality. Freud found such a rift or split occurred in many situations in which the infantile ego was faced with the necessity of constructing a defense against a trauma.

Thus, in transvestism, the dual self-representation reflects a split of the ego in which two mutually incompatible gender identities, male and female, coexist. In turn, disorder of the sense of self, as experienced by the transvestite, reflects his dual self-representations And here is the essential dilemma for the transvestite: he is trying to validate two realities which are ultimately mutually incompatible, two realities which are predicated on a split in the ego and consequently in the sense of self. A considerable portion of the rhetoric in the transvestite press is designed to counter the tension the transvestite experiences from his double self-representations. As a result, many transvestites are militantly committed to the position that they have a richer personality because of their "femme" selves than "normal" people who are relegated to a one-gender role.

OBJECT RELATIONS

Characteristically, transvestites relate relatively well to women and avoid intimacy with men except for other transvestites. Although many authors viewed transvestism as a defense against homosexuality, we see here both a similarity and a profound difference between homosexuals and transvestites. Both groups are uncomfortable in a world made up of two sexes, but each group eliminates a different sex. While some homosexuals live their lives as completely as possible in a world of gay men, whereas transvestites eliminate men, to some degree in reality, and to an extensive degree in fantasy. The point of transvestic life is to live in a society of women. This is evidenced in fantasy, in pornography, and in the social structure previously described. Explanations for this tendency vary, but the observation is crystal clear. In our opinion, the tendency derives developmentally from contrasting views of the pregenital mother: the homosexual sees her as engulfing, and hence avoids her; the transvestite sees her as nurturing, and hence holds on to her. We do not know whether this is an accurate reflection of reality or whether it represents the child's distorted perception of the relationship with the mother.

There are certain relationships on the part of transvestites which provide clues to the characteristic modes of relating. The frequent pairing of transvestites and operated male transsexuals has been noted by Guze (1968) as well as by ourselves (1973). We know of three such instances which eventually led to marriage. Male transsexuals, of course, are men who "succeeded" in becoming women, an actualization of the transvestite's key fantasy. These altered males are particularly attractive to the transvestite because he can so easily, through identification, put himself in their place and vicariously experience their femininity as his own. The following clinical vignette illustrates the complexities of such relationships.

Mr. S., a transvestite, took hormones to grow breasts and was contemplating sex reassignment. In the meantime, he fell in love with Blanche, an operated transsexual. He immediately withdrew from hormones to regain his potency and become Blanche's lover. In this way, he affirmed and stabilized his male identity. Simultaneously, he projected his fantasied female identity onto Blanche and then reincorporated it by identifying with her — a mechanism we call *projective identification*. (We use this term in much the same way as Masud Khan, 1966.) Thus, in effect, Mr. S. seemingly achieved the impossible: he objectified his fantasy of being a woman, but at the same time managed to remain a man. When Blanche ran off with a truck driver, Mr. S., therefore, suffered a double blow. Momentarily, he was unable to sustain either aspect of his identity, male or female: the competitive defeat undermined the former and Blanche's flight removed the latter. As a reparative measure, he reverted to hormones, assumed a predominant female identity, and to reinforce it, became "mother" to two lesbian lovers.

Another mechanism used by transvestites in relating to objects is that of *introjective identification*. This is a mechanism through which a person "takes in" a desirable aspect of another person and then experiences it as his own. The most desirable aspect for the transvestite, of course, is the feminine component of a woman. For this reason, the mechanism can be particularly troublesome for some married transvestites in whom the process of falling in love and living with a woman evokes immense jealousy of her femininity. In such instances, the longing for the loved woman's clothes becomes almost unbearable. In these cases, there is a confusion between *loving* and *becoming*, an observation made by Greenson in his treatment of a cross-dressing effeminate boy (Greenson, 1968). An illustrative example in a transvestite follows.

C. fell in love and married early in life in the hope that he could stabilize his male personality. However, instead of forming a complementary relationship wherein he could enhance his masculinity through enjoying his wife's femininity, C. introjectively identified with her to such an extent that instead of just loving her, he wanted to become her. His jealousy of his wife's clothing and of her biological right to be feminine greatly intensified his own interest in female impersonation. Thus, instead of becoming more masculine, as he had planned, he paradoxically became more feminine. The escalation in C.'s cross-dressing became intolerable to the wife and eventually precipitated the demise of the marriage.

These observations lead us to certain conclusions about object relations in transvestism which can be observed to varying degrees depending on its extent. Transvestites, in common with certain borderline personalities, do not always relate to people as people in their own right, but are prone to contaminate the relationships with components of their own self-representations via projective and introjective identifications. External objects are often denied a separate existence, but are used as weights to maintain the balance of power between the male and female identities as each struggles for supremacy. There is incomplete differentiation between self and external objects; hence, relationships represent a symbiotic condensation of both. For example, lack of separation between self and object is clearly evident in pornographic cartoons of transvestic masochism in which dominant women and transvestites are identically depicted, both dressed in high heels and Merry Widow corsets. It is further evidenced in the name the transvestite assumes for his "femme" identity, frequently the name of an envied woman or a lost love object.

ENACTMENT OF FANTASIES AND THE SENSE OF REALITY

Transvestites, as a group, are variably anhedonic and experience feelings of loneliness and emptiness. They find relief through preoccupation with fantasies and through their enactment. As we stated, it is characteristic that there are periods of activity interspersed with periods of renunciation. Although the fantasies have an obsessional cast in the sense of pervasiveness, they differ from true obsessions insofar as they are not experienced as ego-alien. In fact, the fantasies are a major source of pleasure, ease, and sometimes a prerequisite for orgastic release. As such, they present a constant temptation to withdraw from reality pursuits. As long as the transvestite is not under undue stress, both the preoccupation and the enactments occur in moderation and do not seriously interfere with everyday functions. At times of intense stress, however, the temptation to enact expands to uncontrollable proportions and he is beset by an urgent need to convert the primal fantasy into reality.

The fragility of both reality sense and object relations renders the transvestite unusually vulnerable to external stress. At best, therefore, the transvestic defense system is unstable and easily overwhelmed by threats to masculinity and dependent security, for example, vocational failure, competitive defeat, broken marriage, death of the mother, or birth of a child. In such crises not only does the transvestites's own assertion fail him but he fails to derive security from real objects. He must rely more and more on fantasies and their enactment to alleviate his anxiety. As preoccupation with fantasy escalates, the transvestite's involvement with real objects diminishes even more. In addition, there is great resentment toward real objects, particularly wives, who interfere with fantasy preoccupation. Such estrangement is experienced as a threat to the reality organization of the transvestite. Enactment becomes a way of lending objective validity to his fantasies and thus of reestablishing contact with substitutive real objects, albeit symbolic ones, to replace the objects that have been lost. The internal fantasy, thus objectified, becomes a substitute for the attenuated external reality.

These fantasies solutions cannot be sustained indefinitely, but, for several reasons, are doomed to collapse. Thus, failure of the transvestic defense and consequent renunciation of acting out is often based on the relative inadequacy of the fantasy enactment compared to the fantasy itself.

A masochistic transvestite, with a plethora of transvestic fantasies, had a well-developed fantasy that a dominant woman forcibly cross-dressed him and then bound him with rope. He tried to enact the fantasy in a number of ways, with a prostitute, with a dominant woman who advertised in the sex periodicals, and with a transsexual who had been a drag queen. Much to his dismay, he discovered these enactments much less effective, both in sense of well-being and orgastic arousal, than the unenacted fantasy. This failure was due to his awareness throughout the ritualized enactment that he was not in fact being forced to submit, but rather that he himself was the author of the enacted events. Thus, there was a serious limitation to the illusion of reality.

However, there is a far more profound reason for the pressure toward renunciation of perverse activity. Although acting out is predicated on the need to reestablish contact with substitute real objects and thereby preserve a sense of reality, there is another reality which is simultaneously threatened. Fear of immersion in the transvestic reality is concretized by the transvestite's knowledge that some members evolve into transsexuals. Several transvestites have described virtually the same experience: each felt painfully isolated until he discovered the transvestite network, which revealed to him he was not alone and, in addition, offered the framework for objectification of his fantasy life. The relief was all too brief, since he quickly became frightened of another contingency, namely, that he would sink so deep into the transvestic world that he would lose his male identity. Thus, for most transvestites, there is a point of no return, a point beyond which they will not go.

PSYCHODYNAMIC CONSIDERATIONS

What is the infantile trauma in transvestism that leads to the defense of splitting? Where does the wish to be a woman and the subsequent denial of male identity originate? Transvestism is one of three interrelated gender disorders in men. The other two are transsexualism and cross-dressing, effeminate homosexuality. We are in agreement with other workers (Stoller, 1968; Segal, 1965; Socarides, 1968, 1970; Golosow and Weitzman, 1969; Weitzman, Shamoian, and Golosow, 1970; Gershman, 1970) that these disorders have their roots of origin in the preoedipal period. We have proposed (1974a, 1974b) that all three disorders stem from unresolved separation anxiety during the separation-individuation phase of infantile development. In point of time, we suggested they originated along a developmental gradient, transsexualism first, transvestism and effeminate homosexuality later. The symptomatic distortions of gender and sex reflect different ways of dealing with separation anxiety at progressive levels of maturation.

Thus, transsexuals unconsciously resort to the fantasy of symbiotic fusion with the mother to allay separation anxiety. The final transsexual resolution is an attempt to get rid of this anxiety through sex reassignment, that is, the transsexual acts out his unconscious fantasy surgically and symbolically becomes his own mother. In contrast, effeminate homosexuals and transvestites resort to less-drastic measures, the incorporation of part objects and transitional objects. In the effeminate homosexual, the boy fears engulment and annihilation by the mother. He, therefore, transfers his dependency and sexual needs to a male object. His partner's penis is equated with the mother's breast and incorporated orally or anally as a part object. In transvestism, the female clothes represent the mother as a transitional object and hence confer maternal protection. Later, in the oedipal period, the basis is laid for their eventual use sexually as fetishistic defenses against incestual anxiety.

In transvestites there is evidence of an unusually intense and ultimately unresolved oedipal struggle in which the incestual object persists and oedipal rivalry is perpetuated. Thus, the female clothes simultaneously symbolize the mother as a transitional and incestual object. Not only is the first sexual object one of the mother's garments, but the clothes which transvestites favor when cross-dressing are often out of date, the clothes "which mother used to wear." In some transvestites, as we said earlier, the sexuality gradually drops away, although the cross-dressing continues unabated. With these, one might say there is a regression in which genital heterosexuality is sacrificed in order to preserve the earlier ties to the pregenital mother, both dependent and sexual. Here, then, we have a clue to the meaning of the transvestite's initiation fantasies. The imposition of feminization through cross-dressing relieves him of responsibility for his incestual wishes and thus allays oedipal guilt.

Secondarily, the clothes represent a defensive posture in the oedipal constellation, originally against the father, later against other males. They magically protect the transvestite in two ways: (1) they symbolize an autocastration, a token submission to his male competitors, which wards off their retaliation; and (2) they disguise his masculinity and serve to disarm his rivals. The clothes conceal his penis, the symbol of masculine power, and deny his hostile intent. He therefore feels safe because his rivals do not know that secretly he is plotting their demise. He avoids detection by passing as a woman, which makes it possible for him to risk assertion and thus validate himself as a man.

We have already noted that the transvestite's personality is integrated on an obsessive-paranoid axis and that typically he is irritable, hyperaggressive, and hypercompetitive. We also noted that, in general, transvestites avoid the company of men, except other transvestites. Relationships with men, when they exist at all, are characterized by covert, angry interactions. Passing — not being "read," "getting away with it" — represent an affront to the straight community, particularly the men, in which anger is discharged through contempt ("the straight didn't get it") and the risk is minimized through disguise. In the family histories, as we have said, many fathers were perceived either as verbally abusive or physically violent. We do not know whether this is an accurate appraisal of the family situation as it in fact occurred or whether it is a misperception born out of an increased vulnerability in the oedipal period. We believe that there is an early split in the representation of the mother and that attributes of the bad mother are transferred to paternal images. Maternal shortcomings are often rationalized in terms of paternal demands.

We tend to view the transvestite's female identification more as a reparative condensation of mother and child for purposes of security (Ovesey and Person, 1973), as opposed to an identification with a phallic woman in order to allay castration anxiety and enhance masculine power (Bak, 1968). We believe, however, that both mechanisms exist and that the two are not mutually exclusive. The female identification is fostered not only by a defensive symbiotic bond with the mother, but also to some degree by abhorrence of a masculine identification with a hated father. In this way, the transvestite avoids any actual acknowledgment of his wrath toward his mother, and therefore toward women in general.

Most of the time, transvestic defenses function reasonably well. At times of stress, however, the defenses may fail. Under such circumstances, transvestites frantically step up the pace of acting out. Should such reparative measures fail, they regressively fall back on the more primitive fantasy of symbiotic fusion with the mother. It is at this point that transsexual impulses break out and may go on to a full-blown transsexual syndrome (secondary transsexualism).

CONCLUSION

We have conceptualized transvestism as a disorder of the sense of self characterized by a split in the ego into incompatible male and female gender identities. We have attributed the split to an early identification with the mother as a defense against unresolved separation anxiety during the separation-individuation phase of infantile development. We are well aware that we have not "explained" transvestism etiologically, nor was it our intention to do so. We cannot say why separation trauma results in the type of splitting which is the hallmark feature of transvestism. Splitting, as a Freudian concept (Freud, 1940), can be applied to every neurotic defense. However, we have used splitting in a special sense, similar to Kohut's (1971) notion of a vertical split in the ego in which there are two elaborated identities. It is this formal characteristic of transvestism which we believe links it to such disorders of the self as multiple personality, imposture, and certain types of psychopathy.

REFERENCES

Arlow, J. (1954). Perversions: theoretical and therapeutic aspects. *Journal of the American Psychoanalytic Association* 2: 336-345.

Bak, R. (1968). The phallic woman: The ubiquitous fantasy in perversion. *Psychoanalytic Study of the Child* 23: 15-36.

Beigel, H., and Feldman, R. (1963). The male transvestite's motivation in fiction, research and reality. *Advances in Sex Research*, ed. H. Beigel, pp. 198-210. New York: Norton

Fenichel, O. (1964). The psychology of transvestism. *Collected Papers*, pp. 167-180. New York: Norton.

Guze, H. (1968). Psychosocial adjustment of transsexuals: An evaluation and theoretical formulation. *Transsexualism and Sex Reassignment*, eds. R. Green and J. Money. pp. 153-169. Baltimore: Johns Hopkins Univ. Press.

Freud, S. (1964). Splitting of the ego in the process of defense. *The Complete Psychological Works of Sigmund Freud*, ed. J. Strachey, 23: 271-278. London: Hogarth.

Gershman, H. (1970). The role of core gender identity in the genesis of perversions. *American Journal of Psychoanalysis* 30: 58-65.

Golosow, N., and Weitzman, E. L. (1969). Psychosexual and ego repression in the male transsexual. *Journal of Nervous and Mental Diseases* 49: 328-336.

Greenson, R. R. (1968). Dis-identifying from mother. Its special importance for the boy. *International Journal of Psycho-Analysis* 49: 370.

Guze, H. (1968). Psychosocial adjustment of transsexuals: An evaluation and theoretical formulation. *Transsexualism and Sex Reassignment*, eds. R. Green and J. Money. Baltimore: Johns Hopkins Univ. Press. pp. 153-169.

Jucovy, M. (in press). Initiation fantasies and transvestism. *Journal of the American Psychoanalytic Association*.

Khan, M. M. R. (1966). Foreskin fetishism and its relation to ego pathology in a male homosexual. *Psychoanalysis and Male Sexuality*, ed. Ruitenbeck, pp. 235-268. New Haven: College and Univ. Press.

Kohut, H. (1971). *The Analysis of the Self*. New York: International Universities Press.

Money, J. (1974). Two names, two wardrobes, two personalities. *Journal of Homosexuality* 1: 65-70.

Ovesey, L., and Person, E. (1973). Gender identity and sexual psychopathology in men: A psychodynamic analysis of homosexuality, transsexualism, and transvestism. *Journal of the American Academy of Psychoanalysis* 1: 53-72.

Person, E. (in press). Discussion of "Initiation Fantasies and Transvestism" by M. Jucovy. *Journal of the American Psychoanalytic Association*.

_____ and Ovesey, L. (1974). The transsexual syndrome in males: I. Primary transsexualism. *American Journal of Psychotherapy* 28: 4-20.

_____ (1974). The transsexual syndrome in males: II. Secondary transsexualism. *American Journal of Psychotherapy* 28: 174-193.

Segal, M. M. (1965). Transvestism as an impulse and as a defense. *International Journal of Psycho-Analysis* 46:209-217.

Socarides, C. W. (1968). *The Overt Homosexual*. New York: Grune & Stratton.

_____ (1970). A psychoanalytic study of the desire for sexual transformation ("transsexualism"): The plaster of Paris man. *International Journal of Psycho-Analysis* 51: 341-349.

Stoller, R. (1968). *Sex and Gender*. New York: Aronson.

_____ (1970). Pornography and perversion. *Archives of General Psychiatry* 22: 490-498.

Weitzman, E. L., Shamoian, C. A., and Golosow, N. (1970). Identity diffusion and the transsexual resolution. *Journal of Nervous and Mental Diseases* 51: 295-302.

LIONEL OVESEY, M.D.

DR. OVESEY is a clinical professor of psychiatry at Columbia University where he teaches undergraduates, psychiatric residents, and analytic candidates. He is a practicing psychoanalyst and is a training and supervising analyst at the Psychoanalytic Clinic for Training and Research, Columbia University. He is attending psychiatrist at New York State Psychiatric Institute and Hospital.

ETHEL PERSON, M.D.

DR. PERSON is an assistant clinical professor of psychiatry at Columbia University where she teaches undergraduates, psychiatric residents and analytic candidates. She is a practicing psychoanalyst and is a training and supervising analyst at the Psychoanalytic Clinic for Training and Research, Columbia University.

Empathy and Intuition in Becoming a Psychiatrist: A Case Study

Ronald J. Blank, M.D.

University of Michigan Medical Center

This paper, through the use of the case study, presents the idea that the beginning psychiatrist must often depend on his own native intuition and empathic skills during his early clinical work. A case is presented in detail to show that amid the anxiety, freshness, and inexperience typifying a beginning psychiatrist, a psychotherapeutic treatment that benefits both the patient and the psychiatrist can be carried out. The growth of the patient and the therapist is described over the course of a three-month hospitalization.

THE BEGINNING

If there exists a time in the life of a psychiatrist when he is free from the historical forces of traditional psychiatry that will later serve to shape his own psychotherapeutic style, it is during the first months of his residency. It is here amid the chaos, anxiety, idealism, and anticipation that he is most likely to depend on his intuition and native empathies to serve as the cutting edge of therapy. He will place a high degree of importance on his supervision; yet he will have to act first and later examine his actions as he attempts to learn psychotherapy. As the resident advances further in his training, his native intuition and empathic skills will be carefully buttressed by a host of psychotherapeutic techniques and philosophies, such that he will never re-create those first few months when he had only him*self* to use as the therapeutic tool. Of course, there are some, like Otto Will (1971), who consider this to be one of the primary ingredients for the advanced as well as the beginning therapist. Will considers the

therapeutic situation as being an interpersonal situation in which the tool of the therapist is himself, his personality. This is in the main what he has to use in the psychotherapeutic relationship. To use it well, he must possess some knowledge of himself, the acquisition of which may be discomforting as well as enlightening.

With the foregoing in mind, I would like to outline the treatment (in the hospital by a beginning first-year resident) of a most interesting and challenging young woman. I believe that it demonstrates the use of the beginning therapist's native intuition and empathy backed up by the knowledge and advice of an experienced supervisor. This is not to suggest that the treatment occurred without errors in technique. In fact, it is perhaps these errors seen retrospectively that served as the most important basis for growth on the part of the therapist. Nor does this paper mean to suggest that the beginning psychiatrist has no cognitive framework with which to begin his career. In fact, today's beginner will often bring to his residency a good deal of clinical and theoretical skill, developed during his college and medical school experience. The case is presented with certain critical facts changed to protect the anonymity of the patient and her family.

THE OPENING PHASE

I first made the acquaintance of L. on the morning after her admission. She lay propped up in a hospital bed with an IV slowly running into her left arm. The room was quite dark, and L. looked as though she had been crying for some time. She was wearing flannel pajamas and had her hair tied in a bun on top of her head. I introduced myself, and told her I would be her doctor; I would be her therapist in the hospital. She looked at me with sad eyes. She was a vaguely pretty woman, somewhat plump, but pleasing to look at. She had a childlike appearance, despite her thirty-six years. I asked her how she was feeling and she responded that she felt frustrated and depressed and wanted to die. I asked her about what had happened the night previous, and she said that she did not remember, but she thought that she had tried to kill herself. She then remained silent. I told her that I would be back to see her at half-past three that afternoon, so that we might get acquainted. She agreed to this.

I saw her again at the agreed time. She was dressed carefully in a blue dress, with her hair neatly done, and we spoke for thirty minutes in my office. The patient spoke of her husband, how she had met him, their deteriorating marriage and sexual relationship, and her strong wish to die. I hoped that in the ensuing weeks, through our work together, she would be able to give up her strong wish for death. She again expressed a wish to die, along with feelings of hopelessness, worthlessness, and emptiness. We made an appointment for the following day.

That evening, although I should have been long gone, I found myself lingering in the hospital, half-expecting, and strangely enough, half-hoping, to see a repetition of the previous night's event. On that first night, shortly after her admission by another doctor, the patient had been discovered by a nurse trying to strangle herself with a towel and then with her own hands. She was restrained and no damage was evident. She, shortly thereafter, became unresponsive to verbal commands and was found to be posturing. She then began to hyperventilate for about a minute and then suddenly stopped breathing. Her pulse was found to be strong, but increasing, and her lips seemed to be cyanotic. Mouth-to-mouth resuscitation was begun and the patient was ventilated with an ambu bag. A respiratory arrest was called and a code team arrived. The patient maintained good pulse and blood pressure and soon began to breathe on her own. An EKG was found to be normal as were all other parameters. The chief medical resident responding to the code felt that the patient had undergone a self-induced breath-holding spell or a reactive apnea secondary to her hyperventilation. Having just come to psychiatry from a medical background, I found myself incredulous that a healthy woman could induce a respiratory arrest. Although trusting the admitting doctor's description of the previous night's event, and agreeing with his intervention, I still remained skeptical that it all happened. I found myself consciously wanting to see a repetition of the behavior in order to prove that is was functional and not organic. At this early stage in my career I was engaged in the difficult and still unresolved attempt to give up my so newly earned "medical" view of my patients. Quite frankly I did not believe that the patient had *tried* or come close to committing suicide. It all sounded like an hysterically dramatic happening. Little did I anticipate the behavior that would take place in the patient and the response I would have to it.

It was now the following evening, a warm humid July night. Without being aware of it, this thirty-six-year-old "child-woman" had aroused in me a rescue fantasy that I would later find to be her dominant mode of social interaction with me.

Again L. was trying to strangle herself. Upon entering her room, I saw her lying flat on her back in bed, her face flushed, her eyes shut tightly, her hands clawing at her neck, as she rolled from side to side in her bed. I called her name softly without response. I shouted her name—still no response. I shook her briskly, and finally, I slapped her hard across the face, all to no avail. Clearly she did not wish me to intrude. I forcibly pulled her hands away from her neck and held them at her side. She resisted at first and then seemed to relax.

I spoke to her in what I thought to be my most reassuring voice, trying to get her to relax, open her eyes, and talk to me. Alas, she did not respond. I let go of her hands, and slowly, as if controlled by strings, her hands moved toward her throat, and again she tried to strangle herself. Her hands were removed and she then began to scratch sharply at her body. I was struck by the primitiveness of her attempt and her apparent self-absorption in what she was doing. Whether she was truly in a dissociated or catatonic trance, or whether she was having a hysterial episode was impossible for me to determine.

Again, I restrained her; she was breathing normally, her pupils were reactive to light, and her pulse was strong, but she was still unresponsive to verbal or physical stimulation. Soon after, the patient's respiration became shallow: I called for a stethoscope, ambu bag, oral airway, and laryngoscope. The patient's blouse and bra were removed by a nurse so as to listen for sounds of breathing. It is worth noting that for the second time in twenty-four hours, a doctor was seeing L.'s breasts, something that had been expressly forbidden by the patient's husband when he had signed her into the hospital. At that time he had stated that he refused to allow any male doctor or nurse to view his wife's breasts or unclothed body. He further said he was the only man who had ever seen her body, and that L and he had an agreement that no other man was ever to view her. For that reason, she had never, during their married life, been seen by a male doctor.

As I listened with my stethoscope, her breathing sounds began to diminish, and finally I could not hear them. Neither could I feel air exiting from her nose or mouth, nor see the rise and fall of her chest wall. I looked at my watch and waited. After twenty seconds, I shook her and then slapped her across the face. By this time my own pulse was rapidly increasing. Still she didn't breathe. After about forty-five seconds, she again began to breathe, but in a shallow manner, at the rate of about ten breaths per minute. She again began clawing at her throat.

It was my feeling at this time that L.'s respiratory problem was indeed functional in nature, and with the necessary medical equipment ready, if I should need to intervene, I made the decision to treat her with an ice pack. It allowed me to accomplish a number of effects all at once. First, it served as a firm means of restraint, the patient being tightly packed in sheets. Next, it stimulated her breathing by causing her to shiver. Third, it lowered her body temperature, causing a tranquilizing effect without need to use drugs. Fourth, it allowed her the regressive, yet safe, experience of returning to the womb, the warmth and security therein. Fifth, with preconscious awareness it allowed me to put on a display of unusual treatment technique in front of a group of nurses who were clearly unimpressed with my skills as a psychiatrist. Finally, and only retrospectively, did I realize that it allowed me to again cover the patient's breasts, which had been uncovered in defiance of the husband's taboo, as well as my own in regard to physically examining my own therapy patients.

The patient was packed in ice-cold sheets, after all of her clothes had been removed by a nurse. Quickly, she began to shiver and her breathing became deeper and more rapid. She appeared to relax and after about five minutes she began to mumble about her grandfather. She kept repeating, "I loved him. I loved him." She then began to weep softly. She was still unresponsive to my voice. She remained quiet for five minutes and then suddenly began to struggle in the pack. The facial musculature tightened severely and she appeared very angry. She then began to grit her teeth, making a loud, grinding noise. She remained unresponsive, and then, suddenly started mumbling, "I hate him. I hate him. I hate him," but would say no more. I sat quietly by her side, at times mopping her forehead with a warm towel. She appeared to be undergoing an intense abreactive experience.

After forty-five minutes in the pack, the patient appeared quite peaceful. I decided to attempt to bring her out of her dissociated state with the use of hypnosis, something I had seen demonstrated twice before. If I was going to be omnipotent, and if I was correct in thinking this to be hysterical behavior, I might just as well be as dramatic and magical about it as I knew how. Much to my amazement, she responded, and within a couple of minutes was able to speak with me in a totally coherent manner, without evidence of a frank thought disorder.

She spoke of being frightened. She feared that her husband was angry with her for being in the hospital. She expressed total amnesia for the experience just completed. She then asked me in a pleading voice, "Please let me die, please let me kill myself. I feel empty." She then went on to speak of her hatred of her husband and her mother. She talked of her father, whom she feared she had let down in his dying years, and of her dead grandfather, whom she loved dearly. She then told me that none of the therapists she had ever seen had helped her and told me that I could not help either. Again, she asked me to let her die. I again firmly told her that I would not allow her to die.

The patient, as it turned out, was not to make another suicide attempt during the ensuing nine weeks of her hospitalization. Perhaps there was no further need, for within the first twelve hours of our meeting, she had aroused in me a strong protective feeling, which I would eventually come to fear, as her strong symbiotic needs became clear.

THE USE OF EMPATHY AND INTUITION

In assessing this most important first day of contact with the patient certain responses in the realm of empathy and intuition on the part of the therapist become clear. The approach to this patient, after the standard psychiatric history had been gathered, was one of developing empathy, later to be converted into an intuitive intervention. For the beginning psychiatrist, with little psychotherapeutic knowledge and even less experience, the empathic understanding of the patient—and its conversion via intuition to insight—leads to the therapeutic intervention.

Greenson (1960) in his classic paper on empathy describes this phenomenon as the sharing and partial but temporary participation in the emotional experience of the patient. He states that "the main motive of empathy is to achieve an understanding of the patient." This, more than any other approach to the patient, is what the beginning psychiatrist most often attempts—to understand the patient. He does this at great risk! The new therapist navigates the treacherous straits between detachment on one side and involvement on the other. The therapist may adopt a detached, omnipotent stance or an involved, regressive one. But perhaps the greatest risk for the young therapist is countertransference. As Shapiro (1974) intimates, the therapist's anxiety can "lead him to project his own past relationships and interactions onto the present in the name of empathy, to the detriment of understanding either himself or his patient."

Let us then return to the early phase of this case and examine the interventions made in light of the previous cautions regarding empathy.

Most evident and perhaps most controversial in that some, including the supervisor, would consider it a technical error was the stance I took of an omnipotent rescuer or, as Searles (1967) might suggest, my "Dedicated Physician" role. In a purely empathic response I was identifying with the patient's utter lack of control and through my own countertransference fears instituted the firmest of controls. Not only is it clear that the patient's loss of ego boundaries caused her to experience massive regression, but it instilled in me a fear of losing control of the situation and hence a massive display on my part of omnipotent rescue tactics. Clearly, there were other avenues available to me in dealing with this initial crisis in the treatment. Having read Frieda Fromm-Reichmann's (1950) *Techniques of Intensive Psychotherapy* and seen them used by those who were influenced by her, I used my own interpretation of them in an idealized manner when faced with crisis and lack of confidence. I have no doubt that a more strict medical response to this crisis would have been effective. However, it lacked the idealized vision of a psychological response that I now saw as my major tool as a new psychiatrist.

Empathy in this early phase was in retrospect a process of sharing and experiencing the patient's feelings. It led to periods of identification, countertransference, projection, anxiety, and finally intuitive action. As Greenson (1960) points out "empathy often leads to intuition. You arrive at the feelings and pictures via empathy, but intuition sets off the signal in the analytic ego that you have hit it." Although the empathic response included numerous technical and unconscious therapeutic errors, the intuitive response to exert firm control on a patient who was clammering for safety seemed justified. To have denied it would have risked possible suicide.

THE THERAPEUTIC RELATIONSHIP

Over the ensuing three months, the therapeutic relationship was to unfold. It would involve not only myself and the patient, but her husband as well. It emerged that L. was to make use of symbiosis as a her major defense against impending psychosis. She was, in fact, to transfer her symbiotic needs from her husband to myself. And, as with her husband and her two previous therapists, I was to be seduced into providing the symbiosis she required.

In developing a psychotherapeutic plan, two important outside sources of information became helpful in my approach to the patient. The first was the psychological testing, which was done by a highly experienced clinical psychologist who also served as a supervisor on the case. The results of the test offered me clues, as well as warning signals, in my approach to the patient. In particular, the findings of an underlying potential for psychosis directed me toward a more supportive tack with the patient. The other clue was the psychologist's perception, which was quickly confirmed clinically, that L. had the capacity to readily evince from people a protective and supportive attitude, bordering on the symbiotic. This readily understandable need on her part to evoke this response became one of the more important therapeutic issues in the treatment. Finally, the testing made me aware of certain ego strengths which the patient exhibited and which would serve as points of focus in rebuilding the patient's shattered ego function.

The second key aid in approaching the therapy was the patient's past hospital and therapy records. These provided me with information regarding the successes and failures in her previous treatment plan. This knowledge aided me in avoiding the pitfalls that would certainly have occurred if the prior experience of other therapists had not been available to me. In particular, my decision to keep L. hospitalized for a long period of time, treating her with supportive psychotherapy without allowing her to leave the hospital, plus the enforced separation between the patient and her husband all came out of my knowledge of her past treatment history. Finally, the task of psychotherapy was made significantly easier by the adjunctive use of a phenothiazine, which allowed her to carry on with the often high-anxiety process of psychotherapy.

THE PSYCHOTHERAPY

Psychotherapy over the three and one-half months that I treated L. divided into three phases. When describing the three stages, I will summarize their development and touch on some of the therapeutic and supervisory issues involved.

During the first month, I met with L. daily for 30-45-minute sessions at scheduled intervals. This was to facilitate the formation of an interpersonal relationship and to reinforce reality through limit-setting for the patient. For the first week of treatment she was kept on a twenty-four-hour one-to-one nursing coverage to further reinforce reality and to prevent another suicide attempt. By the second week this was no longer necessary.

Therapy sessions revolved around a more thorough history-taking and a gentle exploration into the current situation. In the second session I told the patient that I would not allow any visitors, including her husband. She seemed visibly relieved by this decision. For the next ten days she was permitted to speak with her husband for ten minutes a day on the telephone. After that they were able to visit daily. In order to allow for this total separation from her husband, it became apparent that I would have to build an alliance with him from the start. He was seen on the second hospital day by myself and a social worker. The husband, J., was a forty-year-old, self-trained musician who ran his own music school. He was a carefully groomed and conservatively dressed man. Indeed, he described himself as conservative, commenting that he was somewhat puritanical. He came across as a very rigid and obsessive person. He stated that he had to have a reason for everything he did. He also asserted that his marriage to L. was unique and involved a total commitment to each other, allowing no individual expression. He explained that there were no individuals in the marriage, only a total working unit. He admitted to making all the decisions for L. and treating her like a child. He was understandably disappointed by my decision not to let him see his wife, but, surprisingly enough, he agreed to abide by my decision.

The meeting with J. brought the first supervisory issue to the surface. My initial internal response to him was, to put it bluntly, one of strong disgust. I felt sure he was totally to blame for L.'s predicament, including her symbiotic attachment to him. My intuition was only partially correct and I needed to be shown where it was wrong. Supervision centered about my seeing his side of the relationship and how the patient herself contributed to its bizarreness. It was pointed out to me that, without a good working relationship with J., he would inevitably sabotage the therapy. I did, in fact, establish a good relationship with him, seeing him once a week for the next two months. And with no little surprise, I can tell you that I developed a warm and genuine fondness for this man whom I originally loathed.

My work with L. soon uncovered a lifelong battle she had fought to maintain her tenuous grip on reality. She described her early years as frequently frightening due to her fear of ghosts and monsters. Her early screen memories were particularly revealing; her first, at age two and one-half was of going away with her family to a mountain cabin where her older sisters continually taunted and scared her by telling her ghost stories. At age four, she described a sleepwalking experience where she got up in the early morning, still asleep, but claiming her eyes to be open, and stated that she looked out the window and saw a herd of cattle grazing on her front lawn. She then returned to sleep. She then stated that she could not tell the difference between what was real and what was imaginary. She commented that it was impossible for cattle to have been grazing on the lawn of her suburban house. During her hospital stay, L., in fact, actually experienced a documentd sleepwalking episode, much like the one described.

The last screen memory, at the age of four and one-half, was of an evening when her parents were out and she was home alone with a baby-sitter. At dusk, some mischievous neighborhood boys started lighting matches on her front porch. She saw them through the front window and became convinced that they were fire-breathing monsters. She became frightened and hysterical and did not settle down until her parents returned hours later. To this day, she could not tolerate her front windows not being covered by drapes as soon as it became dark.

During the first week of therapy, L. was able to tell me in very graphic terms about her depression and her dissociated episodes. She described the depression as a massive, rolling wave coming toward her, ready to overwhelm her and engulf her. She would begin to feel empty and frightened, and sometimes hear internal voices telling her to kill herself. It was a that point that she would take flight from psychosis by withdrawing to a dissociative state.

Another important historical fact that came out in the early session with L. was a history of perceptual distortions, involving depth perception, dating back to childhood. These distortions were confirmed by the psychological testing. One cannot help but wonder how this apparently congenital defect in perceiving reality interacted with her psychological development and her need for symbiotic relationships.

The first month saw the formation of an intense, frightening, and at times, demanding interpersonal relationship. During this time, the patient would frequently ask me, during our sessions, whether I was angry with her. The question usually arose toward the end of a session, but it would often be preceded by silence between myself and her. She would then regard me with a very intense and sensual look on her face. She would seem to become very distant to me, as if in another world. She would then ask me if I were angry with her. I would invariably reply that I wasn't angry with her, that I wondered what it was that made her feel that way. She would without fail respond that it was my silence that made her think that.

These episodes became a supervision issue in connection with trying to understand their meaning, as well as how to respond to them. My own fantasy about this behavior was that this was L., the infant, responding toward me as if to her mother. She and her husband had described L.'s mother as cold and distant and had nicknamed her the "iceberg." One could imagine L. as an infant, responding to her cold, distant mother by internal flight and external seductiveness in an attempt to deal with the lack of maternal love, though still trying to elicit it. My occasional silences and perceived distance must have reminded her of this maternal mode and could only be described by her adult self as being angry and rejecting.

The empathic response that had characterized my early relationship to the patient was now being dismantled by reason. I no longer wanted to be the omnipotent rescuer that I had set myself up to be. In fact, in retrospect she was correct in perceiving my unconscious display of anger. In essence, I was rejecting her and her wish to make me godlike and therefore totally responsible for her existence, be it happy or sad. Clearly, my earliest errors were catching up with me.

However, the errors did serve one useful purpose. The ability of L. to project the transferential part of her anger onto me allowed her to exist within the bounds of reality rather than in the dissociated state she had exhibited during those first nights in the hospital. Clearly, this murderous rage, which she blithely called anger, skimmed beneath the surface, threatening to explode at any important figure who would deny her love.

It was early on decided in supervision that the way to approach L. was not through deep interpretations, which would threaten her tenuous hold on reality. I was therefore faced with having to respond to the episodes with a more supportive, yet helpful, response than merely asking her why she felt that way.

I finally arrived at a compromise between being supportive and being interpretive. When L. would ask me if I was angry with her, I would reply that I was not; still I could understand that she might be confused by my occasional silences and that it was perfectly acceptable for her to find out how I felt by asking me. I had become aware from both the patient and her husband that similar episodes occurred between them during which she would be convinced that he was angry with her and she would become severely depressed. I suggested to her that when she did have these feelings with her husband it would be important for her to check them out with him just as she did with me. Here we see most clearly the significant countertransference error that I, like her husband, was involved in. My empathy and intuition were telling me to let the patient be honest with me. I would ask her, even encourage her, to tell me when she thought I was angry with her and didn't understand why. The reality, however, was that my countertransference anger toward her clearly was being experienced. As a "Dedicated Physician" my superego couldn't tolerate the thought of my being angry with a patient toward whom I was to be ostensibly warm and understanding. Because supervision was not being done on a countertransference basis both myself and the supervisor continued with a blind spot present. I continued to point out to the patient that ambiguous or unstructured situations were difficult for her and that she must continually seek to structure her surroundings in order to feel safe within them. In retrospect, I was talking to my "self."

If my anger toward the patient was a cause for countertransference errors that led to slow and painful recognition of its presence, my erotic countertransference remained something that I could only barely recognize before being banished with conscious intent. It was never mentioned in supervision; yet it clearly confused me and caused me to be defensive with the patient. For a beginning psychiatrist it is perhaps less acceptable to have erotic feelings toward a patient than to have hostile ones. In retrospect, when the patient looked at me with a sensuous gaze and then seemed to dissociate, I too was forced to deny and repress my erotic feelings from my conscious awareness—hence furthering my countertransference errors.

Another important issue that came up during the first two months of therapy was L.'s frequent wish to leave the hospital against medical advice. Each time this would happen it would be as the result of some painful interaction with her husband. Her husband demanded a full report of everything that went on at the hospital, including details of the men that L. talked with, the places she went, and the things that we talked about in therapy. After hearing of her activities, he would often attempt to engender guilt in her. This would renew her fears that he was angry with her and cause her to become severely depressed and withdrawn and finally to ask to leave the hospital. She constantly feared J.'s wrath and the possible loss of her pathological, yet protective, symbiotic relationship with him. On one occasion, I told her that if she tried to leave, I would have commitment papers filed. Again, I was taking the omnipotent stance to assuage my own fear that she would leave the hospital and kill herself. I knew unconsciously that I could not accept the guilt that she had by now induced in me. My intuition and what seemed to be reasonable decisions regarding L.'s management were clearly being guided by my own countertransference problems. To my good fortune, each time she responded well to this enforced structure. However, she was unable to talk about what was happening to her when these episodes would occur.

The second phase of therapy began as a slow process of working through our relationship. I continued to help L. to understand her relationship with J. and her sometimes distorted perceptions of the therapeutic relationship with myself.

TWO VIGNETTES

At this point I would like to describe two vignettes of events which transpired in connection with the clinical work done with L. The first episode occurred early in treatment and is an example of the failure of the therapist to establish empathy and make an intuitive interpretation. The second, ten days later, shows the successful use of empathy in making an intuitive interpretation.

The First Episode

The patient spent the first part of the last session describing how her first leave outside the hospital had gone. Her description of how her husband had wanted her to make love to him led into a retelling of her sexual history and its associated conflicts. Toward the end of the session L. began to talk about her feelings about the relationship with Mr. X. The patient had seen Mr. X in the hospital outpatient psychiatric clinic one year previous to this present hospitalization. She had developed a psychotic transference to this therapist who was a beginning clinical psychology intern. She had fallen in love with him and hoped he would marry her. She now told me that she was totally over her feelings toward him. She had earlier described herself as wanting him at some point to marry her, but knew inside that he would not marry "a neurotic woman as herself."

I looked at the patient who seemed quite engrossed in her thoughts, and said to myself, "She doesn't really mean she's over Mr. X—she's really asking me to help her talk about her feelings toward him." My empathic experiencing of her feelings led me to say to her: "It seems to me that you really aren't over your feelings toward Mr. X. Perhaps you would like to talk more about him?" Shortly thereafter she looked at me and said she was frightened and nervous. She then asked me if I was angry with her. I asked her why she felt that way and she said because I seemed quiet today. I told her that I wasn't angry with her but I was interested in knowing why she felt that way. She said that she was feeling insecure and just now she was beginning to experience a crushing feeling of depression coming over her. As I watched she momentarily dissociated. When she regained contact with me she asked if we could end the session. I said yes!

Clearly, my empathic understanding of her was incorrect and my intuitive interventions had led to her dissociation. Retrospectively, I was able to view my empathic response as defensive in nature. What L. was perhaps saying to me was that, if she really did get over her strong feelings toward her previous therapist, would she or could she develop those same feelings of attachment toward me?

Greenson (1960) describes what I have called the defensive use of empathy as "the loss of control of empathy." He describes the typical situation where a young therapist finds himself experiencing a "sexual or hostile undercurrent of feelings in his patient which then interferes with his capacity for objectivity and understanding." In the name of empathy I was defending myself against the sexual and hostile feelings that I was unconsciously experiencing from the patient.

The Second Episode

During the fifth week, a major breakthrough came when L. was able to talk of her relationship with me. This was the first opening that allowed us to begin to discuss our therapeutic relationship.

The previous two weeks had seen a steady improvement in L.'s feeling of well-being and sense of self. Therapy sessions had become more spontaneous and less frightening for both patient and therapist. With the patient's first overnight pass approaching, she had become moderately depressed and the previous therapy session had brought out despairing feelings of ever getting well. She stated that she did not know what she would do at home, how to take care of her husband and her brother-in-law, who was coming to visit. She continued talking about these vague anxieties. During the middle of the interview, I began to sneeze and started to blow my nose frequently. I did this three or four times. Each time I would begin to do this, she would stop talking and watch me carefully. Finally she said, "I hope you're not getting the flu." I asked her why she said that. She responded first by saying, "Well, many people are getting the flu now, and I hope you don't get it." At this point I experienced what Greenson (1960) calls the "Aha Experience." By this he means the "involuntary and pleasant sensation of suddenly grasping and understanding something hitherto obscure." At this point, I knew empathetically that L. was trying to tell me how afraid she was of becoming symbiotically attached to me. My "analyzing ego" was now able to formulate an intervention to help the patient bring to consciousness that which I intuitively believed she was experiencing.

The following interchange then took place: I said, "What would it mean if I did get the flu?" She finally said, "Well, you might have to stay home from work." I asked her how this would affect her. She became visibly more upset, and finally started to say to me, with much affect, "I don't want this to happen to me again; I don't want it to happen again. Haven't I learned my lesson?" I asked her what she meant by this. Finally, after much difficulty, she said, "I don't want to happen with you what happened with Mr. X" (her previous therapist). I asked her to explain this and she replied, "I don't want to get attached to you." I asked her what it was that made her frightened of being attached to me. She said she was afraid it would ruin our relationship and, therefore, ruin her chances for getting better.

She then started talking about how she was again feeling hopeless about ever getting better. She said she didn't know what to do about her anxieties and her recently developed trouble with sleeping. I expressed to her the fact

that I felt she was trying to get me to rescue her because of what she was saying over the last ten minutes. She looked at me very quizzically. I then said to
her that I would not rescue her, that she must learn to take care of herself.
She seemed somewhat relieved at hearing this and repeated to me, question-
ably, "You will not rescue me, will you?" I said no. By the end of the interview
the patient appeared noticeably less depressed.

This session marked a decisive change in the relationship between L. and
myself. She was able to verbalize her feelings of becoming attached to me, and I
was able to verbalize my feelings that I could no longer rescue her or protect
her, nor would I allow her to become attached to me. What had started out to
be a difficult and depressing session for both patient and therapist had been
turned into a movement of important understanding through the therapist's
use of his empathic feelings toward the patient and his intuition that the patient was reexperiencing an important previous relationship brought out by
her concern for my health. For the advanced therapist a careful awareness
and knowledge of transference and countertransference would have sufficed.
For the beginning therapist the therapeutic intervention depended on an empathic understanding leading to intuitive action.

THE CLOSING PHASE

Finally, let me discuss the closing phase of therapy with L., involving termination and separation. In the sixth week of her hospitalization, a major supervision issue arose around my initial plan to keep the patient hospitalized
for four to six months and do intensive psychotherapy. It was pointed out to
me, and soon became apparent in therapy, that this was not a wise idea. In
fact, it was most pointedly brought to my attention by the patient herself, who
began to talk about Mrs. Y (previous female therapist), and how she really
wanted to go back to her for therapy. A very important part of me was
wounded and felt rejected by this feeling of L.'s, but a more intellectual part
knew that the patient was making a wise decision regarding our relationship.
In the first month of our work, she had become very close to me, and she was
now feeling the need to separate in order to preserve her integrity and her
marriage. In the seventh week, I met with Mrs. Y and she agreed to resume
seeing L. in therapy. She began to see the patient two times per week in her
office, and I cut back my sessions with L. to twice a week and kept them
geared to surface, nonemotional issues. During the eighth week, L. made a
final gesture to test my feelings toward her. Her husband became angry at her
for taking a walk with other patients and a male aid. The next day she asked
to sign out of the hospital. At this time she looked as depressed as when she
had first entered the hospital. That morning she had made remarks to one of
the nurses that she felt like burning her face. She said this would make her ug-

ly so that J. would have no cause to be jealous of other men's attention toward her. She sat in my office wringing her hands and looking tearful. The first feeling that went through my mind was one of panic. I kept thinking that I had failed and all the work was now going down the drain. We were back to where we had started.

I sat there quietly for a moment, thinking. Finally, I took a deep, existential breath, and made the most direct interpretation I had thus far made to her. I told her she was acting like a little child. She had gotten everyone upset by her pouting, her talk of suicide, and her wish to leave the hospital. She had upset the nurses, the doctor, her husband, and even the other patients. I told her she was testing us to see if we really cared and if we would protect her. I let the interpretation fly and sat back to see what would happen. There was silence. She continued to look at the floor. Then slowly, her head came up and she looked me straight in the eye, as an impish grin began to appear on her face. She then said to me, "Doctor, is that really what I'm doing, acting like a little girl? Gosh, I'm sorry, I didn't mean to upset you." She then sat back and smiled. The session ended. I smiled a sigh of relief and relaxed.

As a beginning therapist it was important for me to label the above interaction as *interpretation*, for that would give it the stamp of experience. Again it seems evident that the response was intuitive and based on an empathic belief that the patient could understand what I was saying. But more than that, it was a reasonable response and perhaps for the first time in the therapy one that was honest for me. The countertransference, the blind spots, the reaction formations on my part were becoming evident. What I believe I was feeling can be paraphrased thus:

"God damnit, L., you *do* make me angry sometimes. But, that's okay because my anger won't kill you as you must think your anger has the power to kill. I can be angry at you, have erotic feelings toward you, be upset by you, and yet still be your therapist and help you get better. You don't have to test me like this to prove it."

The next week was spent discussing separation and meeting with L. and J. together. A final issue arose between J. and myself regarding his fear that L. was pregnant. She had not had a period in forty days. She and her husband had both assured me that they had not had sexual intercourse during her hospitalization. I could only reflect to myself that J. needed reassurance that neither I nor other male staff had impregnated his wife. Blood and urine pregnancy tests were negative and nine and a half weeks after her suicide attempt, L. was discharged.

After that, I saw her three times in the outpatient deparment, because Mrs. Y (her therapist) was on vacation. During our first outpatient session, L. appeared dressed in a very tight sweater, her hair down, and in a seductive manner proceeded to tell me what a wonderful person I was, how I saved her life, how she didn't know how she could get along with me, and how much she would miss me. I reminded her of what psychotherapy was. I told her it was an intense personal experience between two individuals—one a patient and one a therapist—which took place in a unique environment. I told her that it had a beginning and an end. I told her that it was often difficult for people that had shared such an intimate experience to say good-bye, and yet this perhaps was the most important part of the experience. I told her that she could not take me with her, but that she could take our psychotherapeutic work with her and use it in the future. Finally, I told her that her work in therapy was only just beginning.

She smiled at me again, telling me what a nice person I was and how much she would miss me. I took a deep breath, trying to think of how far I had developed in this therapy, and told her that it was nice of her to say those things about me, and that I, too, would miss our work together. I then ended the session.

At our last session, L.'s hair was back up over her head and she was dressed in one of her older dresses. We spent the whole session talking about the current state of classical music.

She went back to work for the first time in eighteen months, and though still emotionally shaky, she did well. At our last session I said good-bye to her with a good deal of warm feelings of accomplishment as well as of trepidation. I was not so naive as to think that three months of therapy had changed a lifetime of pathology. The future seemed uncertain and the prognosis guarded, but, as I imagined a father must feel when he sends his favorite daughter off to college far, far away, I had to be stoic and not show my doubts. But for good measure, I gave her a two-month supply of birth control pills and Stelazine.

IN THE END

In presenting this first psychotherapy case of a beginning psychiatric resident, I have attempted to portray both the constructive use of empathy and intuition as well as its erroneous use. I have implied that these assets when properly used and understood can aid another human being in psychological pain. The beginning resident is often overwhelmed by his colleagues and his teachers with a plethora of philosophies and techniques with which he may gird himself during his initial treatment attempts. Certainly, these tend to allay the often distressing anxiety a resident feels when he first attempts to treat a patient without a stethoscope close at hand. It is at this point in his career, perhaps more than at any other, that he is in such close proximity to the tools that can serve him so well throughout his career as a therapist—his own empathy and intuition. However, for these tools to be truly valuable the beginning therapist must be aware of how they can be used erroneously. He must begin to understand his own countertransference problems, his own anxieties, his own defensive structure — all of which can severely interfere with his use of his native qualities. This happens slowly and painfully; it is a process not an event.

In looking back at the therapy with L., I find myself wondering why she recovered. It is clear that very basic errors of a technical nature were made in her treatment. There are times when I am tempted to wonder if it wasn't the phenothiazine and the time spent in the hospital that accounted for the improvement in the patient. In the end, however, I must admit to a growing sense that I, despite my inexperience, played a significant role in the return to a more healthy position that occurred for this patient.

One of the most difficult aspects of becoming a psychiatrist is developing a faith in yourself as a therapist and in your ability to help people toward emotional health. Developing respect for one's own embryonic skills is also a process — not an event. I cannot help but believe that this development of self-respect and faith in one's abilities begins here, with recognizing the importance and potential of the native qualities that one human being can bring to bear toward understanding and aiding another human being in distress.

REFERENCES

Fromm-Reichmann, F. (1950). *Principles of Intensive Psychotherapy*. Chicago: Univ. of Chicago Press.

Greenson, R. (1960). Empathy and its vicissitudes. *International Journal of Psychoanalysis* 41:418-424.

Searles, H. F. (1967). The "Dedicated Physician" in psychotherapy and psychoanalysis. *Cross currents in Psychiatry and Psychoanalysis*, ed. R. W. Gibson. Philadelphia: Lippincott.

Shapiro, T. (1974). The development and distortions of empathy. *Psychoanalytic Quarterly* 43: 4-25.

Will, O.A., Jr. (1971). Psychotherapy and schizophrenia: Implications for human living. Reprinted from Proceedings of the Fourth International Symposium, Turku, Finland, August 4-7, 1971. International Congress Series No. 259.

On Becoming a Psychiatrist: Discussion of "Empathy and Intuition in Becoming a Psychiatrist," by Ronald J. Blank

Robert Langs, M.D.

Clinical Assistant Professor of Psychiatry
Division of Psychoanalytic Education
Downstate Medical Center, Brooklyn

Using the data from Blank's (1976) description of his clinical efforts with his first patient, selected issues on becoming a psychiatrist and psychotherapist are explored. Considered among the motives for entering this profession are opportunities for the therapist to projectively identify into his patients, and to introjectively identify with and contain his patients' psychopathology. The relationship between empathy and intuition on the one hand, and projection and projective identification on the other, is also studied, as is the need for the application of the validating process in confirming all so-called empathic and intuitive responses on the part of the therapist. Counter-transference influences on the experience and use of empathy and intuition are also investigated. The development of therapeutic misalliances and framework "cures," the distinction between transference and nontransference, the constructive elements contained in essentially countertransference-based interventions, the mastery of countertransference difficulties, and the choice of insight-oriented versus noninsightful therapeutic modalities are also discussed.

INTRODUCTION

Specific investigations of the motivations for becoming a psychiatrist and of the psychiatric resident's earliest modes of functioning appear to be quite rare. Because of this, Blank's (1976) description of the psychotherapy of his first patient offers unique data with which to consider some specific issues related to the choice of psychiatry or psychotherapy as a profession. His presentation reveals not only the expressions of inner disturbances inevitably found in the beginning therapist—countertransference problems that he will spend the balance of his career endeavoring to master—but also the kernels of constructive functioning that he will hopefully develop as the basic core of his therapeutic aptitudes.

Using the material offered by Blank, with its inevitable limitations, I will discuss some of the apparent universal issues with which every budding psychiatrist must deal and will focus on the following selected issues (see Langs, 1976a) for a broader discussion of the therapist's functioning) : the motivations for becoming a psychiatrist, and especially their relationship to the mechanisms of projective and introjective identification and the therapist's containing functions; the specific advantages and disadvantages that derive from the therapist's early and relatively naive functioning; the role of the validating process in psychotherapy and in testing out the subjectively identified experiences of both empathy and intuition; the means of early therapeutic "cures" and their relationship to "misalliance cures"; the distinctions between transference and nontransference, and countertransference and noncountertransference; and the functions of the framework of the psychotherapeutic situation.

While I know of no precedent for this attempt to utilize a specific description of a therapeutic interaction as a means of developing observations related to the problems and motives in becoming a psychiatrist, this study has as its heritage a wide range of investigations related to the analyst's nonconflicted (noncountertransference-based) and conflicted (countertransference-based) functioning (see Langs, 1976a, for details). More specifically, there have been several notable general discussions of the motivations for becoming a psychoanalyst and the traits that best serve this profession. Among the most well known of these efforts are the papers by Sharpe (1930), Fleming (1961), and Greenson (1966, 1967). Greenson in particular attempted to define the central genetic experiences and intrapsychic conflicts that contribute to the choice of psychoanalysis as a profession, and he stressed the role of pregenital sadistic drives and various pregenital and oedipal libidinal conflicts, the contribution of primal-scene experiences, the role of various defensive maneuvers, and aspects of identification with the mother. Along different lines, Olinick (1969), in his study of empathy and regression in the service of the other, suggested that a powerful motivation in becoming a psychiatrist derives from a rescue fantasy involving a depressed mother—a thesis that seems especially relevant to the material we shall discuss. All of these authors emphasized the importance of the mastery of such underlying conflicted constellations in the effective functioning of a therapist. With this as a general background, I will now turn to the data offered in Blank's (1976) paper.

THE MOTIVATIONS FOR BECOMING A PSYCHIATRIST

Opportunities to Projectively and Introjectively Identify

Of all the motives related to the wish to be a psychiatrist, I should like to focus on two interrelated determinants: the therapist's wish for opportunities to projectively identify[1] aspects of his own inner conflicts, unconscious fantasies, and introjects into his patients; and contrarywise, his wish to have the opportunity to receive—introjectively identify with—pathological projective identifications from his patients. Related to these motives are the therapist's wishes to have the patient serve as a container for the former's contents and, in addition, to serve as a receptacle for the pathological contents of the patient (Bion, 1962, 1963). These motivations may be adaptive or maladaptive, pathological or nonpathological, openly expressed or defended against, and well managed or sublimated on the one hand, or poorly managed and unsublimated on the other. Before discussing this dimension further, I will turn to selected material in Blank's presentation that relate to these ideas.

In this context, it is of interest that Blank first met his patient while she was receiving an intravenous infusion. She was somewhat older than he and was frustrated and depressed. The therapist's first intervention was offered at their second meeting and in response to the patient's expression of a strong wish to die; he told her firmly that he would not allow her to die.

Here, we see one type of effort at projective identification that is characteristic for many therapist initiates: the need to intervene without permitting the development of derivatives related to the patient's unconscious fantasies and to do so by placing manifestly good contents into the patient. Such an intervention reflects the rather characteristic ambivalence seen in beginning—and even more experienced—psychotherapists in regard to unconscious fantasies and introjects. The selection of psychiatry as a profession relates to the wish to delve into the unconscious fantasies of others, and interactionally, to accept these unconscious contents from the patient into oneself. However, the dread of the primitive aspects of unconscious fantasies and introjects and of the internal damage they will generate often prompts strong defenses within the therapist against such expressions. This leads to many premature interventions and other efforts to shut off the patient's unconscious communications.

In terms of my central thesis, such an intervention unconsciously appears to express several trends within the therapist. First, there is the unconscious need to place good, hopeful, and controlled contents into the patient. However, by making this effort prematurely, the therapist surrounds these good qualities with his own anxiety, so that the projective identification has both positive and negative, helpful and disturbing, aspects. In addition, the intervention serves to disrupt the flow of the patient's associations and unconsciously conveys to him or her the therapist's refractoriness toward being a container for his or her more pathological contents. We may note that Blank's comment came after the patient began to talk about her deteriorating marriage and sexual relationship with her husband—material that may have generated some anxiety within the therapist. Since the patient responded to the intervention with feelings of hopelessness and emptiness, she may have unconsciously detected the therapist's difficulties. While this may seem speculative, it should be noted that patients are extremely sensitive to this component of the therapeutic interaction (Langs, 1976a).[2]

Next, we learn that Blank found himself lingering at the hospital hoping to see a repetition of the previous night's events during which the patient had made a suicide attempt that had necessitated efforts at resuscitation. Among other implications, we see here an intense wish, expressed in a seemingly countertransference-based form, to have an opportunity to directly contain the patient's sickness, so that we may suspect a pathological need to do this. In general, such pathological needs are extremely common among neophyte psychiatrists. These wishes may prompt the therapist to intervene incorrectly and to unconsciously provoke the patient into regressive episodes that the therapist can readily submit to introjective identification and work over within himself.

While we have no data in regard to Blank's unconscious communications to the patient, we learn next that the patient did indeed attempt to strangle herself once again. The therapist's comments in this context afford an opportunity to demonstrate the distinction between projection and projective identification, mechanisms often used by psychiatrists in their interaction with the patient. Blank indicates that he was aware that the patient had aroused in him a rescue fantasy that he later found to be her dominant mode of social interaction with him. However, this unilateral suggestion overlooks his evident parallel needs. Thus, the focus on the patient's need to be rescued is here in part a defensive projection. This could extend into a projective identification in the therapist's interaction with the patient—i.e., in to an actual interactional effort—if he were to communicate to the patient his wishes to rescue her—and there is some evidence that this did indeed occur.

Blank next describes his active efforts in response to the problem he found upon going to the patient. He reacted with a strong appeal, made physical contact with her, and observed her exposed breasts. He had violated a taboo set by his patient's husband, and she responded with a prolonged period of breath-holding, and with further clawing at her throat. Once the patient's respiration had returned, the decision was made to treat her with an ice pack.

The patient then responded by speaking about her grandfather and expressing her love for him, and then her hatred for someone else; she was directly unresponsive to the therapist. Next, the therapist turned to hypnosis to bring the patient out of her dissociated state, and he was amazed to find her responsive. The patient was amnesic and pleaded that she be allowed to die, stating that she felt empty, and then talking of her father whom she feared she had let down in his dying years and again of her love for her dead grandfather. She expressed the concern that the therapist could not help her, and he responded with the reassertion of his determination not to allow her to die.

In his discussion, Blank indicates that he felt quite protective toward the patient and that he had become aware of her strong symbiotic needs. He suggests that he responded empathically to her and with intuition as well, although he notes the danger of projecting aspects of his own past relationships and interactions onto the present situation in the name of empathy (Shapiro, 1974). He viewed himself as identifying with the patient's lack of control and suggested that his empathy led him to offer her the firmest controls available. Blank also expresses a fear of losing control of the situation and acknowledges an aspect of omnipotence in his rescue tactics.

For our purposes, we see in this interaction a situation in which the patient offered herself as an unconscious container for aspects of the therapist's difficulties. The therapist thereby projectively identified into the patient his own symbiotic needs and possibly his own fears on some level of suicidal impulses. For her part, the patient attempted to projectively identify into the therapist aspects of her own self-destructiveness, to which the therapist responded by modifying the classical boundaries of the therapeutic relationship (Langs, 1973, 1976a) — in making physical contact with the patient, observing her breasts, offering her an ice pack, wiping her brow, and then, finally, hypnotizing her. These measures appear to make evident the therapist's own need for symbiosis and fusion, and for the patient to serve as a container for his own inner disturbances. [3]

Throughout this interaction we observe efforts by the therapist to project — i.e., intrapsychically attribute to the patient — and to projectively identify — interactionally place into the patient — aspects of his own inner needs and difficulties. Similarly, we see his repeated efforts to evoke regressive responses in her and his mixed reaction to their occurrence in that he very abruptly responds to these regressive communications with directives that indicate his refractoriness about containing them. The patient generally responded to this with disillusionment followed by a mobilization of her own resources.

I would therefore suggest that in this particular initial interaction, the patient's abrupt recovery reflects the development of a therapeutic misalliance (Langs, 1975a) that was both mutually seductive and hostile, and which gratified the symbiotic needs of both participants, thereby evoking what I have termed a misalliance or framework cure (Langs, 1976a). This constitutes momentary symptomatic recovery based on bilateral unconscious collusion that creates bastions — split off sectors of denied and repressed contents within the bipersonal therapeutic field (Baranger and Baranger, 1966; Langs, 1976a). This relief also stems from gross modifications of the framework which undo the buildup of the patient's pathological intrapsychic fantasies and anxieties. It appears that these vehicles were the primary modality of symptom alleviation in this case. My general clinical experience indicates that this is characteristic of beginning therapists.

The Wish to and Fear of Containing the Patient's Inner Contents

In this connection, two aspects of this material deserve specific discussion. The first relates to the unconscious motives on the part of the psychiatrist as these pertain to his wish to work with unconscious fantasies and introjects—inner contents that are usually viewed in terms of frightening, regressive, primitively sexual and aggressive material. As Greenson (1966) has noted, much of this relates to the child's curiosity regarding the contents of his mother's body, and undoubtedly such voyeuristic interests derive from a variety of specific individual experiences, intermixed with unconscious fantasies drawn from all levels of development.

The characteristic conflicts regarding the exploration of the patient's primitive inner contents are evident in the presentation by Blank. We see both his intense curiosity about his patient's fantasies and his defensiveness; the latter is reflected in efforts to obliterate their communication. It seems likely that the patient introjectively identified with the therapist's fear of her inner contents, and that this is another aspect of the mobilized misalliance cure which enabled this patient to seal off her symptoms. This struggle is handled in a not uncommon manner by invoking the concept of supportive treatment as a means of justifying the obliteration of the patient's unconscious fantasies and introjects. Accompanied with this rationalization is the decision not to do insight psychotherapy and not to offer so-called deep interpretations. [4]

It is quite common for those psychiatrists who dread their patients' inner contents to arrive at a similar rationalization that supports their turning away from any type of insight therapy. The early months in his training provide crucial interludes during which the therapist may choose to allow the patient to speak, or may consciously or unconsciously decide to shut off avenues related to the latter's unconscious communications. Throughout the paper, we see Blank interrupting the patient with some type of general and surface intervention at the very moment when she initiates movement in the direction of her inner struggles. These defenses are a factor in the disillusionment of many psychiatrists in regard to psychoanalytic psychotherapy and psychoanalysis.

In addition, while the therapist avows some struggle with his aggressive impulses with this patient, there is also strong evidence for an overlooked intense erotic countertransference—his examination of the patient and observation of her breasts, his difficulty in recognizing the patient's erotic transference and nontransference responses, his interruptions of the patient each time she approached communications related to himself, his fear of her becoming too dependent on him, and his final "gifts" to her. The therapist's unconscious defenses against his own erotic and hostile countertransferences led him to obliterate the communication of the patient's unconscious fantasies lest they approach these areas—especially the sexual. Put another way, it would appear that because of his own unresolved intrapsychic conflicts, the therapist was especially refractory about containing the contents of the patient's erotic fantasies and her essentially valid unconscious perceptions of the therapist in this area.

These data illuminate the choice of insightful or noninsightful therapeutic modalities by the early psychiatric resident. They clarify common rationalizations for advocating so-called supportive therapy that is actually, in part, designed to obliterate the patient's unconscious contents. There is a concomitant failure to acknowledge the supportive aspects of sound, sensitive interpretations (Langs, 1973, in press). This initial interaction also demonstrates the manner in which patients may invite projective identification by the therapist by offering themselves as containers for particular kinds of pathology that especially threaten the treating psychiatrist. The anticipation of this type of experience also motivates the therapist's choice of profession.

The Wish to Exclusively Possess the Patient

Another motive for becoming a psychiatrist reflected in this material is that of the search for the exclusive possession of the maternal and paternal objects, especially the preoedipal and oedipal mother. Stalemates in long-term psychotherapy and analysis are not infrequently based on the failure to resolve such unconscious wishes. In the material from Blank, these relatively unresolved wishes appear to be reflected in his decision not to allow her any visitors, and in his evident rivalry with the patient's husband for total possession of her. In addition, the therapist's response to the patient's initial suicidal gesture and respiratory difficulties seem to reflect wishes to totally possess and fuse with her. The material suggests symbiotic longings as well as later oedipal-based wishes. These possessive needs are a factor in the therapist's over-identification with, and excessive needs to introject from, his patient. They are also reflected in the therapist's threat to commit this patient should she wish to leave the hospital prematurely.

The resolution of the countertransference-based aspects of these motives is also evident. Blank develops some self-awareness in this area and ultimately informs the patient that he will not rescue her and that she will have to take care of herself. This is then reinforced when he apparently scolds her for behaving like a little child and for testing out whether he cared and would protect her. His display of anger and upset became the medium through which he was able to establish boundaries between himself and his patient that he was otherwise unable to effect. The patient's unconscious perception of the therapist's symbiotic and oedipal needs may well have been reflected in her failing to have her menstrual period; in this way she seems to have lived out fantasies of impregnation that were evident to the therapist, although apparently not interpreted to the patient.

The final expression of these needs for fusion and possession appears in the therapist's sessions with the patient after she left the hospital, while her subsequent therapist was on vacation. We can detect the Blank's sadness in giving up his patient, but we also find indications that he has resolved his more primitive longings for fusion. In these final moments, he conveys his needs for this patient on a more object-related and oedipal level, to which the patient apparently responded favorably. One may theorize that she found considerable relief through her perceptions of these changes in him.

EMPATHY AND INTUITION; PROJECTION AND PROJECTIVE IDENTIFICATION

Validating Seemingly Empathic and Intuitive Experiences

Both Beres and Arlow (1974) and Shapiro (1974) have addressed themselves to the need to utilize what I have termed the *validating process* (Langs, 1976a) to verify the therapist's empathic and intuitive experiences (see Langs, in press for a full review of these topics). In brief, these authors described empathy as an emotional form of knowing through a temporary identification with the patient, while intuition, according to the former authors, tends to involve the more cognitive aspects of immediate knowing. To these aspects of empathy and intuition, I would add the contributions of projective and introjective identification through which the therapist places into the patient aspects of his own inner contents in order to have the patient work them over (in part as efforts to evoke proxies; see Wangh, 1962 and Langs, 1976a), and through which the therapist interactionally takes into himself aspects of the patient's contents for similar processing. These mechanisms may have adaptive and maladaptive aspects, and the distinction between empathy and intuition as valid processes on the one hand, and projections, projective identifications, and introjective identifications on the other is by no means an absolute one. These latter processes are the basis for aspects of empathic and intuitive functioning, so that the validating process must be utilized to determine the extent to which the therapist is involved in their pathological use and the extent to which these are utilized in the service of understanding and interpreting to the patient.

Blank's presentation offers concrete data regarding the failure of many therapists to undertake efforts at validation in response to subjective experiences within themselves that they identify as empathic and/or intuitive. Such a validating process actually must include a careful exploration of the therapist's own subjective reactions and a continued assessment of the patient's associations for fantasied and perceptive responses in the context of the empathic or intuitive experience and the conclusions derived from it. The mate' ial from the patient following a valid empathic or intuitive response will almost always broaden the therapist's understanding of that response and will usually include allusions to helpful figures. In addition, the patient will generally be working over aspects of his own unconscious fantasies, onflicts, and affects as related to the areas in which the therapist is responding empathically and intuitively, and the patient will add specific, additional, previously repressed contents to the initial, more-blurred, empathic or intuitive experience of the therapist (Langs, 1974).

It appears that at this particular stage of his development, Blank generally did not apply such a validating process to his intuitive and empathic experiences. It is evident from the psychoanalytic literature (Langs, in press) that the consistent use of validating measures is relatively rare even among psychoanalysts, and that much work remains to be done in establishing the validating process as the cornerstone of psychoanalytic methodology. In addition, Blank's presentation reveals the readiness with which empathic and intuitive subjective experiences can actually constitute pathological projections, introjective identifications, and projective identifications.

Empathy, Intuition, and Countertransference

In general, Blank attempted to work largely in advance of and without the full use of his patient's associations. In representative fashion, he somewhat narcissisticly relied on his own inner responses without broad efforts at validation; he thereby often fell into difficulty. This involves not only a cognitive problem, but reflects difficulties in containing and working over — metabolizing — the patient's sickness and his need to place his own difficulties into the patient.

The first indications of a brief for empathic response appear when the author states that he empathically identified with the patient's utter lack of control and thereby instituted the firmest of controls. He also states that this led to intuitive action and justified his intervening on the basis of the danger of the patient's possible suicide. Because there was some ground for the therapist's assessment of this patient's difficulty with controls, we cannot view his excessive measures as entirely deriving from his own needs. Instead, this interlude demonstrates how patients lend themselves to the therapist's projections and projective identifications. The degree to which the therapist had actually responded empathically here, and the extent to which his responses constituted a projection and even a projective identification, cannot be fully determined from the data.

It can be pointed out, however, that the concerns about loss of control were utilized in part as a major defense against the recognition of intense aggressive — and especially sexual — unconscious fantasies that seem to have been present in both patient and therapist. Thus, the therapist's empathic response in terms of the lack of control and his efforts to institute general controls were designed in part to shut out specific sexual and aggressive contents and, in addition, to prevent their emerging in the patient's associations--and possibly even in the therapist's subjective awareness. The therapist indicates his own fear of losing control of the situation, without referring to the specific underlying unconscious fantasies—a common oversight. This type of defensiveness appears throughout the therapeutic interaction. Here, the empathic functioning is restricted to a nondescript and general issue as a means of shutting out more specific sexual and aggressive fantasies, and such an approach is reinforced by shutting off the patient's associations and by disregarding the validating process. Similarly, Blank's intuitive responses also served in part the mutual defensive needs of the patient and himself and, in effect, generated a misalliance that afforded some controls and relief to each of them, while bypassing the search for more insightful adaptations.

The Fear of Interpreting

In a not uncommon way, Blank and his supervisor decided to approach the patient without deep interpretations, since these were considered threatening for her tenuous hold on reality. The conclusion was to direct the therapist toward a more supportive role in which empathy and intuition would play a particularly significant part. This seems to reflect a common misconception among therapists regarding the consequences of valid interpretations, viewing them as disturbing to a patient's equilibrium and to his reality testing. Such a concept is based on a failure to appreciate the importance of the capacity to differentiate internal from external reality testing. On this basis, interpretations, when offered in a valid and sensitive manner, with due respect for the patient's fragile ego, actually enhance the patient's capacity for reality testing rather than disrupting it. In addition, this misconception is related to another mistaken view that ego dysfunctions are inherent or innate within the more disturbed patient, and that disruptive unconscious fantasies, memories, and introjects do not significantly contribute to these malfunctions. Clinical evidence indicates that this too is far from the case, and that sensitive interpretations can help to resolve inner disturbances that disrupt the patient's functioning, including reality testing.

The data in the presentation by Blank indicate that these misconceptions tend to be based in part on a fear of the patient's inner world—unconscious fantasies and introjects—and the parallel fear of these aspects of the therapist's inner self. Because of these shared anxieties and avoidances, such a so-called supportive approach actually constitutes a basic therapeutic misalliance in which there are shared defenses against the respective unconscious fantasies and introjects of both participants. Such work, as Blank's paper demonstrates, helped the patient to massively mobilize sufficient defenses or resources to reconstitute her functioning. However, such a "misalliance cure" (Langs, 1975a, 1976a) did not help the patient to resolve her inner conflicts and the underlying basis for her suicidal attempts and severe inner pathology.

These therapeutic decisions to be somewhat supportive and less interpretive led to a so-called empathic and intuitive attempt to let the patient be honest with the therapist. Blank saw this as based partly on a denial of his own countertransference anger which the patient had consciously perceived. As a result of this countertransference difficulty—and the apparently concealed erotic countertransference—there was actually a distinct failure in the therapist's empathic responses to his patient. However, Blank appears to have gradually become aware that he was projecting certain aspects of his own inner difficulties onto the patient and that he was directing his efforts to offer her structure as a means of trying to contain his own aggressive—and he later adds erotic—countertransference impulses. Eventually, he realized that he was struggling with his own guilt and fear of the patient's suicide, and that he was adopting an inappropriate and omnipotent stance because of these worries. Here he acknowledges his countertransference problems as they contributed to his threat to commit the patient when she was ready to leave the hospital prematurely. He also notes that the patient nonetheless responded well to this enforced structure, despite the fact that it was based on his own countertransference anxiety. Here again the therapist's empathic capacities seem actually to have failed him and to have been disrupted by his needs to project onto and projectively identify into his patient. However, Blank's gradual recognition of his countertransference problems suggest a crucual initial movement toward mastery—a point to which I will return later.

The Role of Unrecognized Countertransferences

Blank then offers two vignettes through which he details what I view as the resolution of a misalliance and shared bastion of the bipersonal field established between himself and his patient. These were related to the erotic unconscious fantasies and unconscious perceptions of the patient regarding her therapist, and therefore to her unconscious and conscious erotic transference and nontransference reactions to him (see below). In addition, the vignettes involve the resolution of the therapist's blind spots in this area and possibly some inner working through of his own erotic countertransference.

In this context, Blank reports a session that followed the patient's first leave outside of the hospital. In that hour, she vividly described her erotic fantasies toward her previous therapist. Blank invokes his empathic capacities to point out to the patient that she had not gotten over her feelings toward this previous therapist, despite her belief that she had done so. The author later recognized that he had experienced a general empathic failure to understand the patient, and that initially he had disregarded the associations from the patient that strongly suggested the presence of erotic feelings toward himself. As he worked over this blind spot, Blank came to the conclusion that the patient was concerned about developing feelings of attachment toward himself, as she had experienced with her previous therapist. He then specifically acknowledges efforts to defend himself against both sexual and hostile feelings that he was unconsciously experiencing from the patient, but he did not extend this insight fully into a comparable blind spot in regard to his own sexual and hostile countertransferences.

This sequence is of general interest because it characterizes the work of many psychiatrists who quickly become disillusioned with insight psychotherapy, and it reveals aspects of the basis for this reaction. We see an effort to work empathically without support on the cognitive level and without sufficient use of the patient's specific associations. This vignette reminds us of the dangers of working empathically and intuitively without the full use of the contents of the patient's associations and without a full utilization of the validating process. And the vignette also reveals something of the unconscious basis for these restrictions: the patient was moving toward specifically indicating feelings of love and wishes for marriage in her relationship with her present therapist, and she was hinting at strong sexual fantasies toward him. These responses were evidently mobilized by her separation from the therapist and undoubtedly had other precipitants in earlier sessions with him. Because of the dangers of the patient's and therapist's erotic feelings, we see the therapist attempting to maintain a displacement onto the previous therapist—another bastion of the bipersonal field in which the erotic transference and countertransference is split off and displaced onto the previous therapy and denied in the current interaction.

We see here too the common fear of the patient's erotic feelings toward the therapist, one that is in general far more intense than fear of the patient's aggression. These anxieties mobilize intensive defensive efforts by the therapist; unrecognized, they may lead him away from insight therapy.

Blank's failure to fully recognize and rectify his erotic countertransference, and the related anxieties and defenses, created a situation in which he in part utilized the patient's sickness as a container for his own countertransferences and as a means of projecting, and probably projectively identifying, his inner fantasies into the patient. This too seriously impaired his empathic and intuitive functioning.

The Defensive Use of So-Called Empathic and Intuitive Experiences

As we observe this interaction, it becomes evident that the so-called use of empathy and intuition can actually serve as a defense against the specific cognitive awareness of derivatives of the patient's unconscious fantasies and perceptions. We also see that it is often difficult for the therapist to conceptualize the specific ways in which his empathy and intuition are failing him without the use of cognitive material, so that we come to the conclusion that the beginning therapist who feels a need to rely on his empathy and intuition is at a great disadvantage in his interaction with the patient. The outcome of these failures in empathy, intuition, and cognitive understanding culminated in the session under study with the patient's dissociation and with her abrupt ending of the hour. In part, these responses confirm the present assessment of the therapist's problems (see below).

In the second detailed session, the author describes an "Aha Experience" through which he felt he had empathically recognized that the patient was afraid of becoming symbiotically attached to him. He also indicates that he felt he intuitively understood what the patient was experiencing and describes an intervention in regard to the patient's wishes to be rescued by him that was offered on the basis of those inner experiences. However, this empathic response was not subjected to the validating process. Thus, while it seems to have had a valid component, it also served as another defense against the patient's and therapist's erotic fantasies toward each other. As a result, the patient did not confirm this intervention, though she seemed less upset. This relief may be viewed in terms of the defensive misalliance offered to the patient and the unconscious communications in the therapist's interventions. These latter were to the effect that the therapist was beginning to resolve his unconscious countertransference fantasies and that he would attempt to subject the patient less intensely to them. Thus, while the specific unconscious fantasies within the patient and the therapist were not made conscious or interpreted, the therapist unconsciously indicated some degree of resolution of his countertransference difficulties. This appears to have offered the patient another sector of misalliance cure, based on the therapist's indications to the patient that he no longer wished to possess her.

In the termination phase, the therapist again attempted to utilize his empathic responses. On that basis, he essentially scolded the patient for her behavior, and she responded by apologizing. Here again we find the use of empathy and intuition in the service of obliterating the patient's threatening communications, which at this point again had to do with her feelings toward the therapist. Her hostility was condensed with a continued need to defend herself against her own and the therapist's erotic fantasies, leading to the wish to disfigure herself. These shared defenses against the erotic components of their relationship I have elsewhere (Langs, 1976a, in press) termed *interactional resistances*, while I have considered the patient's symptoms under such conditions to be an expression of an *interactional neurosis* (or psychosis) since they express inputs from both the patient and therapist.

Threatened by this regression and by the fear that he had failed, the therapist spoke based on his own subjective feelings. He indicated to the patient that she seemed to be testing him to see if he really cared and would protect her, and he told her that she was upsetting the staff and himself by her behavior. It would appear that the patient was then able to mobilize her own adaptive resources once she had experienced the sense of helplessness that the therapist projectively identified into her, and that the result of the interaction had been the evocation of a proxy (Wangh, 1962) in which the patient developed adaptive resources that were failing within the therapist. As a general principle, erroneous interventions contain efforts by the therapist to projectively identify into, and evoke proxies from, the patient.

Confirmation of the shared and unresolved erotic problems, and the failures of both patient and therapist to contain the sexual aspects of their interaction, may well lie in the patient's delayed menstrual period. I have postulated (Langs, 1976a) that spillage into the somatic sphere occurs in the context of failures to contain. Unconscious fantasies of impregnation were evident to the therapist, but were not interpreted; instead, physiological confirmation of the absence of the pregnancy was effected. Similarly, there was a referral back to the original female therapist without an analysis of the underlying factors, including its role as a defense against the erotic elements of this interaction. Lastly, in the post-hospitalization interviews, the therapist provided the patient with birth control pills as a possible final uninterpreted means of denying his sexual intentions toward her and of asking her to contain and deny her sexual fantasies toward him.

In summary then, we discover that the therapist's subjective use of empathy and intuition was basically an effort to avoid specific hostile and erotic feelings within his patient and himself. These so-called empathic responses had strong defensive components, and served as a means of managing disturbing unconscious fantasies and interactions through the creation of bastions and sectors of therapeutic misalliance that afforded both patient and therapist strong defensive backup and a modicum of unconscious hostile and erotic gratification. Nonetheless, embedded in these defensive and inappropriately gratifying uses of so-called empathy and intuition were islands of constructive efforts. It is characteristic to find contained in essentially unsound and countertransference-based interventions such nuclei of unconsciously helpful intentions. It is these latter that must be expanded if a therapist is to be appropriately gratified in his work.

The data indicate that the patient's improvement occurred not through insight and the consequent structural change, but largely through the therapist's projective identifications into her of his own concerns about controls, and his own unresolved hostile and erotic countertransferences. The patient responded to these evocations of proxies by developing ego and probably superego responses as a means of coping with these shared difficulties. Theoretically, such misalliance cures and evocations of proxy within the patient are likely to be relatively unstable, although it is possible that there could be structuralization of these changes and long-lasting symptom relief. However, we must be reminded that symptom alleviation through insightful interpretations is far less risky. This avenue would provide the patient with the specific cognitive means for resolving her intrapsychic conflicts, and offer her positive introjective identifications with a nonanxious and truly helpful therapist.

OTHER COMMON PROBLEMS FOR THE BEGINNING PSYCHIATRIST

Unneeded Modifications of the Frame; Framework Cures

It is not uncommon for beginning and more experienced psychiatrists to repeatedly modify the framework of their therapeutic relationship and not specifically explore and interpret the repercussions of these measures (Langs, 1975b). Here, such modifications ranged from Blank's physical examination of the patient, his viewing her breasts, his use of adjunctive measures including cold packs, hypnosis, and medication, and his interviews with the husband. Elsewhere, I have indicated that these modifications in the frame are often, however justified, a reflection of unmanaged countertransferences, and my previous discussion suggests that this thesis appears to be confirmed in Blank's material.

In addition, I will comment on one effort by the patient to effect what I have termed a *framework cure* at a moment of mounting anxiety in both participants—an intensification of the pathology of the bipersonal field (Langs, 1976a). This occurred in the interview after the patient's first outside pass, one that was videotaped by the therapist—another modification in technique. It was evident that the patient at this time was experiencing an intensification of her own—and possibly the therapist's—erotic fantasies. When she expressed derivatives of these fantasies and perceptions in alluding to her relationship with her previous therapist, Blank indicated his incapacity to contain this material as it related to himself by intervening in regard to his predecessor. The patient responded by wondering if the therapist was angry with her. This seems to reflect a perception of the therapist's anxieties and his reactive anger in the face of her erotic fantasies. It also expresses a mobilization of her own hostility in the face of her fears of her own erotic fantasies, as well as her responsive anger to the therapist's failure to understand her. The therapist then modified his neutrality and anonymity by denying the anger, and the patient responded by feeling insecure and with a crushing feeling of depression. She subsequently dissociated and then asked if the hour could be ended, to which the therapist readily agreed.

This interaction demonstrates some of the risks of the therapist's countertransference difficulties and his failures to be truly empathic when it comes to specific erotic and hostile fantasies. The patient unconsciously perceives the therapist's difficulties and attempts to protect herself, experiencing a type of depression that is rather characteristic at such moments. It is just this type of danger that is involved in offering the patient a sector of misalliance in which erotic fantasies are to be split off. It appears that, when the patient recognized that neither she nor the therapist could contain or manage the shared erotic fantasies that were intensifying within the bipersonal field, the patient resorted to a termination of the session as a means of alleviating the mounting mutual anxiety. It is this that I have termed a *framework cure* (Langs, 1976a) in order to designate a type of misalliance cure in which mounting intrapsychic conflict and anxiety is temporarily resolved through a modification in the framework of the therapeutic relationship. In addition, the material suggests that many modifications in technique undertaken by this therapist were designed, however rationalized, to afford a similar type of momentary symptom alleviation.

Distinguishing Transference and Nontransference

Another common problem suggested by Blank's presentation relates to the distinction between transference and nontransference components in the patient's responses to the therapist (Greenson, 1972; Greenson and Wexler, 1969; Langs, 1974, 1976a,b), and the therapist's defensive use of the concept of transference (Szasz, 1963; Langs, 1976a). Blank alludes several times to his relationship with the patient as interpersonal, without attempting to sort out the transference and nontransference components of his patient's relationship to him. He implies that the patient experienced a symbiotic and maternal transference with him, and there are allusions to transference-based anger experienced by the patient toward the therapist and to the patient's concern for the therapist's health that has been displaced from past relationships.

This material provides an opportunity to discuss certain common misuses of the term *transference*. Many therapists think of the patient's relationship to the therapist as transference, and fail to continuously search for and identify nontransference elements in this relationship and in the patient's communications, except in terms of the so-called real relationship between the patient and the therapist. For example, even though Blank acknowledges his own errors in technique, there is the repeated implication that the patient was essentially distorting her reactions to him and perceiving him primarily in terms of past relationships, rather than for the most part reacting to him validly and in keeping with the present interaction. Such a conception will not only lead to erroneous interventions and especially to failures to appreciate the patient's unconscious perceptiveness, but will also prevent the therapist from becoming aware of the extensive consequences of his countertransferences in his relationship with the patient. Often, the concept is used to blame the patient and to make him fully responsible for regressive episodes and other disturbances in the therapeutic interaction, and as a means of denying the therapist's contributions to such interludes.

A closer examination of the material indicates, for example, that the patient's dread of being overly attached to her therapist stemmed not only from her own pathological inner needs, but in a very major way from the therapist's communications to her—e.g., his decision to offer her long-term hospitalization, to refuse her visitors, to examine her physically and become otherwise involved with her, his insistence that he would not let her die, his threat to commit her should she wish to leave the hospital prematurely, his initial lingering and waiting for the patient to regress after his first interview, and finally his strongly protective stance. For this reason, an identification of the symbiotic component of the patient's relationship to the therapist would have to include a scrutiny for both transference and nontransference aspects, and include a full recognition of the therapist's contribution to the patient's reactions. It is for reasons such as this that I have advocated the use of the concept of the bipersonal field as a dyadic situation into which both the patient and therapist place pathological and nonpathological contributions (Langs, 1976a). On this basis, any fantasy within the patient is examined for contributions from each participant, and transference and nontransference components are separated out; there is always an admixture of the two.

Blank's interventions, with their unconscious sexual and aggressive components, contributed to the patient's hostile and erotic fantasies as well. The patient's responses to them included both valid unconscious perceptions of these interventions as well as intrapsychic elaborations and distortions from within herself. On this basis, we might suspect that the patient's discussion of her love and marital wishes toward her previous therapist, which she was now attempting to renounce, contained not only erotic transference elements but also erotic nontransference components in that they related to unconscious perceptions and introjective identification of the therapist's sexual longings for the patient. The patient's efforts at renunciation appear to stem from her appreciation that the therapist was making attempts in this direction—a positive introjective identification—and her own needs for resolution as well. In this context, the therapist's failure to understand the patient's communications in that hour may have prompted the dissociated state within the patient because her unconscious perceptions of the therapist failed to indicate further resolution or a resurgence of his erotic countertransference.

My emphasis here, however, is on the need to separate transference from nontransference components in this patient's communications—and unconscious fantasies about, from unconscious perceptions of, the therapist. As I have indicated elsewhere (Langs, 1976a, b) patients will, of course, elaborate on their unconscious perceptions of the therapist in keeping with their intrapsychic needs and will always distort and color these perceptions, but this does not negate their valid core.

The Constructive Elements in Countertransference-based Interventions

I will conclude my discussion with a consideration of the positive aspects of this therapeutic experience. My prior work (Langs, 1976a) has indicated that in every technical error and every therapeutic misalliance, no matter how predominant the psychopathological contribution from each participant, there are nuclei of adaptive efforts and positive therapeutic intentions. This observation is borne out in Blank's presentation. The phenomenon appears first in his overidentification with the patient and in his extraordinary protective efforts. The positive nucleus here is his determination to rescue the patient, to seduce her in a positive sense that offers her a feeling of being attractive and a hope for life, and to redeem her from her fate of death. The patient apparently unconsciously perceived these aspects of the therapist's work, along with their more destructive components, when she responded to his initial frantic therapeutic efforts with expressions of both love and hate. She seems to have experienced the therapist's countertransference-based need for a symbiotic tie with her both positively and negatively, welcoming it one moment and dreading it the next. Even the therapist's decision not to allow the patient any visitors and to thereby totally possess her had within it a significant wish to protect and cure.

It should be noted, however, that each of these positive nuclei were surrounded by significant countertransference difficulties, and were often overshadowed by these elements. As a result, it seems likely that the therapeutic interaction was in constant danger of being overwhelmed by the therapist's countertransference-based contributions to it. It is these uncertain and tenuous but helpful nuclei that often sustain patients who are in treatment with therapists who avoid interpretations and the comprehension of the patient's unconscious fantasies and perceptions. The resultant therapeutic experience is not unlike that of the patient described: there is an erratic clinical course that is often difficult for the therapist to understand because he is obliterating some of the most significant contributions to these developments.

The Slow and Uneven Mastery of Countertransferences

In the case of Blank, we soon learn that the therapist's empathic responses —
here referring to relatively uncontrolled and defensive uses of empathy — were
being "dismantled by reason." The therapist began to recognize his wish to be
the omnipotent rescuer and recognized some of his countertransference-based
anger and erotic feelings. Blank indicates his belief that his errors enabled the
patient to experience anger toward him and that this kept her within the
bounds of reality and away from a dissociated state — his own communication
that within his errors, there was something useful for the patient. More and
more the therapist was becoming aware of his blind spots and difficulties with
the patient. Despite this, he still threatened her with commitment, thereby
again expressing a countertransference difficulty within which was contained
a need to protect the patient from her self-destructiveness. It may well be that
in this way, he was undoing something of his own unconscious hostility to the
patient as well.

In the first session presented by Blank we see a further awareness of some
aspects of his countertransference difficulties and an effort to struggle with
them. The patient's dissociated state is then seen as the product of the bipersonal field and the therapist acknowledges his contribution to the patient's
psychopathology, thereby implicitly indicating his awareness that this was an
interactional syndrome (Langs, 1976a).

While the therapist's need to deny both the patient's and his own erotic fantasies toward each other is prevalent in the first vignette, in the second vignette Blank begins to recognize that the patient is dealing with feelings toward him. While, as I noted earlier, this neophyte therapist had the characteristic difficulty of separating the transference and nontransference components of the patient's reactions toward him, and while he also continued to
avoid her specific erotic and aggressive fantasies, we see a dramatic bit of personal growth in his capacity to explore the patient's relationship with him.

The patient apparently picks up the unconscious communications from the
therapist that the therapeutic relationship should be explored in terms of dependency and she accordingly confines her efforts to this level. The avoided
bastion concerning the analysis of the therapeutic relationship was modified,
but only to a limited degree. At this juncture, instead of interpreting the
specific unconscious fantasies and perceptions with which the patient was
struggling in her relationship with him, Blank focuses on the issue of rescue
fantasies and indicates to the patient that she must take care of herself. The
latter responds both quizzically and with relief, after which she is left less depressed.

This session was seen as decisive in that the therapist was able to consciously
verbalize aspects of the patient's fantasies toward him, however incompletely.
He was also able to refute his wishes to rescue and protect her. Using his own
native abilities (as Blank put it), he had unconsciously let the patient know

that he was renouncing his symbiotic, erotic, and hostile countertransferences toward her, and that he expected her to mobilize her own resources. The patient's positive response could well be viewed as amounting to a countertransference cure (Barchilon, 1958) in that she then lived out the therapist's wishes. It could also be seen as a transference cure (Oremland, 1972) in that she responded favorably as a result of a transference-based wish to please the therapist. My own preference, however, is to term this a misalliance cure (Langs, 1975a, 1976a) in that it occurs with a minimum amount of insight and with the unconscious participation of both the patient and therapist. This cure utilizes projective identification inasmuch as the therapist placed some of his capacity to renounce into the patient and she introjected and benefited from it. In addition, it included an effort to evoke proxies of adequate functioning based not only on incorporative identifications of the therapist, but on the mobilization of adequate functioning in the patient.

However, the situation then deteriorated somewhat because neither patient nor therapist was able to resolve the specific sources of the disturbances in the therapeutic relationship. A compromise was worked out by returning the patient to a female therapist. The unsatisfactory aspects of this resolution are reflected in the patient's wish to burn her face so as to make herself ugly and affording her husband no cause to be jealous of other men's attention toward her. This is the patient's unconscious perception and fantasy of solving a sexual problem through manipulation.

In the face of mounting tension, the therapist then made what he terms an interpretation to her. We may note that this intervention reflects the common difficulty in conceptualizing the nature of an interpretation as a comment that should allude to the patient's unconscious fantasies and perceptions. The term is often used in a way that also fails to recognize that such an intervention grows out of the therapeutic interaction. As a result, so-called interpretations may contain much that comes from the therapist rather than the patient; the concept may be utilized as a cover for the former's countertransference difficulties.

Blank's comment comes across as a way of scolding the patient and as a means of further denying his countertransferences. As is characteristic of erroneous interventions, there is a projective identification into the patient of both the therapist's renunciation and his disturbance over her regressive behavior. The patient responds by mobilizing her own empathic capacities and more adequate ego functions, thereby apologizing and integrating. Later, when Blank recognizes that his intervention probably was not an interpretation, he once again resorts to the appellation of empathy and takes pride in the honesty of what he communicated to the patient.

The post-hospitalization session reveals a continued need in the patient to support the therapist whom she apparently saw as threatened and attached to her. In the context of the therapist's growing capacity to renounce his overinvolvement with her, he engages in an intellectualized discussion of the nature of psychotherapy and attempts to remind the patient that it should take place in a unique environment. This is an extremely important concept that the therapist seems to have intuitively arrived at; here, his *unconscious intuition* was mobilized in a most adaptive manner. He was of course alluding to the fact that without a unique environment with a specific framework, the patient's intrapsychic fantasies cannot unfold within the therapeutic relationship in a safe and analyzable manner (see Langs, 1976a). The therapist was appealing to the patient to accept the necessary renunciations entailed in maintaining a secure framework for psychotherapy with adequate interpersonal boundaries. While Blank candidly acknowledges some of the pain that he is having in his work with the patient, he now offers symbolic substitutes for himself in suggesting that the patient internalize and take her psychotherapeutic work with her.

Here we see an effort to place a positive introject in the patient. While this is a relatively well-managed and controlled partly countertransference-based response, it nonetheless reveals disturbances within the therapist who is having difficulty in working out his own separation from the patient; it reflects his need to keep a part of himself within her. The final offers of medication, however justified, also may reflect a need by the therapist to place parts of himself into the patient. It is extremely common for therapists to experience intense separation anxieties in terminating their patients, and many deviate unnecessarily at such moments in a countertransference-based effort to manage their own inner distrubance (Langs, 1974, 1975b).

The session ends with a mutual expression of sadness and appreciation, and then a final hour occurs in which all therapeutic work is avoided. The therapist expresses his great state of happiness and views himself as a father sending off his favorite daughter to college. In doing so, we see further indications of his growing capacities for sublimation and control: this fantasy is a far cry from his initial direct and possessive interventions. At the same time, in expressing his favoritism toward the patient and in offering her the birth control pills as an added measure of protection, not surprisingly we see possible continued reverberations of his erotic countertransference and his failures to completely master it.

In all, there is evidence of considerable growth in the therapist, and I strongly suspect that his patient's improvement derived in part from her unconscious recognition that she had been of help to this therapist. The therapist's capacity to *implicitly* accept and utilize the patient's unconscious therapeutic efforts toward him can have strong positive effects on the patient. The patient also introjectively identified with the improved functioning of the therapist and thereby was able to reinforce her own adaptive ego functioning.

We cannot help but feel a deep sense of empathic identification with the therapist's long struggle and ultimate conviction that he had been a help to this patient and with his growing self-esteem and positive feelings about his therapeutic abilities. While in no way wishing to undermine this growing sense of security, it is also crucial that it be based on sound clinical observations and that the therapist develop an ability to appreciate the basis for his patient's clinical improvement. Failure to establish a validating process in this regard will lead to many puzzling disappointments and to the therapist's discouragement. It is for those reasons that I have stressed the contributions of misalliance cure and of the patient's therapeutic efforts toward the therapist, since there was ample reason to view this as part of the basis for this patient's improvement. There was little in the clinical data to indicate that her symptomatic resolution occurred on the basis of cognitive insights and secure positive introjective identifications based on the therapist's interpretive ability. The material, however, demonstrates the extent to which the patient can incorporate good aspects of the therapist in the face of many technical errors and actual failures of empathic and cognitive capacities.

The Choice of Insight-Oriented or Noninsightful Therapeutic Work

In concluding, we may note the manner in which this material has illuminated the motivations and conflicts of the beginning psychotherapist and the influences on his choice of insight-oriented versus noninsightful therapy. Having had the good fortune to be able to cure a patient through sublimated and unsublimated love may well encourage the therapist who believes that his interpretive interventions have contributed to this outcome to search further for such techniques. On the other hand, such a cure may prove frightening and confusing to the therapist and he may turn away from more insightful work. In addition, should the patient not respond favorably to this type of therapeutic endeavor, or should he or she quickly relapse, the anxiety and guilt evoked by the therapist's countertransference difficulties may prompt him to move away from the intimate one-to-one therapeutic relationship involved in insight-oriented treatment.

Perhaps the most important aspect of this therapist's development is reflected in the indications of his capacity to benefit from the therapeutic efforts of, and interactions with, his patient, and his developing ability to modulate and control aspects of his countertransference difficulties. Movement in this direction can provide the therapist with the strength necessary to face both his own inner fantasy life and that of his patient. Such progress can provide the therapist with the courage to move toward greater use of insight psychotherapy and to better handle his patient's unconscious fantasies and perceptions about himself. It becomes clear that the therapist's response to the therapeutic interaction and to the intense intrapsychic pressures that it creates for him is a crucial determinant in his future development. If he is unable to bear the stirrings, and the projections and projective identifications, effected by the patient's behaviors and associations, he will become more and more defensive and endeavor to shut out both the patient and his inner awareness of himself. He will be loath to become a container for the patient's sick contents, since their specific aspects disturb him. He will also be prone to project and projectively identify his own difficulties into the patient, and to seek the therapeutic modalities that will justify these countertransference needs. On the other hand, a growing tolerance for the patient's unconscious fantasies and perceptions, and for his projective identifications, provides the strength through which the further development of an interest in analytically oriented psychotherapy can unfold.

Blank's presentation can profitably take every psychotherapist back to his earliest work. It provides us with a humbling reminder of the anxiety and difficulty that each of us faced in our first therapeutic encounter, and in retrospect may help us to remember many countertransference difficulties that were mobilized in that first therapeutic experience. It gives us all reason to pause and assess the extent to which we have indeed mastered these early anxieties and countertransference difficulties, and helps us to recognize that the struggle to maintain such mastery and to enhance it is part of our everyday therapeutic work.

In terms of empathy, there is a part of every therapist in Dr. Blank, and we can share with him both the limitations of the resolution of his countertransference difficulties and the many moving indications of his budding efforts to master the problems facing every therapist. We are reminded of the human condition—the psychotherapist's condition—and of the fact that it is an eternal struggle to the last moment of which it best can be said that there are those who achieve relative mastery and there are those who are less fortunate.

NOTES

1. Throughout this paper, I will use the term *projective identification* to refer specifically to actual interactional efforts by a given subject to put into a particular object aspects of his own inner state, so as to externally manage them and to evoke adaptive responses for reintrojection. Projective identification is to be contrasted with projection in that the latter is essentially an intrapsychic mechanism, while the former is interactional; both range from primitive to sophisticated forms. The term identification is applied in an unusual manner in the term projective identification; it refers to the subject's continued attachment to—identification with—the contents that he has externalized and to his efforts to evoke an identification in the object. *Introjective identification* refers to the complementary interactional process within the object who takes in contents that have been projectively identified into him by the subject, and who then processes these contents according to his own intrapsychic needs. *Containing functions* refers to the totality of these intaking processes and their inner "metabolization" by the object (see Langs, 1976a for full details).

2. Because of the limitations in the data available, speculations are inevitable, and confirmation of hypotheses, though feasible within limits, will be less elaborate and specific than possible in the clinical situation. In my discussion, I will bypass the therapist's possible use of noninterpretive efforts to develop the therapeutic alliance with his patient, and will focus instead on the basic contributions of valid interpretive work to creating

an insight-oriented alliance (see Langs, in press). Many pertinent issues related to Blank's material will, of necessity, be bypassed in this discussion.

   3. Here, I will not consider the important issues raised by the contributions of ward policy, supervisors, and other "cultural" pressures on Blank's decisions and techniques. These often serve as sanctions for counter-transference-based expressions in the therapist. A consideration of their role is beyond the scope of this discussion, as is the issue of the accepted boundaries of the therapeutic relationship and the therapeutic setting under consideration as compared to the classically defined framework for psychoanalysis and psychoanalytic psychotherapy (for relevant explorations, see Langs, 1973, 1975a, b, 1976a, b).

   4. Here again it will be necessary to bypass a host of additional factors in this decision.

BIBLIOGRAPHY

Barchilon, J. (1958). On countertransference "cures." *Journal of the American Psychoanalytic Association* 6: 222-236.

Beres, D., and Arlow, J. (1974). Fantasy and identification in empathy. *Psychoanalytic Quarterly* 43: 26-50.

Bion, W. R. (1962). *Learning from Experience.* New York: Basic Books.

_____(1963). *Elements of Psycho-Analysis.* New York: Basic Books.

Blank, R. (1976). Empathy and intuition in becoming a psychiatrist: A case report. *International Journal of Psychoanalytic Psychotherapy* 5: 237-252.

Fleming, J. (1961). What analytic work requires of an analyst: A job analysis. *Journal of the American Psychoanalytic Association* 9: 719-729.

Greenson, R. (1962). That "impossible" profession. *Journal of the American Psychoanalytic Association* 14: 9-27.

_____(1967). *The Technique and Practice of Psychoanalysis.* Vol. 1. New York: International Universities Press.

_____(1972). Beyond transference and interpretation. *International Journal of Psycho-Analysis* 53: 213-217.

_____, and Wexler, M. (1969). The non-transference relationship in the psychoanalytic situation. *International Journal of Psycho-Analysis* 50:27-39.

Langs, R. (1973). *The Technique of Psychoanalytic Psychotherapy.* Vol. 1. New York: Aronson.

_____(1974). *The Technique of Psychoanalytic Psychotherapy.* Vol. 2. New York: Aronson.

_____(1975b). The therapeutic relationship and deviations in technique. *International Journal of Psychoanalytic Psychotherapy* 4: 106-141.

_____(1976a). *The Bipersonal Field.* New York: Aronson.

_____(1976b). The misalliance dimension in Freud's case histories. I. Dora. *International Journal of Psychoanalytic Psychotherapy* 5: 301-317.

_____(in press). *The Therapeutic Interaction.* New York: Aronson.

Olinick, S. (1969). On empathy and regression in the service of the other. *British Journal of Medical Psychology* 42: 41-49.

Oremland, J. (1972). Transference cure and flight into health. *International Journal of Psychoanalytic Psychotherapy* 1, 1: 61-75.

Shapiro, T. (1974). The development and distortions of empathy. *Psychoanalytic Quarterly* 43: 4-25.

Sharpe, E. F. (1930). The technique of psycho-analysis. *International Journal of Psycho-Analysis* 11: 251-277.

Szasz, T. (1963). The concept of transference. *International Journal of Psycho-Analysis* 44: 432-443.

Wangh, M. (1962). The "evocation of a proxy": A psychological maneuver, its use as a defense, its purposes and genesis. *Psychoanalytic Study of the Child* 17: 451-472.

ROBERT LANGS, M.D.

DR. LANGS is editor-in-chief of this journal. He is a graduate of the Downstate Psychiatric Institute at Brooklyn, where he currently teaches. He has written on a variety of psychoanalytic topics, including books on the technique of psychoanalytic psychotherapy and the psychotherapeutic and analytic relationships and interactions.

Author's Response to Dr. Langs' Discussion

Ronald J. Blank, M.D.

Despite all of his intellectual and humanistic traits, a beginning psychiatrist quickly finds himself in a confusing matrix of communications. Relating to a seriously disturbed patient is a difficult new experience for which he has had little preparation. I have stated that the beginning resident may attempt to allay his often distressing anxiety by girding himself with a host of newfound philosophies and techniques. I have further stressed that close at hand to the young psychiatrist is a potential ally in his work with the disturbed. This I have termed the psychiatrist's native empathy and intuition.

Langs's paper leads me one step further. That is, it reminds me of the uncertainty with which we use our own internal thought processes and feelings. Langs has underlined the importance of distinguishing transference from nontransference: that is, the patient's reactions to the therapist are far too often seen in terms of past relationships rather than viewed as what actually is occurring in the interpersonal field. Let me then underline for neophyte and expert alike the equally important task of distinguishing in a similar manner between countertransference and noncountertransference.

I·am reminded of Werner Heisenberg's profound theoretical discovery—the uncertainty principle. It is this uncertainty, which remains a cornerstone of current atomic theory, that we as psychotherapists must consider. We find ourselves in a unique interpersonal situation—the patient and the therapist. It is a relationship that has both a reality and an uncertainty; we struggle to understand its many facets. For the psychiatrist, the feelings he experiences must become an ally; they must be personally acknowledged. Some, based on distortions stemming from the therapist, will be found erroneous; Others—those emerging from the interpersonal experience between patient and therapist—will be reality based. In the end, however, one must accept that the interpersonal field, like the atomic field, can be understood only in terms of probabilities and viewed only with uncertainty.

The risk that the beginning psychiatrist and his supervisor run is the facile labeling of feelings as countertransference. It is clear that the process of sorting out countertransference feelings from noncountertransference feelings in a supervisory session is difficult for therapist and supervisor alike. For the therapist it necessitates honesty, risk taking, and the experiencing of pain in regard to his work. For the supervisor it necessitates the skill and the strength to help someone separate real feelings from distorted feelings—just as he himself must do in regard to the supervisee. The challenge remains, then, for the therapist finally to bring understanding to the interpersonal field despite its uncertainties.

Again, I must ask the still unanswered question: Why did the patient get better? Why has she been able to stay out of the hospital for eighteen months when during the previous year she had been hospitalized four times? I return to the uncertainty principle. Perhaps we must accept that the only unchangeable thing about our work is uncertainty. And yet people in therapy do get better. I am left with the belief that we cannot always know with exactness what goes on in the process of psychotherapy. What I can accept is that two people, working together in an interpersonal field, can bring about movement toward emotional health.

ACKNOWLEDGEMENT

I am grateful to Dr. Howard Shevrin for his discussion of the early drafts of this paper. I would also like to thank my colleagues Muriel Tornga and Peter Ash for their insightful comments regarding the final pape:

RONALD J. BLANK, M.D.

DR. BLANK graduated from the State University of New York-Downstate Medical Center and is currently a Resident in Psychiatry at the University of Michigan Medical Center. This is the first of a series of papers dealing with the process of becoming a psychiatrist.

Toward a General Concept of the Therapeutic Process

Paul A. Dewald, M.D.

Clinical Professor of Psychiatry
St Louis University School of Medicine

Medical Director
St. Louis University School of Medicine

Using clinical psychoanalytic theory as a unifying concept, an attempt is made to observe, interpret, and integrate the therapeutic process in a wide variety of psychotherapies. All psychotherapy, regardless of specific form or technique, is viewed as an interpersonal or intrapersonal process, and should be understandable from a psychoanalytic perspective. Ten common factors are selected: structure of the therapeutic situation; the therapeutic relationship; management of anxiety; drives and their derivatives; mechanisms of defense; identification; regression; catharsis and abreaction; external reinforcement; structural change. The various psychotherapies are compared regarding each of the ten factors.

INTRODUCTION

Since Knight's 1949 survey of the psychotherapies the types being practiced have expanded. Client centered therapy (Rogers, 1951), reciprocal inhibition (Wolpe, 1958), operant conditioning (Bandura, 1969), aversive conditioning (Kalish, 1965), rational-emotive therapy (Ellis, 1962), existential therapy (May et al., 1958; Laing, 1965), transactional analysis (Berne, 1961), and gestalt therapy (Perls et al., 1951) are a few of the newer forms of individual therapy. A similar expansion has occurred in the various group therapies (Slavson, 1956; Moreno, 1946; Masters and Johnson, 1970; Lieberman et al., 1973; Sugarman, 1974; Ackerman, 1966) and in applications of group and family process.

These therapeutic procedures have been described in isolation from each other, often with implied or explicit derogation of other modalities (Goldstein and Dean, 1966; Shahakian, 1969). Recently several procedures have been combined in the treatment of specific cases (Birk and Brinkley-Birk, 1974; Birk, 1974; Rhoads and Feather, 1974) and not infrequently patients are treated individually and in groups simultaneously.

The theoretical models advanced to conceptualize the therapeutic process have mostly been narrowly focused, with relatively little effort toward integration among different therapies. Where an attempt has been made to find commonalities among the various treatment approaches (Frank, 1961; Haley, 1963; Porter, 1968; Garfield, 1971; Goldstein and Dean, 1966), there have often been oversimplifications of the naturalistic treatment processes, or research exploration considerably removed from the usual clinical situation. Bergin and Strupp (1972) conclude from their survey that collaborative research among the varying "schools" of psychotherapy is not feasible at this time because of theoretical and technical differences and emotionally held attitudes.

The articulation of conceptual generalizations regarding the therapeutic process in different treatment modalities hopefully might initiate more objective and dispassionate comparison of similarities and differences. Dollard and Miller (1950), Goldman (1956), Murray and Jacobson (1971), Mendel (1972), Bordin (1974), Offenkrantz and Tobin (1974), Strupp (1975), and Tseng and McDermott (1975) are among those making such attempts.

My attempt will be to use clinical psychoanalytic theory to observe and interpret the therapeutic process in various different treatment forms, and hopefully develop some general concepts about them. It should be possible to observe all the different forms of psychotherapy as intrapersonal and interpersonal human phenomena understandable from a psychoanalytic perspective. Much of the confusion in the present scene stems from claims of exclusiveness or expediency. But any comprehensive concepts of the therapeutic process must be able to account for at least some beneficial results in *all* of these different approaches. Some of the current modalities of treatment are listed in Table 1.

TABLE 1

Individual Psychotherapies

Psychoanalysis
Psychoanalytically oriented therapy
Supportive therapy
Behavior modification
   Systematic desensitization
   Methods based on learning theory
      Operant conditioning
      Aversive Conditioning

    Assertiveness training
    Paradoxical intention
    Relaxation therapy
  Client-centered therapy
  Transactional analysis
  Psychotropic drug therapies
  Hypnotherapy and narcosynthesis
  Existential therapy
  Gestalt therapy

Group Psychotherapies

  Psychoanalytic group therapy
  Supportive group therapy
  Milieu therapy (particularly for hospitalized patients)
  Marathon group therapy
  Psychodrama
  Transactional analysis
  Family therapy
  Social action group therapy
  Sexual therapy

Individual Treatment not labeled Psychotherapy

  Medical management by the nonpsychiatric physician
  Counseling

Group Treatment not Labeled Psychotherapy

  Alcoholics Anonymous
  Alanon
  Weight Watchers
  Daytop, Synanon, and other drug addiction programs
  Medical management groups
  Activity groups
  Sensitivity groups

The therapeutic process in the various forms of psychotherapy can be compared from ten component psychodynamic perspectives. These will be considered separately here, but in the actual clinical situation there is much interrelationship between them.

STRUCTURE OF THE THERAPEUTIC SITUATION

Every therapeutic method has its own structure as the framework within which the participants will function. This structure includes such things as whether the situation is identified formally as psychotherapeutic, or as a non-psychiatric or nontherapeutic venture (sensitivity groups, Alcoholics Anonymous, Weight Watchers, marital or pastoral counseling, etc.) ; the physical setting (a medical office or clinic, vs. an informal group room, vs. a swimming pool in an idyllic location) ; the frequency and duration of sessions (brief, infrequent, or irregular sessions, vs. a 50-minute session multiple times per week, vs. continuous 24-36 hour sessions) ; individual vs. group arrangement; emphasis on verbal vs. nonverbal behaviors; physical contact between group members, or patient and therapist, etc. These types of structural factors influence the participants' expectations and the nature of the therapy.

THE THERAPEUTIC RELATIONSHIP

Treatment always involves a relationship between the participants. In some therapies the relationship and interactions are the focus of conscious attention, and their understanding is actively part of the process (psycho-analysis, Gestalt therapy, transactional analysis, sensitivity groups, psycho-analytic group therapy, etc.). In others, the therapeutic relationship may be recognized and used by the therapist, who does not focus the patient's attention on it (various supportive treatments, counseling, operant conditioning, client-centered therapy, etc.). In still other forms of therapy neither therapist nor patient consider their relationship to be an active force in the therapeutic process (drug-oriented therapies, behavior modification, social action groups, etc.).

In all forms of treatment the therapist (or the therapeutic group) manifests real and observable behavior which indicates to the patient whether he is accepted, understood, and treated consistently and considerately. Such behavior also tells much about the therapist's interests, skill, and sense of confidence in himself and in the treatment. Even therapists who attempt to implement the same type of treatment vary in skill, experience, and the capacity to work effectively with patients. These outwardly manifest therapist variables influence the ultimate outcome, and contribute to the establishment of rapport and the consolidation of a working alliance.

In addition, every therapeutic relationship offers the potential for the patient to develop transference reactions toward the therapist and the treatment situation. The types of feelings, attitudes, values, defenses, wishes, expectations, etc., that are experienced toward the therapist and therapeutic situation are specific to the individual patient as a function of his past experience, psychopathology, and personality organization. But their intensity and level of consciousness during treatment are also a function of the therapist's theoretical orientation, behavior in the treatment process, and the structure of the treatment situation.

Other things being equal, the factors which will tend to *intensify* conscious awareness of transference reactions include

1. Personal anonymity and suspension of external manifestations of the therapist's real self and values
2. Relatively constant neutrality toward the patient's behavior and material
3. Abstinence toward the patient's derivative transference wishes and expectations in the therapeutic situation
4. Regular, prolonged, and frequent scheduling of therapeutic sessions.
5. Active interest in transference phenomena as they become manifest
6. Interpretation of resistances against emerging transference feelings, along with interpretation of the nature and significance of the content of the transference reactions when appropriate technically
7. The therapist's acceptance of the transference distortions without anxiety and without a personal need to correct them

Factors which tend to *diminish* the intensity and conscious awareness of the patient's transference responses include

1. Irregular, infrequent, or brief therapeutic contacts
2. Interaction with the patient in a reality-oriented fashion
3. The therapist actively expressing his real self, values, and emotional reactions
4. Ignoring the transference and its manifestations, and/or allowing or strengthening the patient's defenses agains its conscious emergence
5. Actively gratifying the derivative transference wishes in the treatment situation
6. Rapidly and actively correcting transference distortions if they emerge

Transference responses and their importance in treatment occur on a continuum of intensity and degree of consciousness. Some treatment methods in their concepts and technique ignore or minimize the role of transference (drug-oriented therapy, behavior modification, client-centered therapy). Other therapists may make use of the transference potentials and experiences, but do not explore or focus conscious attention on them (supportive individual or group therapies), and instead permit the transference responses to remain at an unconscious level. Such transference responses may be used selectively to gratify or modify unconscious wishes, strengthen defenses, change moral values, etc., sometimes with the therapist's conscious awareness and intent, and at other times without the therapist being aware of this element in the treatment process.

In treatment methods using symbolic or derivative expression and/or satisfaction of transference phenomena (transactional analysis, psychodrama, marathon group therapy, etc.) interactions between patient and therapist are experienced as actual reality-oriented situations in the present. The patient reacts behaviorally in the "here and now," in hopes that he will find his previous conflicts and expectations of danger (along with his inhibitions and/or other pathological responses) inappropriate and that new, more effective responses can be learned.

In those therapies that emphasize more direct experience of pathogenic conflict situations (some forms of sexual therapy, physical contact between therapist and patient, physical contact between group members, situations involving critical attack by the group upon the patient, etc.), the patient re-experiences as a current immediate reality the transferred conflicts and relationships which had produced various types of neurotic responses. However he now has the active support of the therapist and/or group, with gratification of transference wishes for love and acceptance varying directly with the degree to which he develops more adaptive behavior patterns.

In the analytic forms of therapy, the transference relationship is limited to the verbalization of feelings and fantasies by the patient, and is used by the therapist as a vehicle for the conscious mobilization of previously unconscious conflicts as part of the therapeutic process. This reaches the level of transference reactions in the analytically oriented psychotherapies, or of the fully developed transference neurosis in psychoanalysis.

But in all forms of psychotherapy, including those whose technique and rationale ignore the phenomena of transference, a significant element of the therapeutic interaction is a function of the transference relationship even if it remains unconscious to both the patient and the therapist.

THE MANAGEMENT OF ANXIETY

The role of anxiety and other signal affects in the development of psychopathology is central in psychoanalytic theory. Each therapeutic modality has its own method and rationale for managing the patient's experience of anxiety.

Some forms of psychotherapy suppress or minimize anxiety through logical and rational exhortation and strengthening the patient's capacity for reality testing. Others aim at strengthening the patient's psychological defenses against anxiety. One effect of tranquilizers or antidepressant drugs is to reduce the intensity of unpleasurable affective experiences. As a result secondary mechanisms of defense previously utilized to minimize or avoid anxiety will be less intensely required, in turn permitting a reduction in the intensity of the neurotic symptoms and/or character traits. Other forms of therapy aim at suppression of anxiety through manipulation of external environmental factors which may contribute to psychic disequilibrium as additional stresses upon ego capacity for adaptation, or as precipitating events which have associational connection to the intrapsychic conflicts.

Other treatment modalities (behavior modification, learning theory, sexual therapies, reality therapy, supportive therapy) encourage the patient gradually to experience increasing increments of anxiety in situations which previously had evoked a major response. A graduated series of fantasied or real experiences is presented to the patient, beginning with one which stimulates minimal anxiety and, as mastery occurs, proceeding to the major stimulus of the symptoms. The intention is to allow the patient to master anxiety-provoking situations in relatively small, graduated steps, analogous to the desensitization treatment of an allergy. The presence of the therapist during these experiences offers the simultaneous support of an unconsciously loved, protective parental transference figure, analogous to a parent helping a child face and master situations of fear.

In psychoanalysis and the analytically oriented therapies, a somewhat similar process of desensitization occurs. The underlying anxiety-producing intrapsychic conflicts are progressively mobilized in incremental steps tolerable to the patient, and anxiety is maintained at a level which will not overwhelm him. By repeatedly experiencing the emerging conflicts, the patient is increasingly able to tolerate the anxiety (and other unpleasurable affects) without the previously established automatic and unconscious use of multiple defense mechanisms. In this sense the process of desensitization itself is similar to that used in behavior modification therapies, except that the desensitization is aimed at the *unconscious* anxiety-producing intrapsychic conflicts, while in behavior modification the focus is on their *conscious* external derivative manifestations.

In those group and individual therapies where regression and pressures on psychological defense mechanisms are actively and continuously operative, the patient is pushed to master anxiety through "practicing" new overt behaviors and methods in the therapeutc situation, accompanied by active reinforcement and gratification when he has been able to tolerate anxiety more effectively and to change his behavioral response to it.

In the nonsuppressive forms of therapy, one basic hypothesis is held in common. The patient is asked to face the anxiety-producing situation, whether at the level of its unconscious manifestations in behavior therapy, or at the level of conscious fantasied danger situations in the analytic approaches, or as active behavioral mastery of an immediate conflict-producing interaction as in the transactional therapies. The assumption is made that if the patient is willing and able to do this, then through his own personal experience he will "learn" that he can master and tolerate the anxiety, realistically assess the danger, and thereby no longer respond to it with inappropriate behavior patterns.

THE DRIVES AND THEIR DERIVATIVES

Another factor in all therapeutic methods is the management of drives and drive derivatives, both at unconscious and preconscious levels. Other things being equal, frustration of unconscious drive derivatives by the therapist tends to intensify the underlying drive, thereby causing it to come closer to conscious awareness; gratification of such derivatives temporarily tends to reduce their intensity, thereby permitting more effective defense and continued maintenance of the underlying drive at an unconscious level.

Those analytic therapies which seek to evoke conscious awareness of conflicts associated with the underlying unconscious drives generally utilize a consistent pattern of transference frustration. The result is a gradual intensification and emergence of the drives in their many manifestations, so they can be consciously experienced, inhibited behaviorally but expressed verbally, subjected to rational consideration, thus leading to ultimate conflict resolution.

In the transactional, sensitivity, sexual, and other forms of therapy involving physical contact, nudity, and various degrees of sexual encounter, derivatives of drives from infantile and childhood sexual phases are gratified in various forms of manifest behavior. The same is true regarding aggressive drives directed toward the therapist, other members of a group, or inanimate objects, where overt behavioral expression of the drive derivatives may be encouraged. Once such derivatives have been expressed, the therapeutic forces of identification, catharsis, and reinforcement (to be discussed below) are applied.

In supportive individual and group psychotherapies, drive derivatives such as passivity, dependency, exhibitionism, voyeurism, hostility, competitiveness, etc., are frequently gratified by the therapist or by the group process. For example, a medication taken orally may involve gratification of unconscious drive derivatives regarding the therapist's concrete interest, magic fantasies, or libidinal and/or aggressive oral incorporation, etc. Or a therapist giving concrete advice, showing manifest active liking for a patient, or telling personal things about himself, etc., may gratify dependent, voyeuristic, competitive, or other drive derivatives. The meanings of such gratifications will usually be left unconscious in the patient, and therapists who do not accept such unconscious implications are unaware of the derivative gratifications that are occurring.

Programs such as Alcoholics Anonymous provide gratification of passive-dependent drive derivatives when the new member is considered, and treated like, a "baby" by his sponsor and initially is given money, food, care, lodging, etc. He becomes the center of sustained attention and is accepted in the group by virtue of his pathology.

THE PSYCHOLOGICAL MECHANISMS OF DEFENSE

Management of the psychological mechanisms of defense is another variable in comparing currently practiced psychotherapies. In psychoanalytic theory the unconscious use of psychological defense mechanisms to avoid anxiety and maintain intrapsychic conflicts at unconscious levels is well known.

In dynamic supportive psychotherapy the therapist responds in ways which strengthen the patient's already existing defenses or introduce new defenses compatible with the existing overall defensive organization, in order to establish a more stable dynamic equilibrium. Examples include intellectualized interventions for patients who resort to isolation, encouragement of hobbies or other substitute activities for patients spontaneously embracing displacement, vacations for those with dependency needs, work and doing for others in patients employing reaction formations against dependency wishes, fostering new identifications, strenghtening of rationalizations, etc.

Those treatments which deny intrapsychic conflict and emphasize a sociological or biological etiology strengthen psychological defenses such as denial, repression, and rationalization. Group therapies such as AA or Weight Watchers which deny any psychiatric disturbances or intrapsychic conflicts do the same thing.

Behavior modification therapies stress that phobic, obsessional, sexual, or other symptoms are the sole pathogenic process and deny underlying unconscious psychopathology. They thereby strengthen mechanisms such as repression, denial, displacement, undoing, reaction formation, etc., utilized by the patient in symptom formation, and reinforce the patient's defensive organization.

In psychoanalytic and analytically oriented insight-directed therapies, whether individual or group, the therapeutic process includes gradual reduction of defenses by bringing the existence of these mechanisms to conscious awareness in the patient. As part of the working alliance the patient gradually decreases the intensity and automatic use of these defense mechanisms. He voluntarily tolerates the anxiety thus mobilized in order that underlying conflicts previously defended against can now emerge more clearly into consciousness and be subjected to rational attempts at conflict resolution or adaptation.

Other forms of psychotherapy involve more active, rapid, and intense or sustained pressures on the defensive organization to circumvent them or to create situations of pressure to renounce their use. Hypnosis or narcosynthesis permit a bypassing of the patient's defenses through temporary alteration in his state of consciousness and ego integration. In some group therapies social pressures are forcibly brought to bear upon the individual member, demanding active renunciation of previous defenses with reward by acceptance into the group when the defenses are renounced, as contrasted with rejection if they are maintained.

A variant of this approach is the marathon group which deliberately adds factors of fatigue and concentrated repetition to the previously described group pressures. The rationale for these vigorous pressures upon defensive structures is that expression of the previously warded-off drives, feelings, and conflicts can occur when the defenses are thus forcibly reduced, thereby permitting an attempt at reorganization with active encouragement by the group for new methods of adaptation and interaction.

THE ROLE OF IDENTIFICATION

Ego and superego identification and its management is another variable among the different forms of psychotherapy. It may be positive and libidinal, or entail an identification with the aggressor as a result of anxiety and/or fear.

For ego functions this may result from the therapist acting as alter ego for the patient (as in neighborhood clinics for disadvantaged people) by actively intervening in the latter's life situation, or interceding with bureaucratic authority, with employers, etc. The therapist actively does things of which the patient himself is incapable (thus recreating a "good" parent-child relationship), thereby providing a model for imitation, and he encourages the patient to follow his example as a more effective mode of interaction and adaptation.

In some of the behavior modification approaches, the patient is encouraged to imitate and ultimately internalize the therapist's attitudes toward anxiety and toward the symptoms. This identification is actively reinforced by appropriate therapeutic rewards. In the active group psychotherapies the patient is encouraged to identify with the group and to accept as his own (through positive approval and reinforcement) the methods and mechanisms by which the therapist, the group, or its individual members approach psychological and emotional problems. The same is true in assertiveness training, therapy based upon modeling procedures, and psychodrama, which actively teach the patient to imitate, practice, and learn new behavior patterns.

In supportive individual psychotherapy the therapist frequently presents himself as a model for the patient, indicating ways in which he (the therapist) might approach, conceptualize, or deal with problems and encouraging the patient to imitate him in those functions and ultimately to internalize him as a new model.

In the analytic forms of treatment, identification with the therapist's analyzing functions and ways of looking at psychological problems occurs, and becomes part of the therapeutic alliance, reinforced indirectly through the therapist's interest and/or approval. However, in these forms of therapy the aspects of identification which involve more personal modes of function or personality characteristics are usually interpreted as resistances against independent self-development and are not actively encouraged by the therapist.

Identification in superego functions is another important element in the therapeutic process. In individual analytic therapy the patient's transference reactions include projection onto the therapist of previously active superego functions, anticipating from the therapist the various punishments or rewards that had been part of the patient's intrapsychic organization. The therapist maintains a relatively benign neutrality, neither condemning nor rewarding various behaviors, value systems, or thought processes. Repeatedly expecting a positive or negative reaction from the therapist, the patient receives neither and is forced to see his expectations as arising intrapsychically, to reevaluate their current appropriateness, and gradually to establish hiw own positive and negative value systems.

In analytic group processes, the members of the group are usually not as consistently nonjudgmental and neutral as is the therapist in individual treatment. However, the collective group values tend to be more benign and appropriate than those of the individual patient, and sharing of guilt-producing experiences and feelings makes the individual member feel less alien.

In supportive individual therapy the therapist may present himself as actively approving or disapproving of the patient's behavior and feelings. By actively becoming a superego model (presumably more effective and reality-oriented than the patient's), he is encouraging the patient to identify with him in these functions.

In nonanalytic group therapies there is an active use of group pressures (either positive acceptance and reward, or criticism and threat of exclusion) as a means of encouraging the patient to accept the group's value systems and moral precepts. This is an important factor in currently practiced sexual therapies, where the patient's neurotic inhibition is frequently the result of anticipated condemnation, shame, guilt feelings, punishment, etc., concerning his sexual impulses. In the frequently practiced model of male and female cotherapists working simultaneously with a couple, the therapeutic situation recreates the childhood family constellation, with potential transferences from both the mother and father actively available. But the patient couple, instead of receiving the anticipated guilt-producing criticism, condemnation, or punishment for sexual expression, rather find the parental superego transference

figures actively pleased and positively rewarding for sexual success and gratification. This encourages identification with the therapists as new superego
models and modification of previously guilt-producing superego functions.

Client-centered therapy is another example of the nonjudging and benign
superego model. The patient frequently anticipates critical or rejecting responses by the therapist, but when these are not forthcoming it forces him to
reevaluate his expectations and anticipation. He can then internalize the
therapist's benign and accepting attitudes toward the psychological material
expressed.

The limitations to the therapeutic utilization of identification include the
patient's continuing reliance on an external model (the individual therapist
or the group), and not infrequently this requires continuing active contacts to
maintain the new identification. However, if by virtue of the new identification a more gratifying adaptation is achieved, it may become self-reinforcing.
In this way identification can at times induce significant and lasting change.
Another limitation, however, may be in inhibition of the patient's development of his own potentialities if these are significantly different from those of
the therapist or group.

THE MANAGEMENT OF REGRESSION

Regression and its management is another factor observable in all the different therapeutic modalities. Regression may be related to the drives and
their derivatives, the superego processes, or the ego functions. It does not necessarily occur to the same degree in each group of psychic functions, and
there is wide variability in both the degree of regression accompanying the illness, and the capacity to tolerate therapeutically induced regression as part of
the treatment process.

The presumption in those therapies that foster regression as part of the
therapeutic process is that earlier levels and forms of conflict may thus emerge
into consciousness, in order that they can be managed or resolved in accordance with the overall procedure. The therapist's and/or group's capacity to
tolerate regressive manifestations and to assist the patient in reversing the regressive process when the therapeutic session ends are important in the management of these phenomena, and will often determine whether or not they
have ultimately beneficial effects.

In psychoanalysis and analytically oriented psychotherapy such regression
is made possible through the patient's trust in the therapeutic alliance, is encouraged through the therapist's interventions, and is perceived by both as
part of the treatment. Its usual chief manifestations are the emergence of the
transference phenomena, and the depth and intensity of the regression will in
part determine whether these remain as transference reactions or whether

they develop into a full transference neurosis. In analytic group situations, such regression is usually manifested by intensifying transference reactions both to the therapist and to the other group members.

In some of the transactional forms of group or individual therapy, in psychodrama, and in some of the variants such as primal scream therapy, regressive behavior is even more vigorously induced, encouraged, and actively reinforced. The therapeutic intent is the promoting of catharsis and abreaction of previously repressed and unconscious affective components of the patient's life.

At the other extreme are those therapies (supportive individual and group psychotherapy, behavior modification, therapy based on the use of psychotropic drugs, reality therapy, client-centered therapy) which oppose the inducement of regression and its accompanying phenomena. In these approaches the thrust of treatment is usually focused on "here and now" problems, feelings, or behavior, rather than on earlier levels of conflict. The same is true in therapies based on learning theory, where reinforcement is offered only for progressive behavior patterns, with either negative reinforcement or the absence of positive reinforcement in instances of regressive behavior patterns.

In group settings such as AA or an inpatient milieu program, regressive behavior may be initially accepted and tolerated as a means of establishing positive rapport. But once such rapport is firmly established, the therapeutic efforts are then directed toward opposing further regression and toward promoting more progressive behavior patterns.

CATHARSIS AND ABREACTION

Another variable involves the encouragement and utilization of catharsis and abreaction as therapeutic tools. In the various forms of behavior modification, therapies based on learning theory, drug-oriented therapy, and supportive group treatment, catharsis and abreaction are not considered significant therapeutic factors, in keeping with the general theoretical conceptualizations that underly these therapeutic approaches.

Dynamically oriented supportive psychotherapy may encourage catharsis and abreaction in connection with already-conscious memories or experiences, but responses which are unconscious and defended against are left unexpressed.

Hypnosis and narcosynthesis promote catharsis and abreaction of repressed memories and experiences on the premise that when the painful affective tensions have been discharged during altered states of consciousness, the memories and experiences themselves can then return more readily to consciousness for rational integration.

In psychoanalysis and analytically oriented forms of psychotherapy, cathar-sis and abreaction are used as part of a broader therapeutic process in that they contribute to an emotionally meaningful, affective, "real" psychological experience for the patient. They represent one means of exposing and desen-sitizing the patient's repressed memories and conflicts, with the ultimate goal of structurally modifying and/or integrating them through conscious under-standing and working through.

Other forms of therapy (transactional analysis, psychodrama, primal scream therapy, etc.) utilize catharsis and abreaction to reduce the intensity of conflict and foster a more comfortable psychic equilibrium through the discharge of affective tensions. The patient's willingness to undergo this type of response is actively rewarded by the therapist, or by the participants in a group experience. But ordinarily this is not followed by systematic explora-tion of the nature and implications of the conflicts and relationships which had produced the previously warded-off affects.

THE ROLE OF EXTERNAL REINFORCEMENT

Another distinguishing feature among the various modes of therapy is the use of active external reinforcement for appropriate behavior. The omnipres-ent potential for all therapeutic situations to stimulate conscious or uncon-scious transference reactions endows the therapist or group as an external superego force for the patient. In this transference role, the therapist or group may wittingly or unwittingly offer the patient rewards for behavior consonant with their own values, and withhold such reward if the patient's behavior does not meet criteria set by the therapist as appropriate and adaptive.

A series of reinforcing activities ranges from tangible tokens or gifts, through physical contact, hugging, and "stroking," to verbal encouragement, praise, or indications of pleasure, and at the other end of the spectrum con-sistently neutral therapeutic interest or verbal response. What is reinforcing for one patient may have different effects with another.

The effects of reinforcement are related to the nature of the transference and the emotional significance which the therapist or group have for the pa-tient. Therapies using persistent reinforcement often require the continued presence and activity of the reinforcing agent and involve dependence upon an authoritarian or parental figure to control behavior. To that extent they tend to reduce the patient's freedom of choice. But if the use of reinforcement causes the establishment of more fulfilling and satisfying behavior patterns, the new gratifications may in and of themselves serve as continuing reinforc-ing agents.

In analytic therapies whose goal is to promote the patient's independent judgment and control of behavior, the therapist attempts to remain neutral and to avoid *active* reinforcement of the patient's behavior patterns, thus fostering self-directed choice by the patient. However, given the general situation of relative transference abstinence in these forms of therapy, minor cues may assume greater importance and inadvertant external reinforcement may still occur through the therapist's verbal or nonverbal interventions. The therapist must be alert to these factors and deal with them as part of the treatment process.

THE CONCEPT OF STRUCTURAL CHANGE

Claims that only psychoanalysis can produce lasting structural change in an individual's personality have generated much emotional debate. In psychoanalytic theory the concept of psychic structure refers to individual or groups of mental functions which are relatively automatic and stereotyped, and have a slow spontaneous rate of change. Core psychic structures are those sets of mental functions established in the infantile and early childhood phases of psychological development, while derivative structures are their progressive modifications and subsequent development.

The variable among the different forms of therapy lies in the breadth of structural changes taking place, and in the depth of change in the sense of preconscious *derivative* vs. unconscious *core* psychic structures.

In psychoanalysis the goal is permanent modification of the infantile and early childhood core structures, and the therapeutic situation and process are uniquely designed to permit access to them in ways that allow such change to take place. All other forms of psychotherapy deal with derivative psychic structures and organization which are closer to conscious awareness. Psychoanalysis also involves the broadest possible reorganization of core as well as derivative psychic structures. In other forms of therapy goals are more narrowly focused upon specific behavior patterns, conflicts, or symptoms. And those forms of therapy based on theoretical models that do not accept unconscious intrapsychic disturbances focus upon only the most conscious and manifest derivative psychic structures.

But in all therapies if any psychological process which was previously stereotyped, automatic, and only slowly changeable has been permanently modified as a result of treatment a change in psychic structure has occurred. This may include any function, behavior pattern, fantasy, defense mechanism, identification, moral precept, type of object choice, etc. This is in contrast to a therapeutic outcome where there is no demonstrable change, or where the previously existing psychological processes again recur when the therapy is terminated, or those therapeutic situations where a change in one aspect of the patient's psychic behavior is accompanied by a reciprocal increase in some other neurotic manifestation.

DISCUSSION AND IMPLICATIONS

There has been no attempt in this presentation to make comparative assessments concerning therapeutic efficacy among the various forms of psychotherapy available today. It is highly unlikely that any one form of therapy will ever become equally applicable or effective with all different types of patients. Nor is it likely that the same therapeutic goals can or should be set for everyone who seeks treatment. Even patients who fall into the same clinical diagnostic groups will show significant variables in many specific areas of psychological functioning which will influence their accessibility and responsiveness to different forms of treatment. Not only do patients present widely varying individual differences, but therapists too show great variation in personality, skill, experience, confidence, understanding, and capacity for effectiveness, even among those sharing a common theoretical viewpoint.

In an ideal clinical situation the setting of treatment goals should take account of the multiple detailed variables involved. Within such a framework, it should become possible eventually to establish explicit indications and contraindications for each of the available treatment modalities. And it should then become possible to select for the particular patient that form of therapy most likely and expeditiously to achieve the individually established treatment goals.

It would be my hope that an attempt at unifying concepts of the treatment process, such as the one presented here, will stimulate others to apply different theoretical perspectives to the spectrum of psychotherapies without oversimplifications. And hopefully such combined attempts can hasten the day when the choice of therapeutic modality is based upon the needs and potentialities of the patient rather than the prejudices and allegiances of the therapist.

REFERENCES

Ackerman, N. W. (1966). *Treating the Troubled Family*. New York:Basic Books.

Bandura, A. (1969). *Principles of Behavior Modification*. New York: Holt.

Bergin, A. E., and Strupp, H. H. (1972). *Changing Frontiers in the Science of Psychotherapy*. Chicago: Aldine-Atherton.

Berne, E. (1961). *Transactional Analysis in Psychotherapy*. New York: Grove Press.

Birk, L. (1974). Intensive group therapy: An effective behavioral-psychoanalytic model. *American Journal of Psychiatry* 131:11-16.

———— and Brinkley-Birk, A. W. (1974). Psychoanalysis and behavior therapy. *American Journal of Psychiatry* 131:499-510.

Bordin, E. S. (1974). *Research Strategies in Psychotherapy*. New York: Wiley.

Dollard, J., and Miller, N. E. (1950). *Personality and Psychotherapy*. New York: McGraw-Hill.

Ellis, A. (1962). *Reason and Emotion in Psychotherapy*. Secaucus, N.J.: Stuart.

Frank, J. D. (1961). *Persuasion and Healing*. Baltimore: Johns Hopkins Press.

Garfield, S. L. (1971). Research on client variables in psychotherapy. *Handbook of Psychotherapy and Behavior Change*, eds. A. P. Bergin and S. L. Garfield. New York: Wiley.

Goldman, G. (1956). Reparative psychotherapy. *Changing Concepts of Psychoanalytic Medicine*, eds. S. Rado and G. E. Daniels, pp. 101-114. New York: Grune & Stratton.

Goldstein, A. P., and Dean, S. J. (eds.) (1966). *The Investigation of Psychotherapy*. New York: Wiley.

Haley, J. (1963). *Strategies of Psychotherapy*. New York: Grune & Stratton.

Kalish, H. J. (1965). Behavior therapy. *Handbook of Clinical Psychology*, ed. B. B. Wolman. New York: McGraw-Hill.

Knight, R. P. (1954). *A Critique of the Present Status of the Psychotherapies—Psychoanalytic Psychiatry and Psychology*, eds. R. Knight and C. Friedman. New York: International Universities Press.

Laing, R. D. (1965). *The Divided Self*. Baltimore: Penguin Books.

Lieberman, M. A., Yalom, I. D., and Miles, M. B. (1973). *Encounter Groups: First Facts*. New York: Basic Books.

Masters, W. H., and Johnson, V. E. (1970). *Human Sexual Inadequacy*. Boston: Little Brown.

May, R., Angel, E., and Ellenberger, H. F. E. (1958). *Existence: A New Dimension in Psychiatry and Psychology*. New York: Basic Books.

Mendel, W. M. (1972). Comparative psychotherapy. *International Journal of Psychoanalytic Psychotherapy* 1:117-126.

Moreno, J. L. (1946). *Psychodrama*. New York: Beacon Press.

Murray, E. J., and Jacobson, L. I. (1971). The nature of learning in traditional and behavioral psychotherapy. *Handbook of Psychotherapy and Behavior Change*, eds. A. E. Bergin and S. L. Garfield. New York: Wiley.

Offenkrantz, W., and Tobin, A. (1974). Psychoanalytic psychotherapy. *Archives of General Psychiatry* 30:593-606.

Perls, F. S., Hefferline, R. F., and Goodman, P. (1951). *Gestalt Therapy*. New York: Julian Press.

Porter, R. (ed.) (1968). *The Role of Learning in Psychotherapy*. "A Ciba Foundation Symposium." Boston: Little Brown.

Rhoads, L. M., and Feather, B. W. (1974). The application of psychodynamics to behavior therapy. *American Journal of Psychiatry*. 131:17-20.

Rogers, C. R. (1951). *Client Centered Therapy*. Cambridge, Mass: Riverside Press.

Shahakian, W. S. (ed.) (1969). *Psychotherapy and Counseling*. Chicago: Rand McNally.

Slavson, S. R. (ed.) (1956). *The Fields of Group Psychotherapy*. New York: International Universities Press.

Strupp, H. H. (1975). Psychoanalysis, "focal psychotherapy," and the nature of the therapeutic influence. *Archives of General Psychiatry*. 32:127-135.

Sugarman, B. (1974). *Daytop Village: A Therapeutic Community*. New York: Holt.

Tseng, W., and McDermott, J. F., Jr. (1975). Psychotherapy: Historical roots, universal elements and cultural variations. *American Journal of Psychiatry*. 132:378-384.

Wolpe, J. (1958). *Psychotherapy by Reciprocal Inhibition*. Stanford, Calif.: Stanford Univ. Press.

PAUL A. DEWALD, M.D.

DR. DEWALD is medical director of the St. Louis Psychoanalytic Institute and a training and supervising analyst for the St. Louis and Chicago institutes. He is also clinical professor of psychiatry, St. Louis University School of Medicine. He is the author of Psychotherapy: A Dynamic Approach, and The Psychoanalytic Process.

The Misalliance Dimension in Freud's Case Histories: I. The Case of Dora*

Robert Langs, M.D.

Clinical Assistant Professor of Psychiatry
State University of New York
Downstate Medical Center, Brooklyn

This paper presents an effort to identify sectors of therapeutic misalliance between Freud and his patient Dora based on modifications in the framework of the analytic relationship and situation. Use is made of a template based on the current ground rules and boundaries of the patient-analyst relationship, and three deviations from this template are identified in Freud's analytic work with Dora. The intrapsychic and interactional sequelae of these deviations in technique for Dora and for the course of her analysis are traced out. The consequent sectors of misalliance are identified and the participation of both Dora and Freud is described, as are their respective, largely unconscious efforts to modify these areas of unconscious collusion. Stress is placed on Dora's unconscious perceptions of the actual implications of Freud's modifications in the frame. The role of Freud's failure to rectify these deviations and to analyze their implications for Dora are considered, including their influence on the patient's premature termination of her analysis.

INTRODUCTION

In the past decade or so, there has been a growing interest in developing a well-rounded and comprehensive understanding of the patient-analyst relationship. Among the many issues that have been explored in the course of these endeavors, one segment will be considered here on the basis of a restudy of one of Freud's case histories, that of Dora (Freud, 1905a; see also Langs, in press b,c). My focus will be on problems in the establishment and maintenance of the therapeutic alliance, and the development of a particular type of disturbance in sectors of this alliance that I have termed "therapeutic misalliances" (1974, 1975a, 1976, in press a). In particular, the contribution of

*This paper is the first in a series of three prepared for the volume, *Freud and His Patients*, edited by Mark Kanzer and Jules Glenn. I am indebted to both for their helpful editorial suggestions.

deviations in the basic ground rules and boundaries of the analytic situation and their relationship to the development of sectors of misalliance will be explored. It will be my main hypothesis that modifications in the basic framework of the analytic relationship evoke intense responses in the patient, and that these characteristically offer him a basis for potential sectors of misalliance with the analyst. It will be my goal to return to Freud's case histories in search of support or refutation of this hypothesis, and to examine the implications of my findings. In order to concentrate on this task, it will be necessary to bypass many other contributing factors to the material that I will study, and I will be able only briefly to counterbalance my focus on misalliance with references to the indications of positive segments of therapeutic alliance between Freud and his patients (Kanzer, 1952, 1975; Zetzel, 1966).

We may broadly define the therapeutic alliance as the conscious and unconscious agreement, applied in subsequent actual work, on the part of both the patient and analyst to join forces in effecting symptom alleviation and constructive characterological changes through insight and inner structural change on the part of the patient. In contrast, therapeutic misalliances constitute interactions that are designed either to undermine such goals or to achieve results on some other basis (Langs, 1975a). Therapeutic alliances and misalliances constitute a continuum, and, at any given moment, one or the other may predominate. While often difficult to distinguish, this differentiation is important since sectors of misalliance entail transference gratifications, shared defenses, and mutual acting out, even though they represent mutual and misguided efforts at cure. The determination of the presence of a misalliance is based on a careful and repeated scrutiny of the patient's associations and behaviors, and the analyst's subjective awareness. This type of assessment —which I have termed the validating process (Langs, 1976, in press a) —is repeatedly carried out during the course of an analysis and it serves as an indicator of the direction taken by the analytic work at a given moment. The recognition of misalliance is important in that their development undermines sectors of the basic psychoanalytic work and compromises aspects of the outcome of the analysis. It is therefore essential that they be resolved if insight and structural change are to be maximally achieved for the patient. In fact, the development of sectors of misalliance are inevitable in any analytic experience, and their recognition and analytic resolution are among the most insight-producing and growth-promoting experiences for the patient—and at times, for the analyst as well.

While investigating therapeutic misalliances, it was found empirically that they are often based on deviations in the analyst's usual stance and on errors in technique (Langs, 1973a, 1974, 1975a,b, 1976, in press a). These findings led to a reconsideration of the framework of the psychoanalytic relationship and of the indication for, and complications evoked by, deviations or parameters of technique (Langs, 1975b). The attempt was made to establish the distinction between valid deviations from those that prove detrimental to the analytic process and are, therefore, best classified as technical errors. Related to this problem is the issue of how to best establish and maintain the therapeutic alliance (Stone, 1961, 1967; Greenson, 1965, 1967, 1971, 1972; Greenson and Wexler, 1969; Arlow and Brenner, 1966; Zetzel, 1956, 1958, 1966-1969; Heimann, 1970; Kanzer, 1975; Arlow, 1975; Langs, 1975a, b, in press a).

In brief, my own clinical observations have indicated that the therapeutic alliance is best maintained and developed through a firm, though not rigid, adherence to the basic ground rules of analysis and through a sensitive maintenance of the psychoanalytic framework. This includes the establishment of a sound therapeutic stance and the use of interpretations; in general, noninterpretive measures of all kinds prove detrimental and the source of misalliances.

In this context, I attempted (1975b, in press a) to define the present, empirically derived optimal ground rules of the psychoanalytic situation. I included the following: set fees, hours, and length of sessions; the fundamental rule of free association with communication occurring while the patient is on the couch; the absence of physical contact and extratherapeutic gratifications; the analyst's relative anonymity and the use of neutral interventions geared primarily toward interpretations; and the exclusive one-to-one relationship with total confidentiality. I found that in most clinical situations — including the treatment of adolescents — it was more therapeutic to adhere to these basic ground rules and to offer interpretations to the patient, rather than to deviate under any conditions short of an emergency. Further, all modifications of these ground rules, even when prompted by necessary human responsiveness or an emergency situation, universally evoked intense responses in the patient. If these went unrecognized and unanalyzed, they tended to have detrimental effects on the analysis and on the patient.

These earlier findings were not considered a brief for rigidity, but they indicate the importance of the framework of the analytic relationship and the great influence on the patient of any modification in this basic area. It was concluded that the manner in which the analyst establishes and maintain the boundaries and framework of the analytic relationship reflects important aspects of the management of his own intrapsychic state and fantasies, including their countertransference aspects. Further, the proper management of the framework implicitly offers the analyst as a constructive figure for unconscious identification by the patient, and creates the conditions for the most viable and uncontaminated unfolding of the patient's transference projections and neurosis — and their interpretation and modification. On the other hand, impairments in the management of the framework and unneeded deviations in technique tend to inappropriately gratify and offer maladaptive defenses to both patient and analyst, promoting pathogenic interactions and identifications. I concluded that the present ground rules and boundaries of adult (and adolescent) psychoanalysis contain within them an optimally viable and valid basic hold for the patient (Winnicott, 1965) and a corresponding setting for the unfolding of the analytic work.

With these observations and hypotheses in mind, I restudied Freud's case histories. I reasoned that if my main conclusions were valid, and if these basic tenets had stood the test of time and could be viewed as fundamentally sound, it would also be possible to look to the past and apply the current ground rules of analysis to Freud's work—despite the fact they did not represent his own framework. In this way, I would have an opportunity to test hypotheses developed from current clinical observations and possibly develop further insights concerning them. Thus, I proposed to use the current set of ground rules as a template to be applied to Freud's work, so that each time he intervened in a manner that did not fit with the present framework, I would observe the consequences of the "deviation" and its repercussions for the patient.

In taking this backward look and applying current standards to Freud's work, I recognize the extent to which he experimented with the ground rules and maintained a consistent search for more effective therapeutic principles. It would be difficult to delineate a consistent set of rules by which Freud worked, and I will not attempt to do so here. Further, his case histories in no way incorporated a detailed account of Freud's analytic technique or of the sessions with his patients. We are therefore faced with a number of limitations to this exploration, and yet it seems possible to benefit from Freud's early ingenious efforts to develop a viable psychoanalytic technique and to learn from the apparent mistakes that he inevitably made. Thus, despite the inherent difficulties, the attempt to test current hypotheses based on a retrospective study of Freud's material offers an unusual opportunity to ascertain the extent to which the management of the framework of the psychoanalytic relationship meaningfully contributes to the therapeutic experience of the patient. With these ideas in mind, let us now consider Freud's (1905a) analysis of Dora.

THE CLINICAL MATERIAL

In studying the case of Dora for misalliances, I am not embarking upon an entirely original research. Erikson (1962) utilized aspects of this analysis to develop his conceptualization of reality and actuality both in the analytic situation and for the individual in his life. In attempting to demonstrate that actuality—defined as "the world verified only in the ego's immediate emersion in action" (p. 453)—differed for Dora and Freud, Erikson was stud-

ying a dimension of misalliance from his own vantage point. Before comparing his findings with my own, however, I will present some pertinent clinical
material.

A review of Freud's paper on Dora indicates that there were two main "deviations" — by present definition — and one related minor one in analytic technique utilized by Freud and two types of misalliances which developed between himself and Dora, formed partly on the basis of these deviations. Specifically, Freud had treated Dora's father for syphilis and also knew her father's sister and brother; in addition, Freud knew Herr K., the man who had
attempted to seduce or marry Dora and who also had referred Dora's father to
Freud. Freud's presentation suggests that Dora's father spoke to him directly
about her prior to the analysis and that he communicated with Freud after
the analysis had been completed, and possibly did so during the three months
in which the analysis was in progress as well. In these ways, Freud did not
maintain the one-to-one relationship with Dora that many analysts would
currently establish (Langs, 1973a), and these various third parties to the a-
nalysis — directly and indirectly — appear to have become important factors in
the outcome of the analytic experience.

A second area of deviation related to Freud's special interest in Dora's sexual material — a modification in neutrality — while a third and more minor
"deviation" occurred when Freud experimented with Dora by pointing to a
book of matches that he had brought into his consultation room; the role that
this maneuver played in the analysis will be discussed presently.

In this context, then, the first sector of misalliance between Dora and
Freud related to the manner in which she entered analysis. Her father
brought her to Freud with the evident intention that the latter should actively
intervene on the father's behalf so that Dora would no longer press him to give
up his affair with Frau K. As Dora's father gave Freud a history of her problems, he said: "Please try and bring her to reason" (Freud, 1905a; p. 26).

Dora, for her part, apparently entered analysis in order to convince Freud
that her assessment of the situation with her father was correct and in all likelihood she also hoped to persuade Freud to intervene for her with her father so
that he would give up his mistress (Erikson, 1962). Thus, Dora began treatment in the hope of establishing a misalliance in which Freud would help her
to manipulate her father and disrupt his relationship with Frau K. As additional evidence that this was among Dora's motives for seeing Freud, we may
note that she had threatened suicide and was first brought to Freud for analysis after a quarrel with her father on this very subject.

Dora was also suffering from a multiplicity of hysterical symptoms and
wished to find symptomatic relief from these maladies. In all likelihood, this
contributed to segments of a viable therapeutic alliance with Freud that fostered the development of the positive aspects of their therapeutic endeavors.

However, in addition to possibly being prepared to resolve her inner conflicts and symptoms through the analytic efforts developed by Freud, it appears that Dora also hoped to alleviate these difficulties through the special assistance that she sought from him. Thus, it seems likely that Dora's conscious and unconscious motivations for analysis, and her conscious and unconscious fantasies related to the means through which she would find symptomatic relief, contributed both to sectors of alliance and misalliance with Freud. This is typical of patients entering analysis, and much depends on the analyst's response.

For his part, Freud was aware of Dora's intended misalliance and while he did not specifically interpret and analyze it, rather early in the analysis (p. 42) he pointed out to Dora that her illness was intended to detach her father from Frau K. In so doing, he added that she would recover if this were a-chieved, but that he — Freud — hoped that her father would not yield in the face of Dora's symptoms, since this would provide her with a most dangerous weapon. This intervention preceded by a short time the appearance of Dora's first dream which conveyed her intentions of terminating her analysis. Freud's comment may have contributed to these intentions, since he was, in effect, unconsciously indicating to Dora his unwillingness to participate in her intended misalliance, doing so without providing her insight into the meanings of the misalliance and without offering — however indirectly — alternative methods of resolving her difficulties. In a sense, this may be seen as an early effort by Dora to effect a "misalliance cure" (Langs, 1975a, 1976, in press a) —noninsightful symptomatic relief effected with the help of Freud. The latter's comment indicates the extent to which he sensed the power of such "cures" and recognized them to be antianalytic. This interaction and the areas of developing misalliance should, however, become clearer after we outline Freud's apparent contributions to them.

Freud was, of course, interested in helping Dora to alleviate her hysterical symptoms through insight into the unconscious fantasies on which they were based. However, he also indicated in his presentation that there were other motives which prompted his interest in Dora, and these had the potential for creating sectors of misalliances that could also disturb the analysis. They are evident in one of Freud's pivotal statements (p. 31) : "I was anxious to subject my assumptions [i.e., regarding sexuality] to a rigorous test in this case." As we know, Freud had recently written *The Interpretation of Dreams* (1900) and was learning to apply his new theories about dreams and neurosis clinically. Furthermore, he was working on his "Three Essays on the Theory of Sexuality" (1905b) and was also most eager to test out his hypotheses regarding infantile sexuality in his clinical work with his patients. As Freud himself later stated (1912), therapeutic zeal and vested interests of this kind can prove disruptive to an analysis — in our terms, can create misalliances. Erikson (1962) has written of these concerns as part of Freud's quest for genetic truth. Erikson contrasted it with Dora's search for historical truth, as related to her then current realities and to the fidelity of those close to her; this served as a means of establishing her identity as a young woman.

Let us now briefly follow some of the highlights of Dora's analysis with a focus on the threads woven out of Freud's "deviations" and the potential efforts toward misalliance of both Freud and Dora. The first communications from Dora — as reported by Freud in his paper — alluded to an attempt at seduction by Herr K. when she was fourteen years of age; this had preceded by two years the scene at the lake with Herr K. during which he had proposed to her. The latter incident had prompted Dora to rupture her relationship with him and intensified her efforts to separate her father from Frau K. In an earlier experience, Herr K. had arranged to be alone with Dora, and had kissed her, evoking a reaction of disgust. Dora was frightened and Freud considered this to be an abnormal reaction; he very quickly brought out her awareness of erections in men.

From the vantage point that we are considering, it would appear reasonable to formulate the hypothesis that Freud's personal acquaintance with Dora's father and Herr K. contributed to a very early and intense erotization of her relationship with Freud, one that was communicated in a relatively thinly disguised form in this first communication. If we remember that Dora's father had turned her over to Herr K. as a kind of payment for his relationship with Frau K., we can immediately recognize a very striking parallel between that situation and Dora's initial relationship with Freud. While it is true that Freud failed throughout this analysis, as he readily acknowledged and discussed, to interpret Dora's transference (i.e., primarily genetically — or intrapsychically — based) feelings and fantasies toward him, the additional fact that Freud was closely identified in reality with Dora's father and Herr K. undoubtedly contributed to her conscious and unconscious perception of this relationship (Langs, 1973b). It would therefore be difficult and incorrect to attribute this initial, and the subsequent rather pervasive, erotized relationship with Freud entirely to transference factors. There were strong kernels of reality at the roots of Dora's inner responses to Freud that were embedded in the latter's relationships with these two men and in the actual stance that Freud took with Dora in the analysis. His ready acceptance of sexuality and his very early emphasis (intervening and questioning) on this area undoubtedly heightened Dora's belief that Freud was in some ways not unlike her father and Herr K. Freud's intense interest in specific sexuality — amounting to a relaxation of his neutrality — seems to have contributed to a misalliance with Dora which she (unconsciously?) perceived very strongly in sexual terms (Langs, 1975c).

This delineation of the role of possible unconscious perceptions of Freud and of the interactional dimension of Dora's responses to him help to clarify her ongoing intrapsychic conflicts and unconscious fantasies. A patient's reactions to the analyst are always a mixture of reality—as it exists and is perceived—and fantasy, transference and nontransference. Only by specifying the actual nature of the ongoing interaction with the analyst, and especially the implicit and explicit meanings of his interventions and failures to intervene, can one establish the components of reality and fantasy in the patient's reaction to him (Langs, 1973b, 1975c, 1976, in press a).

The relative neglect of reality factors in the patient-analyst relationship (see also Greenson, 1972) and of nontransference elements was not only characteristic of Freud's technique at the time of his analysis of Dora, but persists to the present day. Freud tended to neglect the interaction between himself and his patients, and the percipitants of primarily transference reactions therein. With Dora, he was quite slow to recognize the transference reactions in her communications, and he tended to quickly link them to genetic material without a full appreciation of the implications for his current relationship with his patient (Kanzer, 1966). We can still learn a great deal from the consequences of these oversights in Freud's work with Dora.

To return more specifically to my discussion of this analysis, the case history indicates that Dora expressed other concerns that were related to the manner in which she entered analysis and to the fact that Freud knew her father. She spoke of how a governess had pretended affection for her while in reality preferring her father; eventually she dropped Dora. This may be an indirect representation of her concerns in her relationship with Freud. She may even have fantasied that Freud's primary allegiance was to her father and that there was an unholy alliance between the two. For her part, the patient continued to attempt to prove that the scene by the lake had been a reality and not her fantasy, and Freud concluded—undoubtedly conveying this to Dora —that she was being completely truthful. As a possible reward for this affirmation, Dora told Freud that she believed that her father was impotent and acknowledged her awareness of fellatio. Freud then quickly interpreted Dora's love for her father and for Herr K., but she denied being attracted to the latter. It was in this context that the first dream was reported.

In it, a house is on fire and Dora's father is standing beside her bed and wakes her. She dresses quickly but her mother wants to stop and save her jewel case; her father says, "I refuse to let myself and my two children be burnt for the sake of your jewel case" (p. 64). They hurry downstairs and as soon as Dora is outside, she wakes up.

This dream had first been dreamed three times at the lake after Herr K.'s attempt to either seduce or propose to her. It is striking that in his analysis of this dream, while Freud alluded to the concept of day residues, he neglected the task of determining the specific day residues for this dream—the adaptive tasks or stimuli which had prompted it (Langs, 1973a). Since they undoubtedly included major percipitants from Dora's ongoing relationship with Freud, this suggests that Freud had a blind spot for Dora's feelings toward him — the so-called transference — since the dream, even retrospectively to Freud, very clearly conveyed Dora's thoughts of fleeing the analysis and her fantasies that she was once more in danger sexually with Freud as she had previously been with Herr K. (a repetition of the initial theme of the analysis).

The manifest dream itself and certain of Dora's associations illuminate the theme of misalliance in that her mother wanted to save her jewel case, but her father wanted to save his children. The associations to the jewel case related to Dora's virginity, which she had felt had been threatened by Herr K.; she apparently felt similarly threatened by Freud. While the unfolding genetic history provided clues as to the development of the intrapsychic fantasies and needs within Dora that prompted her to sexualize her relationship with Freud and to respond to his technique in an erotic manner, our main efforts here will continue to focus on the generally ignored contributions made by Freud to these sexual anxieties and fantasies, and to the misalliance with which Dora was concerned. In this regard, the dream seems to reflect Dora's anxiety regarding Freud's intense interest in her sexual fantasies, his close association with her father and Herr K., and her responsive determination to flee the analytic situation.

The continuum and intermixture of alliance and misalliance is suggested by the apparent dual roles in which Freud was placed in this dream: seducer and protector. This provides evidence that in addition to the sector of misalliance between Freud and Dora, there were important areas of alliance and continued hopes in the patient that Freud would rescue her from her plight, both inner and outer. Further, the manifest dream was concerned with alerting and adaptive responses to danger. On this basis, and in keeping with Dora's subsequent associations, we may also postulate that the dream was prompted by unconscious perceptions of the misalliance and was reported to Freud as part of an effort to call it to his attention and to assist him in resolving it (Langs, 1975a, 1976). It therefore appears that Dora was attempting to save her analysis at the very juncture that she was thinking of abandoning it — a response that is characteristic of patients faced with sectors of misalliance with their analysts.

Dora's associations to this dream eventually led to the fact that Herr K. had taken the key to her bedroom and had left her unprotected from his intrusions. Freud interpreted her intentions to escape from Herr K.'s persecution, but did not develop a comparable theme for her relationship to himself. Eventually, the anxieties were traced to her feelings toward her father, who actually was the middleman in both situations. Freud was also able to point out that Dora was frightened by her readiness to submit sexually to Herr K.

and needed to flee him because of this—though he again did not allude to the analysis.

It was in this context that Freud attempted his experiment of placing matches were Dora could see them from the couch. When she could see nothing, Freud pointed to the matches and examined how fire was tied to fears of bed-wetting, and they went on to establish that she had indeed been a bed wetter in her childhood. Here Freud's interest in the genetic truth and in sexuality deflected him from verbalizing Dora's current anxieties and fantasies, although his behavior did demonstrate an unconscious appreciation of some of the current stimuli for her fantasies and associations. Unconscious perceptiveness of this kind is often evident in otherwise deviant or erroneous interventions of analysts (Langs, 1976). In addition, Freud was unconsciously acting out something akin to Dora's very fear of an uncontrolled analytic situation—fire—therebe sharing this fantasy with her. It is of interest, in view of my finding that deviations in technique almost always evoke attempts by analysands to evoke further deviations (1975b), that Dora later responded with two symptomatic acts of her own—the hiding of a letter from, and thereby playing secrets with, Freud, and playing with a reticule during a session. This latter reflected her masturbatory fantasies and, undoubtedly, her mounting sexual anxieties in the analytic situation and her unconscious perception of Freud's behavior. We may view Freud's use of the matches and Dora's behavior with the letter and reticule as a sector of misalliance in which nonverbal communication and acting out—actually, acting in—was permitted in lieu of verbal communication.

Freud's experiment led to a most revealing addendum to the first dream: Dora had smelled smoke. Freud then connected the dream to himself, since he was prone to use the phrase that there could be no smoke without fire; yet when she directly objected to this intervention, Freud appears to have dropped it. It may well be that here both he and she shared a defensive misalliance—a displacement away from their relationship. Freud did, however, return to this area in a small way when he interpreted Dora's wish to yield to Herr K. and to have a kiss from him, suggesting that she also wished to be kissed by himself. In this context, Freud later made the general comment that transference fantasies cannot be proven—something that seems to reflect his skepticism and difficulties in this area.

Freud then adds that the dream had actually been reported when he and Dora had been working on the topic of masturbation. He next reports that Dora knew of her father's syphilitic diagnosis by virtue of the fact that she had heard her father talking about it after he had seen Freud. She had connected this illness with her father's loose behavior and we can see again how Freud was, for Dora, undoubtedly identified with her father and with his style of life. Freud did attempt then to tentatively suggest to Dora that he must remind her of Herr K., but he did not consider the possibility that his behavior, in being similar to that of Herr K., was a factor. There is a general tendency in the psychoanalytic literature on so-called transference phenomena to ignore this latter aspect (Langs, 1974a, in press a).

The second dream, one that is far more complex than the first, alludes to Dora being in a strange town and then going into a house where she finds a letter from her mother that refers to Dora's having left without her parents' knowledge. She learns that her father is dead and asks about a hundred times: "Where is the station?" receiving the answer, "Five minutes." She sees a woods and then asks a man who replies, "Two and a half hours more." She refuses his company and then sees the station that she is seeking in front of her, but she cannot reach it. She feels anxious and then is at home where a maid opens the door and replies that her mother and the others are already at the cemetery.

As indicated by Dora's associations and Freud's analysis, this dream had many allusions to the scene at the lake as well as to Dora's plans to terminate her analysis. Freud delineated three unconscious fantasies in the latent content of this dream: revenge on her father, defloration by force, and waiting until a goal is reached. Associations led to pregnancy fantasies and to sexual curiosity.

In the third session in which this dream was being explored, Dora announced her intention to terminate at the end of the hour. Her associations indicated that, in doing so, she was identifying with a governess toward whom Herr K. had made advances and who had succumbed, only to be rejected later by him. Despite her anger, the girl had waited around, hoping that Herr K. would pursue her, although he never did. Still ignoring the "transference" implications of this dream and associations, Freud used it to finally convince Dora that she had been deeply hurt by Herr K. who had used similar language in approaching both Dora and the governess. Freud added that it was this hurt that had prompted her to flee from Herr K.—all the while secretly hoping that he would pursue her and convince her that his intentions were sincere. In a sense, by accepting Dora's decision to terminate and by not analyzing the meanings of this decision, Freud enabled Dora to reenact the incident with Herr. K.—with one important modification: she was now the aggressor and Freud was the victim. This type of shared acting out of conscious and unconscious fantasies is another common form of misalliance.

In his discussion of the analysis, Freud indicated his awareness that Dora was attempting to have him ask her to continue and to thereby provide her with the substitute gratification that she longed for. In stating this, he was alluding to another kind of misalliance that Dora sought to live out with Freud, one in which she would spurn him and he would ask her to remain. This would have entailed the bilateral enactment of another unconscious fantasy related to the experience with Herr K., and, while Freud did not gratify this misalliance, he also did not interpret it. In all, Dora lived out her revenge on both her father and Herr K., as well as undoubtedly some direct hostility toward Freud, in terminating in the manner that she did.

Freud emphasized that his failure to master the transference was an important factor in Dora's abrupt termination, although he did not ascribe to it the prime importance that he gave to his failure to explore Dora's homosexual fantasies. He did state, however, that "Owing to the readiness with which Dora put one part of the pathogenic material at my disposal during the treatment, I neglected the precaution of looking out for the first sign of transference" (p. 118). He then goes on to say that Dora, "kept anxiously trying to make sure whether I was being quite straightforward with her, for her father 'always preferred secrecy and roundabout ways'" (p. 118). We see here Freud's own awareness that his special interest in Dora's sexual material had contributed to his neglect of the transference; his comments also seem to reflect his unconscious realization that Dora had strongly identified him with her father, although he does not trace this to the role that her father played in introducing Dora to him. We see that, to the very end, this "deviation" in technique contributed to Dora's "transference" fantasies, and to the premature interruption of her analysis; Freud's overriding interest in having her confirm his theories of infantile sexuality is also reaffirmed here as a source of misalliance and flight.

In concluding his presentation, Freud describes Dora's return visit some fifteen months after her termination. As Erikson (1962) emphasized, Freud stated that he immediately knew that she was not in earnest, thereby reflecting some difficulty that remained within him regarding his relationship with her. In that last interview, Dora described how five months after termination, at the time of the death of one of Herr and Frau K.'s children, she had confronted everyone and was vindicated. The timing of her visit to Freud, however, related to a facial neuralgia that she had developed after she had apparently read about Freud's promotion to professor. Without considering why she returned to see him at the time that she did, Freud "forgave" Dora for not letting him cure her more fully and the interview ended.

Erikson (1962) suggested that Dora's vengeance seemed to Freud to be acting out, and that this assessment may have been a factor in his feeling that she was not interested in pursuing further analysis with him. Further, to extend Erikson's discussion of the importance of establishing a sense of fidelity so as to assist Dora in affirming her feminine identity, we can see that Freud's involvement with Herr K. and her father impaired both his image as a person with whom his patient might identify in a more healthy manner and as the analyst who might help her achieve a sense of identity based on a strong sense of fidelity. As Erikson noted, Dora's first dream assigned to her father the role of a hoped-for protector, a role that she had no doubt transferred to Freud, but then had difficulty in maintaining.

DISCUSSION

To summarize, the case of Dora suggests that Freud's "deviation" from present technique, through which he accepted a patient under the circumstances of having previously treated her father and having known the man who had attempted to seduce her, along with his continued contact with this patient's father during and after the analysis, violated the one-to-one quality of the analytic relationship. In doing so, it threatened the sense of confidentiality necessary for a proper analytic atmosphere and confounded Dora's image of Freud. This deviation in technique runs like a clear thread throughout the analysis and is directly related to the premature termination enforced by Dora, who fled Freud in a manner very similar to her flight from Herr K. The material strongly suggests that she was never able to sufficiently differentiate Freud from her father and Herr K., and was never clear as to Freud's motives for seeing her and as to the underlying basis for his interest in her sexual fantasies.

This special interest, which modified Freud's neutrality, prompted a second sector of misalliance between him and Dora, and placed undue emphasis on the patient's sexual associations and on the efforts to search out the genetic dimensions of her infantile sexual life. This was perceived by Dora as strongly seductive and quickly linked to her father and Herr K., and was further reinforced by the fact that Freud had made the diagnosis of her father's syphilitic infection. Dora was also unable to overcome the suspicion that Freud was directly involved in a misalliance with her father and carrying out the latter's wish to deter her from disrupting his relationship with Frau K. or that Freud was to serve as a new potential substitute lover.

From the material available to us, it is unclear how effective interpretations of Dora's conscious and unconscious perceptions of Freud's tendencies toward misalliance would have been, since their realistic core could only be partially modified through the necessary first step of rectification (Langs, 1973b, 1974a, 1975a, 1976). Clearly, when such interpretations were not offered, Dora terminated her analysis, possibly because of her uncertainty regarding Freud's intentions and because of her own temptations to submit to the potentially erotic misalliance.

For her part, Dora intended another kind of misalliance with Freud, one through which she could prove the veracity of her contentions. While a good deal of her initial communications to Freud unfolded along these lines, when he indicated his belief in her and his hopes that she would not use her symptoms as a weapon against her father, Dora seems to have shifted her focus to her own sexual anxieties and fantasies, and to her response to the erotic stir-rings evoked in part by Freud. When these were not interpreted to her and her fears of losing control sexually apparently mounted, she terminated her analysis to protect herself—another latent meaning of her first dream.

In all, then, major unanalyzed "deviations" in technique in the case of Dora proved central to the premature termination of this analysis. They con-tributed to an exhibitionistic-voyeuristic and erotized sector of misalliance which went uninterpreted and was resolved only through Dora's premature termination. It may well be that when Dora realized that she could not gratify her intended manipulative misalliance with Freud, she terminated in order to do the job herself—something she accomplished several months later.

The determination of reality and fantasy in Dora's relationship with Freud is a very complex one (Langs, 1973b, in press a). Because of Freud's acquain-tance with Dora's father and Herr K., her erotic fantasies toward Freud had a significant kernel of truth to them, although they were not founded on direct-ly seductive behavior by Freud. On the other hand, the latter's intense interest in Dora's sexual material readily lent itself to the development of conscious and unconscious fantasies of sexual interest in his patient.

As I have shown elsewhere (1973a, 1973b, 1974a, 1975c, 1976), patients are exquisitely sensitive to the slightest deviation in technique and to any un-due interest in a particular area on the part of the analyst. Such responses are based on conscious, and more usually unconscious, perceptions of this interest which are largely veridical—though never totally undistorted—and exten-sions of these realities into intrapsychically determined fantasies on the part of the patient are the rule. It is also not uncommon, as seems to have been the case with Dora, for certain patients to retreat, regress, and to become mo-mentarily less communicative—except in regard to the deviation itself—when faced with modifications in the framework of the analytic situation (Langs, 1975b, 1976, in press b,c; Viderman, 1974), especially when these are un-recognized and unanalyzed with the patient. Thus, Dora's second dream and the associations to it seem far more confused than in the case of the first dream, though both manifestly and latently reflect a variety of conscious and unconscious fantasies with which she was struggling.

I would speculate that both Freud and Dora engaged in unconscious efforts to modify the sectors of misalliance—respective, unconscious attempts at cure (Langs, 1975a, 1976). Freud's use of the matchbook may have unconsciously conveyed his recognition that the analytic interaction was a major source of anxiety and disturbance for Dora, even though his manifest use of this meas-ure was primarily for reconstruction. Dora's first dream may be viewed as an unconscious effort to alert Freud to the misalliance and to her unconscious perceptions of her analyst's apparent difficulties with her—an effort to a-waken Freud to these problems. Along with her associations, this dream also became the vehicle through which she attempted to communicate to Freud her unresolved "transference" fantasies and possibly her unconscious perceptions of his unresolved countertransference difficulties as well. Freud's capacity to benefit from these unconscious efforts by Dora found their ultimate fulfillment in his recognition of the role of transference fantasies and resistances in her — and in all — analysands, though he failed to make this discovery before she left. The universal unconscious capacity of patients to teach and "cure" their analysts (Langs, 1976, in press a) thereby found a most exquisite expression.

We see, then, that misalliance and alliance tend to intermix and that patients — as well as analysts — have the unconscious need to both maintain and resolve them. Early efforts toward misalliance are inevitable in patients; their analysis and modification by the analyst, who does not participate in them or who is capable of their rectification and interpretation should they occur, offers a significant therapeutic experience for the patient — and analyst.

Finally, I wish to note that the study by Viderman (1974), which I discovered after completing this paper, offered, in part, a similar though more general approach to some of the issues discussed here. Viderman suggests that Freud failed to establish a clearly defined "analytic space" for Dora's analysis and that he did not create "classical conditions" for her treatment. He argues that the analysis ended prematurely because Freud's and Dora's words did not resonate, or accrue meaning, in this poorly demarcated clinical situation and that an unresolvable resistance was established. Thus he views Dora's premature termination as largely a consequence of Freud's failure to establish clearcut ground rules and boundaries for her analysis. My own observations support this aspect of Viderman's position.

SUMMARY

Using as a template the ground rules and boundaries of the patient-analyst relationship, as they are generally established in contemporary adult — and in some quarters, adolescent — psychoanalytic practice, the case of Dora has been studied as to deviations from current standards as set by Freud at that time. Three such deviations were identified and their consequences investigated in an effort to demonstrate that such modifications of the analytic framework contributed to sectors of therapeutic misalliance between Dora and Freud. The intrapsychic repercussions of the misalliances for Dora were investigated, and an effort was made to describe both her participation in them, as well as her — and Freud's — unconscious efforts to modify them. The consequences of Freud's failure to consciously recognize these sectors of misalliance and to modify them in actuality, as well as to analyze their implications for Dora, were considered, as was their influence on Dora's premature termination of her analysis.

REFERENCES

Arlow, J. :1975). Discussion of Mark Kanzer's "The Therapeutic and Working Alliances." *International Journal of Psychoanalytic Psychotherapy* 4: 69-73.

_____ and C. Brenner (1966). Discussion of Elizabeth R. Zetzel's "The Analytic Situation." *Psychoanalysis in the Americas*, ed. R. Litman, pp. 133-138. New York: International Universities Press.

Erikson, E. (1962). Reality and actuality. *Journal of the American Psychoanalytic Association* 10: 451-474.

Freud, S. (1900). The Interpretation of Dreams. *Standard Edition*. Vol. 4 and 5.

_____(1905a). A fragment of an analysis of a case of hysteria. *Standard Edition* 7: 1-122.

_____(1905b). Three essays on the theory of sexuality. *Standard Edition* 7: 125-243.

_____(1912). Recommendations to physicians practicing psycho-analysis. *Standard Edition* 12: 109-120.

Greenson, R. (1965). The working alliance and the transference neurosis. *Psychoanalytic Quarterly* 34: 155-181.

_____ (1967). *The Technique and Practice of Psychoanalysis*. Vol. I. New York: International Universities Press.

_____ (1971). The "real" relationship between the patient and the psychoanalyst. *The Unconscious Today*, ed. M. Kanzer, pp. 213-232. New York: International Universities Press.

_____ (1972). Beyond transference and interpretation. *International Journal of Psycho-Analysis* 53: 213-218.

_____ , and Wexler, M. (1969). The non-transference relationship in the psycho-analytic situation. *International Journal of Psycho-Analysis* 50: 27-40.

Heimann, P. (1970). Discussion of "The non-transference relationship in the psychoanalytic situation." *International Journal of Psycho-Analysis* 51: 145-147.

Kanzer, M. (1952). The transference neurosis of the Rat Man. *Psychoanalytic Quarterly* 2: 181-189.

_____ (1966). The motor sphere of the transference. *Psychoanalytic Quarterly* 35: 522-539.

_____ (1975). The therapeutic and working alliances. *International Journal of Psychoanalytic Psychotherapy* 4: 48-73.

Langs, R. (1973a). *The Technique of Psychoanalytic Psychotherapy*. Vol 1. New York: Aronson.

_____ (1973b). The patient's view of the therapist: reality or fantasy. *International Journal of Psychoanalytic Psychotherapy* 2: 411-431.

_____ (1974). *The Technique of Psychoanalytic Psychotherapy*. Vol. 2. New York: Aronson.

_____ (1975a). Therapeutic misalliances. *International Journal of Psychoanalytic Psychotherapy* 4: 77-105.

_____ (1975b). The therapeutic relationship and deviations in technique. *International Journal of Psychoanalytic Psychotherapy* 4: 106-141.

_____ (1975c). The patient's unconscious perception of the therapist's errors. *Tactics and Techniques in Psychoanalytic Therapy*, ed. P. Giovacchini. Vol. 2. New York: Aronson.

_____ (1976). *The Bipersonal Field*. New York: Aronson.

_____ (in press a). *The Therapeutic Interaction*. New York: Aronson.

_____ (in press b). The Misalliance dimension in Freud's case histories. II. The rat man. *Freud and His Patients*, ed. M. Kanzer and J. Glenn. New York: Aronson.

_____ (in press c). The misalliance dimension in Freud's case histories. III. The wolf man. *Freud and His Patients*, ed. M. Kanzer and J. Glenn. New York: Aronson.

Stone, L. (1961). *The Psychoanalytic Situation.* New York: International Universities Press.

_____ (1967). The psychoanalytic situation and transference: Postscript to an earlier communication. *Journal of the American Psychoanalytic Association* 15: 3-58.

Viderman, S. (1974). Interpretation in the analytic space. *International Review of Psycho-Analysis* 1: 467-480.

Winnicott, D. W. (1965). *The Maturational Processes and the Facilitating Environment.* New York: International Universities Press.

Zetzel, E. (1956). Current concepts of transference. *International Journal of Psycho-Analysis* 37: 369-376.

_____ (1958). Therapeutic alliance in the psychoanalysis of hysteria. *The Capacity for Emotional Growth*, pp. 182-196. New York: International Universities Press, 1970.

_____ (1966). Additional "notes upon a case of obsessional neurosis." *International Journal of Psycho-Analysis* 47: 123-129.

_____ (1966-1969). The analytic situation and the analytic process. *The Capacity for Emotional Growth*, pp. 197-215. New York: International Universities Press.

Psychotherapists' Passivity— A Major Training Problem

Gerald Roskin, M.D.

Director, Adult Outpatient Clinic
Department of Psychiatry
Long Island Jewish-Hillside Medical Center
New Hyde Park, N.Y.

Charles J. Rabiner, M.D.

Chairman
Department of Psychiatry
Long Island Jewish-Hillside Medical Center
New Hyde Park, N.Y.

A major problem encountered in the early psychotherapy training of psychiatric residents, psychologists, and social workers is the tendency for the student to take an inappropriately passive and silent role. Rather than actively engage patients in a therapeutic alliance, beginning students have the tendency to remain withdrawn and inarticulate. This often reaches extreme proportions and may later significantly block treatment progress.

Clinical vignettes are presented to show the range and variety of hyperpassive behavior in psychotherapy training and the potential crippling and destructive effects on the treatment process. This is not to imply that there is no danger in excess activity on the part of the therapist. Indeed, not all silence need be destructive. However, detachment, withdrawal, and excess silence—attitudes often fostered by our training programs—can be markedly destructive to both patients and treatment.

Psychodynamic factors causing this situation are reviewed. A variety of methods and strategies are recommended for dealing with it. If the supervisor remains alert, the problem can be significantly resolved before it interferes with treatment. In this way, the student will be helped to overcome one of the major early hurdles of training.

INTRODUCTION

Many facets of the teaching of psychotherapy have been well covered in the literature. Various papers have dealt with patients' silence in the psychotherapy situation (Weisman, 1955; Zeligs, 1961; Loomie, 1961; Greenson, 1961). A less commonly studied phenomenon, however, is the problem of dealing with therapists' silence and passivity during the early stages of their training.

Much emphasis is placed on teaching the neophyte general concepts of psychoanalytically oriented psychotherapy and on understanding psychodynamic formulations of particular patients. Less attention is paid to the very real problem of what the trainee is to do while he is attempting to absorb and integrate all of this knowledge. Often the young therapist, when placed in a situation he is unable to master resorts to the old adage, "first do no harm." In terms of the psychotherapeutic situation, this becomes translated into silence and passivity on the part of the beginning resident. It seems natural for the beginner to assume that active intervention on his part may have deleterious effects on a patient and that to withdraw and do and say nothing amount to a relatively harmless tactic. In actuality, this may not be the case.

It should be kept in mind that silence and passivity are not the same. Silence on the part of the therapist can have a constructive and meaningful role in treatment. However, it can also be misused and be very destructive.

The silence of the therapist can be interpreted as having a variety of meanings — assent, rejection, support, objective inquiry, watchful expectation, indifference, even seduction, anger, love, and protection, and the lot (Greenson, 1961; Nacht, 1963; Brockbank, 1970). It is essential that early on the therapist-in-training learn that communication takes place on a variety of levels and that silence is a very definite form of communication having a significant effect on the course of the psychotherapy. To assume one will be on safer ground by being passive and silent often proves fallacious and destructive.

SOME CLINICAL VIGNETTES

Example One

A twenty-one-year-old college student was referred for treatment by her parents. They felt that her isolation and withdrawal paralleled the behavior of her sister who at the time of this referral was a patient in our Day Hospital Program. From the beginning of the treatment it was clear that the patient resented being forced into therapy by her parents but felt that she had no choice other than to obey them. Because of this she volunteered little information and remained silent for long periods of time in the therapy. The resident, who had just begun to do treatment in the Outpatient Clinic, brought the problem of the patient's silence to supervision. The supervisor indicated that the patient obviously resented being forced into therapy and suggested that the therapist pursue an active course and engage the patient on any level available rather than sit back and wait for the latter to produce information. When the therapist asked the patient questions and attempted to interact with her, she became animated, shared her daily activities, and the silence ended. As soon as the patient began to talk, however, the therapist ceased to interact and adopted a passive-silent position. The patient responded to this by becoming silent again. Each time the resident presented the case and was encouraged to become more active, he did, and in response, the patient became more active. Each time the resident withdrew, the patient withdrew. This pattern continued until eventually the patient withdrew from treatment altogether. The resident, aware of his difficulty in maintaining an active position stated, "I actually felt more natural when I was talking to the patient but I also felt that it was not really psychotherapy and my job was to sit back and listen."

Discussion

In this example, the therapist was *consistently* unable to become active, which was what this patient needed in order to engage in a *beneficial and productive* therapeutic relationship through relating and talking. Despite the therapist's awareness of this, he seemed helpless to alter the situation. A variety of issues may have been functioning to block him: a view of the role of therapist as detached and inactive, with a concomitant disparaging of activity as a bona fide role; anger at the patient for her demanding this activity from him; anger at the supervisor for requiring it; etc.

Example Two

A psychiatric resident, who had just started to see outpatients in therapy, had begun treating, on a once-a-week basis, a moderately depressed man in his late thirties. He had seen him for two sessions. At the time of the third session the resident went into the waiting room and found his patient asleep. He thought for a moment and decided to go back into his office. He sat in his office with the door open for about twenty minutes. He then came out and saw that the patient was still sleeping. He mulled the situation over for a few moments and then walked back into his office.

About three minutes before the end of the appointment (it was scheduled as a forty-five-minute session), the patient awakened and walked into the therapist's office. He apologized and was somewhat upset because he had fallen asleep. The therapist politely accepted his apologies but noted that there were only about two minutes left to the appointment, and that, because of his schedule, he could only see the patient for two minutes. The patient asked why the psychiatrist had not awakened him. The resident parried with, "What are your thoughts about this?" The patient got very angry, walked out in a rage and never returned to treatment.

The therapist contended, spontaneously, that he did not feel guilty about this whole situation because during the whole time that he was sitting in his office he was thinking about the patient and considering all the possible dynamics of the patient's being asleep.

Discussion

The psychiatric resident in this situation felt very uncomfortable taking the role of waking the patient. This would be "feeding the patient" and thus, in the mind of the resident, "not therapy." The resident may well have felt relieved not to have to be bothered seeing the patient, but also clearly felt guilty about the whole incident (note the spontaneous negation that he did not feel guilty because he devoted the time of the session—in his mind—to the patient). There was also considerable anger with the patient for his demands on the therapist that the "pure model" of psychotherapy be abrogated. But although the resident won the battle he lost the war, for the patient quit the therapy altogether.

Example Three

A psychiatric resident, early in his training, was treating an eleven-year-old boy who was caught up with his mother in a passive-aggressive struggle. The child was doing poorly at school, mainly because he was not paying attention in class and refusing to do any homework. There were no organic or learning disability problems and it was clear that the child was in an intense struggle with his mother by whom he felt exploited and manipulated. He was withholding to get back at her.

The resident rather aimlessly played with the child for eleven months, saying little of moment and never getting involved dynamically with meaningful issues. Suddenly, the resident realized that he had only one month of treatment left (four sessions). He had to review the case with his supervisor and realized that the case had gotten nowhere. The battle between mother and child was continuing unabated—to the detriment of all.

The resident in the four remaining sessions became very active. He confronted the patient with the dynamic struggle the patient was engaged in with his mother. To the resident's shock, the boy began to actively work with this material. The patient articulated very clearly his anger at his mother and how he was getting back at her. The resident was stunned by the child's ability to articulate the important dynamics and was shocked and gratified as the relationship between the boy and his mother improved and the passive-aggressive manipulative struggle between them began to abate. The resident felt that if he hadn't suddenly become aware that he had done nothing the "treatment" could have gone on interminably with little or no result.

Discussion

Why the resident, in this example, did nothing for the first eleven months of treatment is not entirely clear. Fear of working dynamically with the child, fear of harming him, and fear of losing him as a patient seemed to be factors. At any rate, under pressure from his supervisor he suddenly, in the last month of treatment, began to actively confront the boy with his dynamic understanding of the major problem area, and the patient responded by working meaningfully in the treatment and applying this understanding to his outside life situation in a constructive way. This is a good example of how active — albeit belated — supervisory prodding can lead to constructive activity on the part of the therapist.

Example Four

A resident was treating a young college woman who kept complaining that the office seemed very cold. He asked her what she meant by that, and she kept insisting that the room was freezing. He continued to press for associations to the feeling of being cold or freezing and the patient brought forth no associations other than to reiterate her complaint that the room was terribly cold. When this material was presented to his supervisor, the latter asked the resident what the temperature of the room actually was. The resident responded that it was, indeed, extremely cold because the window had been left open by the previous therapist and it was the middle of the winter. The supervisor asked the resident why he didn't close the window and the latter was rather puzzled. He stated that he thought his job was to understand all that goes on in therapy and that to close the window would be "acting in" the treatment.

Discussion

Often, our training deemphasizes the importance of reality as a factor in the productions of patients and in the ebb and flow of the treatment process. In the foregoing example, the therapist ignored a pressing reality (the cold) in order to "do therapy." How can we explain the blatant poor judgment in this situation of a bright, intelligent, conscientious resident? A misplaced fear of "acting in" is the therapist's explanation. We have here an example of a quite common distortion of the psychoanalytic psychotherapeutic model. This assumes that therapy occurs in a "pure culture" and that the impact of reality on the therapeutic situation is nil — or minimal. In fact, there is no "pure therapy"; all therapy occurs in the context of more or less pressing realities and these must be given their proper due if the treatment is not to become a grotesque mockery (Stone, 1961).

Example Five

A psychiatric resident, early in his outpatient work, was treating a twenty-six-year-old man because of depression and premature ejaculation. For the first six months of treatment the resident took a "silent analytic" stance; this was apparently fostered by the resident's supervisor. Through this period of treatment, the patient had a slight improvement in his depression but his premature ejaculation was unchanged. The therapy consisted, mainly, of a battle between the patient and the therapist. The patient felt the therapist was too silent, too nongiving, and not helping him. The therapist saw all this as resistance and felt the patient was unproductive and wanted to be fed. The therapy was going nowhere.

After six months of treatment a new supervisor was assigned. The new supervisor took a much different position than the former one. He told the resident that the patient's feeling that the therapist was too silent was not resistance but reality. The therapist had been waiting for the patient to "come to his own insights." The new supervisor strongly urged that the therapist talk more, and that he *tell the patient* what he knew about the patient's problems, behavior, and dynamics. As the therapist put it, "The therapy became more conversational. I became more relaxed and a therapeutic alliance was established. We began working together rather than fighting all the time. Previously, he would come in, lay something on the table, and wait for me to give something in return. We were always fighting over giving."

With the new more active stance, the therapy moved significantly over the next six months of treatment. The patient was discharged with substantial improvement in his depression and complete cessation of his premature ejaculation.

Discussion

This example speaks for itself. We would only add the qualification that we are not stating that silence or a passive stance is inherently ineffective. It was in the foregoing example, but this, as in our other examples, was due to a misapplication and misinterpretation of the psychoanalytic psychotherapeutic model.

Example Six

A psychiatric resident was treating a twenty-one-year-old obsessive-compulsive college student. He had seen her on a twice-a-week basis for about a month when she began to get increasingly depressed and anxious. After about three weeks of treatment, she recalled some sexual fantasies and possible erotic experiences with her father during her childhood. A week went by and this material was not brought up again. Then, in a session, she mentioned a dream in which she was in a car with the therapist, although she didn't know where they were going or "what there was between us in the situation." At around this time the patient began to eat very compulsively. She became increasingly anxious and depressed and began having thoughts of scratching her wrists with a knife.

The supervisor suggested to the therapist that perhaps the patient was struggling with sexual and/or dependent wishes and fantasies in relation to him. The therapist did not believe this and at the same time was quite anxios about bringing up this subject so early in the treatment. The patient continued to deteriorate, becoming more depressed and more anxious. Her obsessive-compulsive behavior worsened. She was unable to do her schoolwork because she found herself unable to concentrate and she became more and more agitated with compulsive thoughts of hurting herself.

Under pressure from the supervisor, the therapist began to explore her feelings toward him, in particular her sexual thoughts about him. The patient then began to speak of how angry she was at the therapist for what she experienced as his rejection of her dependent, affectionate, and sexual needs. She also indicated that she had been afraid that *he* was afraid of these feelings within her. As the feelings welled up she had become more and more angry and frustrated and began to punish herself because of such "evil" feelings and wishes. As he encouraged her to discuss this she began to feel that these were not so evil and that she could talk about them without anything happening in reality in relation to such wishes.

Over the course of several weeks, as these matters were discussed, her depression and anxiety were relieved and her compulsive eating and thoughts about harming herself disappeared.

Discussion

In this example it would seem that feelings and attitudes on the part of the therapist toward the patient were inhibiting his expressing to her his understanding of her difficulty. The patient experienced this as his fearing her as well as his rejecting her, and her condition deteriorated. When—*with pressure, support, and reassurance from his supervisor*—the therapist opened up these issues in the treatment, there was a rapid subsidence of symptomatology. Whether or not the clinical improvement was due to clarification and ventilation (abreaction) or actual interpretation, the important factor here was active intervention rather than passive silence.

Example Seven

A twenty-eight-year-old truck driver was referred for treatment because of acute anxiety attacks. He was unable to work because he became panicky when he was with a group of men. He would frequently faint in their presence, for no apparent reason. His history was significant in that he had always been a Don Juan prior to and following his marriage. On the basis of a variety of data from the sessions, the supervisor suggested that the resident begin to explore the patient's fears and feelings in relation to homosexuality. The resident ignored this advice and kept passively listening to the patient. The patient kept complaining about his anxiety and fainting. The supervisor continued to prod the resident into introducing the issue of homosexuality but the resident avoided it. As time went on the patient went downhill, restricted his activities to staying at home, and, after failing to improve with several medications, was hospitalized.

The supervisor continued to insist that the resident explore the homosexual fears of the patient (which continued to be suggested by considerable material from the treatment). After all else had failed, the resident, in a very difficult situation because he knew of nothing further he could do — and as a last resort — brought up the issue of homosexuality. Initially, the patient became very indignant. However, he then began to seriously consider and explore his thoughts and feelings in relation to this issue. Slowly, the anxiety attacks began to diminish, he continued to improve, and his symptomatology abated. He returned to work and was able to resume a normal life.

When asked why he had resisted raising the issue of homosexuality at an earlier stage of treatment the resident responded that he had no conviction that the anxiety was, indeed, based on homosexual urges and, therefore, would not bring it up. He simply didn't believe it. He gained conviction when he saw it work.

Discussion

Other issues on the part of the therapist besides lack of conviction may have blocked him from bringing up the homosexual problem. And here, too, we are not sure that the symptoms subsided because of ventilation (abreaction) or interpretation. The case data are not clear on this point. But again, it is *activity* rather than passivity that seems to be of moment in turning the tide clinically.

DYNAMICS OF THERAPISTS' PASSIVITY

What are the causes of the situation as outlined. Why are our psychotherapy students so passive? Multiple factors are involved.

Anxiety and Fear of Making a Mistake

This seems to be a most important element. An error of omission appears preferable—to most psychotherapy students—to one of commission. There is a fear of being criticized by supervisor and/or patient for having said the wrong thing, and this fear usually outweighs any apprehension about failing to say the right thing. Some supervisors encourage this passivity by focusing their supervision more on criticism of active interventions by the therapist rather than pointing to their lack. It is less likely that a silence will be criticized; indeed, silences are usually not reported as such and are therefore not available as material in the supervisory process.

There are two kinds of feelings that patients display toward the therapist that are avoided by the neophyte. first, there is the reality response of anger or annoyance on the part of the patient as being misunderstood; this can be unsettling to a beginning therapist. But these feelings are not too different from similar feelings toward physicians in other specialties of medicine. Second—and this is new and different—is the transference that develops. Although beginning therapists are given an intellectual awareness of transference, it is most difficult to describe before the fact. The dependent, hostile, and/or erotic feelings patients develop in the psychotherapy situation must be experienced firsthand. Confronted with these feelings, and not always able to distinguish between reality feelints and transference feelings, the therapist freezes; he chooses to do nothing and takes a position of withdrawal. If strong countertransference feelings also develop, they amount to another confusing issue for the new therapist to handle. Once again he may deal with his chagrin and confusion by retreating to what appears to be a safe distance.

Fear of Patient's Anger

This may occur in relation to an intervention specifically verbalized or a potential intervention that the therapist may have in mind. If he anticipates that his remark will anger, hurt, offend, or upset the patient in any way, he may hold back.

Related to apprehension over making the patient angry or offending him is a fear of harming him and this often amounts to a fear of hurting the patient with hiw own (i.e. the therapist's) aggression. Indeed, the therapist-in-training may carry this a step further by punishing the patient with his silence. He resents the patient's demands upon him and resents giving to the patient. Thus, when he should speak he is silent—and the patient squirms. This passive-aggressive mode is seen frequently in our experience. In a sense, this is an active, angry silence.

Fear of Patient's Positive Feelings

Fear of provoking anger goes hand-in-hand with what may be an equally inhibiting fear of stimulating positive feelings on the part of the patient in response to a given intervention. The psychotherapist-in-training may be quite frightened of exciting the patient's dependent or erotic wishes. In the last analysis, this may boil down to a fear on the part of therapist of his own erotic and dependent impulses toward the patient.

Identification with Hyperpassive Role Models

A variety of identifications are involved in the hyperpassivity we have described. For example, "My own analyst doesn't do this for me so why should I do this for my patient?" or, "Why should I give what I don't get?" One may speculate that, at a deeper level, there may be identifications with nongiving, cold, stony parents. Thus the therapist-in-training, with his silence, may be paying back his parents for their lack of giving to him.

Lack of Belief in the Therapeutic Process

The overly passive, reticent psychotherapy resident is often struggling with a lack of belief in the psychotherapeutic process itself. His philosophy is therefore that the best thing is to do nothing. This is carried a step further when the resident attempts to undermine the treatment through his passive silence. This makes the patient's condition worse and thus proves that the supervisor is wrong and therapy is no value. One may speculate that, on a deeper level, his parents are being devalued and therapeutic failure functions as a retaliation. Thus, his passivity makes a mockery of treatment.

Sociocultural Factors

Further, it may be that we are dealing with significant cultural and social factors here, with a whole generation of passivity, as it were. This is an era of psychotherapy trainees brought up on television and demand-feeding. Our students expect and often demand spoon-feeding; they want didactic courses and they don't want too many patients to treat. The Protestant ethic and the work ethic seem to be dead, and the kind of hyperpassivity that we have described may be part of this phenomenon.

Lack of Understanding and Knowledge of Psychotherapy

The young therapist-in-training may really not understand what goes on in therapy and attempts to hide this lack of comprehension of the therapeutic process under a mask of hyperpassivity. He may be afraid to ask the supervisor for direction because it exposes this ignorance, and thus he hides behind a veil of passivity.

GENERAL DISCUSSION

While most of our psychotherapy training teaches the beginning therapist to listen, sometimes we can cause problems with this approach. Taken to an extreme, the misuse of silence can be a destructive element in the therapeutic process. We are not, of course, attempting to criticize the utilization of any and all silences in treatment. There is no question of the value of appropriate silence by the therapist in the treatment process. Further, as our examples have shown, the therapists were misusing silence, based either on counter-transference difficulties or other problems and misconceptions.

In order to teach the beginning therapist to overcome his natural inclination to be inactive, several direct steps must be taken. Frequently, the beginner will identify with the supervisor. Therefore, it follows that a supervisor who sits back quietly and makes relatively few comments and expects the resident-in-training to "present the case" will wind up with a resident who is likely to act in a similar way with his patients. Just as there is nonverbal communication between patient and therapist, there is nonverbal communication between instructor and student (Nacht, 1963; Brockband, 1970). The young resident, with his silence, may then be treating his patient in a manner similar to the way he is being treated by his supervisor, and thus a kind of conspiracy of silence is perpetuated.

It is necessary for the supervisor to constantly stress the positive results of actively interacting with patients. Nor should the *negative effect* of the resident's *lack of intervention* be overlooked. Since an intervention is an actuality, while a missed opportunity to say something is only a possibility, there is the obvious difference between an error of omission and one of commission. The supervisor must be wary lest he give the resident the message that it is dangerous to intervene. If the instructor balances his comments about the resident's interventions with comments about his failure to intervene, the resident is less likely to remain passive in his conduct of therapy.

Frequently, as discussed above, students will be silent because they honestly do not know what to say. It is certainly expected that a beginning therapist will have difficulty always understanding the patient's communications. However, not every response to the patient must necessarily be an interpretation based on a dynamic-genetic understanding of the entire case. Simple questions used to clarify the patient's communications may be used to convey interest on the part of the therapist to the patient. One should encourage the resident not to wait until everything becomes crystal clear, because this will often take an inordinate amount of time; the treatment may falter significantly before the therapist has the chance to understand all.

A major factor involved in the silence and passivity of the resident is the latter's experience as a patient. If the resident is involved in a classical psychoanalysis, there is a natural tendency for him to identify with the analyst and treat his patients in a manner similar to the way in which he is being treated. When this happens it is the function of the supervisor to point this out directly to the resident and to attempt to differentiate psychotherapy from psychoanalysis. The average clinic patient has a much different psychological makeup than the average resident as well as there being a different level of sophistication. Residents must constantly be reminded of this; they must not assume that all patients are to be treated alike. The expectation of the clinic patient in terms of activity on the part of the therapist is quite different from a psychiatric resident's expectation in his own analysis.

As residents gain experience there is generally less reluctance to involve themselves with patients. They learn that nothing terrible happens if they make a mistake and they begin to take a more realistic view of treatment. Also, they gain a sense of conviction that what they are saying to the patient makes sense and *helps*, and this enables them, in turn, to make more interventions. However, in the early stages of training it is to be expected that residents will lack conviction concerning the therapeutic process. Therefore, it is imperative that the supervisor remain alert to this problem and attempt to anticipate its occurrence before it interferes with the therapy. As the learning process evolves and the resident comes to believe in the value of therapy, the problem of passivity as a direct result of lack of conviction will diminish.

SUMMARY

In this paper we have attempted to demonstrate that psychotherapists' passivity is a major stumbling block in treatment and in learning the psychotherapy process. We have given a number of examples illustrating this phenomenon and have attempted to show how destructive it can be to patients and to treatment.

Traditionally, the psychoanalytic stance employs a good deal of silence on the part of the therapist. We are not—explicitly or implicitly—trying to make any criticism of the psychoanalytic model of psychotherapy. Rather, we are critical of the distortion of this model by students, and perhaps certain teachers and practitioners. Our impression has been that beginning students, in their anxiety and fear, may hide behind this model and use a misinterpretation of the model defensively to help handle a variety of fears, conflicts, countertransference issues, etc. Unfortunately, some of our more experienced practitioners may be doing likewise. An awareness of this problem is a crucial first step toward its correction.

NOTES

1. This example was given to us by Dr. Robert Dickes, to whom we express our thanks.

REFERENCES

Brockbank, R. (1970). On the analyst's silence in psychoanalysis: A synthesis of intrapsychic content and interpersonal manifestations. *International Journal of Psycho-Analysis* 51:457-464.

Greenson, R. (1961). On the silence and sounds of the analytic hour. *Journal of the American Psychoanalytic Association* 9:79-84.

Loomie, L. S. (1961). Some ego considerations in the silent patient. *Journal of the American Psychoanalytic Association* 9:56-78.

Nacht, S. (1963). The non-verbal relationship in psychoanalytic treatment. *International Journal of Psycho-Analysis* 44:328-333.

Stone, L. (1961). *The Psychoanalytic Situation.* New York: International Universities Press.

Weisman, A. S. (1955). Silence and psychotherapy. *Psychiatry* 18:241-260.

Zeligs, M. S. (1961). The psychology of silence. *Journal of the American Psychoanalytic Association* 9:7-43.

GERALD ROSKIN, M.D.

DR. ROSKIN is director of the Adult Outpatient Clinic in the Department of Psychiatry at the Long Island Jewish-Hillside Medical Center. He is an assistant professor of clinical psychiatry at the medical school of the State University of New York at Stony Brook and past president of the Nassau Psychiatric Society. His major interests are in psychotherapy process and the development of psychiatric treatment programs.

CHARLES J. RABINER, M.D.

DR. RABINER is presently chairman of the Department of Psychiatry at the Long Island Jewish-Hillside Medical Center and associate professor of psychiatry at the Medical School of the State University of New York at Stony Brook. He received his psychiatric training at Kings County Hospital, Downstate Medical Center, in Brooklyn. He has contributed numerous articles to the literature in the fields of hospital and community psychiatry, evaluation of programs, and psychosomatic medicine.

Related Issues in Childbearing And Work: Two Clinical Studies of Professional Women

Rosemary Marshall Balsam, M.D.

Assistant Clinical Professor of Psychiatry and Staff Psychiatrist
Yale University

A common structure is described in two women's experience in central aspects of their professions and in their thoughts and feelings about motherhood. For example, a scientist's fascination in experimentation with cells in developing embryos is linked with wishes to experiment with the fertility of her own body, and an artist describes connections between the conflicts in finishing and showing her paintings and the conflicts in allowing her infant to separate from her body in the birth process.

Historical clinical material from once-weekly psychoanalytically oriented psychotherapy is used to trace some of the dynamics common to the major themes.

INTRODUCTION

Some women who have professions talk about an analogy between what they want and experience in central aspects of their work, and what they want and experience in important aspects of childbearing and mothering. The topic could have a wide scope, and a similar analogy may be found among many men too. This paper will be confined to clinical material and a discussion of two women, a scientist and a painter, who were seen for a year in once-weekly psychoanalytically oriented psychotherapy.

I would like to concentrate on the parallels between the goals, the related psychological terms of the work and motherhood situations, and the similar affective tone and language used to describe both aspects of these patients' lives. Abbreviated historical material will be presented, because this may shed some light on how the parallels came to coexist in each woman.

Because the therapies are brief in terms of time spent with the patients, of necessity the material is unsatisfactory in terms of specific unconscious fantasies, early memories, and more developed transference reactions which would be maximally enlightening and result in less speculation regarding the psychodynamics. Nevertheless the central idea may prove interesting. I do not wish to include a review of the literature on this matter at the moment because it is so wide, diffuse, and obliquely related to the central idea. It ranges from stress laid upon social and historical issues influencing contemporary life of women to the early psychoanalytic literature which seems to view careers in women only as a flight from womanhood. Here, more in tone with developing modern psychoanalytic views of feminine psychology, I would like to draw attention to overall family historical influences and the adaptive aspects of the girl child's developing career interests. That is not to diminish in any way the interwoven pathological aspects which are also present.

CASE ONE

This young woman was a thirty-year-old, married college researcher and teacher in physical chemistry. At the time she was seen she had no children, but she and her geneticist husband planned to start a family within the following two years when their careers were established. They had been married five years.

Ms. R. was an active, enthusiastic, pretty, shy, stylish, and very bright young woman whose research was of high quality. She entered therapy because she wanted a place in her life where she could talk about her role as a woman. Anxiety at faculty meetings interfered with her administrative ability, and she felt unable to speak her opinions with clarity. She was worried that this might interfere with her chances for promotion.

Family History

Ms. R. was the only child of a professional couple from the Midwest. Her pharmacist father died when she was six months old, and within a year her schoolteacher mother married a man who was a laboratory assistant in a local industry. Shortly after the marriage he stopped working, and subsequently took transient laboring jobs. He was alcoholic, chronically depressed, and stayed at home a lot and read science fiction. After seven years they had another daughter, who was beautiful, irresponsible, and unintelligent. The patient was often called upon to baby-sit and was resentful of the parents' attention to this child. Her stepfather openly favored his own daughter. However, he encouraged the patient in her scholastic interests, which he said were admirable. The mother derided his encouragement of his stepdaughter, saying his opinion about everything was worthless. Nevertheless, the mother and the patient tended to side together, often against the stepfather and younger sister.

The patient was constantly worried about her stepfather's withdrawal and the state of his mental health. Her vision of her real father was that he would have been emotionally strong and supportive of her and her mother. In fact, the mother often so described her first mate, and was often angry. She felt she had chosen a poor substitute for her former husband. There was covert competition as to who could get more attention from the stepfather, even if it meant fighting with him.

The patient and her mother had a very close relationship, the patient being very dependent on the latter, and the mother hovering closely over her daughter to save her from the "bad influence" of her stepfather and younger sister. At puberty the patient buried herself in her schoolwork, had no school friends of either sex and little chance for communication at home. She geared her efforts toward going away to college.

The negative maternal transference involved fears that I as a woman psychiatrist would be critical of her ambition, her anger, and her sexuality, in fact most of her strong feelings. Mother was seen as repudiating of any messiness, lack of self-control, and the patient's evolving sexuality. Maternal support of her schoolwork was often enmeshed in other issues between the two.

For example, on the issue of the conflict between childbearing at the moment and her work, the following interchange took place early in therapy:

Patient: My last experiment worked out very well. I was sure it would fail. . . . You know that . . . I feel anxious about telling you it succeeded for some reason . . . I expect you to be angry.

Therapist: Should I be angry?

Patient: Well, yes. After all I know you have kids. You must believe in women having children. You must despise me for not getting pregnant after all this talking I've done about my wishes. . . . You think I'm a nothing woman because I'm so involved in my work. . . . But then you work too. I keep forgetting that. Maybe I despise myself.

Therapist: Or me?

Patient: The thing I despise you for is for not putting me right on those issues. You should know what's right for a woman and what's wrong . . . Your children will end up not knowing what's right from wrong. I'm taking time away from them.

Therapist: As if I didn't choose to be here with you right now.

Patient (relieved): Yes. My mother was so busy all the time. She was always talking about having more babies—she really wanted a boy she said. While we'd be working on math problems she'd say how unhappy she was with Daddy and how she'd wish my father was alive. I think I'd be very angry with her and despise her for not getting what she wanted.

Therapist: It would get lost for you that you wanted help for you right then and she'd offered help.

Patient: Yes, I'd feel so guilty. I couldn't satisfy her no matter what . . . I'd dream a lot about having a boy baby myself . . . I was terrified of boys in reality. I wanted to be better than her, have a better marriage. I was so sorry for her. I used to cry at night feeling so sorry for her (cries). And angry—so angry now I realize. Like with you at the beginning of the hour. I'm afraid people will give me no credit for what I do if I've twisted their ear off saying how afraid I am that it won't be satisfactory. I was angry and afraid in case you'd say, "I told you so—what was the big deal?"

The interchange has many meanings at different levels. In general it serves to illustrate the patient's feelings of being unsatisfactory, both as a woman and as an academic. Projection of her debasing attitude upon herself and her anger and pity of her mother show themselves here in the transference. The twelve-year-old good math student with concerns about her sexual development was lost in preoccupations, in fantasy, evolving from the mother's inviting her to be her confidante. The love for her mother provoked intense wishes to provide all for her, and in every area the little girl fell short. Her anger about both being used in this way and her feelings of being inadequate to the tasks were turned against herself in self-accusation.

Marriage

The patient and her husband, who was her first lover, and sometime lab partner, were married when they were graduate students. She and her husband cared for each other and each showed evidence of trying to accommodate the other. She was nonorgasmic at the beginning of the marriage and was tentative about initiating sexual relations. After two years she became orgasmic regularly and was more comfortable in sexual experimentation. She was hesitant about her anger and more open with loving feelings in the marriage. Her husband was restricted in expressing his love and more open with his anger. From time to time she felt she was clinging to him emotionally, being too demanding and keeping him from his academic work. In turn he felt excluded from, and jealous of, some of her work associations. Both wanted children, but wanted more time to work on their relationship together and their professional lives.

Current Career

The patient was ambitious, in the sense that she wanted to be at the top of the academic hierarchy. She was competitive and had at times vehemently vied for honors, feeling most dejected if she were not first in the class (even if objectively someone else deserved it more). Promotion would mean that she had "made it in a man's world," which would be a matter of pride for her. She was the only woman on the faculty of her department. She readily expressed admiration and envy of men in her profession. She viewed them as more assured, more charismatic, and less sensitive to criticism. She said she wanted to be more like that herself. In her students' opinion, much learning went on in her class. However, she regarded their views with some denigration, doubting whether her willingness to be involved with them was the "right way to get ahead."

Her peer and senior colleagues regarded her with a seriousess she appreciated. Most of these relationships were not intense. Anxiety at faculty meetings emerged when a particular peer was present to whom she was sexually attracted. He made sexualized comments to her, which both annoyed and flattered her, but raised deeper doubts; she wondered if her status with the faculty was due only to her being female and sexy.

This man was also her academic inferior and his job was in the balance. Her guilt about her anger at his behavior was also unconsciously connected with anger in comparable situations with her stepsister who consistently failed in school.

Career History

At first she said that her scientific career was meant to emulate her father's career. It was also partly rooted in pleasing her mother, so verbal about disappointments in her expectations of the stepfather's laboratory interests at the time of their marriage.

The mother was the career person in her life as she grew. She was an energetic teacher who took a great interest in her pupils. The patient had early ambitions to be like her, was taught by her, and was proud of her. The patient's interests were in an area of physical chemistry having to do with protein synthesis in developing cells. It would entail doing scientific experiments she compared to building blocks and doing mathematics in the company of her mother. The patient said she emulated her mother's care and attention concerning the students' development in her teaching. She was particularly interested in the protein matrices in the cells of embryos. Beneath this was a fascination about people's genetic makeup: what biophysical elements in the brain contribute to making people different — what they inherit from their parents, and in particular how the cerebral components can be damaged and give a person propensity to mental illness. Her nature-nurture questions began early with comparisons of herself and her stepsister. Her interest in basic biological makeup and survival of the fittest reflected a whole background of enigmas in trying to understand her biological father's death, her stepfather's depression, the sexual relationship of her parents, and her own position and worth in the family. She said, for example, "My stepsister and I both came out of the same womb. How can my father's sperm and one month's cells of my mother's ova emerge as *me* and another combination with a different father emerge as my sister?"

Fantasies Re Childbearing

About having her own babies some day (four in all) she had specific fantasies. She wanted to see if her body "would work," with her husband taking part in this sexual experiment. Would her cells be receptive and give fruit with her husband's sperm? Would the baby be normal? Her basic worry that it would not was connected with unconscious fears of being punished for being sexual and aggressive. In bearing children she hoped to be able to conceive more than twice. She said she needed to have a boy baby. He must be "perfect." She hoped to bring him up so that he would not be subject to depressions (or, possibly, at a deeper level, death). For example, she had read psychological studies, and planned to breast-feed him for at least a year. With her husband's help she hoped to respond a great deal to him in early infancy. She felt guilty that she did not do enough for the stepfather to help his depressions (and possibly her own father, to keep him alive). After this she wanted a girl baby. She too would be perfect No dichotomies would be created in her upbringing as to "prettiness" versus "academic ability." She would try to treat them equally. She would cook with her children, and would enjoy teaching them the wonders of detail in nature to be discovered around them. She also looked forward to the executive challenge of working out ways with her husband to care for the children and being able to carry on her work, which she loved.

The connecting ideas between this patient's career and her ideas about mothering were the following:

1. Investigating the basic nature of cells after conception. *In work*: Pursuing a direct experimental way.
   In having babies: Performing a sort of experiment with her body to see if it "would work."
2. A biological search for truth and perfection.
   In work: Looking for conditions under which cells are damaged or are whole and functional.
   In having babies: Seeing if the entire baby could be perfect as produced by her body, and in the early care of the infant to master the nature-nurture problem.
3. Having the opportunity to outdo her mother and both fathers.

In work: Being promoted, to be a respected and admired academician.
In having babies: Conceiving more than once and having a boy and girl in order to redo her own upbringing, through she and her husband doing a better job than the parents.

The parallel and interwoven threads of each aspect of her life are demonstrated in this summarized way and reflect in descending order the intensity of the goals as they unfolded in therapy.

CASE TWO

The next patient is presented in a similar manner, though individually her concerns were very different. This woman was a twenty-eight-year-old graduate student who was a talented painter. She also taught art. Married, with a nine-year-old child, she wanted to have another child someday.

Mrs. M. was an intense, energetic, articulate, tall and slender blonde woman. She came to therapy because of depression related to marital problems. She felt locked into an unsatisfactory alliance and felt that her daughter's needs were what maintained the marriage.

Family History

Mrs. M. grew up in the Midwest in a small, conservative community where a set social code seemed to her to dictate the family's behavior. Her father was an engineer of local repute, and her mother a housewife who had longings to be a psychologist, but had given up further education the day of her marriage. The mother had had ten pregnancies and the patient was the oldest of three living daughters. Her siblings were twins six years younger than she. The mother pleaded and enjoined all her daughters to have careers to "save" them from the burdens of child-rearing. She had been psychotically depressed before becoming pregnant with the patient and had many episodes of severe depression while the patient was growing up. The mother was also a "secret" alcoholic. The father, while he praised the girls' traditional charms, also encouraged their education, partly to foster self-sufficiency and partly through wanting them to have absorbing outside interests to compensate for their troubled homelife. He himself overworked professionally. Both parents wanted a scientific career for their oldest daughter, and she displeased them by "frittering away" her time with artistic pursuits. They avidly opposed her independence in every area and restricted her activities to math and science homework.

The patient, feeling unwanted and peripheral in all areas at home, often sought the refuge of her paternal grandparents' home. They were more emancipated and hence adjudged enemies of the parents. They had a substantial art collection. The patient went to live with them in adolescence. In their company she needed to fight less for her own ideas and freedom of feeling and behavior.

Marriage

The patient married at seventeen in the midst of a family battle, without her parents' consent, and came to the East with her husband, who was a brilliant, hardworking, mathematics student about to enter college. In the beginning she assumed a very dependent position which coexisted with depression after her tumultuous separation from home. She felt very lost in her new adult role. Her daughter was born the following year. The birth of the baby stimulated a great deal of growth in self-confidence. When the child was two, Ms. M. became a college student and graduated cum laude when the child was six. After this she took up painting very seriously and went to graduate school. The parenting of the child was equally shared, but vigorously conflicted, because each parent adopted a philosophy at either end of a scale of permissiveness. This went along with a gradual alienation between the couple. Over the years each had made thwarted efforts to understand the other, accept each other's friends and differing points of view about life-style. But both felt the marriage to be stultifying in its current form.

Current Career

This patient was ambitious, in the sense that she wanted to gain recognition, to display her work, and to experience some gratification for all the canvasses to which she privately gave her energies. Ms. M. had conflicts about exhibiting her painting, feeling it was too personal and that, if the audience disapproved, it would be akin to deriding a precious part of her soul or body. However, she tackled the problem with perseverance and sought the interest of the galleries in her work. The situation made her anxious, and she had to take a more aggressive stance than was comfortable for her, to compensate for her insecurity. Some of her problem she related to opposing views of her parents on what was proper behavior for a young girl. Her father had encouraged her to show off for company ordinarily monopolized by adults, while the mother had disapproved, saying that girls should be demure. Other aspects of the conflicts involved anticipated shame and excitement in showing paintings in fantasy to her parents, when she had formerly regarded the work as her own secret activity. There were other levels concerning unconscious feelings and views of her impulses and body, in relation to herself and her parents, being displayed for scrutiny. The second formal exhibition of painting was easier than the first. Her confidence grew concerning the appropriateness and value of what she had to show.

Her peer group was mainly composed of dedicated painters and craftsmen. She tried out new ideas with them and they shared their work, finding mutual support and constructive criticism. Her daughter was popular with this group; they all were fascinated with the child's art and encouraged her. Her daughter found visiting art shows exciting. However, her mathematician father disapproved, couching the situations as being too overstimulating.

Career History

Tracing some feelings about the patient's career in a schematic way, as a young child she was often perplexed, alienated from and angry with her mother, who was vociferous, domineering, and intensely demanding while drunk. The father seemed to side with her in private, but relinquished support of her in the presence of her mother, of whom he seemed afraid. The patient revolted strongly sometimes, but often simply went off to her room where she painted. Among her subjects were abstract forms of large, furious women with babies—babies attached bodily to the mother in every dimension. Two very dominant parents figured as well in the early works. Usually, she said, the main effects in her painting were her own internal rage and particularly her mother's potential for annihilation. Occasionally there was delicacy and beauty but only at the periphery. Her paintings were hidden in locked closets in her room at home.

In her grandparents' home she found peace. They lived a bicycle ride away. They were always interested in her works. Grandfather had a studio and did some sculpture. His wife had a kiln, and did pottery. The three artists worked together, and the grandparents often talked of how the patient could be famous someday. She talked with them about feeling different and left out of her immediate family, and about her hopes for the future.

She was lonely and had little out-of-school contact with friends. She fantasied sitting with imaginary friends, sharing her views on art. Her grown-up friends would be unusual, colorful people who would fully respond to her.

Fantasies About Childbearing

Her main wishes from childhood were to be a painter, have twin children, and become a teacher. She wanted more closeness to her sisters, but they did everything they were told to do and often sided with the parents against their rebellious older sister. The patient had longed for them to be born, and subsequently had been quite aggressive with them.

In puberty her fantasies about motherhood became more formed. She saw her children as four-year-olds, highly creative, painting, writing, being guided and taught by her in a sharing way, while she appreciated their individuality, even though they were twins.

Her adult feelings and experience of her first baby, and longings for another, were important in her description. A major investment in this area was the creative biological art of "keeping within my body a few cells which will multiply, be molded, remolded and given form." After saying this in one hour, she started and said, "Isn't that what I said more or less about how I paint?" Her paintings, she said, started off as concrete images and gradually became more and more elaborated, as if they took on a momentum and power of their own. The initial images came "unplanned in a sense" and the patient merely recognized the urge to paint a canvas. On one level the process was a disciplined action, but, in the molding and reworking, the creation seemed not altogether under her control and the forms took on more and more vitality of their own. Looking at them afterward, sometimes it was as if they had come from a force outside her. "Sometimes I might start another one on a related set of images—or totally afresh and the process renews itself. This connection sounds to me in part like the ideas I have had about conceiving, bearing and raising a child."

Before her baby was born she was full of fears, especially specific doubts of being able to go into labor and deliver the baby. She enjoyed the pregnancy, and felt she wanted to cling to the fullness and sensations of keeping the baby to herself, privately within her body forever. (Her baby was, in fact, overdue.) Another fear involved mothering a child adequately. In particular, she had anxieties about breast-feeding, again along the lines of a wish and fear of holding on to the milk and being unable to part with it. She anticipated that feeding once begun, weaning could be difficult.

Her paintings before her pregnancy and while the child was an infant were often left unfinished. Her experience of successfully nursing the infant she associated with an ability to sustain a painting until she felt it finished.

The connecting ideas between this patient's career and her ideas about mothering were the following:

1. Being responsive to something being taken in from the outside, which grows and is molded while she is partly responsible and partly not responsible.

   In work: The acceptance of an inspirational idea, working and reworking it on canvas in a process experienced as partly within and partly without her conscious control.

   In having babies: The biological act of receiving sperm in conception, and allowing her body vegetatively to bring the child to fruition through a process of ever-differentiating growth.

2. The conflicting urges to keep or to give the finished product while it is still psychologically attached to herself.

In work: Her fight to overcome her urge to keep the paintings to herself, against her urge to display them for admiration and help her gain public recognition, and thereby her self-recognition and self-differentiation.

In having babies: Her fears before the birth about being unable to allow the infant to separate in the birth process, and fears of being unable to suckle the infant, thus keeping the milk all to herself, as against her urge to give the child to the world in birth and nurture the infant toward its own self-sufficiency.

3. The wish to share and have an influence upon a person while remaining separate.

In Work: The intellectual companionship of a student peer group, a group who would be touched by her ideas but essentially use them as a basis for discussion of their individual ideas.

In having babies: Ideas about having four-year-old twins to teach, but simultaneously to enjoy their individuality in expressiveness.

DISCUSSION

From the psychoanalytic point of view, a person's chosen profession often meshes conscious, preconscious, and unconscious goals in such a way as to allow him or her maximal opportunities to reexperience satisfactory areas from the past and rework conflicted positions from his or her developmental heritage. Aspects of a person's sexuality can be interwoven in and run parallel with certain actions, hopes, fears, wishes, and needs expressed about his or her career. In the specific clinical material about these two women, one could consider the analogies presented through asking some of the historical meaning surrounding these connections. Some of the themes they are trying to establish and work out in their adult womanhood are represented in these two areas of their lives.

Having a career was stressed for each woman while growing up. The scientist's mother and stepfather were involved in struggles in which the fact of having a career was focussed upon as representing value, personal growth, and power in the family. These factors combined with family judgments about not wasting time, being useful to society, and a person's ability to be independent. The mother's career meant a great deal to her, but it was used in a chronic, angry battle with her second husband to stress his academic inferiority as evidence of personal inferiority. Not having a career became associated for the patient with being a weak, useless person. This was a worry in the child's mind possibly because of the reality of her stepfather's sitting around drinking at home, inviting devaluation and suffering from depression. The same parent, with his low self-image, also supported the idea of careers. For the patient to be scholastically successful was a way of pleasing herself and both of her unhappy parents. There was therefore an urgency in the child's environment to develop ideas early about being a professional, so that she could value herself as a person, please mother in particular and not incur her anger. Unconsciously this position could have been used by both mother and daughter to avoid oedipal intensity and rivalry. Any overt positive feelings of closeness the patient had to the stepfather was interpreted by the mother as signs of disloyalty to her, thus further strengthening by guilt the preoedipal mother-daughter bond. Having a successful career was also associated with the patient's early feelings of what is expected of an adult woman. As well, it was colored by admiration of her image of her dead father. The usual traditional sexual dichotomy related to the man only having a career in the family did not apply to this patient. Identification with the mother in having a career was therefore important. Possibly an unconscious search for her dead father impinged upon her, too, in exploring a career in science.

The artist's family influences to be professional were equally strong. The father had his established career and enjoyed it. He particularly wanted his oldest daughter to do something scientific, like himself. This work ideal for his child was linked to his conflicts with his own artistic father toward whom he was embittered. The daughter could go along with the father's wishes for a career up to a point, but she seemed more influenced by her grandparents. For her, there was less tension surrounding them, and a conscious wish to be like them flourished. Her identification with both grandparents was stimulated, too, by her anger at the father and rejection of his orthodox principles. The mother constantly stressed having a career as a projection of her own ego-ideal upon her daughter. The pressure was powerful, and mother was such a disappointing figure in so many ways that the patient rebelled vigorously. Her early marriage seemed partly a response to parental insistence on a set career path. However, in her adolescent revolt, identifying with the aggressor, the patient unconsciously repeated her own mother's early marriage, pregnancy, and giving up her own possibility of college while turning to investment in her husband's career to fulfill this wish for herself. It was only after the patient's pregnancy, which seemed to strengthen her ego development, that the earlier experience with her grandparents began to find expression and add impetus to her natural talents. Thus the encouraging attitudes as well as the battles with adult members of the family of both sexes, for two generations, were represented in the psychological background of this woman's professionalism.

At what point in each woman's development the career ideas became so linked with ideas about having babies must remain unclear in this material available from once-weekly therapy. Did the career expectations develop before her fantasies or producing children? Or did the baby precede the career ideas? Or did they develop more or less in parallel? The latter seems possible, since at age two to three both children would be expected to be full of infantile fantasies about their bodies as potentially being capable of producing babies, and curious about adults as sexual beings. Concurrently, the career adults were importantly engaged in their work and satisfactions therein and in disagreements with other important members of the family about these career issues. These difficulties were representative of the parents' own conscious and unconscious conflicts, which involved their children's sexuality and the simultaneous projection of certain academic expectations upon these offspring. Perhaps a parallel development in the ideation could contribute partially to these women's parallel conflicts underlying their conscious unquestioned expectations and convictions of becoming professional women and mothers.

The overall tone of the scientist's wish to have four babies, and thus fulfill a supersuccessful need as an adult woman, has the same quality of urgency and necessity as fulfilling a successful image in her career. Stretching herself maximally academically and as an adult sexual woman was what she most wanted. Perfection was a common goal, with the watchful expectation that something could go wrong at any time. Her detailed work used to great advantage her obsessional tendencies and desire to control the unexpected. At this point her baby plan could be controlled too, as it was in the future and in fantasy. She felt that her need to have everything as defined as possible—in talking about her husband almost as a lab partner in the sexual experience and her functioning in her everyday work—was connected with feelings that adults had drawn her into much that was beyond her control. She also had uneasy feelings about being vaguely responsible for unfortunate events and that it was up to her to make things right. Her father's death was untimely and out of her control. Her mother's pregnancy and being replaced by another baby at a point when she was very dependent on the mother created a trauma. Her mother's worries were constantly her burden, as if she were responsible. The mother's demands upon her became more like asking her little girl to be a substitute husband. From the point of view of feeling too childlike for the pressures, when she knew at some level that it was an adult man's place, the patient developed an acute sense of inadequacy and doubted her power to achieve anything, especially in human relationships. She was also disappointed, angry, and left out with her stepfather, who reinforced her sense of inadequacy by favoring his own daughter so openly. These were forces which urged her more fervently to solve scientific problems, an arena where at least she could be safely in charge of some of the conditions and search by herself to eradicate flaws. Her fortés of investigation and intellectual curiosity were two of the bulwarks against her feelings of being inadequate. Her need to be academically excellent and be acclaimed was strong, since it would amount to a more global self assurance that she could do something well. Speculatively, the sense of bodily damage reflected in her baby fantasies, combined with fantasies of being a "supergirl," proving her fertility over and over again, could be connected unconsciously with an idea that in being a girl she was already damaged, as in the case of castration fears. Feelings of inadequacy and damage could also be linked to an unconscious notion (frequently described in children for whom a parent dies early) that her own birth had killed her father, that she was a very destructive angry, person who "deserved" the damage and punishment. Her body, therefore, had to behave as a perfect apparatus to dispel many unknown fears.

The patient was very taken with the idea of being a "better person" than anyone in the family—a better, more academically successful and more fertile woman than her angry, devaluing mother who was conflicted about her sexual relations and whom the patient felt contributed to her father's lack of success; a cleverer and more fertile woman than her libidinal, flighty stepsister; a better "father" then her stepfather in having a career that both he and mother could admire and in having a boy baby and thus speculatively her own better penis, achieved in a womanly way. In fantasy her son's emotional makeup would exceed her stepfather's. In a sense, in growing up she considered herself a failure as either a girl or a boy, so that the fantasy of needing a boy child unconsciously represented choosing the more "perfect" sex in her way of thinking, a boy who might have less need to compensate for the inadequacies with which she viewed herself burdened.

The artist's overall tone in her career and in having babies suggested one of a fascination with the vicissitudes of growth toward separateness. There seemed an implicit question as to how a separated object could or would be valued in the outside world, and whether it might be safer self-contained.

In consideration of the parallels which the painter described, a close analogy between creating artistically and libidinal sexual energy is well documented in the analytic literature. The creativity of men has been linked with wishes in women to bear babies, and the impulses involved are often talked about in terms of sublimation. The connections between drives and impulses in both areas of this woman's life are here more inferred than demonstrated, with more emphasis on the object relations involved.

The first aspect in the parallel, the patient's wish for conception both in biological and outwardly creative terms, seems very much like the description of Kris (1964) of an artist's feeling about the moment of inspiration, the sense of being taken over by something outside of one's own control. The following stages of molding and giving form could be interpreted on oral, anal, or genital levels. The language used about the artist's paintings could represent symbiotic desires, wishes, and fears of anal withholding or genital functioning in its active or passive nature in producing a baby. Other aspects of the analogy could more generally be dynamically related to her difficulties in development and interaction between her and the family.

The patient grew up in intense ambivalent involvement with a mother who was psychotically depressed. In the close company of a mother who was needy and engulfing, she must have often doubted her capacity for separateness. Both parents' hindrance of her independence, in her behavior and even in her own ideas, stimulated doubts about her autonomy and her ability to produce something of value by herself. Her separateness was almost a guilty secret, shared by her more supportive grandparents. Clinging fiercely to the privacy of her early artwork served to stave off parental reaction which she feared could be damaging to either her or her paintings. She felt the creations too transparently demonstrated her anger, hatred, and fear of mother and father, but especially mother. These conflicts were carried over in her fear of criticism in setting up her first exhibition of paintings, in particular. As in the collection of paintings, the act of conception and her pregnancy could be viewed as a successful way of keeping the details of something of great moment to herself quite secret. Her expectations of not going into labor and being overdue could reflect inhibitions about exhibiting her private creation, the baby, in the delivery room. In both her views of paintings and babies there is a theme of ambivalence about psychologically separating from them, as if they were both bodily attached to her—the baby even in the weaning process. In the separation, as was the case with her parents, unconsciously she possibly expected much anger and resentment. It is interesting that her survival of the turmoil of primitive feelings and fantasies in the pregnancy and her pride in successfully delivering the baby girl spurred on her development and sense of identity as if she proved that it was possible for mother and child to separate and still remain whole. Shortly after, she was able to go to college. The new ability to complete her paintings at this time suggested her increased sense of boundaries for herself, willingness to relinquish a work and recognize its value on its own. Uncertainty about her ability to maintain her boundaries and fears of her potential for regression were possibly reflected in the age of the children in her fantasies. Intuitively, she may have perceived and been afraid of desires for and fantasies of fusion expected in the relationship of the mother to the newborn infant. This was bypassed by allowing herself only fantasies of four-year-old children, in whom individuality would already be established. The ideas of having twins, as well as re-creating a possibility for closeness with her sisters, also could have posed a special opportunity for her in the management and mastery of identity diffusion, between each of them and herself. The wish to teach students seemed of a similar flavor. The need for a supportive peer group seemed to be increased by her longings for people who would appreciate and regard her separateness, a repetition of supportive aspects on the part of her grandparents. The wish to be a teacher also seemed linked with her identification of her grandparents' sharing their craftmanship with her, while supporting her autonomous development in the same field.

In fulfilling their destinies as defined by themselves and their families, both women thus experienced conscious convictions of becoming career women with children, while parallel underlying conflicts existed. Other conflicts of a practical nature took a minor role (though much of the literature about professional women emphasizes these), e.g., how their lives could be managed to include both roles, or what supports were available for them in the environment. As the artist had had the experience of having a baby, it was clearer how the two areas were ego-syntonic and how the anticipation in fantasy had evolved in reality and had furthered some of her aims for herself. She wanted to have another baby someday to reexperience some of the satisfaction and explore other dimensions within herself, although she was unsure if she wanted her present husband to be the child's father. The scientist had yet to test herself in the arena of childbearing, so that for her there were many intriguing hypotheses, questions, and feelings to be explored when she felt ready for that experience. However, meshing areas of the psychological goals were present even in anticipation.

ACKNOWLEDGMENT

I would like to thank Roy Schafer, Ph.D., for his helpful comments during the writing of this paper.

REFERENCE

Kris, E. (1964). *Psychoanalytic Exploration in Art*. New York: Schocken Books.

ROSEMARY H. BALSAM, M.D.

DR. BALSAM received her medical degree in Belfast, Northern Ireland, and trained there in psychiatry. She was a member of the Royal College of Physicians of Edinburgh and the Royal College of Psychiatrists in London. She is on the staff of the Yale Student Health Services in New Haven and is in private practice. She is a candidate at the Western New England Institute for Psychoanalysis.

The Ellsberg Psychoanalytic Situation

Victor Bernal y del Rio, M.D.

Director, The Puerto Rico Institute of Psychiatry
at Hato Rey Psychiatric Hospital

The author proposes to explore an event that received nationwide publicity through the Watergate investigation: the burglary of the office of a Los Angeles psychoanalyst believed to be treating Dr. Daniel Ellsberg. A brief questionnaire, with an accompanying letter, was mailed to all members of the American Psychoanalytic Association. It requested voluntary information on the reaction of their patients to the aforesaid particular event. The results of the study were then evaluated as serving hopefully an indirect inquiry into psychoanalytic practice. This paper is based on an adjusted sample of 861 respondent psychoanalysts, who reported on a total of 5,074 analysands. The resultant figures indicate that a high percentage of the analysand sample was silent concerning the office break-in during the eight-week period following the national publicity given the event. Of the small percentage of analysands that did present material concerning the event, the survey found that they were the patients of only 84 analysts of the entire sample of 861.

The absence of reference to the Ellsberg Affair in so many patients may have been due to (1) the fact that analysts create an analytic situation which has a basic quality of interference such that events of this kind do not get communicated, and (2), more important, the fact that analysts through some defensive need failed to take cognizance of references to the Ellsberg Affair in dreams or in the latent content of the associations of their patients.

A "natural" psychoanalytic experiment has been studied, and the results are offered for consideration.

INTRODUCTION

I submit that an incident germinal of a "natural experiment" occurred on April 24, 1973; it concerned the sudden revelation of Daniel Ellsberg's link to psychoanalysis and psychiatry. This produced the Ellsberg psychoanalytic situation, where in turn led to the creation of a national psychoanalytic perimeter event.

We shall summarize the Ellsberg Affair as follows: Dr. Ellsberg, a former State Department official, openly admitted that, in keeping with his opposition to the United States government's role in the war in Vietnam, he had given a copy of classified government documents, to which he had access, to the American press. This event was followed by (1) the immediate publication of these papers (a secret government study of the Vietnam war) by four national newspapers; (2) the indictment by the government of Dr. Ellsberg;

and (3) the scheduling of a trial in Los Angeles to be presided over by Judge Matthew Byrne. (The trial has since been completed.)

More particularly, by the Ellsberg psychoanalytic situation we mean the following: In September 1971, burglars were assigned to enter, and did enter, in search of records, the California office of Dr. Lewis J. Fielding, who was understood to be treating Dr. Ellsberg psychoanalytically. This was thoroughly publicized, beginning April 27, 1973, through newspaper, radio, and television coverage, and it received national prominence and extraordinary publicity in relation to Watergate.

Thus it became widely known that the politically controversial Dr. Ellsberg had been under "psychiatric treatment" (communication media consistently used the word *psychiatric*; the word *psychoanalytic* was seldom used); that therapists traditionally keep records of therapeutic sessions; and that such records might be made accessible to others through theft and unauthorized reproduction for public use.

By using the term "psychoanalytic perimeter event" I mean to acknowledge any event, occurrence, chance encounter, coincidence, or fringe happening that may enter into the psychoanalytic situation. Perimeters take place, by definition, on the periphery of that situation. Some remain on the emotional periphery; others, however, come to have a part in the emotional nucleus, or transference neurosis.

Perimeter events may originate in or around the analyst's office. For example, they may occur in changes in office decor or location, absences or latenesses of the analyst, or alterations in the appearance or demeanor of the latter—the analyst might be wearing a cast as the result of an accident, for example. Perimetric events may also originate outside the office, such as through fringe contacts, chance social encounters, public appearances of the analyst, through talks, lectures, or publications. The analyst may become a public figure and appear in the news.

A perimeter event may have intense pertinence to the creation of the initial transference and the therapeutic alliance. To speak somewhat figuratively, the indicated perimeters generally assume orbits equidistant at all points from the center. Frequently, however, they may adopt elliptical orbits, offering no interference in their apogee and only occasionally in their perigee. Ordinarily, such a constellation of factors does not produce an analytic *interference*, as may be the case with a parameter, but occasionally the perimetric events become part of the analytic situation.

I can offer an example from my own practice. Five years ago, close relatives of mine were involved in a locally prominent catastrophic airplane accident. In connection with that disaster, my name and my picture were given first-page exposure in the local newspaper. The accident was mentioned by all my analysands; it was also part of their dream formation.

Semantic confusion may be avoided if we recall here that, as defined in *A Glossary of Psychoanalytic Terms* (ed. B. E. Moore and B. D. Fine, 2nd ed., 1968) : "A psychoanalytic *parameter* is a term relating to an aspect of psychoanalytic technique. It conceptualizes departures from a hypothetical baseline, namely, the classical analytic technique, in which interpretation is the exclusive technical tool." As defined by Eissler (1958), on the other hand, a parameter is *any technical action* of the analyst, other than interpretation.

Not all perimeter events are of the same cathectic accountability. A study of the contents of a perimeter event may provide some inkling as to its possible interference in the psychoanalytic situation. This will depend on its closeness, descriptively or dynamically, to primal relations or to the primitive transferences. A classification of perimeters might even be produced someday. The perimeter is brought into the psychoanalytic situation either directly or in some disguised form.

I am, of course, indebted to many writers for this concept, especially to Greenson and even more so to Stone (1961), who has written: "The ordinary accidents of life, the confidences of apartment-house employees, social conversations, professional meetings and publications, sometimes (if one's life is more spectacular) the newspapers, provide abundant interesting data about the analyst, if not always accurate, objective or thorough. In smaller communities, direct observations may be a common-place of 'everyday life.' " Yet Stone seems to be mainly concerned with the *management* of some situations, while neglecting (I believe) to name and categorize the entire range of such orbital happenings.

On the other hand Weiss, in a recent paper, refers to them as "special events," but offers examples only from his own practice. The present paper deals with an event of nationwide publicity which could serve as the core for the formulation of a psychoanalytic perimeter event amenable to comparative study.

THE STUDY

It was on April 27, 1973, that Judge Byrne released the initial information about the burglarizing. This immediately reached all national news media and remained front-page information for many weeks following.

I waited with an increasing sense of frustration for my analysands to mention the Ellsberg Affair; yet any reference failed to appear, and I was quite taken aback. It seemed to me altogether unbelievable that a patient who was himself involved in a closely comparable undertaking, upon being made aware of a well-publicized burglary, with some possibly ominous implications for him, could fail to take note of such a parallel. This I thought might be attributed to the patients' local insularism and perhaps their political status. I thereupon proceeded to turn to "mainland" analysts in order to discover how their analysands had reacted.

On June 24, 1973, two months after the official revelation of the burglarized office, I mailed a letter and a questionnaire (see Figures 1 and 2) to the entire membership of the American Psychoanalytic Association (Revised Roster 1971-1973). By early July, a total of 1,383 such communications had been mailed, along with a return stamped envelope.

FIG. 1

June 24, 1973

Dear Colleague:

Certain events of national importance with specific timetables (i.e., the assassination of President Kennedy, the eastern seaboard power failure) crystallize into an engram with specifics of time, place, etc. A person does recall where he was, what he was doing, etc. In 90 percent of my analytic practice at the time it was rapidly reported and has appeared in dreams consistently.

With the arrival on the scene of the now well-publicized para-Watergate Affair and ultimate disclosure of the burglary of the office of Doctor Ellsberg's psychiatrist, I expected the same mass reaction. I have been surprised by the total lack of involvement of my patients on the subject — one which seems to me would have so much bearing on their own situation. I can report that 100 percent of my ten analytic patients have never mentioned the Ellsberg situation, it has not appeared in the manifest content of dreams — and as far as I can detect, it has appeared in but one instance in an indirect or symbolic reference. In lieu of this — and to compare findings — I am asking fellow members of the American Psychoanalytic Association to respond to three questions.

Would you be so kind as to take a few minutes from an already overcrowded schedule and answer the enclosed.

Gratefully,

VICTOR BERNAL Y
DEL RIO, M.D.
Member A. Psa. A.

FIGURE 2

VICTOR BERNAL Y DEL RIO, M.D.
Member A. Psa. A.

June 24, 1973

1. Of (x number) _____ patients in psychoanalysis under my care (x number) _____ have mentioned the breaking into the office of Dr. Ellsberg's psychiatrist.

2. (x number) _____ have mentioned dreams with a manifest content of direct reference concerning the breaking into the office of Dr. Ellsberg's psychiatrist.

3. (x number) _____ have mentioned dreams with symbolic reference to the breaking into the office of Dr. Ellsberg's psychiatrist.

Name can be omitted if desired: _____ M.D.

Geographical   East USA _____   West USA _____

Location   Mid USA _____   South USA _____

Remarks: _____

             _____

             _____

The total response received, within 4 weeks (see Table 1), was 861, or 62.25 percent of the 1,383 questionnaires that had been mailed. (It should be noted that no follow-up reminder was sent.) Colleagues have commented on this truly phenomenal response, and it can interpreted in various ways. Was it that the Ellsberg Affair had provoked extreme interest and curiosity in the psychoanalytic community, turning the response to my inquiry into an exception in the current tendency *not to answer* mailed inquiries? Other factors may also have to be taken into consideration. The envelopes were coming from an insular setting, namely, Puerto Rico, which always produces a certain curiosity. They were also coming from a small and unknown institute, and that sometimes produces a desire to help by answering.

TABLE 1

Statistical Data

	Analysts	%
Number questionnaires sent	1,383	100
Number answered questionnaire received	861	62.25
Answers statistically sterile	60	6.9
Answers statistically useful **n** = 861	801	93.03
Answers signed or identified	597	69.33
Answers unidentified = 861	264	30.66
Answers with remarks	433	50.25
Answers without remarks	428	49.75

Total Number of analysands 5,074 reported by 861 analysts

ANALYSIS OF THE DATA

Among the 861 answers received, 801 were useful for our study: that is, there were 60 respondents who were no longer practicing (whether through retirement or for other reasons), but who were kind or interested enough to return the questionnaire anyway, along with an explanatory note about the absence of information. Of the replies, 597 were signed or identified in some way. Such a readiness for identification (69.3 percent), which has been unheard of in analytic circles and runs counter to our well-established practice of anonymity, in addition to indicating the great interest in and cathectic importance of this material, may prove dynamically relevant.

Four hundred and thirty-three answers (50.2 percent of the total) were accompanied by remarks. Moreover, 300 respondents demonstrated in diverse ways their interest in obtaining the results of this study. Although I shall be making use of some of the answers in my theoretical formulation, I shall not be able to do justice to their incisive pertinence, or to the wealth of dynamic "knowhow" they evidenced. The answers alone could stimulate many pages of theoretical speculation.

The phenomenal response, the number of expressions of interest in the results, the accompanying remarks, and the signed or identified inquiries — all these point toward a concern on the part of the analytic community. The failure to report material brought by patients would thus have to be evaluated carefully. Both analysts and patients had been subjected to an unavoidable deluge of input by the news media. If we were to judge the reaction of analysts themselves to this event, we might well have to declare it to be a highly sensitive one. I may note in passing that it would have been fruitful for "in depth" study to have included in the questionnaire some reference to the *analyst's own* dreams during this period, as was suggested by some of my correspondents. Unfortunately, I was not alert to this possibility at that time. Thus, our sample consisted of 5,074 patients, as reported in treatment by 801 respondents (see Table 1).

Of these 5,074 analysands, however, only 671 (13 percent) had been reported as mentioning the Ellsberg situation; that is 4,403 (87 percent) had made no direct mention of it.

TABLE 2

Statistical Data

	Analysands	%	Analysts
Number directly mentioning the Ellsberg psychoanalytic affair **n = 5,074**	671	13	Reported by 294 analysts
Reported not mentioning	4,403	87	
Total analysands	5,074		

The absence of direct mention is noteworthy by itself. Closer examination reveals even more interesting figures: the 671 analysands who did mention the break-in were reported by only 294 psychoanalysts. Four hundred and ninety analysts (61 percent of those responding) reported *no direct mention and no dreams* concerning the Ellsberg Affair, on the part of *any* of their patients. Seventeen analysts reported *no direct mention* by patients, although they did report *some dream material.*

One hundred thirty-three analysts reported *one single analysand* of theirs as mentioning the incident. This leaves us with 161 analysts to account for 538 analysands who mentioned the break-in. Furthermore, 77 analysts reported *two analysands each*, as directly mentioning the break-in; that added up to 144 patients, and leaves us with 84 psychoanalysts respondents reporting 394 analysands, *three or more of whom mentioned the incident* (see Table 3).

TABLE 3

Analysis of Data

	Analysts	Analysands
Reported verbal mention by one patient	133	133
Reporting verbal mention by two patients	77	144
Reporting verbal mention by three or more patients	84	394
	294	671
Reported verbal or dream material	311	———
Reported no verbal mention but some dream material	17	———
Reported no verbal mention and no dreams	490	———
Reported no verbal mention	507	4,403

Of 5,074 analysands, 79 were reported as mentioning dreams with *manifest* content referring to the Ellsberg Affair; this constituted 1.5 percent of the total. Four thousand nine hundred ninety-five patients (93.5 percent) were reported as presenting *no dreams with manifest content* referring to the affair. Thirty-six analysts reported 79 patients with such manifest content dreams, these being 0.4 percent of the total, but 765 (96 percent) of the total number of analysts) reported *no* patients presenting dreams with a manifest content that referred to the affair. The 79 analysands who did report dreams with manifest content were divided among the 36 analysts in the following fashion: 21 analysts reported *one* patient in their practice as producing such a dream; 9 reported *two* patients as producing such a dream; and 6 analysts reported *more than two* such patients. Thus, 6 psychoanalysts reported 40 analysands who mentioned manifest content dreams (see Table 5).

TABLE 4

Statistical Data

	Analyst	Analysands
Reported patients with a manifest content dream	36	69
Reported patients with dreams with a latent content	63	134

TABLE 5

Statistical Data

	Analysts	%	Analysands	%
Reported one patient with dreams with a manifest content ($n = 801$)	21	3 ($n = 5,074$)	21	.46
Reported two patients with dreams with a manifest content	9	1	18	.35
Reported more than two patients with dreams with a manifest content	6	1	40	.71
Total:	36			
Reported dreams with a manifest content	36	5	79	.015
Reported dreams with a manifest content	765	95.5	4,995	98.4
Total:	801		5,074	
Reported patients with no verbal mention but with manifest content dreams	6	1	10	.19

Thus, of 5,074 analysands, 134 (2.6 percent) were reported as mentioning *dreams* with a latent content referring to the Ellsberg Affair; whereas, 4,940 patients (97.4 percent) appear to have reported *no* such dreams. We need to take note of the difference between the 79 analysands who mentioned manifest content dreams and the 134 analysands who were reported as producing latent content dreams. Sixty-three analysts (7.8 percent) reported dreams with a latent content by patients, while 738 analysts (92.2 percent) reported *no* patients bringing in dreams with such latent content. Note the difference between the 36 analysts who reported manifest content dreams by patients, and the 63 analysts who reported latent content ones by their patients.

Is it possible, one may ask, that many analysts, although consciously very aware of the Ellsberg Affair, through some defensive scotoma need, failed to take account of manifest dreams referring to loss or theft?

One hypothesis concerning symbolic representation of burglary in dreams would relate to the theft of sexual partners. The two famous such burglaries occurring in history and mythology concern the abduction of Helen by Paris and the ensuing Trojan Wars, and that of the Sabine women by the Romans. I am, of course, aware of the famous mythological theft of fire by Prometheus, purportedly to present it as a gift to man. But, I am not put off by the "charity" hypothesis and consider it to be within the context of agression, namely patricide. Prometheus steals the fire in order to annihilate the gods, mainly Zeus, who later indulges in a pertinent paternal act of revenge.

Of the 63 analysts who reported 134 latent content dreams, 34 reported *one* patient with a latent content dream, and 17 reported *two* patients in the same category; thus it was 12 analysts who reported 68 patients with latent content dreams (see Table 6).

TABLE 6

Statistical Data

	Analysts	%	Analysands	%
Reported patients with dreams with a latent content	63	10	134	3
Reported no patients with dreams with a latent content	738	90	4,940	97
Total:	801		5,074	

TABLE 6 (cont'd)

Statistical Data

	Analysts	%	Analysands
Reported one patient with dreams with a latent content	34	5	34
Reported two patients with dreams with a latent content	17	2	34
Reported three or more patients with dreams with a latent content	12	1.5	68
Reported patients with no verbal mention of latent content dreams	14	1.6	24

To sum up: *84 analysts reported a total of 394 patients as directly mentioning the incident—that is, approximately 5 patients per analyst. Six analysts reported a total of 40 patients who produced a dream with manifest content related to the incident—that is, 6 patients per analyst. Twelve analysts reported 68 patients with dreams that had a latent content referring to the incident—that is, 6 patients per analyst.*

Six is the average number of analysands per analyst. Thus we may conclude that, for a very small part of the sample, *all patients of certain analysts referred in one way or another to the Ellsberg situation.* We also can say conversely that this particular group of analysts heard and reported their patient's references to the Ellsberg situation.

The data thus shows that, of 801 analysts reporting on 5,074 patients, the majority, 520 analysts (64.9 percent), were producing an analytic situation of sufficient similarity for their patients all to behave in a similar fashion. Eighty-four analysts (10.5 percent of the total number) were producing an analytic situation in which the Ellsberg Affair appeared conspicuously. This exception, 84 analysts, producing a psychoanalytic situation in which 394 analysands behaved so differently from their counterparts, with regard to this national psychoanalytic perimeter event, must be considered carefully. Our immediate concern, however, is with the 520 analysts whose patients made *no* mention of it.

Naively but characteristically, some respondents tried to explain the lack of reference to the Ellsberg Affair among their analysands by admitting, "I do not take notes and my patients know it." That statement, or something like it, was made by 40 respondents.

Other respondents were not at all impressed by the lack of concern on the part of their patients with the Ellsberg Affair. Their argument was that patients in analysis are *usually not concerned enough with current events* to bring such issues into the psychoanalytic situation. One wonders whether such an argument is really tenable in view of the possibility, to be discussed later, that the psychoanalytic situation may itself be responsible for a patient's lack of reference to such events.

Some colleagues also commented on the differences as being due exclusively to geography. This theory was the delight of a number of my respondents, who ascribed to the locale truly formidable powers. It is true that a pocket of positive responses existed in Washington, D.C., and Los Angeles, as anticipated, because of problems of job tenure or political contamination, or nearness to the burglary site; but strangely enough, a subpocket of negative responses also occurred a few blocks from the actual burglary site. Some analysts in the same block as Dr. Fielding reported zero answers in items 1-3 (figure 2), while others reported a high positive response. The analyst whose offices were at the actual burglary site reported, as expected, a 100 percent involvement of his patients. A look at the tables of geographical differences (see Tables 7 and 8) shows approximately the same percentages of analysts as in the general response, *on all questions asked.*

TABLE 7

Analysis of Data

GEOGRAPHICAL DIVISION		SENT	RECEIVED	%
East USA		930	540	58
Mid USA		262	171	65
West USA		190	149	78
Foreign		1	1	
	Total	1,383	861	

TABLE 8

STATISTICAL DATA - FURTHER GEOGRAPHICAL DATA

	ANALYSTS	%	ANALYSANDS
East USA			
Reporting 0 Verbal Response	309	62	—
Reporting 1 Verbal Response	82	16	82
Reporting 2 Verbal Response	53	10.72	106
Reporting 3 Verbal Response	50	10.12	—
	494		
Mid USA			
Reporting 0 Verbal Response	112	68	—
Reporting 1 Verbal Response	26	15.9	26
Reporting 3 Verbal Response	13	7.9	26
Reporting 3 Verbal Response	13	7.9	—
	164		
West USA			
Reporting 0 Verbal Response	82	57	—
Reporting 1 Verbal Response	31	21	31
Reporting 2 Verbal Response	12	8.4	24
Reporting 3 Verbal Response	18	12	—
	143		

I shall at this point make a slight detour, in order to report what can only be called a "slip of the pen." Forty-one analysts reported a higher figure for the number of patients who had referred to the break-in than they gave as the total number of their patients. That is, they inverted the figures in the blanks of item 1 in the questionnaire. I regard this as a "slip of the pen" and my statistical report has corrected the slip. I offer no theoretical commentary on this slip, although it very much interests me. Perhaps wiser colleagues than I may offer some theoretical explanation. Interestingly, there was only one analyst from the Far West guilty of this inversion. Finally, there were 104 analysts who reported analysands that did refer to the Ellsberg Affair, but they did not report their total number of analysands, reflecting our usual secrecy as to the number of analysands being treated by us.

THEORETICAL CONSIDERATIONS

This inquiry may have proven so far to be more productive as to questions than answers. We may start with this question: Why was the Ellsberg situation referred to only by a total of 671 analysands, only 13.2 percent of the 5,074 in the sample?

Referral to the Ellsberg Affair of some patients with some analysts must, for its evaluation, be placed in relation to the phase of analysis of the particular patient. Different importance should be ascribed if mention of the Ellsberg Affair was made by patients at the inception, middle, or final phase of the analysis. Patients do vary in their perception and report of perimeter events.

A few years ago, an example occurred in my practice which may have some bearing on this. I was stung on the forehead by a wasp. As the result of a violent allergic reaction, my face became swollen. Unable or unwilling to cancel, I saw my entire patient load. Most of my analysands on the couch that day did not mention the swelling at all. Perhaps this could be ascribed to the subliminal aspect of visual stimuli, as they walked from the door to the couch under very subdued lighting conditions. Two analysands who were terminating their analysis, however, did refer to my condition as they entered the dimly lit office. The following day, when I thought my facial swelling was hardly discernible, a sitting-up patient in psychotherapy mentioned the disfigurement.

On the other hand, a borderline patient in intensive psychotherapy (five times per week), sitting in front of me in a well-lighted office, and at the time in severe narcissistic regression, spent her entire 45 minutes without mentioning my rather obvious facial change. In her involvement with herself, she communicated verbally entirely within the circle of her "preoccupations." A striking change in my physical being was devoid of any significance at the time. On the other hand, this patient had occasionally verbalized her concern for my thinness. In her upbringing, the utmost importance had been given to feeding, thus reinforcing the original hierarchical organization of "big = better" so as to make it mean "fat = healthy." This is a very common equation; in fact, it is almost universal. This patient, on seeing my swollen face, may have translated it into the thought that I was gaining weight, and thus been reassured rather than disturbed.

Back to our central theme. We can easily say that the positive answers in individualized cases reported above may have been due to job tenure (politically sensitive jobs), or to excessive exposure to the material (journalists, writers, etc.), or possibly even as a result of geographical location. Why was it, however, that an event *so pertinent to the reality situation of every analysand* did not become a conscious psychoanalytic perimeter among the great majority? Why did 4,405 analysands (86.8 percent out of 5,074) *not even so much as mention* the Ellsberg case? Mass denial may perhaps be posed as the commanding mechanism behind these findings. But the material also failed to appear in dreams, which would be expected if denial were the mental mechanism in action.

We must turn to the analysts themselves. Could it be that the analysts failed to witness and identify latent references to the Ellsberg Affair both in the verbal expression and in the dream material of their patients? Although consciously well aware of the Ellsberg matter, and, even like myself, looking for it intently in the production of the patient, could they have failed to recognize and hence left uninterpreted this material, thus failing to take cognizance of an important part of the psychic activity of their patients? The desire to compare my patients' experiences to those of other analysts became the impetus for this study. The impasse may have been related to my own failure to grasp or hear pertinent latent content and to interpret it. The expressed interest of analysts in the result of this study may also be of the same nature. This defensive need on the part of the analyst not to hear the patient's latent material regarding the Ellsberg Affair may have been due to: (1) political stances; (2) a lack of them on the part of the analyst; (3) to other "scotoma" regarding burglary and theft as financial interchange continues to be such an important and yet mostly undisclosed part of our psychoanalytic situation.

The avoidance of mention of the Ellsberg Affair by so many patients may very well be the result of an unconscious interchange between analyst and patient, the analyst having failed to recognize the material as it was introduced indirectly by the patients. Analysts may have felt threatened by the possibilities of a repetition of the Ellsberg situation in their own offices and analytic practices. Analysts of course keep records, usually not very well secured; thus guilt on the part of many analysts and mistrust in many analysands may explain the avoidance of the subject.

We must also take cognizance of the ancient talmudic dictum: "The person who steals from a thief is not guilty" and use it to theorize. Concretely, stealing is the removal or abduction of property, always to be equalized by retrieval or punishment. Both Ellsberg and the burglars may have been seen on identical terms, or Ellsberg may have been seen as a thief and the burglars as retrievers. Robin Hood and other modern Robin Hood-like sagas offer themselves for parallel considerations.

The identification possibilities of the situation were with (1) Dr. Ellsberg; (2) with the burglars; and (3) with Dr. Ellsberg's analyst and his tribulations, etc., and through him with "my analyst" and "me." Identification with the victim or the aggressor would depend on the particular makeup of each patient or on the patient's material under analysis at that time. Patients may have felt entirely secure as far as their analysts were concerned, or regarded themselves as simply not "important" enough for anybody to employ such measures as burglary in order to accomplish an exposure of them.

If we take note of the fact that the John F. Kennedy assassination, as well as those of Martin Luther King and Robert Kennedy, were often referred to from the couch (which was apparent from my experience and from some of the remarks in the questionnaire, personal communications, etc., but has not yet been the result of an inquiry), we can propose a rather succinct theoretical explanation of the different dynamics involved in those instances. The assassination of a young leadership figure who is both beloved and charismatic is so clearly reminiscent of the "killing of the father," and the equation of "father = analyst" is so intense in the transference, that the equation "Kennedy = father = analyst" inevitably appeared in direct references, manifest and latent dream content, sometimes for many years. The use to which the material was put by each analysand, had to do chiefly with his situation in analysis (phase) and to the particularities of his oedipal resolution.

While the killing of the leader (father-analyst) is related to the inevitable blueprints of transference formation (primal relations), and eventually plays a part in all transference neurosis, the burglarizing of records cannot be equated with those "original blueprints." Secrecy and confidence, as well as the violation of these by burglary, are rather sophisticated intellectual entities, devoid of representations in the primal relations.

If we also take note of the fact that the 1968 eastern seaboard "blackout" [1] was mentioned quite often in analysis, we must once again draw a comparison. Darkness (the night) has to do with the very earliest and most deeply emotional experiences of the human being, and results in the inevitable equation of "darkness = heightened danger = uncontrollable fear = anxiety."

Reference to the Ellsberg case by some analysands may, as we have already noted, be attributed to the particular phase of analysis, geographical location, or job tenure. If a satisfactory explanation does not emerge from these categories, however, we must look to the psychoanalytic situation itself. Differences in the behavior of patients may well be the result of differences in the analyst's own approach to the situation, insofar as it is the *analyst* who is the creator and guardian of the "psychoanalytic climate," through the use of well-known "facilitators" (many of which are, descriptively, abstentions).

We are therefore forced to take a close look at one final and perhaps crucial matter: how did it happen that only a small number of analysts had been producing or cultivating a "psychoanalytic climate" in which the Ellsberg situation was able to appear conspicuously? What relevance can be discovered in the different psychoanalytic situations created and maintained by diferent analysts? Is what we are faced with the result of *basic modifications in technique*? To obtain the answer to these questions, we would have to address ourselves at least to the 10 percent of the total sample of analysts who reported the Ellsberg material as having been referred to by their analysands. It might be possible to address a questionnaire to, or to interview, 81 analysts regarding these differences. By contrast, questioning 720 analysts, or the entire membership, once again would be a gargantuan undertaking. Further research could be accomplished by

1. Soliciting voluntary self-identification of those analysts in whose practice the Ellsberg situation was mentioned conspicuously or consistently.

2. Through questionnaires, interviews, etc., looking into the particulars of the "psychoanalytic upbringing" of these particular analysts: their personal analysis, training experiences, supervision, professional life, selection of patients, personal life-style, political thinking, etc.

The differences noted above could have been the outcome of particular reactions by the analyst, positive or negative, to the entire Ellsberg Affair, flowing from the specific character of the analyst's political thought and practice. The events involved may have provoked, for example, too much or too little activity in the psychoanalytic situation on the part of the analyst. As a consequence of his unconscious motivation, the analyst would have been producing minute modifications in technique, which would either enhance or make more difficult the formation of a psychoanalytic perimeter.

If investigation were able to bring to light discernible, explainable, and codifiable *modifications of technique of this sort* on the part of analysts, it could be of immense value to the psychoanalytic field. It might make possible the introduction into the psychoanalytic situation of material close to some analysand's life-style, material that had until then been forced to enter only in the guise of perimetric events when stimulated.

We must declare that decisions about *scientific* methodology cannot be made by a *democratic* process, by considerations of *popularity*. We may eventually find that our silences in regard to certain areas of material actually stem from strong countertransference biases on our part which we have unwittingly imposed on our patients.

The reaction of analysts and patients to the Ellsberg matter offers intriguing theoretical possibilities. As suggested earlier, the high percentage of answers from analysts in this study, the inclusion of remarks by them, and requests from them for the results of the study, would seem to point to great interest on their part. An individual analyst could conceivably have identified with Dr. Ellsberg's analyst and reacted with realistic concern, inasmuch as privacy is a "tool of the trade."

To have discovered that our professional activities had been menaced by illegal invasion should logically have led to a mammoth collective protest on our part. Our profession, however, has remained relatively silent regarding this, although it touches upon one of the fundamental questions of the profession's existence, as well as on the basic tenets of its practice. This silence at the group level so far may very well be an inappropriate extension of the useful and necessary silence in the analytic situation. Only one of my analyst correspondents expressed this concern directly; interestingly enough, he is not now in private practice.

Identifying with the patient (Dr. Ellsberg) —which probably many of us had already done—could in this case have been tied in with a particular political stance. The *homo politicus* is rather subdued in analysts, and the profession has consistently withheld itself from political involvement or identification. It should be noted, however, that nearly five thousand analysands are reported as having responded with an identical "lack of concern." The analytic population is, of course, one very particular portion of the general population; nevertheless, there is no reason why this should preclude a substantial number of politically alert and concerned persons. We could perhaps declare the reported lack of reaction to be part of a *general* political apathy on the part of the population as a whole, or hypothesize that bombardment by the communication media actually fails to make any impact on the general public. One might also suggest that people had, by that time, become "fed up" with political issues. Yet, for the analysands, the political elements reflected in the Ellsberg Affair had been transformed by the burglary into a matter of *personal danger to them*.

We also have to consider the fact that the burglary eventually boomeranged. There might have been other developments, if some records had been openly publicized as a result of it. Patients in the midst of negative transferences might have seized upon such an event to express anger, bitterness, betrayal, etc., this time directed against their own analyst, or the profession as a whole.

Some colleagues have suggested that patients in psychotherapy may have referred to the Ellsberg situation more often, and I therefore extended the study to inquire into the experiences of psychotherapists. I sent similar letters with enclosed questionnaires to a geographically matched equal number of board-certified psychiatrists who were *not* members of the American Psychoanalytic Association. The number of responses equaled those received from psychoanalysts.

I want to make it clear that I am not prepared to assert that possible technical variations in methods between 80 analysts and 800 has proven to be more advantageous therapeutically. As physicians, we attend with care to the performance of numerous qualitative or semiquantitative skills in a highly uniform fashion. Early in our training, we learn the art of auscultation, and the consistency with which physicians describe what they hear is astounding. Just as medicine can take pride in its ability to impart the knowledge of such skills unchanged, so can those who train psychoanalysts.

The thrust of this study, however, has been to take note of the implications of what has emerged as an important question. With regard to perimeters of *wide scope and possibly deepgoing significance*, stemming from a *general social experience* that touches on many different analysands at once, our uniform "psychoanalytic climate," the *unspoken milieu* in the midst of which the psychoanalytic situation, *whatever the technique involved*, takes place, may have shown itself, in the results of this study, to be generally unamenable to the introduction of the patient's intrapsychic reactions to such events—in short, of such *material*—into the psychoanalytic situation.

Can it be that a "national psychoanalytic perimeter" is a misnomer? If so, we all need to examine whether or not we, as analysts, have relegated to the perimeter what may very well be, among some of our present patients, close to the heart of their conflicts. Still they have tacitly agreed, at the silent but unmistakable behest of the analyst, to exclude these very things from the material that will be dealt with as *relevant* to the joint resolution of those conflicts.

In short, does not our present uniform approach, and the uniform training based on it, need to be *uniformly expanded*, so as to include what Freud once described as the psychoanalyst's own "silent" (or "blind") areas? For more and more of our patients, and certainly the newest among them, these areas may by no means be blind. It may be we *ourselves* who have continued to keep such areas "off the couch," and who now need to take steps to assure our patients that these elements of their psychic experience have every right to be there too.

NOTE

1. In May 1968, the entire eastern seaboard was subjected to a mammoth power failure, lasting for a period of approximately 24 hours.

REFERENCES

Fenichel, O. (1941). Problems of psychoanalytic technique. *Psychoanalytic Quarterly*,
Freud, S. (1912). The dynamics of the transference. *Collected Papers* 2:301-355. London: Hogarth Press.
Glover, E. (1935). *The Technique and Practice of Psychoanalysis*. Vol. I. New York: International Universities Press.
Greenson, R. (1967). *The Technique and Practice of Psychoanalysis*. Vol. I. New York: International Universities Press.
_____, & Wexler, M. (1969). The non-transference relationship in the psychoanalytic situation. *International Journal of Psycho-Analysis* 5:27-39.
Shafer, R. (1959). Generative empathy in the treatment situation. *Psychoanalytic Quarterly* 28:342-373.
Stone, L. (1961). *The Psychoanalytic Situation*. "Freud Anniversary Lecture Series." New York: International Universities Press.
Weiss, S. (1975). The effect on the transference of "special events" occurring during psychoanalysis. International Journal of Psycho-Analysis. pp. 56, 69.
Wolfenstein, M., and Kliman, G. (1965). *Children and the Death of a President*. New York: Doubleday.

VICTOR BERNAL Y DEL RIO, M.D.

DR. BERNAL is a graduate of the Columbia Psychoanalytic Clinic, New York. He holds a variety of teaching positions in Puerto Rico and New York and is an active committee member for the American Psychoanalytic Association. He has published on a variety of subjects including the problems of ethics.

Conservatism and Liberalism: A Psychoanalytic Examination of Political Belief

J. Alexis Burland, M.D.

Philadelphia Psychoanalytic Institute
Philadelphia, Pennsylvania

A review of the historical development of conservative and liberal thought reveals contradictory basic assumptions: the former views man as essentially evil by nature, and places its priorities upon self-restraint; the latter views man as essentially good, and with unlimited capabilities, and celebrates his efforts at creating a perfect society for himself. Three clinical vignettes are recounted in which the patient's intrapsychic organization found support from a harmonious political philosophy. It is suggested that conservatism and liberalism offer the individual an ideological resolution to the narcissistic injuries he experiences as a consequence of life's inevitable and developmentally determined disappointments.

> "An individual is much more influenced in his appraisal of a political situation by his traditional background, his economic state and class, his prejudices and his personal animosities, than by cool and objective, impersonal considerations."
>
> —*A Glossary of Psychoanalytic Terms and Concepts*
> Moore and Fine, 1968

INTRODUCTION

To the psychoanalytically knowledgeable observer, man has little ability to be completely objective when examining the social and political situation and prescribing for it. In *The Coming Crisis of Western Sociology* (1970) Prof. Alvin Gouldner wrote, allegedly to the astonishment of academic sociology, "Whether or not it 'should be,' social theory is always rooted in the theorist's experiences." He went on to say: "Sociologists must surrender the human but elitist assumption that *others* believe out of need whereas *they* believe because of the dictates of logic and reason." He pointed to what he called "background assumptions," implied but never explicitly stated in all sociological theory, which imbue any given theory with a subjective quality of "validity" for those who espouse it. He said of these assumptions: "they are not originally adopted for instrumental reasons. . . . They are not selected with a calculated view to their utility. This is so because they are often internalized (by the theorist) before the intellectual age of consent." It is of interest that this notion should be so startling some eighty years after *Studies in Hysteria*.

This paper concerns one aspect of political belief, the conservatism-to-liberalism continuum. The historical development of conservatism and of liberalism will be briefly sketched, and their respective literature, past and present, examined. Three clinical vignettes will then be presented from cases in which political belief and activity expressed attempts at compromise solutions to developmental conflicts, and to demonstrate the extent to which the political view adhered to was well suited to its task.

Though for reasons of clarity of exposition conservatism and liberalism will be discussed in either/or terms, it is to be understood that in actuality "pure" conservatives, or liberals, are rare indeed, as anyone conversant with current events is well aware. Similarly, no direct parallel is implied with Republicans or Democrats, of course, both political parties containing within their ranks conservative and liberal elements.

THE LITERATURE OF CONSERVATISM

The birthdate of classical conservatism is generally conceded to be the year of the publication of Edmund Burke's *Reflections on the Revolution in France* — 1790. The eighteenth century saw the culmination of great changes in social structure. The middle class had been born. Men of humble background had been achieving social, economic, and intellectual prominence for the first time. Increasingly the common man (as opposed to the gods, or royalty, or religious figures) had been portrayed in the arts, and, as Edmund Wilson has pointed out, history became more concerned with recording the average citizen's activities and less with merely chronicaling those of the aristocracy. "Rationalism" and "science" celebrated man's intellectual potential and his growing mastery over the forces of nature. The notion was born that there could be social progress (Arendt, 1969), that Everyman's lot could be improved, if not perfected.

The French Revolution was a product of these phenomena, and Burke reacted with alarm to it. As one writer put it: "Burke, as he regarded humanity, is ever asking himself, How are these men (revolutionaries) to be saved from anarchy?" (Kirk, 1960). The cornerstone of Burkean conservatism is the never ending contest between man's basically anarchic nature and God's supernatural order. "Social tranquility" is maintained, therefore, by the exercise of certain virtues to tame man's nature in obedience and acquiescence to God's order. Burke distrusted the new rationalism that believed it could improve upon God's formula for the social order. "If society is treated as a simple contraption to be managed on mathematical lines . . . then man will be degraded into something much less than a partner in the immortal contract which unites the dead, the living, and those yet unborn, the bond between God and man." He saw disappointment as the inevitable result of the new social activism. He wrote in defense of the class system:

> You would have had a protected, satisfied, laborious and obedient people, taught to seek and to recognize the happiness which is to be found by virtue in all conditions; in which consists the true moral equality of mankind, and not in that monstrous fiction, which, by inspiring false ideas into men destined to travel in the obscure walk of laborious life, serves only to aggravate and embitter that real equality, which it never can remove; and which the order of civil life establishes as much for the benefit of those whom it must leave in humble state, as for those whom it is able to exalt to a condition more splendid, but not more happy. . . . If veneration is eradicated by sophistication [life will become a] continual battle between usurpation and rebellion. . . . Radicalism . . . levels all emotions, placing all sensations on a common plane of mediocrity, erasing the moral imagination which sets men apart from the beasts. . . . Learning will be cast into the mire, and trodden down under the hoofs of a swinish multitude."

Rather than "sophistication," or the new "science" of "rationalism," Burke believed in what he called "prejudice":

> Prejudice is of ready application in the emergency; it previously engages the mind in a steady course of wisdom and virtue, and does not leave the man hesitating in the moment of decision, skeptical, puzzled, and unresolved. Prejudice renders a man's virtue his habit; and not a series of unconnected acts.

Referring also to the personal qualities of "high character, strong intellect, good birth, and practical shrewdness," Burke wrote, in an often quoted phrase,

> So long as these endure, so long the Duke of Bedford is safe, and we are all safe together—the high from the blights of envy and the spoilations of rapacity, the low from the iron hand of oppression and the insolent spurn of contempt.

Burke did not see the social order as being in need of "perfection," of alteration. He believed that a divine intent ruled the society of man, by means of forces that man cannot fathom. Human reason alone could not, therefore — *must* not — be trusted. The mysteries of "traditional" life were to be venerated (this has been called "conservative enjoyment"). Civilized society requires orders and classes. The only true equality is moral equality, not material equality. Society longs for leadership.

It is man, rather than the social order, that is in need of correction. One contemporary conservative author has written, "Man is not entirely corrupt and depraved, but to state that he is, is to come closer to the truth than to state he is essentially good" (Kirk, 1969). Another writes,

> If educated properly, placed in a favorable environment, and held in restraint by tradition and authority, he may display innate qualities of rationality, sociability, industry, and decency. Never, no matter how he is educated or situated or restrained, will he throw off completely his other innate qualities of irrationality, selfishness, laziness, depravity, corruptibility, and cruelty. [Rossiter, 1962].

The prescription for man is the exercise of certain "primary virtues." These include wisdom, justice, temperance, industry, frugality, piety, honesty, contentment, obedience, compassion, and good manners. Duty comes before pleasure, self-sacrifice before self-indulgence. *Prudence* above all others is central, involving a mixture of caution, deliberation, discretion, moderation, calculation. Education's task is to teach us to think, to survive, to ply a trade, to enjoy leisure; it is basically a conserving, civilizing process "conveying to us all our share of the inherited wisdom of our race, training us in morality and self-discipline, fostering in us a love of order and a respect for authority" (Rossiter, 1962). Man *can* govern himself, but there is no certainty that he *will*. Man needs, therefore, help from education, religion, and tradition; he must be counseled, encouraged, informed, and above all checked. Men are unequal, and can never be made equal; the social order is constructed so as to take advantage of these ineradicable natural distinctions and bring about a reconciliation between classes rather than their eradication. Man must submit to the inevitability of the class structure. The aim of conservatism, to quote Burke, is "the preservation of the Constitution of Civilization."

This all too brief summary of classical and contemporary conservative philosophy brings to mind a few preliminary conclusions. Conservatism is psychological in orientation due to its emphasis upon man's intrapsychic struggle between anarchic instinctual pressures and the exercise of self-control over them. Its view of man is rather bleak. He is seen as his own worst enemy, the instigator of his downfall rather than a victim of external pressures. The Good

Life is offered as a possibility, without guarantee, for which one must work hard. There is pessimism as to the perfectability of man and skepticism as to his capacity to master either himself or nature, science and rationalism notwithstanding. The reward one works for is a sense of community, a oneness, a mystical union with a Divine Providence. The natural order has been ordained, and man must adjust himself to it. Self-esteem depends upon mastery over one's self, not mastery over the environment.

THE LITERATURE OF LIBERALISM

Liberalism was also born in the eighteenth century as a by-product of the complex of forces that led Western civilization from an agrarian to an industrial society and gave birth to the middle class. But in its celebration of the common man's innate goodness and capacity to master all forces of his environment, it is in marked contrast to conservatism.

It is this sense of celebration of man that is most striking in the literature of liberalism — celebration of the common man's newly gained middle-class prosperity, his newly gained success at achieving material comfort, and celebration of his hitherto unrealized capacity for scientific exploration and invention.

Whereas conservatism invoked religion as its final authority, the proponents of liberalism invoked the authority of science in their efforts to "prove" its social and political assumptions. The physical sciences were prominent among those borrowed from. For example, starting with the proposition that all reality is matter in motion seeking that which aids its motion, Hobbes (see Girvetz, 1963) made the leap to asserting that society could be viewed as also reflecting this natural law, that men are all therefore *by nature* singlemindedly self-seeking, and if left undisturbed and uninhibited are bound to succeed in achieving their individual ambitions. Further, as their ambitions themselves reflected natural law, they were inherently noble. Bentham (see ibid.) took a slightly different tack, however, to make a similar point. Starting with another and seemingly contrary proposition from the physical sciences, he argued that man, like all matter, was by nature *inert*, and moved to action only by the promise of pleasure and/or the avoidance of unpleasure. He elaborated so complex a system by which man determines the relative chances of achieving pleasure vs. unpleasure that his theories were nicknamed the "hedonistic calculus." The conclusion "proved" was, again, that man needs but be left free from external restraint to achieve his ambitions, which are assumed to be pleasurable. A basic assumption underlying much of the liberal theory — an assumption against which Burke railed — was that society could be viewed atomistically, that it could be understood (and mastered) as simply a conglomeration of atoms of similar (if not identical) individuals. In short, classical eighteenth-century liberalism claimed a "scientific" justification which viewed each individual as calculatedly and rationally seeking to serve his own best interests, in particular to achieve prosperity, and held that this reflected natural laws with which one should not tamper. Governments were eyed with suspicion and relegated strictly to the role of protector against external interferences. In marked contrast to the view of conservatism, man and his works were held to be good by nature, and his downfall lay in the hands of external forces.

The indigent, however, contradicted the basic assumption of self-interest and the motive force of material, gain and the unequal distribution of wealth and finally the great depression in America contradicted the assumption that the unfettered self-interest of the individual and the good of the state were in natural harmony. Liberal theory accordingly went through a major revision and, in contrast to its initial distrust of government, assumed its current profile with the pivotal role of the welfare state concept.

Of interest in the literature describing this theoretical revision is the extent to which the original sociological premises were minutely reexamined. The discussions are not altogether sound examples of logic, but are convincing as expressions of the continued conviction that rational thinking by scientific individuals can fathom social pressures and devise formulas for the perfection of society. The concepts of egoism (Hobbes) and hedonism (Bentham) were discarded in the face of inspirational and biographical material pointing to a basic altruism in man. The assumption of man's basic inertia was replaced by the proposition that man finds a natural pleasure in work (e.g., by John Dewey, as quoted in Gervitz). Whereas man's *ir*rationality was conceded in the light of historical events, as one theorist wrote: "Proper recognition by the liberal of the irrational factors in conduct renders them subject to use and control" (Girvetz, 1963). In summary, then, man changes from the hedonistic, calculating, rational, inert creature of the eighteenth century, expressing natural law and therefore best left alone. He becomes instead, in the nineteenth-century view, the altruistic, hardworking individual, in control (at least potentially) of the irrational side of his nature and capable of devising a government-supervised formula for the perfection of society.

Material equality, by means of governmental management, or the "redistribution of wealth" is the feature of the ideal society most stressed in the revised literature; this is in striking contrast to liberalism's initial insistence that man in his efforts to achieve wealth should be left entirely to his own devices. The problem in accounting for the indigent is resolved by seeing them as victims of external social pressures, which latter are correctable by means of governmental activity.

In contrast, then, to conservatism's preoccupation with social order, liberalism from its inception, and despite its revisions in theory, has been concerned primarily with man's wish for material gain. Furthermore, whereas conservatism stands in awe of God's superordinate wisdom, liberalism celebrates man's (and in particular *common* man's) limitless capabilities and scientifically based wisdom. To quote Thoreau in *Walden* (1854): "Man's capacities have never been measured; nor are we to judge what he can do by any precedents, so little has been tried." Liberalism is social as opposed to psychological in its focus upon external pressures and their manipulation and in its minimization of the role of individual intrapsychic conflict. Individual responsibility, so important in conservative thought, is also minimized, and communal responsibility is stressed. Liberalism is instrumental as to its orientation, placing a value upon expediency in its efforts to perfect society. Science replaces religious faith. It is optimistic and forever striving for something better. The demand for change is a constant feature of its belief in the perfectability of society. Man is good and deserving by nature, and the gratification of his wishes is viewed as of primary importance.

SOME CURRENT CONSERVATIVE AND LIBERAL VOICES

Compare the writing styles in the following two quotations:

> On seeing it (a newly erected billboard above the local drugstore) my father was seized with indignation, which he communicated to us at dinner. Activists that my older brother and sister were, they promptly volunteered to go out and burn the sign down. My father's allegiances were in conflict. On the one hand, he himself had once been a revolutionary, or rather counter-revolutionary. . . . On the other hand, he was the conservative who believed in law and order. The dialectic did not yield altogether convincing results: We were to do no such thing. *However,* he said, if the town of Sharon itself rose in popular uprising against the billboard and marched against it, our sympathies would clearly be on the side of Sharon.

and

> I want to be tried not because I support the Natural Liberation Front — which I do — but because I love long hair. Not because I support the Black Liberation Movement, but because I smoke dope. Not because I'm against a capitalist system, but because I think property eats shit. Not because I believe in student power, but that the schools should be destroyed. Not because I'm against corporate liberalism, but because I think people should do whatever the fuck they want, and not because I'm trying to organize the working class, but because I think kids should kill their parents. Finally, I want to be tried for having a good time and not for being serious. I'm not

angry over Vietnam and racism and imperialism. Naturally, I'm against all that shit, but I'm *really* pissed 'cause my friends are in prison for dope and cops stop me on the street because I have long hair. I'm guilty of a conspiracy, all right. Guilty of creating liberated land in which we can do whatever the fuck we decide. . . . Guilty of trying to overthrow the motherfucking senile government of the U.S. of A. I just thought you ought to know where my head was at, PIG NATION. . . .

If I had to sum up the totality of the Woodstock experience I would say it was the first attempt to land a man on the earth.

Reich, some fifty years ago, brought the analyst's attention to the fact that the *form* of his patients' communications revealed basic character structure even more than their *content*. The above two quotations, the first from the Right and the latter from the Left, from William Buckley (1969) and Abbie Hoffman (1969), respectively, serve to illustrate some of the differences in writing style that characterize the literature of the two persuasions.

It is striking in how many ways the writers of each persuasion are alike in the form of their communications. For instance, compare the following words from Russel Kirk (1960) with Buckley's, or with Burke's:

Along with the consolations of faith, perhaps three other passionate human interests have provided the incentive to performance of duty by ordinary men and women: the perpetuation of their own spiritual existence through the life and welfare of their children; the honest gratification of acquisitive appetite through accumulation and bequest of property; the comforting assurance that continuity is more probable than change—in other words, men's confidence that they are part of a natural and social order in which they count for more than "the flies of a summer." With increasing brutality, the modern temper . . . has ignored these longings of simple humanity. Thus frustration distorts the face of society as it mars the features of individuals. . . .

No mere defender of the establishment of the hour, the true conservative is loyal not to factions, but to norms; thus, with Ben Johnson, [Shakespeare] scourges the naked follies of the time. Every age is out of joint, in the sense that man and society never are what they ought to be; and the great poet feels himself born to set the time right—not, however, by leading a march to some New Jerusalem, but by rallying to the standard of the permanent things.

Note the aristocratic tone. These conservative writers speak from a position of "high character, strong intellect, good birth, and practical shrewdness," to repeat Burke's words. Their prose is often dense, filled with frequent references to authors and events not exactly at the fingertips of the average reader. The density in part seems to result from a cautiousness that leads them to seek so diligently the right word, the right turn of phrase, and then to qualify and requalify it in such an attempt at exactness that its purpose is defeated: obfuscation in the name of clarity. There is a quality of joylessness, even in the sentimental and humorous anecdote related by Buckley, for instance. Instead there is a sarcastic and ironic tone, a dark cast, a *weightiness*. There is a static quality to its sense of resignation, and stasis makes for heavy reading. To read these authors is often to be reminded that duty comes before pleasure.

Although the writings of the Left appear at first glance to be more of a mixed bag, again the similarities outweigh the differences. Abbie Hoffman's words, for instance, might sound quite different at first glance from these of Robert Kennedy (1968):

> Our answer [to the world's problems] is the world's hope: it is to rely on youth — not a time of life but a state of mind, a temper of the will, a quality of the imagination, a predominance of courage over timidity, of the appetite for adventure over the love of ease. . . . It is a revolutionary world we live in. . . . [There is danger in] futility, the belief that there is nothing one man or one woman can do against the enormous array of the world's ills — against misery and ignorance, injustice and violence. Yet many of the world's great movements, of thought and action, have flowed from the work of a single man. . . . There is no basic inconsistency between ideals and realistic possibilities, no separation between the deepest desires of heart and mind and the rational application of human effort to human problems.

Or consider these words by Paul Cowan, describing his sixth of seven proposals representing the "minimum necessary" for the "survival" of America (McReynolds, 1970):

> (6) Establish new communities, "liberated zones," in cities or sections of states. There we can build the kind of humane institutions we believe in — schools, hospitals, child-care centers, old peoples' homes, mental institutions that are dedicated to serving people. Our loyalties will not be to the piggish United States, but to people throughout the world. In such communities, we will have to learn to transcend the racism, egotism and product addiction that we have developed during our lives in the culture of greed — to undergo personal revolutions that parallel the political revolution we are trying to bring about. If we can create such communities and defend them, people throughout the country will relate to them enthusi-

astically, see them and the politics and the life style they represent as vi
brant alternatives to the horrors of Nixonia.

In the words of all three authors the liberal creed is revealed in the tone o
optimism, the sense of promise, the hopefulness, the spirit of crusade. Wheth
er the goal is "doing whatever the fuck we decide" or wrestling with "the enor
mous array of the world's ills" or "building humane institutions" there is ar
uncritical assumption of a "happy ending."

There is also a strong conviction of each author's own personal innocence
The enemy is without, not within: *Out* in "pig nation," not *within* Abbie
Hoffman. Likewise Robert Kennedy clearly did not number himself among
the timid and not youthful, nor does Paul Cowan's use of the editorial "we"
conceal his conviction that he has *already* undergone a personal revolution a
opposed to those *others*, in "Nixonia," who have not.

One feels much less oppressed while reading the authors of the Left. The
writing is in fact often entertaining. And one feels *good* inside; altruistic and
loving feelings are mobilized, and a sense of innocence and personal impor
tance is shared. The "enemy" is without, and seems readily defeatable.

In the writings of both conservatism and liberalism the "background as
sumptions," as Gouldner (1970) called them, tend to overshadow the pure
logic of their arguments. One feels he is reading propaganda rather than
science, or inspirational material sufficiently sectarian that it could move only
members of its own congregation. That the thoughts expressed are primarily
personal and subjective could not be more clear, nor that the attempts at jus
tification and rationalization are largely secondary elaborations.

CLINICAL MATERIAL

"Betty," "Steve," and "George" are not meant to serve as examples of "typ
ical" conservatives or liberals. All three spontaneously used political action
and thought as an arena in which to express and work through their individ
ual needs and conflicts and spent much time in their treatment focusing on it.
As will be seen, for each their specific political orientation was uniquely suited
to the specifics of their intrapsychic organization. They serve, therefore,
merely as examples of the confluence between individual need and generally
available schools of thought. The nature and dynamics of this confluence will
be discussed after the clinical material has been recounted.

Betty

Betty entered analysis at age nineteen complaining of feeling unattractive
and unalluring as a woman and of self-consciousness and insecurity in social
relationships. She felt needy, but attempts at getting her needs met were

somehow unsuccessful. Fantasies, sexual and otherwise, were intense, frequent, often sadistic, but ungratifying. She felt driven to eat, to shoplift, to compete, to prevail, to succeed. In contrast to her feelings of insecurity she was an excellent student, a scholarship winner, a college "campus leader." She gave the impression to others of hypercompetence with her "cocksure" manner, in a somewhat masculine way coming on strong with her intellectualisms, assuming control of the situation. The surface appearance was that she plunged into things boldly on impulse, letting the pieces fall where they might. Yet, on closer inspection, one could sense the terrified little girl underneath, longing to be directed and cared for, confused and helpless. One felt pushed and pulled by her.

Initially she spoke in glowing terms of her family. Both parents had histories of involvement in liberal activities, including the "intellectual communism" of the thirties. Both were children of minory group immigrants, and both left their respective (and different) religions. Nondirection, independence, and "liberality" were stressed at home. "Progressive" child-rearing practices were used. Betty's own political commitments and activities (sit-ins against the war, storming of the Pentagon, etc.) were initially seen by her as a continuation of her parents' commitments and activities.

At the very start of analysis, Betty voiced the manifestly phallic-oedipal wish to have a sexual experience with a man in order to "become a woman." She saw herself as unambivalent in her efforts to achieve such a relationship and therefore could not account for her inability to do so. Similarly, in the analysis itself, she believed herself to be motivated only for success, and energetically and rather innocently presented voluminous, intellectually quite reasonable "free associations" about her thoughts and daily activities. In the name of "self-help" she quit college, relinquishing what she saw as a nonfeminine, longstanding competition with her scholastically oriented older brother and rather scholarly father. She aggressively seduced a young man in order to achieve her first sexual experience and "become a woman" (of note was the fact that she fellated him). She was rearranging her life—changing the outside, as she put it, to change the inside.

Her illusory transference (Nunberg, 1955) was such that she felt already "cured." She talked glowingly to her friends of her psychoanalysis. In the analytic sessions themselves, however, the denial revealed in the flood of intellectualized pseudoassociations and long, convoluted, unanalyzable dreams made clear how terrified and resistant she was and how desperately she needed to be unaware of it.

Her first major insight was achieved around a dream, the associations to which made clear her underlying wish not so much for genital penetration, but rather to be held, rocked, cuddled, and, in particular, fed. The dream concerned a "cherry," first associated to as slang for female genitals, but then

associated to as food, with recollections of being given sweets by her mother
and then finally of being comforted by her mother when she was upset. In an
effort to resist the significance of this insight, she aggressively pushed for het
erosexual activity. She literally seduced a man into having intercourse with
her; she felt like her "insides were being torn out" and was terrified by the ex
perience.

Hand in hand with the uncovering of her anxiety about the analytic situa
tion in these early months of the analysis, she reconstrued her childhood. To
her surprise she rediscovered how frightened and insecure she had actually
felt as a child, and how beneath the mask of "progressive" nondirection from
her parents she had sensed coldness and rejection. To her, "nondirection"
had been experienced as absence of support and guidance. To compensate, at
one point in her childhood, she fantasied a trio of elder women, a "commit
tee" which she imagined oversaw all her activities, and which she needed to
please at all times. In the transference she continued to deny her clinically ob
vious dependency. She had "no feelings" toward the analyst, he was a "func
tionary," a "technician." She reacted with consternation when friends began
to point out how her analysis was changing her. She grew to realize she had
counted on her analyst being impotent, a wish she acted out in her preference
at that time for homosexual boy friends.

As her awareness of her helplessness and dependency deepened, increasing
ly her anger came to the surface. While pleading to be loved by a man, she
raged at them endlessly and delighted in belittling their efforts to give her
what she wanted. Her erotized hostile-dependent attachment to her father
was reconstructued, with her need for, and scorn of him. She said to an in
secure young man during intercourse, "Oh, have you put it in already? I
didn't notice." In the transference, she pleaded to be understood and com
forted, but was angrily silent for hours, came late to sessions, fell behind in
payment of her bill, and talked precipitately of leaving town. She felt totally
the victim, however, and saw her rage as therefore justified; she saw little
need to contain or moderate it. Although the material continued to be pre
sented in manifestly phallic-oedipal terms, the prephallic, more infantile
quality of her demands was obvious.

She recalled at this time a vivid fantasy from childhood. While riding in the
back seat of a car, she would imagine a gigantic scythe extending outward on
both sides, leveling everything in its path. The fantasy was accompanied by
intense feelings of omnipotence.

Her rage at the analyst continued to grow stronger as did her associated
feelings of dependency upon him. She demanded she be allowed to be totally
dependent upon him; he was to do all the work of the analysis; she was not
even to have to pay for it. She further demanded she be allowed to rage
against him. Her rage she felt to be her only sense of strength; it was her

ower, and her penis. It was all she had to combat the narcissistic mortifica-
on of being so utterly powerless and alone. Caught between her intense
ependency and her need to rage against her passivity and helplessness, she
lt the analysis was deadlocked. The only solution she could envisage was for
ie analyst to beat her into submission, forcing her to "grow up." As she put
, "*Make* me grow up! . . . But I *refuse* to grow up!"

Although initially her feelings were directed mainly at her father, in time
ie was able to see how much it was her mother she was raging against. She
ad turned to father for mothering, and to rescue her from mother. The
edipal father was then a fusion of mother image *and* father image, as was the
nalyst in the transference.

For several months this struggle took the shape in the analytic material of
er ambivalence about penetration. Genitally, though she believed she sought
, she discovered how much she feared the invasion of her body, and how
uch she fantasied the invisible internal meeting of the organs as a violent
nd destructive event. She saw the penis as a destructive organ, and felt in-
nse penis envy. Through the interpretation of the transference neurosis,
owever, a deeper and more significant dynamic to this fear was found to be
regenital. She felt the analyst's interpretations as attempts not only to pene-
ate her psyche, but to take it over, to fuse with it so that her and her ana-
st's minds were one.

As these issues were worked through, she came to realize the intensity of her
ependency upon her mother and her fear of being "swallowed up" by her
iother's own ambivalent neediness. Aspects of her early childhood relation-
iip with her mother were rediscovered, and she realized how depressed and
mote her mother had seemed to her, a bottomless pit into which she feared
ie would fall if she allowed herself to open up to her or to give of her love to
er. Her mother was seen as powerful, and Betty felt torn between the wish to
ecome a part of that power and the fear of disappearing if she dared to ven-
ire into it. So she closed herself off, so to speak, and concomitantly her
roblems with obesity had begun. Compulsive, episodic overeating was her
lution to her feelings of neediness. Food was all she allowed to enter into her
-not mother's love, not interpretations, not penises. Rage was her other
mpensation, an ejecting mechanism to discharge tension as well as a source
 gratification of infantile megalomanic, narcissistic needs. As she lay on the
uch, silent, obstinate, closed tight, ungiving, she felt both protected from
ie analyst, safe from his influence, and satanically powerful. She recalled on
ie occasion, rather suddenly, the final scene to her scythe fantasy: herself,
one, standing amid a desolate sea of rubble of her own making. In it she felt
oth very small and very powerful — but very alone.

Throughout the analysis her political activities ran as a thread. She saw her
lationship with society as a parent-child relationship. Her avidity for the

cause of civil rights was imbued with a deep sincerity that stemmed from he
feelings of disappointment with her parents. The violent activities of the mor
militant black organizations (in which she participated on several occasions
allowed her vicarious expression of her rage at her parents. The crimes sh
felt society perpetrated against her were twofold: First, it did not *care* abou
her; it did not see her needs as important. She put it well in describing he
feelings while participating in the famous storming of the Pentagon: "I coul
just see all those big fat-cat generals with all their medals sitting up there i
that huge granite building. And not one of them cared about how awfully
felt!" cond, she resented being held responsible for her own actions, in particu
lar, for the destructiveness of her rage. She felt it unjust that it was up to he
to see that her anger was sufficiently contained, that those upon whom she de
pended were not repulsed or destroyed. Near the end of the analysis, whe
termination was under discussion, she had a dream in which her anger, in th
guise of an explosive black lover, suddenly broke loose and destroyed he
world. In her associations she saw how she had turned to the analyst to cor
tain her rage for her, and to play the role of villain—i.e., attacker, rejecto
and withholder—to justify and therefore make self-syntonic her destructiv
activities. Politically, she shared Abbie Hoffman's demand to do "whateve
the fuck I want," and in the militancy of Women's Liberation and Civ
Rights sought and found a policitcal platform which *encouraged* violence
even saw it as noble. As will be elaborated in the discussion that follows th
clinical material, she sought to end her disapointment in her parents/th
world by changing the world (unconsciously, her parents), while simultar
eously denying the very rage that motivated her.

George

George entered analysis as a young adolescent complaining of multipl
phobias, in particular regarding recitation in the classroom. He was timi
with his peers, but his superior intelligence, verbal wit, and seemin
sophistication were seen as charming and winning by adults, with whom h
got along well. His symptoms dated from early latency. He complained bitte
ly that his parents had not gotten help earlier for him, and did not compr
hend his distress; he demanded that they assume direction over his activitie
so as to lead him out of his plight. His parents were politically liberal, bu
nondirective as parents, however, and tended to throw decisions back in h
lap. He had—as is true with all phobics—many self-imposed restrictions c
activities aimed at avoiding phobic situations. For example, utilizing his abi
ity to get along well with adults, he had arranged with his teachers speci;
classroom privileges to avoid the recitations he feared the most.

The first months of analysis saw a rapid diminution of most of the presen
ing symptoms. His fear of recitation gave way gradually to an almost flambo

nt exhibitionism. He soon became a campus leader, in fact, and a central figure in political and social protest activities. In analysis all was wonderful. He talked of the analyst as his friend, and referred to him by his first name. He came eagerly to each session during which he would chat charmingly and volubly. Increasingly he presented blatantly symbolic material relating to phallic masturbatory preoccupations and castration fears. He dreamed of tall pillars that toppled. He rubbed pencils up and down the shaft until they leaped out of his hand. He stroked his neck up and down and then spat out small quantities of saliva. All of this material was presented humorously and innocently" as though it had no meaning to it. He made no attempt to translate" it. He did not listen to himself, "forgetting" what he said as soon as he had said it, forgetting what he did as soon as he had done it. Running comments by the analyst, and end-of-the-session summaries, were seemingly ignored.

After some six months of analysis a gentle suggestion was made that this material was symbolic and seemed on the surface to relate to masturbatory concerns. George reacted over the ensuing weeks with surprising intensity to this confrontation. He cried. He insisted that it was disgusting to even consider the possibility that such a "filthy" and "degrading" practice would be on anyone's mind. A man, he felt, sought sex with a woman. Masturbation was "sick" because the masturbator was so involved with himself.

This distaste for masturbatory self-preoccupation gradually generalized to include any preoccupation with one's self, or with what one felt within one's self. The patient expressed anger at having any feelings at all. He deprecated all subjectivity, such as that devoted to art or poetry criticism. He alternately denied any fantasy life, or refused to relate his fantasies because they were too fleeting and he feared contradicting himself. He sought a life governed totally by objectively verifiable and utterly consistent *fact*. All interpretations and confrontations were subjected to "courtroom" cross-examination, in which each word had to be substantiated with "hard fact." Analysis was deprecated as a ridiculous pastime in which "crazy" meanings were invented for meaningless bits of behavior, such as entering the office right foot first. He feared being "brainwashed" by incorrect interpretations through which wrong ideas would be put into his head. Much of the time he insulted the analyst or was silent or did homework. Occasionally he would lie down on the couch and go to sleep. Yet as he angrily "spat out" the analysis, the subjective experience of the analyst in the countertransference was of being drained by his dependency. During these months George's functioning outside of the office continued to improve.

His political views came to the fore as an arena in which he fought out his transference neurosis. His view crystallized into two major complaints against the "Establishment": First, no one listened to him. He complained that his objections about the "senseless" war in Vietnam and "senseless" laws against marijuana were being ignored. In school, the curriculum, he felt, ignored his needs; his teachers put his future in jeopardy by stuffing his head with irrelevant lies and half-truths. In the transference he complained that the analyst ignored his demands to terminate the analysis, or alter the schedule to better fit in with his, or even heed his insistence that psychoanalysis was folly. Second, he complained that too much was expected of him, that too much responsibility for his fate was placed on his own shoulders. This was the era in which there was a social agency for everyone. The analysis was to be his. As he put it in one of the complex similes he invented to avoid talking directly in terms of the transference: If he bought a train ticket, and the train crashed, and he was thrown out of it into a huge mud puddle, and he was cold, wet, and uncomfortable, he would still refuse to get up out of the puddle, even if totally physically able to do so, because in selling him the ticket, the train company had assumed total responsibility for his safety and comfort. And further, he would refuse even to ask for help, for he insisted that not only his needs be met, but that the very fact of neediness itself must be erased from existence. He was to be helped automatically and only because it was objectively fair and just that he be helped.

As this hostile-dependent material was worked through, there were increasing references to food. He described his past idiosyncracies of diet; for years when younger he would eat only hot dogs or peanut butter. He spoke of his great concern over the cleanliness of all he ate. His disappointment in and distrust of his mother were central in this material with much focus on his mother's technique in preparing meals. He was also sensitive to the textures of food; for instance, he would not eat cake because it felt too dry in the mouth.

He fantasied that whatever food might cross his mind as he headed home from school would be the one his mother chose to serve that night. In related fantasies, he imagined a "money tree" that would rain dollar bills on him just at the moment the thought crossed his mind he would like to have some money, and at no other time. He also fantasied an analysis in which his sessions would be held, instantaneously, when he wished, and at no other time.

He described in a session a comic strip he had written for the school paper. He ordered the analyst not to interpret it because it had no "hidden meaning." It told of a cowboy and his beloved horse, trapped by Indians. It was necessary for the cowboy to kill the horse and eat him to survive. The one to pity, the story went, was not the horse, but the cowboy since he was alive to feel regret and guilt for his actions. In a session shortly thereafter, he expressed the wish that one could eat, perhaps, in one week all one needed to eat throughout life, so that hunger would be eradicated forever.

As this pregenital, more regressed material was worked through, the conflict over his exhibitionistic phallic-aggressive strivings, which the phobia had also expressed, grew more prominent in the analytic material. He spoke of wanting to give people "The Word," to "lay them *low*" with the brilliance of his ideas as he stood before them. He saw his ideas as destructively powerful; his intellect was to him a rare and deadly weapon, a trait shared by all the men (i.e., not the women) in his family; it made him superior to his peers, but also, therefore, apart from them, and in danger of their jealousy and wrath. He quoted the adage: The bigger you are, the harder you fall. He alternated in his schoolwork between success and failure, reflecting his ambivalence over the aggression and retaliatory dangers implicit in his mental prowess. Throughout this period in the analysis, his father was an important figure in his associations and it was made clear the extent to which father was a substitute mother and, therefore, *not* to be oedipally defeated.

Following a weekend in which he labored long and hard on a term paper with results that greatly pleased him, he entered a period of depression in which he mourned the imperfections of the world. He expressed disappointment that in the analysis he had to use *words* to convey his thoughts to the analyst; how much better it would be, he said, if his and his analyst's minds were one, so that each would know exactly what the other thought and felt at the very moment of the thinking and feeling of it. As a disappointed idealist, to borrow from Wilde, he became for a while quite cynical.

The final months of the analysis dealt with the resolution of the transference neurosis. George talked of the latter in terms of his being the analyst's "nigger." The political implications, in an era of civil rights, were clear. Intrapsychically, the choice of term was overdetermined. It expressed symbiotic wishes and fears, anal sadistic passive and active wishes and fears, and the negative oedipal configuration so prominent in the dynamic structure of his phobic neurosis. There was much emphasis put upon the political note, however, of his deserving to be "freed," which he saw more as a restructuring of the social order than as an issue of state of mind. "Welfare statism" served as a useful metaphor for George, relating to both his identity and his expectations of the world. As will be described in the discussion which follows the clinical material, it served as a compromise solution to his conflicts about independence — allowing dependency gratification, but from a position of strength.

Steve

Steve was seen in twice weekly psychotherapy for six years. He was brought for treatment as a young adolescent because of school failure. From the start he impressed one as a polite, "sweet," rather asexual young man, well-mannered and attentive, very eager to please, very afraid of offending. His complaints were of feeling inhibited, hypersensitive, depressed, and frustrated. Although he made an effort to conceal it, he was also angry. His anger was expressed primarily in passive-aggressive behavior, and outbursts during which he'd go up to his room, slam the door, and beat his pillow. Anger vis-a-vis others was expressed often also in tears and protestations of helplessness.

His mother had committed suicide during a postpartum depression when he was a little over one year old. He and his two-years-older brother were reared by their grandparents and the maid. The father's business kept him preoccupied and frequently away. Steve grew up in the shadow of his older brother, an openly defiant and rebellious boy. Steve was the "good" boy. Yet his father seemed to him to prefer the older son; Steve believed this was because he was blamed for the death of his mother. In Steve's mind, his father was intolerant of any show of anger or defiance on his part.

The school failure reflected Steve's passivity, but only in part; another factor was his older brother's scholastic problems. As a displaced oedipal figure, the older brother was an object of intense competitive strivings, but he could not be bested; Steve elected self-imposed failure. Further, Steve felt that his brother was his one ally, his sole source of support and love in the family, and he feared he would lose his love if he succeeded where his brother had failed. Steve's school failures reflected his efforts at holding onto whatever interpersonal nutriment he could find.

This was revealed in the transference as well. Steve developed dependent wishes toward the therapist which acted as a transference resistance. Steve saw himself as affection starved, but as "bad," and all evidence of independence, aggression, or sexuality had to be concealed lest the therapist be repelled. He manufactured a false front of "niceness"; though the resultant "friendship" was therefore spurious, it was, to Steve, better than nothing.

Politically, Steve was conservative. He spurned long hair and the styles of dress popular among his more "radical" classmates. He was adamant in his condemnation of "drugs" (though he drank and smoked), and had no patience for the rebelliousness and social protestations of the political activists at his high school. Though he grew to be aware of his own capacity for hedonism and defiance, he saw these traits as "bad ones," and so limited their exercise to appropriately clandestine occasions rather than the chauvinistic ones.

He viewed those things that stood between himself and what he wanted as being internal, as facets of his personality, and so saw manipulation of himself —or of his image—as the means best suited to realize his ends. He came to realize through therapy a deep conviction that he had killed his mother and, thereby, repelled his father, and he was not eager to make the same mistake another time. He saw his relationship to society in similar terms: his security depended upon his exercising self-restraint. The political philosophy of conservatism was in keeping with these views: he was by nature "evil," and the exercise of the cardinal virtues was his one hope for salvation.

DISCUSSION

Many authors, from Freud on, have expressed the "human dilemma" in terms of the struggle to transform paradise lost into paradise regained, as Sandler (1960) phrased it. The latter goes on to say:

> With increasing discrimination between the self and other schemata, the child comes to realize that his early, pleasurable, narcissistic state of union with the mother is threatened. He suffers a lowering of the libidinal cathexis of the self, with consequent narcissistic depletion, and, as Freud puts it, he needs to restore the state of "a real happy love, which, corresponds to the primal condition in which object-libido and ego-libido (we would now say self-cathexis cannot be distinguished."

Mahler (1961, 1966, 1968) has written extensively about this subject. In the rapprochement subphase of the separation-individuation process, there is an "unavoidable, predetermined growing away from the previous state of 'oneness' with the mother. This loss—the necessity for a more or less gradual relinquishing of claims upon the need-satisfying symbiotic object—implies the gradual giving up of the more or less delusional fantasy of symbiotic omnipotence." The rapprochement child learns in his day-to-day confrontations with reality of the

> very large number of obstacles that stand in the way of his magic omnipotent wishes and fantasies. . . . The world is not his oyster; he has to cope with it on his own, every so often as a relatively helpless, small, and lonesomely separate individual . . . [he] comes to realize his love objects are also separate individuals. . . . His inability to recreate the "omnipotent unity" of his earlier life he can only regard as [mother's] withholding from him an omnipotence which she possesses but which he is no longer permitted to share.

Mahler has used the term "the mother of separation" to refer to a mother insofar as she appears to the child to be omnipotent, but not withholding.

The dissolution of the symbiosis is a nuclear challenge to the integrity of the self-esteem of the developing ego. There are other developmentally determined challenges to the self-esteem system as well. A sequence can be formulated for these challenges:

1. Dissolution of the symbiosis and consequent loss of delusional infantile megalomanic omnipotence.
2. Anger, with its consequences, when directed at love objects, and retaliatory fears.

3. Discovery of castration, whether already castrated or capable of being castrated in the future.
4. Oedipal defeat.
5. Guilt, with its limiting effect upon behavior, and its attendant self-blame.
6. Discovery of the inevitability of "growing up," the passage of time, and eventual death.
7. In puberty, the relative weakness of the ego vis-a-vis the drives.
8. In young adulthood, intimacy and sexual object love, with its limiting effect upon autonomy.

Betty, George, and Steve presented initially with manifestly oedipal symptomatology. Betty complained of oedipal defeat: i.e., she was unattractive as a woman, unalluring, and wanted a man but "somehow" couldn't get one. As was revealed during regression in the transference, her disappointments had begun much earlier with her mother's remoteness, and then with her struggles to contain her aggression. Her disappointment over being penisless was accompanied by anxiety over the ease with which she could figuratively castrate the important men in her life (her father and brother, and later the analyst) —again, her difficulty in containing her now phallic-competitive aggression. Oedipal defeat was intolerable in as much as she had arrived at the oedipal level already narcissistically wounded, limited in her ability to tolerate frustration and contain anger, and prone to regress to hostile-dependent attachments. Acceptance of the penis into her vagina invoked oral-symbiotic wishes, with attendant fears of loss of self in the symbiotic fusion. Her problems with guilt, her fear of growing up, and her frustration over the relative weakness of her ego vis-a-vis her id were also suggested in the brief extracts from her long and complex analysis.

George's presenting phobia manifestly expressed phallic-oedipal exhibitionistic and competitive fears. Again, in the analysis the underlying disappointments over the loss of the symbiotic love object and the later struggles with containing his anger were uncovered. His oedipal-competitive strivings with his father were contaminated by preoedipal hostile-dependent ones. Identification with his father (or with the analyst, in the transference) was proscribed because it implied, regressively, symbiotic fusion and loss of separateness and individuality, as well as the gratification of oral-aggressive cannibalistic impulses. He also clearly demonstrated fears related to the weakness of his ego vis-a-vis the drives in puberty.

Steve's chief complaint was more an expression of his disappointment in himself over his, to him, inexplicable acceptance of castration. The material from his therapy revealed his inability to live comfortably with the intensity of not only his phallic-oedipal but also his anal-sadistic and oral-symbiotic urges.

Anna Freud (1949) wrote of the ego's main task as the reconciliation of the demand for gratification made by the instinctual urges with the actual conditions existing in the environment. The ego, she wrote, when confronted with frustration may decide to disregard the claims of the inner world and utilize repression, or it may decide to disregard outer reality and utilize denial. The ego may choose to submit to the claims of the outer world and oppose the instinct, or it may choose to submit to the claims of instinct and revolt against the outer world. She concludes: "What we call character formation is, roughly speaking, the whole set of attitudes habitually adopted by an individual ego for the solution of these conflicts."

The conservative and liberal political schools of thought offer to their adherents consistent sets of attitudes parallel to the alternatives described by Miss Freud.

The conservative submits to the claims of the outer world, to the needs of the community and to the inequities of life, and chooses to oppose the instincts, placing a high value on self-control and self-denial. The liberal submits to the claims of the instincts, places his highest priority on the gratification of his needs, and chooses to oppose the disappointing reality as it exists and mold it into what he believes it ought to be.

Conservatism offers gratification of longings for a return to the symbiotic, omnipotent fold in the sense of mystical oneness with a Supreme Providence. Rage is appeased by this substitute gratification, and bound in the self-inhibitory and repressive activities of ego and superego. The liberal obtains gratification for his symbiotic yearnings in his concern for the welfare of all and in his sense of shared "goodness" with his fellowman. Rage is appeased by the promise of the perfect society, and destructive energies are bound in his active assault upon the presumed inequities in the existing social structure.

In his struggles to oppose instinctual pressures, the conservative is made most anxious by any show of instinctual gratification. The birth of conservatism resulted from Burke's anxiety in the face of man's "anarchic" impulse and his violent restructuring of society. Burke saw safety only in *order*, "only so long as the Duke of Bedford be safe." The conservative fears around him what he fears within himself.

The liberal fears most the mother of separation. Normal Mailer (1968), writing about himself in the third person during the storming of the Pentagon, describing his reaction of horror to the impersonality of the troops: "He would not stand a chance with this Marshal—there seemed no place to him where he'd be vulnerable: stone larynx, leather testicles, ice cubes for eyes . . . Brother!" Abbie Hoffman (1969), writing of those who first settled in Haight-Ashbury, describes the omnipotent but withholding and indifferent Establishment in these words: " . . . an educational system void of excitement, creativity and sensuality. A system that channeled human beings like so many laboratory rats with electrodes rammed up their asses into a highly mechanized maze of class rankings, degrees, careers, neon supermarkets, military industrial complexes, suburbs, repressed sexuality, hypocrisy, ulcers and psychoanalysis." David McReynolds (1970), field secretary of the War Resistors League, wrote: "Revolutions . . . are caused . . . by the indifference and inhumanity and inflexibility of existing institutions." The liberal fears, and seeks to eradicate, the specter of the unresponsive, indifferent, tuned-*out* but sovereign and governing authority, that which he feels excludes him from the seat of narcissistic omnipotence, to borrow the phrase Mahler used in referring to the mother of separation.

The conservative in his attempts to maintain self-control resists regression, whereas the liberal seeks it. Abbie Hoffman (1969) writes: "They heard from their mothers over and over again about being *respectable* and *responsible* and, above all, *reasonable*. . . . The work that the kids saw around them was so odious, so boring, so worthless that they came to regard WORK as the only dirty four-letter word in the English language." Norman Mailer (1968) discusses the point well:

One marched on the Pentagon because . . . because . . . and here the reasons became so many and so curious and so vague, so political and so primitive, that there was no need, or perhaps no possibility to talk about it yet, one could only ruminate over the morning coffee. . . . Politics had again become mysterious, had begun to partake of Mystery; that gave life to a thought the gods were back in human affairs. . . . The new generation believed in technology more than any before it, but the generation also believed in LSD, in witches, in tribal knowledge, in orgy, in revolution. It had no respect whatsoever for the unassailable logic of the next step; belief was reserved for the revelatory mystery of the happening where you did not know what was going to happen next; that was what was good about it.

In this description of a rather far-left political view—though one quite widely publicized—one can see the promulgation of regression to a level of functioning commensurate with the preseparated and preindividuated infantile ego— as though to live thus is to have regained symbiotic paradise.

Violence is the outcome of the breakdown of either system. To the conservative, the punitive and oppressive "violence of the right," "law and order," is mobilized when all other defenses against the anxiety-provoking anarchic impulses fail. As Burke put it in one of his better-known paragraphs, "Society cannot exist unless a controlling power of will and appetite be placed somewhere; and the less of it there is within, the more there must be without. It is ordained in the eternal constitution of things, that men of intemperate minds cannot be free. Their passions forge their fetters." "Intemperate minds" would today support liberalized abortion laws, legalization of marijuana, abolition of antipornography laws—all issues which have stirred up a "law and order backlash."

To the liberal, violence is mobilized by what Hannah Arendt (1969) calls the rule of nobody: when, in efforts aimed at restructuring the social order more in harmony with his individual needs, the individual runs into a bureaucratization so great that there is no one with whom to argue, no one to whom one can present one's grievances. The "Establishment" is the euphemism currently in vogue, and, as indicated above, its similarity to the mother of separation in the eyes of those who believe themselves to be disenfranchised seems unmistakable.

Schools of political or social belief can be seen, then, to function for the individual as supports and reinforcers of certain ego-defensive and adaptive attitudes. The same can probably be said by generalization of all isms, whether religious, moral, political, or otherwise. In fact, it can be said that the sincerity and depth of conviction of the individual adherent is always a reflection of the extent to which his own personal intrapsychic attitudes are reinforced by whichever school of thought he adheres to; similarly, the lasting power of any ism must depend upon its ability to support these attitudes in a sufficient number of individuals to maintain an adequate following (see Oremland, 1974, for a similar view).

Betty, in radical liberalism, found a platform harmonious with her inability to contain adequately her intense rage at life's disappointments, and a program of activity aimed at altering her world so that the pain of her narcissistic mortifications would lessen—changing the outside to change the inside, as she put it. For George, welfarism—his own personal "social agency"—promised a return to the symbiotic paradise he had had to leave, and through its promise of collective as opposed to individual responsibility he sought relief from the heavy burden of independently mastering his own sexual and aggressive needs. Steve found in conservatism a platform harmonious with his fear of his own anarchic urgings and the promulgation of a way of life compatible with his own. He experienced "conservative joy" and a boost to his self-esteem through the exercise of mastery over himself. For each, it was the basic assumptions about man and the world implied by their political view which gave it the stamp of validity in their eyes, assumptions in harmony with their own. Further, participation in the perpetual, ongoing debate between political factions in our society afforded each the opportunity to work through and master their own ambivalences and crystallize and solidify their views of reality, their self-esteem systems, their defensive structures, and their identities.

SUMMARY

The historical development of conservative and liberal political philosophies were briefly traced. Conservatism is based on the proposition that man is by nature evil, and life inequitable, and therefore places the higher value upon self-restraint and submission to a less-than-ideal reality. Liberalism instead celebrates man and his capacities, and views life as inequitable only insofar as man has failed to perfect it. The highest value is, therefore, placed upon social activism and the restructuring of institutions. Three clinical cases were presented in which the intrapsychic organization of the patient found support in political orientation. In one, a woman's rage at the mother of separation found support in the anti-Establishment violence of the sixties. In another, an adolescent's reluctance to accept the dissolution of symbiosis found support in welfarism. In a third, a young man who lost his mother in infancy and blamed himself found solace in the self-restraint demanded by a conservative philosophy. It was proposed that political and social philosophies reflect an individual's resolution to life's disappointments, starting with the narcissistic mortification associated with the discovery of separateness in the rapprochment subphase of separation-individuation.

REFERENCES

Arendt, H. (1969). *On Violence*. New York: Harcourt.
Buckley, W. F., Jr. (1969). *The Jeweler's Eye*. New York: Putnam's.
Freud, A. (1949). Aggression in relation to emotional development; normal and pathological. *Psychoanalytic Study of the Child* 3-4: 37-42. New York: International Universities Press.
Freud, S. (1914). On narcissism: An introduction. *Standard Edition* 14:67-102. London: Hogarth, 1957.
Girvetz, H. (1963). *The Evolution of Liberalism*. 2d ed. London: Collier-Macmillan.
Gouldner, A. (1970). *The Coming Crisis of Western Sociology*. New York: Basic Books.
Hoffman, A. (1969). *Woodstock Nation*. New York: Vintage.
Kennedy, R. F. (1968). *To Seek a Newer World*. New York: Bantam.
Kirk, R. (1960). *The Conservative Mind*. 2d ed. Chicago: Regnery.
Mahler, M. (1961). On sadness and grief in infancy and childhood: Loss and restoration of the symbiotic love object. *Psychoanalytic Study of the Child* 16:332-351. New York: International Universities Press.
_____(1966). Notes on the development of basic moods: the depressive affect. *Psychoanalysis—A General Psychology*, ed. R. Loewenstein, pp. 152-168. New York: International Universities Press.
_____(1968). *On Human Symbiosis and the Vicissitudes of Individuation*. New York: International Universities Press.
Mailer, N. (1968). *The Armies of the Night*. New York: New American Library.
McReynolds, D., et al. (1970). Are we in the middle of the second American revolution? *New York Times Magazine*.
Oremland, J. D. (1974). Three hippies—A study of a late-adolescent identity formation. *International Journal of Psychoanalytic Psychotherapy* 3:434-455.
Reich, Wilhelm (1949). *Character Analysis*. (1926-1948). New York: Orgone Inst. Press.
Rossiter, C. (1962). *Conservatism in America*. 2d ed. New York: Random House.
Sandler, J. (1960). On the concept of superego. *Psychoanalytic Study of the Child* 15: 128-162. New York: International Universities Press.

J. ALEXIS BURLAND, M.D.

DR. BURLAND is in the practice of child, adolescent, and adult psychoanalysis. He had his psychiatric training at Temple University Medical Center and St. Christopher's Hospital for Children, both in Philadelphia. His psychoanalytic training was undertaken at the Philadelphia Psychoanalytic Institute, on whose faculty he now serves. He is also a consultant to various social agencies dealing with foster care services and community mental health projects.

Homogamous and Heterogamous Marriages

David M. Moss III, Ph.D.

The Center for Religion and Psychotherapy
Chicago, Illinois

Ronald R. Lee, Ph.D.

Garrett-Evangelical Theological Seminary
Evanston, Illinois

This paper explores two marital constructs set forth by Peter Giovacchini. The first is based on a symbiotic reenactment in which the investment of both partners is tenacious and reciprocal, an attachment which Giovacchini refers to as a "character object" relationship. It represents intrapsychic homogamy. In the second construct, this deep form of attraction is absent and the dyadic bond is superficial, frequently transitory. The latter couples do not require an elementary, intrapsychic bond but do share particular defensive traits or symptoms. Thus these unions are termed "symptom object" relationships and are characterologically heterogamous.

By means of a group case study approach, this distinction was statistically supported. Furthermore, it was found that homogamous marriages stay in treatment longer, maintain a lower divorce rate, and respond best to individual psychoanalytic psychotherapy. Heterogamous marriages, by contrast, show a higher divorce rate and tend to leave therapy prior to termination. The research also suggests that the initial treatment of choice for this type of marriage may well be conjoint or group psychotherapy.

INTRODUCTION

The phenomenon of spouses clinging tenaciously to bankrupt marriages, even when much destructive behavior is involved, has been explored by a number of therapists for nearly thirty years. Bion (1957) and Klein (1946) focused on the projective identification involved in these dyads. Brodey (1959) described the dynamics of many of these marriages through the concept of externalization. Piers and Singer (1953), Lynd (1961), and Lewis (1971) point to the shame-guilt binds that keep such relationships cemented. Giovacchini (1958) stresses the homogamous nature of the character structure of these spouses.

We first discovered the "tenacious marriage" through clinical experience which led to a group case study to determine differences in treatment response between characterologically homogamous marriages and those which are characterologically heterogamous (Moss, 1974). We believe that these distinctions are important for the strategies involved in marital therapy. We will present the following: (1) unidentified clinical examples of tenacious marriages; (2) theoretical background of the study; (3) methodology; (4) study results; and (5) conclusions.

A basic or central purpose behind our research was to take a particular set of concepts or models which were derived from patients in psychoanalysis and to investigate those constructs by means of another approach. While the focus of the study was validation, the reader must keep in mind that our results do not, by themselves, lead to definite conclusions. However, they do add a dimension which *augments* some important psychoanalytic insights and, hopefully, point up certain methodological factors which have been previously overlooked in the treatment of marital maladjustment.

CLINICAL ILLUSTRATIONS

Mr. and Mrs. A had been married ten years. As a thirty-six-year-old night clerk in a large hotel, Mr. A played the role of an inadequate male. Mrs. A, a thirty-four-year-old public school teacher, was the overadequate female. At a counseling center's staffing, they both were diagnosed as having a "depressive-neurotic/passive-aggressive" personality. After participating in a couples group for a year, they had established separate addresses, had nearly finalized their divorce, and were well on their way to establishing new, separate lives. They then terminated from the therapy group. About six months after the divorce, the wife returned for therapy, complaining that she felt acute loneliness and an inability to deal with her divorced state. In describing her situation, it was obvious that while a legal change had taken place, her relationship with her ex-spouse was the same as before. He called her daily; they dated; they fought about finances and child-rearing practices; and periodically they had intercourse, without birth control measures.

Mr. and Mrs. B, a couple in their late forties, had a similar type of schizoid personality structure. Both came from mixed immigrant backgrounds. During their twenty-two years of marriage, they had managed to build two small low-budget apartment complexes. After being in treatment for three months, they dropped out. Nearly two years later, they were again referred to the center by their lawyer because of the wife's constant threats of suicide if her ex-husband moved out. At that time, they had been legally divorced for fifteen months. They maintained separate telephones, automobiles, and expense accounts, but neither was interested in different living quarters. Moreover, they had no conscious intention of remarriage. Each claimed to "despise" the other.

Mr. and Mrs. C, in their late twenties, differed somewhat from the other two. Married for four years, they were divorced during their individual treatment at the center. Both were diagnosed as having "depressive-neurotic/obsessive-compulsive" personalities. Following termination, the husband moved to another city to practice tax law. After a year he called for a long distance referral. He complained about his sleep difficulties and his preoccupation with sexual fantasies regarding his ex-wife. He attributed his problems to the season: it was a time which corresponded to the anniversary of his mother's death, his marriage, and the divorce. A referral was made. Soon after his wife called for a follow-up interview. Unknown to her husband, she was planning to remarry a mutual college friend, a tax accountant, whom she described as having many of the same personality traits as her former husband.

The unconscious persistence of these three relationships pointed up the deep investment and symbiotic tie of each couple. It seemed that their intrapersonal needs contributed to the continuance of a conjugal relationship — in spite of divorce. The dyadic maintenance persisted respectively in fact, fantasy, and repetition. In the final instance, it was expected that remarriage would reflect or duplicate the first marriage. All three of the object relationships were characterologically homogamous; that is, both spouses had the same character structure.

These cases led to thinking about possible differences between characterologically homogamous marriages and those which were characterologically heterogamous, that is, where the spouses had different character structures. What follows is a report of a study of forty-five couples who were separated as to homogamous or heterogamous marriages based upon a diagnosis of character structure. However, because the study leans heavily on theory developed by ego psychologists, especially Giovacchini (e.g., 1965, 1967), we will first present a brief summary of this theory.

THEORETICAL BACKGROUND

The original work of ego psychologists focused heavily on the concept of symbiosis. This term, coined by a biologist, initially referred to an association in which two different organisms lived together in a close spatial and physiological relationship (DeBary, 1879). Its present meaning is broader: a reciprocally dependent or *mutual* relationship. This relationship is initially a maternal-neonate dependency which is internalized and introjected, thus becoming the prototype of subsequent intimate relationships of which marriage is one.

Among the studies investigating symbiosis and marital interaction, the most complete and articulate were done by psychoanalyst Peter Giovacchini.

The bulk of his work in this area attests to a homogamy of character structures based on a symbiotic reenactment. Prior to his work other thinkers addressed themselves to mate selection and marital interaction based on a deep psychological "sameness," but no one has done so definitively. For example, in 1925 Jung (1970) claimed that marital partners selected each other because of a basic similarity. Winnicott (1965), Spitz (1965), and Mahler (1968) also supported a deep homogamous trend that was intricately involved with early mother-child relations. Spitz (1965), like Benedek (1956), related this specifically to symbiosis. Klein (1937) came close to reiterating this point:

> Psycho-analysis shows that there are deep unconscious motives which contribute to the choice of a love partner, and make two particular people sexually attractive to each other. The feelings of a man towards a woman are *always* influenced by his *early* attachment to his mother. But here again this will be more or less unconscious and may be very much disguised in the manifestations.

From the outset of his work Giovacchini believed that the insights gained from ego psychology could promote an understanding of the psychic operations involved in marital dyads. In turn, the deep and intimate ties that create such a relationship might contribute considerably to our knowledge about the operation of the ego in general. Furthermore (1965), "any study of the ego eventually leads us into a study of object relations." "Married partners are a particular example of an object relationship" (1958).

Working from a hierarchial concept of object relations—Erikson's (1963), for instance—Giovacchini noted: "Insofar as every relationship contains all elements of its development, even the most mature object relations contain some degree of earlier adaptive techniques." For example, when a person has developed sufficiently to be able to execute some autonomy in selecting an object" there must be reasons arising from past relationships that cause him to select that particular person." If the relationship is characterized by strife, "is one of disharmony, then the likelihood that he has stumbled upon it accidentally is minimal" (1965).

That marriage is a special type of object relationship can be understood from several viewpoints. One immediately perceived function of object relations is their adjusive potential, which frequently can be considered in view of intrapsychic conflict and/or characterological defect.

As we have seen, writers like Mahler (1968) and Benedek (1956) explain that life involves a symbiotic stage of mother-infant interaction that is characterized by considerable mutual dependency. The psychic impression of this experience forms the basis of later interpersonal relations, especially when the mother's relationship with the child is a "total" one during the early neonate periods.

Giovacchini's earliest writings (e.g., 1958) explore the interaction of dyads characterized by a high degree of mutual dependence. Using the case study method, he found marriage to be a complex dyadic phenomenon in which many basic similarities of character structure and epigenetic crises were revealed. Building a theory of marital interaction on the symbiotic process discussed thus far, Giovacchini said that in a marriage "the needs of one partner for the other are *equal*." This is not necessarily the same as the original maternal-neonatal dependency, "but it has some resemblance to the initial symbiosis. . . . Early fusion with the mother, although global, nevertheless represents an embryonic self-image." As a person matures, this *imago* is altered, but the primary experience remains set in the unconscious perception of mother, world, and self.

> The initial symbiosis has undergone a series of refinements and progressive development lending to an expansive sense of self. . . . A person seeks a spouse whom he values in the same way he values himself. The elements of the earlier symbiosis continue to operate even in so-called 'mature' object relationships, but they are expansive rather than constrictive because the symbiosis has undergone considerable organization. The person finds that, in order to value another person, he must know how to value himself, and he must rediscover in the other a valued part of the self." [1965]

Giovacchini's work also shows that "the psychopathology of the married person is identical or equivalent to that of the spouse" (1958). Frequently the couples who manifest such similarity have a "total" emotional involvement with each other based on massive projections that are vital for their individual psychic survival.

He goes on to note that, when each partner requires the total personality of the other partner in order to maintain intrapsychic equilibrium, the marriage lasts regardless of its health.

> In spite of bitter strife and turmoil the marriage lasts, and even though it may seem constantly on the brink of divorce, the observer recognizes that divorce is unlikely. [1965]

This is because of the characterological involvement between the husband and wife, an intense and reciprocal type of object attraction that Giovacchini refers to as a *character object relationship*.

However, not all marriages establish an equilibrium on this basis. Giovacchini distinguished a second group as exhibiting *symptom object relationships*, which differ from the marriages described in that the marital bond is transitory and superficial: these marriages frequently result in divorce, and

the need of one spouse for the other is less intense than that described in connection with character object relationships.

The partners do not require the total personality of each other; each must
have only a particular trait or symptom to serve the other's defensive needs.
Frequently, such a patient has had several marriages in which each spouse
had a common denominator, so to speak, but in other respects differed
markedly.

> This relationship represents the personification of a defensive need. There
> may be similarities in the manifest expression of some defenses [but there
> are] differences in underlying personality organization. . . . Involvement
> of the partners is partial. . . . One partner needs only a particular attri-
> bute of another. [1965]

In contrast, character object relationships involve a projection of self-representation onto the spouse which then makes the establishment of intrapsychic
and marital equilibrium possible. Regardless of the level of fixation, the
spouse is essential to the maintenance of that level, so that homostasis can be
achieved. The function of the marital object relationship can be generalized
to include marriages which have only a minimum of psychopathology. "Object relationships are not only important determinants of emotional development, but once optimal development has been achieved they continue to be
vital for the maintenance of ego integration" (1967).

From the standpoint that the initial fusion with the mother leads to an integrated ego with a coherent identity, Giovacchini writes that the symbiotic element" can

> be considered in terms of its *positive* differentiating potential rather than in
> terms of its defensive psychopathological implications.
>
> The neonate's dependence upon the mother is total. If the mother re-
> lates to her child as a whole object during the stage of symbiotic fusion (a
> situation analogous to a Character Object Relationship), the child may
> develop a well-differentiated autonomous ego. The well-developed ego pos-
> sesses a coherent self-representation that views itself as a whole object and
> also responds to external objects as whole objects in the same fashion the
> mother related to the child during early developmental stages [1967].

An indication of this rudimentary reenactment of fusion is the similarity of
character structures in marital partners. We might also add that the extent to
which one spouse "fits" the role assigned to him may determine the stability of
the object relationship. Stable marriages emphasize the durability of such a
projection. The spouse has been conceptualized as being the recipient of the

projection of the self-representation. The introjection of the spouse self-representation image is instrumental in reinforcing the general ego coherence and the identity sense in particular.

Giovacchini holds that the marital relationship is a situation in which a "passage" of psychic energy occurs. This passage entails a movement through an external object representation and then a return to that initial structure which leads to preservation of a functioning ego. He concludes:

> More advanced states of psychosexual and characterological development view the object as a whole object, and the introjective projective process is continuous. The self-representation is projected in toto onto the spouse and then is introjected back into the ego, often with a positive integrative outcome. In the marital relationship the projection of the self-representation onto the spouse is equivalent to the synthesizing aspects of converting object-libido into ego-libido. Finding someone with whom one can feel in complete harmony is an experience that both enhances and maintains self-esteem. Complete harmony is, of course, a fictional ideal state but there are relative degrees of such an integrated equilibrium [1967].

METHODOLOGY

The method of investigating these two types of marital dyads based on character structure relied on a group case study approach. The research setting was the Community Pastoral Counseling and Consultation Center of Lutheran General Hospital, a small out-patient service which offers treatment primarily to the northern suburbs of metropolitan Chicago. The region is broad in its range of social classes, but the center's applicants are usually from the middle socioeconomic classes.

In many respects, such as education and economic status, the applicants of the center are a "culturally selected group" (Howard and Orlinsky, 1972). Furthermore, their ethnic backgrounds do not show much variation. For example, the center received very few requests from Jewish couples and no applications from black or Mexican-American populations. Thus, the nature of this study's population is basically homogamous.

The study consisted of forty-five couples. They were selected from a pool of seventy couples interviewed by the center's staff. The process of selection fundamentally consisted of a simplified rating procedure for each couple. The center's intake report served as the principal mode of supplying data for four professional raters to evaluate. When three out of four raters independently agreed in their analysis of the character structure of each of both spouses in a marriage, the couple was accepted as a unit of the experimental population. The raters were given the individual case histories in a random order and thus did not know the marital dyads.

For each patient a psychiatric history was recorded in careful, routine fashion (e.g., Masserman, 1952). While such an evaluation does not have the in-depth conviction acquired from an examination of the transference neurosis during psychoanalytic regression, psychodynamic formulations made on the basis of professional interviewers do have some validity, especially when they can be comparatively reviewed.

The raters used the nomenclature of *The Diagnostic and Statistical Manual'* of the American Psychiatric Association to evaluate each individual's intake staff report. All of the raters were psychoanalytically orientated psychotherapists. Three were Ph.D.'s and the fourth was a senior psychiatrist on the hospital's staff. When the raters agreed on the diagnosis of a particular client, that individual was tentatively accepted for the study. Again, this was done for both males and females without the raters knowing the marital relationships. When both spouses had interrater agreement, they were accepted as subjects for final evaluation as homogamous or heterogamous. A chi-square analysis was then carried out on the character structure combinations.

Having established the homogamous and heterogamous marriages of the sample, we next decided to test whether the homogamous couples remained longer in treatment because of their tenacious object-attachment qualities. It was reasoned that if such spouses invested more in their marriages, such an investment would become a major component in the therapeutic transference. Since fifteen of the forty-five couples were still actively in treatment, the remaining fifteen homogamous and fifteen heterogamous couples were compared by their mean number of treatment sessions and the difference between the means subjected to a *t*-test.

With a 2 x 2 chi-square test, these same thirty couples were compared for psychological improvement using the independent ratings of the therapist and therapist's supervisor. To facilitate this rating, both raters were given a simple termination evaluation questionnaire, the first part of which dealt with degrees of growth during treatment. The second part of the termination evaluation gave data on divorce, thus allowing a comparison by character structure on this dimension.

RESULTS

Although the American Psychiatric Association offers a selection of eleven personality disorders, only six characterological types were used by the four raters. Table 1 lists those categories and, to their right, records their individual frequencies and proportions.

TABLE 1
Characterological Categories

	INDIVIDUAL FREQUENCIES	PROPORTIONS
1. Paranoid personality	9	.10
2. Schizoid personality	5	.06
3. Explosive personality	1	.01
4. Obsessive-compulsive personality	35	.39
5. Hysterical personality	3	.03
6. Passive-aggressive personality	37	.41
	$N = 90$	1.00

After these ninty people were individually rated, they were rearranged as couples and grouped into two characterological camps, homogamy and heterogamy. Table 2 lists the frequency of homogamous character types.

TABLE 2
Characterologically Homogamous Dyads

CHARACTER TYPES	FREQUENCY
1. Paranoid personality	3
2. Schizoid personality	1
3. Explosive personality	0
4. Obsessive-compulsive personality	12
5. Hysterical personality	0
6. Passive-aggressive personality	12
	$total = 28$

Table 3 records the various combinations of character types involved in the heterogamous dyads.

TABLE 3
Characterologically Heterogamous Dyads

CHARACTER TYPE COMBINATIONS	FREQUENCY
1. Obsessive-compulsive personality passive-aggressive personality	8

2. Passive-aggressive personality   2
    obsessive-compulsive personality
3. Explosive personality   1
    obsessive-compulsive personality
4. Paranoid personality   3
    hysterical personality
5. Schizoid personality   1
    passive-aggressive personality
6. Obsessive-compulsive personality   2
    schizoid personality

                                                           total = 17

Using the data of Table 4, an investigation was conducted in order to cal-culate the expected number of homogamous and heterogamous character structure combinations. The basic principle involved in such an investigation is the Law of Independent Probabilities for Two Events: the joint occurrence of two events in the product of the occurring probabilities of each event.

The chi-square examination of character structure combinations (Tables 1 and 2) showed that the probability of their occurrence was not due to chance. The observed breakdown of twenty-eight homogamous dyads and seventeen heterogamous couples was compared to the expected breakdown of fifteen and thirty. Table 4 portrays the chi-square evaluation of this comparison. The result, 16.90, proved to be significant at the .05 level.

TABLE 4

Marital Character Structure

	HOMOGAMY	HETEROGAMY
		$N = 45$
OBSERVED	28	17
EXPECTED	15	30

$X^2(1) = 16.90\ p$ "less than" .05

That is to say, *the mating of similar character structures was unlikely to be a fortuitous occurrence.*

Turning to another set of results, the reader will remember that the sample used thus far contained two clinical classes, those who were currently engaged in therapy and those who had discontinued treatment at the center. At the time of their rating, fifteen out of the forty-five couples were still participating in either individual, conjoint or group marital psychotherapy. Generally speaking, these three therapeutic modalities were evenly distributed among the couples. For the most part, these couples were in the process of working through their interactional difficulties and deciding whether or not they were going to continue their marriage. The remaining thirty couples were no longer being seen at the center. They had either terminated with their therapist or dropped out of treatment. They were "inactive" as far as formal psychotherapy was concerned.

The thirty inactive couples were independently rated by their therapists and supervisors on (1) psychological improvement while in therapy, and (2) their marital status at the time treatment ceased. In every instance, the therapists and clinical consultants agreed. Collectively, these results showed that for seventeen couples one or both spouses reflected "favorable psychological improvement." The collective figures for marital persistence showed that eighteen couples were still married at the time they left the center. Twelve had either separated or finalized their divorce. When divided into characterological categories, it was found that both homogamous and heterogamous marriages were equally represented. Table 5 categorically estimates the improvement of the reduced sample.

TABLE 5
Psychological Improvement by Character Structure

	FAVORABLE PSYCHOLOGICAL IMPROVEMENT	LITTLE OR NO PSYCHOLOGICAL IMPROVEMENT
CHARACTEROLOGICAL HEMOGAMY	7	8
CHARACTEROLOGICAL HETEROGAMY	10	5

N = 30

$$X^2(1) - 1.22 \; p \text{ "greater than" } .05$$

The results support the null hypothesis, which contends that there is no difference between the two characterological categories as far as therapy is concerned: neither type is more amendable to psychotherapy.

Length of therapy was a different issue. The same thirty couples varied noticeably in the duration of their treatment. Table 6 records the number of sessions for couples that were active in therapy at the time of the project, as well as those who had either temporarily discontinued, dropped out, or effectively terminated.

TABLE 6
A Characterological Presentation
of Number of Treatment Sessions

HEMOGAMOUS DYADS			HETEROGAMOUS DYADS	
Couple Number	Number of Sessions		Couple Number	Number of Sessions
7	16		2	20
8	21		3	7
14	44		4	4
16	38		6	10
18	16		9	7
21	42		15	21
23	26		19	9
24	4		25	19
29	31		26	1
31	24		27	5
33	27		32	14
35	19		34	5
37	9		36	31
38	25		41	4
39	17		45	17

$$T = 359$$
$$N = 15$$
$$\overline{X} = 23.93$$

$$T = 184$$
$$N = 15$$
$$\overline{X} = 12.26$$

$$t = 3.26$$
$$p \text{ "less than" } .01$$

That is to say, characterologically, homogamous dyads stayed in treatment longer than heterogamous couples. As we will see, this longevity parallels the trend of marital persistence.

Again, using the reduced sample, a categorical examination of the marital status revealed that twelve of the homogamous couples were together at the time they left the center and three had separated and/or divorced. To a lesser degree, the opposite trend could be seen in characterologically heterogamous couples. As the X2 is significant the results support the idea that characterologically homogamous couples find it more difficult to get a divorce.

TABLE 7

Marital Status on Leaving Treatment

	MARRIED	SEPARATED DIVORCED	
CHARACTEROLOGICAL HOMOGAMY	12	3	15
			$N = 30$
CHARACTEROLOGICAL HETEROGAMY	6	9	
	18	12	

$$X^2 (1) = 5.0 \ p \text{ "less than" } .05$$

Of the three characterologically homogamous marriages which did divorce, two couples were still living together at the time of the study.

DISCUSSION

It will be seen from Table 1 that 80 percent of the diagnoses of individuals fell into two categories: obsessive-compulsive personality and passive-aggressive personality. Considering the middle-class, white, Protestant nature of the hospital's catchment area, the high proportion of these two categories was not surprising. However, the 3 percent figure for hysterical personality was unexpected. This could be because of a collective diagnostic bias of the raters, but is more likely a product of the nature of both the counseling center and the referral sources. The counseling center, run by ministers trained to the Ph.D. level, receives most of its cases by referral from parochial ministers in the area. It has been the experience of the authors that ministers in the parish find hysterical persons interesting, often easier to work with and, therefore, are more reluctant to refer them.

The reader may also have second thoughts regarding the proportion of homogamous marriages discovered by our research. A potential criticism might be that the diagnostic approach used throughout this report was characterological rather than phenomenological. By phenomenological diagnosis we mean personality evaluation by means of certain clusters of behavioral traits and symptoms, not a finalized grouping of those clusters under a single

characterological category (e.g., Giovacchini and Borowitz, 1974). We believe, however, that if a phenomenological mode of diagnosis had been used
instead of the standard nomenclature of the American Psychiatric Association an even greater proportion of homogamous dyads might have been evidenced. (On the other hand, there are critics who argue the reverse—that a
characterological diagnosis cannot be established on the basis of tests and interviews. Obviously, the authors do not agree with such a position but are
aware of its existence.)

Furthermore, we have, at this time, no way of knowing whether the results of
Tables 2 and 3 reflect the proportion of characterologically homogamous
marriages in middle-class suburban communities, or whether our study reflects a larger proportion of homogamous marriages because members of this
type of marriage are more likely to seek treatment. The data of the study
supports the notion that homogamous marriages are more tightly bonded
than heterogamous ones. Their partners have fewer divorces and stay longer
in treatment.

Characterological homogamy does not necessarily yield "sickness" or
"health." It refers to a mutual investment across a continuum of adjustment.
Such clients may be more prone to apply for marital therapy simply because
they have more invested in the marriage. Such an investment, it is contended,
is due to a deep psychological homogamy. By comparison, characterologically heterogamous marriages show a tendency toward divorce because the investment in the object relationship is not as total.

Several treatment generalizations arose from this characterological distinction. First, when one considers the nature of a characterologically homogamous marriage, the most beneficial form of treatment may be individual psychotherapy for each spouse. In some cases this mode may be accompanied by
periodic conjoint sessions with both therapists present. The purpose of such
meetings would be to help the couple learn some *inter*actional tools in a controlled setting. By a sparing use of conjoint treatment, we think homogamous
spouses will be better equipped to gain psychological distance and take steps
toward greater individuation.

When the emphasis is placed on analytic treatment the client has the opportunity to deal with some *intra*psychic features that are projected onto his
or her mate. It enables a characterological focus to be maintained. If divorce
occurs during the process of therapy, grief work or mourning can be done. If
remarriage is a subsequent option, the clients' needs for a particular kind of
object relationship can be explored. In this way the pathological ramifica-
tions of what Greene (1968) calls a "sequential marriage" can be worked
through.

One of the characterologically homogamous couples used in this study illustrates these points. The patient, a thirty-two-year-old office manager, came

to the center with her husband because of "marital friction." They listed their major problems as the husband's angry reactions toward his wife's interest in work and books. He also complained about her disregard for his standards (e.g., punctuality and domestic cleanliness). Her central complaint, apart from his anger, was that his job frequently entailed out-of-state projects that were assigned with little or no notice. Both were diagnosed as exhibiting "depressed neurosis in an obsessive-compulsive personality trait disorder."

The husband, then ten years older than his wife, had been married once before. His former wife, like his mother, had dominated him and he had felt "pushed around for most of [his] life." When he married his present wife he "swore that would never happen again." She, on the other hand, was used to being controlled by males, particularly her father. She had tolerated this through an immersion in books until she got married. While the issue of control was central in conjoint therapy, they progressed slowly, learning mostly some basic interactional skills. After twenty-three sessions the therapist saw than conjoint therapy had become a stalemate. Just at that point the husband provoked his wife into leaving home by losing their savings at jai alai. Both discontinued treatment and were divorced a few months later. The husband was not heard from again.

About two years after the divorce the wife called requesting analysis. She had been involved in two affairs since her conjoint treatment, both with salesmen she described as "very much like her former husband." Because of her recent experiences and current pain, motivation was high. Individual therapy moved quickly and after a year she had worked through many of her needs to be involved with rejecting men. Her relationship with her dying father, an overseas Protestant (fundamentalist) missionary, was closely explored. Often when anticipating rejection and criticism on the part of the therapist, her anger emerged. An analysis of the transference involved her feelings toward her father's erratic presence and judgmental attitudes. By investing herself in men like her father she was unconsciously attempting to relive her childhood in order to gain the love she had missed. Therapy continued for another year, and eighteen months after her termination she telephoned to say that she was contemplating marriage to a man whom she saw as unlike her father and the other men with whom she had been involved.

While our contention is that homogamous couples would be best treated with concurrent individual therapy, it may be that an interactional or conjoint psychotherapy could supply the appropriate initial treatment for characterologically heterogamous couples. Conjoint therapy will help such spouses become aware of the basic differences or similarities in their personality structures and thereby help them place themselves in a better position to decide whether they want to continue to live with each other or strive to make changes.

Through clinical observations of our sample we have found that hetero-gamous marriages seem to respond better to either group or conjoint modes of treatment. Naturally, if there is too much individual pathology in a hetero-gamous marriage, group or conjoint modes of treatment cannot be expected to be sufficient. However, extensive group or conjoint treatment of a hetero-gamous marriage seems to be a necessary foundation before individual work can take place if the preservation of the marriage is a factor. Further, with heterogamous marriages, individual treatment will also need consistent inter-spersing of conjoint sessions to maintain the marriage bond and hence the marriage option. While these suggestions are rather speculative, and obvious-ly need further study, they seem even now to offer insights to marriage thera-pists who are currently being forced to make treatment choices. Of course, psychoanalytic treatment focuses upon the individual, and the marriage is simply another aspect of external reality in which the therapist does not intrude.

We realize these treatment suggestions are in need of some kind of verifica-tion. They are rooted, as we have pointed out, in Giovacchini's (1965, 1967) marital models, character object relationship and symptom object relation-ship. We have referred respectively to these dyads as homogamous and heter-ogamous marriages. Our study has supported this distinction at a characterol-ogical level. Giovacchini's observations of this phenomena grew out of long-term psychotherapy with individuals, that is, with one part of a marriage. Our study included a moderate sample of couples where both spouses were given an independent diagnostic evaluation based upon a thorough, lengthy case history.

SUMMARY

Using ninty persons (forty-five couples) on whom three clinicians had reached concordance after independent diagnosis, there was evidence to sup-port Giovacchini's (1965, 1967) position that characterologically homogam-ous marriages, where both spouses have the same character structure, show greater bonding qualities than heterogamous marriages, where the spouses have different character structures. In other words, the former reflect a stronger tenacity than the latter.

Homogamous marriages stayed longer in treatment, showed a lower divorce rate, and seemed to respond better to individual treatment; hetero-gamous marriages showed a higher divorce rate and tended to need more con-joint or group treatment or both. The heterogamous and homogamous char-acterological distinctions seems to be important for the strategies involved in marital therapy.

REFERENCES

Benedek, T. (1956). Psychobiological aspects of mothering. *American Journal of Orthopsychiatry* 26:272-278.

Bion, W. (1957). Differentiation of the psychotic from the non-psychotic personalities. *International Journal of Psycho-Analysis* 38:266-275.

Brodey, W. (1959). Some family operations and schizophrenia. *Archives of General Psychiatry* 1:379-402.

DeBary, A. (1879). *Die Erscheinung de Symbiose.* Strasbourg: Trubner.

_____(1879). De la symbiose. *Review of Internal Science.* 3:

Erikson, E. (1963). *Childhood and Society.* New York: Norton

Freud, A. (1949). Aggression in relation to emotional development: normal and pathological. *Psychoanalytic Study of the Child* 3/4:37-48.

_____and Burlingham, D. (1944). *Infants Without Families.* London: Allen & Unwin.

Giovacchini, P. (1967). Characterological aspects of marital interaction. *Psychoanalytic Forum* 2: 7-30.

_____(1965). The classical approach. *The Psychotherapies of Marital Disharmony,* ed. Bernard Greene. New York: Macmillan.

_____(1958). Mutual adaptation in various object relationships. *International Journal of Psycho-Analysis* 34:1-8.

_____and Borowitz, G. (1974). An object relationship scale. *Adolescent Psychiatry,* Vol. 3, eds. S. Feinstein and P. Giovacchini. New York: Basic Books.

_____(1966). Psychopathological aspects of the identity sense. *Psychiatric Digest* 26:31-41.

_____(1961). Resistance and external object relations. *International Journal of Psycho-Analysis* 40:246-254.

_____(1972). The symbiotic phase. *Tactics and Techniques in Psychoanalytic Therapy,* ed. P. Giovacchini. New York: Aronson.

Greene, B. (1970). *A Clinical Approach to Marital Problems.* Springfield, Ill.: Thomas.

_____(1968). Sequential marriage: repetition or change. *The Marriage Relationship,* eds. S. Rosenbaum and I. Alger. New York: Basic Books.

_____(ed.) (1965). *The Psychotherapies of Marital Disharmony.* New York: Macmillan.

Hollingshead, A., and Redlich, F. (1958). *Social Class and Mental Illness.* New York: Wiley.

Howard, K., and Orlinsky, D. (1972). Psychotherapeutic process. *Annual Review of Psychology* 23:615-668.

Jessner, L., et al. (1955). Emotional impact of nearness and separation for the asthmatic child and his mother. *Psychoanalytic Study of the Child* 10: 353-375.

Jung, C. (1970). Marriage as a psychological relationship. *Collected Works,* Vol. 17. Princeton:

Klein, M. (1937). Love, guilt and reparation. *Love, Hate and Reparation.* London:

_____(1946). Notes on some schizoid mechanisms. *International Journal of Psycho-Analysis* 27:99-110.

Lewis, H. (1971). *Shame and Guilt in Neurosis.* New York: International Universities Press.

Lynd, H. (1961). *Shame and the Search for Identity.* New York: Harcourt, Brace.

Mahler, M., et al. (1968). *On Human Symbiosis and the Vicissitudes of Individuation,* Vol. 1, Infantile Psychosis, New York: International Universities Press.

Masserman, J. (1952). Psychiatric supplementation of the medical history and physical examination. *Diseases of the Nervous System* 13:8-15.

Moss, D. (1974). A clinical application of Giovacchini's model of marital interaction. Unpublished Ph.D. dissertation, Northwestern University, Evanston.

_____(1973). Dialogue at Maresfield Gardens: An interview with Anna Freud. *Pilgrimage: The Journal of Pastoral Psychotherapy* 2:2-7.

Piers, G., and Singer, M. (1953). *Shame and Guilt: A Psychoanalytic and Cultural Study.* Springfield, Ill.: Thomas.

Pollock, G. (1964). On symbiotic neurosis. *International Journal of Psycho-Analysis* 45: 1-30.
Spitz, R. (1965). *The First Year of Life: A Psychoanalytic Study of Normal and Deviant Development in Object Relations.* New York: International Universities Press.
Winnicott, D. (1965). *The Family and Individual Development.* London: Hogarth.

DAVID M. MOSS, Ph.D.

DR. MOSS is an Episcopal priest affiliated with the Center for Religion and Psychotherapy of Chicago and the Chaplaincy Program at Northwestern University. He is an Associate Editor of **Pilgrimage: The Journal of Pastoral Psychotherapy** and is presently completing a book entitled **Dialogues in Psychoanalysis and Religion.**

RONALD R. LEE, Ph.D.

DR. LEE is a Methodist minister and registered psychologist in Illinois. He is Professor of Pastoral Psychology and Director of Counseling at Garrett-Evangelical Theological Seminary. He is also a member of the Graduate School faculty of Northwestern University and Chairman of the Human Subjects Committee of Evanston Hospital.

Symbiosis and Intimacy

Peter L. Giovacchini, M.D.

Clinical Professor
Department of Psychiatry
University of Illinois College of Medicine

The symbiotic phase of development is crucially involved in determining the nature of psychopathology as well as promoting psychic processes that are involved in creative activity and intimate object relationships.

In a well-established object relationship, the partners relate to each other in a symbiotic fashion. From the analysis of married persons (and some clinical material is presented in this paper), the author concludes that the fundamental character structure, psychopathological or otherwise, of each spouse is identical. Exceptions to this conclusion exist, but here one is dealing with an object relationship that is superficial and transitory.

Symbiotic fusion regularly occurs in creative activity and empathic intimate relationships.

INTRODUCTION

Psychoanalysts are showing increasing interest in studying early developmental phases. Many patients seeking psychoanalytic treatment seem to be suffering from very severe psychopathology; consequently, knowledge about primitive mental operations and defenses becomes particularly meaningful in helping us understand patients and dealing with them psychotherapeutically.

The investigation of infantile psychic constellations often leads to insights about so-called higher mental operations, such as creativity, intuitiveness, empathy, and intimacy. There is an interplay between primitive psychic processes and achievements which requires high degrees of perceptivity, differentiation, and interpretation.

It is this interplay which I wish to explore further here. Rather than dealing with the combination of primitive elements and secondary process factors found in creative endeavors (Giovacchini, 1965, 1971), I now prefer focusing upon object relations. Some of my focus will be on marital object relationships, since in such interactions one has the opportunity to study the gamut of psychic processes involved in long-lasting relationships in which there are greater or lesser degrees of intimacy. How one partner is used by the other and how the mutuality maintains the marital pair's psychic equilibrium should shed considerable light on the nature of both constrictive defenses and structuralizing processes. I will discuss the marital interaction, although marriage refers only to a legal state; the important factors are the depth of involvement between the partners and the duration of the relationship.

LINES OF DEVELOPMENT

The study of particular object relationships will emphasize that emotional development can be viewed in terms of an hierarchal sequence. This is a fairly obvious approach, but recently a variation has been introduced. Kohut (1966, 1971) prefers what has been called a double axis theory which preserves a structural hierarchy, to be sure, but which postulates separate lines of development for such reality-attuned functions as sensitivity, introspection and empathy on the one hand and commitment and object love on the other. These distinctions are important because they are elaborated in the context of primitive mental states and developing capacities and defenses that lead to special types of transference in the therapeutic setting.

If one is to remain consistent within Kohut's theoretical framewrk, then one has to assume that the part of the ego that develops certain capacities and the part which eventually relates to objects have to be kept separate from each other. If not, there is no point in postulating separate lines of development which, in my mind, obscures the interaction of the primitive and sophisticated within the psyche rather than clarifying it.

If the mind develops from a state in which it cannot recognize its own boundaries to one where it can sensitively perceive and become intimately involved with the external world, then it is reasonable to assume that earlier mental operations become amalgamated into higher systems and contribute to their functioning.

The developing psyche learns more and more how to distinguish between its parts, the outer world, and how it relates to the outer world. There is a reciprocal relationship between self-perception and the ability to make sensitive discriminations, and the ability to relate to the outer world. The ability to perceive reality and to interact comfortably with the environment requires psychic energy, one might say narcissistic energy or ego-libido. Without sufficient energy, object relations are not possible. Thus, one can postulate a continuum; object relations can be traced back to their narcissistic precursors which make development possible and which, in turn, continue to develop.

As involvements with the self become more sophisticated, they make possible more sensitive and intimate object relationships. There is a reciprocal interaction between the self and the outer world, a positive feedback, so to speak, where the self becomes enriched by object relationships, and object relationships, in turn, are enhanced by a progressively structured self. To speak of separate lines of development tends to obscure these subtle structuralizing relationships.

Freud (1911, 1914) traces libidinal development from an initial stage of autoerotism where no operative ego exists to primary narcissism where there is some rudimentary ego cohesion and then to secondary narcissism and finally object relationships, the ego acquiring greater unity throughout this developmental sequence. Kohut (1971) differs regarding some aspects of this sequence but accepts the progression from autoerotism to primary narcissism. Both Freud and Kohut believe that the psyche progresses from a fragmented state to more highly differentiated, organized ones. What begins in a disparate fashion comes under the dominance of a unifying force, as occurs when component instincts are subjected to genital dominance. This is an integrative and cohesive process.

Kohut's lines of separate development begin, however, when the disparate autoerotic instincts are organized to the extent that they are directed toward a rudimentary ego. In other words, there is a progression from unintegrated component instincts seeking independent erogenous gratification to a psyche that has achieved some unity in that some ego exists, the stage of primary narcissism. Thus, Kohut postulated separate instincts becoming unified and then dividing into two separate lines of development. It seems conceptually inconsistent to postulate separation, which always represents some loss of organization, as part of normal development. At best this would be a defensive and regressive process.

In psychoanalysis, insofar as the elements of the mind are ordered in a hierarchal sequence, all theories, in a sense, are single-axis. There can be only one line of development, a progression from the global and amorphous to the discrete and structured. The structured end of the spectrum may encompass many areas which involve all types of interactions and relationships between parts of the psyche and between the ego and external objects. These various areas may be compared to branches radiating outward from a main stem, but they are not separate stems.

The outcome of Kohut's separate lines of development, the separation of narcissistic development from the development of object relationships, also raises some questions. The progression from narcissism leads to such higher functions, to repeat, as sensitivity and the capacity for introspection, empathy, and intuitiveness. The end points of object relationships are commitment, object love, and intimacy. If one is to remain consistent in such a theoretical framework, then there must be a part of the psyche that develops certain capacities and another part which relates to objects, and these two parts have to be kept separate from each other; otherwise the concept of separate lines of development becomes meaningless and superfluous. However, it is difficult to view such qualities as sensitivity and empathy as having different origins than commitment and intimacy. It would seem that they are fundamentally of the same cloth.

DEVELOPMENTAL THEORY

This paper will develop the thesis, through the presentation of clinical material, that in well-developed object relationships as well as in the exercise of such higher functions as creativity, a variety of mental mechanisms operate, some of which are characteristic of and originate during early phases of development. Consequently, it is germane to reexamine our concepts of what are considered psychopathological mechanisms and what constitute aspects of normal development.

Freud (1911, 1914) postulated a sequence from autoerotism to primary and then secondary narcissism, and finally from part objects to whole object relations. He described primitive mentation and postulated the existence of a megalomanic stage, a phase of magical and omnipotent wish fulfillment characteristic of early stages of development. True, he first referred to megalomania in the context of psychopathology, of paranoia (Freud, 1911), but later he included megalomania as an aspect of normal narcissism (Freud, 1914). The omnipotent aura of infantile narcissistic phases is typified by such expressions as "his majesty the baby." When frustration of this omnipotence occurs, as it must because physiological needs can never be perfectly met nor can hallucinatory wish fulfillment fulfill except for a limited time, the child uses projective defenses in order to protect himself from hatred which tends to overwhelm him. Here we might have a paranoid picture. All of this occurs very early and these primitive reactions are revived by the regressions of later psychopathology.

In my mind, many of the arguments leveled against Melanie Klein apply to the above formulations as well. I am referring to attributing complex mental operations to an unformed and immature psyche. Magical manipulation, omnipotence, megalomania, grandiose feelings are very complicated states and reactions which go far beyond the limited mentational capacity of the neonate. To feel persecuted or to ascribe all evil to something or someone outside the self presupposes the ability to make some distinction between the self and the outer world as well as the capacity to evoke subtle and sensitive feelings. This appears especially incongruous when one notes that the infant cannot as yet smile and because of the state of myelinization of the nervous system we assume his reactions are restricted to diffuse feelings of comfort or discomfort.

Freud (1915) believed that hatred is an early affect and signifies a response to frustration. What causes frustration is bad and has to be ejected. Spitting is the prototype of the expulsion of disturbing forces and this is a factor at the very beginning of the developmental timetable. This formulation is quite similar to Klein's (1946) concept of the paranoid-schizoid position, as being part of normal development rather than a psychopathological vicissitude.

Freud did not postulate the existence of elaborate fantasies, fantasies that Klein believed were typical of paranoid-schizoid and depressive positions. Still, he considered grandiose and paranoid orientations as manifestations of the narcissistic stage, his first step in the ladder of the sequence of psychosexual development. So even though Freud did not elaborate on content, he still described complicated mechanisms which could evoke fantasies that would have a certain degree of complexity-certainty requiring more structure than is possible in a preverbal ego state.

Thus, it would seem that certain modifications are required to make our concepts about emotional development consistent with biological data, since ego states dominated by megalomania, grandiosity, and paranoiac ideation are frequently found in the transference regressions of many patients or as important orientations which characterize object relationships. Their position in the developmental hierarchy has to be ascertained. First, however, I will outline a scheme of emotional development which requires only a minimum of adultomorphization.

At the very beginning of extrauterine life, the neonate must be considered somewhat amorphous, mentationally speaking, and his feelings and perceptions must be, at best, vague and indefinite. A nervous system which is, to some extent, unmylinated and which responds in a global fashion as demonstrated by positive Babinski and Moro reflexes is not yet capable of making fine discriminations or of much mental activity. Perhaps one can best describe this earliest phase as *prementational*, a phase which is predominantly physiological in orientation. How long it lasts, that is, how long before some mentational activity develops, is difficult to ascertain. As some experimental evidence suggests, it is probably of very short duration, perhaps a matter of only days.

One can assume that the child very soon begins to recognize states of comfort and discomfort and then that some type of activity can alleviate the latter. He does not yet discriminate between what emanates from within himself and what emanates from the environment. The environment is only dimly perceived, if it is perceived at all. To some extent, the infant "believes" that he is the "source" of what is happening. Of course, he does not "believe" anything of the sort. I am adultomorphizing in the same way that I have accused Freud and Klein of doing. The infant cannot as yet have any beliefs and he certainly can have no notions as complicated as etiological connections. He cannot even hold anything in his memory system without the reinforcement of an external perception. I am emphasizing, however, that the neonate, because he is still neurologically immature as well as experientially naive, has very little notion of anything happening anywhere, especially in the outside world. For our purpose, it is important to realize that he has no concept as yet of an external object being relevant to his comfort or discomfort, but he recognizes that there are forces and activities which have some bearing on the establishment or disruption of psychic equilibrium. This phase could be called a *preobject stage* and may be comparable to what Freud referred to as primary narcissism insofar as there is some awareness of a self that can be both needful and gratified, but very little awareness of anything else separate from one's feeling state.

From this phase, the psyche progresses to the acquisition of the ability to have part-object relations and finally to whole-object relations. This sequence may sound familiar and self-evident, but the various qualities and mechanisms attributed to these phases, such as megalomania and paranoid projection, I believe, justify this recapitulation and further clarification.

I return to the question of where to fit these qualities and mechanisms in the developmental hierarchy. Since clinicians encounter them so often in the transference regressions of analytic patients, this question is particularly germane. Furthermore, if one is to investigate the primitive antecedents of intimate object relationships, this task becomes even more relevant.

The qualities of omnipotence and megalomania that Freud viewed as the essence of his beginning phase, I believe are defensive adaptations which develop later and then become part of the regression back to earlier traumatic fixations. They represent techniques designed to deal with disturbances in the developmental sequence. Rather than viewing omnipotence and megalomania as the essence of early phases of development, I believe that, in actuality, he was describing complex defensive techniques that could not possibly have been constructed by an ego that is associated with an immature central nervous system.

Melanie Klein has been criticized for the same reasons when she considers the paranoid-schizoid and depressive positions as stages of normal development occurring around the ages of two and six months respectively. She attributes the concepts of good and bad, destroying and being destroyed, as well as the affects of rage and fear to projective and introjective mechanisms, which are the essence of the paranoid position. Rescuing, reparation, and ambivalence are characteristic of the depressive position which normally occurs around the age of six months, when the child supposedly begins to perceive whole objects.

By making some revisions in Freud's developmental scheme and considerably more in Klein's, they can continue being used to help us understand our severely disturbed patients as well as helping us to develop further our concepts about object relationships. If the qualities of omnipotence and grandiosity are eliminated as aspects of normal development, then Freud's stages of primary and secondary narcissism are not too different from my prementational, preobject, and object-related stages. The latter place greater emphasis on object relationships than did Freud. Klein, on the other hand, concentrated on both internal and external objects but confused psychopathological reactions with normal developmental processes.

Viewing development in the terms just described has clinical and technical implications about narcissism and those entities that have been considered narcissistic character disorders. Quite obviously, Kohut's (1971) concept of narcissism characterized by grandiosity and omnipotence as a developmental stage with its independent progression is meaningless in this context (see Kernberg, 1974). In fact, narcissism, insofar as it involves self-love or grandiosity, has no place in early development.

Later in development, because of trauma or perhaps healthy integration, ego states emerge that can be conceptualized as narcissistic. With psychopathology, narcissism is a defensive overcompensatory defense and character trait designed to protect an ego which feels vulnerable, has low self-esteem, and finds itself unable to cope with the exigencies of the outer world. As an outcome of normal development, healthy narcissism, as Federn (1952) so long ago described, is characteristic of an ego that is confident of its abilities and enjoys its capacity to function and relate to reality, an ego that is attaining the attributes of its ego-ideal. I believe this regularly occurs with creativity (Giovacchini, 1965).

Healthy narcissism, in the above sense, is the outcome of a relatively nontraumatic and comfortable symbiotic phase, one which promotes structuralization and individuation rather than fixation. Now, I wish to discuss symbiosis and the achievement of healthy narcissism, to repeat, a self-representation that is confident of its adaptive abilities and enjoys high levels of self-esteem, in the context of object relationships.

The symbiotic phase can be considered a transitional one between a preobject and an object, or more precisely, a part-object phase. The mother-child, that is the nurturing, combination is experienced as a unit during symbiosis. In order to fuse with someone, the infant must have some awareness, dim and vague as it may be, of someone or something to fuse with, since distinctions between animate and inanimate are, for the most part, rudimentary. Some kind of discrimination must momentarily take place before the nurturing source becomes part of the neonate's psychic world.

The first beginnings of self-esteem, in my mind, develop during the symbiotic phase. The child begins to gain security that his needs will be met and this state of confidence is somehow related to what Winnicott (1953) called transitional object and transitional phenomena.

If the mother's need to mother is synchronized, so to speak, with the infant's need to be nurtured, a state of satisfying fusion between mother and infant is possible. The mother senses the child's needs since they have really become part of her own needs. In the same fashion, the mother's response to the child's needs have become part of the child. In other words, the mother's nurturing activity is introjected, and here we have the transitional situations Winnicott so aptly described.

To repeat, the symbiotic phase is a transitional one between a preobject stage and a stage where part-object relationships are dominant. It is during this transitional phase that transitional phenomena occur. The child begins to develop the confidence that he can meet his own needs. Of course, this is an illusion, but, as Winnicott states, it is an illusion that is not challenged when mothering is so delicately attuned to the infant's needs.

The child's confidence is based upon the acquisition of the maternal introject. Winnicott considered this introject to be a part-object, the breast, and insofar as the infant believes it is his own creation, Winnicott calls this process primary psychic creativity. The projection of this introject results in the transitional object.

This introject can also be viewed as a modality, a functional modality which represents the nurturing function. Thus, in a smoothly balanced symbiotic relationship, the infant fundamentally has the security that his needs will be met without needing to recognize his dependency upon an external object for survival. Since the ego is still relatively nonstructured at this stage, it is not characterized by complex feelings of omnipotence; rather, the child achieves some rudimentary feeling of satisfaction without the disruption that would accompany experiencing his needs painfully since he cannot anticipate gratification. Needs and gratification are still primarily physiological in nature and disruption is probably not accompanied by structured affects. However, frustrated infants show signs that could be interpreted by the adult as rage and, perhaps at times, one can detect signs of anxiety or, more precisely, terror. Rage then would be a sign of an unsatisfactory symbiotic relationship insofar as the fusion has not led to the achievement of, one might say, the transitional phenomenon, or in my terms, a seemingly independent nurturing modality. The child does not develop self-confidence in his ability to have his needs met and in his psychic integrity or, not to attribute more to the infant's mentality than it can sustain, he does not develop the anlages that will lead to self-confidence and self-esteem.

Such an infant develops feelings of vulnerability and helplessness and concern about survival instead of healthy self-confidence. He may develop compensatory omnipotence as a defense against vulnerability. In healthy development, on the other hand, the infant is free from concerns about survival and from feelings of vulnerability and helplessness, and also free from megalomanic grandiose defenses against vulnerability and helplessness; instead he feels optimism and self-reliance, and turns to the outer world and external objects with confidence.

Preoccupation with the external world rather than exclusive absorption with the self is an important aspect of creative activity. However, this does not mean that one activity replaces another; it is not simply a matter of an increase of libido directed toward the outer world at the expense of ego-libido. On the contrary, both the self and the outer world are highly cathected. During the creative act, both a symbiotic and object-directed modes of relating are simultaneously operating. However, it is not the purpose of this paper to pursue the topic of creativity extensively. It is mentioned merely to highlight the interplay of psychic mechanisms originating in early developmental stages with mechanisms characteristic of mature emotional functioning. This occurs in creativity and, as I shall emphasize, is concerned also in the development of intimate object relationships.

In an intimate object relationship all levels of the personality are involved. The self-reliance that is the consequence of a firm establishment of the nurturing modality acquired during the symbiotic phase will direct itself toward a sexual object and manifest itself by taking care of a cherished person. Taking care, however, does not mean forcing the partner into a dependent relationship with its accompanying helplessness. Rather, it refers to meeting another person's needs without threatening either partner's autonomy. The giver can become the recipient, individual ego boundaries can be lost through fusion, and yet the partners retain their basic identity even as they are merging with each other.

The study of the role of the symbiotic phase of development in leading to and maintaining later object relationships is a potential source of insight about the structure and psychodynamic balance of intimacy and intimate object relationships. As in all psychoanalytic investigations, these factors can be studied in the therapeutic setting which allows inferences to be made from psychopathological distortions.

CLINICAL MATERIAL

Some marriages, those which have endured for many years, highlight the mutually adaptive elements of object relationships. The following example illustrates how the marital relationship supported the psychic integration of each partner, an integration based upon psychopathologically constructed defenses. Furthermore, the sequence of events in the external world precipitated by the analytic process reveals striking aspects about the character structure of each partner and how they specifically relate to each other.

The patient, a woman in her middle thirties, had been married for almost twelve years when she sought treatment. Actually, it was her husband who insisted upon analysis and he made the initial telephone call in order to arrange an appointment.

He felt concerned about the effects of a move from their hometown to Chicago would have on her emotional stability, a move that was apparently dictated by a change in employment. Moving away meant moving away from her family, especially her mother.

The patient did not object to seeing me, she did not resist the idea of analysis. She had, in fact, been aware of growing tension and occasional waves of anxiety which she, too, attributed to moving to a large, strange, and perhaps unfriendly city.

She was immaculately groomed during our first interview. She was poised and her demeanor was sophisticated and graceful. However, it seemed to be a pose because she would, from time to time, burst into tears as she was discussing some sensitive aspects of her life and relationships. She would then apologize and attempted quickly to pull herself together. Regaining her composure became more difficult as the session continued and by the end of our time, she seemed drained and disheveled. Apparently, talking about herself had been a great strain.

Oddly, I did not feel any strain and this seemed strange to me. I will return to my reaction later, that is, when I describe how I came to understand it in context with what the patient revealed about herself.

Thus, in the space of one session, the patient became reduced or rather reduced herself from an apparently self-sufficient, confident woman, to a frightened helpless person. Still, she was eager to continue treatment in spite of the traumatic reaction to our first interview. From that point on, she melodramatically revealed how inept, clumsy, insensitive, and miserable she felt. She believed that without support, specifically the support of her mother and husband, she would not be able to sustain herself, and now her mother was not available to her in this strange and lonely city.

Her mother was described as a beautiful and highly competent, efficient woman. By contrast, the father was a passive, withdrawn person whose role was clearly to be the mother's vassal. She came from a rich and aristocratic family and he also came for a socially prominent family but one that had become impoverished because of the imprudent investments of his fickle and alcoholic father. The patient's father was totally dependent upon his wife and he only went through the motions of earning a living by pretending to be a financial consultant.

The patient's husband was described as an aggressive, outgoing person who in many ways seemed similar to her mother. From her description, at times it seemed that his aggression had acquired qualities that might make it more appropriate to call it sadism. Apparently, he had total charge of the household and dictated how everything, such as the arrangement of meals, the raising of the children, and even the selection of his wife's wardrobe, should be done.

As stated, the patient emphasized her weakness. She had been a sickly child and was frequently bedridden. It is not to this day clear, however, 'what diseases in addition to the usual childhood ones she actually suffered from. She was said to be delicate and fragile and her family, including her husband, treated her as if she were a china doll. As I looked at her, I noted a frail quality to her demeanor but it was ephemeral. I could not sustain such an image in my mind.

Nevertheless, in one respect, I became aware of impulses to protect her. Her description of her mother's imperious manner and her husband's intrusive arrogance roused me to want to side with her as the downtrodden and exploited one and to liberate her from such tyrannical influences. Still, I was not comfortable with these feelings.

I gathered that the patient was, to some extent, being manipulative in her unabashed and open display of weakness and fragility. I somehow felt that part of this feebleness was designed to control others who prided themselves because of their exhibitionistically displayed strength. Consequently, I indicated that part of what she was describing was a facade, one which, in a paradoxical fashion, led to the subjugation of others rather than herself. I stated that I believed she also wanted to control and manipulate me. I had recalled my initial lack of strain when she displayed her helplessness.

To my surprise, she agreed; she offered no resistance to my interpretation. In fact, she was pleased, and then she began relating episodes which were meant to confirm it. For example, she mentioned a very traumatic experience which occurred when she was about eight years old. She returned home from school unexpectedly because her teacher felt she should not stay in class because of some flu symptoms. She found her mother in the bedroom in a disheveled, confused state, muttering gibberish and, all in all, presenting a picture of sordid degradation, a marked contrast to her usually regal composure. The maid finally became aware of the patient's presence and quickly whisked her out of the room. Later the patient learned that her mother was an alcoholic who usually drank herself into a stupor by early afternoon and then slept until the evening, when she went through an elaborate ritual of pulling herself together. The patient was very much aware of her mother's vulnerability and helplessness, but she both suppressed and repressed it because it had a traumatic impact upon her.

She uncovered similar weaknesses in her father and also in her husband. The father was always depicted as an ineffectual person but her husband had seemed to be a bulwark of strength. Gradually a somewhat different picture was formed during the course of treatment. Her husband, the son of a wealthy industrialist, was tolerated in the business simply because he was the son of the president of the firm. His transfer to another city was made to appear as if it were a promotion, but, in actuality, he was removed from the main office to a position with an impressive title but with little meaning or responsibility. A sinecure had been created for him with the purpose of shoving him off to one side, relegating him to the background, to be rid of his clumsy interference and ineptness. It also became apparent that in spite of his strutting aggressivity, the patient was really in charge of the household. However, she had a strong and vital need to appear helpless.

At the same time that she was pointing out the paradoxical elements of the personalities of her husband and her mother, she continued focusing upon how inept she felt. She did, indeed, feel helpless, and the first year of analysis was characterized by many sessions of clinging dependency and tearful appeals for help. Her confusion was augmented by mine because neither of us knew exactly what she meant by help (see Giovacchini, 1975).

She seemed to regress even further during therapy than she had prior to entering treatment. To some extent, even her personal habits deteriorated and she seemed so distressed, presumably because of her separation from her mother, that it seemed that hospitalization might be necessary. She complained bitterly and desperately of not being able to define herself; in essence, she was suffering from the miserable anguish of a lack of identity. It was peculiarly striking, especially in view of his later behavior, that her husband never raised his voice in protest. He was forbearing, encouraged her to continue treatment at all costs, and showed no reaction to the way her chaos disrupted the household. His attitude toward treatment during these trying times seemed to be that of the perfect supportive relative.

I also did not feel perturbed by the patient's seemingly desperate situation, but I was not able to accept it at face value as I was led to believe her husband did. The patient was suffering intensely but there still seemed to be some purpose to it rather than it being just a regressive disintegration. I gradually gained the impression from the patient's associations and dreams that, among other things, she was testing me to see if I could withstand the onslaught of her total helplessness and vulnerability.

I was struck by the extent of the patient's inhibitions. As stated, she felt completely "paralyzed" and her phobias kept her tied to the house. The only time she went out was when the husband or a neighbor drove her to my office. I also felt that she had a need to keep destructive feelings under control and feeling helpless was the outcome of the repression of murderous rage. I interpreted her weakness as designed to protect me from the onslaught of what she believed was unmanageable anger. She agreed and was pleased that I was not afraid of her. I had survived both her helplessness and the underlying hostility.

The patient gradually regained a competent, composed demeanor and began functioning in her everyday life. For several months, she was pleased with our relationship, but the serenity of the treatment relationship was in striking contrast to what was occurring in her marriage.

Now she no longer needed her husband to drive her to sessions or to take care of the household. At first, he had no apparent reaction; certainly, he did not express any pleasure at his wife's recently acquired integration.

He now made no reference to analysis, whereas previously he had always been concerned about her getting to sessions and, in general, encouraged her. As his wife's behavior continued improving, he began making remarks about the length and ineffectiveness of analysis. This was followed by complaining about the cost of treatment, although there never had been a financial problem.

My patient had very little reaction to both his overt and covert attacks against analysis. She conjectured that her husband was expressing some fundamental problems of his own. However, her friendly attitude toward me disappeared and she began criticizing her analysis and me.

She started questioning the rationale and method of analysis much in the way her husband did. This was followed by a period where her attacks were much more personal than those of her husband. She reached a crescendo; she moved from a generalized intellectual and didactic antianalytic attitude to fierce personal attacks on my integrity and competence. She was critical of my furniture, clothes, and appearance, as well as eloquent in exposing what she called the shaky and perhaps fraudulent basis of the psychoanalytic method. From time to time she succeeded in making me feel inept and helpless.

She seemed to be echoing her husband's protests. I believe that, for defensive purposes, she had identified with her husband's attitudes. I expected that the marriage would have gained strength in the unity of husband and wife against analysis and, for a short while, this was the case.

According to the patient, her husband's behavior was becoming increasingly agitated. In addition to attacking me, attacks which now seemed to have reached paranoid proportions, he also found it difficult to carry on his everyday activities. He had paralyzing attacks of anxiety, was unable to go to work, and even found himself afraid of driving and leaving the house. In other words, he seemed to present a picture identical to his wife's prior to her treatment and during the first year of treatment.

By contrast, the patient was calm, perceptive, and efficient. Even though her attacks on me continued to be devastating, she seemed to be achieving considerable relief from them, and at no time did she even consider stopping treatment. Her demeanor indicated she was deriving considerable benefit from the therapeutic relationship.

As her husband's helplessness and dissolution increased, he redoubled his irate outpourings against analysis. He insisted that she stop treatment.

Whereas previously he had merely implied that she should not continue seeing me, he became direct and demanding, insisting that treatment was ruining her. The ludicrousness of his position was highlighted when she demonstrated that for the first time in her life she was able to function autonomously. He then pleaded on financial grounds but this was equally feeble since his father furnished him with all the money he needed and the patient had money of her own, more than enough to live comfortably and support analysis.

The husband became totally incapacitated and had to be hospitalized for four months. The patient continued improving and she saw herself as a "very well put together person."

Still, in spite of behavioral improvement, she viewed treatment as a vital necessity. Her attacks on me were mitigated as she recognized that she was projecting hateful parts of herself in the transference. Attributing all the negative views of herself to me enabled her to deal with the more positive, competent aspects of the self-representation. However, there was much to analyze even about her improvement since much of it depended upon having someone around, such as a husband or therapist, who could carry her inferiority. She also identified with her mother's imperious facade, a rather shaky basis for a truly confident, well-integrated self-representation.

Her improvement vacillated in a remarkable fashion with her husband's. He was discharged in a much improved state. The patient's behavior then deteriorated, but less than it had previously. The husband once more became indulgent and tried to baby her—even literally, by using baby talk or cuddling her in lieu of sexual advances. However, as she said, she could no longer "play the game."

I need not discuss the further course of her therapy since it is not relevant to the thesis to be developed. I will merely refer to the fact that the patient no longer needed someone inferior onto whom to project feelings of inner badness and to whom she thereby could feel defensively superior. She also no longer feared the destructive potential of her all-pervasive rage, which caused her to demean herself and feel impotent and helpless, and which had been a defense against her fear that she could destroy people such as her husband. She felt herself able to get closer to others rather than, as in the past, when, whichever role she played, inferior or superior, she had to isolate herself and maintain distance, because to do otherwise would have been tantamount to destroying or being destroyed in terms of her psychic integration.

Regarding the marriage, the patient had secured a sufficiently stabilizing identity such that the former pathological interplay with her husband was no longer necessary. She made it quite clear that terminating treatment was going to be her decision, not his. He had two options, to adjust to a different marital equilibrium or to dissolve the marriage. He requested that she ask me for the name of a colleague he might see. He went to see the person to whom I referred him and has remained in analysis for many years. The marriage also continues but on an entirely different basis than prior to therapy.

DISCUSSION

This case presentation highlights the importance of a particular object relationship in maintaining psychopathological stability. It also permits the formulation of a generalization regarding intimate ties, that is, lasting relationships, regardless of the presence or absence of significant psychopathology.

Perhaps the outstanding feature of my patient's adjustment was the role the marriage played in determining her dominant ego state. One can think in terms of the identity sense or the self-representation in particular. The self-representation can be viewed in terms of its integration, confidence, and self-esteem, that is, its positive aspects or, at the other end of the spectrum, in terms of weakness, helplessness, and inability to function, its negative aspects. The patient and her husband demonstrated the interplay between negative and positive aspects of their identity systems and total ego integration as they determined the balance of the marital relationship. As far as one could ascertain from the wife's material, it was apparent that the husband supported himself, that is, maintained his self-esteem, by feeling superior to his wife. Viewed from the perspective of introjective-projective mechanisms he rid himself of the bad aspects of the self by projecting them into his wife. She, in turn, responded by acting helpless; her husband's projection reinforced the negative aspects of her self-image and they came to the fore. Among other things, the dominance of helpless and vulnerable parts of the self protected the wife from being overwhelmed by murderous rage. She protected herself from a destructive superego by being impotent to destroy emotionally significant external objects. In addition she avoided being inundated by her anger, which would have meant loss of control and psychic dissolution.

The analysis later revealed that the patient was afraid that valued parts of herself had to be protected from her destructiveness so they had to be hidden; that is, they had to be dissociated from general ego integration. She also had the fantasy that if others found that she possessed something precious, they would steal it from her.

In treatment, the relationship between husband and wife reversed. When the patient was not functioning, the husband was the perfect model of forbearance and understanding. He never complained. However, when the patient's psychic equilibrium shifted, he did his best to sabotage the treatment (see Giovacchini, 1975). Realizing that his efforts were going to be fruitless, he developed exactly the same symptomatology that brought his wife to treatment. He was no longer able to project because his wife was no longer willing to serve as a recipient of his projections. Now, he had to cope with the helpless aspects of his self-representation, one that was identical with the wife's, since he was not able to use customary projective defenses to protect himself from it.

The patient's familial constellation is instructive and reveals how she developed certain aspects of her identity sense. She was always faced with deceptive situations. Her mother's strength was only a matter of surface appearance. Beneath her imperious, regal assurance was a weak alcoholic who disgusted the patient. The patient identified with both aspects of her mother's identity, but these antecedents are not of particular interest for this paper.

This patient, I believe, produces further evidence for what I have come to regard as the symbiotic basis of intimate object relationships. In previous publications (1975) I have emphasized the similarities of character structures in relationships that have endured. Moss and Lee (1976) present us with data from other areas besides psychoanalytic treatment which support this formulation.

Symbiosis and Object Relationships

I will briefly outline the main features of the symbiotic theory of object relationships and some of the data from which conclusions have been reached. I believe this is necessary if I am to continue with the discussion of the contribution of early developmental levels, such as the symbiotic stage, to such higher-order qualities of object relationships as intimacy, and how methods of relating are also instrumental to processes such as creativity.

Psychoanalyses of marital partners have led me to the conclusion that marriages that have lasted for many years—I do not care to be more exact—are symbiotic in nature. I am using the word symbiotic in the original sense in which De Bary (1879) used it, as well as retaining its use to designate a particular developmental phase (Benedek, 1959). De Bary stressed the mutually adaptive aspects of a symbiotic relationship. The need of one partner for the other is equal; the partners need each other for their survival. Symbiosis as a developmental phase seemingly does not involve equality of needs. The child cannot live without the mother, but the mother could exist without the child. Once motherhood has occurred, however, one wonders about the mother's psychic survival if she were deprived of the mothering relationship.

The data obtained when something disrupts a symbiotic relationship reinforce the conclusion that the relationship is symbiotic and give us considerable information about the character structure of the partners. As stated, I am referring to marital partners, but the same conclusions apply to all close relationships, such as those of unmarried lovers who have lived together for years or homosexual partners who have had a lasting relationship. As occurred with the patient I presented, behavioral roles are often reversed, the weak partner becomes strong and vice versa. This is particularly striking in the spouses of alcoholics. When one spouse, for whatever reason, gives up drinking, the other spouse often may begin. This is known as complementarity; the behavior and orientation of the partners complement each other. Freud (1915) referred to complementary polarities such as active-passive and sadist-masochist.

My patient's symptoms or character traits seemed to complement those of her husband. Whereas he was strong, she was weak; he was competent, and she could not function; and, in general, their relationship was highlighted by its polarities. Still, the reversal of roles stressed basic similarities.

There are other types of relationships — at least they seem different on the surface — which more directly stress the similarity of character structures of the partners and point to the symbiotic quality of the emotional tie. The behavior, defenses, and character traits of the two partners are, in essence, identical rather than complementary. Both may have the same phobias, for example, and thereby neither partner demands that the other face some fearful situation. Similarly, other activities, perhaps guilt-provoking ones, can be avoided and others which have defensive significance can be pursued.

With my patient, in contrast, the patient's phobias sometimes protected the husband from facing the existence of a similar phobia. The patient, when she felt helpless, would become panicky in crowds and was extremely fearful of being beyond a specific distance from her home. She could not attend parties or company functions. Since the presence of the wife was, more or less, mandatory, the hudband could not attend these parties either, and he could then blame his wife for his lack of advancement or, more precisely, his inability to achieve rapport with his peers and subordinates. When his defensive facade crumbled it became obvious that he suffered from exactly the same anxieties and phobias as did my patient.

Complementary relationships and those characterized by phenomenological similarities emphasize totality of involvement in object relationships. Both types of relationships are based upon similarities of underlying character structure. Since defenses and character traits are similar, it is plausible to assume that they are based upon identical basic conflicts and structural and developmental defects. In many instances where the other partner has been analyzed, as occurred with my patient's husband, this has invariably proven to be the case. I have used the term *character object relationship* to refer to the total involvement of these partners with one another.

Are there exceptions to the generalization that, in long-standing relationships, the total character structures of the partners are identical? Certainly there are situations which could justifiably prompt the question. For example, a middle-aged scientist had had many marriages, around five, and was seeking treatment because he was about to get involved again, a relationship which he believed would suffer the same fate as his previous marriages. It turned out that this was prudent prognostication.

The longest any marriage had lasted was about a year. Among his wives, there were no basic common characteristics as I might have expected if I assumed that the character structures of married partners are similar. The woman he married during treatment proved to be a schizophrenic and finally had to be institutionalized. The description of his first wife indicated, by contrast, that she was in no way severely disturbed. She seemed to be a rather well-integrated hysterical character. His other wives seemed to have varied character sructures with lesser or greater degrees of psychopathology. How these different women were related to his needs seemed at first puzzling.

His relationship with his mother, as would be expected, shed light upon his seemingly mysterious and colorful choice of wives. Apparently she frequently had psychotic episodes. The patient emphasized how she could suddenly and without warning swing from one mood to its opposite. He recalled an incident during childhood when his mother was petting the cat and then the cat jumped off her lap and ran outside. She rushed for a shotgun and blew the cat in half. With him, too, she could be loving and then attack him, verbally or physically. He never knew what to expect from her.

The women in his life had one feature in common; they were unpredictable. Even though their character structures varied, their behavior was punctuated by surprising quirks. The patient needed to solve the puzzle of the unpredictable woman. He had to find women who presented him with such a problem, one that could be found in different personality structures. His choice of profession was also, to some extent, a reflection of his need to solve the unfathomable riddle. Otherwise, he felt vulnerable. Each marriage was, in a sense, a reliving of the vulnerable situation with his mother, and, as Freud (1920) would say, he was abosrbed by the compulsion to repeat the original trauma in order to master it. This theme determined the course of his life and, since each wife only served a circumscribed defensive need, there was not much to anchor the relationships.

Here is an instance where the needs of the partners for each other were not equal. It was learned that his schizophrenic wife attached herself to him in an anaclitic fashion, a need for total dependency and magical salvation. He, in turn, was trying to reinforce his defenses against his mother's unpredictable mood swings. In other words, he only needed a particular segment of the wife's personality rather than her whole character structure. As long as she behaved unpredictably, it did not particularly matter upon what psychic foundations this was based. There was not sufficient mutuality of needs for his marriages to survive.

This type of object relationship can be called a *symptom object relationship* in contrast to relationships where the partners are totally involved, which I have called character object relationship. In a symptom object relationship only one facet of the partner's personality, which is manifested in behavior, is required for the psychic stability of the other partner; whereas in a character object relationship an intermeshing and fusion of all levels of the psyche maintains stability. Symptom object relationships, on the other hand, endure, although sometimes miserably, until something such as therapy upsets the equilibrium.

The analysis of a married person does not usually lead to divorce, although it does happen. The spouse may seek analysis, as happened with the husband of my patient, or he may be able to adjust to a new equilibrium. In the latter case, without formal analysis, the spouse is able to achieve higher levels of psychic integration, to keep pace with the partner's analytic progress. The relationship itself may have an integrative effect.

Psychic Equilibrium and Fusion

Symbiosis, as a developmental phase, is characterized by fusion. If marital and other deep object relationships are based upon symbiotic ties, this should not be construed to mean that all such relationships indicate a fixation at the symbiotic level. On the contrary, fixation points are as varied as are personality configurations, but there is a sufficient amount of symbiotic element to account for similarities of character structure. When psychopathology is present, difficulties in the symbiotic phase will become manifest in the transference regression. They may not be particularly significant with some fairly well-integrated psychoneurotic patients, but with patients suffering from severe characterological problems the significance of this stage becomes increasingly prominent.

The symbiotic phase of my patient was disturbed. There is evidence that her mother used her as a narcissistic extension insofar as she projected all the hateful parts of herself onto her daughter. Such fusion is a frighteningly destructive experience.

Often such patients withdraw in order to protect themselves from being destructively engulfed. Then the picture is schizoid. Still, they can form certain kinds of object relationships because the defenses against fusion need not exclude all such relationships.

There are many different types of object relationships which involve various psychic levels and developmental stages. There is a spectrum from catatonic withdrawal, where external objects presumably are completely excluded to minimal involvement as seen in "as-if" personalities (Deutsch, 1942), to relationships which permit some degree of closeness, but also a defensively constructed interaction which allows partial and guarded fusion. My patient could allow herself to relate to her husband's and mother's facade of omnipotence. She could allow her depreciated and hateful self to fuse with elements of the external object's self-representation in order to be rescued. Meanwhile, the more valued aspects of herself were dissociated, kept out of the mainstream of her ego organization and thereby protected from both her destructive self and from being dissolved in a destructive fusion state which would be a recapitulation of the infantile traumatic symbiotic phase.

Thus, partial fusion can become an effective defense against total fusion which is experienced as annihilating. Some patients who are obviously severely disturbed seem, nevertheless, to have the capacity to participate in open, deep, and meaningful relationships. They often achieve such depths of involvement in group situations. In analysis one observes, however, these seemingly meaningful relationships seldom last. Some patients may exclaim how sensitively involved they may be with someone, but then without any continuity may terminate one relationship and form a similar alliance with someone else. In the transference regression such patients are terrified of fusion, and indicate that their involvement is a pseudo type and that what appears as closeness is, in reality, a pseudofusion.

Although these patients seem to have intimate object relationships, this is a facade. Khan (1964) has developed the thesis that perversions are designed to prevent or to defend against true intimacy. Perverse sexual behavior is a ritual where inhibitions seem to have been obliterated, but, in actuality, all psychic investments have been deflected to the soma and the partner is treated in a mechanistic fashion, as a robot or masturbatory equivalent, that is, as a part of the self rather than an autonomous human being. Here again, there is an intense fear of fusion which is indicative of a disturbed symbiotic phase.

Intimate Object Relationships

Intimate involvement supposedly reaches its peak when orgasm is experienced with a beloved sexual partner. Ego boundaries are dissolved and result in blissful ecstatic fusion. Thus, fusion is an important psychic mechanism which is fundamental to the achievement of true intimacy in a loving and mature object relationship.

The effects of disturbances of early developmental levels are reflected in psychopathology but they are also instructive and add to our understanding of how modes of psychic functioning which originated in childhood contribute to the highest levels of mature functioning. As stated, the ability to fuse is an example of such a mechanism and, insofar as fusion begins with the symbiotic phase, the role of symbiosis, that is the mutually adaptive aspects of symbiosis, can also be emphasized in nonpathological relationships. Instead of thinking exclusively in terms of similar types of psychopathology, one can think preponderantly in terms of identical character structures in relationships which are more or less normal.

In a psychopathologically established symbiosis, the mother uses her child to maintain a defensive stability. The child may represent a narcissistic extension of her hated self and becomes a receptacle for her destructiveness, vulnerability, and feelings of inadequacy. The child is, in a sense, engulfed by the mother and its autonomous potential is submerged. As occurred with my patient, such a symbiotic stage is traumatic, and later in life the patient finds fusing with an external object terrifying. As discussed, at best only a pseudo-fusion can be tolerated.

The outcome of a comfortable symbiotic phase, one where the mother's needs blend with the child's, is different. The child develops self-confidence and moves toward external objects and situations with pleasurable anticipation rather than dread. These qualities, in my opinion, originate with the establishment of the transitional situation.

Winnicott (1953) described the transitional object as occurring when there are, as yet, no clear-cut distinctions between the inner world of the psyche and the outer world. Still, the child is vigorously interacting with the mother. This can easily be identified as a symbiotic setting.

According to Winnicott, the child incorporates some aspect of the mother, the breast, as a part object. The child, however, believes he has created his own introject and the mother, because she is so perfectly in tune with his needs, does not disturb this illusion. This is called the transitional phenomenon, and the partial projection of this introject leads to the formation of the transitional object.

The child needs to be cared for and fed, and the mother, to preserve her motherliness, a fundamental aspect of her identity system and self-esteem, needs to feed and care for him. Consequently, the nurturing modality becomes part of the child's memory system and is firmly established as an introject, the part-object breast Winnicott refers to. Because such an introject is so smoothly and unobtrusively incorporated, the symbiotic fusion, where distinctions between the inner and outer world are dim, remains undisturbed. As a result, the child need not acknowledge the nurture came from the external world. The child believes he has created his own introject, that is, fundamentally created the transitional situation. Winnicott called this sequence primary creativity.

Because he has established an introject, a functional introject of the nurturing modality, the infant feels secure that he can meet his own needs. This is a source of self-esteem and self-confidence. With further psychic differentiation, the child and later adult derives pleasure in his ability to care for himself, one which gradually develops as he is able to avail himself of helpful experiences from the outside world. Knowing that inner needs can be met causes him to become further involved with external objects. His attitude is generous.

Involvement and generosity are enhanced by the recapitulation of the symbiotic phase. A comfortably experienced symbiotic phase, as is understandable, would cause one to enjoy the fusion experience rather than being terrified by it.

In contrast to the psychopathological situations described earlier, these healthier personalities project the good rather than the bad parts of their personality as they fuse with an external object or, to be less mechanistic, with a cherished beloved. This represents true intimacy, since there are no barriers that block interaction and still each partner retains autonomy even as they are merging. This type of relationship is nondefensive, or at least to a greater extent, nondefensively constructed.

The participation of earlier phases of development is significant even for relatively stable and mature object relationships. Insofar as symbiotic modes of attachment are involved, the identical nature of the character structures of the partners is again emphasized. Projection of good parts of the self requires a suitable recipient for their projection. Insofar as such intimate relationships are characterized by an interplay of fusion and mutual projection, both partners have to be especially adaptive to each other's projections and this can occur only if the partners are fundamentally similar.

Intimate object relationships enhance both partners. There is, so to speak, a positive feedback sequence. By projecting valued parts of the self and not feeling threatened by making such a projection, because the psyche has sufficient self-confidence and largesse not to feel vulnerable and depressed, both partners benefit. The psyche values the self and through the projection is enabled to value others. The subsequent fusion leads to further increase in self-esteem.

To recapitulate, to project good things onto someone else is an act of generosity, since the person is, in a sense, giving away something that is valued. The external object is then valued not only because of what is projected but the subject is helped by such a projection to discover parts of the partner which he can cherish. The height of intimacy is experienced through fusion, where the subject gives the object his esteemed qualities and at the same time absorbs similar qualities from the partner. The emergence from the fusion, as with the "hatching" (Mahler, 1969) from the symbiotic phase, results in enhancement of the self-esteem of both partners.

Thus, an object relationship leads to higher states of integration for both partners. Something similar happens during a creative act. In creativity, there is projection of something valued which stems from the transitional situation insofar as the subject believes that this aspect of himself has no antecedent which he has incorporated from the external world. Most frequently what he has created is a unique and novel positioning and association of external percepts, combinations which had no counterparts in reality. Actually, to speak of projection here involves a very loose use of the term because usually there is no external object, no person. Still, the creator experiences what is happening to him as a projection; he is putting something of himself into what he feels as an outside situation, whether it is something concrete or an abstract idea. As with an intimate object relationship, fusion and defusion is a regular occurrence in creative activity.

One final distinction is warranted. In both intimate love relationships and creativity, self-confidence runs high and states of fusion may be experienced as blissful and ecstatic. These ego states should not be confused with the megalomania and grandiosity that is characteristic of severe psychopathology. True, there may be some surface similarities, hence the equation between madness, being in love, and creativity, but the psychic mechanisms involved are fundamentally different. As discussed at the beginning of this paper, megalomania and omnipotence are defensive regressions resulting from emotional maldevelopment, whereas intimacy and creativeness are the outcome of a comfortable symbiotic phase and a well-established transitional situation.

SUMMARY

The study of object relationships teaches us that early stages of development continue to participate prominently in determining the quality of later ties. In order to appreciate more fully how primitive psychic structures and processes influence sophisticated adaptations, I described various stages of normal and pathological emotional development. I view omnipotent wish fulfillment and megalomania as defensive adaptations stemming from relatively late developmental levels rather than normal primitive emotional stages.

The symbiotic phase proves to be crucial in determining the quality of later object relations. In long-lasting relationships, such as some marriages, the partners are symbiotically attached to each other and their personality structures are identical.

True intimacy is based upon the mutual capacity to project valued parts of the self upon the loved one and then to achieve pleasurable fusion. The fusion is gratifying and in a positive feedback fashion leads to higher levels of ego integration for each partner.

NOTE

1. This article was written after I read the article by Moss and Lee appearing in the present volume. Their study caused me to extend some of my earlier formulations.

REFERENCES

Benedek, T. (1959). Parenthood as a developmental phase. *Journal of American Psychoanalytic Association* 7: 389-417.

De Bary, A. (1879). *Die Erscheinung der Symbiose.* Strasbourg: Trubner.

Deutsch, H. (1942). Some forms of emotional disturbances and their relationship to schizophrenia. *Psychoanalytic Quarterly* 11:301-321.

Federn, P. (1952). *Ego Psychology and the Psychoses.* New York : Basic Books.

Freud, S. (1911). Psycho-analytic notes on an autobiographical account of a case of paranoia (*denentia paranoides*). *Standard Edition* 12:3-85.

_____(1914). On narcissism—an introduction. *Standard Edition* 14:67-105

_____(1915). Instincts and their vicissitudes. *Standard Edition* 14:109-140.

_____(1920). Beyond the pleasure principle. *Standard Edition* 18:7-64.

Giovacchini, P. L. (1965). Some aspects of the ego ideal of a creative scientist. *Psychoanalytic Quarterly* 34:79-101.

_____(1970). The need to be helped. *Archives of General Psychiatry* 22:245-251.

_____(1971). Characterological factors and the creative personality. *Journal of the American Psychoanalytic Association* 19: 524-542.

_____(1975). *Psychoanalysis of Character Disorders.* New York: Aronson.

Kernberg, O. F. (1974). Further contributions to the treatment of narcissistic personalities. *International Journal of Psycho-Analysis* 55:215-228.

Khan, M. M. R. (1964). The function of intimacy and acting out in perversions. *Sexual Behavior and the Law,* ed. P. Slovenko. Springfield Ill.: Thomas.

Klein, M. (1946). Notes on some schizoid mechanisms. *Developments in Psychoanalysis,* ed. J. Riviere. London: Hogarth, 1948.

Kohut, H. (1966). Forms and transformations of narcissism. *Journal of the American Psychoanalytic Association* 14:243-272.

_____(1971). *The Analysis of the Self.* New York: International Universities Press.

Mahler, M. (1969). *On Human Symbiosis and the Vicissitudes of Development.* New York: International Universities Press.

Moss, D., and Lee, R. (1976). Homogamous and heterogenous marriages. *International Journal of Psychoanalytic Psychotherapy* 5:

Winnicott, D. W. (1953). Transitional objects and transitional phenomena. *International Journal of Psycho-Analysis* 34:89-97.

PETER L. GIOVACCHINI, M.D.

DR. GIOVACCHINI is clinical professor in the Department of Psychiatry at the University of Illinois College of Medicine and is in private psychoanalytic practice in Chicago. He is a fellow of the American Psychiatric and the American Orthopsychiatric Associations, and a member of the American Psychoanalytic Association. He is author of **Psychoanalysis of Character Disorders**, coauthor of **Psychoanalytic Treatment of Characterological and Schizophrenic Disorders**, editor of **Tactics and Techniques in Psychoanalytic Therapy**, and coeditor of **Annals of Adolescent Psychiatry**. In addition, he is a member of the Editorial Board of this journal.

Psychological Unevenness in the Academically Successful Student

Thomas H. Ogden, M.D.

The Tavistock Clinic, London

Among students seen in psychoanalytic psychotherapy, there is a group who present the paradoxical clinical picture of great academic success alongside of quite primitive features in other aspects of their psychological functioning. This article offers an early developmental formulation of this aspect of these students. A clinical description of these patients is presented, including the observation that for each the early mother-child relationship seems to have been characterized by a predominant focus on maternal needs. A case history and summary of therapy of one of these students is discussed. Aspects of the mother-child relationship are explored by means of historical data, memories, and, most important, through various transference and countertransference manifestations. The nature of this early relationship is then discussed in terms of the work of Donald Winnicott and Masud Khan. Finally, an overview of therapy is presented along with a discussion of some forms of resistance and some countertransference problems that often arise in the course of therapy with such students.

There is within the population of undergraduate and graduate students, an intriguing and poorly understood group of students who present the paradoxical picture of very high academic achievement alongside of some very primitive features in other aspects of their functioning. These students very often seem to be involved in long-standing, dependent kinds of relationships with a strong narcissistic orientation. However, it is not so much that these academically successful students present a specific kind of deficit in other areas of functioning; rather, it is the unevenness of psychological functioning itself that seems to characterize them. By "unevenness" I am referring to a discontinuity in maturational levels of functioning, either between different areas of functioning (e.g., an incongruity between capacity for cognitive functioning and capacity for mature object relations) or within a given area of functioning (e.g., kinds of object relatedness demonstrated by a given student). In this paper there will be an attempt to offer a genetic formulation of this apparently paradoxical aspect of these students.

The subject of unevenness of psychological functioning in the high-achieving student has not been focussed on as such from the point of view of possible early developmental determinants. There is a body of literature that addresses this general area, but it tends to focus either on the dynamics of the "underachieving" "gifted" student (Newman, et al., 1973; Gowan, 1957; Miller, 1961; Shaw and McCuen, 1960) or on the psychological problems entailed in being a "gifted" or "talented" student (Schafer, 1960; Torrance, 1960; Keiser, 1969).

CLINICAL ASPECTS OF ACADEMICALLY SUCCESSFUL STUDENTS

The basic clinical feature that this group of students shares is a marked unevenness in psychological functioning, with one aspect of this unevenness being a capacity for great academic success. Such students demonstrate highly developed cognitive skills and equally well-developed abilities for abstract thought and certain types of verbalization. But beyond that, they give one a sense of their adeptness at perceiving and responding to the conscious and unconscious demands and needs of professors, deans, etc. This includes their sensitivity to the fears and anxieties of teachers and their ability to know exactly when their own knowledge, intellectual assertiveness, or other aspects of themselves begin to frighten a teacher or make that teacher experience uncomfortable feelings of rivalry, inadequacy, or sexual anxiety.

In the therapy, in a very subtle way, one often senses that one's moods, wishes, and anxieties are being accurately sensed and responded to. This is not at all in an overt or obsequious form. For instance, I came to a session with one of these students (a medical student), questioning my competence as a therapist. The failure of a patient earlier that morning to show up for her appointment had left me feeling that I was somehow mishandling her therapy. The session with the medical student later that morning was an unusual one in that he was preoccupied with doubts about his own ability to perform as student editor of a medical journal. Formerly, his intellectual competence had never been an issue. In addition, there was the curious insertion of "ya' know" at the end of almost every sentence, and the frequent repetition of the question, "Do you know what I mean?" He seemed to be asking if I ever felt that way. The patient then began to talk at great length, and in a rather pressured way, about the marvellous progress that therapy had helped him make. I noticed that I was enjoying hearing him talk that way. I finally began to wonder whether the patient had sensed my worry about competence and was now trying to reassure me that I had done a good job with him. I pointed out to the patient how hard he was working to convince me he was making progress. He was relieved that I recognized that. He said that he had felt he had been laboring very hard at something during this session, but didn't know what, and still wondered why he felt he had to convince me of his progress. In subsequent sessions, this phenomenon reappeared again and again, and could eventually be discussed in terms of the patient's keen attentiveness to my internal state and his attempts to ameliorate any worries or problems he sensed.

Another striking feature of these students is their heavy reliance on their ability to study and in other ways function academically as a basic organizing aspect of their personality. School holidays are often very difficult times for these students due to the loss of this organizing dimension of their work. Also, any compromise whatsoever in cognitive functioning is experienced as devastating. One such student described his experience on being started on a low dose of Trilafon by a previous therapist as the most frightening experience of his life. There were no extrapyramidal or other noticeable organic side effects, but because he could not study as effectively, he felt that his mind was paralyzed and he felt excruciatingly vulnerable and helpless.

The kinds of relationships these patients become involved in seem to be predominantly of two types. Some become enmeshed in long-standing dependent relationships where the patient feels that his very being is tied up in the other person and he could not imagine how he could live without that person. One freshman, who I would include in this group, took a serious overdose of barbiturates upon being dropped by the girl friend he had dated since junior high school. He said afterwards that every facet of his thoughts and his life seemed intertwined with her. Alternatively, other students of this group tend to become involved in a large number of short-term relationships that are terminated as soon as the patient begins to feel any degree of involvement with the other person. These patients often expressed the fear of being "swallowed up" by a long-term relationship or of losing their freedom to "be themselves" if involved with another person.

A DEVELOPMENTAL VIEW

It is not immediately apparent that the patients presenting the clinical picture described have anything at all in common. And yet, one cannot work with these students without feeling that something profoundly similar is occurring in the transference and counter-transference. In the course of my work with them, I gradually came to the formulation that this similarity derives from their having in common a specific deficit in an essential aspect of their early relationship with their mother: there is evidence that the needs of the mother were the predominant focus of the mother-child relationship, with very little importance placed on the feelings and needs of the child.

In several cases there was a history of maternal depression beginning within the first two years of the patient's life, with the patient and mother sharing the fantasy that it was the patient's talents, especially verbal ones, that would keep the mother alive. In one of these cases, both parents had suffered the loss of their own mother within months of the patient's birth. The father handled his grief with massive denial while the mother turned to the new baby for solace and relief.

Two other patients presented histories of parental divorce within the first three years of life. In both of these cases the child in question was singled out from among the other children as the only person who could fill the void experienced by the mother.

In other cases the evidence for the focus on maternal needs is more subtle. In some cases, one learns of it through the manner in which the patient recounts childhood memories. Such patients devote almost exclusive attention to their mothers' problems and concerns while omitting any mention of their own feelings.

There are also cases where the patients present already-conscious memories of a childhood filled with worry over the mother's difficulties and the feeling that nothing is more important than "making life easier for Mom."

However, as will be seen in the following case discussion, the most important source of information about the nature of the mother-child relationship is the transference and countertransference. The patient who will be discussed is a twenty-five-year-old single, white, female law student, who sought psychotherapy because she was getting very little pleasure out of anything she did and because she felt unable to sustain a meaningful relationship, especially with a man.

from a small city on the Pacific Coast. Her father left one job after another and abandoned the family when the patient was six months old. He quickly remarried and made no further contact with his former wife and children. The patient's mother was a chronically "gloomy" person who on rare occasions could not get out of bed all day. However, she was able to perform her work as a librarian with great skill.

The patient was singled out as the one person who could understand the problems and worries faced by the mother. The patient and her mother talked for hours at a time about the difficulty of being a divorced woman in a small city and about the intense anger the mother harboured toward her former husband and all other men. The patient's mother seemed to love talking in this way with the patient, and gave the patient the feeling that it was the one pleasure in her life. The patient was told by her mother that she was verbally precocious, and they dated these discussions back to a time before the patient was five years old.

The patient did extremely well in school but had difficulty making friends. Instead, she found it easier to be with teachers and was considered a teacher's pet. In early adolescence, the patient began to take school with deadly seriousness and became totally immersed in her work to the exclusion of social contacts.

The patient found leaving home to go to college very difficult and continued to retreat into her studies. Over the next six years, she had a series of brief sexual relationships. Each of these ended with the patient furious at the man involved. The patient would then reimmerse herself in academic work, from which she derived little satisfaction, although she was doing exceedingly well. As this pattern repeated itself over and over, she began to feel that the anger she felt toward these men had more to do with herself than with the men involved. She began to be afraid that she would never be able to have a sustained relationship with a man. She also began to be aware that nothing in life seemed to give her any real pleasure. It was at this point that she sought psychotherapy and was seen in once-a-week therapy for a year.

Initially, the patient talked at length about her childhood, but the focus was almost exclusively on the problems and worries faced by her mother: how to raise three children on her own; how to survive without a husband in a world that requires that you have one; what to do with all the anger she felt toward her former husband and all other men. Almost all the feelings in the hours were connected with the patient's empathic comments about her mother's predicament.

After several sessions I made the following comment: "You've given me a very vivid picture of what life was like for your mother when you were a child, but I almost never hear about what you were feeling." The patient said that she did not understand how I could say that because it felt to her as if all she had been talking about was how she was feeling. But then she began to think back over what she had just been talking about and was jolted by the recognition that it had not occurred to her that she might have had any feelings at all aside from her concern over her mother's problems.

During the school vacation following that session, the patient became extremely anxious about a fear that she knew was "irrational": she imagined that she would be stopped by the police and would not be able to properly identify herself and would be taken to jail. The patient coped with this anxiety by immersing herself in her studies, which significantly calmed her.

In the next session she said that the anxiety she had felt during the week of not being able to identify herself was the same feeling she had had in the last session when she tried to locate her own feelings as a child. As therapy proceeded, she began to view her discussions with her mother about her mother's problems as symbolic of the nature of their relationship. At one point she said quite sadly, "I *was* my ability to talk to her in that way." Over the next several

months, it became clear to the patient that she had been filled with the fear
that if she were to stop providing her mother with this kind of talk, her
mother would have become hopelessly depressed and would have killed her
self, and "that would have been the end of me too—what would have become
of me without a father or a mother?"

These themes repeatedly recurred in the transference in various forms over
the course of the therapy. This patient would again and again ask me what I
was thinking. There was a sense at the beginning of therapy that she could
only define herself in terms of my thoughts, feelings, worries, and problems.
Later in the therapy, when another dimension of this emerged, I said to her
that I thought she was worried that I was depressed and that she might have
to keep me alive with her talk in the way she had done with her mother.

Also, this patient would repeatedly instruct me on issues of therapeutic
technique. It gradually became clear that she felt that my own style was dic
tated entirely according to what would make me feel comfortable and with
absolutely no attention to what was best for her.

As these themes emerged through the transference and were discussed in
terms of her relationship with her mother, the patient began more and more
to experience her feelings as distinct from her mother's and from mine. The
repetitious request to know what I was thinking decreased markedly and on
one occasion she was even able to say she didn't give a damn what I thought
she would have to miss a session.

In addition, as the patient experienced herself as more separate, she began
to feel intense resentment toward her mother for "using" her with so little re
cognition of her as a child who needed to be a child and "not a psychiatrist or
a husband." The patient said she also deeply resented me for luring her into
becoming dependent on me. At that point in therapy, I felt it was important
not to rush in with an interpretation which might have undercut her right to
have feelings different from mine and her right to be angry at me. Instead, I
simply acknowledged her right to her feelings.

Late in the therapy she looked back on the instructions about technique
that she used to give me and laughingly justified this by saying, "After all, I've
been in this business for twenty-five years, which is a hell of a lot longer than
you have."

As the patient began to consolidate her experience of having feelings of her
own, distinct from her mother's and mine, she was then open to feeling the af
fectionate side of her fantasies about her father and found that she could ex
perience real warmth toward men for the first time in her life. This appeared
very poignantly in the therapy, when, toward the end of treatment, the pa
tient cried and told me that even though she still wasn't sure she could trust
me, she had a great deal of love for me. The therapy ended because both the
patient and I were moving away from the city we were in.

This patient's history, as well as the various transference patterns that merged, seem to give strong indication that the mother's internal state ormed the focus of this mother-child relationship. A basic need of this mother was for the child's empathic talk, which was demanded with an implicit threat of suicide or extreme emotional withdrawal. There was practically no recognition of other aspects of the child. Verbal and intellectual capacities developed precociously and seemed to flourish while other aspects of development remained rather primitive. The process of separation from the mother was incomplete, and developing capacities for mature object relations suffered greatly. In addition, the development of a sense of real feeling, originating from within, was severely impaired.

A THEORETICAL CONTEXT

The work of Donald Winnicott and Masud Khan provide an important theoretical context for the clinical work just described.

Winnicott (1945, 1948, 1949, 1951, 1956, 1958) sees normal development as predicated on the mother's ability to provide reliable and empathic responsiveness to her infant's unique physiological and psychological needs. The mother who is "not good enough" cannot be accepting of, or responsive to, the infant's spontaneous gesture and substitutes one of her own which requires the baby's compliance. Also there can be maternal failure to dose and regulate external stimuli, and this results in what Winnicott calls "impingements" which interfere with the infant's internal sense of continuity of his earliest, most rudimentary sense of self. Winnicott believes that such impingements interrupt normal ego development. The infant's ego development is not allowed to proceed according to its own pace appropriate to the maturity of the rest of the developing personality organization (see Anna Freud, 1965, on the importance of the coordination of the rates of maturation of the different developmental lines). Instead, precocious, and as a result, less-integrated, defensive organization occurs in an effort to meet, comply with, and defend against impingements.

Such failures in mothering result in what Winnicott called a false self personality organization, where there is a lack of sense of internal realness, aliveness, uniqueness, and continuity of experience, where functioning is based on compliance with external demands and on attempts to rid the self of instinctual experience (see H. Deutsch, 1942, on "as if" character for another way of talking about a related personality organization).

A series of papers by Masud Khan (1963, 1964, 1969) serves to further refine Winnicott's conception of compliance to maternal needs. In these papers Khan introduces the concept of "cumulative trauma", which involves the exposure of the infant to repeated impingements of a given type and which results in a fixed pattern of compliance to the mother. Over time, cumulative

trauma results in premature awareness of the mother as separate and as hav
ing her own needs, wishes, and demands. The infant responds by establishing
a precocious "pseudo-independence" that give him just enough separatenes
to read the mother as a partially separate object. However, this early differen
tiation of self and object is won at the price of an underlying and persistin;
profound dependence on the mother. Her needs and wishes are not seen a
clearly distinct from those of the self, and the child's orientation to her is es
sentially as an extension of himself (see Greenacre, 1959, on "focal symbiosis
for a discussion of limited symbiotic union of mother and child). There is i
pressure on the infant for early development of defenses so that he can protec
himself against the extremely frightening premature awareness of his mothe
as a separate object.[1]

With regard to the group of students under consideration, one could view
the early demand upon these patients to focus almost exclusive attention on
the needs of the mother as representing an impingement. When repeated over
time, one could see this as constituting a cumulative trauma. The precociou;
development of verbal and intellectual capacities by these patients could ther
be seen as having developed in response to this early "pressure" on ego devel
opment.[2] This precocious intellectual functioning would represent a
premature defensive organization which is necessarily brittle because it is so
poorly integrated into the pace of the development of the other aspects of the
personality. One could also understand the difficulty in self-object differen
tiation faced by these patients as having arisen out of the mother's need for
the child to develop only enough separateness to understand and respond to
her spoken and unspoken needs.

I have come to view the quality of uneveness of psychological functioning in
these patients as an accurate and carefully balanced representation of the
paradoxical dual nature of the mother-child relationship that they experienced. On the one hand, these were intellectually and verbally advanced children who held a rather "privileged" and important position in relation to
their mother. And yet, underlying this, their part of the relationship was
characterized by joyless compliance and pseudo-independence.

ASPECTS OF THERAPY

The case described earlier in this paper is quite representative of the important issues that often arise in therapy with this group of patients. In a schematic way one could say that the initial stages of therapy centred around a
clarification of the nature of the maternal focus in the mother-child relationship. This was done through consistent attention to its various transference
manifestations and through a discussion of the historical data.

This early work made it possible for the patient to make gains in the area of separation-individuation as reflected in 'the way she began to feel more the author and owner of her own feelings. Only after this had been achieved, could the patient then begin to explore the feelings she herself did have, which included her anger at her mother. This anger in turn gave further impetus to the process of separation from the mother (Jacobson, 1964). Once his separation from the mother had been consolidated to some extent, the patient could experience a sense of triumph as she began to explore a range of feelings to which her mother was almost totally closed. This involved the patient's ability to experience and accept both sides of her ambivalent feelings toward men.

Even though each therapy takes its unique form from the patient being seen, I have been impressed by the way the "logic" of the presented sequence of movements seems to hold true in a general way among this group of patients.

I would like to conclude by turning attention to some countertransference problems and to some forms of resistance that often arise in the course of work with this group of patients. These students evoke several countertransference difficulties grounded in the specific nature of their pathology. One such problem results from the fact that it is very easy for us to form strong identifications with these patients, since we as psychotherapists are "academic" people, strongly invested in the importance of talk, and vitally interested in understanding and talking about other people's internal states, with little verbal focus on our own. If not fully recognized, an overly strong identification can interfere with the patient's development of distinct self-object differentiation, which is such an essential aspect of work with these students.

A second countertransference problem may arise because of the adeptness of these patients at "reading" and complying with the conscious and unconscious needs of the therapist. This can result in a false sense that the therapeutic alliance is developing well and that the patient is working satisfactorily in just the kind of exploratory psychotherapy that the therapist likes to do best. If the therapist becomes aware that he is being "read" in this way, it may make him feel manipulated, and, as a result angered at the patient for "duping" him. Being read in this way may also make the therapist feel the anxiety and discomfort connected with feeling like an open book that can be read, including one's innermost secrets.

In the course of therapy with these students, one must be careful not to duplicate the early pathogenic interaction by beginning to see them as special patients. They can be very engaging and can, through their highly developed verbal skill, distinguish themselves as outstanding patients, singularly capable of insightful, richly associational thought. There is very often the demand for an extra session, a changed appointment, or some other acknowledgment of special status that has been earned through their outstanding verbal produc tions. To acquiesce to such demands can be gratifying to the patient on on level, but can also be experienced as a repetition of early experiences whic may have involved the overvaluation of his verbal ability to the exclusion o other more age-appropriate, less-compliant aspects of his personality.

Finally, these patients frequently demonstrate tremendous resistance t exploring the "successful" aspects of their functioning as possible sources o difficulty. Such resistance is understandable in terms of the view of the patho genic interaction proposed which involves an ego-syntonic compliance on th part of the infant that served to reduce tension both within the infant an within the mother. These students often feel that, if anything, their academi abilities represent the one bright spot in their lives, the one area where thing are going well. So the idea of exploring this last refuge is felt to be extremel dangerous. It is important to keep in mind that the strength of this resistanc derives from the centrality of academic functioning as a basic organizing as pect of the personality of these students. For this reason, the resistance mus be approached delicately and at a pace set by the patient.

CONCLUSION

In this paper, an early developmental understanding has been brought t the paradox posed by the psychological unevenness of the high-achieving stu dent. This early focus is not meant to imply that there are not equally impor tant contributions made on other levels of development to a clinical pictur such as the one presented.

The early developmental material discussed here is intended to help con struct the genetic formulations that one continually elaborates and revises over the course of a therapy. These formulations become counterproductive i they divert the therapist's attention from what the patient is currently dealing with or if they are used to offer premature genetic interpretations. However, if used judiciously, such formulations can enhance the therapist's awareness of aspects of the therapeutic relationship that may otherwise go unnoticed.

NOTES

1. In discussing the work of both Winnicott and Khan it is important to distinguish the concepts of im pingement and cumulative trauma from that of age-appropriate frustration. The latter has an essential role ir several developmental processes: Rubinfine (1962) and Jacobson (1964) stress the importance of age-appropri ate frustration in the normal development of aggression and self-object differentiation; Kris (1962) emphasizes its role in structural formation; and Mahler (1961) and Parens (1971) discuss its place in the process of separa tion-individuation. In may be that the damaging effects of impingement and cumulative trauma derive in par from the way they preclude the facilitating role of age-appropriate frustration in these areas of development.

2. It is interesting to note the finding of Newman, et al., (1973) that, in half of the poorly achieving, "gifted" children they studied where there was precocious development of speech, they also found that the mother had been depressed during the child's first year of life and experienced her husband as aloof and nonverbal. These mothers turned to the infant for companionship and eagerly anticipated the time when their infant would learn to talk.

REFERENCES

eutsch, H. (1942). Some forms of emotional disturbance and their relationship to schizophrenia. *Psychoanalytic Quarterly* 11:301-321.

reud, A. (1965). *Normality and Pathology in Childhood*. New York: International Universities Press.

owan, J. C. (1957). Dynamics of the underachievement of gifted students. *Exceptional Child* 24:98-101.

reenacre, P. (1959). On focal symbiosis. *Dynamic Psychopathology in Childhood*, ed. L. Jessner and E. Pavenstedt, pp. 243-256. New York: Grune & Stratton.

acobson, E. (1964). *The Self and the Object World*. New York: International Universities Press.

eiser, S. (1969). Superior intelligence: Its contribution to neurosogenesis. *Journal of the American Psychoanalytic Association* 17:452-473.

han, M. M. R. (1963). The concept of cummulative trauma. *Psychoanalytic Study of the Child* 18:286-306.

_____ (1964). Ego-distortion, cumulative trauma and the role of reconstruction in the analytic situation. *International Journal of Psycho-Analysis* 45:272-279.

_____ (1969). On symbiotic omnipotence. *The Privacy of the Self*, pp. 82-92. New York: International Universities Press, 1974.

ris, E. (1962). Decline and recovery in the life of a three-year-old. *Psychoanalytic Study of the Child* 17:175-215.

1ahler, M. (1961). On sadness and grief in infancy and childhood: Loss and restoration of the symbiotic love object. *Psychoanalytic Study of the Child* 16:332-351.

1iller, M., ed. (1961). *Guidance for the Underachiever with Superior Ability*. Bulletin 25, U.S. Department of Health, Education and Welfare.

1ewman, C. J., Dember, C., and Krug, O. (1973). "He can but he won't": A psychodynamic study of so-called "gifted underachievers." *Psychoanalytic Study of the Child* 28:83-129.

'arens, H. (1971). A contribution of separation-individuation to the development of psychic structure. *Separation-Individuation*, ed. J. McDevitt and C. Settlage, pp. 100-112. New York: International Universities Press.

tubinfine, D. (1962). Maternal stimulation, psychic structure, and early object relations: With special reference to aggression and denial. *Psychoanalytic Study of the Child* 17:265-282.

chafer, R. (1960). Talent as danger: Psychoanalytic observations on academic difficulty. *The College Dropout and the Utilization of Talent*, ed. L. Pervin, L. Reik, and W. Dalrymple, pp. 207-222. Princeton, N.J.: Princeton Univ. Press.

haw, M. and McCuen, J. (1960). The onset of academic underachievement in bright children. *Journal of Educational Psychology* 51:103-108.

'orrance, E. P. (1960). Personality dynamics of under-self-evaluation among intellectually gifted college freshmen. *Talent and Education*, ed. E. P. Torrance. Minneapolis: Univ. of Minnesota Press.

Vinnicott, D. W. (1945). Primitive emotional development. *Collected Papers: Through Pediatrics to Psycho-Analysis*, pp. 145-156. London: Tavistock 1958.

_____ (1948). Pediatrics and psychiatry. *Ibid.*, pp. 157-173.

_____ (1949). Mind and its relation to the psyche-soma. *Ibid.*, pp. 229-242.

_____ (1951). Transitional objects and transitional phenomena. *Ibid.*, pp. 229-242.

_____ (1956). Primary maternal preoccupation. *Ibid.*, pp. 300-305.

_____ (1958). The capacity to be alone. *Maturational Processes and the Facilitating Environment*, pp. 29-36. New York: International Universities Press.

THOMAS H. OGDEN, M.D.

DR. OGDEN is currently an Associate Psychiatrist in the Adult Department of the Tavistock Clinic, London. While a fellow in psychiatry at Yale, he worked at the Yale Student Mental Hygiene Clinic. This paper was awarded honorable mention in the 1975 William C. Menninger Award Competition. Dr. Ogden has published previously in this journal on his psychotherapeutic work with a cerebral palsied patient (Vol. 3, No. 4, 1974).

Peter Shaffer's *Equus*—A Psychoanalytic Exploration*

Julian L. Stamm, M.D.

Training and Supervising Analyst and Lecturer in Psychiatry
Division of Psychoanalytic Education
State University of New York
Downstate Medical Center

In this paper on **Equus**, an attempt is made to explore from an analytic point of view the psychodynamics of the protagonist, Alan, and his therapist, Dysart. Both the preoedipal and oedipal aspects are discussed. The main thesis of my remarks are aimed at revealing how the author seized upon a real event, namely the blinding of horses by an English lad, and has woven this into his own fantasies. It is emphasized that the playwright in addition employed various sophisticated ego functions that enabled him to express these fantasies in Greek mythological terms (the oedipal myth and the voyage of Agamemnon). The final work then comprises a true creative effort, since, as I mention in my introductory remarks on the creative process, it employs both primary and secondary process thinking and symbolism. The final synthesis represents an eloquent mythopoetic expression and combination of id and ego (autonomous ego functions).

INTRODUCTION

Much has been written about the mentally ill artist driven to create. Some have spoken about instinctual drive tension that motivates the artist, or attribute the creative effort in geniuses such as Goethe and Van Gogh to a defensive maneuver that enables the individual to keep his mental illness in a dormant state (Eissler, 1965). Philosophers like Hofstadter (1974) talk about the appropriation of otherness in our culture, taking it into one's self and making a creative gestalt out of the new bond.

For several decades, increasing attention has been paid to specific functions of the ego (Hartmann, 1955; Kris, 1952; Kubie, 1962), such as the sensitiv-

*Presented as part of panel including P. Shaffer, J. Glenn, and S. Gifford before the Association for Applied Psychoanalysis, June 1975, and included here in a slightly edited version.

ity of perception, the importance of cognition, and the capacity for imagery and fantasy that enables the artist after elaborate synthesis to create. Greenacre (1957) has spoken of the artist's collective alternates and his love affair with the world.

I ally myself with those who insist that, in the creative process, instinctual tension and/or conflict is the driving, motivating force. I also hold that without the secondary elaboration of the ego no creative product would be born. Further, in the creative product, we are witnessing a mythopoetic synthesis (Slochower, 1965, 1974). I therefore tentatively suggest (Stamm, 1976) that "any stress or conflict of an intersystemic or intrasystemic nature amongst the various agencies of the mind acts as an unconscious motive for creativity."

This unconscious source is usually of instinctual drive origin (not necessarily neurotic). It is this conflict or tension that provides the driving force to create. Should the conflict be too intense or overwhelm the ego then the creativity will cease.

This may explain why a Van Gogh, driven by conflict, was attempting to ward off his psychosis by discharging his pent-up libido and aggression through his artwork; yet ultimately his ego was overwhelmed by his psychopathology, and he succumbed to psychosis. His art, therefore, might be said to have acted partly as a defense against his illness.

In certain instances, as in the case of Goethe (Eissler, 1963), even a neurotic or psychotic predisposition, if relatively circumscribed, may act as a stimulus toward creativity, provided it does not invade too many ego functions and hence destroy creative activity.

Conflict is only one factor in creativity. In addition, the creative artist or scientist has at his disposal heightened sensory modalities that include an exquisitely sensitive capacity to perceive his surroundings, translate them into fantasy, and then rework the fantasies through various autonomous (conflict-free) functions of the ego such as linguistic and symbolic expression to achieve an original synthesis.

In addition, the artist is capable of using his regression into fantasy in a controlled way, and therefore has available to him the flexible interchange and fusion of both primary and secondary process.

In conclusion, it would be both naive and oversimplistic to attribute creativity to either instinctual drive derivations or to the operation of the ego alone. Each plays a crucial role and must blend with the other to produce an original work.

Psychopathology, itself, is not the source of creativity. When it is controlled and of minor degree it may function as a motivating force and is invariably expressed in the artwork in disguised mythopoetic form. When too prominent, it tends to overwhelm the ego and creativity ceases.

To quote from "Creativity and Sublimation" (Stamm, 1967) :

Creative expression is motivated by conflict, invariably driven by instinctual tension, nurtured by the inheritance and development of hyperacute sensory modalities which have become ingrained attitudes through habit (secondary autonomy). Creative expression can then become a vehicle for the discharge of tension on all levels subserving instinctual demands, secondary autonomous functions, defense functions, and both the reality principle and pleasure principle. . . .

The one common denominator for creative people is their drive, their incessant need to express themselves. . . .

The energic force in many instances remains primitive, at times almost untamed. It would probably overwhelm the ego were it not discharged and dissipated via the creative act itself.

It is this latter tendency, the capacity for a symbolic mythopoetic synthesis that represents the artist's unique contribution, i.e., his ability to abstract, symbolize, and depersonalize — in such striking contrast to the psychotic and neurotic, who personalize and concretize their fantasies.

Perhaps, we should refer to the sublime, partial taming of instinctual drives rather than a clear cut deaggressivization and delibidinization of them. All great works of art are endowed with a panoply of aesthetic ambiguities that stimulate unconscious resonance and empathy in the beholder.

THE EMPLOYMENT OF MYTHOPOESIS

As Slochower (1970) states,
"Man is a symbolic species. . . .Symbolic transformation is nuclear in artistic creativity and sublimation." And further, "The greater promise of creativity in our day lies in those writers and artists whose work has found expression in the plumbing of mythic motifs. Mythopoesis provides the artist with a basic means by which he can establish contact with the buried springs of man's creative genius."

It is my contention that, in the writing of his play *Equus*, Shaffer has done just that. In his portrayal of the character of the psychiatrist, Dysart, and his patient, Alan, the author has seized upon an ugly crime (the blinding of six horses) perpetrated by a disturbed adolescent and woven this into symbolic and mythic expression, reviving for us the Greek tragedy of Oedipus, the voyage of Agamemnon, and the indirect, subtle reference to the pagan Greek gods.

His capacity to seize upon a simple, true event and to weave this into a highly complex, psychological play gives eloquent expression to my introductory comments on creativity. That is, his achievement lies in his ability to depersonalize inner conflict, project it in the form of fantasies, distort further by means of symbolic and mythic association, while at the same time arousing the audience's curiosity and stirring them emotionally, and ultimately achieving an exquisite blend of mythopoetic, symbolic, aesthetic ambiguity.

It is also my contention that while inspiration may be a stimulus to creativity in many instances, it is not a sine qua non. For example, writers such as Shaw compulsively wrote a few pages every day. One does not gain the impression that a driving, frenzied inspiration stirred him on. To make matters more complex, Vincent Van Gogh was frequently in a frenzied state and abandoned himself for days and weeks on end to his artwork.

It has also been suggested that too much happiness and relaxation offer a poor matrix for creativity. But what about a lover transported by his ecstatic state who composes an ode to his sweetheart?

How shall we construe the relationship between therapy and creativity? Will curing a patient destroy his creativity? This has never been established. In fact, most often the opposite holds true. Given a severe neurosis or incapacitating mental illness, effective therapy will release the latent, creative talent and permit it to develop of its own. In other words, once an individual has begun to create, the creative function becomes ingrained in his ego and develops an autonomy of its own. An artist such as Shaffer is capable of utilizing past experience, fantasy and conflict, and molding them into a creative gestalt.

I believe that my analysis of the play will bear testimony to these introductory remarks.

ANALYSIS

Equus is a brilliant play depicting many motifs. It is the creative expression of an unusually gifted, psychologically minded playwright, who is capable of striking his unconscious chords on many levels and presenting them to us in art form.

The following is a brief account of some of the highlights of the play. Alan is a seventeen-year-old English lad who has been legally accused of blinding six horses with a boot clip. Because of the apparent irrationality of the act, he is referred by his attorney, Heather, to a psychiatrist named Dysart. Alan is the son of a lower-middle-income English couple. His mother is a former schoolteacher, rather prim, austere, and devoutly religious. The father is a printer, somewhat irreligious, and punitive toward Alan. He comes from a lower socioeconomic background than the mother. The impression is that Alan's parents are incompatible and that the mother has a disparaging attitude toward the father.

Dysart, the psychiatrist, is depicted as a middle-aged successful therapist, who is incompatible with his wife, sexually frustrated, and suffering from a barren marriage. He longs to escape from his work and agrees reluctantly to accept young Alan as his patient. Jill is a young woman who tends horses in a stable and who is instrumental in getting Alan a job there. Later she attempts to seduce him.

This paper explores the dynamics of Alan's psychopathology, leading to his blinding of six horses, the nature of his sexual aberration with respect to horses, as well as his distorted object relationships. In addition, the psychiatrist's relationship with Alan is examined.

Dysart's identification with Alan, and the dramatic unfolding of the play, are foreshadowed in the introductory dream in which the therapist's unconscious fantasies are reawakened by Alan's criminal, perverse acting out. The dream, therefore, constitutes the prologue of the play.

The dream takes place on the very night Dysart has met Alan, learned about his pathological behavior, and agreed to take him on as a patient.

> I'm a chief priest in Homeric Greece. I'm wearing a wide gold mask, all noble and bearded, like the so-called Mask of Agamemnon found at Mycenae. I'm standing by a thick round stone and holding a sharp knife. In fact, I'm officiating at some immensely important ritual sacrifice, on which depends the fate of the crops or of a military expedition. The sacrifice is a herd of children: about five hundred boys and girls. . . . On either side of me stand two assistant priests, wearing masks as well: lumpy, pop-eyed masks, such as also were found at Mycenae. . . . As each child steps forward, the priests grab it from behind and throw it over the stone. Then, with a surgical skill that amazes even me, I fit in the knife and slice elegantly down to the navel, just like a seamstress following a pattern. I part the flaps, sever the inner tubes, yank them out and throw them hot and steaming on to the floor. . . . It's obvious to me that I'm top as chief priest. It's this unique talent for carving that has got me where I am. The only thing is, unknown to them, I've started to feel distinctly nauseous, and with each victim, it's getting worse. . . . Of course I redouble my efforts to look professional — cutting and snipping for all I'm worth: mainly because I know that if ever those two assistants so much as glimpse my distress — and the implied doubt that this repetitive and smelly work is doing any social good at all — I will be the next across the stone. And then, of course, the damn mask begins to slip. The priests both turn and look at it — it slips some more. They see the green sweat running down my face — their gold pop-eyes suddenly fill up with blood — they tear the knife out of my hand . . . and I wake up.

Some Analytic Speculations About Dysart's Dream:

The day residue preceding the dream may be assumed to encompass Dysart's conversation with Heather, Alan's attorney, and her description of Alan's crime — the seventeen-year-old boy's seemingly senseless blinding of six horses, and Dysart's initial encounter with Alan.

The violence of Alan's act stirs the psychiatrist's own sadomasochistic fantasies. At the same time, there is his wish to escape from the ennui of his work. More than that, he has doubts about himself and, as we learn later, is deeply frustrated over his barren marriage. A cultured man, feeling entrapped, Dysart takes flight into fantasy and in his dream becomes preoccupied with his beloved Greece; but he is also the high priest, the God-healer, who is enslaved by his work and his own limitations and must now take on another case, exhausted as he is.

Toward the end of the dream, the psychiatrist's mask has slipped, symbolizing his exposure to the two priests, and expressing his own regressive identification with Alan and the reawakening of his own oedipal conflict disguised in sadomasochistic form. The two assistant priests with pop eyes obviously represent a condensation during sleep of his perception of Alan's description of the horses watching him, now linked up with his own oedipal and primal scene fantasies — looking and being looked at. Their pop eyes filled with blood also depict Alan's crime of blinding the horses and Dysart's unconscious wish to destroy his own parents for exposing his guilt as well as his threat of castration. The theme of both parents is also triggered by the anticipation of seeing Alan's parents during therapy and his further identification with Alan. The upsurge of his sadistic fantasies, like Alan's, may on the deepest level be aimed at the maternal figure, i.e., the desire to seek vengeance on his wife-mother.

The homosexual theme is also displayed in the dream in terms of the sadistic interrelationships between the high priest and his "double" assistants who "emasculate" him at the end by tearing the knife out of his hand.

In the dream, Dysart is wearing the gold mask of Agamemnon — the conquerer of Troy, brother of Menelaus, and son of the accursed Atreus, later murdered by his own wife, Clytemnestra.

The child sacrifice depicts his regressive doubts about his own work as well as the gratification of his sadistic fantasies fanned by the tale of Alan's horse torture. His work as a therapist is translated into Greek mythological terms. He becomes the king about to embark on his voyage toward intellectual freedom and disavows his psychiatric work with children. To do so, he sacrifices them on the altar of therapy as Agamemnon sacrificed his daughter, Iphigenia, to appease Athena, so that he might set forth to conquer Troy and recapture Helen. However, Dysart, like Agamemnon, is accursed. He, too, is identified with Alan and must pay the penalty for his murderous wishes against his wife, who represents his mother. He, too, is threatened with death by the priests, ready to supersede him at the slightest indication of weakness. Here, too, is the thinly veiled oedipal aspect of the dream—the destruction depicted later in the play of the father-king by the son.

To sum up, in this dream we witness the regressive masochistic wish of the therapist, Dysart, totally identified with his suffering patient, Alan.

Alan's crime plays on the unconscious fantasies of Dysart, who, steeped as he is in pagan Greek mythology, translates Alan's oedipal crime and masochistic need for expiation into Greek mythological and biblical themes.

Hence, the dreamwork represents an eloquent mythopoetic symbol of the entire play—namely, the ultimate wish to become the Christ figure and be destroyed like him.

Dysart, because of his longing to escape and his love of Greece, unconsciously identifies himself as a godlike mortal, in the figure of Agamemnon. Agamemnon, in turn may be equated with the Chirst child and Alan— doomed to suffer.

This is foreshadowed in Dysart's associations immediately after the dream when he states to Alan's attorney, Heather: "It's that lad of yours who started it off. . . . It's his face I saw on every victim across the stone. . . . He has the strangest stare I ever met. It's exactly like being accused, violently accused."

In short, we have the playing out of the author's masochistic wish in identification with Christ, and disguised further in Greek mythopoetic terms. This is perhaps the hallmark of a true creative endeavor.

Alan Strang's Psychopathology

How shall we understand Alan's passion for horses? Does it represent a simple displacement of oedipal desires analogous to Freud's "Little Hans" or is it something far more malignant, bordering on perversion and/or psychosis?

Alan's love for horses became all-consuming. When viewed psychoanalytically, it must be considered a deep-seated aberration—sexual love for an animal. It is also based on a perverse fantasy since it expresses almost a total displacement from a human relationship. Even more, when Alan was attempting sexual intercourse with Jill, at the height of his lovemaking, he could only envision the head of Nugget, his beloved horse, for arousal and satisfaction. I quote from the play:

When I touched her [Jill] I felt him. Under me . . . his side, waiting for my hand. His flanks . . . I refused him. I looked right at her . . . and I couldn't do it. When I shut my eyes I saw him at once. The streaks on his belly. I couldn't feel her flesh at all. I wanted the foam off his neck. His sweaty hide. Not flesh. Hide. Horse hide. Then I couldn't even kiss her.

Obviously, his obsession with horses stood in the way of his capacity to achieve a mature relationship with a woman.

His love of horses began as a little boy when his own mother had delighted in describing to him the equestrian exploits of his uncle, with bowler hat and jodhpurs, depicting the gentlemen rider. She also read to him a story about a horse named Prince, as well as daily Biblical readings from Joab about the sufferings of Jesus and the fierce cavalry charge. The description of the cavalry charge and the horse's foaming at the mouth conveyed a sadomasochistic connotation.

We are also told that Alan had a photograph of Jesus in chains at the foot of his bed before which he would kneel nightly. One day, after observing this, the father destroyed the painting and Alan became distraught. Then the father replaced it with the picture of a horse. The latter thereupon became a substitute for Jesus in chains and the object of Alan's nightly worship. In fact, the father describes how he caught Alan lying prostrate before the horse's picture.

The sadomasochistic fantasy is further reinforced by the unconscious fusion between the picture of the horse given him by the father and the picture of Jesus in chains, resulting in the father's becoming a sadistic, punitive character in Alan's eyes (His father had destroyed his beloved painting). Also, the sufferings of Jesus were referred to daily in the mother's biblical readings. Further, the horse's bit is a symbol of Jesus in chains. The horse then becomes identified with Jesus and his suffering and with Alan.

What can be surmised from these events? During Alan's early childhood, he was exposed to pictures, stories, and fantasies about horses. Moreover, these symbols were reinforced by the mother's emphasis on them. It was his mother who read to him about the horse Prince and described his uncle as a gentleman rider. The latter in conjunction with the theme of Jesus and the father's gift of the picture of a horse replacing that of Jesus in chains add the masculine and masochistic component to the perverse fantasy expressed in Alan's love for horses.

Given the material of the play, how shall we construe the fusion component extant throughout? Mother and baby Alan must have been far closer than the author permits us to believe. Because the mother was disenchanted with the father, who she felt was intellectually and socially incompatible with her, she showered her attention on her only child, Alan. She fed him, touched him, and read to him about horses. The term horse, equ-us, may be understood ontogenetically as an equation of "horse" and "us," "mother" and "me"—a primary identification.

Horse and rider are one. The formula then becomes horse = rider = Alan. Mother, the reader, is also unconsciously linked with Alan and the horse. I suggest that the final fusion fantasy - Alan, Mother, Father, and horse.[1]

Therefore Alan, long before he entertained any oedipal fantasies, must have been influenced by these early pregenital experiences with the mother and father, culminating in a marked fixation on sadomasochistic and fusion fantasies.

Oeidpal Aspects of the Horse Mania

When Alan was six he was exposed to a horse named Trojan on the beach. He was very excited by the ride on the horse which the rider let him take. There was now added his identification with the father and the oedipal theme, since the man on Trojan was an unconscious substitute for the father. Since horse is unconsciously equated with the fusion of the mother and himself, at this point the positive and negative oedipal theses are added to the previous preoedipal themes, reinforcing the bisexuality, and enhancing his passionate cathexis for horses. The theme of the rider and the horse Trojan may also be construed as a displaced screen memory for earlier primal scene fantasies. All these oedipal derivatives apparently were far more threatening to Alan and had to be repressed in favor of the far less dangerous preoccupation with his passion for horses and his emphasis on looking and being looked at.

Scopophilia is a very prominent theme throughout the play. Dysart is obsessed with looking at the horse's head, his eyes, and at Alan. We meet Alan looking at horses and being looked at in t rn. Later on, Alan and Jill are viewing a movie of a nude girl when his own father comes in to peek. Father and son catch each other. The father's interest in observing the nude woman shocks Alan and reawakens his oedipal fantasies, his rage toward his father, and the concomitant guilt and castration anxiety. The latter is corroborated in the unfolding of the plot; that is, shortly after the movie episode, Jill attempts to seduce Alan in the stable, but Alan becomes terrified at the sound of the horses and fears that they are looking at him — a regressive projection of his own oedipal guilt. Jill is unconsciously equated with the mother. This results in his panic and impotence — the denouement of his castration anxiety. However, in defense, he strikes out blindly, projecting his own oedipal guilt and murderous rage onto the horses. At this point, the horses become his punitive father, whom he must destroy. He then proceeds to blind six horses with the boot clip he has been given. (The number six may also be linked to his first experience with Trojan on the beach at age six, at a time when he was struggling with his oedipal conflict that finally culminated in a regressive zoophilia.)

The blinding of the horses, therefore, not only symbolizes his revenge against his father and his wish to castrate him, but on another level, since he is unconsciously fused with the horse, he is symbolically destroying himself — out of a sense of guilt. He is also acting out his narcissistic humiliation turned inwardly against himself and then directed against the horses. In the play, the audience actually witnesses Alan tearing at his own face and eyes.

The blinding of the horses can also be considered a displacement from Alan's hostility toward Jill and his mother. Only a few moments before he had been impotent with Jill, and, as a result of his narcissistic humiliation, threatened her; but instead finally vented his wrath upon the spying horses.

Why the riding at night galloping through the meadows? The riding at night in secret must also constitute a perverse acting out of his early childhood masturbation fantasies related to horses, screening the underlying oedipal conflict. The passion for horses has now become a perverse fantasy since his evocation of the horse has become a prerequisite for his lovemaking, and the horse is the main focus of his love.

Concomitantly with his passion for horses, Alan retreated from life and from people. In fact, with the final discharge of his murderous rage culminating in the emotional blinding of the horses, his sense of reality and reality testing are lost, and he sinks into a transient psychotic state, thus achieving revenge against the mother and father.

SOME FURTHER COMMENTS ON THE RELATIONSHIP BETWEEN THE SEXUAL PERVERSION, FUSION FANTASY, AND COMPONENT INSTINCTS

In many instances, the audience is exposed to a description of Alan's erotic love play with Nugget. This consists of caressing Nugget's body, kissing him, embracing him, and feeling his foaming mouth against his own neck, or Nugget's warm body against his own naked body as they surreptitiously ride through the night. Time and time again, he expresses the wish for union with the horse. "We are one" — rider and horse, Mother and he. Two halves joined in one. Throughout the play, the twinning and fusion are frequently evident, even involving Alan's rhymes about Doublemint Gum. [2, 3, 4]

In this play, the component instincts are also everywhere in evidence: touching and being touched; scopophilia, exhibitionism, and the marked sadomasochistic fixation.

Alan's Faulty Object Relations and His Horse Mania

Dysart glorifies Alan's passion for horses, actually lamenting his own sterile marriage and wondering whether by curing Alan he will destroy the latter's capacity for happiness. Here, of course, the author is expressing his doubts about the wisdom of attempting psychological cure, a much debated current issue and a rationalization that every individual has a right to cling to his illness, insanity, perversion, and even more the right to commit suicide should he choose to. Another common fear is that with the approach to so-called normalcy, the patient's creativity may be destroyed.

This is a common fallacy. For while most analysts would agree that creativity is born of conflict (not necessarily actual mental illness) the ultimate origins of creativity are highly complex and involve many ego functions as well as instinctual derivations. These, in turn (Hartmann, 1955), develop a secondary autonomy and continue to survive as newly built-in psychic structures. A simple example would be the driving of an automobile. Even if we should analyze each movement comprising our ability to drive, this would in no way destroy our capacity to drive, which has become an ingrained habit.

It is obvious to all that Alan suffered from a severe poverty in his object relationships. He is depicted as a loner, with markedly negative feelings toward both parents, without intellectual interests and primarily obsessed with his love of horses.

Thus Alan's character is seriously warped and his emotional growth markedly stunted. Hence when Dysart deplores the fact that in curing Alan he may destroy his happiness is he not employing a denial of his own misery and failing to grasp the malignancy of his teenage patient's illness: an adolescent who is egocentric in the extreme, withdrawn, incapable of mature love and clinging desperately to his outmoded, polymorphous, perverse infantile fantasies? Whether he is an overt pervert or struggling with perverse masturbatory fantasies is of no great importance. Of far greater significance is his terrible suffering and flight from life.

The Mythopoetic Theme

The whole horse complex becomes woven into biblical and Greek mythology (Slochower, 1974).

Nugget is God and associated with the earlier biblical stories about the cavalry charge and mother's reading about the horse Prince.

But, the horse is also linked unconsciously to Trojan—the horse and rider on the beach—and the charging steed riding mystically out of the sea.

The Agamemnon theme is also mythopoetic and brought in through Dysart. Agamemnon is a king, a mortal descendant of God, like Christ, and who is accursed because of the sins of his father Artreus.

Alan and his family are also accursed. The theme of horse and rider on the beach is later repeated in Alan's nightly rides through the misty meadows, representing the climax of his fusion fantasy. He and Nugget are one—both halves—finally united - both rising out of the mist of mother sea and ultimately melting as one identity into its seething spray. [5]

The whole play, then, seizing upon Greek and biblical symbolism articulates the author's fantasies in mythopoetic terms. In short, a simple event in real life—namely, the blinding of a horse—is woven into a highly emotionally charged, symbolic event. In so doing the author has resorted to fantasy, symbolism, mythology, and aesthetic ambiguity—thus utilizing the tools of creative expression mentioned in my introductory remarks.

NOTES

1. Perhaps in part a projection of the playwright's own twin fantasy (see the paper following by Glenn). In addition, a vivid family romance fantasy is also expressed when Alan chants the genealogy of his horse as he kneels before the picture in his bedroom and is overheard by the father: "Prince begets Prance, Prance begets Prankus and Prankus begets Flankus." The mother is said to have read him such a genealogical list, stirring his own romance fantasy and making himself into a prince.

I suggest that this family romance fantasy served Alan as a partial restitution attempt to cope with his adolescent identity crisis. An outgrowth of the fusion fantasy, it enabled him to glorify himself. He had now become one with his golden horse, Nugget, the son of Prince. He, too, by flight into reverie had become a prince.

2. It is tempting to speculate like Glenn that the author's own twinship is now depicted in the play.

3. In respect to this fusion fantasy, Freud (1905, p. 136) refers to the deviation of the sexual object and the popular view reflected in the poetic fable expounded by Aristophanes in Plato's Symposium, which tells how the original human beings were cut into two halves—man and woman—and how these are always striving to unite again in love.

4. Further (ibid. 7, p. 148), Freud refers to the marked variation in the choice of sexual objects even applying to sexual intercourse with animals.

5. Glenn (1974a) has drawn attention to the fusion fantasies of both Peter and Anthony Shaffer and has suggested that the authors' own twinship and desire for fusion were dramatically played out in their creative productions (see Glenn, 1974b).

I, on the other hand, do not subscribe to the view that Shaffer's own twinship was crucial, but believe that Alan's fusion fantasies represent a far more primitive type of symbiosis—the kind of primitive narcissism illustrated in borderline states and psychotics, expressing the unconscious wish for a primary identification.

REFERENCES

Eissler, K. R. (1965). *Goethe: A Psychoanalytic Study 1777-1786*. 2 Vols. Detroit: Wayne State Univ. Press.

Freud, S. (1905). *Three Essays on Sexuality. Standard Edition*, Vol. 7.

Glenn, J. (1974a). Twins in disguise: A psychoanalytic essay on *Sleuth* and *The Royal Hunt of the Sun*. *Psychoanalytic Quarterly* 43, 2: pp. 295-301.

———(1974b). Anthony and Peter Shaffer's plays: The influence of twinship on creativity. *American Imago* 31, 3: pp. 270-291.

Greenacre, P. (1957). The childhood of the artist. *Psychoanalytic Study of the Child* 12:47-72.

Hamilton, E. (1940). *Mythology: Timeless Tales of Gods and Heroes*. New York: New American Library, Mentor Books.

Hartmann, H. (1955). Notes on the theory of sublimation. *Psychoanalytic Study of the Child* 10:9-29.

Kris, E. (1952). *Psychoanalytic Explorations in Art*. New York: International Universities Press.
Kubie, L. (1962). On sublimation. *Psychoanalytic Quarterly* 31, 1:73-79.
Rosner, S., and Abt, L. E., eds (1974). *Essays in Creativity*. Croton-on-Hudson, N.Y.: North River Press.
Shaffer, P. (1974). *Equus and Shrivings, Two Plays by Peter Shaffer*. New York: Atheneum.
Slochower, H. (1970). *Mythopoesis*. Detroit: Wayne State Univ. Press.
Stamm, J. L. (1967). Creativity and sublimation. *American Imago* 24, 1 and 2: pp. 82-97.
_____(1969). Camus' stranger: His act of violence. *American Imago* 26, 3: pp. 281-290.
_____(1971). Vincent Van Gogh: Identity crisis and creativity. *American Imago* 28, 4: pp. 363-372.
_____(1976). Creativity. *Psychiatric Foundations of Medicine*, ed. G. Balis, R. Grenell, J. Mackie, E. McDaniel, and L. Wurmser. London: Butterworth. In press.

JULIAN L. STAMM, M.D.

DR. STAMM is training and supervising analyst and lecturer in psychiatry, Division of Psychoanalytic Education, State University of New York, Downstate Medical Center, and adjunct clinical assistant professor, New York Hospital-Cornell Medical College.

"Pop" Psychoanalysis, *Kitsch*, and the "As If" Theater: Further Notes on Peter Shaffer's *Equus**

Sanford Gifford, M.D.

Associate Clinical Professor of Psychiatry
Harvard Medical School

This paper is intended as an examination of Dr. Stamm's (1975) paper and of Dr. Jules Glenn's discussion of Peter Shaffer's previous work. Its premise is the futility of subjecting **Equus** to a traditional psychoanalytic investigation, as a product of the playwright's unconscious, when the play represents a skillful, highly conscious use of analytic cliches to manipulate the audience. This phenomenon, however, and the play's great popularity prompt some reflections on the nature of kitsch, or false art, and its differences from authentic drama. The experience of kitsch can be identified when the spectator feels coerced by exaggerated, unconvincing theatrical devices, and fails to experience genuine empathy with the characters in a play. In the experience of authentic tragedy there is some element of voluntary surrender, of suspension of disbelief with full consent of will, as in the Aristotelian concept of catharsis. Shaffer's play is discussed as an illustration of this distinction and its relation to pseudoemotionality, the impostor syndrome, and the "as if" personality. In conclusion, the play's failure to evoke a genuine emotional response is explained by interpreting **Equus** as an "as if" tragedy.

INTRODUCTION

I have read Dr. Stamm's (1975) thoughtful, painstaking analysis of Mr. Shaffer's (1973) latest play with great interest and I can agree with many of his interpretations. But my concern is with somewhat different issues, and I am afraid that we are engaged in the solemn scientific ritual of flogging a dead horse. Dr. Stamm's exegesis follows the established tradition of applied psychoanalysis, beginning with Freud's studies of Leonardo and Ernest Jones' of

*Presented at a meeting of the Association for Applied Psychoanalysis, New York, June 13, 1975, and slightly edited for this journal.

Hamlet. But to follow Dr. Stamm any further, in marshalling the full-scale apparatus of analytic interpretation, we run the risk of overkill. If Mr. Shaffer's skillful entertainment is given the same serious scrutiny that great works of art are subjected to, we are engaged in breaking a butterfly upon a wheel. My aim is not to denigrate *Equus* for failing to be a great play, nor to disparage its author for failing to equal the Greek tragedians, but to emphasize a difference between two kinds of artistic intention.

Mr. Shaffer has constructed *Equus* with a proficient command of modern theatrical technique, Greek mythology, and the popular analytic concepts most familiar to present-day audiences, although he has disclaimed (Buckley, 1975) any knowledge of analysis. He has used his equipment quite consciously to manipulate the spectator, who may be excited, titillated, and forcibly "entertained," but who fails, in my experience, to be deeply moved. This is not a failure in aspiration, as if Mr. Shaffer had striven to write a great tragedy and missed the mark, but amounts to a difference in intention. *Equus* brilliantly succeeds in creating exactly what Mr. Shaffer apparently intended: a new theatrical sensation. Since the play is a Christmas pudding, intentionally stuffed with mythological and psychoanalytic plums, there is no need for us, as analysts, to pull them out and misidentify them as the products of the author's unconscious. Thus *Equus* sets the critic a different task from the usual analytic studies of the unconscious forces that move us in *Hamlet* or *Antigone*.

Mr. Shaffer's admirers may protest that all playwrights, great and small, have made conscious use of the dramatic conventions and theatrical devices of their time, their knowledge of ancient myths, and their own intuitive understanding of unconscious forces in human nature. I would certainly agree with this, and I would not deny that Mr. Shaffer has an unconscious, nor with the fact that both his writings and his audiences are influenced by it. But I am suggesting that what we react to in *Equus* is so consciously chosen for its specific effect that we are confronted with a different kind of critical problem. I would also emphasize, as I wrote elsewhere (1974), that my criticism of the play was not based on a distaste for theatricality as such nor on an overly fastidious concern about clinical verisimilitude. Nevertheless, since my view is with the minority, amid widespread critical acclaim, I will try to define the grounds for my opinion more clearly. Admittedly all critical judgments ultimately rest on individual, subjective reactions, but I was reassured, by at least one other dissenting voice, that my response to the play was not hopelessly idiosyncratic. This exception was John Simon's (1975) review, which stated, in vigorous, sweeping, bravura strokes, some of the objections that I had made in my own tentative, nonprovessional way. In one short sentence, he summed up the critical problem: "The play pullulates with dishonesty." Nothing more need be said and further discussion is unnecessary or, at best, superfluous. But since so much has already been written, only the rarest of critics could stop with a one-line review.

In a performance of *Equus*, we are faced with two principal choices. If the play is consigned to a special category of "entertainment" or popular melodrama, its skillful construction, imaginative production, and first-rate acting obviously deserve praise. If *Equus* is subjected to the same criteria applied to other "serious" plays, it is seen to fail by excessive cleverness, by an overload of technical virtuosity. I believe the audience was manipulated rather than ennobled by the violent emotions so diligently generated on the stage. This writer felt coerced by its special dramatic effects, rather than being allowed to surrender to theatrical illusion with full consent of the will. In being *forced* to experience certain strong feelings, without a *voluntary* suspension of disbelief, we recognize that we are reacting to a species of kitsch rather than high art.

In this lies the play's essential dishonesty: *Equus* is kitsch impersonating a serious play. The fact that it very nearly succeeds, at least for a large audience, reflects our deepest yearnings for a new tragedy in a lean theatrical year. Other reasons for its popularity have been ably analyzed by Mr. Simon, including the appeal to affluent "liberals" of madness as a pseudoradical cause, against the familiar perils of social conformity. I would also comment on the play's comforting but false message that equates artistic creativity with mental illness, and psychotherapy with a nonsurgical form of lobotomy. In addition, there are the voyeuristic pleasures of observing the psychiatrist's private miseries, which reveal, not surprisingly, the same crippling sexual conflicts as his patient's. Naturally all this is good news to an audience that contains a sizable number of both analysts and patients, artists and would-be-artists, many of whom welcome a rationale for keeping their cherished symptoms, if they are in treatment, or continuing to avoid treatment, if they are not.

II

This prompts a consideration of the more general nature of kitsch, how it differs from high art, and the various ways in which *Equus* illustrates the problem. Critics traditionally have identified many elements in the aesthetic response we recognize as engendered by false rather than authentic art, and only a few of them can be mentioned. In painting, Gombrich (1954) analyzed a repellent nineteenth-century salon nude in terms of its excessive, quasi-photographic, technical skill. He interpreted the unbridled softness and smoothness as a facile erotic and oral gratification, in the manner of foods that are too sweet or mushy, and noted the spectator's passivity, requiring no effort at visual integration. The clinical equivalent of false art is hysterical pseudoemotionality. Siegman (1954) and other analysts have pointed out the qualities of insincerity and inordinate or inappropriate affect in this syndrome, which resembles the *tragedie larmoyante* of the postclassical French theater. Collingwood (1938) made a distinction between "art as magic," in which the emotions aroused by religious rituals are a preparation for action, and what he called the "amusement art" of substitute gratification, in which emotions are discharged in harmless make-believe instead of action. "An aphrodisiac," he wrote, "is taken with a view of action; photographs of bathing girls are taken as a substitute for it." (This could lead to a consideration of pornography as a special form of kitsch.)

My own emphasis, on the unwilling manipulation of the audience, subsumes many of these elements in false art: the excess of theatrical artifice, that leaves so little work to the imagination, and the passivity of the spectator, whose emotions are coerced by spectacular dramatic devices. In this sense Mr. Shaffer's play has the same relation to tragedy that an electric vibrator has to a natural sexual experience: excessive stimulation, mechanically applied to a passive subject, requiring little active participation.

Another element in kitsch — and to me constituting the major flaw in *Equus* as a moving experience — is the failure to establish some basis of identification between the characters and the audience. Pornographic pictures provide an extreme example, in which the "actors" are pure machines, automata with strangely vacuous expressions. They are "busy little sexual engineers," and their actions are reduced to disembodied anatomical parts, *disiecta membra* detached from recognizable bodies. The same effect is achieved in the surgical amphitheater by the use of drapes, where only small portions of breasts, bellies, and genitalia are exposed. This form of dehumanization is both necessary for asepsis and also helpful to the surgeon in performing his dispassionate task.

The problem of dehumanization is a well-documented one in wars and concentration camps, which depend for their effectiveness on a delicate balance between horror and compassion. Excessively gruesome details elicit self-protective reactions of shock and anesthesia. An excessive magnitude of devastation, beyond the scope of our imaginations, reduces the victims to inhuman form, as in those hecatombs of corpses stacked like firewood. In either case, our capacity for experiencing pity is blocked by the absence of a concrete human object for sympathetic identification. Effective examples that move us to compassion are those that provide human details, like Cartier-Bresson's well-known photo of the Chinese baby, or, at the simplest level, the individual "human interest story."

The failure of *Equus* to evoke full compassion is somewhat more ironic, because Mr. Shaffer clearly intends us to identify with most of his characters, and certainly with both the psychiatrist and his patient. (Perhaps the psychiatrist's offstage wife, the "lady dentist," as Mr. Simon pointed out, and the boy's father, are the only intentionally "unsympathetic" characters.) But in my experience the necessary ingredients of empathy, sympathy, and pity through identification simply failed to come together. I left the theater dry-eyed and disappointed, as if mountains of theatrical virtuosity, brilliant acting, and high-sounding rhetoric had labored in vain, to produce a mouse of triviality, a tiny, banal and completely untruthful squeak of a message. I wondered why much simpler, more hackneyed pieces of theatrical machinery could elicit real tears, that long-looked-for suspension of disbelief. I recalled a really good performance of *Traviata*, for example, or even the old Garbo film of *Camille*, when the audience was moved to tears by the most primitive devices known to the Western stage. Or, recalling a recent play that used many technical innovations, I asked myself why *Sticks and Bones* had seemed the most moving and powerful theatrical experience in a decade. I concluded that *Equus* had failed to move me, not because the psychiatrist and his patient were not clinically plausible, but because they were unconvincing as human beings. As bloodless instruments created to manipulate our feelings, "thought you may fret me, yet you cannot play upon me."

III

Let me restate the problem in different, more serious terms, perhaps more appropriate to this occasion. *Equus* can be identified as kitsch, rather than an unsuccessful but sincere attempt at high art, because it fails the traditional Aristotelian test of tragic catharsis: purification through pity and terror. Mr. Shaffer evokes terror, in various ingenious forms, quite effectively, but he seems incapable of stirring pity through empathic identification with the protagonists of his play. If this failure to evoke pity is also a more general characteristic of false art, Aristotle's time-honored concept suggests some further thoughts. Ancient and imperfect as we may find his original definition of "catharsis" in *The Politics* — Aristotle's promised fuller exposition has not survived — he also wrote elsewhere (*The Poetics*) of tragedy as an "imitation, not of men but of action or life, of happiness and misery." This implies the necessary element of unreality, of theatrical convention, the reminder that we are witnessing players on the stage rather than "real" life. The two passages can be interpreted as complementary, deriving from Aristotle a definition of an effective theatrical experience as a balance of two forces, the arousal of powerful emotions and the simultaneous reduction of their intensity.

The phenomena that illustrate this balance of forces, to maintain an optimal level of affective stimulation, have been discussed in various forms by art critics, analysts, and neurophysiologists. Even before Freud had fully developed his concept of the ego as a self-regulatory system, his notion of the "stimulus-barrier" dealt with defenses against perceptual excitation, which disrupted ego function at excessive levels or even shut off perception itself. The well-known conventions of the Greek theater, like those of our own stage, screen, or television image, reduce stimulation and allow us to experience powerful emotions at safe levels of arousal. Insufficient arousal results in boredom, and excessive stimulation evokes shock, distress, or anesthesia. If events are "too real," our own defenses against ego disruption are mobilized, in the form of distaste, noncomprehension, boredom again (of a different, irritable kind), or a simple desire to leave the theater.

Examples of this balance are even more vivid in the visual arts. Bernini as a sculptor, for example, arouses powerful emotions by his technical virtuosity, but he maintains an element of illusion and abstraction that keeps his works within the canon of high art. Decadent forms of baroque art, by contrast, exceed the acceptable boundaries of illusion, as in Spanish colonial crucifixions, with waxen flesh, artificial blood and tears, "real" hair and eyelashes which are fascinating as high camp, a form of kitsch. The same distinction can be made among contemporary neorealists, as with John de Andrea's *Boys Playing Soccer*, in which the exact replication of human bodies is repellent, while Nancy Grossman's magnificent *Captive*, of black leather and zippers, preserves the necessary affective distance by powerful abstraction. The contrast illustrates the difference between sculpture and the effigies in a waxworks museum.

Returning to *Equus* for illustrations of this balance, Mr. Shaffer seated a symbolic audience, in a quasi-surgical amphitheater on the stage, partially to reduce the affective distance. Thus the audience only *seems* to be involved in the stage action, unlike plays with extensive interpenetration between actors and spectators. Mr. Shaffer's stylized chorus of horses also served to reduce intensity of feeling by abstraction, although I eventually found the masks and hooves rather tiresome. The play's two climactic scenes, the boy masturbating on horseback and the naked sexual encounter in the stable, were obviously intended to arouse the strongest feelings. Of the two, the first was a successful *coup de theatre*, while the second seemed gratuitous and unnecessary. Perhaps the failure of the nude-scene was because, paradoxically, naked bodies on the stage always look more like waxworks than human flesh and blood.

IV

I would now like to comment briefly on Dr. Glenn's discussion of the twin motif in the writings of Anthony and Peter Shaffer. As a twin-researcher myself, I have followed Dr. Glenn's earlier papers (1974a, 1974b) with great interest. At the midwinter meeting of the American Psychoanalytic Association, when he presented the first one, on *Sleuth* and *The Royal Hunt of the Sun*, I was inspired to make some rash comments from the floor, offering to guess the respective birth-weights of Romulus and Remus. From our observations (Fox, et al. 1965; Gifford, et al. 1966) on individual differences within pairs of healthy monozygotic infant twins, I became especially interested in the early developmental aspects of twinship. Like Dr. Glenn and our predecessors in twin-research, our observations found a fascinating interplay of attitudes toward similarities and differences within genetically identical twin pairs. These represented a wide variety of solutions to both the unusually intense rivalry and the unusually close emotional attachment between twins. These variations in twinship patterns included defensive fantasies of absolute equality, as well as complementarity and separate identity. The outcome reflected an interaction between constitutional similarities and differences on the part of the pair, and their parents' selective attitudes toward them. The range of variation spanned a continuum. There were a number of monozygotic pairs raised as fraternal twins whose parents attached great importance to modest constitutional differences. In other monozygotic twins, substantial intrapair differences were denied by their parents and the twins themselves, through a defensive fantasy of absolute equality or identity. This pattern of solution relieved both their parents' guilt about favoring one twin over the other and the twins' own intense competitive conflicts. In our series there were no fraternal pairs raised as monozygotic twins, as if the much greater constitutional differences facilitated the development of separate, individual identities.

Dr. Glenn's studies have found rich and imaginative illustrations of these variations in all the plays of Peter Shaffer and in the relationship with his twin brother Anthony Shaffer. When I saw *Equus*, however, without having read Dr. Glenn's last paper which deals with it (1974c), I found surprisingly little thematic material suggesting twinship. There were frequent fantasies of fusion between horse and rider, the boy being inside or part of the horse, but this imagery has other, more general, pregenital sources than twinship alone. In actual twins, fantasies of fusion, of being half of a once undivided unity, are rare and relatively late manifestations of intrapair differentiation, evolving in latency and adolescence out of the twins' preexisting relationship and the influence of popular beliefs and scientific knowledge about the biology of twinning. Even after reading Dr. Glenn's persuasive discussion of the special relationship between the psychiatrist and patient, their similar sexual conflicts and the psychiatrist's envy of his patient's symptomatic solution to these conflicts, I am not altogether convinced. I wonder, again, whether this theme reflects unconscious derivatives of Mr. Shaffer's twinship or primarily his need for dramatic symmetry, which is quite consciously used for polemic purposes, to suggest that the psychiatrist is as sick as his patient.

In conclusion, my enthusiasm for Shaffer's work as a test object for theories about twin relationships, which Dr. Glenn's early papers had imparted to me, has been chilled by my experience with *Equus* itself. Once again, the high proportion of conscious artifice, as well as a pervasive sense of insincerity, makes me skeptical and extremely cautious in speculating about unconscious derivatives of Mr. Shaffer's relationship with his brother.

After reading Mr. Tom Buckley's lively and informative biographical sketch of Mr. Shaffer (1975), however, I cannot resist one speculation about the origins of this sense of insincerity, as well as the theme of deception and trickery that Dr. Glenn demonstrated so clearly in his discussion of Mr. Shaffer's earlier plays. In Mr. Buckley's article, I learned that the Shaffers were *fraternal* twins, whose mother had an unusually strong need to dress them alike. Thus she treated them *as if* they were monozygotic twins, that is, as more nearly identical than they actually were. In our observations on healthy same-sex fraternal twins, several pairs indicated a sense of being "false twins," that is, not identical but masquerading as such, as if only "identical" twins were authentic. Whether a fantasy of this kind was shared by the Shaffers, leading to a highly developed interest in imitation, impersonation, and transposed identities, it would be tempting but reckless to speculate, without fuller and more reliable developmental data. Clinical descriptions of these identity conflicts, however, are to be found not in the twin-literature but in Helene Deutsch's studies of the impostor (1955) and the "as if" personality (1942). And in this sense, the failure of *Equus* can be summed up as an "as if" tragedy.

REFERENCES

Aristotle. *The Politics*, trans. T. A. Sinclair. London: Penguin, 1962. 8. 7.

_____.*The Poetics*, trans. K. A. Telford. Chicago: Regnery, 1961. 2. 6.

Buckley, T. (1975). "Write me," said the play to Peter Shaffer. *New York Times Magazine*, April 13.

Collingwood, R. G. (1938). *The Principles of Art*. Oxford: Clarendon.

Deutsch, H. (1955). The impostor: Contribution to ego psychology of a type of psychopath. *Psychoanalytic Quarterly* 24:483-515.

_____ (1942). Some forms of emotional disturbance and their relationship to schizophrenia. *Psychoanalytic Quarterly* 11:301-321.

Exhibit (1972). "Recent Figure Sculpture," Fogg Art Museum, Cambridge, Mass., Sept. 15-Oct. 24.

Fox, H. M., Gifford, S., Valenstein, A. F., and Murawski, B. J. (1965). Psychophysiology of monozygotic male twins. *Archives of General Psychiatry* 12:490-500.

Gifford, S. (1974). Review of *Equus. New York Times*, December 15.

_____, Murawski, B. J., Brazelton, T. B., and Young, G. C. (1966). Differences in individual development within a pair of identical twins. *International Journal of Psycho-Analysis* 47:261-268.

Glenn, J. (1974a). Twins in disguise. A psychoanalytic essay on *Sleuth* and *The Royal Hunt of the Sun. Psychoanalytic Quarterly* 43:288-302.

_____(1974b). Twins in disguise II. Content, style and form in plays by twins. *International Journal of Psycho-Analysis* 1:373-381.

_____(1974c). Anthony and Peter Shaffer's plays: The influence of twinship on creativity. *American Imago* 31:270-292.

Gombrich, E. H. (1954). Psychoanalysis and the history of art. *International Journal of Psycho-Analysis* 35: 401-411.

Shaffer, P. (1973). *Equus*. London: Deutsch.
Siegman, A. J. (1954). Emotionality: a hysterical character defense. *Psychoanalytic Quarterly* 23:339-354.
Simon, J. (1975). Hippodrama at the psychodrome. *Hudson Review* 28:95-106.
Stamm, J. L. (1975). A psychoanalytic exploration of Peter Shaffer's play, *Equus*. Read at the Association for
    Applied Psychoanalysis, June 13.

SANFORD GIFFORD, M.D.

DR. GIFFORD teaches at Harvard Medical School and at the Boston Psychoanalytic
Society and Institute, where he is librarian and chairman of the Archives Committee.
He is on the staff of the Peter Bent Brigham Hospital, where his interests include psy-
choendocrine research, developmental studies of healthy twins, and the history of psychoanalysis and preanalytic psychiatry.

Alan Strang as an Adolescent: A Discussion of Peter Shaffer's *Equus**

Jules Glenn, M.D.

Clinical Associate Professor of Psychiatry
Chairman of the Child Analysis Section of the Division of
Psychoanalytic Education
Downstate Medical Center
State University of New York

Psychoanalytic knowledge of adolescence helps us to understand the protagonists of Peter Shaffer's play **Equus**. Alan Strang, the seventeen-year-old who maimed six horses, has undergone a retreat from oedipal wishes to narcissism typical of teenagers. His fragile attempts at achieving a sound sense of identity are undermined when his seeking of a nonincestuous object produces panic and impotence.

Dr. Dysart, the psychiatrist who envies his patient's passion, and fears hurting him through treatment, displays in an exaggerated way countertransferences often seen in therapists of adolescents. In addition, his doubts have some foundation in that the treatment he employs, catharsis, can encourage primitive defenses and the outpouring of uncontrolled, unneutralized drive derivatives. This is more likely to prevent adaptive creativity than the cure the doctor dreads.

Finally, some technical problems in dealing with sublimations in psychoanalysis (which is not Dr. Dysart's form of treatment) are discussed.

INTRODUCTION

One of the approaches that comprise the field of applied analysis is to study a character of a play as if he were a real person and not simply the creation of an artist. In this paper, I will follow in the footsteps of Julian Stamm (1975), who has already examined the personality structure of Alan Strang, one of the protagonists of Peter Shaffer's *Equus*, and the reactions of Dr. Dysart, his psychiatrist. In attempting this analysis I fear that I am tackling one of the most ominous perils in applied analysis. There is danger that the analyst's fantasies will determine his interpretations, unrestrained by the rigorous control

*This paper in modified form was presented as a discussion of Stamm (1975) at the June 13, 1975, meeting of the Association for Applied Psychoanalysis.

inherent in the analysis of a real person. Freud (1900, 1905-6, 1907, 1916), who analyzed the conflicts of character in Hamlet, Richard III, Macbeth, and Gradiva, limited himself to studying *aspects* of their personalities. Similarly, I will focus on what I consider a central issue: Alan Strang as an adolescent patient. In restricting myself to the application of firm, proved psychoanalytic knowledge of adolescent development and pathology to this fictional teenage patient, I will refrain from attempting a complete analysis of every trait that Shaffer attributes to Alan. Furthermore, I will deal only with those aspects of the psychiatrist's reaction to his patient which entail the usual responses to adolescent patients.

There are other approaches as well. [1] (1) An analyst may study an author's traits, seeing how they show up in his creation's content and form. It has been repeatedly demonstrated that literature and art involve the projection of an artist's tensions, conflicts, fantasies, and characteristic defenses and adaptive mechanisms. (2) An analyst may also study those characteristics of an artist's personality that enhance his mysterious creative abilities. This is usually done with a recognition that the inherent core of creativity may never be revealed, that only reinforcing influences can be analyzed. (3) Further, one may assess the audience's responses to the artistic product, the audience's aesthetic experience. This tradition is as old as Aristotle's *Poetics*, in which he states that the audience, experiencing pity and terror, undergoes an emotional catharsis as it watches and engages in an excellent play.

I have previously studied *Equus* and other plays by Peter Shaffer from these latter three points of view (Glenn, 1974a, b, c). In these papers I demonstrated that the author, being a twin, often portrays characters who manifest the traits of twins. I have observed for instance that in many of his plays two protagonists who are similar become increasingly alike as they identify with each other. The main characters are often bound in an intensely ambivalent relationship typical of twins. They often attack each other, yet love and complement each other. A fantasy that twins are half-people leads to a preoccupation with halves and doubles. I also offered the hypotheses that twinship may enhance an artist's creativity and that the audience may react aesthetically to the disguised twins in a play.

In the present paper I will discuss the psychology of adolescence and its manifestations in Alan Strang's pathology, the nature of the treatment used in *Equus*, Peter Shaffer's suggestion that psychotherapy interferes with creativity, and Dr. Dysart's countertransference to Alan as an adolescent.

A SYNOPSIS OF *EQUUS*

The focal relationship in Peter Shaffer's play is between the characters of the psychiatrist, Dr. Martin Dysart, and his seventeen-year-old patient, Alan

Strang. The disturbed boy had been brought to him for treatment in a hospital following a violent outburst during which he blinded six horses with a metal spike. The youth is taciturn and uncooperative at first, and the psychiatrist's interviews with his parents provide a great deal of background information which clarifies the nature of the disorder and its origin. We learn that there is an ideological conflict between the parents. The mother is a devout Christian who fosters her son's religious interests by reading to him from the Bible. The father is an anticlerical socialist. He forbids television to his son and attempts to inculcate in him a work ethic, urging him to read, study, and be productive.

When the boy was twelve, Mr. Strang, who opposed his wife's religious indoctrination, removed from the wall in front of Alan's bed a portrait of the chained Jesus being beaten as he carried the cross to Calvary, a picture that the boy had purchased. For a few days thereafter Alan cried incessantly. He recovered his composure when his father replaced the picture of Christ with a photograph of a staring horse. Then, eighteen months before Alan's hospitalization, his father was dismayed to discover Alan bowing before this picture, beating himself, and chanting Bible-like phrases, "Prince begat Prance . . . and Prance begat Prankus . . . " (p. 49), etc.

The father could not thwart his son's mythopoetic urges. Alan's love for Jesus was transformed into a fascination with horses. A number of experiences had led to this preoccupation. Mrs. Strang's family had an equestrian tradition. She repeatedly talked of her grandfather's attachment to horses and had told Alan stories about a horse, Prince, that only one child could ride. Alan recalled with excitement the time that an elegant young man, after his horse had rushed at the six-year-old Alan, lifted him to his shoulders and galloped with him. The boy became outraged when his parents interfered and his father pulled him off the horse causing him to fall. In addition, his mother reported that Alan had been attracted to *equus*, the word he used as a generic name for horses, "because he'd never come across one with two *u*'s together before" (p. 32).

Because of his intense interest, Alan acquired a position as a stable helper. Although he pretended not to ride horses, he actually did so secretly, riding naked at night. He imagined that the horse, Equus, would say to him, "Ride me . . . Mount me, and ride me forth at night . . . I see you" (p. 65). and that Equus would save Alan by bearing him away.

The psychotherapy proceeds uncertainly. At first the patient refuses to talk. Instead he sings television commercials, including, in the original British version, his favorite, the advertisement for Double Diamond beer:

> Double Diamond works wonders,
> Works wonders, works wonders.

Double Diamond works wonders, works wonders
for you! [p. 21]

In the American production, a commercial for Double Mint Gum, a popular one in the United States, replaced this:

Double Your Pleasure
Double Your Fun
Try Double Mint, Double Mint,
Double Mint Gum.

Eventually, therapist and patient establish a temporary *modus operandi*. Alan agrees to reply to the psychiatrist's questions if the physician responds to his; they are to answer in turns. Early in the treatment Alan asks Dr. Dysart whether he engages in intercourse with his wife. The psychiatrist, infuriated, refuses to see the boy for a period of time. The answer, we later learn, would have been no. The audience's learning of Dr. Dysart's lack of sexual passion foreshadows Alan's description of his own potency problem, and clarifies aspects of the doctor's envy of his patient.

We come to see that the two protagonists are similar in many ways. Dr. Dysart is fascinated by Greek mythology, while Alan has developed his own mythology based on the worship of Equus. However, Dr. Dysart believes that the boy has succeeded where he has failed. Alan lives his myth with passionate conviction, while the psychiatrist merely reads about Hellenic culture and makes occasional uninspired visits to Greece. His envy of Alan is complemented by his fears of injuring him. Just as the boy is impelled to injure horses, so the psychiatrist is plagued by impulses to cut. Dr. Dysart describes a dream in which he, as a sacrificial priest, removes children's hearts. He views the treatment itself as a destructive process; perhaps by removing Alan's symptoms, curing him, he will deprive him of something vital. So great are his observations that Hesther, the magistrate who sent Alan to Dr. Dysart, has to urge him to continue the treatment.

The psychotherapy relies heavily on the cathartic recovery of memories. In order to impel the patient to produce material Dr. Dysart hypnotizes him and urges him to overcome resistances by talking into a tape recorder while alone. Dr. Dysart tricks the patient by giving him a placebo which he pretends will make him reveal the truth; in addition, paradoxically, he reveals the trickery to the patient.

As the treatment progresses, the patient acts out his ecstatic desire to ride the horse and to fuse with Equus. Alan imagines himself saved by Equus as the horse bears him away, shouting, "Two shall be one" (p. 65). Alan shrieks: "I want to be *in* you! I want to BE you forever and ever!—*Equus, I*

love You! Now! Bear me away! Make us One Person!" At this point in the play
the horse is both a substitute for Christ and a father surrogate to whom he is
ambivalently attracted, whom he loves and flagellates.

Much of the play is presented in a stylized manner, but the penultimate
scene is starkly realistic. Alan recalls having been introduced to sexual intercourse by Jill, the twenty-year-old who had obtained the job in the stable for
him. The seduction occurs after the pair are discovered by Mr. Strang at a
pornographic movie to which Jill took Alan. Alan is disturbed at being caught
watching the film by his father and also at his father's seeing the obscene
show. Realizing that his father, whom he had imagined ascetic, has earthly
desires, Alan becomes disillusioned with his father — and his mother.

As Alan vividly remembers the events leading to his stabbing the horses, the
audience sees Jill take Alan to the stable, where he and she undress. Fearing
that the horses might see him during intercourse, Alan insists on locking them
out. Alan and Jill attempt intercourse in the stable as the sounds of the horses
are heard in the background. The boy at first states that he enjoyed superbly
successful sex relations. But when Dr. Dysart contends that he is lying, Alan
admits to his impotence. Panicky, he imagined the horses looking at him and,
in reaction to this, he stabbed a sharp grooming instrument into the horses's
eyes after crying, "Equus . . . Noble Equus . . . Faithful and True . . . God-
slave . . . Thou — God — Seest — NOTHING!" (p. 102) Having blinded the
animals, Alan collapses to the ground, stabbing at his own eyes.

This exciting recollection and the associated abreaction leads the psychiatrist to predict that the boy will soon be cured. Then, in a final soliloquy, Dr.
Dysart expresses his dissatisfaction with the result. Alan will now be free of
pain and be normal, but he will have lost his passion and his poetry. The physician has harmed his patient. "I stand in the dark with a pick in my hand,
striking at heads" (p. 105).

DISCUSSION

In attempting to analyze Alan Strang I feel the need for some incontestable
fact on which to anchor my speculations. As I have indicated, the fact around
which I will organize my discussion is that Alan Strang is an adolescent. Certainly we have sufficient knowledge of that developmental stage to help us
evaluate and understand the complexities of the play.

It is typical of adolescence [3] that there is an increase in the intensity of
drives, both the aggressive and libidinal urges. This comes from bodily
changes and the increase in hormones that occur at puberty. With the increase in drives, there is both great attraction and antagonism to one's parents. Since the possibility of actually achieving tabooed and dangerous oedipal wishes is so great, the teen-ager must mobilize potent defenses to stem

their power. One such mechanism is to turn away from the parents, to find new objects for gratification; the mechanism obviously contains an adaptive value. Alan attempts this in his romance with Jill. But his love for her is clouded by oedipal images and prohibitions and accompanying intense anxiety. Impotence and the tragic mutilation of the horses occur as a consequence. Alan fails in his attempt to find a nonincestuous object so Jill becomes a tabooed oedipal object.

Another means of warding off the overwhelming oedipal wishes of adolescence is regression to narcissism, i.e., to an early stage of development in which one loves oneself or an extension of oneself. In the symbiotic stage the child pictures himself as fused with his mother much as Alan fantasizes himself fused with the horse he rides. In later derivative fantasies one may wish for a twin, a double, or a mirror image. Derivatives of Alan's wishful fantasy of being a twin are seen in his preoccupation with doubles. He recites the Double Diamond beer jingle in the original play and the Double Mint Gum commercial in the American version. He is fascinated by the generic name *Equus*, containing two *u*'s juxtaposed. (Alan's mother makes this latter point in the play.) The twin fantasy also shows up in Alan's desire to be like the therapist, to alternate with him in asking and responding to questions, and in his interest in horses, creatures with whom he might fuse, so that "two shall be one" (p. 65).

The reader will realize that this construction springs from the characteristics of the protagonist and will not at this point be considered as Shaffer's projection. The regression to narcissism and the appearance of fantasies of fusion enable the teen-ager to achieve disguised oedipal gratification while gratifying preoedipal wishes for union. Hence Alan's becoming one with a horse is at once an expression of oedipal and preoedipal desires for intimacy with his mother.

Narcissistic wishes and fantasies are typical of adolescence. They find expression in a spectrum of phenomena including adolescent convictions of omnipotence; wishes for omnipotentiality; teenage idealism; desires to experience feelings of fusion which are gratified by ingesting such drugs as LSD and marijuana. Even sadomasochistic relationships may contain a narcissistic element. Alan's withdrawal, his self-preoccupation, his desires to fuse with horses, his latent homosexuality, the fantasy that he was twin that I have postulated—all of these are derivatives of narcissistic regression typical of the age. That the narcissism is more intense in Alan than in most teenagers can be attributed to more intense and threatening oedipal wishes in the boy and to a greater degree of fixation at pregenital levels of development than occurs in most children.

Because marked regression is frequent in teenagers, it is often difficult to establish an adolescent patient's diagnosis. Often the diagnosis can be determined only after the treatment clarifies how firmly an oedipal constellation has been established, the severity of the distortions of the Oedipus constellations, and the degree of preodipal fixation and arrest. Even in schizophrenics one sees the appearances of an Oedipus complex in adolescence, but the content may be bizarre, the distorting influence of early developmental stages extreme, and the propensity to regression uncontrolled. Because Shaffer is a playwright, not a clinician, he did not find it necessary to provide the data necessary for me to decide Alan's diagnosis. Hence I have limited my speculations in this regard. Rather than dwell on diagnosis I have emphasized the dynamics and developmental characteristics typical of his adolescent stage. Parenthetically, however, I will add that it appears to me that Alan was at least borderline and probably psychotic.

Of course there is more to adolescence than drive aspects. Alan is an adolescent futilely searching for a firm identity. Identity formation (Erikson, 1963; Blos, 1962), a prime task of this developmental stage, consists of attaining a sense of oneself as a more or less integrated individual, different and separate from others. To accomplish this, the young person reorganizes his family traditions and his identification with other significant persons into a coherent whole. He develops a feeling of continuity with the past and a sense of a future with a purpose. If his ideals and plans are achievable and adaptive, his identity is more likely to remain stable. Stability is also more likely when the psychic energy invested in the sense of identity is largely neutralized.

As we learn in the course of the play, Alan's father is a rigid moralistic but antireligious socialist who works as a printer. Although Alan's incorporation of his father's prohibitions into his personality has an inhibitory effect, I believe his father's moral influence also appears in Alan's religious system in which Equus is God, the Father. However, for the most part Alan's inability to identify with his father predominates. He could not tolerate being a salesman of electrical appliances, a position similar to his father's job as a seller of printed matter. Further, he could not allow himself to be a student and reader as his father and mother were. His father bemoans the fact that Alan prefers watching TV to reading. Although Mrs. Strang, a teacher, is more tolerant of Alan's intellectual failures, both parents wished he had become a scholar.

Alan's mother's affirmative influence on his mythopoesis is more apparent. Mrs. Strang's grandfather had been an aristocratic equestrian, a member of a horsey family. Through her stories about horses she encouraged her son to continue in this tradition. She also tried to imbue him with her Christian fervor by reading him the Bible. Alan identified with her and her values despite his father's intense antagonism to nobility and religion. Finding his mother's ethos compelling but unacceptable, Alan invented his own personal religious system which included in a disguised form both his mother's religious passion and family tradition. Equus, the horse, became the god with whom he fused. This substituted for the Christian God with whom Jesus (whom Alan identified with) united and was one.

His pagan fantasies and rites had to be hidden from all. He rode his horse *secretly* at night, not only because the perverse nature of these acts had to be kept secret. His riding the horse while *naked* indicated the erotic nature of his conscious and unconscious fantasies. In addition, his identity, in which he was similar to and different from his parents, had to be kept quiet. Each parent would have been shocked by his rejecting their respective *Weltanschauungen*.

Alan's pagan identity broke down (identity diffusion occurred, Erikson, [1963] would say) under the influence of his attempt to achieve tabooed oedipal gratification with Jill. For many people oedipal fantasies reinforce a sense of identity. Feeling like his father can be a central organizing factor in a boy's identity formation. But for Alan identification with the father is forbidden and dangerous, cathected with libidinal and aggressive energy. Father is the prohibiting watcher whose piercing eyes had to be destroyed in a displaced attack on Equus. The horse also represented Jill-mother who had to be fused with and penetrated sexually. Alan was uncertain about his gender identity and hence a latent homosexual—a negative oedipal—penetration was involved also. Once the identity structures were invaded by these oedipal elements cathected with raw libidinal and aggressive energy, they failed to sustain the patient. Already fragile, Alan's identity formation was shattered after he attempted intercourse in the stable in the presence of his god-horses, after seeing his father watching the obscene movies and in turn being seen by his father as he, Alan, watched. His disillusionment with both his parents after catching his father at the skin flick, although it seemed to free him, also contributed to his narcissistic regression and, related, his identity diffusion. Such disillusionment in adolescence often leads to regression to primitive states in which one imagines fusion with idealized parental imagos (Kohut, 1971).

Adolescence, as is well known, is a period in which there is often a creative surge. It is a sad fact that often when adolescence passes, imagination becomes less marked and life becomes more humdrum, less vibrant. The factors that make adolescence a creative period include the increase of drives we have discussed. There is tremendous pressure to produce derivatives of such drives; artistic activities are important means of achieving this. The advance in cognition that appears with adolescence (the stage of formal operations, as Inhelder and Piaget [1958] call it) enables youth to produce more coherent art forms while imagination and hypothesis formation bloom. At the same time that the teen-ager becomes more able to use abstract logic and secondary processes he is able to (often has to) regress so that primary process thinking can appear. The proper balance and sequence of primary and secondary process thinking can enhance creativity. This involves regression in the service of the ego (Kris, 1952) and the capacity to snap back and utilize secondary processes for optimal and artistic organization (see also Hartmann, 1964).

Narcissism can feed the creative process in several ways. The urge for fusion with objects, the confusion of self- and object-representations results in greater projection, identification, and empathy; these can all be helpful in creativity.

The creativity of the adolescent can be adaptive or it may fail in this respect and succeed only in the creation of pathological thought. Alan's creative urges could not be channeled to produce artistic daydreams that even a limited audience could share. Instead they led to a tragic action which ended in criminal prosecution and hospitalization.

This leads us to the prime philosophical question that the play raises. Can the therapeutic work of the psychiatrist interfere with the worship, the passion, the imagination, the creativity of the patient? Is such an interference inevitable? Dr. Dysart fears that, through his treatment, he will destroy his patient's mythopoetic capacity. When I saw *Equus* the audience applauded every speech that indicated that this was true, that the restraints of civilization were indeed harmful; and the audience was strangely silent when Hesther argued that Dr. Dysart could save his patient from the torture of his symptoms.

Indeed the author of the play (Shaffer, 1975) made three palpable points in the discussion of *Equus* at the Association for Applied Analysis. (1) He thought that Dr. Dysart's arguments were more compelling than Hesther's because Dr. Dysart is a more complex and interesting person. (2) Society ordinarily produces ordinary, uninspired people who lack passion and worship. Although Alan Strang possessed but modest creative capacities—he was certainly no genius, no Mozart—these did exist and manifested themselves in the fantasies which he carried out in action. He succeeded in his disturbed way in elevating himself above the stultified mass of the general population. Psychiatric treatment, while relieving him of his symptoms, also would deprive him of the modicum of passion and worship that he possessed. As a result of treatment, Alan would become dull like most people in our society. (3) Shaffer did not believe that successful treatment could result in an adaptive displacement of passion to other areas. The treatment could only crush the creative urge, destroying it completely.

Shaffer presents both sides of the argument. Hesther favors the psychiatric cure while Dysart worries about its ill effects. But the author tilts the scale so that the menace of psychotherapy is emphasized. He makes Dysart more interesting and the audience sympathizes with his fear of injuring the patient.

I would like to make several comments which I hope will clarify some of the issues. First we must recognize that the treatment used in the play is not psychoanalysis but is another form of psychotherapy. The author never calls it psychoanalysis, but many people who have seen the play believe it is.

In psychoanalysis the patient freely associates and the analyst makes interpretations to help him understand himself. This does not happen in the play. The doctor hypnotizes the patient. He tries to trick the patient, with the use of a placebo for instance, rather than remaining straightforward and honest as an analyst would be. Under such circumstances the transference or transference neurosis could not be analyzed, an essential of psychoanalysis. In fact, Dr. Dysart offers few interpretations, and these were intended to prod Alan to repeat his traumatic experiences emotionally. The audience may, as Stamm (1975) and I have, make their own interpretations, but the doctor of the play does not. This of course is artistically potent, but it is not psychoanalysis. In fact, if the author presented an actual psychoanalysis, the play would certainly not be the hit that *Equus* is. Without condensation and artistic alteration such a play would be an aesthetic disaster.

The treatment that Dr. Dysart carries out is one in which the cure depends on abreaction or catharsis, on the remembering, with an intense emotional counterpoint, a traumatic precipitating event and traumata from childhood or later. This is similar to the treatment that Freud (Breuer and Freud, 1893-5) developed prior to his markedly modifying it in the creation of psychoanalysis. Like Breuer and Freud Dr. Dysart used hypnosis to encourage catharsis. but, as I say, the treatment in *Equus* is not psychoanalysis. Freud abandoned his earlier abreactive treatment (which he used in conjunction with interpretations) as being limited in the degree of help it could provide.

Such treatment can be dangerous in that the patient may be encouraged to surrender mature defenses and may resort to primitive defenses instead. There may be an uncontrolled outpouring of emotion that will not stop. A serious psychosis may be precipitated or prolonged. If so, creativity, in the sense of being able to produce an organized product, will not be enhanced. Instead wild chaotic, psychotic fantasies would be unleashed. Abreaction treatment is especially perilous to adolescents who normally regress and then snap back to more mature functioning. Abreactive treatment interferes with the balance between regression and recovery. It encourages primitive expression rather than maturity. It encourages identity diffusion, confusion of self-representation and object-representation at the expense of firm identity formation. In teenagers who are in danger of failure to return to mature functioning such treatment may result in a sustained psychotic state.

Not only adolescents who are prone to regression, but borderline or psychotic patients (which may well include Alan) as well, do poorly when subjected to treatments encouraging regression without providing the interpretations necessary for recovery.

On the positive side, such a treatment as Dr. Dysart prescribed might be successful in that the patient might fantasy the therapist a powerful magical doctor with whom he could fuse; if the patient can thus fortify himself without developing paranoid ideation, he may recover from a serious illness. If then the doctor encourages the patient to be creative (and if the patient has the inherent capacity), the outcome from the point of view of developing an artist may be admirable. Such urging, whether overt or implied, might result in a superego alteration in which creativity becomes an ideal rather than forbidden. You will note that Dr. Dysart, although he did *act* the omnipotent godlike doctor and offered himself as a sane substitute for Equus, did not *feel* all-powerful. Nor did he encourage his patient's creativity.

In my opinion Dr. Dysart, aside from his countertransference and counteridentification, had good reason to worry about the outcome of his treatment. I don't think that, even allowing for the artistic distortions of the treatment that were necessary to produce a convincing but not altogether realistic play, the therapy would have worked at all. Dr. Dysart's anxiety was justified but misplaced. Instead of fearing that he would cure his patient of his painful symptoms but remove his passion and his creative powers, it would have been more realistic for him to worry lest Alan's disorganization blossom while he failed to achieve constructive creativity.

As for psychoanalysis 4 itself: Can we say with confidence that it would never interfere with creativity? Psychoanalysis consists, as I have said, of the patient's freely associating and the analyst helping the patient to understand himself. To achieve this the defenses as well as the drives are analyzed and the transference must be interpreted.

Very often the interpretation enables the patient to reorganize his defenses in a more adaptive way, so that too much energy is not utilized in controlling conflict and fighting drives. Then not only are symptoms alleviated, but energy is released for creative purposes. Pathological passion can be transformed into truly creative ardor.

Since, however, sublimation involves the use of defenses, the analyst may often avoid analyzing defenses that support creative activity (Bornstein, 1949). Nevertheless, when there is a breakdown in the sublimation, analysis can help to restore it.

For instance, an adolescent patient of mine, a superb musician, could produce beautiful sounds with his French horn. There were indications that this was a sublimation of his desire for freedom of expression on the pot. His being toilet trained quickly and cruelly by his aunt when his mother was ill at the age of two and one-half had so distressed him that he started to stutter. The stuttering was his displaced way of saying he would not let the BM out as others demanded. His French horn playing was his triumphant way of saying that he would do it his way, beautifully and powerfully. At one point unfortunately he started to produce stutterlike sounds while playing his instrument.

Although previously no interpretations of his sublimation were made, it was now interpreted. He was stuttering on the horn in order to rebel against demands for anal compliance that had first occurred when he was an infant. This interpretation enabled him to play well again.

Psychoanalysis is a potent treatment; interpretations can support or interfere with sublimation, with creativity. In some cases the incapacitating neurosis of the patient may have invaded the autonomous ego functioning, so that there is no way interpretations can be made that exclude recognition of sublimation. Sometimes such interpretations will result in the patient's being aware of things in such a way as to interfere with his creativity. This is rather rare. Usually apt interpretations of sublimation have a helpful influence and not an obstructive one. My experience has been that psychoanalysis, properly applied, most often frees energy for creativity. A patient's fear that the analyst will hurt him or take something from him can generally be analyzed and unconscious antecedents uncovered.[5] A therapist's fear of injuring his patient may have many determinants. In this paper I will emphasize certain countertransferences that often occur on the part of therapists of adolescents.

As I have said, Dr. Dysart feared he would destroy Alan's passion, his worship, and his mythopoetic powers. The doctor envied his patient's possessing these valuable assets which he felt he himself lacked. He envied Alan's ability to live his fantasies, to carry them out in action. Condemning himself for his "own eternal timidity" (p. 79), he imagines Alan accusing him, saying, "At least I galloped. When did you?" (p. 79) Whereas Dr. Dysart could read about Greece or visit it properly but not passionately, he could not realize his wish to immerse himself in the primitive pagan world. Although Alan was impotent, Dr. Dysart nevertheless appeared to envy his sexuality.

Here we see common reactions of an adult to an adolescent: idealization and envy.

There is much for an adult to envy in a teenager. Youth has life ahead while the adult's is closer to the end. The adolescent is nearing his peak, while the grown-up's powers are waning. The adolescent is often taller, stronger, sexually more driven, more imaginative, more confident, feeling capable of all, omnipotential. He will soon replace his father. Who would not wish for these powers? The adult has decided he cannot accomplish all, cannot be the Renaissance man, and has committed himself to limited accomplishment. Longing for a past time when all was possible, he may well envy youth.

Although this picture of the adolescent is accurate it is incomplete. Youth is also often tortured, limited, impotent, often unable to achieve anything because of a desire not to yield in any possible field of accomplishment. Youth is often driven to dangerous action, anxious and wary. Adolescents are in the process of giving up their attachments to their parents and hence are depressed and lonely, frightened of old and new ties.

Adults often forget the details of their adolescence. Instead of remembering the pain, the grown-up may idealize his past and recall only its glory.

Such is Dr. Dysart's plight. Having restricted his life in a commitment to medicine, he envies his patient's powers. Having failed to achieve full potency and an ideal happiness, he is jealous of the adolescent's distorted sexuality and his powerful passion. Being envious he wishes to harm his patient and fears it. Dr. Dysart's dream expresses the wish to be like Alan, but it also depicts the forbidden wish of an envious man to cut his patient's soul.

Now let us return to Alan Strang and to Peter Shaffer. We have seen that Alan as an adolescent regressed to a narcissistic state which involved desires to fuse, to have a double, and to be a twin. Peter Shaffer's vivid dramatic depiction of Alan's particular conflicts is possible because the author drew on observations of the world about him. He incorporated and modified a true story that he had heard about a boy who blinded horses (Buckley, 1975). He utilized his knowledge of psychiatry and sought the help of physicians to clarify his thoughts about therapeutic processes. He also drew upon his own past and present inner experiences, as an adolescent in the past and as a twin in the past and present. His sources may well be largely unconscious but they are powerfully used. His conscious and unconscious reservoir of experiences from the past enabled him to write a vivid and compelling play in which adolescence and unconscious narcissistic fantasies stir the audience. His capacity to fuse knowledge gained from the world about and inner experiences is one of the hallmarks of that elusive, inherent capacity for creativity that we keep trying to understand.

NOTES

1. See Eissler (1968).

2. This summary is a modification of the description of *Equus* that appeared in Glenn (1974c).

3. The reader is referred to the following articles and books for detailed studies of adolescence: Blos (1962), Erikson (1963), A. Freud (1958), S. Freud (1905), Glenn and Urbach (in press), Pumpian-Midlin (1965), Spiegel (1951, 1958).

4. I am not implying that psychoanalysis would be the appropriate treatment for Alan. More would have to be known in order to make a proper decision about his therapy. Possibly psychoanalytically oriented therapy and/or medication would be necessary for his recovery.

5. Often fantasies of being deprived of food or mother, of having anal products removed, or of being castrated lie behind fears that the analyst will harm the patient. Projection of aggressive wishes may also create such fears.

REFERENCES

Aristotle. *De Poetica*, trans. I. Bywater. *The Basic Works of Aristotle*, ed. R. McKeon. New York: Random House, 1941. (There are many other editions of this work.)

Blos, P. (1962). *On Adolescence: A Psychoanalytic Interpretation*. Glencoe, Ill.: Free Press.

Bornstein, B. (1949). The analysis of a phobic child. *Psychoanalytic Study of the Child* 3/4: 181-226.

Breuer, J., and Freud, S. (1893-5). *Studies on Hysteria. Standard Edition*. Vol. 2. London: Hogarth, 1955.

Buckley, T. (1975). "Write me" said the play to Peter Shaffer. *New York Times Magazine*, April 13, 1975.

Eissler, K. R. (1968). The relation of explaining and understanding in psychoanalysis: Demonstrated by one aspect of Freud's approach to literature. *Psychoanalytic Study of the Child* 23: 141-177.

Erikson, E.H. (1963). *Childhood and Society*. 2nd ed. New York: Norton.

Freud, A. (1958). Adolescence. *Psychoanalytic Study of the Child* 13: 255-278.

Freud, S. (1900). *The Interpretation of Dreams. Standard Edition*. Vols. 4 and 5. London: Hogarth, 1953.

_____ (1905). Three essays on the theory of sexuality. Ibid. 7: 125-245. (1953).

_____ (1905-6). Psychopathic characters on the stage. Ibid. 7: 303-310 (1953).

_____ (1907). Delusions and dreams in Jensen's *Gradiva*. Ibid. 9: 1-96 (1959).

_____ (1916). Some character types met with in psychoanalytic work. *Ibid*. 14: 309-333 (1957).

Glenn, J. (1947a). Twins in disguise: A psychoanalytic essay on *Sleuth* and *The Royal Hunt of the Sun. Psychoanalytic Quarterly* 43: 288-302.

_____ (1947b). Twins in disguise II: Content, form and style in plays by Peter and Anthony Shaffer. *International Review of Psychoanalysis* 1: 373-381.

_____ (1974c). Anthony and Peter Shaffer's plays: The influence of twinship on creativity. *American Imago* 31: 270-292.

Glenn, J., and Urbach, H. Adaptive and non-adaptive action in adolescence. To be published in *Directions in Psychoanalysis*, ed. S. Orgel and B. Fine. New York: Aronson.

Hartmann, H. (1964). *Essays on Ego Psychology*. New York: International Universities Press.

Inhelder, B., and Piaget, J. (1958). *The Growth of Logical Thinking from Childhood to Adolescence*. New York: Basic Books.

Kohut, H. (1971). *The Analysis of the Self*. New York: International Universities Press.

Kris, E. (1952). *Psychoanalytic Explorations in Art*. New York: International Universities Press.

Pumpian-Midlin, E. (1965). Omnipotentiality, youth and commitment. *Journal of the American Academy of Child Psychiatry* 4: 1-18.

Shaffer, P. (1973). *Equus*. London: Deutsch.

_____ (1975). Discussion of Stamm (1975).

Spiegel, L. (1951). A review of contributions to a psychoanalytic theory of adolescence: Individual aspects. *Psychoanalytic Study of the Child* 6: 375-393.

_____ (1958). Comments on the psychoanalytic psychology of adolescence. *Psychoanalytic Study of the Child* 13: 296-308.

Stamm, J. (1975). A psychoanalytic exploration of Peter Shaffer's play, *Equus*. Read at the Association for Applied Analysis, June 13.

JULES GLENN, M.D.

DR. GLENN is clinical associate professor and chairman of the Child Analysis Section at the Division of Psychoanalytic Education, Downstate Medical Center, SUNY. He is a graduate of the New York Psychoanalytic Institute. His papers include studies of twinship, the psychology of women's testicular cathexis, and Freud's cases. Currently he is editing a book on child analysis technique.

Equus and the
Psychopathology of Passion

Jacob E. Slutzky, Ph.D.

Diplomate in Clinical Psychology, A.B.P.P.
Private practice, Roslyn Heights, N.Y.

Peter Shaffer's play **Equus** is discussed in terms of its views on the concept of passion. The major characters show clear indications of psychopathological expressions of passion. Alan's pathology is highlighted by his psychotic identification with Equus and his blinding of the horses. Dr. Dysart's pathology is seen in his greatly inhibited sense of passion. He envies Alan's passion and shows "countertransference" toward treating him. Both characters are studied in terms of level of object relations, ego functions, and unconscious fantasy.

Equus is ostensibly a play about the psychiatric treatment of an outwardly docile, highly disturbed adolescent boy, Alan Strang, who one night unexplainedly blinded six horses. The audience is let into the private world of the boy, his parent's influence on him, and his consuming fascination with horses, particularly an imaginary horse Equus.

As the play unfolds, the events immediately preceding Alan's blinding of the horses is told. While working as a stock clerk during the week, Alan works at a stable on the weekends, cleaning the stall and grooming the horses. However, every three weeks, in the middle of the night, he secretly rides one of the horses in an intense passion-filled ritual, the object of which is complete merger with the horse. In his work at the stable he meets a young woman who ultimately attempts to seduce him there one night. The feelings subsequently aroused in him culminate in his panic-stricken blinding of the horses.

Parallel to the character study of Alan, the audience is confronted with a simultaneous study of the psychiatrist, Dr. Dysart, who is called upon to treat him. He is portrayed as middle-aged, disillusioned, emotionally distant, unhappily married, and sexually impotent. He doubts the efficacy of his work and seems incapable of forming committed human relationships. The doctor is reluctant to treat Alan because he envies in him what he terms the boy's "passion," in stark contrast to his own sterile life, fearing that treating him will remove all traces of passion in the boy's life. The "treatment" consists largely of hypnotic and abreactive techniques portrayed in a highly dramatic style.

Mr. Shaffer states in his introductory note on the play that *Equus* is his attempt to interpret the event in some entirely personal way . . . to create a mental world in which the deed could be made comprehensible." As his story is told, he communicates the message that passion is irreconcilable with adaptation to reality, that integration is virtually impossible and that psychotherapy removes passion.

The author presents Alan's primitive narcissistic ritual as an expression of passion and has the doctor envy the boy's passion. This parallels a tendency in contemporary society to glorify relatively direct instinctual expression and to confuse primitive mergers for a deep sense of loyalty, personal commitment, and love. Alan and Dysart are both faced with the task of modulating aggressive drives and forming human relationships. Alan is portrayed as solving this problem by becoming the centaur while the doctor becomes the mythologist.

The dissatisfaction in the doctor's life may be seen as a mirror of dissatisfaction in middle-aged adults of today, whereas Alan's becoming overwhelmed in passion may well be seen as expressing the struggle of young adults in our society to forge a new world. There is a tendency in both groups to fantasize about how things might have been or might become, especially when satisfactions in personal relationships and work are missing and depressive moods prevail.

The purpose of this paper is to explore from the framework of ego psychology:

1. The play's treatment of passion.
2. Alan's pathological expression of passion as seen in his psychotic identification with Equus and his blinding of the horses.
3. Dysart's pathological inhibition of passion as seen in his envy of Alan's passion, his reluctance to treat him ("countertransference"), and his choice of abreaction as a form of therapy.

Both characters will be studied in terms of level of object relations, ego functions and unconscious fantasies.

PASSION

Passion is generally defined as an intense emotional experience involving a total sense of emotional abandon and usually a temporary loss of control. The term "passion" can best be understood in terms of a specific context. The suffering of Jesus following the Last Supper is described as his Passion, and plays depicting this theme are known as Passion plays. There is also the frequent usage of the word *passion* to denote an intense level of sexual or aggressive emotional experience as in crimes of passion. Furthermore, collectors are said to have a passion for books, art, or other subjects. The range of meanings covers all aspects of emotional experience from the most primitive to the most mature and from the pathological to the generative.

It is surprising that there is very little psychoanalytic literature dealing specifically with the concept of passion in any of its aspects. What few articles do exist generally do not take into account structural thinking and deal primarily with psychopathological aspects of passion. Applying structural thinking to the psychoanalytic theory of affects, Jacobson (1971) emphasized that all affects are ego experiences and may arise from intrasystemic, intersystemic, and combined sources of tension. The key element as to whether any affect, simple or compound, including passion, is pathological or healthy would seem to rest on the level of ego development, which is closely related to the level of object relations.

At the most primitive level passion would be the manifestation of intersystemic tension such as rage. At the most developed level, passion would be the integration of both intra- and inter-systemic tensions as experienced in the heights of love and in creative work. Whether both primitive and mature forms are appropriately termed passion is open to question. Michel (1971) introduced the term "symbolic passion" to denote passion for passion's sake and "true passion" as an organizer of thought and action. [p. 423]

Mature passion can be understood as an intense emotional experience blending diverse aspects of overlapping libidinal phases, raw and modulated aggression, and varying stages of object relatedness. The essential determinant for experiencing passion on a mature level is the capacity of the ego to value the full range of human experience without disabling fear of regression or archaic retribution. Prior to the attainment of individuation, particularly while a symbiotic level of object relationships prevails, passion can largely be experienced at the level of primitive intersystemic-id discharge as is seen in Alan. There is no cohesive sense of self and there is the ever-present danger of fragmentation. While there is evidence in the play to suggest that Dysart has progressed beyond this level, he does not seem to have maintained his individuation.

Alan and Dysart illustrate two manifestations of the psychopathology of passion. Alan shows a deficiency of control of passion in his merger with E-quus and his blinding of the horses. Dysart manifests an inhibition of passion in his life. He fears that treating Alan would bring him closer to his own stifled and feared passion and transform the boy into his (Dysart's) passionless life.

Although Dr. Dysart uses the term "passion" as a primitive expression of affect, it should be kept in mind that the difference between primitive and mature passion is as vast as the difference between lust and love. The differentiation is that lust represents drive dominance, with little regard for the object and for ego controls, while love requires a deeply cathected object and modulation of the drive by the ego.

Both major characters will be studied in terms of their psychopathology of passion with a focus on such elements as level of object relations, level of ego development, and the nature of their unconscious fantasies. Shaffer's view that passion and adaptation to reality are irreconcilable will be discussed in the context of the material on Dysart.

ALAN

In the course of the play, material is presented concerning Alan's parents, the quality of his life, the factors relating to his attachment to Equus, and his blinding of the horses. Alan is described as a rather lonely boy, with no friends to speak of and closely tied to his parents who seem a little too old to have an adolescent son. Alan's level of object relations is profoundly primitive as is his psychosexual development and level of ego functioning. His primary process thinking and inability to differentiate reality from fantasy resembles the clinical picture found in schizophrenia.

Alan's relationship with others is narcissistically experienced and all "objects" are archaic self-objects rather than "true" objects. Kohut (1971, p. 51) describes true objects as "objects loved and hated by a psyche that has separated itself from the archaic objects, has acquired autonomous structures, has accepted the independent motivations and responses of others, and has grasped the notion of mutuality."

In Mahler's (1968) terms, Alan's level of object relations would be described as primarily symbiotic. Alan's mother is depicted as possessive and almost clandestine in the quality of her relationship with him. She is overly permissive and involved in a "conspiracy" with Alan, inspiring him in religion in opposition to her husband who is an avowed atheist. Alan's father is portrayed as externally stern, and self-righteous, but basically ineffectual, hypocritical, and sadistic. In the absence of a strong relationship with his father, Alan not only succumbs to a predominantly symbiotic relationship with his mother but regresses further to a delusional psychotic identification with an imaginary horse he names Equus.

The horse becomes a self-object and represents a fusion of his mother's expressed interests in both Jesus Christ and in horses. The quality of fusion between Equus and Jesus is conveyed by the following lines from the play (pp. 49-50):

Alan: Prince[1] begat Prance . . . And Prance begat Prankus! . . . And Prankus begat Flankus! . . . Flankus begat Spankus . . . And Spankus begat Spunkus the Great, who lived three score years! . . . And Legwus begat Neckwus . . . And Neckwus begat Fleckwus the King of Spit . . . And Fleckwus spoke out of his chinkle chankle . . . And he said, Behold — I give you Equus my only begotton son.

The father relates that following his overhearing Alan in the above soliloquoy he observed the boy putting a string in his mouth and beating himself with a wooden coat hanger as if he were both horse and rider. Alan's passion for Equus may be truly described as autoerotic.

It is interesting to note Spitz's (1962) observation that during infancy, where the mother-child relationship was problematical (as it inevitably is in children who do not develop decisively beyond the symbiotic phase), specifically genital play tends to be rare and that other autoerotic activities tend to replace it. For Alan, the horse became the focus of his autoerotic activities.

While the horse has been previously utilized primarily as a representation of the father, as in Freud's (1909) first published case of child psychoanalysis, "Little Hans," this symbolism probably cannot be applied in Alan's case. Little Hans had a clearer sense of self, had a strong relationship with his father, related well to his environment, and showed specific fantasies and a specific symptom (phobia) rather than an elaborate private world. At Alan's level, the horse conveys a more primitive undifferentiated representation.

The failure to develop decisively beyond experiencing all objects as archaic self-objects (Kohut) or beyond the symbiotic level (Mahler) significantly impairs the development of psychological structures to autonomously perform "drive regulating, integrating, and adaptive functions . . ." (Kohut, p. 51). Alan's failure to develop the capacity to experience others as separate individuals has left him with the heavy burden of drive regulation, both sexual and aggressive. His apparent dullness probably reflects the depression experienced by turning his aggression inward while his violence was the outward expression of his pent-up feelings for which he had grossly inadequate means of adaptive discharge. His archaic superego and faulty ego development led to his experience of guilt on a very harsh primitive level rather than as a signal affect leading toward control of aggression.

It is interesting to consider the possible dynamics leading to Alan's passion for Equus and his subsequent blinding of the horses. While Alan admitted to cleaning the stables and grooming the horses, he conveyed the impression of being uninterested in riding to guarantee the perpetuation of his autoerotic ritual. Ferenczi (1933) related a pathological quality of surreptitiousness and a tendency to form enslaving sadomasochistic relationships to the aftermath of primal scene observation and to actual seduction during early childhood.

While the views appear quite germane to understanding Alan, it is imperative to keep in mind Alan's overall primitivity. These same experiences in an individual at a higher level of psychosexual development, object relatedness, and psychic structure can be reacted to in other terms, as will be shown in the discussion of Dysart.

At Alan's level of primitivity he probably would understand the primal scene as two individuals merging into one. His mother had told him a story of Crusaders on horseback who were thought by the infidels to be one being, rather than a distinct horse and a rider. His fascination with a bloody picture of Christ, given him by his mother, may be an indication of his interpretation of the primal scene in sadomasochistic terms. Children react to their observation of the primal scene according to their developmental levels, and it is not unusual for them to attempt to master the trauma of such observation through their play. One child may act out fantasies of being beaten, and another will become uncontrollably aggressive. One child will play at being an animal, such as a horse, and another will become the horse.

Rather than calling forth castration anxiety, the event may evoke the terror of annihilation and may be defended against by merger as seen in Alan or by isolation as will be seen in Dysart. His wish to merge with Equus, which becomes the guiding passion in his life, is an expression of his reenactment of the primal scene.

In the course of the play there is ample material to indicate that Alan is furious with both parents. At one point in the play after Alan has confessed his merger with Equus to Dysart, his mother comes to pay him a visit and he throws his tray at her. She complains of his staring at her which she takes to be accusatory. In the seduction scene Alan fears the horses staring at him and becomes even more uncontrollably violent with them. Fenichel (1945, pp. 71-74) points out that "very often sadistic impulses are tied up with scoptophilia: the individual wants to see something in order to destroy it." Furthermore, being seen or stared at can be understood as being destroyed.

Immediately preceding the seduction scene and the blinding of the horses, Alan unexpectedly meets his father at a pornographic movie. This leads to his recognition of his father as being sexually frustrated and having feelings of his own. However, his vague recognition of his enslavement to Equus and his dim awareness of another's feelings come too late. Alan could only experience life in terms of merger. He could not differentiate easily between self and other and was enmeshed in his fantasy of merger with Equus.

Alan's blinding of the horses followed Jill's attempt at seducing him at the stable and his inability to perform sexually. He states that wherever he looks, even when he closes his eyes, all he can see is Equus and he is absolutely terrified of Equus seeing him. In terms of his sadistic trends he equates seeing as destroying and being seen as being destroyed.

Another factor that must be considered in Jill's seduction of Alan is her intrusion on Alan's deeply ingrained mode of relating to others only as archaic self-objects. The need to guard this mode of experiencing life is probably based on a fear that failure to do so could only lead to complete fragmentation. Perhaps on one level Alan wished to have sexual relations with Jill, but to do so threatened him with imminent self-destruction.

Under these circumstances his blinding of the horses rather than killing them may be seen as a primitive attempt at self-cure enabling him to have a relationship with Jill while retaining his merger with Equus, but on a more controlled basis. In a sense the blinding of the horses also is an expression of his primary process thinking that "if you don't see it, it didn't happen."

DR. DYSART

The play presents material about Dr. Dysart in the form of his autobiographical statements, his reactions to his encounter with Alan, and by his reporting a dream after meeting Alan and learning of the latter's "crime." The character of Dr. Dysart resembles the clinical picture seen in obsessional neurosis, chiefly on the basis of his inability to integrate affect and thought, although there is also a depressive undercurrent to his personality. He is middle-aged, a child psychiatrist in a provincial hospital in England, unhappily married, and childless. Dysart seems stunned by his loveless relationship with his wife, his sexual impotence, and perhaps above all his secret of a very low sperm count. As Alan had to keep his riding secret, Dysart had to keep his very low sperm count secret.

Dysart's sense of passion is greatly inhibited. He is uninvolved sexually with his wife and is psychologically as well as biologically impotent. His attitude toward his work takes on a mechanical, technical quality, and he cannot relate closely :o other people. Yet, he has fantasies of an adventurous life and his dream, as will be seen, indicates his conflicts with aggression. He does show some compassion for Alan, however, and ultimately treats him. However, he is deeply involved in maintaining a sharp split between his affects, thoughts, and his overt behavior.

It is clear that his meeting Alan has struck a responsive chord and his unconscious fantasies, as discussed by Arlow (1969) and Beres and Arlow (1974), resonate with Alan's. It was suggested earlier in the paper that Alan's merger with Equus and his riding the horse may be understood as a primitive reenactment of the primal scene. Dysart's defense of isolation can be understood as a response to primal scene observation as well. At his higher level of overall development, however, his response to the same trauma would probably have been experienced more specifically as castration anxiety rather than as a fear of annihilation in the case of Alan. His defense of isolation can be seen as based on a need to keep distance in order to forestall the inevitable castration he associates with almost any degree of closeness.

His heavy usage of isolation places him under profound emotional strain. The sharp blow to his narcissism by virtue of his biological impotence has probably augmented whatever depressive moods may have previously been present. In addition, obsessional tendencies have probably been amplified and can be seen in his doubting the efficacy of his work and the meaning of his life. His isolation seems based on averting the anxiety generated by unconscious fantasies and early traumata.

It is this defense of isolation which is really championed when Dysart expresses the view that passion (affect) and adaptation to reality cannot be reconciled. The implication that psychotherapy removes passion can better be understood as his dread that psychotherapy will remove the experience of a sense of passion as an isolated affective fantasy and compel him to express his passion in terms of true object relationships. His use of isolation and the concomitant inhibition of passion in his life can be seen in the contrast between his fantasies and reality, in his dream and in his method of psychotherapy.

Dysart is quite interested in ancient Greece and has visited Greece on holiday. But the contrast between his fantasies about ancient Greece and his actual trips with suitcases crammed full with Kaopectate and advance booking of hotels for every night is striking. The author's usage of the doctor's dream after meeting Alan, is quite revealing. While Alan expresses his violence overtly in a break with reality, Dr. Dysart does so in terms of his dream, which follows:

I'm a chief priest in Homeric Greece, I'm wearing a wide gold mask, all noble and bearded, like the so-called Mask of Agamemnon found at Mycenae. I'm standing by a thick round stone and holding a sharp knife. In fact, I'm officiating at some immensely important ritual sacrifice, on which depends the fate of the crops or of a military expedition. The sacrifice is a herd of children: about five hundred boys and girls. I can see them stretching away in a long queue, right across the Plain of Argos. I know it's Argos because of the red soil. On either side of me stand two assistant priests, wearing masks as well: lumpy, pop-eyed masks, such as also were found at Mycenae. They are enormously strong, these other priests, and absolutely tireless. As each child steps forward, they grab it from behind and throw it over the stone. Then, with a surgical skill which amazes even me, I fit in the knife and slice elegantly down to the navel, just like a seamstress following a pattern. I part the flaps, sever the inner tubes, yank them out and throw them hot and steaming on to the floor. The other two then study the pattern they make, as if they were reading hieroglyphics. It's obvious to me that I'm tops as chief priest. It's this unique talent for carving that has got me where I am. The only thing is, unknown to them, I've started to feel distinctly nauseous. And with each victim, it's getting worse. My face is going

green behind the mask. Of course, I redouble my efforts to look professional—cutting and snipping for all I'm worth: mainly because I know that if
ever those two assistants so much as glimpse my distress—and the implied
doubt that this repetitive and smelly work is doing any social good at all—I
will be the next across the stone. And then, of course, the damn mask begins to slip. The priests both turn and look at it—it slips some more—they
see the green sweat running down my face—their gold pop-eyes suddenly
fill up with blood—they tear the knife out of my hand . . . and I wake up.

Assuming his encounter with Alan to be the significant day residue, and
recognizing the limitations of interpreting the dream largely in terms of its
manifest content, Dysart's dream may be understood as follows:

The contrast between his killing the children and his initial lack of affect is
startling. Yet his apparent lack of affect breaks down and he begins to feel
nauseous. His concern then is to hide his distress and lack of belief in the value
of his work. But he cannot carry it off; his mask (defense) slips; and his knife
is taken away from him. The dream can be understood as an expression of
Dysart's castration anxiety which he defends against by attempting to hide his
affective experience (sense of passion) utilizing the defense mechanism of isolation.

Dysart is a very troubled man who is completely disillusioned with his work
and who seems to be overwhelmed by the emotional strain it places on him.
He doubts himself and is terrified of facing his underlying primitivity and
castration fears. He is stirred up by the aberrations of the patients he is called
upon to treat, and his own fear dictates that he cover up their wounds as
quickly as possible so as to preclude the possibility of confronting the conflicts
within himself.

Dysart's lack of ability to strive toward personal fulfillment, which is a
major aspect of the inhibition of his sense of passion, clearly relates to his fear
of confronting his personal "chamber of horrors." He envies Alan not only his
emotional release but his perception of Alan's primitive ritual as a capacity
for passion which he cannot find within himself. His envy of Alan's passion
can be viewed as his gross misunderstanding of the youth's attachment to
Equus as a mastery of castration anxiety and his blinding of the horses as a
capacity for aggressive discharge.

He states in the dream that his face is turning green under his mask. He is
becoming nauseous by the work but he cannot let anyone know. This is so
reminiscent of the deeply troubled person who is terrified of confiding the
depth of his rage and self-doubts to another lest he be found incompetent and
insane. In general, the fear of self-knowledge probably stems from a feeling
that at bottom there is a psychotic core to the personality, which, if confronted, will lead to total annihilation. The only thing for the doctor to do, as

for so many people, is to "make the best of it." This the doctor does with his loveless marriage and his work in a provincial hospital.

The presentation of the psychiatrist as a human being in deep personal trouble, rather than as a paragon of emotional perfection, seems to have had great interest for many viewers of the play. One of the chief requirements for an effective psychotherapist is his capacity for empathy, which can be understood as incorporating a capacity for passion. While Dysart clearly had an initial empathic reaction to Alan, he lost control of his empathy. Greenson (1960) describes this failure as a tendency to become too intensely involved in the emotional lives of patients so that the position as observer cannot be readily regained. Uncontrolled empathizers "tend to identify or act out or have strong instinctual reactions, all of which interfere with their ability to observe and to analyze" (p. 420).

For Dysart to treat Alan therapeutically would require the capacity to face the fear generated by his early observations. Thus he utilizes abreactive techniques to spare himself the pain otherwise required. The approach is very much in vogue today and can be seen in behavioral therapies as well as "primal" therapy. These therapies have one thing in common, an emphasis on emotional release without working toward making the unconscious conscious, a defense which serves the pathological needs of both therapists and patients.

Empathy, like capacity for passion, can only be used constructively in psychotherapy when there is a continuing process of individuation. It is suggested that impairments of this process unresolved by the therapist's own psychoanalysis, if any, compound the possibilities for countertransference reactions, in terms of heightened vulnerability to shared unconscious fantasies with patients and in the inability to differentiate the patient's needs from one's own. Countertransference is seen as not only based on unconscious libidinal or aggressive feelings toward the patient, but as reflective of a flaw in the therapist's quality of his object relatedness. It is this failure to experience empathy while retaining the capacity to observe and analyze which is presented so dramatically in the personage of Dr. Dysart. He reads his own lack of capacity for passion into his patient's primitive autoerotic ritual and joins Alan in his secret riding, his sexual failure, and his blinding of the horses.

CONCLUDING OBSERVATIONS

There is a clear need for psychoanalytic study of the concept of passion in terms of psychopathology and in normal development. The play presents two examples of the psychopathology of passion. In keeping with his overall lack of differentiation and need for merger, Alan manifests a welding of primitive wishes, fears, and actions. Dysart shows a gross inhibition of passion related to his strong usage of the defense mechanism of isolation. While differentiating self from other, he maintains his emotional detachment from others.

Alan's merger with Equus seems so primitive that his blinding of the horses, in the context of his seduction by a stable girl, precludes an oedipal interpretation of the event. The blinding seems a product of the turmoil experienced by individuals at primitive levels who are confronted with stimuli calling for more mature responses than they are capable of.

Dysart's inhibition of passion prompted significant countertransference reactions and demonstrates the importance of an emotionally satisfying life situation for the psychotherapist. In considering the qualities which contribute to the therapist's effectiveness, following Greenson's (1960) discussion of empathy, it would seem that there is a close relationship between a therapist's capacity for empathy and his capacity for passion. Dysart's inhibition of passion was expressed in the impairment of his empathy in that he could not allow himself to remain sufficiently the analytic observer while he shared emotionally with Alan.

Equus has been criticized by many mental health professionals as being antipsychotherapeutic. In the sense that it expresses a dread of uncovering painful material and despairs of the possibilities for integrating passion and adaptation to reality the criticism may be accurate. But it can also be seen as a deeply moving artistic portrayal of very powerful resistance to psychotherapy. Enabling emotionally tormented, creative individuals to find the means to work through their resistances and become meaningfully involved in treatment poses an important challenge to psychoanalysts and psychotherapists.

ACKNOWLEDGMENT

The author would like to thank Dr. Robert Langs for helpful suggestions in the course of preparing this article.

NOTE

1. The name of a horse in a favorite story told by his mother.

REFERENCES

Arlow, J. (1969). Unconscious fantasy and disturbances of conscious experience. *Psychoanalytic Quarterly* 38: 1-27.

Beres, D. (1962). The unconscious fantasy. *Psychoanalytic Quarterly* 31:309-328.

_____, and Arlow, J. (1974). Fantasy and identification in empathy. *Psychoanalytic Quarterly* 43:26-49.

Fenichel, O. (1945). *The Psychoanalytic Theory of Neurosis*. New York: Norton.

Ferenczi, S. (1933). Confusion of tongues between adults and the child—the language of tenderness and of passion. *The Selected Papers of Sandor Ferenczi, M.D.*, Vol. 3, pp. 156-167. New York: Basic Books.

Freud, S. (1909). Analysis of a phobia in a five year old boy. *Standard Edition* 10:3-149.
Greenson, R. (1960). Empathy and its vicissitudes. *International Journal of Psycho-Analysis* 41:418-424.
Jacobson, E. (1971). *Depression, Comparative Studies of Normal, Neurotic and Psychotic Conditions.* New York: International Universities Press.
Kohut, H. (1971). *The Analysis of the Self.* New York: International Universities Press.
Mahler, M. (1968). *On Human Symbiosis and the Vicissitudes of Individuation.* New York: International Universities Press.
_____(1971). A study of the separation-individuation process: And its possible application to borderline phenomena in the psychoanalytic situation. *Psychoanalytic Study of the Child* 26: 403-424.
Michels, R. (1971). Student dissent. *Journal of the American Psychoanalytic Association* 19:417-432.
Shaffer, P. (1974). Equus. *Equus and Shrivings, Two Plays by Peter Shaffer.* New York: Atheneum.
Spitz, R. (1962). Autoeroticism re-examined: the role of early sexual behavior patterns in personality formation. *Psychoanalytic Study of the Child* 17:283-315.

JACOB E. SLUTZKY, Ph.D.

DR. SLUTZKY is a diplomate in clinical psychology, A.B.P.P., and conducts a private practice in Roslyn Heights, N.Y. He was formerly director of clincial research, Children's Treatment Center, New York City, and Luther E. Woodward School, Freeport, N.Y.

Discussion of Papers on Equus

J. Alexis Burland, M.D.

Faculty, Philadelphia Psychoanalytic Institute

Three points are discussed concerning **Equus** and the preceding papers: (1) Because a play is not a free association obtained within the context of the analytic situation it is most difficult to "analyze." (2) The central theme of "passion" in **Equus** would seem to relate to the vicissitudes of infantile omnipotence, as noted in both the content of the play and the process of playwrighting. And (3) in **Equus**, the playwright not only creates a reality out of a fantasy, but "tricks" the audience into being a participant in the scopophilic activities depicted.

INTRODUCTION

I will limit my discussion of Peter Shaffer's *Equus* and the preceding four papers to three topics: the difficulties inherent in the psychoanalytic interpretation of literature, the issue of "passion," and the nature of the creative process.

There are inherent dangers in psychoanalytically studying a work such as *Equus*. Some of the preceding authors have identified these dangers and skirted them; others have done neither. For one thing, content analysis without the accompanying free associative data, while entertaining and often stimulating, is a risky business at best, bordering on "wild analysis." A product for the commercial theater is quite different from productions on the couch in the analytic setting. Though both playwright and analysand have unconscious mental processes, as well as an ego engaged in the processes of verbalizations, secondary elaborations, etc., their purposes are quite different. An actual dream, for instance, during the course of analysis bears little relationship metapsychologically to a written dream created as part of the life of a fictitious character; how then can one "analyze" conscious invention as though it were dreamwork? Some of our authors do not share my view on that, I will admit.

The issue is an important one in psychoanalysis; it touches on the critical question of technique: Is psychoanalysis a process done *by* the analyst *to* material given him by his patient, or is psychoanalysis something done within the patient's head with the guidance and assistance of the analyst? If the former, any mental production can be "analyzed" by anyone trained to decode the latent from the manifest; if the latter, without the therapeutic alliance, without the aim on the part of the patient to understand in greater depth, despite resistances, the workings of his unconscious mind, real psychoanalytic work cannot proceed. It is not as either/or an issue as the question suggests, of course. There are enough similarities in the human condition between us all that it is possible to understand the latent meaning of manifest material in many situations; but there is a difference between identifying general areas of shared human concern, and elucidating specific dynamics unique to one particular individual.

A further problem inherent in viewing a work of art from an analytic perspective is revealed in the variety of diagnoses given Alan Strang by our four authors: from psychoneurosis, with an oedipal-based conflict, to schizophrenia! The "solution" is obvious: Alan Strang does not really "exist" and has *no* diagnosis. He was created by a nonclinician in order to serve certain artistic and theatrical functions. Being true to the descriptive categories of the official A.P.A. nomenclature was not one of the playwright's major purposes. As a sensitive and perceptive human, he has created a character who does resemble certain kinds of recognizable people, but his theoretical constructs are not those of a clinically trained psychoanalyst. The people he creates in his dramas are not, nor are meant to be, exact replications of reality. Though he uses flesh-and-blood actors, who themselves *are* real enough, in fact from a functional viewpoint he uses materials akin to the portrait painter: strokes and colors and shapes that approximate a surface similarity to reality. Because the bodies of actors *look* more real than tubes of oil paints does not alter this basic element of the playwright's creative endeavors.

I hasten to add: In the program notes to the New York City production which I saw the playwright states he consulted with a psychiatrist in the writing of the play. Where the psychiatrist's input ends and Mr. Shaffer's input starts is not made clear; nor is it clear from the play. But my assumption remains the same: Mr. Shaffer was not primarily interested in depicting a psychiatric case study. It is perhaps for this very reason that the problem of Alan Strang's "diagnosis" exists. If he reflects some part of the playwright projected outward into the character, some parts of past acquaintances, some parts of insights and serendipitous accidents that occurred during the rehearsal of the original production—all of which is at least likely—certain diagnostic criteria appropriate to these real-life fragments will be recognizable. Although I observed a preponderance of clinical data relating to the so-called narcissistic character disorders, with very little that I recognized as oedipal-based psycho-neurotic structure, to attempt to pin any single diagnostic label on a nonper-son — on an impressionistic portrayal of some of the surface features of an imagined character — remains an exercise in futility. It also seems inappropri-ate as part of a critique of a *theater* piece.

As to the issue of "passion," I agree with Dr. Slutzky that that is an area that calls for further exploration. Current writings concerning ego develop-ment and problems of narcissism illuminate many facets of the subject, how-ever. In the performance of *Equus* that I saw I, too, noted that the audience reacted with much feeling, and a strong sense of partisanship, toward Dr. Dy-sart's view that "passion" is akin to creativity, and psychiatric "cure" is equiva-lent to the extinction of both. Approaching the issue from a vantage point other than one related to Alan Strang's *or* Dr. Dysart's "diagnosis," the "pas-sion" Dr. Dysart saw in Alan and so sorely missed within himself can be understood as a subjective sense of *infantile omnipotence*. In the course of human psychological development, infantile omnipotence suffers a severe re-versal when, during the rapprochement subphase of the separation-individ-uation process, cognitive development makes obligatory the child's awareness of his separateness from his mother. The mother is viewed at first as still re-maining omnipotent, but now excluding the child from sharing in it. Our awareness of our mortality starts at that time, and in the years of life that fol-low we are all increasingly educated as to our "ordinariness" and less-than-godlike status. The quasireligious, mythopoetic, ecstatic obsession of Alan Strang, and Dr. Dysart's painful sense of his ordinariness, would seem to re-flect the author's interest in this developmental milestone and his use of *Equus* as a vehicle for its presentation in the form of a dialogue on the subject. It is a subject many authors, philosophers, poets, and artists have dealt with. Ham-let and Macbeth mused upon the subject, as did Wagner's Hans Sachs, Strauss's and von Hofmannsthal's Marschallin, and Eliot's J. Alfred Prufrock, to name but a few.

Mr. Shaffer's yearning for the recapture of a sense of infantile omnipotence is clearly stated by Dr. Dysart; but in the play the harsh realities of the ordin-ary win out — in the past for Dr. Dysart and in the future for Alan Strang. It is in this that Mr. Shaffer would seem to aspire to the tragic insofar as the tragic can be equated with an awareness of life's inevitable disappointments and the gaps that exist between man's aspirations and what in fact he can accomplish. Whether Mr. Shaffer has succeeded in this is a matter for debate. My person-al feeling is close to Dr. Gifford's: Mr. Shaffer, his actors, and the director fail to create on the stage characters of sufficient weight to carry such a heavy burden.

This brings me to my final point related to one aspect of the creative pro-cess as demonstrated by *Equus*. In a note in the program, it is stated that Mr.

Shaffer heard about the actual blinding of some horses by a stable boy. He was instantly gripped by the thought of such an act, and felt compelled to create the play *Equus* in response to it, as *his* "explanation" for the crime he heard about. As I understand it, he could find out nothing more about the actual event; the play, therefore, with the exception of the act of the blinding of the horses, is totally Mr. Shaffer's creation. It is of interest that such information should be contained in the program; never before at the theater have I seen in the program such a statement as to the playwright's inspiration.

Something in the brief statement of the crime, without details, must have struck a sympathetic note with something personal within the playwright. What that something personal was, we of course do not know, and cannot know without the playwright's assistance. He felt compelled to give it a shape, in the form of a drama, and to give it reality in the form of real actors on the real stage. In other words, a fantasy was generated, with an effective quality suggesting many pre-conscious and unconscious roots, and the act of play-wrighting was in effect an act of making a reality out of a fantasy. A painting, a novel, certainly a play are *circumscribed realities*; as such, their creation must contain as an element the recapture of a sense of infantile omnipotence, a sense of constructing reality as opposed to being confronted and challenged by an autonomous reality of its own making. In this, the very act of play-wrighting itself would seem to touch on a subject central to the content of the play, namely, the vicissitudes of infantile omnipotence and the narcissistic deflations of the rapprochement crisis. The fact that, as reported in the *New York Times*, the young actor who played Alan Strang when *Equus* first opened in New York lived with the playwright points even further to the creation of reality from fantasy: from fantasy, to drama, to actual cast of characters, to relationship in real life with the central character in the form of the actor who portrays him.

As an audience, therefore, we are asked to witness a self-inflating, even autoerotic act. Any creative artist asks as much: look at me and the reality I create. The audience supports the narcissistic overidealization of the artist by purchasing tickets to the performance of his play, and by lionizing him. The papers which appear in this journal, and this discussion of them, all contribute to this lionization.

In the case of *Equus*, we are even asked to participate in a most subtle way. As Dr. Stamm points out, the scopophilic element is most prominent in the play. The act of blinding the horses, because of what they had seen, is most interesting in light of the fact that Dr. Dysart tricks Alan into letting him see the same thing, in the process of making the audience also a witness to it. The nudity on stage, although not quite as shocking—or shall I say eye-catching?—as it once was, is nevertheless a dramatic technique which maximizes the audience's sense of seeing something so personal that one feels he is intruding.

One is thus made even more aware of one's scopophilic participation in Mr. Shaffer's fantasy-made-into-a-reality.

Our scopophilic impulses are aroused and gratified, and for some in the audience I am sure this was a pleasure, for others a source of anxiety, and for most, a mixture of both. But in the process of thus gratifying certain instinctual wishes, the experience of witnessing Mr. Shaffer's creation takes on certain connotations that cannot help but effect one's overall reaction to it. Objectivity is lost, and the sense of the tragic is diminished by one's feeling tricked into participating in an essentially perverse interaction. An impotent and depressed psychiatrist and a deranged adolescent do not at best offer comfortable models for identification for the majority of the audience; finding oneself suddenly a participant in their interaction makes identification with them only more uncomfortable. It is almost as though the audience is given the alternative of being actively perverse or resisting doing so.

For the sense of the tragic to prevail, there must be an admixture of noble intentions of human frailty. The latter element is most evident in *Equus*; the former is nowhere to be found. It is just this lack of noble intention, particularly when coupled with the playwright's ability to theatrically entrap the audience into participating in what might be called an ignoble interaction, that ultimately weakens the play.

To summarize, attempting to interpret psychoanalytically the content of a drama such as *Equus* is fraught with difficulties since a work of art is not a free association obtained within the psychoanalytic situation. The major theme of *Equus* relates to the rapprochement subphase deflation of infantile omnipotent narcissism and the yearning for its reestablishment thereafter. A real-life event seems to have stimulated certain fantasies in the playwright's mind which he made into a reality—the staged drama—recapturing in this process of constructing reality some sense of infantile omnipotence. The audience participates by overidealizing the artist. In the case of *Equus* due to the very form of the play, the audience is "tricked" into being a scopophilic participant in the reality the playwright has created; whereas, this may make for exciting theater, it takes away from the sense of the tragic which the play might have achieved.

J. ALEXIS BURLAND, M.D.

DR. BURLAND is a child analyst who works extensively wth adolescents. He has also been for over thirty years an inveterate theatergoer. He is a member of the Editorial Board of this journal.

Intersecting Languages in Psychoanalysis and Philosophy

Louis Agosta, Ph.D.

Member, Philosophy Department
University of Chicago

Research Associate
Center for Psychosocial Studies

The introduction establishes a general view of the literature in which philosophers have profited from their encounters with analysis. It provides a frame within which to present more specific ideas about the method and language of psychoanalysis as viewed by philosophers.

The method of interpretive reconstruction is unfolded from its original context of Freud's archaeological analogy. Further, the vocabulary of reconstruction, which is an intimate part of this analogy, is employed by Anna Freud in her discussion of defense mechanisms. Texts are cited and explicated. Meanwhile, the method of reconstruction is given independent, though related, application in the work of R. G. Collingwood, an archaeologist-philosopher-historian.

The juxtaposition of Freud and Collingwood suggests that the methods of philosophy and analysis are more alike than the particular problems they try to solve. Both methods are oriented toward solving the problem of discovering meaning amid absurdity. The introduction of two specific examples lends substance to this claim.

In the final section on the practice of interpretation, the question is raised as to how the introduction of the method of reconstruction affects the debate about the epistemological status of psychoanalysis as a science. Psychoanalytic knowledge shows itself to be more like that available to the historian than that accessible through physical theories. Still, physics and analysis can be compared. One must look to the interpretation of symbols. In psychoanalysis, giving an interpretation—in which nonsense becomes understandable—is a form of explanation. This methodological result suggests a conclusion about the relation between metapsychology and clinical practice.

INTRODUCTION

The interest of philosophers in the language of psychoanalysis is motivated by a number of considerations. Questions of method are particularly important.

Philosophers wonder in what way the problems and techniques of the two disciplines may be parallel and complementary. The following questions are typical of the most urgent issues that have occupied philosophers in relation to their own field. Why does one's sanity come into doubt in the treatment of deep perplexities about the self in its relation to the external world and other selves? How does amnesia, or forgetfulness, contribute to the emergence of philosophic confusion? In what way is the treatment of a philosophic problem a therapeutic enterprise?

The way these issues emerge in Wittgenstein's *Philosophical Investigations* is instructive. Each remark is an occasion for reflection on the use and misuse of philosophy:

> We feel as if we had to repair a torn spider's web with our fingers. [1945, p. 46, par. 106]
> The work of the philosopher consists in assembling reminders for a particular purpose. [1945, p. 50, par. 127]
> There is not a philosophical method, though there are indeed methods, like different therapies. [1945, p. 51, par. 133]

Philosophers are far from unanimous about Wittgenstein's contribution, except to say that it's immense. He continually combats intricate skeptical doubts with common sense and uncommonly clear diagnosis of the perplexity. With the promise of self-knowledge on the horizon, Wittgenstein sets out to map the limits of what can be said from within the bounds of language (1921, p. 149, par. 6.5). But the discipline of his project is not supposed to be a substitute for life itself. Both his writings and the example of his own life show that the solution to the problem of the meaning of life is to be found only in living every single day (Janik and Toulmin, 1973, pp. 204ff.).

Our sanity is clearly at stake in skeptically questioning the existence of the external world as Descartes does in his *Meditations on First Philosophy* (1642). This provides a paradigm of the kind of intricate doubt that Wittgenstein tries to undercut. Like every good analyst, he appreciates that one cannot solve all one's problems by direct confrontation. It is necessary to employ a method which discloses implicit presuppositions. Otherwise what is at first an exercise in radical doubt becomes a tormenting inability to escape isolation and solipsism.

Husserl's *Cartesian Meditations* takes up the skeptical challenge and attempts to repair the torn web of the subject's relations with others. He uses the method of "analogical apperception." The *alter ego* is sketched as a self-like-me in the analogical transference of a familiar scheme to a new situation (1970, pp. 112-113, 119). Husserl's contribution is the study of the attachment and division between subjectivites in terms of intentionality (1970, pp. 106ff.).

Turning now from phenomenology to ordinary language philosophy, John Wisdom compares the reiterated doubt of the skeptic to the compulsive questioning of the obsessional type of neurotic (1953, p. 288). He then offers a positive program for philosophy. Philosophic method consists in unmasking the hidden dimension of problems, which are structured like riddles and paradoxes. The philosopher wins peace of mind and autonomy in the face of doubt by revealing what's disguised, by disclosing the implicit.

Philosophic paradoxes emerge because we forget the context of use in which our concepts were first formed. The task of "assembling reminders" aims at overcoming this amnesia. Here there is a significant parallel, which goes back to Plato's *Meno*, between the languages of Freud and Wittgenstein. When learning is defined in terms of recollection, the thinker's project becomes one of struggling against forgetfulness (*Meno*, p. 81d).

The therapeutic dimension of philosophy attempts to give the ultimate philosophic questions—those of freedom, God, and immortality—a proper place in thought. They lie at the limits of conceptual intelligibility. These questions inevitably transcend the limits of any language whose field of reference is sense perception. They are undecidable through use of our finite senses.

Questions about such supersensuous objects as freedom, God, and the immortal self (soul) are the proper subject of metaphysics. Nevertheless, they are questions whose consideration enriches life. They press forward for reflection at crucial times no matter how often science correctly demonstrates them to be unsolvable. They show man in his most anxious and vulnerable moments as he faces death, life, and the finitude of his time in the world of men. If approached with the right method—perhaps that of Socratic midwifery (*Theaetetus*, p. 150b)—the engagement of these questions yields that hard-to-attain philosophic treasure, self-knowledge.

Further incentive for philosophers' interests in psychoanalysis is provided by significant philosophic interpretations of Freud's works. In what is basically a confrontation between Freud and Marx, Herbert Marcuse focuses on the dialectics of guilt and cultural discontent. He extends the notion of repression to the collective enterprise of production and consumption. According to him, the prevailing mode of the reality principle is the performance principle. He deserves credit for representing analysis not as a mere epistemological exercise but as a method of healing and personality change. The transformation of analysis into a method of social change that criticizes this prevailing mode of the reality principle and formulates an alternative is a more questionable move than the former. His ultimate vision is one of replacing the rationality of performance, based on scarcity, with a higher rationality of creativity, based on abundance. In the end Marcuse admits that Freud's psychological categories have been transformed into political ones (*Eros and Civilization*, 1955, pp. viii, xvii).

From another perspective, Paul Ricoeur provides a detailed reading of
Freud in an essay on interpretation (*Freud and Philosophy*, 1970). The argument of this work is based on a careful study of texts, and outlines the way in
which analysis is a "mixed discourse." The dynamic approach of the conflict
of forces, with its constancy principle, is summarized under the term "energetics." The method of interpretation, the deciphering of dreams and symptoms as the recollection of meaning, is called "hermeneutics." These two
styles of discourse are complementary: hermeneutics without energetics is
empty; but energetics without hermeneutics is purposeless. The ultimate inseparability of these two forms of discourse corresponds, in philosophic terms,
to the dualism of the body and the mind. Energetics is the field of biological
drives and forces in conflict, while hermeneutics (interpretation) is the focus
of human meaning, intention, and purpose. This dichotomy recalls George
Klein's distinction between two different analytic theories (1973). According
to Klein, "serious incompatibilities" exist between the thermodynamic model
in metapsychology and the unlocking of meaning by interpretation in clinical
practice (1973, p. 107). We'll consider Klein's proposed solution below in
light of his assertions about Freud's philosophy of science.

Finally, questions about the method of psychoanalysis often engage philosophers of science. A significant part of this discussion focuses on the dichotomy between theory and observation in science and analysis (Nagel, 1959;
Hartmann, 1959). Both philosophers and analysts are bewitched by a particular view of the experimental method in science. It's easy to forget that the
theories of today are the special cases of tomorrow. We should assemble reminders that the distinction between theoretical language and observational
language has as much to do with a particular philosophic interpretation of
science as with the actual practice of the scientific method. Here the work of
one philosopher and historian of intellectual disciplines deserves recognition
(Toulmin, 1953, 1972). Toulmin distinguishes between the rationality characteristic of the logical relations between the elements of a formal system of
explanation and the rationality of human conduct as purposive practice
(1972). He transforms the distinction between theoretical and practical reason (Kant, 1787, 1788) into terms of the collective variation and selection of
concepts. Here philosophy has an important contribution to make to psycho-
analysis' own self-portrait in reflection on the relation between theory and
practice, metapsychology and technique of interpretation. We'll return to
this point, and consider some relevant literature (Klein, 1973; Mischel,
1974) in a later section.

So far the purpose of this introduction has been to establish a general view
of the literature in the field. The remarks were deliberately programmatic
and suggestive of the way in which philosophers have profited from their encounters with psychoanalysis. Furthermore, the task has been to provide a

frame of reference within which to present more specific ideas about the method and language of psychoanalysis as viewed by philosophers. The following sections will be less general and focus more directly on areas where Freud's discourse intersects with that of important philosophers. But two warnings are necessary. First, "intersection" means "overlap" not "identity." The point is not to reduce Freud to Wittgenstein or Collingwood—or vice versa. Rather it is to amplify, enrich, and illuminate the two disciplines, while preserving the integrity and independence of each. Only if one is secure in one's own integrity is "letting go" possible in dialogical encounter. Second, the following entails nothing either in favor or against laying the philosopher down on the analyst's couch. Following the example of Wisdom (1953) there has been a tendency to do this among philosophers themselves. Although I recognize the validity of such an approach, I don't follow it here. Rather, my main objective is to foster a fruitful interdisciplinary dialogue between philosophy and psychoanalysis in which there is mutual reciprocity and self-revelation.

ARCHAEOLOGY AND ANALOGY

Freud's analogical comparison of the method of interpretation with archaeological reconstruction forms the focus of various intersecting fields of discourse. Language about the temporal genesis of structures of the mind intersects with language drawn from the spatial representation of physical ruins. The incommensurability of discourse whose reference is temporal succession with discourse whose reference is spatial extension sets a limit to the validity of this analogy.

Still Freud's archaeological analogy is of interest because it's an intermediate mode of discourse, constituting a middle level between abstract metatheoretical models and the concrete practice of specific interpretations. The analogy is valuable as a transitional construct mediating the switch from theory to practice.

The first occurrence of this analogy that I've been able to find is in the early paper "The Aetiology of Hysteria" (1896). Freud writes of an explorer entering an unknown region:

> Imagine that an explorer comes in his travels to a region of which but little is known and that there his interest is aroused by ruins showing remains of walls, fragments of pillars and of tablets with obliterated and illegible inscriptions. He may content himself with inspecting what lies there on the surface and with questioning the people who live near by. . . . But he may proceed differently; he may come equipped with picks, shovels, and spades, and may . . . make an onslaught on the ruins, clear away the rub-

bish and, starting from the visible remains, may bring to light what is buried. If his work is crowned with success, the discoveries explain themselves . . . the many inscriptions, which by good luck may be bilingual, reveal an alphabet and a language, and when deciphered and translated may yield undreamed-of information about the events of the past, to commemorate which these monuments were built. *Saxa loquuntur!* [1896, p. 192]

Thus the stones speak! Meaning is discovered amid otherwise random fragments, unintelligibly absurd. In the context of his paper, Freud is arguing against the technique of asking the patient's relatives about possible sources of neurosis and even against the uncritical acceptance of what the patient tells. Understanding the neurosis is analogous to trying to decipher and translate an inscription in an unknown tongue.

Freud seems to allude to the case of the Rosetta stone, though this slab bore a trilingual inscription—Egyptian hieroglyphic, Egyptian demotic (popular script), and Greek. Here decipherment was possible because one of the languages, Greek, was already known. Comparison of the texts allowed some of the symbols to be identified, and in this lay the beginning of the translation of hieroglypic, which was previously considered undecipherable (Forde-Johnston, pp. 50-51). Similarly, the work of the psychoanalyst is furthered by the factor of overdetermination. The same message is repeated in the context of many different complexes, and the same complex repeats many different messages. This element of redundancy facilitates decipherment of the meaning of symptoms.

Freud's commitment to the archaeological analogy can be appreciated in the fact that some thirty-four years later he is still employing it for the teaching of psychoanalysis. When Freud needs a way of representing the unconscious aspects of the mind in relation to consciousness, he turns to the analogy of the ancient city (1930, p. 69). It is no accident that he speaks about one particular city, namely, Rome. Of course, this choice is determined by personal preference. But furthermore Rome is the "eternal city." Likewise the unconscious is "timeless": the primary processes of the unconscious are not altered by the passage of time.

Here Freud's language intersects explicitly with that of Wittgenstein. The analogy of the ancient city is used by Wittgenstein to illuminate the historical accretion of the forms of speech that convey men's thoughts:

Our language can be seen as an ancient city: a maze of little streets and squares, of old and new houses, and of houses with additions from various periods; and this surrounded by a multitude of new boroughs with straight regular streets and uniform houses. [1945, p. 8, par. 18]

Language is an ancient city with new and old figures of speech and forms of expression. The historical accumulation of these forms of speech and action (or language games) is represented by the patchwork of old and new streets and houses. The suggestion is that language houses our thoughts. Furthermore, the emphasis on avenues and streets implies that language is the vehicle that gives direction to thought. (In Rome street signs meaning "one way" read *senso unico*. Thus direction and sense are intimately related.) Language channels and directs the course of thought in a way analogous to the relation between the traffic channeled by the streets and squares.

The language of science is made of straight, regular streets. Philosophy consists of old and new houses with additions from various periods. Perhaps psychoanalysis is an avenue running diagonally through town, cutting across many major thoroughfares. All these different language games crisscross like avenues and streets. In themselves they are neither true nor false. The crucial test of validity is the practioner's ability to use them to get where he wants to go.

Of course, Freud's use of the ancient city analogy is different than Wittgenstein's. He wants to teach that in mental life nothing which has once been formed can perish (1930, p. 69). But the introduction of the analogy of Rome's defensive walls has interesting consequences, of which Freud may have been only peripherally aware. He does not introduce the topic of psychic defense mechanisms; but the analogy is admirably suited to exemplify such a topic:

> We ask ourselves how much a visitor, whom we will suppose to be equipped with the most complete historical and topographical knowledge, may still find left of these early stages in the Rome of today. Except for a few gaps, he will see the wall of Aurelian almost unchanged. In some places he will be able to find sections of the Servian wall where they have been excavated and brought to light. If he knows enough — more than presentday archaeology does — he may perhaps be able to trace out in the plan of the city the whole course of that wall . . . . [1930, p. 69]

Although primitive psychic structures and defenses have been replaced by modern ones, still the foundations remain. Here the intersection of discourse about spatial walls with that about psychic defense mechanisms is furthered by the semantic richness of the concept of defense. The task of the archaeologist is to reconstruct the physical defense perimeter of the city. Likewise the practice of analysis involves the retrospective reconstruction of the ego's defensive operations (A. Freud, 1936, p. 28). "Defense" becomes the focal term of the analogy between the ancient city and the personality. The focus is what the elements of the analogy share. It is that through which the analogy yields results.

Now let's turn to another text. Freud compares himself to a conscientious archaeologist:

> In the face of the incompleteness of my analytic results, I had no choice but to follow the example of those discoverers whose good fortune it is to bring to the light of day after their long burial the priceless though mutilated relics of antiquity. I have restored what is missing, taking the best models known to me from other analyses; but like a conscientious archaeologist I have not omitted to mention in each case where the authentic parts end and my construction begins. [1905, p. 12]

There is a parallel relation between buried relics and forgotten memories. We can schematize this relation formally according to the proportion: *buried/relics = forgotten/memories*. But the analogy is not merely formal. There is a common focus of meaning through which the equal sign (" = ") has significance. That focus is the method of reconstruction, which allows one to restore what is hidden to integrity and wholeness in a context of meaning.

The forgotten memories represent what is behind the repression barrier on the right-hand side of the proportion. Reconstruction amounts to a recollection of meaning (Ricoeur, 1972, p. 28). Otherwise unintelligible fragments are reinstituted in a complex totality, which is posited as the original matrix of their meaning.

The method of reconstruction is oriented toward interpretation. Reconstruction is a global concept embracing many particular interpretations of dream symbols, associations, screen memories, slips of tongue and pen, symptomatic behavior, etc. Reconstruction is the total story in which the mechanisms of displacement, condensation, reversal into opposite, allusion, and consideration of pictorial representation find application. Reconstruction necessarily goes beyond the given fragments, but it must always proceed from them and return to them. The relation of the individual parts to the whole must be a coherent one. Every fragment must find a place in the unified gestalt. A fragment doesn't become intelligible until it is related to a larger context of meaning, which it either supports or disconfirms. Random fragments are inadmissible in a coherent and adequate interpretation.

Freud again uses the language of reconstruction in his late paper "Construction in Analysis" (1937), where he says of the analyst:

> His work of construction, or, if it is preferred, of reconstruction, resembles to a great extent an archaeologist's excavation of some dwelling-place that has been destroyed and buried or of some ancient edifice. . . . Just as the archaeologist builds up the walls of the building from the foundations that have remained standing, determines the number and position of the columns from depressions in the floor and reconstructs the mural decora-

tions and paintings from the remains found in the debris, so does the analyst proceed when he draws his inference from the fragments of memories from the behavior of the subject of the analysis. [1937, p. 259]

This way of characterizing the practice of making interpretations is taken over by Anna Freud. The problem is that one cannot obtain knowledge of mental phenomena until they impinge on the sphere of the ego, which is the seat of observation. The operation of defense is not accessible until it is loosened and undone in the working-through process of analysis. This points toward the indispensability of reconstruction for understanding the relation between the various psychic institutions. According to Anna Freud,

> All the defensive measures of the ego against the id are carried out silently and invisibly. The most that we can ever do is to reconstruct them in retrospect.

> Only the analysis of the ego's unconscious defensive operations can enable us to reconstruct the transformations which the instincts have undergone. [1936, pp. 8, 26]

In this context the language of reconstruction represents an intermediate discourse between the metapsychological institutions of id, ego, and superego and the interpretive practice of undoing defenses. The metapsychological institutions provide a theoretic model of dynamic forces in conflict. The practice of undoing defenses involves a confrontation with the ambivalence of human emotions emerging in the context of the transference relation, where the analyst and analysand are purposively engaged in seeking the answers to questions of their own formulation. The method of reconstruction is valuable as a transitional function mediating the move from discourse about the causal efficacy of forces in conflict to discourse about human emotions and purposes.

Now the languages of philosophy and analysis intersect again in the specific field of the method of reconstruction. Collingwood offers some reflections on the practice of reconstruction in the context of the history of philosophy and aesthetics (1938, p. 107). Besides being a philosopher of art, metaphysics, science, and history, Collingwood was an expert on the history of Roman Britain. Thus he was a practicing archaeologist. He made important contributions to the understanding of the function of Roman fortifications in Britain thanks to his capacity for empathizing with the intentions and purposes of their builders (1939, pp. 128-130). Collingwood developed a method of analysis for discovering truth amid the apparent absurdity and falsehood of mistaken philosophic theories:

An erroneous philosophical theory is based in the first instance not on ignorance but on knowledge. The person who constructs it begins by partially understanding the subject, and goes on to distort what he knows by twisting it into conformity with some preconceived ideas. . . . If the truth which underlies it is to be separated out from the falsehood, a special method of analysis must be used. This consists in isolating the preconceived idea which has acted as the distorting agent, reconstructing the formula of the distortion, and reapplying it so as to correct the distortion and thus find out what it was that the people who invented or accepted the theory were trying to say. [1938, p. 107]

Thus philosophic theories have the structure of symptoms: they are compromise formations. The compromise is between truth, such as it is, and preconceived ideas or prejudice. Collingwood doesn't mention another equally important point, namely, that the theory's capacity of representation may be inadequate to express the truths and modes of knowledge over which the theory ranges. Thus an element of distortion would be inevitable in setting up any formal system.

The reader may well feel that Freud himself could have written the foregoing quote, with certain appropriate substitutions. Compare the text with one from Freud, published at about the same time:

The essence of it is that there is not only *method* in madness, as the poet has already perceived, but also a fragment of historical truth. . . .

Just as our construction is only effective because it recovers a fragment of lost experience, so the delusion owes its convincing power to the element of historic truth which it inserts in the place of rejected reality. [1937, p. 267]

The delusions of the narcissistic neuroses (1917, pp. 422ff.) are an attempt to reestablish contact with a reality that has been rejected and lost. Insofar as they contain an element of historic truth, they represent a distorted attempt at a cure or recovery (1915, p. 203).

Let us schematize the interdisciplinary analogy implicit in this comparison of Freud and Collingwood. We come up with the following proportion: *erroneous philosophic theory* = *knowledge* = *delusion* = *historic truth*. The area of intersection is defined by this analogy is the method of construction as means of discovering meaning amid absurdity. The focal meaning, which makes the analogy a source of insight, is the construction through which the separation of error and knowledge, distortion and truth, can be attained.

Until the philosopher invents and applies his formula of reconstruction, the theory on which he is working may seem riddled with contradictions and unintelligible paradoxes. But the formula of reconstruction enables him to grasp the nucleus of truth that the author was trying to express. Likewise, without reconstructive analysis, the delusions of psychiatric patients seem absurd. The analyst's method of reconstruction loosens the apparent absurdity through the assumption that the delusion is a distorted reflection of some psychic or interpersonal reality. However maladaptive the delusion may be in the long run, it is still a way of mastering anxiety that is immediately present and destructively overpowering. The method of reconstruction respects the delusion. This is the first step in discovering the experience for which the delusion is a substitute. Then the method of reconstruction places the historic dimension in perspective and lays out the kernel of truth as well as the husk of illusion.

EXAMPLES

At this point the best way of amplifying the method of reconstruction is by means of examples. I would like to lay out the way in which neurosis can express a kernel of historic truth in terms of Freud's Dora (1905). My remarks are based on a close reading of this case history, and they presuppose to some extent familiarity with the complex personal relations obtaining in Dora's universe of family and friends. I want to argue that one of Dora's central fantasies, in terms of which many of her symptoms are emotional ambivalences become intelligible is just this: "Sexual intercourse makes one sick."

This last statement, then, is the formula of distortion. How did I arrive at it? To paraphrase Collingwood, Dora's hysterical symptoms are based not on ignorance but on knowledge. She formed an understanding of the relations between the sexes based on the model of the relationship obtaining between her mother and father. But her mother married a man with venereal disease and contracted it from him. The mother reacted to the infection by becoming very strict, even compulsive, about cleanliness. She developed what Freud calls a "housewife psychosis" (1905, p. 20). Dora's fantasy that intercourse makes one sick is based on an unwarranted generalization from the one exceptional case of her parents.

Obviously, Dora's problem is not so much a matter of faulty logic as of faulty models on the basis of which to reason. The nucleus of historic truth at the foundation of Dora's unconscious fantasy about the relation between sex and sickness is her correct perception of her mother's relation to the father. The historic truth is experienced realistically by the mother: "Sexual intercourse makes one sick [if one's partner has venereal disease]." This is the formula of distortion with the kernel of historic truth reinstated.

This is the point at which the reconstruction is no longer supported by specific facts and is transformed into a story. In order to reconstruct Dora's (mis) perception we must hypothetically consider the effect on Dora of experiencing her mother's reaction to infection from the father. How was this state of affairs transmitted from parents to child? Whether they know it or not, parents continually teach their children in a form which uses no words, namely, by their example. What is a conscious reality for the parents (i.e., sexual intercourse can be a source of syphilis) must be redescribed as an unconscious fantasy in the child. And unless this fantasy is tested against reality by being expressed, it remains detached and isolated. As a source of anxiety, such fantasy gets split off, and so remains descriptively unconscious.

There is textual evidence in the story of Dora to support my view about the formula of distortion in Dora's fantasy life. According to Freud:

> To Dora that must mean that all men were like her father. But she thought her father suffered from venereal disease — for had he not handed it on to her and her mother? She might therefore have imagined to herself that *all men suffered from venereal disease*, and naturally her conception of venereal disease was modelled upon her one experience of it — a personal one at that. To suffer from venereal disease, therefore, meant for her to be afflicted with a disguisting discharge. [1905, p. 84; italics my own]

It is a short step from Freud's proposition about Dora's fantasy "all men suffered from venereal disease" to the view "sexual intercourse makes one sick."

Unfortunately, this text is problematic for other reasons. Freud seems to imply that Dora's father handed his venereal disease on to her, that the disease was hereditary. But this was a view he later qualified and rejected in light of advance in medical research.

But Freud may have unwittingly hit upon the truth anyway. Dora's father did hand his symptom on to his daughter, only it was psychically, not physically, determined. As a psychically determined symptom Dora's vaginal catarrh (leukorrhea) is a compromise formation. It is an inflammation of the sexual membrane expressing ambivalence about sexual intercourse in light of Dora's fantasy about the proximity of sex and sickness. On the one hand, it expresses sexual arousal in an obvious way — the tissue is swollen and excited. A substance is discharged in preparation to receive the male. On the other hand, the symptom expresses a rejection of the idea of intercourse — the discharge is an infected, moi bid one (1905, p. 84).

The otherwise enigmatic and recalcitrant symptom of a catarrh is intelligible as the expression of the wish to copulate incestuously with the father and the simultaneous expression of a punishment for this forbidden wish. Under this interpretation Dora's catarrh would be an example of hysterical venereal disease. But this symptom would also be typically overdetermined as an identification with the father, for she has the same disease as the father, as well as the expression of the wish to replace the mother in intercourse with the father.

Thus, this symptom is simultaneously a defense *against* and an expression *of* her fantasy that intercourse makes one sick. The symptom is based on both knowledge and ignorance; in order to decipher it, one must understand the scope and limits of the reality of Dora's interpersonal universe in relation to her fantasy life. The result is somewhat ironic. Whoever attempts to sketch the conditions of knowledge also maps the limits of his or her own self-ignorance. Whoever seeks the treasure of self-knowledge also discovers the sting of distortion and disguise.

Now let us turn from psychoanalytic discourse to philosophic discourse in order to give another brief example of the method of reconstruction.

Consider the following philosophic mini-theory: "Existence is perceived by the mind." On first reading this proposition may not seem false, but rather just plain absurd. So much the better for my purposes of illustrating how reconstruction discovers meaning amid apparent absurdity!

In order to discover the formula of distortion one must have enough respect for the integrity of our theory to ask: "What is the knowledge on which this (seemingly) absurd remark is based?" There is an implicit analogy concealed by the form of this remark. In explicit terms, one perceives colors with the eyes, smells with the nose, sounds with the ears, tastes with the tongue, etc. This much is given.

If we take the analogy one step further, then the formula of distortion emerges. The mind perceives particular patterns of sensations through the instrumentality of the sense organs; yet what is that instrument through which the mind perceives such universal attributes as existence and nonexistence, identity and difference, unity and multiplicity? The analogy leads us to the conclusion that the mind doesn't need any sense organ to perceive these attributes, and is its own organ in this respect. The formula of distortion is just this: "Existence is the same kind of attribute as those attributes accessible to us through the senses." This leads to the absurd attempt to perceive existence as one perceives the physical properties of objects. And in order to succeed we must posit "mind" as an organ analogous to our eyes, ears, nose, etc.

When we apply our formula of distortion to the original mini-theory, then the knowledge on which the theory is ultimately based becomes accessible. What the propostion "Existence is perceived by the mind" really attempts to teach us is just this: Knowledge isn't reducible to perception. Knowledge and perception are not the same. Perception is of individual attributes—particular objects of sensation—but knowledge also involves universal attributes—abstract properties like existence, identity, unity, etc.

Thus the reconstruction of an apparently meaningless formula discloses a surprising depth—the distinction between individual and universal. This is possible because the mini-theory summarized the conflicting requirements of an analogy between sense perception and abstract conception. The intersection of discourse about sensible particulars and conceptual universals led to a compromise that incorporated both knowledge and ignorance. (For a more detailed discussion of the mini-theory in its historical context see Plato, *Theaetetus*, pp. 184b-186e, from which the basic idea of the above paragraphs is drawn.)

The introduction of the two examples, one from a classical psychoanalytic text and the other from a classical philosophic text, suggests the following conclusion about the method of reconstruction. The method entailed is one of problem solving. At the beginning is a state of initial uncertainty. A recalcitrant symptom (Dora's vaginal catarrh) or an unintelligible maxim ("Existence is perceived by the mind") evokes a state of puzzlement. The question of meaning arises. Do these phenomena make sense? The search begins for a "formula of distortion." This is a principle for decoding the apparently incomprehensible elements of the problem. It is a criterion according to which nonsense can be transformed into a meaningful answer to the initial question.

A process of trial and error is the only way for deciding between alternative formulas. In the case of Dora's symptom alternative formulas might include the following. Instead of being an expression of a disguised wish to have intercourse with the father, Dora's symptom is intelligible as (1) hereditary veneral disease, (2) due to her masturbation, or (3) due to intercourse with an infected male. Freud actually does seem to suggest something like (1) and (2) at times. However, he later rejected (1) on the basis of advances in medical research. The second variation is dismissed in light of the fact that many girls masturbate without succumbing to a vaginal catarrh, much less hysteria. Thus (2) is clearly not a sufficient condition for the symptom in question. (This does not exclude the validity of some sort of principle of "somatic compliance" [1905, pp. 40-41], that a necessary condition of hysteria is the cooperation of the physical body with psychically determined meanings.) Finally, the third variant is eliminated in virtue of Dora's own testimony. In reporting her sexual experiences to Freud she recalled that Herr K. made sexual advances and tried to kiss her (1905, p. 28). She broke off the encounter due to a violent feeling of disgust. This goes against the interpretation of her symptom as due to intercourse with a man infected with V.D. We can indeed conceive of the possibility that she was deflowered and infected some time between age fourteen (when the first unsuccessful attempt at seduction occurred) and eighteen (when she came to Freud), and furthermore managed to keep it a secret from Freud. But none of the available textual testimony supports this reconstruction in terms of a real venereal infection from without.

Instead we are left with the task of deciphering Dora's symptom in terms of intrapsychic fantasies and interpersonal relations. The meaning of her symptom is made more intelligible as the expression of a disguised wish to copulate with her father and a simultaneous punishment for this wish. The proposed formula of distortion in operation here is Dora's belief, a belief of which she need not have been consciously aware, that sexual intercourse makes one sick. This notion further contributes to solving the problem of why she felt disguist when Herr K. embraced and tried to kiss her. A transformation of desire into the anticipated sickness occurred in terms of her expectations that the consequences of intercourse would be infection.

Of course, we must admit that the variation and selection process of trial and error does not lead to absolute knowledge. The point is to show how the method of reconstruction is an instance of problem solving. We must admit the possibility that if a particularly compelling alternative reconstruction is offered in the future, then a given question will have to be reopened, and a decision reached as to whether the present solution is false or a limiting case of a more general principle.

A reflection of this kind can also be made about the solution of the problem presented by our philosophic maxim, "Existence is perceived by the mind." Here the formula of distortion summarizes a lot of thought that isn't evident in the account as it's presented above. At first I thought the formula of distortion was "Knowledge and perception are not the same." But I realized that this statement was rather the result yielded by the application of a formula that I hadn't yet discovered. In other words, I discovered the answer to the meaning of the problem *before* I obtained the principle of translation according to which the answer is justified. This just means that I knew the solution before I could say how I arrived at it. This is often, though by no means always, the case in problem solving by the reconstructive approach.

Now let's take a moment to summarize the results of the last two sections before proceeding to the final ones. Various texts were cited in which Freud employs an analogical comparison of the method of the practicing analyst with the method of the archaeologist. This employment can be found in his early (1896, 1905) as well as his late writings (1930, 1937). Furthermore, the vocabulary of reconstruction, which is an intimate part of the archaeological analogy, is employed by Anna Freud (1936) in her discussion of defense mechanisms.

Meanwhile, the method of reconstruction is given independent, though related, application in the work of Collingwood. The focus of the relation is once again the archaeological analogy. Collingwood generalizes the method of reconstruction from archaeology to philosophy. He engages the task of overcoming the distortion inherent in false theoretical constructs, which nevertheless disguisedly express a dimension of correct knowledge. Disentangling knowledge from ignorance requires reconstructing the formula of distortion.

The juxtaposition of Freud and Collingwood suggests that the methods of philosophic and psychoanalytic thought are much more alike than the particular problems that each discipline treats. The methods of both are oriented toward discovering meaning amid apparent absurdity.

The introduction of two specific examples lends substance to this claim. The examples represent problems. Although the subject matters presented are incommensurable, the methods of treating them are comparable. In both cases, the methods of reconstruction involve problem solving. So the methods of philosophy and psychoanalysis chart a course of discovery to the limits of intelligibility. They suggest longitudinal lines on a globe, parallel on the equator but convergent at the poles.

In the final sections, the question is raised how the introduction of the method of reconstruction affects the debate about the epistemological status of psychoanalysis as a science. Here the practicing psychoanalyst must remind the philosopher that analysis is not only a theory of knowledge (epistemology) but also (and indeed primarily) an approach to personality change and a way of alleviating suffering. At the same time, philosophic reflection on the method of reconstruction can help bridge the gap between metapsychological theory and clinical practice, and guarantee the methodolgical integrity of the discipline. These and related topics now become the points of discussion.

THE PRACTICE OF INTERPRETATION

One of the main points of initiation of the debate about psychoanalysis as a science was the exchange between Heinz Hartmann and Ernest Nagel (Hartmann, 1959; Nagel, 1959). Taking off from Nagel's philosophic remodeling of the kinetic theory of gases, Hartmann compared psychoanalytic metapsychology to just such an axiomatic system of propositions. The basis of the comparison was the fact that neither molecular interactions nor processes in the unconscious are directly accessible to perception. Nevertheless we have indirect confirmation of the existence and efficacy of these phenomena in such effects as temperature, pressure, and change in volume, and dreams, symptoms, and slips (respectively). Nagel countered by attempting to point out inconsistencies in metapsychology. He claimed that the "correspondence rules" or "operational definitions" for relating theoretical to observational terms were loosely formulated, and that the economic point of view was just a metaphor (Nagel, 1959, p. 40).

This debate was reopened by Ricoeur's presentation of *Freud and Philosophy* (1970). There his strategy consisted in applying the terms of a general question about the epistemological status of the humanistic disciplines (or *Geisteswissenschaften*) to the specific field of psychoanalysis. He advanced the thesis that psychoanalysis is *not* an observational science (1970, p. 358). This may seem enigmatic at first. However, it does not imply that the analyst is prohibited from using his eyes. Rather, it means that the analyst's use of his eyes (and ears and other senses) is different than the use any scientist makes of his perceptual organs in an experimental setting. Ricoeur's thesis should be taken to imply an opposition to modeling therapy on the research laboratory. The comparison of psychoanalysis with the physical sciences should not be taken too far. Ricoeur then attempts to turn his thesis, which is allegedly a criticism in the hands of the opponents of analysis, into a counterattack against the logical positivist interpretation of science.

Let's take a step back and put matters in perspective. The philosopher Wilhelm Dilthey (1833-1911) distiguished the natural sciences and the humanistic disciplines according to the principles of knowledge on which they were founded. The former employs mechanical explanations of the causal interconnections between phenomena, while the latter aims at understanding human purposes and intentions in an intersubjective context. Dilthey proposed to complement the mathematical foundation of the natural sciences with an historical foundation for the humanistic disciplines. The understanding of language, art, and cultural expressions of human subjectivity happens through the interpretation of these phenomena in their historical milieu. (For an account of Dilthey's work see Palmer, 1969, pp. 98-123.)

Even before Dilthey, Immanuel Kant (1724-1804) attempted to demonstrate that mechanical explanations must be complemented by an account of purposefulness in order to intelligibly encompass the rule-governed organization of living beings. Kant's thinking, however, was more cautious than Dilthey's. He insisted that purposefulness was a function of our finite human understanding and, in fact, a limitation to it. Indeed purposefulness was a form of the subject's reflection, not a determination of the object (Kant, 1790, pp. 233-234, par. 79).

Ricoeur draws explicitly on this tradition but is otherwise original in applying its terms to psychoanalysis. A positive thesis is implied in saying that analysis is not an observational science. The alternative is that analysis is a science of interpretation. It employs the method of reconstruction for solving questions of meaning. From this perspective, analysis is as much (if not more) like archaeology and history than like physics or biology. One might easily overlook this if one remained at the level of a theoretical system of deductively linked propositions. Instead one must look at the method that's practiced.

Relying on Dilthey's distinction between causal explanation and understanding purpose, Ricoeur states his case:

Analytic experience bears a much greater resemblance to historical understanding than to natural explanation. Take for example the requirement put forward by epistemology of submitting a standardized set of clinical data to the check of a number of independent investigators. This requirement presupposes that a "case" is something other than a history, that it is a sequence of facts capable of being observed by many observers. [1970, p. 374]

Clinical practice is oriented toward problem solving in a genetic context. It is not a form of experimental research. In any case, analysis is clearly not an observational science in the sense that the molecular theory of gases is one. The latter has the restriction and the privilege of defining its object of inquiry in a setting where independent investigators can repeat, check, and publically control the reporting of data. In comparing analysis with archaeology, Freud gives us warrent for saying that the study of the individual life history is an historic discipline in a broad sense.

(For reasons of his own Hartmann rejects the archaeological comparison. One suggestion is that this is intended as a criticism of Wilhelm Reich, who saw analysis exclusively as a peeling of historic layers of the personality. The issue is complicated by Hartmann's explicit acknowledgment of the value of the "reconstructive approach," independent of the arachaeological analogy. See Hartmann, 1959, pp. 8-9.)

In addition, Freud notes that neurotics are usually unable to give an ordered history of their life in its relation to their illness (1905, p. 16). This happens due to actual fear and shame of revealing certain events as well as genuine amnesia, which serves the purposes of the unconscious.

We must remember that a case history is precisely that, a *history*. It's a unique sequence of events. This sequence is not capable of being repeated or of being repeatedly observed by many investigators. The events are accessible only through the interpretive reconstruction of memories, dreams, associations, and related reflections. Without reconstruction there may be a calender of events. The events hang together thanks to the method of the chronicler, descriptively labeled "scissors-and-paste" history by Collingwood (1946, p. 278).

In a sense, the spontaneous reports, the free associations of the analysand are like the historian's "sources" or, as they used to be called, "authorities." The critical historian questions, cross-examines, and revises his sources. If he is not only critical, but also scientific, then he realizes that the false statements in his sources are as important as the true ones. Men's blind spots reveal the dimensions and scope of their limited situations. For the historian, the reports provided by the men and women engaged in living their lives' time (the "authorities") are not yet evidence. A selection process must first occur through the posing of questions that the historical thinker wants to answer. Random information is constituted as evidence in juxtaposition with questions that are answered through it. Evidence is what answers questions.

Similarly, in psychoanalysis random free associations are not evidence. Neither is observable behavior or symptoms evidence. In this connection, it's significant that the same overt behavior, the same symptom, can have many different meanings. Psychoanalytic questions seek to reconstruct meaning, not describe behavior. (The description of overt behavior is not a specifically analytic task, though it may be a necessary condition of one.) What then is evidence in the analytic field where fantasies are as important as — and indeed more important than — objectives states of affairs? A tentative closure to this question is won by taking a clue from the historian. A select part of the mass of analytic discourse and behavior is constituted as evidence through its answering questions about the patient's (implicit and explicit) intentions, purposes, projects, and desires. Once again, evidence is what answers questions.

This thesis leaves the field open for the possible introduction of uniquely psychoanalytic modes of transmitting information. Of particular relevance here is the concept of empathy. The analyst perceives the affects of the analysand through empathy, which, as I understand it, is a special use of the sense organs involving both distance *from* and participation *in* the emotional life of the other person. A detailed consideration of the literature on this topic can further the task of defining the specificity of psychoanalytic evidence. (See, e.g., Kohut, 1959, 1971; Modell, 1973.)

The questions and answers of the psychoanalytic setting unfold in a situation that is intermediate between the naive naturalness of everyday life and the manipulative artificiality of the laboratory. Clinical therapy is a practice governed by rules of its own. On the one hand, these rules are more rigorous than those of everyday life. One must try and tell everything, no matter how trivial or embarrassing. At the same time, clinical practice is more flexible than scientific experimentation. Human beings have to be respected as ends in themselves and not mere means to attaining metatheoretical knowledge. In short, the therapeutic situation is a dialogical one, in which human existence, not properties of an object, is under scrutiny. With simple devotion to the phenomena, the analyst turns his "evenly hovering attention" toward the analysand's "free associations" as they emerge (Freud, 1912, pp. 111-112). This is a way of initiating understanding. A life story, a case history, unfolds between these two poles of communication. Questions are posed and answers sought to solve problems that are intimately personal, yet no less universal for all that.

Here is the point at which psychoanalysis goes beyond history. Even if analysis can be classed with history for epistemological purposes, still the practice of analysis uses history as a means to an end of its own. In undertaking the compilation of a life history, in uncovering an archaeology of the subject, the therapist is engaged in an enterprise oriented toward alleviating human misery. The patient must not only remember the past, but he must also transcend it. In the words of Shakespeare, the patient and therapist must "pluck from the memory a rooted sorrow. . . . "

Now some may object that, without really taking Nagel's criticisms seriously, we've plunged into an alternative way of representing psychoanalysis in comparison with history, not physics. This objection is warranted, and we must retrace our steps to eliminate this shortcoming. The reason for postponing this consideration was not to repress Nagel's views, but rather to prepare the way for an intelligible reconstruction of them.

According to Nagel, theoretical knowledge consists of a system of propositions, deductively linked by valid logical inferences. Scientific method involves specifying observable events or processes as the meaning of otherwise unobservable theoretic terms through "correspondence rules" or "operational definitions" (Nagel, 1959, p. 40). Thus scientific method is a technique of relating theoretical terms to observational terms.

However, this way of representing the scientific method is questionable. The view of scientific method that emerges here is too narrow. It is, in fact, not a scientific method, but the method used by a particular philosophic view of science to analyze theoretical constructs. The trap into which we are led is one of conceiving of scientific rationality in the form of a system of deductively linked propositions. The result is preoccupation with the distinction between theoretical terms and corresponding observational ones. We forget that the correspondence is arrived at in terms of practical techniques and operations. That is to say, theoretical terms are applied to observations in the context of practice.

For the practicing scientist, theory and observation are more intimately related than the discussion of Nagel and the language of operational definitions would have us believe. Experimental evidence is theory laden. Random observations have no place in science.

The history of philosophy offers us a lesson here. Kant understood that theory and observation are separable only for a transcendental idealist, not an empirical realist. He gave a valuable clue for representing the relation between theory and observation in his maxim: "Thoughts without content are empty, intuitions without concepts are blind" (1787, p. 93). Following this formula we can say: Theory without content is empty, observations without theory are blind. Similarly, Wittgenstein went in search of an example of pure observation, unalloyed by any theoretic or conceptual determination. He didn't find pure seeing. Instead he found "seeing as . . . " (1945, p. 200). He always found the "echo of thought in sight" (1945, p. 212). Even the most primitive perception is already structured by thought as this or that.

Scientists do not make accidental observations, but constrain phenomena to answer questions of their own formulation. Once again, evidence is what answers the investigator's question. When Galileo, for example, let balls roll down an inclined plane, he had already mathematically anticipated the curve they would describe. The parabola is the shape yielded by the spatial interpretation of the algebraic function for acceleration under the influence of gravity, $F(x) = \frac{1}{2}at^2$. He was cross-examining his witness, in this case nature herself, to test out his mathematically based conjecture.

It is instructive to consider that Galileo was giving a physical interpretation to a mathematical formula of the form, $F(x) = x^2$. Similarly, the molecular theory of gases consists in an interpretation of Newton's second law of motion (net force = rate of change of momentum) in the closed system of a volume, V, within a limited temperature range. The result is a function relating the pressure exerted by the molecules' mass and velocity to the temperature in terms of the kinetic energy of the system.

These examples should upset our complacency somewhat. They imply the breakdown of the neat dichotomy between the natural and humanistic sciences from an unexpected direction. The natural sciences are more humanistic than we thought. The interpretation of symbols is a source of meaning in both!

The point is that there are indeed important parallels between the methods of psychoanalysis and physics, even in the most theoretical aspects. But these parallels emerge at the level of the practice of interpretation, not in terms of the artifical distinction between theory and observation. (Two qualifications are needed. One, no one wants to claim that dream symbols have the atemporal invariability of the symbols of the language of mathematics. Dream symbols are inevitably culture bound. Two, the use of mathematical models in physics is not free historic change. Mathematics provides absolute certainty only as long as it is disconnected from the contingencies of empirical situations. Physics remains an empirical science subject to the vicissitudes of future variation.)

This digression into the philosophy of science was necessitated by the objective of making sense out of the comparison between the molecular theory of gases and psychoanalytic metapsychology. This comparison was initiated by Hartmann and developed by Nagel. Unfortunately, both men are bewitched by a preconceived notion of scientific method. Their formula of distortion (see pp. 515-516) represents scientific method as mapping unobservable terms (e.g., molecules or unconscious process) onto observable ones (e.g., pressure or dreams). The reconstruction of the sense of their dialogue consists in showing that interpretation has a positive role to play in the method of the physical sciences, where there is a practical inseparability of theory and observation.

In a way, this discussion has the consequence of deepening our perplexity about the relation between psychoanalytic metapsychology and the case histories of clinical therapy. Here the gap between theory and practice seems greater than in the natural sciences. Some psychoanalysts resist theorizing, are quite antipathetic toward metapsychology, and even ignore it, but they are still skilled at helping patients to overcome their problems and regain their personal integrity and well-being.

One paper that contains an engaging proposal on how to deal with this gap
is George Klein's "Two Theories or One" (1973). In effect, Klein argues that
the gap would be eliminated if one pole of the opposition was discarded.
Klein suggests that the economic and dynamic points of view of the metapsychology are really a veiled extension of the physiologizing effort of Freud's
1895 "Project." Klein argues that, although Freud abandoned this particular
form of the neurological program, he never gave up the idea. But this effort
to find a neurological model is actually an obstacle to the development of the
psychoanalytic enterprise. According to Klein, psychoanalysis is most
intimately related, not to biology, but to the work of the dramatist and novel-
ist (and historian), for it focuses on the intentional structure of human encounter, conflict, and understanding (cf. Klein, 1973, pp. 115, 126, and
Ricoeur, 1970, p. 375). There are really two psychoanalytic theories presently. One is oriented toward "unlocking meaning" (1973, pp. 109, 113). The
other aims at a general psychological theory in which behavior is explained
causally, ultimately in terms of physiological mechanisms (1973, pp.
106-107). Klein proposes that this latter theory be abandoned and replaced
with further efforts toward developing "experiential" and "functional" concepts (1973, p. 110) in the clinical setting.

Klein's presentation is loaded with valuable material. He finds great sympathy with the reconstructive themes of this paper in locating the essence of
the psychoanalytic method in "unlocking meaning." Klein's representation of
the "two theories" of analysis definitely intersects with Ricoeur's distinction
between energetics and hermeneutics. There is a further intersection of
Ricoeur and Klein in that both turn to the model of the historian in contrasting the clinician with the experimenter (through Klein actually suggests several alternatives).

In addition, Klein's interest in research designs using data germaine to the
psychoanalytic setting recalls C. G. Jung's word associations tests (1907).
Certainly the time has come to update the criteria of responsible knowledge
that are available to the investigations of the research analyst (see Klein,
1973, p. 128).

Unfortunately, the force of Klein's proposal is undercut somewhat by the
fact that at least two of his three statements about Freud's assumed philosophy of science are open to serious question.

Klein asserts that Freud's philosophy of science assumed that "concepts of
purposefulness and meaning are unacceptable as terms of scientific explanation" (Klein, 1973, p. 104). However, in discussing slips, as we will see, Freud
talks in terms of double intentions. In fact, Freud argues vehemently against
those who want to reduce these slips to mere organic aberrations. Such a reduction serves the interests of resistance, though it is not always an example of
resistance to cite organic compliance with psychic acts. Freud says that slips

are "psychic acts," arising "from mutual interference between two intentions" (1915, p. 60). Furthermore, he believes that this thesis *explains* slips in a way that no appeal to organic influences can. He says that his explanation of errors as psychic acts has

> won for psychology phenomena which were not reckoned earlier as belonging to it.
>
> Let us pause for a moment over the assertion that parapraxes are "psychic acts". Does this imply more than we have already said—that they have a sense? I think not. . . . The question will then be whether the particular mental phenomenon has arisen immediately from somatic, organic and material influences—in which case its investigation will not be a part of psychology—or whether it is derived in the first instance from other mental processes, somewhere behind which the series of organic influences begins. It is this latter situation that we have in view when we describe a phenomenon as a mental process, and for that reason it is more expedient to clothe our assertion in the form: "the phenomenon has sense". By "sense" we understand "meaning", "intention", "purpose" and "position in a continuous psychical context". [1915, pp. 60-61]

Here Freud doesn't even pay lip service—as he occasionally does elsewhere—to the idea that an organic explanation will eventually be found. He is clearly interested in establishing the autonomy of psychology vis a vis physiology. He sharply distinguishes the field of psychological investigation from the region of organic influences, which are shoved away "somewhere behind" the field of mental phenomena. The autonomy of psychoanalytic psychology is secured in orienting itself toward phenomena that have meaning or sense.

Klein's second assertion about Freud's philosophy of science asserts that Freud assumed that an acceptable explanation had to be purged of teleological implication (Klein, 1973, p. 104). The status of this assertion turns on what Klein means by "teleology." If teleology just means purposefulness, then this second statement is a positive form of the first one. And it's corrected along with the first one, too. However, if Klein is alluding to Freud's strictly antivitalist theory of life, then it may be allowed to stand. A complete discussion of the issues would entail an adequate decision about the theory of life implicit in *Beyond the Pleasure Principle*, and this cannot be engaged in at this late point.

Klein's third assertion maintains that Freud assumed that purposive regularities would eventually be described through the use of purely physiological models (1973, p. 104). But this is open to serious question even at the point of the origins of psychoanalysis. Very early on Freud recognized that hysterical symptoms are rooted, at least in part, in the hysteric's ideas. He says: "Hysteria behaves as though anatomy did not exist as though it had no knowledge of it" (1893, p. 169). A physiological explanation is clearly impossible where there is no "anatomical lesion." There is certainly some involvement of the organism. But the leison is "dynamical" and "entirely independent of the anatomy of the nervous system" (1893, p. 169).

If this were not enough to show the limits of physiological investigation, there is the further fact that hysterical paralysis corresponds to the popular conceptions of anatomy: "It takes the organs in the ordinary, popular sense of the names they bear" (1893, p. 169). Freud never denies that "somatic compliance" is a necessary, though admittedly insufficient, condition of neurosis. But he also never forgets that what the body or soma complies *with* has the character of the popular psyche's conception of anatomy, not the scientist's specialized theory. The point is that physiology is inadequate to explain hysteria. The psychic contributes something to the intelligibility of the phenomena in question, and analysis claims its own proper field as the unmasking of this often hidden contribution.

Admittedly, Klein's abstract of Freud's alleged philosophy of science is only a limited part of his paper. It is the weakest part, but perhaps not the most important part. In the end, his conception of psychoanalysis is not that far from the present structure of the discipline. Once Klein has abandoned the dynamic and economic (i.e., the more metphorical) aspects of metapsychology, then he finds that he must stretch his notion of clinical theory to accommodate some clinically relevant concepts that were previously stationed there. Instead of two theories, Klein gives us one theory with two kinds of concepts.

According to Klein, clinical concepts are divided into experiential and functional concepts, intra- and extra-phenomenological ones (1973, p. 110). It's a generalization, but an accurate one, to say that this division represents a distinction between concepts that are experience-near and those that are experience-distant (respectively). Concepts such as projection, introjection, repression, and the ego's other defense mechanisms operate as autonomous processes independently of the subject's immediate experiential awareness. But these functions are a "part of his reality" (1973, p. 111). Presumably they are a part of the subject's reality, for they serve to transform and bind anxiety (an experiential phenomenon) in a way that furthers adaptation. These mechanisms are classified by Klein as "functional concepts" (1973, p. 110).

The problem is that Freud often engages in a use of language involving both dynamic forces in conflict and meaningful purposes, both mechanisms and intentionalities (Mischel, 1974 has documented this extensively). Freud talks about forces and intentions in the same breath. For example, he does this where the phenomena of psychology are described as ". . . signs of an interplay of forces in the mind, as a manifestation of purposeful intentions working concurrently or in mutual opposition" (1915, p. 67). No matter how often one tries to suppress the language of dynamic forces in conflict, it re-emerges. Even Klein admits this. After successfully rooting out any mention of physiological mechanisms (at the level of psychoanalytic explanation), he still needs to reintroduce "the dialectic of directed forces to which a person is subject" (1973, p. 115). Psychoanalysis cannot do without its dynamic metaphors, whether one draws them from the context of physiology as Freud or from the context of drama and history like Klein.

Strictly speaking, Freud doesn't recognize, or at least doesn't adhere to, the classic distinction between mechanical, causal explanation and understanding purposeful intentionality (see p. 523). In mixing the language of forces and meanings, Freud also mixes the corresponding explanations and understandings. For Freud, it is an explanation to discover (through interpretation) that an apparently absurd slip, dream, or symptom is understandable, i.e., has a meaning. Interpretation is one way of showing that certain phenomena, apparently unintelligibly subject to chance, do not escape the deterministic network (1901, p. 239). Interpretation is a form of explanation which seeks understanding amid absurdity. (Klein is basically in agreement with this view, though he sometimes gives the impression that he's revising Freud's view rather than describing it [1973, p. 116].)

The introduction of the method of interpretation into the debate about the epistemological status of psychoanalysis as a science has three significant consequences. (1) Psychoanalytic knowledge shows itself to be more like that available to the historian than that accessible through theories in physics. The approach to knowledge in analysis and history is reconstructive. (2) Psychoanalysis and the physical sciences do have a comparable area of intersection. But this comparison is not available through the distinction between theory and observation. One must rather look to the level of the interpretation of symbols as a source of meaning in both. (3) In psychoanalysis the distinction between explanation and understanding breaks down. Giving an interpretation, in which what was nonsense becomes understandable, is a form of explanation.

CONCLUSION

We still have to say something about the relation between metapsychological theory and the case histories of clinical practice. Can we find an alternative way of bridging the gap between theory and practice short of eliminating metapsychology itself? The key insight here consists in realizing that, although there may be many psychoanalytic theories, there is still only one psychoanalytic method.

On the one hand, we have metapsychological theory with its various perspectives, which can always discover adequate causes to determine every example of behavior. And even if some examples escape the deterministic network, the legitimate task of metapsychology is the reduction of behavior to causal mechanisms. On the other hand, clinical practice deals with the purposes, conflicts, and goals of human behavior in its intersubjective and dialogical aspects. Here the task is to reveal the meanings of symptoms, to understand their relation to the patient's interpersonal environment, and to restore the patient's well-being. People are not causal mechanisms. However mechanistic the theoretical consideration of symptom formation may aspire to be, the practice of undoing symptoms still relies on discourse about human intentions and purposes.

The solution to the problem of how to bridge the gap between theory and practice consists in realizing that the link is a methodological one. The method of interpretive reconstruction traverses the distance between mechanical explanation and human understanding. It seeks understanding amid seeming nonsense as a form of explanation. The reenactment and mastery of the breakdown of this distinction is the solution to the problem.

The method of interpretive reconstruction is an invariable function that links the variable metatheories to clinical practice. Here the theories are rather like those mathematical formulas that acquire physical meaning in being interpreted in a spatiotemporal context (see p. 527). The application of a metapsychological model requires its reconstruction on the basis of the materials already available in the case history to which it is being applied. This reconstruction is a transitional function mediating the application of theoretical structures to practical processes of therapy. It's therefore a kind of reasoning involving both theory and practice.

Only one more point. In a sense, all theories are alike, whether in philosophy or psychoanalysis: they come too late to change the world, they can only reflect it. But the goal of therapy is precisely that, to change the world by changing the people who dwell in it. The practice of therapy aims at answering the desperate needs of personal disintegration and confusion with the antidote of self-knowledge. Macbeth's desperate question is transformed into an assignment; the task is to

> minister to a mind diseased,
> Pluck from the memory a rooted sorrow,
> Raze out the written trouble of the brain,
> and with some sweet oblivious antidote
> Cleanse the stuff'd bosom of the perilous stuff
> Which weighs upon the heart.

ACKNOWLEDGEMENT

I am grateful to Dr. Robert Langs and Professors S. E. Toulmin and P. Ricoeur for reading earlier versions of this paper and making useful suggestions. I alone am responsible for its remaining imperfections.

REFERENCES

Collingwood, R. G. (1938). *The Principles of Art*. London: Oxford Univ. Press. 1972.

_____(1939). *An Autobiography*. London: Oxford Univ. Press, 1969.

_____(1946). *The Idea of History*, ed. T. M. Knox. London: Oxford Univ. Press, 1969.

Descartes, R. (1642). Meditations on first philosophy. *Descartes: Philosophical Writings*, trans. G. E. M. Anscombe and P. T. Geach, pp. 59-109. London: Nelson, 1966.

Forde-Johnston, J. (1974). *History From the Earth: An Introduction to Archaeology*. Greenwich, Conn.: New York Graphic Society, 1974.

Freud, A. (1936). *The Ego and the Mechanisms of Defense*. New York: International Universities Press, 1946.

Freud, S. (1896). The aetiology of hysteria. *Standard Edition* 3:191-221. London: Hogarth.

_____(1901). *The Psychopathology of Everyday Life. Ibid.* Vol. 6.

_____(1905). A fragment of an analysis of a case of hysteria. *Ibid.* 7:7-122.

_____(1912). Recommendations to physicians practicing psychoanalysis. *Ibid.* 12: 109-120.

_____(1915). The unconscious. *Ibid.* 14: 166-215.

_____(1916-17). *A General Introduction to Psychoanalysis. Ibid.* Vol. 16

_____(1930). Civilization and its discontents. *Ibid.* 21: 64-145.

_____(1937). Construction in analysis. *Ibid.* 23:257-269. (*Please note*: there may be an occasional variation in translation where the author used the available paperback edition.)

Hartmann, Heinz (1959). Psychoanalysis as a scientific theory. *Psychoanalysis, Scientific Method and Philosophy: A Symposium*, ed. S. Hook, pp. 3-37. New York: New York Univ. Press, 1964.

Husserl, E. (1970). *Cartesian Meditations: An Introduction to Phenomenology*, trans. Dorion Cairns. The Hague: Martinns Nijhoff.

Janik, A., and Toulmin, S. (1973). *Wittgenstein's Vienna*. New York: Simon & Schuster.

Jung, C. G. (1907). The psychology of dementia praecox. *Collected Works* 3:1-154. Princeton: Princeton Univ. Press, 1960.

Kant, I. (1781-1787). *Critique of Pure Reason*, trans. N. K. Smith. New York: St. Martin's, 1929.

_____(1788). *Critique of Practical Reason*, trans. L. W. Beck. Indianapolis: Bobbs-Merrill, 1956.

_____(1790). *Critique of Judgment*, trans. J. H. Bernard. New York: Hafner, 1968.

Klein, G. S. (1973). Two theories or one? *Bulletin of the Menninger Clinic* 37,2:99-132.

Kohut, H. (1959). Introspection, empathy, and psychoanalysis. *Journal of the American Psychoanalytic Association* 7,3:459-483.

_____(1971). *The Analysis of the Self*. New York: International Universities Press.

Marcuse, H. (1955). *Eros and Civilization: A Philosophical Inquiry into Freud*. New York: Vintage, 1955.

Mischel, T. (1974). Understanding neurotic behavior: from "mechanism" to "intentionality." *Understanding Other Persons*, ed. T. Mischel. London: Blackwell, 1974.

Modell, A. H. (1973). Affects and psychoanalytic knowledge. *Annual of Psychoanalysis* 1:117-124.

Nagel, E. (1959). Methodological issues in psychoanalytic theory. *Psychoanalysis, Scientific Method, and Philosophy: A Symposium*, ed. S. Hook, pp. 38-56. New York: New York Univ. Press. 1964.

Palmer, R. E. (1969). *Hermeneutics*. Evanston: Northwestern Univ. Press.

Plato. *Meno*, trans. W. K. C. Guthrie. *Collected Dialogues*, ed. E. Hamilton. Princeton: Princeton Univ. Press, 1971. (Please note: the pagination in the references in this paper is based on the standard page subdivisions of H. Estienne (ed. 1578), usually available in all editions.)

_____. *Theaetetus*, trans. F. M. Cornford. *Ibid*. (See note above.)

Ricoeur, P. (1965). *Freud and Philosophy*, trans. D. Savage. New Haven: Yale Univ. Press, 1970.

Toulmin, S. (1953). *The Philosophy of Science: An Introduction*. New York: Harper Torchbooks, 1960.

_____(1972). *Human Understanding*. Vol. 1. Princeton: Princeton Univ. Press, 1972.

Wisdom, J. (1953). Philosophy and psycho-analysis. *Classics of Analytic Philosophy*, ed. R. R. Ammerman, pp. 285-294. New York: McGraw-Hill, 1965.

Wittgenstein, L. (1921). *Tractatus*, trans. D. F. Pears and B. F. McGuinness. New York: Humanities Press, 1971. (The references to this text are to both page and paragraph.)

_____(1945). *Philosophical Investigations*, trans. G. E. M. Anscombe. New York: Macmillan, 1971. (References are to both page and paragraph.)

LOUIS AGOSTA, Ph.D.

DR. AGOSTA has been associated with the University of Chicago as a student and member for the past seven years. He is presently preparing a book on the intellectual history of the concept of empathy in philosophy and psychology.

A Cross-cultural Test of the Freudian Theory of Circumcision

Michio Kitahara, Fil. Dr.

University of Maryland
Far Eastern Division
Tokyo

Freud's thesis that circumcision is a symbolic substitute for castration as a result of the Oedipus conflict was tested by examining 111 societies (see the note to Table 1). The result shows that circumcision is likely to be found in societies in which (1) the son sleeps in the mother's bed during the nursing period in bodily contact with her, and/ or (2) the father sleeps in a different hut, reducing his influence on the son as a superior and competing male. Since these two factors seem to intensify the son's oedipal attachment to the mother, the data are compatible with Freud's theory. Bettelheim's theory of circumcision is less fully formulated, and only when we assume that males significantly reduce their vagina envy after puberty rites is his theory compatible with the data.

According to Freud, circumcision is a symbolic substitute for castration. In his discussion of the Oedipus complex, Freud states that a son experiences anxiety when he loves his mother because he believes in the possibility of castration as an external threat. A little boy is often told that his penis may be cut off at the time of his early masturbatory activities, and this makes him feel that the danger of castration is real (1973, p. 119). Freud also suggests the possibility of a phylogenetic memory trace in order to explain the existence of the fear of castration. He says, "during the human family's primaeval period castration used actually to be carried out by a jealous and cruel father upon growing boys" (Ibid. See also Freud, 1949, pp. 92-93, fn. 11; Bonaparte, 1949, p. 482). Freud goes on to say that the custom of circumcision, which is often a part of puberty rites among nonliterate peoples, is a symbolic substitute for castration. When a son is circumcised, there is an expression of his subjection to the father's will (1939, p. 192; 1949, pp. 92-93, fn. 11).

The idea of considering circumcision as a symbolic substitute for castration has been supported, among others, by Nunberg and by Fenichel. Fenichel thinks that a puberty rite promises privilege and protection to a son in return for his obedience, and this arrangement is enforced on the son in the form of circumcision as a symbolic castration (1945, p. 364). The significance of circumcision in puberty rites as a means to resolve conflict between sons and fathers has been pointed out by Reik. He thinks that the problems of incest and parricide are dealt with through such rites. The circumcision rites prevent incest, and the symbolic killing in these rites prevents parricide (1958, p. 99 ff.).

Bettelheim has presented a different theory of circumcision, in which men's envy for women's sexual organs and their functions is emphasized. In the history of psychoanalysis, this idea of "vagina envy" (Bettelheim, 1954, p. 20) has been repeatedly mentioned. Freud states that everyone has a bisexual tendency (1950, p. 197). Nunberg says that dissatisfaction with one's own sex is found among both highly civilized and nonliterate peoples (1949, p. 1), and Roheim (1953) thinks that the myths concerning the Milky Way indicate ambisexual symbolism. According to Fromm (1951, p. 233), men are envious of women, and Landauer (1931, p. 178), Chadwick (1925, pp. 61-62), and Jacobson (1950, p. 142) all indicate men's desire to bear children. Klein says that a son feels inferior to his mother after identification with her because of his inability to bear children (1948, pp. 206-207). In Zilboorg's opinion, men's vagina envy is more fundamental than women's penis envy (1944, p. 290). By following Jung's ideas, Neumann (1949) emphasizes the importance of the archetypal mother figure and men's desire for, and fear of her, influence.

By following this line of thought, Bettelheim suggests that circumcision symbolizes men's envy for women's sexual organs and their functions (1954, p. 56; also ch. 10). Such phenomena as transvestism, placing of a plug in the anus among the Chagga males to imitate menstruation, and couvade, in which a man simulates his wife around the time of her parturition, are all seen as expressions of men's envy for femininity (Bettelheim, 1954, chs. 7 and 8). Among the Arunta of Australia, in addition to circumcision, boys must undergo the operation of subincision, in which the urethra is cut open along the posterior part of the penis, as part of the puberty rite. In Bettelheim's opinion, the purpose of subincision is to make the incised penis resemble the vulva, and the bleeding due to this operation, when it is repeated, simulates menstruation (1954, p. 112).

However, Bettelheim does not explain circumcision in a satisfactory way. On the one hand, he thinks that by means of circumcision, men get women's functions symbolically, and on the other, he also thinks that the exposed glans emphasizes masculinity as a result of circumcision. Bettelheim also does not rule out other reasons for circumcision. Nevertheless, he seems basically to assume that circumcision is due to men's envy for femininity (1954, ch. 10).

In essence, then, there are basically two psychoanalytical theories of cir-

cumcision. According to Freud, circumcision is a symbolic castration resulting from the Oedipus conflict, and according to Bettelheim, it is an expression of men's envy for the woman's sexual organs and their functions. The
purpose of this paper is to consider these two theories by means of cross-cul-
tural data on circumcision. If we compare these two theories, however, we
recognize that Bettelheim's is rather vaguely formulated, especially in regard
to the matters of how men themselves look at circumcision and whether or not
vagina envy is persistent throughout a man's life. For this reason, the emphasis will be placed on the examination of Freud's theory, and some comments
will also be made on Bettelheim's hypothesis.

PROBLEM

The custom of circumcision is not universal. But at the same time, it is not
limited to only a few societies in the world. According to one study, it is practiced among 65 percent of the societies in Africa, 39 percent in Oceania, and
3 percent in Eurasia. It is absent among the societies in the rest of the world
(Whiting, 1964, p. 511, Table 1).
The geographical incidence of circumcision and its frequency of occurrence in the world in this manner suggest two things. One is that circumcision
is not a peculiar custom which was started totally by accident. Since it is practiced in many vastly different societies, it may be reasonable to assume that
this custom has some functional meaning to the practising societies and their
members, whatever that meaning may be. The other point is that, since circumcision is present in some societies and absent in others, some have certain
factors which increase the possibility of the practice, while the same factors
are missing in others.
If the Freudian theory of circumcision is seen in terms of these two assumptions, a problem emerges which requires serious attention. That is, if circumcision is a symbolic substitute for castration because of the Oedipus conflict,
the son's relations with his parents may have something to do with its presence
or absence. Even if the Oedipus complex may be universal, it is conceivable
that, depending on the extent of closeness between mother and son, the intensity of that complex may vary. If the relationship between mother and son
is indeed very close, the latter is likely to develop a very strong attachment to
the mother, and this may increase the likelihood of circumcision. On the
other hand, if this relationship is more distant, the son may not develop a
strong attachment, and as a consequence, the incidence of circumcision is
likely to be less frequent. In brief, the presence or absence of circumcision can
be studied in terms of the intensity of the son's oedipal attachment.
Anthropologist J.W.M. Whiting and his associates recognized the possibilities of this approach and have presented an interpretation of circumcision in

which a modified version of the Freudian theory is used (Whiting, et al., 1958). According to them, among the societies in which the nursing baby has close bodily contact with its mother due to exclusive mother-infant sleeping arrangements and/or a long postpartum sexual taboo, circumcision is likely to be present, compared with societies in which the baby does not have such a close relationship.

These two factors considered by Whiting and his associates, namely, the presence or absence of exclusive mother-infant sleeping arrangements and also of a long postpartum sexual taboo, can certainly be considered to affect the extent of the son's oedipal attachment. According to one custom, the nursing baby sleeps in the mother's bed in bodily contact with her while the father sleeps in another bed, and according to the other, a taboo prohibits sexual intercourse between a man and wife after childbirth, sometimes even as long as two years or more. In practice, these two phenomena tend to coexist, and when there is an exclusive mother-infant sleeping arrangement, there is likely to be a postpartum sexual taboo, and vice versa.

However, in a later publication, Whiting abandoned this approach in favor of a different interpretation in which the son's incorrect identification with his mother, instead of the oedipal conflict, is considered the key factor (Burton and Whiting, 1961). In this new approach, circumcision is seen as a rectifying mechanism when the son envies the mother's status and makes an incorrect identification with her rather than with the father, because of the closeness between mother and son. In a still later publication, protein deficiency in diet was taken up as an additional problem (Whiting, 1964).

In the opinion of the present writer, Whiting's first approach using the extent of oedipal attachment between the mother and nursing infant for predicting the presence or absence of circumcision is potentially a fruitful one. At the same time, it must be said that this approach is rather crudely and incompletely conceived, and it has not been justly formulated, tested, and evaluated (see Norbeck, et al., 1962). Above all, it is necessary to look at the problem of the oedipal conflict in a wider perspective: it is possible to think that there are two important factors affecting the intensity of the son's oedipal attachment. First, there is the extent of bodily contact between mother and son. This is the factor recognized and discussed by Whiting and his associates. In addition, it is also possible to look at the relationship between father and son. If the extent of contact between mother and son is assumed to affect the intensity of the Oedipus complex, the extent of contact between father and son may also affect it. Whiting and his associates do not consider this problem, but in view of the nature of the Oedipus complex as conceived by Freud, this relationship ought to be taken into account.

There is good reason to assume the importance of the father-son relationship. According to one study, among polygynous societies in which the family consists of husband, wives, and children, if each co-wife lives in a separate quarter with her children, males are significantly more likely to be circumcised and/or segregated at puberty (Kitahara, 1974). In terms of the Freudian approach, this finding can be interpreted as follows. If a co-wife lives in her own quarter with her children, sons are likely to have significantly less social contact with the father, compared with the situation in which the co-wives live together in the same quarter with their husband and children. A decrease in contact with the father is likely to mean an increase in contact with the mother, and the son's oedipal attachment may be intensified as a result. In addition, if the son has little social contact with the father in his everyday life, he may not feel the threat of the father as a superior and competing male figure, and this facilitates his freer attachment to the mother. Therefore, when each co-wife lives in a separate quarter with her children, there are these two mechanisms which may intensify the father's desire to castrate the son. This is carried out in a symbolic form as circumcision.

The key point of this approach is that the relationship between father and son becomes crucial in reference to the possibility of circumcision when they have less frequent contact between them due to the separate quarters for co-wives. In this sense, at least, it is desirable to add the problem of the father-son relationship in examining circumcision. Therefore, it may be reasonable to assume two factors which are to be considered. One is the factor of the mother-son relationship, and the other is that of the father-son relationship. They may be presented as two propositions.

Proposition 1: When the mother and son sleep in the same bed in bodily contact, the son's Oedipus attachment to her increases.

Proposition 2: If the father does not stay in the living quarter where the mother and son sleep, the son's Oedipus attachment to her increases.

METHOD

In order to examine the Freudian theory of circumcision in terms of the two propositions stated, Whiting's data (1964) on circumcision were used. This is an informative source in which the sleeping arrangements for father, mother, and baby are indicated. In all 177 societies are listed, but 31 must be discarded because of the lack of information on circumcision or sleeping arrangements. Also, many of these are geographically too close to each other, and in order to avoid the danger of including societies which are practically the same due to extensive diffusion in the past, the "three degree rule" suggested by Murdock (1967, p. 4) was applied: whenever two societies were too close geographically, the less informative society was eliminated. If they were identical in this regard, one of them was chosen randomly. In this way, 35 societies were eliminated additionally. The final sample thus obtained consisted of 111 (see Table 1).

These societies were then scrutinized by checking the information in Column 6 (most common type of sleeping arrangement for father, mother, and baby), Column 9 (sleeping distance between father and mother in monogamous situation), and Column 10 (sleeping distance between father and mother in polygynous situation), included in Whiting's data (1964). Since the mother and baby sleep at least in the same hut in all cases, when the father and mother do not sleep in the same hut, there is approximately as much distance between the father and baby as between the father and mother. Similarly, when the father and mother are described as sleeping in the same hut, this necessarily means that the father and baby sleep in the same hut. In this way, the distance between the father and baby as well as the distance between the mother and baby were determined. In many societies, two kinds of sleeping arrangements (one for monogamy, the other for polygyny) are possible, and whether a given society is basically monogamous or polygynous was determined by using Column 14 (family organization) of the *Ethnographic Atlas* (Murdock, 1967).

In accordance with propositions 1 and 2, there are two factors both of which dichotomize the data. One is whether or not the mother and baby sleep in the same bed, and the other whether or not the father and baby sleep in the same hut. On this basis, four types of sleeping arrangements for father, mother, and baby are possible. Table 1 shows the classification of the data into these four types.

In Table 1, two symbols are used for the two types of sleeping arrangements. When father, mother, and baby (hereafter abbreviated as F, M, and B respectively) are separated from each other by an ampersand, they sleep in the same hut, and when they are separated from each other by a solidus, they sleep in different huts. When both of these two symbols are absent, they sleep in the same bed in bodily contact.

RESULTS

From Propositions 1 and 2, five hypotheses were derived, and they were tested against the data. To begin with, it was reasoned that if the possibility of circumcision increases (1) when the mother and son sleep in the same bed, or (2) when the father does not sleep in the same hut where the mother and son sleep, among the societies in which both of these two factors are present (MB/ F), the frequency of circumcision is greater, compared with the societies in which only one of the two factors is present (MB & F or M & B/F). The frequency of circumcision in these societies in turn is likely to be greater com-

TABLE 1
Four Types of Sleeping Arrangements
for Father, Mother, and a Baby

Number of Societies

		Circumcision Absent	Circumcision Present
Type I	(MB & F)	35 (a)	9 (b)
Type II	(MB/F)	10 (c)	19 (d)
Type III	(M & B & F)	32 (e)	1 (f)
Type IV	(M & B/F)	4 (g)	1 (h)

F = father, M = mother, and B = baby. When M, F, and B are separated from each other by an ampersand they sleep in the same hut; when they are separated from each other by a solidus they sleep in different huts. The absence of these symbols signifies that they sleep in the same bed.

The names of the 111 sample societies in these cells are as follows:

a. Lamba, Miao, Okinawa, Andamanese, Semang, Trukese, Ifaluk, Papago, Tarahumara, Mixtecans, Aymara, Mataco, Timbira, Nama, Nuer, Ainu, Chukchee, Japanese, Bhil, Balinese, Marshallese, Yaruro, Trobriands, Copper Eskimo, Chiricahua, Tarascans, Siriono, Callinago, Tapirape, Witoto, Yagua, Yaghan, Nambicuara, Trumai, Tenetehara

b. Amhara, Songhai, Silwa, Samoa, Marquesans, Tuareg, Murngin, Aranda, Kwoma

c. Pondo, Bemba, Nyakyusa, Rundi, Ashanti, Katab, Tanala, Malaita, Kurtatchi, Bush Negro

d. Somali, Yao, Fang, Mongo, Mende, Tiv, Nupe, Azande, Ila, Hausa, Wolof, Lesu, Lovedu, Chagga, Kikuyu, Bambara, Mossi, Dahomeans, Dorobo

e. Lapps, Lepcha, Coorg, Maria Gond, Kapauku, Kaska, Kutchin, Cuna, Carib, Araucanians, French, Yankee, Bulgarians, Serbs, Koryak, Burmese, Maori, Aleut, Kwakiutl, Klamath, Tubatulabal, Ute, Cheyenne, Crow, Ojibwa, Omaha, Delaware, Micmac, Hopi, Mosquito, Tehuelche, Apinaye

f. Rwala

g. Ganda, Yurok, Sanpoil, Cagaba

h. Lau

pared with the societies in which the two factors are absent (M & B & F). Hypothesis 1 was tested from these reasonings as a preliminary investigation.

> Hypothesis 1: Circumcision is most likely to be practiced among the societies in which (1) the mother and son sleep in the same bed, and (2) the father does not sleep in the same hut where the mother and son sleep; it is least likely to be practiced among the societies in which both of these two factors are absent; and the societies in which only one of the two factors is present lie in between in this regard.

Hypothesis 1 was tested by comparing the societies of Types I, II, III, and IV (Table 1). The result shows that circumcision is found among 64 percent of the Type II societies (MB/F), and only 3 percent of the Type III societies (M & B & F). Among the Type I and Type IV societies (MB & F and M & B/F), the frequency of circumcision is 22 percent and 20 percent, respectively. This is clearly in agreement with the prediction, and Hypothesis 1 was supported.

Since the result of testing Hypothesis 1 suggests that the factor of mother-son sleeping arrangements is associated with circumcision, by controlling the distance between the father and son (B & F), the two forms of mother-son sleeping arrangements were compared (MB vs. M & B).

> Hypothesis 2: If the mother and son sleep in the same bed and the father sleeps in the same hut where they sleep, the son is more likely to be circumcised, compared with the situation in which the mother and son do not sleep in the same bed and the father sleeps in the same hut.

Hypothesis 2 was tested by using the societies of Types I and III (MB & F and M & B & F). The result shows that there is a significant association between a close mother-son relationship and circumcision (p less than .024; Fisher's test, one-tailed) suggesting that when the son has bodily contact with the mother as he sleeps, the intensity of his Oedipus attachment increases.

The same problem was examined by increasing the distance between the father and son (B/F). In this case too, it is conceivable that when the mother and son sleep in the same bed (MB), the son is more likely to be circumcised. But since the father does not sleep in the same hut, the possibility of social contact between the father and son is likely to decrease significantly. This further means that, as a consequence, the mother and son are likely to increase the interaction between them, regardless of whether or not they sleep in the same bed. When they interact more, the son may increase his oedipal attachment to the mother, without worrying about the threat of the father as a superior and competing male figure. In this situation, it is conceivable that the matter of bodily contact between the mother and son may become less decisive in regard to circumcision. This means that, when the father does not sleep in the same hut, the association between the factor of mother-son sleep-ing arrangements and circumcision is not as significant as in the situation in which the father sleeps in the same hut. Therefore, Hypothesis 3 was tested.

Hypothesis 3: If the father sleeps in a separate hut, the factor of bodily contact between the mother and son is more weakly associated with circum-cision, compared with the situation in which the father sleeps in the same hut.

In order to test Hypothesis 3, the societies of Types II and IV were com-pared (MB/F vs. M & B/F). The association is in the expected direction, but it is not significant enough (p less than .08; Fisher's test, one-tailed), sug-gesting that when the father sleeps in another hut, the son's oedipal attach-ment is almost equally strong whether or not he sleeps in the mother's bed. Since the association is significant when the father sleeps in the same hut, as the result of testing Hypothesis 2 indicates, Hypothesis 3 was supported.

Both Hypotheses 2 and 3 deal with the situation in which the factor of so-cial contact between father and son is controlled. By reversing this, two hy-potheses can be formulated in which the factor of bodily contact between mother and son is considered controlled.

Hypothesis 4: When the mother and son sleep in the same bed, if the fa-ther does not sleep in the same hut where they sleep, the son is more likely to be circumcised, compared with the situation in which the father sleeps in the same hut.

Hypothesis 4 was tested by comparing the societies of Types I and II (MB & F vs. MB/F). The results shows a very significant association (p less than .00014; Fisher's test, one-tailed). This finding suggests that when the father sleeps in a separate hut, the threat of the father as a superior and competing male figure decreases significantly and the son develops a strong oedipal at-tachment to the mother as a consequence.

According to the result of testing Hypothesis 2, when the father sleeps in the same hut where the mother and son sleep, if the mother and son do not sleep in the same bed, the son is significantly less likely to be circumcised. Therefore, it is possible to think that in this sleeping arrangement (M & B), the son's oedipal attachment is less intense, compared with the arrangement in which they sleep in bodily contact (MB). This further implies that when the mother and son do not sleep in the same bed, the distance between the fa-ther and son is likely to be much less important compared with the situation in which the mother and son sleep in the same bed. Thus Hypothesis 5 was tested.

Hypothesis 5: If the mother and son do not sleep in the same bed, the factor of the distance between the father and son is more weakly associated with circumcision, compared with the situation in which the mother and son sleep in the same bed.

In order to test Hypothesis 5, societies of Types III and IV were compared in regard to the frequency of circumcision (M & B & F vs. M & B/F). No significant association was found between the two types of societies (p less than .99; Fisher's test, one-tailed). Since the association is significant when the mother and son sleep in the same bed, as the result of testing Hypothesis 4 indicates, Hypothesis 5 was supported. This suggests that when the mother and son do not sleep in the same bed, the son does not become intensely attached to the mother. As a consequence, the matter of whether or not the father as a superior and competing male figure exists in the same hut becomes unimportant.

DISCUSSION

The results of testing the five hypotheses indicate that Freudian theory of circumcision is not incompatible with the empirical data. If the father sleeps in the same hut where the mother and son sleep, whether or not the mother and son are in the same bed becomes the key factor in predicting the presence or absence of circumcision. Here, the bodily contact between the mother and son is significantly associated with the practice of circumcision. The presence of the father in the same hut is a factor working against circumcision, and if he sleeps in a different hut, the possibility of circumcision becomes significantly greater. In this case, it makes little difference whether or not the mother and son sleep in the same bed. When the mother and son do not sleep in the same bed, whether or not the father sleeps in the same hut is irrelevant to circumcision.

These findings can be seen in terms of the Freudian frame of reference as follows. When the father sleeps in the same hut where the mother and son sleep, his presence as a superior and competing male prevents the son from developing an intense oedipal attachment, and it is intensified only when the son sleeps in the mother's bed. But if the father does not sleep in the same hut, his influence on the son decreases significantly, and the son feels less threat of a competing male, compared with the situation in which the father sleeps in the same hut. In addition, interaction between the mother and son increases, and as a consequence, the son easily develops a strong oedipal attachment and the matter of sleeping arrangement becomes less relevant. When the father recognizes the son's strong oedipal attachment to the mother, circumcision is performed as a symbolic castration. But if the mother and son do not sleep in the same bed, the son is less likely to develop a strong oedipal attachment, and, for this reason, whether or not the father sleeps in the same hut becomes irrelevant to circumcision.

If we try to examine Bettelheim's theory, there exists the problem of whether or not a man retains his vagina envy throughout his life. Although Bettelheim (1954, p. 56) says that, for both boys and girls, puberty rites symbolize the acceptance of socially determined sex roles, he does not state to what extent puberty rites are successful in this regard. In order to examine his theory by means of the data we have, then, it is necessary to specify his formulation.

First, it is conceivable that males are more or less envious even after puberty rites. In this case, a puberty rite may reduce the intensity of vagina envy, but it nevertheless continues to exist in a man's mind. In this situation, the father's vagina envy is more likely to be conveyed to the son when he sleeps in the same hut, compared with the situation in which the father sleeps in a different hut. This suggests that the son's vagina envy is intensified by a close contact with another envious male. This further implies that the son is more likely to be circumcised if the father sleeps in the same hut. But the result of testing Hypothesis 4 does not support this.

Second, if males change after puberty rites in regard to their vagina envy and acquire a more positive attitude toward their own sexuality, the father may influence the son in terms of developing more interest and pride in male sexuality if they live in the same hut. Also, when the father shows a more positive attitude toward the male sexual organs, the son may become envious of the father's larger penis. As a result, the son's vagina envy may be reduced. These reasonings imply that if the father sleeps in the same hut, the son is less likely to be circumcised. Indeed, the results of testing Hypotheses 1 through 5 are all compatible with this interpretation. In brief, Bettelheim's theory can be supported by the data we have only if we limit it by assuming a change on the part of males after puberty rites.

CONCLUSION

Freud's theory of circumcision as a symbolic substitute for castration has been, insofar as the data used in the present study are concerned, well supported. Probably one virtue of this theory is that it is easy to recognize the meaning of circumcision in reference to castration as conceived in the oedipal conflict. If castration is too harsh a measure to be taken by the father, the removal of only a small portion of the son's sexual organs is a compromise between father and son. The father may recognize that bleeding due to the removal of the son's prepuce symbolizes a damage to the son and a victory to himself. The son may be able to accept circumcision when he realizes that the prepuce is totally unnecessary for his sexual functioning, and that it may also signify a new status as an adult male.

Bettelheim's theory is less fully formulated, and in order to test it, it is necessary to say whether or not men change their vagina envy after puberty rites. That is, only when we make an additional assumption that men give up or at least significantly reduce such envy after puberty rites, the available data are compatible with this theory. If man has an archetypal need of transitional rites in order to become a new person, as discussed by Henderson (1967), Bettelheim's theory can be interpreted from this angle.

REFERENCES

Bettelheim, B. (1954). *Symbolic Wounds: Puberty Rites and the Envious Male.* New York: Free Press.

Bonaparte, M. (1949). *The Life and Works of Edgar Allan Poe.* London: Imago.

Burton, R. V., and Whiting, J. W. M. (1961). The absent father and cross-sex identity. *Merrill-Palmer Quarterly of Behavior and Development* 7, 2:85-95.

Chadwick, M. (1925). Die wurzel der wissbegierde. *International Zeitschrift fur Psychoanalyse* 11.

Fenichel, O. (1945). *The Psychoanalytic Theory of Neurosis.* New York: Norton.

Freud, S. (1939). *Moses and Monotheism.* New York: Knopf.

_____(1949). *An Outline of Psychoanalysis.* New York: Norton.

_____(1950). *Collected Papers.* Vol. 5. London: Hogarth.

_____(1973). *New Introductory Lectures on Psychoanalysis.* Middlesex, Eng.: Penguin.

Fromm, E. (1951). *The Forgotten Language.* New York: Holt.

Henderson, J. L. (1967). *Thresholds of Initiation.* Middletown, Conn.: Wesleyan Univ. Press.

Jacobson, E. (1950). Development of the wish for a child in boys. *The Psychoanalytic Study of the Child* 5.

Kitahara, M. (1974). Living quarter arrangements in polygyny and circumcision and segregation of males at puberty. *Ethnology* 13, 4:401-413.

Klein, M. (1948). *Contributions to Psychoanalysis, 1921-1948.* London: Hogarth.

Landauer, K. (1931). Das menstruationserlebnis des knaben. *Zeitschrift fur Psychoanalytische Padagogik* 5.

Murdock, G. P. *Ethnographic Atlas.* Pittsburgh: Univ. of Pittsburg Press.

Neumann, E. (1949). *Ursprungsgeschichte des Bewusstseins.* Zurich: Rascher Verlag.

Norbeck, E., Walker, D. E., and Cohen, M. (1962). The interpretation of data: Puberty rites. *American Anthropologist* 64:463-485.

Nunberg, H. *Problems of Bisexuality as Reflected in Circumcision.* London: Imago.

Reik, T. (1958). *Ritual: Psychoanalytic Studies.* New York: International Universities Press.

Roheim, G. (1953). The Milky Way and the esoteric meaning of Australian initiation. *Drives, Affects, Behavior,* ed. R. M. Loewenstein. New York: International Universities Press.

Whiting, J. W. M. (1964). Effects of climate on certain cultural practices. *Exploration in Cultural Anthropology,* ed. W. H. Goodenough. New York: McGraw-Hill, pp. 511-544.

Whiting, J. W. M., Kluckhohn, R., and Anthony, A. (1958). The function of male initiation ceremonies at puberty. *Readings on Social Psychology,* eds. E. E. Maccoby, T. M. Newcomb, & E. L. Hartley. New York: Holt, pp. 359-370.

Zilboorg, G. (1944). Masculine and feminine. *Psychiatry* 7.

MICHIO KITAHARA, FIL. DR.

DR. KITAHARA received his Fil. Dr. from the University of Uppsala, Sweden, and currently teaches at the University of Maryland, Far East Division, Tokyo. He is interested in psychoanalytic study of sociocultural phenomena.

Sartre's Contribution to the Understanding of Narcissism

David B. Klass, M.D.

Research and Clinical Director
Manteno Mental Health Center
Lecturer in Psychiatry
University of Chicago

William Offenkrantz, M.D.

Professor of Psychiatry
University of Chicago

As a means for presenting Sartre's insights into the narcissistic problems of the self, we have used his phenomenological system as articulated in **Being and Nothingness** (1943) to illuminate these issues in the personality of Roquentin, the hero of his novel **Nausea** (1938). Roquentin attempts to stabilize his fragmenting self and to avoid "nausea" by using three mechanisms which Sartre argues maintain the self from drowning in the objects of the self. These are "reflection," "temporality" (continuity through time), and "being-for-others" (how we experience another's view of ourselves).

In Sartre's conception of being-for-others lies many clinically useful insights which can be used to explain both the structure and the instability of the transferences seen in the treatment of narcissistic personality disorders. Sartre demonstrates by implication that the patient must maintain (by using bad faith, i.e., disavowal) that the therapist is acting freely, or these transferences collapse. Thus, the patient must feel he is the unique and special "occasion," of any warmth, empathy, or compliments. A case example is included to illustrate these issues of freedom and bad faith.

One of the authors (D.K.) became interested in the philosophy of existentialism as it relates to clinical problems of narcissism when he observed that several of his patients with narcissistic personality disorders might find kindred spirits in the heroes of certain existential writers. Review of the literature revealed that one of these authors, Sartre, in his major philosophic work, *Being and Nothingness* (1943), had attempted an in-depth explication of some of the problems of narcissistic object relations—which are "lived" by his hero Roquentin in the novel *Nausea* (1938). We hope it will add to the current understanding and treatment of narcissistic personality disorders if Sartre's own explanations of Roquentin's turmoil are made available to the psychoanalytic reader. In order to do this, we will consider Roquentin's diary in

Nausea as clinical material. We shall then refer to the relevant sections of *Being and Nothingness* which "explain" the portion of *Nausea* under examination. We shall also add our own case material.

Nowhere in *Being and Nothingness* did Sartre specifically state that this philosophic work bears the explanatory relationship to the character in *Nausea* we are suggesting here. However, it seems clear in the structure of these two works that this relationship exists. This conclusion is supported by the similar observation of H. Barnes, the translator of *Being and Nothingness* (p. XIX), in her introduction to the work.

SUMMARY OF *NAUSEA*

This novel is in the form of a diary supposedly kept by Antoine Roquentin, a historian working on a monograph dealing with the Marquis de Rollebon. The fictional framework is that the journal has been found among Roquentin's papers and is now being published posthumously. At the time the diary was begun, Roquentin was thirty years old and had lived at Bouville, the marquis's birthplace, for almost three years while he worked on this biography. Sartre was actually thirty-three when the book was published.

The act of beginning the diary is prompted by a disquieting experience that Roquentin cannot explain to himself. On the beach at Bouville he picks up a pebble and is suddenly overcome by a sense of nausea. "It was sort of a sweetish sickness" (p. 10). In order to overcome this nausea (a feeling clinically familiar in patients experiencing a fragmented sense of self and often accompanied by feelings of emptiness and purposelessness), Roquentin attempts a series of maneuvers to stabilize his sense of self. The act of writing the diary (which is the novel) induces in him a state of hyperreflection. He turns to his own past in an effort to give himself a feeling of continuity through time. But most important, he repeatedly and unsuccessfully tries to reestablish his self by depicting the Marquis de Rollebon as an imposing figure whom he could look up to and in whose "presence" he could feel exalted. The biography is given up when these repeated attempts continue to fail.

He then attempts a similar relationship with an acquaintance, the "self-taught man," who is engaged in reading the entire contents of the Bouville library. The man's fatal flaw is also quickly found: misguided humanism. When this attempt at idealization also fails, the nausea returns. Subsequently, in a state of extreme tension, Roquentin wanders into a garden where he is overcome by the absurdity of all existence but suddenly understands the "meaning" of his previous experiences—and the nausea diminishes. He decides he no longer has any ties to Bouville and returns to Paris to see his former love, Annie. His effort to reestablish an old bond with her fails and they separate permanently. He returns to Bouville to settle his affairs and, after attempting unsuccessfully to help the self-taught man avoid public humiliation in the town library, he leaves Bouville for the final time. He has decided to write a novel.

THE SELF

In this study, we will focus on the means which Roquentin uses to stabilize his self and escape the feeling of nausea. First, we must understand what Sartre means by the "self." Since his conception is totally phenomenological, it does not include any unconscious aspects. The self (being-for-itself) for Sartre is equivalent to the "no-thingness" of consciousness. It is often experienced as a "lack," striving to fill itself or coincide with itself in the future — always unsuccessfully (*Being*, p. 77). Consciousness, or the self, always has within it an object which has *thinglike* properties, i.e., identity, essence. By object Sartre means anything within consciousness such as ideas, images, etc. Thus when a person looks at a painting the object of self is the painting. Sartre points out that there is a tendency for the self to merge with its objects. Thus, the self can lose itself in its objects "as ink is absorbed by a blotter" (*Being*, p. 777).

One unusual aspect of Sartre's conception is his view of the specific mechanisms which allow the self to maintain its integrity from its objects. These mechanisms are what Sartre calls the three "ekstases" (standing out from). Although the self is no-thing, it must for survival always be potentially separable from its objects. The three ekstases permit this: they are "reflection," "temporality" (the sense of ourselves through time), and "being-for-itself-for-others" (the experience we have of how others regard us). Reflection and temporality are complex concepts in the philosophy of phenomenology, thus our treatment of them will be brief. However, within the concept of "being-for-itself-for-others" is contained Sartre's description of what Kohut later called the narcissistic transferences. To explicate this, we will first examine in some detail Roquentin's relationships both with Rollebon and the self-taught man, with occasional references to clinical practice and psychoanalytic and aesthetic theories concerning the self.

SUPPORTS OF THE SELF

Reflection

Reflection is the process by which consciousness (the self) tries to adopt an external point of view toward itself. Thus, one may try to think about what one was thinking about. On the very first page of the novel, the hyperreflectiveness of Roquentin becomes clear.

The best thing would be to write down events from day to day. Keep a diary to see clearly—let none of the nuances or small happenings escape even though they might seem to mean nothing. And above all, classify them. I must tell how I see this table, this street, the people, my packet of tobacco, since those are the things which have changed. I must determine the exact extent and nature of this change. [*Nausea*, p. 1]

His continuous description of his subjective experiences is reminiscent of the hyperreflectiveness of many patients whose sense of self is unstable. In fact, diaries such as Roquentin's are not uncommon in the life histories of people with narcissistic conflicts who become authors. Reflection stabilizes the self by temporarily reestablishing its separateness from its objects. For example, if one is engrossed in looking at a painting and has no "self-consciousness," one can always regain self-consciousness by reflecting. "Oh, here I am, looking at this painting." Transiently, then, consciousness is separated from the painting. In the process of reflection, one also becomes aware of the ineffable presence of the ego, i.e., the sense of "I" the agent or actor.

Temporality

According to Sartre, the sense of the continuity of time from past to present and the anticipation of the future is a support for the self. In subsequent periods of pain following his early disillusionment with Rollebon, and before giving up the biography completely, Roquentin attempts to find inner cohesion by evoking memories of exciting adventures from his own past.

For a hundred dead stories there still remains one or two living ones. I evoke these with caution, occasionally, not too often, for fear of wearing them out. . . . I must stop quickly and think of something else. [Unfortunately, however,] My memories are like coins in a devil's purse. When you open it you find only dead leaves. I build memories with my present self. I am cast out, forsaken in the present. I vainly try to rejoin the past: I cannot escape. [*Nausea*, pp. 32-33]

Earlier, however, we find him temporarily reintegrated with an establishment of a more cohesive self. This has occurred through listening to music.

A few seconds more and the Negress will sing. It seems inevitable, so strong is the necessity of this music; nothing can interrupt it, nothing which comes from this time in which the world has fallen; it will stop of itself, as if by order. [*Nausea*, p. 22]

After the last chord has died away he writes, "What has just happened is that the nausea has disappeared. When the voice was heard in the silence, *I felt my body harden* and the nausea vanish" [*Nausea*, p. 22, italics added]. The relationship of music to time has been sharply expressed by Susanne Langer:

> But music spreads out time for our direct and complete apprehension, by letting our hearing monopolize it—organize, fill and shape it, all alone. It creates an image of time measured by the motion of forms that seem to give it substance, yet a substance that consists entirely of sound, so it is transitoriness itself. *Music makes time audible, and its form and continuity, sensible.* [1953, p. 110]

That listening to music helps with the cohesion of the self is familiar from clinical experience with schizophrenic and narcissistic patients. However, Sartre's concept of temporality and Langer's views of music suggest a mechanism for this. In addition, the attempt to strengthen the sense of time as a support for the self is seen in the practice of using calendars, clocks, etc., in the rooms of elderly patients to prevent deterioration of the sense of self. Variations in the sense of self occurring concurrently with alterations in the sense of the passage of time are also seen with psychedelic drug use.

Being-for-Itself-for-Others

The use of reflection, and attempts to establish a sense of time, give Roquentin only very temporary solace from the pain of his fragmenting self. Throughout the novel the principal means by which he seeks to stabilize the self are familiar to psychotherapists from the treatment of narcissistic personality disorders. Roquentin tries to establish Rollebon as a superhuman character in whose omnipotent presence he could feel special.

> His part was to have an imposing appearance. . . . I no longer existed in myself, but in him; I ate for him, breathed for him, each of my movements had its sense outside, there in front of me, in him. [*Nausea*, p. 98]

In another of Sartre's novels, *The Reprieve* (1945), there is an additional description of this same position of the self relative to the other.

> I was both transparent and opaque, I existed in the presence of a look. . . . "I am seen, therefore, I am." I need no longer bear the responsibility of my disturbed and disintegrating self; he who sees me causes me to be; I am as he sees me. [*Reprieve*, p. 405]

Sartre's explication of how such relationships with others support the self depends on understanding what the other is in relation to the self. Consider that one is sitting on a park bench. The world as one sees it consists of objects within one's visual field. For Sartre, these objects of consciousness are *thing-like* and have their essence or significance bestowed on them by the consciousness which sees them. But now, consider this same scene upon the arrival of another person. At first one *captures* him with one's gaze and wonders about his *identity*. Is he a painter, a doctor, etc.? Like other objects of consciousness, any significance, essence, or identity [1] he has is bestowed on him *from the outside*, by being seen. This means of bestowing significance is crucial to the understanding of phenomenology. A striking example of this, again drawn from *The Reprieve*, is the following:

> For one instant, on that June evening when I elected to confess to you, I thought I had encountered myself in your bewildered eyes. You saw me, in your eyes I was solid and predictable; my acts and moods were the actual consequences of a definite entity. And through me you knew that entity. I described it to you in my words, I revealed to you facts unknown to you, which had helped you to visualize it. And yet you saw it, I merely saw you seeing it. For one instant you were the heaven-sent mediator between me and myself, you perceived that compact and solid entity which I was and wanted to be in just as simple and ordinary a way as I perceived you. [*p.* 405]

Returning to the example of the park scene, we must now examine the "other side" of the bestowing-of-significance-by-being-seen. As time passes, the thought crosses one's mind: "What is *my* significance, essence, or identity from *his* vantage point?" Suddenly this scene has taken on a perspective which Sartre describes thus:

> Suddenly an object has appeared which has stolen the world from me. Everything is in place; everything still exists for me; but everything is . . . fixed in the direction of a new object. . . . The apperance of the Other in the world corresponds . . . to a . . . sliding of the whole universe, to a de-centralization of the world which undermines the centralization which I am simultaneously effecting. [*Being*, P. 384]

With the realization that one has taken on "thinglike" qualities for the other, Sartre makes the crucial observation that this is experienced with shame.

> Shame is the feeling of an original fall, not because of the fact that I may have committed this or that particular fault, but simply that I have "fallen"

into the world in the midst of things and that *I need the mediation of the Other* in order to be what I am. [*Being*, p. 366, italics added]

This existential shame accompanies the appreciation that there is an aspect of my being which derives its significance from my sense of how others see me. This Sartre calls "being-for-itself-for-others," or, as he often puts it more simply, "being-for-others."

Sartre makes the important point that this being-for-others is always out of control and in the hands of others. He describes Kafka's novels and particularly "K's" world view as a literary example of this experience [*Being*, p. 355]. He insists that being-for-others is always revealed to us with strong affect, either shame or defensive pride.

To repeat, shame is the painful realization that we are dependent on others to give us a sense of identity. The opposite of shame, and for Sartre the only other attitude with respect to the other which is not defensive, is arrogance (l'orgueil) : the realization that others feel shame when captured within one's own gaze. Defensive pride (fierté) is also closely related to shame, but is a reaction to it. In defensive pride a person has an aspect of his identity bestowed on him by another by virtue of his being an object for the other. However, he then "attempts to make use of it in a return shock so as to affect him [the other] passively with a feeling of admiration" [*Being*, p. 386]. Defensive pride as a support for the self is not described in *Nausea* but will be illustrated by a clinical example in the final section of this study.

At this point, several warnings are appropriate. Sartre's system, like all systems of psychology derived from introspection, contains idiosyncrasies which may not permit easy generalization. This is because any paradigm derived from introspection must bear a relationship to the mind of the individual doing the introspecting. For a system to permit generalization, it needs the modifications that must occur as other persons begin to use it.

It is relevant to point out that Sartre believed it was not possible to make value judgments, i.e., construct essences, give meaning or significance to one's thoughts, actions, or feelings on one's own. Meaning would come from the outside, from one's impression of how others regarded such acts, etc. Most would agree that the significance of one's thoughts, acts, or feelings are at first what significant important others bestow on them from the outside during childhood. In most well-integrated persons, this is then internalized. For Sartre, however, complete internalization is never possible and without the presence (actual or fantasied) of others one is never able to attach value judgments or qualities to oneself.

This state of affairs is probably crucial in what we call the narcissistic personality disorder, where one is strongly dependent on others to perform this function. However, one might argue that, even when a well-integrated person is doing no more than giving some thought, action, or feeling of his own a positive or negative value, he is transiently taking the position of the other with respect to himself (see also George Herbert Mead [1934] in this connection).

If the *I* (ego) is an ineffable presence available upon reflection, then the *me* is our experience of what the other "sees" when we are captured within his or her gaze. It is that which Sartre speaks of as the "being-for-others." It, unlike the self, has *thinglike* properties. The mechanisms by which the *me* supports the self is described by Sartre in (*Being*, pp. 376-382).

CONFLICTS WITH OTHERS

For Sartre there is no peace possible with the other. Although the latter is crucial, he creates feelings of shame (and sometimes defensive pride) in us. When captured within the other's gaze we become objects; yet this is the only way we can have substance or significance. Similarly the other, captured within our gaze, is an object and he derives any significance he may have from our "seeing" him. Thus,

> First, the Other *looks* at me and as such he holds the secret of my being, he knows what I *am*. Thus the profound meaning of my being is outside of me. . . . The Other has the advantage over me . . . but I can turn back upon the Other so as to make an object out of him in turn since the Other's objectness destroys my objectness for him. [*Being*, p. 473]

These two basic attitudes ("me an object," "he an object") toward the other are circular. Sartre feels an alternation occurs because we can "never place ourselves concretely on the plane of equality [with the other]" [*Being*, p. 529].

Sartre believes that any attempt to maintain a *fixed* position over time relative to the other, as a means of overcoming the circularity referred to above, is a defensive way of maintaining oneself because it is always at the expense of one's freedom. It does, of course, permit a person to escape from tension engendered by his responsibility for his own existence.

ROQUENTIN AND ROLLEBON

The relationship Roquentin strives to establish and maintain with Rollebon in order to reduce this tension corresponds to Sartre's *first basic attitude* relative to the other.

If one begins by placing oneself in the position of the "being looked at," we experience the Other as possessing us. . . . The Other holds a secret—the secret of what I am. He makes me be and thereby possesses me, and this possession is nothing other than (my) consciousness of (his) possessing me" [*Being*, p. 475]

Thus when Roquentin recalls how he had first "met" M. de Rollebon, in the pages of a "book of 'Germain Berger'," he reveals how he is "possessed" by the marquis.

I re-read with melancholy this note of Germain Berger. It was by those few lines that I first knew M. de Rollebon. *How attractive he seemed and how I loved him after these words! It is for him, for this manikin that I am here.* [*Nausea*, p. 12, italics added]

THE INSTABILITY OF THE FIRST BASIC ATTITUDE

However, Roquentin's relationship with Rollebon is precarious. The foregoing passage was written when slippages had begun to occur within the relationship (i.e., "manikin"). The relationship can only confer on Roquentin a substantial *me* and thus support his self when his stance with respect to the marquis is as if he (Rollebon) were a God: "that is the recognition of my being-an-object before a subject which can never become an object" [*Being*, p. 385]

Moreover, Roquentin must feel that he is the "unique and privileged object" of his subject (*Being*, p. 479). Here is where the trouble lies. Rollebon must be the flawless god and Roquentin the privileged slave. But as he studies the life of the marquis further, he comes across more qualities which make him less godlike.

For example, he is forced to face the possibility that Rollebon participated in an assassination (*Nausea*, p. 15). Immediately thereafter he asks himself the painful question, "Can we believe that absurd legend that Rollebon disguised himself as a midwife . . ." (for the assassination)? Upon confronting himself with this less-than-godlike behavior in his idol, the author feels "bored to tears" by Rollebon. This is followed by a disorganization of the self (*Nausea*, pp. 16-18). He describes vividly the experience of every feature of his face as his experience of it undergoes a fragmentation. He can no longer "understand" his own face in the mirror, but can only feel it "through a dumb, organic sense." This culminates two hours later with, "Things are bad! Things are very bad; I have it, the filth, the nausea" (*Nausea*, p. 18).

Thus as blemishes are found in his subject, the supportive aspect of the relationship suffers. Also, when Roquentin does not feel his relationship with the marquis to be uniquely privileged, again the support for the self becomes tenuous. This is exemplified in the following passage, when he catches himself believing a lie and wishes Rollebon would not lie to *him*.

> I feel full of ill-will towards this lying little fop; perhaps it is spite: *I was quite pleased that he lied to others but I would have liked him to make an exception of me; I thought we were thick as thieves and that he would finally tell me the truth.* He told me nothing, nothing at all; nothing more than he told Alexander or Louis XVIII whom he duped. It matters a lot to me that Rollebon should have been a good fellow. Undoubtedly a rascal: Who isn't? But a big or little rascal? I don't have a high enough opinion of historical research to lose my time over a dead man whose hand, if he were alive, I would not deign to touch. [*Nausea*, p. 58, italics ours]

After this, he finally gives up Rollebon for the last time and understands what he wanted within the relationship.

> M. de Rollebon was my partner; he needed me in order to exist and I needed him so as not to feel my existence. I furnished the . . . existence . . . His part was to have an imposing appearance. . . . I no longer existed in myself, but in him; I ate for him, breathed for him, each of my movements had its sense outside, there, just in front of me, in him: I no longer saw my hand writing letters on the paper, I saw the Marquis who had claimed the gesture as his own, the gesture which prolonged, consolidated his existence. I was only a means of making him live, he was my reason for living, he had delivered me from myself. What shall I do now? Above all, not move, not move. . . . Ah! I could not prevent this movement of the shoulders. . . . The thing which was waiting . . . has pounced on me, it flows through me, I am filled with it. It's nothing: I am the Thing. Existence, liberated, detached, floods over me. I exist. [*Nausea*, p. 98]

A "clinical correlation" is relevant here. This "transference" as it existed between Roquentin and Rollebon is a common state of affairs seen by therapists treating narcissistically disordered patients. Sartre's work can help explain the instability of these transference situations. For such a transference to be maintained, the patient must not only feel he is in the presence of a flawless person, but also that he is the most central and important "object" for the therapist. Thus flaws discovered in the therapist by the patient tend to destroy the godlike illusion. As Kohut (1971) has described in some detail, the patient suffering from a narcissistic personality disorder may establish an "idealizing transference" in which his experience of the therapist can be summarized as, "You are perfect, and I am part of you." The instability of this kind of relationship is evident when the patient's control over such another (self-object) person is disturbed, either by the therapist's physical absence, e.g., over weekends, or emotional absence, as by a failure of empathy. The patients undergo a variety of typical regressive phenomena when confronted by these "flaws." We believe Sartre's observation that such a person must feel himself to be the unique and privileged slave of his god in order to maintain this relationship offers a new insight into the details of these patients' lives.

Thus it is possible to understand another class of therapeutic interventions which, in a more subtle way, interfere with the idealization. These are interventions which remind the patient that he is not in reality the unique and privileged slave of the therapist master, that he is not the special object of any empathic response from the therapist. They inform the patient that the therapist is not a source of perfection and therefore create an unempathic distance from what the patient needs: a perfect self-object sensitive as if by magic to the patient. These interventions convey this information by exalting the patient's own status, which, at such a moment, disrupts the patient's bliss. (A case example will be given in our section on clinical applications.)

Sartre analogizes to the situation between lovers to convey this point. Just as a lover must have the feeling that any love bestowed on him by his beloved was given totally by the free will of the beloved (not coerced or manipulated) [see *Being*, p. 470], so also the patient must not let himself realize that this need and wish for warm empathic regard is the reason the therapist is empathic. To realize this is to be the subject for the therapist-as-object, and the relationships crumble.

Such a transference could never exist, given this high degree of precariousness, if not for what Sartre calls "bad faith." This mental mechanism, a "lie to oneself within a single consciousness" or disavowal, is related to what Kohut (1971) has called a vertical split in the ego and what Kernberg (1967) refers to "as mutual denial of two independent areas of consciousness. . . ." It permits the patient to disavow (for a time) the dissonant components of the relationship and thus to use the relationship to stabilize his self. However, the disavowal is in itself unstable because no part of that which needs not to be known is fully unconscious, in the same sense as the memories of infantile experiences which only exist behind the true repression barrier.

ROQUENTIN AND THE "SELF-TAUGHT MAN"

Roquentin's search for a figure to rescue him from himself is not over after he gives up Rollebon. On the second day after the "great Rollebon affair is over," Roquentin lunches with the self-taught man, who, when he had first been described (*Nausea*, p. 30), had had the potential for idealization. At that time, Roquentin had said, "I study him with a sort of admiration. What will-power he must have to carry through, slowly, obstinately, a plan on such a vast scale" (to read all the books in the municipal library in alphabetical order). Now, in his effort to recover from the fragmentation resulting from the final giving up of Rollebon, he meets with the self-taught man for lunch. However, the latter reveals that he is committed to humanism, a philosophy for which Roquentin has only contempt. As Roquentin begins to question him he feels "something had died between us." As his attempted idealization fails to materialize, he expresses this in the thought, "His love for people is naive and barbaric, a provincial humanist" (*Nausea*, p. 122).

THE INSTABILITY OF THE SECOND BASIC ATTITUDE:
THE SUPPORT OF THE SELF BY MAKING ONESELF
THE SUBJECT AND THE OTHER AN OBJECT

With a failure of Sartre's "first attitude" toward the other, a patient may move into the "second attitude" in an attempt to stabilize his self. This attitude is the therapist as the object, with the patient as the subject disavowing any possibility of needing the therapist. This is the position Roquentin takes for a time with the self-taught man. He becomes cold and contemptuous, looking *at* him from a distance, pitying him, "I *study* the self-taught man with a little remorse" [*Nausea*, p. 121]. However, Roquentin does not have enough "bad faith" to maintain this stance for longer than a few moments and again suffers nausea. Sartre describes this defense as indifference toward the other.

> In a sense I am reassured, I am self-confident; that is, I am in no way conscious of the fact that the Other's look can fix my possibilities and my body. I am in a state the very opposite of what we call shyness or timidity. I am at ease; I am not embarrassed by myself. . . . This state of blindness can be maintained for a long time, as long as my fundamental bad faith desires; it can be extended — with relapses — over several years, over a whole life; there are men who die without — save for brief and terrifying flashes of illumination — ever having suspected what the Other is. [*Being*, p. 496]

Sartre feels that this indifference, which is the end result of building up oneself as a subject and making the other into an object, is really the practice of a "sort of factual solipsism" where others are seen as "forms which pass by in the street." "People are then broken into their functions for me and I learn how to manipulate them like things" (*Being*, p. 495). However, when the other is always an object for me, I must accept the tension of being free and responsible for myself, without any help from the other. In addition, "my constantly making an object out of the Other puts me in a paradoxical position where I feel I wish to appropriate something from him (his freedom)"

[*Being*, p. 495), but I cannot let myself ever know this. For such awareness would be then to recognize the fact that he does have this freedom (and can turn me into his object). Thus again we have run into bad faith, because I must disavow this truth in order to keep my tension low.

As an additional defense against the wish to make the other a subject for me the object, Roquentin could have chosen "evil for evil's sake." This defensive, grandiose posture, which disavows the other's importance, is described by Sartre in the following way: "Black masses, desecration of the host, demonic associations, etc., are so many attempts to confer the character of object on the absolute subject. . . . Then I 'make God suffer,' I irritate him" (*Being*, p. 386].

Kohut in similar vein writes: "The flaunting of omnipotent unrestricted activities and the delinquent's pride in his skill of ruthlessly manipulating his environment serve to buttress his defenses against becoming aware of a longing for the lost idealized self-object" (1971, p. 166).

For Roquentin, it would seem no defenses are left after the final disillusionment with the self-taught man: "You must love people. Men are admirable. I want to vomit and suddenly, there it is: The Nausea." This time however it has never been so strong.

> So this is Nausea: This blinding evidence? I have scratched my head over it! I've written about it. Now I know: I exist — the world exists — and I know that the world exists. That's all. It makes no difference to me. It frightens me. Ever since the day I wanted to play ducks and drakes. I was going to throw that pebble, I looked at it and then it all began: I felt that I existed. Then after that there were other Nauseas. . . . But it had never been as strong as today. [*Nausea*, pp. 122, 123]

He wanders away from the self-taught man and as his regression deepens, words lose their significance as symbols.

> Things are divorced from their names. They are there, grotesque, head-strong, gigantic and it seems ridiculous to call them seats [he is sitting on a seat] or say anything at all about them: I am in the midst of things, nameless things. Alone, without words, defenseless, they surround me, are beneath me, above me. They demand nothing, they don't impose themselves: They are there. [*Nausea*, p. 125]

This is a form of regression which seems identical with what Freud (1915) described as a person begins to experience a withdrawal of psychotic proportions. He then undergoes a most profound loss of connection with the experiences in his unconscious — and attempts to recapture this lost world of inner experiences by preoccupying himself with the words that symbolize the lost experiences.

In such a state of extreme tension, Roquentin arrives at a park and drops onto a bench between chestnut trees, where the climax of the book occurs — leading to a reorientation of Roquentin's life.

In what follows (pp. 126-135), we find a clue to the process by which Roquentin achieves a more secure sense of self and the correlated ability to function once more.

> And suddenly, suddenly, the veil is torn away, I have understood, I have seen. I can't say I feel relieved or satisfied; just the opposite, I am crushed: Only my goal is reached: I know what I wanted to know; I have understood all that has happened to me since January. The nausea has not left me and I don't believe it will leave me soon; but I no longer have to bear it, it is no longer an illness or a passing fit: It is I. [*Nausea*, p. 126]

However, this is no longer the despairing note of ultimate regression. I has become a means to something else:

> This moment was extraordinary. I was there, motionless and icy, plunged in a horrible ecstasy. But something fresh had just appeared in the very heart of this ecstasy; I understood the Nausea, I possessed it. To tell the truth, I did not formulate my discoveries to myself. But I think it would be easy for me to put them in words now. The essential thing is contingency. I mean that one cannot define existence as necessity. To exist is simply to be there; those who exist let themselves be encountered, but you can never deduce anything for them. *I tried to overcome this contingency by inventing a necessary, causal being.* But no necessary being can explain existence: Contingency is not a delusion, a probability which can be dissipated; it is the absolute, consequently, the perfect free gift. All is free, this park, this city and myself. When you realize that, it turns your heart upside down and everything begins to float . . . no one has any rights; they are entirely free. [*Nausea*, p. 131, italics added]

However, this does not explain to *our* satisfaction how Roquentin reconstitutes himself even though there are no more episodes of nausea. Because when Roquentin gets up to leave the garden, he comments:

> I got up and went out. Once at the gate, I turned back. Then the garden smiled at me. I leaned against the gate and watched for a long time. The smile of the trees, of the laurel, meant something; *that was the real secret of existence.* [*Nausea*, p. 135, italics added]

From the point of view of what has come before (p. 131, cited above), the comment "that was the real secret of existence" is a paradox. How could existence have a meaning, secret or otherwise, if it were simply contingent? However, from the standpoint of his narcissistic needs, the point is crucial. We believe that Roquentin may have established a relationship in which nature is the omnipotent other. This relationship has a somewhat mystical quality to it. Corresponding to Roquentin's experience with the smile of the garden in *Nausea*, is a section in *Being and Nothingness* describing la viscosite (the "sliminess"). Here Sartre (1943b, p. 803) says, "La Viscosite m'a renvoye mon image," i.e., the sliminess has returned my image to me. We believe he is speaking of the earliest amalgam of the self and the objects of the self. Sartre not only calls the sliminess "an ideal being which I reject with all my strength and which haunts me as *value* haunts my being" [*Being*, p. 778] but also says "Thus I am enriched from my first contact with the slimy, by a valid ontological pattern beyond the distinction between psychic and non-psychic, which will interpret the *meaning of being* and of all the existents of a certain category" [*Being*, p. 779, italics added].
ry" (*Being*, p. 779, italics added).

The author feels that his "image" (how he experiences what others see in him) has been returned to him. He is now more in control of his image (his "me"). Whether he has truly internalized his image or is now using "nature" as a mirror which continually reflects it back to him is ambiguous. However, Roquentin's greater stabilization following this experience is confirmed by his visit the next day to Annie, his former love. Whereas in the past he had tried to play his part well in her universe of "perfect moments," which grew out of the "privileged situations with a rare and precious quality" that she had been creating since her childhood, he no longer found himself trying to fit into her universe [*Nausea*, pp. 147-148].

The question must remain open as to how lasting this change will be. All we are sure of at the end of the novel is that he intends to write a novel, presumably the one we are reading.

CLINICAL APPLICATIONS

There are two aspects of the transference relationships with narcissistic personality disorders which emerge from Sartre's discussion that have not been described by other writers on the subject. These are the issues of specialness within the idealizing transference and the double disavowal needed to maintain defensive pride, i.e., the mirror transference (*Kohut*, 1971). We will illustrate these with a case history.

Mr. A was a twenty-four-year-old student who entered psychotherapy (with D.K.) three times a week with symptoms of severe depersonalization, derealization, and an inability to work constructively in school. By the end of the first month of treatment, he had established an idealizing transference. He often spoke of how powerful and perfect this therapist was by comparison to his three previous, and now depreciated psychiatrists. On one occasion when the telephone rang, he imagined it was a call summoning the therapist to the White House. There was great symptomatic improvement with stabilization of functioning which lasted until one day when, by chance, he met the therapist in the hall of the office building. The therapist greeted him warmly, and the patient failed to arrive for his next two appointments. He arrived for the third in what was later described as a state of extreme depersonalization and was nearly mute. He nodded his head affirmatively to the therapist's inquiry as to whether the chance meeting occasioned the regression. As he slowly composed himself, he painfuly revealed that, when he saw the therapist in the hall, the thought crossed his mind that the therapist was only attentive to him in the sessions because he was being paid. If he were not a paying patient, he could only expect that the time and energy the therapist spent with him would be comparable to the hall encounter. In other words, he, the patient, was not the special occasion of the therapist's attention. His sudden realization that he paid for the therapy destroyed the possibility that the therapist was a totally free agent who bestowed his favors on him completely outside the patient's sphere of control. Thus, the therapist's attention could not be accounted for simply because the patient was "there."

At the time this occurred, the therapist had not yet understood the crucial problem explained above concerning the illusion of the therapist's freedom. The therapist tried to be empathic concerning A's hurt feelings, but the regression continued. In retrospect, it now seems apparent that the therapist's attempts to "understand" simply made the situation worse. The patient had the feeling that any move the therapist made was not in the therapist's capacity as subject but as the patient's object: the patient's need was influencing the therapist. Slowly over several weeks the patient composed himself and the severe fragmentation with depersonalization diminished. Presumably, the elapsed time permitted him to reestablish his disavowal and maintain that he was again the privileged slave of his omnipotent master.

After one year, the transference took shape in another form. A's self-esteem was higher, he was working well in school and again winning chess matches (his favorite pastime when not reading and writing papers). During these times of high self-esteem, A would display to the therapist his substantial intellectual capacities by discussing famous literary works. If the therapist made any comment which sounded in the least complimentary, the support for A's self would cease and he would become contemptuous and fragmented. The therapist was taking great pains not to go beyond what Kohut (1971) had called "simple mirroring," but it seemed that this patient had discovered, by seeing a book on the therapist's desk, that they had a shared interest in one particular literary area. From then on A had taken great pains to avoid any discussion on this topic. However, he could never escape the possibility that, even with the other nonrelated literature he discussed, he was covertly seeking, and by manipulation getting, a mirroring response. A could not believe that the mirroring came freely since his disavowal (he "didn't care" how the therapist felt about his talents) was always in danger, when he questioned himself. In *Being and Nothingness* (p. 386), Sartre describes in detail how, with defensive pride, the prideful person must disavow any wish to have a compliment bestowed on him; again it must be experienced as given freely.

However, another illusion must be maintained in defensive pride. The prideful person has, at the moment of the "compliment" by the other secretly established his superiority over the other. But how did the quality which was being displayed before the other arise? In Sartre's system it can only have arisen from the other in his capacity as subject, conferring the quality. A's further problem with feeling pleasure in exhibiting himself to the therapist revolved around this issue. It soon emerged that no matter how good he was able to feel about his intellectual capacities, he sensed that they were available to him only because of the treatment. He needed the therapist to be able to use them. This need had to be disavowed or else the compliment was experienced as the therapist's complimenting *himself*. Until the details of these fantasies emerged, A had to walk a tenuous tightrope tied at both ends by his bad faith, a defense which often failed him because of his intense wish not to delude himself.

CONCLUSIONS

"Explanation" has always been of key importance in classical psychoanalytic technique and theory. Narcissistic problems of the "self" have recently emerged as needing a comprehensive explanatory system. To satisfy this need, we now offer Sartre's system. His system bears certain resemblances to Kohut's (1971), and to a lesser extent Kernberg's (1967, 1970), but in many respects it is novel. Probably one reason it has not already been taken into account by those studying the problems of narcissism, is that Sartre's writing (in *Being and Nothingness*) is relatively impenetrable. Like other phenomenologists, his terms are often obscure. However, once the system is grasped, one is impressed by its simplicity. Not only are all of its components easily available to introspection, but the relationships between the components are easy to grasp. The self is consciousness trying to "fill itself up." The me (being-for others) is what is experienced when one is captured within the other's gaze. The "supports of the self" number only three (temporality, reflection, and being-for-others) and there is only one "defense mechanism," i.e., "bad faith."

There are some potential drawbacks to the system — at least for the psychoanalyst. First, the system is "sociological" or interpersonal in its scope and not intrapsychic. Psychoanalytic systems of explanation seek reasons for thoughts, actions, and feelings *within* the person. Sociological systems look to the *outside* for such reasons. Psychoanalytic systems invoke the individual's past life in explaining present structures (or lack of them). Sartre's phenomenological system operates within the present only. In fact, he strongly asserts that the present situation in which a person finds himself will govern how he *experiences* his past. Thus. the past cannot act in the present, but its significance is, in fact, continuously reconstructed by the present self. Psychological determinism is strongly repudiated by Sartre (*Being*, p. 79). Not only can he not find evidence for it withing introspection but he accounts for its appeal "as a reflective defense against anguish" (engendered by freedom) and a "faith to take refuge in."

Sartre in his approach was not trying to elucidate conflicts within individuals, but was describing a philosophic system which *he* could grasp upon introspection. Sartre was only trying to describe how it was for him to deal with others, how they impinged upon his self, and he then universalized his own feelings. His method thus was not empirical. He was not engaged in a logical-positivistic approach to "data," but was involved in an explication of what it was to have a self in confrontation with the other. Happily, he described this state of affairs within himself so well that the reader not only catches a glimpse of the author himself, but can extend the structure to a subclass of individuals who have conflicts with others paralleling Sartre's description.

NOTE

1. "Identity," "meaning," "significance," "essence," and "value" are related terms. They can apply only to the objects of a consciousness.

REFERENCES

Freud, S. (1915). The unconscious. Standard Edition 14: 161. London: Hogarth, 1957.

Kernberg, O. (1967). Borderline personality organization. *Journal of the American Psychoanalytic Association* Vol. XV, No. 3, p. 670.

_____(1970). Factors in the psychoanalytic treatment of narcissistic personalities. *Journal of the American Psychoanalytic Association* Vol. XVIII, No. 1.

Kohut, H. (1971). *The Analysis of the Self.* New York: International Universities Press.

Langer, S. K. (1953). *Feeling and Form.* New York: Scribner's.

Mead, G. H. (1934). *Mind, Self, and Society,* ed. with intro. C. W. Morris. 18th ed. Chicago: Univ. of Chicago Press, 1972.

Sartre, J. P. (1938). *Nausea,* trans. L. Alexander; intro. H. Carruth. 16th ptq. New York: New Directions, 1964.

_____(1943a). *Being and Nothingness,* translated with intro. H. E. Barnes. 5th ptq. New York: Washington Square Press Pocket Books, 1971.

_____(1943b). *L'etre et le neant.* Paris: Gallimard.

_____(1945). *The Reprieve,* trans. E. Sutton. New York: Vintage, 1973.

DAVID B. KLASS, M.D.

DR. KLASS is currently research and clinical director of Manteno Mental Health Center, a lecturer at the University of Chicago, and in private practice. He obtained his undergraduate and medical degrees in Winnipeg, Canada, and was a resident in psychiatry at the University of Chicago from 1967 to 1970. Dr. Klass is pursuing research in areas of philosophy which he hopes will shed some light on difficult clinical problems in psychiatry.

WILLIAM OFFENKRANTZ, M.D.

DR. OFFENKRANTZ is professor of psychiatry at the University of Chicago, where he was director of residency training from 1957 to 1969. He is a member of the teaching faculty at the Chicago Institute for Psychoanalysis. He is a graduate of both the Chicago Institute and the William Alanson White Institute in New York. He has published studies on psychoanalytic psychotherapy, dream research, and problems of the therapeutic alliance in a combined treatment-research analysis.

Notes from the Couch: From Psychoanalysis to Psychotherapy

A REVIEW OF THE LITERATURE

W. W. Meissner, S.J., M.D.

Boston Psychoanalytic Institute

The present review provides a survey of works written on the subject of psychotherapy and the development in the field within the last decade.

- Tarachow, Sidney. *An Introduction to Psychotherapy*. New York: International Universities Press, 1963. ($3.45) 376 pp.
- Greenson, Ralph R. *The Technique and Practice of Psychoanalysis*. Vol. 1. New York: International Universities Press, 1967. ($15.00) 452 pp.
- Dewald, Paul A. *The Psychoanalytic Process: A Case Illustration*. New York: Basic Books, 1972. ($15.00) 668 pp.
- Saul, Leon J. *Psychodynamically Based Psychotherapy*. New York: Aronson, 1972. ($20.00) 842 pp.
- Paul, I. H. *Letters to Simon: On the Conduct of Psychotherapy*. New York: International Universities Press, 1973. ($12.50) 341 pp.
- Langs, Robert. *The Technique of Psychoanalytic Psychotherapy*. Vol. 1. New York: Aronson, 1973. ($15.00) 659 pp.
- Langs, Robert. *The Technique of Psychoanalytic Psychotherapy*. Vol. 2. New York: Aronson, 1974. ($15.00) 552 pp.
- Bruch, Hilde. *Learning Psychotherapy: Rationale and Ground Rules*. Cambridge, Mass.: Harvard Univ. Press, 1974. ($8.95) 150 pp.
- Balsam, Rosemary, and Balsam, Alan. *Becoming a Psychotherapist: A Clincal Primer*. Boston: Little, Brown, 1974. ($12.50) 319 pp.

Each has its relative merits, which I shall discuss in due course, but it may be useful to set this review in a more specific context, that of the general problem of the application of psychoanalytic principles to the development of psychotherapeutic techniques. The problem arises from the transition between the rich understanding of the therapeutic process which is derived from psychoanalytic experience and the amplification or adaptation of that under-

standing to the area of psychotherapy. The latter area is considerably broader
than the narrow confines of psychoanalysis. Moreover, its practitioners are
under considerable pressure in these times to apply skills and techniques in
the interests of a resolution of psychological difficulties on a broad scale.

In a previous context, the problem of the translation from psychoanalytic
experience and theory to the broader realms of psychodynamic psychotherapeutic work could be cast in the following terms:

> Psychoanalytic psychiatry has been mainly derived from the findings of
> traditional psychoanalysis. These findings, however, include not only the
> results of successful analysis but also the knowledge which has been gained
> through therapeutic failures. The contemporary Freudian would thus
> agree that traditional analysis is no longer regarded as the sole or even the
> best therapeutic technique for every type of mental disorder. He will often
> agree that the establishment and utilization of a sound relationship be-
> tween doctor and patient may be a primary goal in some forms of therapy.
> He would, nonetheless, explain his therapeutic techniques in the light of his
> understanding of contemporary psychoanalysis. He would in addition still
> maintain that traditional psychoanalytic techniques, based on interpreta-
> tion of the transference neurosis, remain the treatment of choice for a wide
> range of clinical conditions. Contemporary psychoanalytic theory and
> practice thus recognize the need for technical modifications in many cases
> and in many types of clinical disorder. [Zetzel and Meissner, 1973, p. 14]

The problem is one which is staggering in its implications and difficulty. It
is interesting to recall, however, that it is not one of which the founder of psychoanalysis was unaware. Freud (1919) addressed himself to this problem in
considering the lines of advance of psychoanalytic treatment. He gazed as it
were into his crystal ball and, prophetlike, foresaw the advancing course of
psychoanalysis in future years. He noted that the number of psychoanalysts
was necessarily small and that, even if each one of them devoted themselves
intensively to the treatment of patients, they could in fact only treat a small
number. This effort could hardly make a dent in the vast amount of neurotic
misery in the world. In addition, economic necessities limited the availability
of treatment to the relatively well-to-do who were accustomed to choosing
their own private physicians. Under such conditions, psychoanalysts could do
little for the wider social strata which also suffered from the scourge of neuroses.

But looking through the mists of time, Freud foresaw that the number of
analysts would eventually increase considerably. He also envisioned a time in
which the conscience of society would awaken to the fact that the poor have as
much right to assistance with mental afflictions as they might have for the

lifesaving help of surgery. He fantasied that institutions or outpatient clinics would be set up where analytically trained physicians could provide treatment for the afflicted populace without charge. With this vision confronting him, Freud commented:

> We shall then be faced by the task of adapting our technique to the new conditions. I have no doubt that the validity of our psychological assumptions will make its impression on the uneducated too, but we shall need to look for the simplest and most easily intelligible ways of expressing our theoretical doctrines. We shall probably discover that the poor are even less ready to part with their neuroses than the rich, because the hard life that awaits them if they recover offers them no attraction, and illness gives them one more claim to social help. Often, perhaps, we may only be able to achieve anything by combining mental assistance with some material support, in the manner of the Emperor Joseph. It is very probable, too, that the large-scale application of our therapy will compel us to alloy the pure gold of analysis freely with the copper of direct suggestion; and hypnotic influence, too, might find place in it again, as it has in the treatment of the war neuroses. But, whatever form this psychotherapy for the people may take, whatever the elements out of which it is compounded, its most effective and most important ingredients will assuredly remain those borrowed from strict and untendentious psycho-analysis. [1919, pp. 167-168]

One of the problems, of course, is that the people who are most qualified to address themselves to this area of concern are specifically the psychoanalysts. Correspondingly, they are also the people whose experience is less intense in other realms of psychotherapeutic intervention to which Freud drew attention. This is obviously less true in the context of intensive one-to-one psychotherapy than it is in other areas. Nonetheless, there is need for the amplification and application of psychotherapeutic principles from nonanalytic perspectives.

It is terribly important, however, in the evolution of such an effort that it not put itself in the position of being isolated from the gold that can be derived from the application of psychoanalytic insights. There is an urgent need in the contemporary state of the science and art of psychotherapy for psychoanalysts to be more actively involved in other realms of psychotherapeutic effort than the strict practice of psychoanalysis itself or the more broadly conceived area of psychoanalytically oriented psychotherapy. Correspondingly, there is an increasing need for collaborative effort and communication between analysts and practitioners in other areas of the spectrum of psychotherapies in order to further the integration of analytic insights and perspectives with other emerging and more experimental realms of therapeutic intervention.

The problems arise not only in the adapting of psychoanalytic principles to the broader realm of psychotherapeutic applications, but also from the social, economic, and political milieu within which the practice of psychotherapy is carried out. The question at this juncture in the history of psychiatry and psychotherapy is whether such extrinsic factors will be able to provide a congenial environment within which the psychotherapeutic model can effectively operate, or whether the most that can be anticipated will be a kind of uneasy and hostile tolerance. We can return to this question later.

I would like briefly to examine the individual volumes that we are considering. The earliest contribution was published over a dozen years ago by Sidney Tarachow (1963), and by this time is well known to students in the field. It is written under the strong influence of ego psychology and in the context of training psychiatric residents in a hospital setting. Much of the material is cast in the form of teaching conferences in which there are often stimulating interchanges between the teaching psychiatrist and his residents. In the course of these exchanges, there is much of merit in the discussions, including a theory of the therapeutic relationship. In Tarachow's view, the therapeutic interaction starts as a real relationship which is then transformed into a therapeutic situation by the imposition of a therapeutic barrier. The therapeutic barrier transforms the real situation into an "as-if" type in which transference can develop. But the inherent need for a real object must be overcome by the imposition of a barrier which settles a therapeutic task on both patient and therapist. The therapist imposes such a barrier by means of interpretations. Interpretation interferes with the reality and with the acting-out of unconscious fantasies.

There are some conceptual difficulties. Interpretation serves to shift the real relationship into a transference neurosis. But the lines between transference neurosis and transference psychosis do not seem to be clearly drawn. Transference neurosis is described in terms of loss of reality contact, domination of unconscious fantasy without real interaction with the therapist, and overriding irrationality. On the other hand, the conceptual tools for clarifying the relationship between transference effects and the therapeutic (working) alliance are not available, so that the discussion of real aspects of the therapeutic relationship is muddied. Few analysts today could agree that "the state of 'transference' which exists in psychotherapy cannot be differentiated from an ordinary real relationship." In effect, Tarachow's formulations are caught between more or less dichotomous concepts of transference neurosis (psychosis?) and real relationship which allows minimal flexibility in technique or approach.

In his approach, therefore, to psychotic patients, Tarachow emphasizes the reality of the therapist to the patient and the reality of the therapeutic relation to both. Such patients cannot tolerate the "as-if" situation. My impression is that the lack of theoretical concepts to adequately formulate the inter-action of alliance and transference factors leaves the more extreme and polar-ized options of dichotomizing real vs. fantasy elements in the therapeutic in-teraction. While it is true that psychotic patients often require greater struc-ture in the therapeutic situation which may call for greater activity on the part of the therapist, the choice between a "real" relationship and a fantasied transference relationship cannot be maintained.

This more dichotomozed approach—real vs. fantasied—creates a tension which may be reinforced by bifurcating pressures generated within the hos-pital environment. This latent tension—perhaps more obvious here than in other discussions in this series of books—takes place between the insight-gen-erating techniques of a psychoanalytically oriented approach and the thera-peutic demands imposed by a hospital setting and a patient population to whom the insight approach is less readily applicable. The tension emerges as a result of the efforts to work psychotherapeutically with such patients and the demands for active intervention and management in the hospital setting.

In the context of hospital treatment, in which relatively sicker patients are being treated, the distinction is much more forcefully and decisively drawn between therapy and management. Currently, the pressures created by the numbers of patients (particularly the numbers relatively resistant to psycho-therapeutic intervention), the availability of resources, not to mention fiscal restraints and the emphasis on cost effectiveness generated by political and economic concerns, shift the emphasis to increasing the effectiveness of man-agement techniques, short-term hospital stays, etc., with a corresponding de-emphasis on psychotherapeutic efforts.

Published in 1967, Greenson's book is specifically and unequivocally a book about psychoanalysis itself, and not about the adaptation of it to a broader range of psychotherapeutic efforts. It is nonetheless a landmark in the litera-ture of psychoanalytic technique, the work of a wise, experienced, and free-spirited psychoanalyst. It will undoubtedly be read and studied by analysts, but it also can be warmly recommended to students of psychotherapy. Green-son provides a clear and expressive treatment of basic principles and concepts which underlie the analytic approach to therapy. He brings to his discussions a refined sense of the complexities and range of forms in which such princi-ples come into play within the psychoanalytic context. He does not attempt to bridge the gulf between the strictly psychoanalytic perspective and the prob-lems of its adaptation to psychotherapy. Nonetheless, the psychotherapist will find the author's articulations of the interplay between the working alliance and the emergence of transference phenomena particularly useful.

The concept of alliance was originaly introduced by Elizabeth Zetzel (1956) as a clarification of those aspects of the analytic relationship which could not strictly be included under the terms of transference. Greenson focused these aspects of the therapeutic relationship in terms of the "working alliance." The working alliance stresses the patient's willingness and capacity to work purposefully in collaboration with the therapist in the treatment situation. Greenson, along with others who have written on the therapeutic or working alliance, regard this capacity for maintaining an effective working relationship with the therapist as a sine qua non of the therapeutic situation.

The addition of the concept of alliance clarifies a number of elements in the therapeutic relationship and provides us with a more flexible and nuanced understanding of the therapeutic relationship which considerably facilitates the adaptation of analytic concepts to the psychotherapeutic medium. It also serves to bring into clearer focus the issues of reality, and particularly the real relationship, that obtains between therapist and patient in a way which was never before possible. It is the ambiguity in these concepts that Tarachow (see above) was forced to struggle with in his attempts to adapt analytic concepts to the treatment of psychotic patients. The articulation of the notion of alliance allows us to balance the interplay of real and unconsciously determined fantasy elements in the therapeutic situation to achieve a broader spectrum of therapeutic objectives.

Thus it can be more readily envisioned that an emphasis on reality factors need not take place in the therapy to the ultimate detriment of the mobilization and therapeutic correction of more unconsciously derived fantasy-related content. All forms of psychotherapy must attend to, balance, and integrate in varying proportions the interplay between alliance and transferential factors in order to achieve a maximal therapeutic result. This balancing differs not only with the level of psychopathology, but also varies from patient to patient, and from therapist to therapist.

In addition, this modified way of looking at the therapeutic process allows us to see a variety of approaches to the therapeutic context in terms of the balance of emphasis on alliance or transference factors. Generally speaking, psychotherapeutic approaches tend to focus on and emphasize alliance and reality factors while they play down in varying degrees the impact and focus on transferential issues. The opposite tendency would take hold in the psychoanalytic context as such and in long-term, intensive, psychoanalytically oriented forms of psychotherapy. Nonetheless, the issues inherent in the therapeutic and working alliances, their relationship to forms of transference, and the refinement of these concepts and the understanding of their elaboration in the therapeutic context remain matters for continuing discussion and study (Dickes, 1975; Kanzer, 1975).

The publication of Paul Dewald's book on the psychoanalytic process (1972) provides us with a unique opportunity. Dewald's own purpose in publishing this extensive material from a single psychoanalysis was to provide a phenomenology of mental functioning as it occurs in clinical psychoanalysis, to provide data which would hopefully offset the frequent accusation against analysis that the material in the mind of the patient is often a result of suggestion by the analyst, and finally to illustrate the central importance of the transference neurosis in the analytic process.

The degree to which these objectives have been accomplished is questionable. First of all, it should be said that this kind of material is rarely made available in any form. Consequently, the effort is laudable and has its own inherent value. The short comings of the present attempt stem from the fact that the material here, perhaps unavoidably, is selected and compressed. Dewald's reflections on this process are often illuminating, but they are the more polished and elaborated reflections based on his later reconstructions of the material. The impression is left that he is in command of the material from beginning to end — a state of mind foreign to most practicing analysts.

Moreover, he seems to demonstrate an insensitivity to the narcissistic and more primitive object-relations conflicts identifiable in the patient's material. The outcome of the case, in fact, suggests that some of these issues were untouched in the analytic work, so that significant transference residues remain unresolved in the patient's experience. At the same time, the role of oedipal structural conflicts is well displayed and skillfully interpreted. Nonetheless Dewald's courageous attempt to present this material offers us a more flesh-and-blood account of the way in which various factors involved in the analytic process — transference neurosis, therapeutic alliance, insight, support, suggestion, etc. — play themselves out in the concrete analytic situation.

Leon Saul's book, published in 1972, is the fruit of considerable clinical experience, but unfortunately I find it to be a "fat" book. His formulations tend to be somewhat abstruse and diffuse, and the writing seems at times rambling. Moreover, I found the ideas often more confusing than clarifying. There is a musty smell about much of it, and I became gradually aware that its corridors are haunted by an old ghost by the name of Franz Alexander.

In the attempt to adapt the psychoanalytic approach to the exigencies of psychotherapy, Saul is one of those who moves in the direction of amplifying factors that have to do with the real situation, both in the patient's life and in the therapy, as against the transference and fantasy elements. Consequently, his technical approach is larded with a variety of active and interventionist techniques. He is much more liable to employ forms of confrontation, suggestion, advice giving, directives, encouragement, assurance, and other forms of ego-supportive and noninterpretive techniques. His emphasis on shortening the course of therapeutic work and reinforcing the faltering neurotic ego seems to consistently run the risk of minimizing the unconscious fantasy-related dynamics and of reducing the role of analytic understanding as an important therapeutic factor.

In terms of the emphasis on alliance factors, generally speaking the reinforcement or strengthening of the alliance requires a relatively greater degree of activity from the therapist, but this activity is specifically directed to the mobilization and engagement of the patient's capacities to enlist more effectively with the therapist in the work of the therapy. Essential to the notion of alliance, then, is the sense of the patient's active participation in the doing of the therapy, actively accepting responsibility for the course and outcome of the therapy through his collaboration with the therapist. One of the difficulties with the more active approaches recommended in Saul's book is that they may not have the effect of consolidating and enriching the therapeutic alliance, but may rather serve to undercut alliance factors. Thus the therapist's active intrusion on the patient by way of suggestion, giving advice, and continual reassurances may force the patient into a position of therapeutic compliance which serves the ends of symptomatic mollification, but at the same time stifles the potential for inner growth that is the more central and purposeful concern of psychotherapy. The approach here often seems to be a combination of manifest problem-solving and the power of positive thinking.

Saul's clinical approach bears the unmistakable stamp of the Alexander influence. There is considerable emphasis placed on techniques intended to circumvent the more patient and time-consuming approaches of psychoanalysis, with compensating emphasis placed on the "corrective emotional experience." Moreover, the problem is compounded by the tendency to regard as psychoanalysis any kind of technical intervention that can be formulated in psychoanalytic terms. Consequently, the author subsumes under the rubric of psychoanalysis short-term therapeutic interventions as well as longer courses of psychotherapy, paying little regard to technical parameters having to do with whether or not the patient is on the couch, how many times the latter is seen in the course of a week, how long the sessions may be, or what the relative activity or interventional stance of the therapist might be.

More problematic, however, is the tendency to manipulate the transference or to use it for "leverage" in promoting change in the patient rather than the more traditional approach via interpretation. This is consistent with Saul's basic shift in emphasis to corrective emotional experience. The risk is that aspects of transference remain unanalyzed and unresolved. The effect may manifest variants of transference cure, but from a purist viewpoint any contamination of the gold of the analytic perspective produces a less valuable alloy. Such techniques undoubtedly have their place, but Saul leaves us unclear as to what the place is. My own experience suggests that the psychotherapy of more difficult and primitive patients leaves ample room for such parameters, and that they have a place in most cases, but a more selective and restrained application than Saul suggests. They are most useful when they help overcome severe resistance, acting out, or characterological defects. In the context of psychoanalytic psychotherapy, they must always be examined, interpreted, and put in proper perspective.

My own feeling is that more careful discrimination concerning the purpose and rationale of specific techniques is needed to bridge the gap between psychoanalytic and psychotherapeutic approaches. The lumping of such diverse approaches and technical variations together as if representing a unitary approach may be more confusing than clarifying, particularly for young therapists who are struggling to derive an understanding not only of the appropriateness of particular techniques in given clinical contexts but also a guiding rationale in opting for one technique in preference to other possible ones.

Since there is much clinical wisdom in the pages of this book, Saul's work strikes me as a good example of the skilled and experienced clinician who functions at a high level of professional competence but whose articulation of his approach falls short of his technical achievement. Consequently, this is not a book that I would recommend to beginning therapists in the process of learning their trade. What is lacking specifically is a coherent theory to support a rationale for technical modifications and an indication how and when such modifications might be employed.

I. H. Paul's *Letters to Simon* make charming and congenial reading. While not as comprehensive in scope as Saul's or Langs's volumes, it manages to cover a fair amount of ground. The format of the book is a series of letters addressed by the experienced psychotherapist to his young nephew Simon, who is beginning to learn about psychotherapy. There is an easy blend of didactic material, clinical vignettes, avuncular advice, and wit and wisdom.

All of the foregoing volumes have something to teach. For example, Tarachow's book highlights the need for imposing a task on the patient in the context of considering psychotherapy as a process that requires engagement and work on the part of both patient and therapist. Saul contributes an emphasis on the need to adapt to the patient and to modify one's theoretical stance in the interest of therapeutic effectiveness.

The *Letters to Simon*, on the other hand, convey a sense of the specialness of the psychotherapeutic context and the need for patience, restraint, and for maximizing the patient's autonomy within the therapeutic relationship. After having made his way through his extended correspondence, Simon would have a good sense of therapeutic attitude, of the gulf that separates psychotherapy based on analytic principles from therapies based on encounter, manipulation, or behavior modification, and would have a stock of solid technical advice. But he would have little sense of the impact of unconscious factors, the interplay of fantasy and reality, and the technical handling of transference. Where Simon's uncle comes through is in his particular emphasis on the centrality of therapeutic understanding and its contribution to the patient's growth in autonomy. In contrast to Saul's approach, the interpretive function of the therapist does not fade into the background.

The Langs work (1973, 1974), from many points of view a most admirable treatise, focuses specifically on psychoanalytic psychotherapy. Consequently, Langs is talking about patients who are taken into psychotherapy for lengthy periods of time, are seen in psychotherapeutic interviews two or more times each week, and display a relatively broad range of neurotic and characterological pathology. This includes the primitive range of borderline and narcissistic character pathologies. While the principles of psychoanalytic psychotherapy are capable of extension to the treatment of the psychoses, Langs pays relatively little specific attention to this area.

The text is clearly and well written, with an abundance of apt clinical illustrations which form the basis for often-illuminating discussion. The theoretical context out of which Langs writes is that of developed ego psychology, strongly influenced by the adaptive perspective of Hartmann, which provides a clear conceptual context in which specific techniques having to do with resistances, analysis of defenses, transference phenomena, and the vicissitudes of the therapeutic alliance are discussed in detail. Particularly praiseworthy is his capacity to link the multiple aspects of technical intervention on the part of the therapist with the need for a basically nonjudgmental and ultimately interpretive stance, both on the part of the therapist and the patient. Moreover, he continually links the interpretive posture and the dynamics of the interpretive process to the underlying therapeutic alliance in ways which make this aspect of psychoanalytically oriented psychotherapy vital and pertinent. The book is a solid and distinguished contribution to the technical literature.

Perhaps more consistently than in the case of any of the other authors in this group Langs makes explicit use of psychoanalytic model, and succeeds in keeping the relevant dimensions of the analytic model in operative focus. When dealing with the elements of regression and transference distortion, he is mindful of the elements of the real relationship between analyst and patient and of the importance of maintaining the therapeutic alliance. When focusing on alliance factors, he is sensitive to transference interferences and the expression of the latter. The result, in my opinion, is that his dealing with clinical material becomes more nuanced and balanced. The resources of the more complex analytic model permit a more measured and explicit attention to the balance of transference and alliance issues and their more effective integration with more peripheral aspects of the therapeutic process.

This approach sets in relief the problems that arose in earlier and more limited approaches. Both the Tarachow volume and the contribution of Saul lacked a more explicit and sophisticated theoretical base on which to articulate their therapeutic rationale. Langs's consistent application of his model allows him to operate more effectively within the range of what Loewenstein called "variations" of technique, rather than in terms of technical deviations. The telling area in which this discrimination expresses itself is in the handling of therapeutic misalliances. Here Langs's approach is consistently analytic, although clearly adapted to the exigencies of the psychotherapeutic context, and in a type of situation which most challenges the analytic format. His rationale is explicit and his sensitivity to countertransference dimensions is consistently maintained. The theoretical premises for specific noninterpretive interventions are clear. Moreover, such interventions are uniformly related to the ultimately interpretive function and role of the therapist. In contrast, Saul seems to apply the analytic model less consistently and gives the impression that he abandons it more readily, without providing us with a coherent sense of the reasons, indications and intentions of such deviations.

The final volumes in this selection are short, introductory works intended as a guide for the novice psychotherapist's first steps. Dr. Bruch (1974) brings to her little introduction to psychotherapy a wealth of clinical acumen and experience. Her discussion of the psychotherapeutic encounter is enriching and insightful, and her brief treatment of psychic development useful. Unfortunately, the text tends to become somewhat diffuse at points so that the effectiveness and clarity of her thinking suffers, but not enough to dissuade one from opening oneself to an educative experience in the reading of this thin volume.

Bruch's orientation to psychotherapy is rooted in the work of Harry Stack Sullivan and his successor, Frieda Fromm-Reichmann. Consequently, the theoretical framework is only loosely psychoanalytic, and tends to orient itself more specifically in terms of an interpersonal perspective. This orientation tends to sacrifice the approach to and understanding of intrapsychic processes and conflicts. The focus falls on patterns and methods of relating between the patient and significant objects in his life and between patient and therapist. This is not quite the same as a more analytic concern with object relations, in which infantile patterns of dependency and relating are reactivated as specific unconscious derivatives within the transference and alliance. The object-relations elements underlie and influence patterns of interpersonal interaction, but they are not the same. Consequently, Bruch's account pays little attention to matters of transference or countertransference. Such dimensions are unquestionably embedded in the flow of interpersonal exchange, but they are not specifically focused. Ultimately, a more satisfactory and complete account of psychotherapy will have to embrace the intrapsychic determinants as well as the interpersonal aspects in an integrated understanding. Bruch's brief introduction does not attempt or reflect such an integration.

The Balsam book (1974) is intended as a memorial to the late Alan Balsam, to whom the inspiration and initiation of the book is due. The efforts of his wife have not fallen short of the mark. The book is specifically a primer for the beginning and learning psychotherapist and it fulfills its purposes admirably. The language is direct, uncomplicated, explicit, fluid, and comprehensible. The approach throughout is sensible, balanced, judicious, and sensitive to the complexities and infinite nuances of the psychotherapeutic encounter. The orientation is sensibly psychodynamic and focuses on the practical and pragmatic aspects of dealing with patients and structuring the psychotherapy situation. The operative model is essentially psychoanalytic, judiciously adapted to the therapeutic context.

Every chapter has its merits and rewards. The opening chapters were the work of Alan Balsam and reflect a rich, sensitive, and balanceᴄ approach to the problems of orienting the beginning therapist to the therapy situation and helping him to situate himself usefully in the initial phases of therapy. One is rewarded by a very sensitive and useful chapter on the use the therapist can make of his own affective responses to the patient—contributed to in part by Henry Grunebaum. Other extemely practical chapters take up questions relating to money and fees, issues of termination, approaches to brief therapy, and the problem of recognizing and dealing with both suicidal and homicidal impulses. There is also an insightful section on insurance and third-party payment and the therapeutic problems it involves. Dr. Rosemary Balsam also comments on her experience in the British National Health Service. There is little in these chapters that will not be helpful to beginning therapists.

The last section focuses on the effect of certain aspects of the therapist's own life on the therapy. Successive chapters deal with the therapist's love attachments, age, illness, or a death in the practitioner's family. Unique in this volume, and delightfully sensitive and sensible, is a chapter on the pregnant therapist. It is the first such consideration that I have ever seen in a book on psychotherapy. In short, the Balsam book is an outstanding contribution and one that can be highly recommended to beginning and learning therapists.

As indicated, with the exception of Greenson's, which deals specifically with the techniques of the psychoanalytic process itself, these books are all the fruits of the efforts of experienced psychoanalysts to address themselves to the general problem of applying psychoanalytic principles to the broader context of psychotherapeutic technique. Perhaps the most successful effort is that of Langs, but even here the context of application is one which requires a fairly intensive and long-standing therapeutic relationship in order for its applicability to be most effective. Thus Langs is relatively clear about his formulations regarding psychotherapeutic technique, but his clarity may have been facilitated by the fact that the context of therapy he envisions lies relatively close to the psychoanalytic end of the therapeutic spectrum. Consequently, he is able to provide a clearer and more consistent concept of what psychotherapy involves and correspondingly employs a more focused model of the therapeutic process which derives more immediately and more consistently from the analytic frame of reference. The writer who veers more deliberately toward the active and interventionist end of the spectrum is Saul, and while his contribution is to be applauded for its intent, he muddies the waters by trying to collapse the distance between the short-term, focused, actively interventionist end of the spectrum and the opposite, more specifically psychoanalytic end.

If there are inherent difficulties in this area of exploration and endeavor having to do with the extension of psychoanalytic principles to psychotherapy, there is an overriding consideration which indeed Freud could not have prognosticated and which may constitute a basic threat to the entire enterprise. When Freud gazed into his crystal ball and tried to envision the practice of psychoanalysis in future years, he came prophetically close to describing something like the current situation in many of our mental health clinics and hospitals. This is particularly true in the public sector. If we recall Freud's vision (see above), he described a situation in which the right to treatment was universally established and in which third-party subsidization was the economic framework within which psychotherapy would be practiced. That imaginary situation has become a reality in our time, and it may become more of a reality as time passes.

Unfortunately, there are contingencies that Freud could not have envisioned in 1919. It is one thing to consider the difficulties of providing a psychoanalytically based form of psychotherapy for economically disadvantaged strata of the population whose real encumbrances are a considerable problem and for whom the treatment would be conducted under conditions of minimal or no payment. But it is quite another to consider the problems raised by the specter of a health care system under which the conditions of regulation and surveillance are such that the basic principles of the psychotherapeutic relationship and intent are counteracted and undermined.

A matter of pressing and deep concern to all professional workers in the area of psychotherapy—whether they be individual psychotherapists, psychoanalysts, group therapists, or whatever—is the demand for regulation and intervention of third-party participation, whether in the form of insurance carriers, as is now often the case, or of government regulatory processes, which may well be the case in the near future. The demands placed on the psychotherapeutic relationship are specifically those of review of treatment and the inherent threat to confidentiality which that poses.

The inherent necessity for confidentiality in the therapeutic relationship is implicit in all of the approaches being discussed here. Some authors are explicit about it. The strongest statement comes from Langs: "The introduction of a third party on any level into the patient-therapist relationship is a deviation in the ground rules that has major consequences for the patient and the therapy" (p. 185). This regulatory impact on the psychotherapy tends inexorably in the direction of increasing the scope of third-party intrusion. The escalation of insurance costs and claims imposes considerable fiscal con-

straints which force carriers to tighten regulations and criteria for acknowledging claims. In my own experience, I have met the direct demand for
copies of personal records on patients under the threat of refusal to recognize
the patient's legitimate claim. This is a form of legalized blackmail. Patients
are also compelled, often without realizing the implications, to sign release-
of-information forms under similar pressures. When one adds to this burden
the problems imposed by computerized information-retrieval systems — with
all the problems of inadequate safeguards, permanence of information stor-
age, ease of retrieval (even by unscrupulous or criminal operatives) — the
problem assumes monstrous proportions.

It must be recognized that these infringements of confidentiality amount to
primary alterations in the structure of the psychotherapeutic relationship.
As such, they constitute serious deviations in technique which can only undermine the effectiveness of psychotherapy. A useful frame of reference for regarding the effects of such deviations has been provided in a subsequent paper by Langs (1975). He points out that the manner in which the therapist
goes about establishing and maintaining the ground rules and structure of the
therapeutic situation provides important communications to the patient.
Deviations in technique distort the therapeutic relationship and serve to introduce inappropriate gratifications and repetitions of pathogenic object relationships. Under these circumstances, the door is open to countertransference
distortion and the influence of serious therapeutic misalliances. Wherever the
ground rules and boundaries of the therapeutic relationship are not maintained, there is ripe ground for pathological projections, pathogenic introjections, unconscious fantasy, and conflicts to be reenacted in such a way as to be
congruent and justifiable within the therapeutic relationship — and consequently *not* available to effective interpretation and therapeutic resolution.

The question that all this raises in my mind is whether the psychotherapeutic contract and its associated relationship, which lie at the heart of any
psychotherapeutic effort no matter what the modality of treatment involved,
can be tolerated by such an overriding regulatory framework. We may be
faced with the possibility that the psychotherapeutic effort can only be carried
on in a context of completely private and noninsurance-supported collaboration of doctor and patient. Tensions already exist in the area of private insurance support for psychotherapy and/or psychoanalysis. Demands of insurance carriers for patient information readily infringe on the area of confidentiality and the privileged area of therapist-patient communication.

The specter of government regulation and intervention in this field, along
with the accessibility of computerized records, offers a grim vision of a process
of federal or quasi-federal regulation within which any form of authentic psychotherapy (toward which all of the present volumes address themselves) may
be an impossibility. The danger is of a politicization of the psychotherapeutic

process—an inherent and intolerable contradiction. However repugnant such a contamination of the psychotherapeutic context by politics may seem, observers of the practice of psychiatry behind the Iron Curtain suggest that such a regimen has become a fact of life in those countries. Moreover, social pressures toward similar outcomes are at work in our own social fabric. The priorities in the emerging framework of health care delivery are clearly on the side of fiscal policy and politics, rather than in the direction of preservation of the essentials of the psychotherapeutic relation and an effort in making that preserve of authentic freedom and autonomy more readily available to broader reaches of the population.

The effects of current efforts in this area seem to be bent on restricting the availability of the psychotherapeutic approach to smaller and smaller groups of more privileged and affluent patients. Thus psychiatric intervention is being pressured in the direction of active disposition and manipulation which is totally foreign to the psychoanalytic attitude and ultimately an irreconcilable violation of psychoanalytic principles. We can only hope that in the future, the riches that are contained in such books as those we are reviewing will not symbolize a relatively unavailable resource for the affluent few, but that they might become a source of help and enrichment for the more impoverished many.

It seems inevitable that under such social and economic pressures some compromises will have to be made. If the conslusion can be drawn from this review that the most adequate model for psychotherapeutic interventions of all kinds is a thoroughgoing psychoanalytic model, appropriately adapted and modified to meet a wide range of forms of psychopathology and socioeconomic contexts, then we must take care that the vitality of such an alloy (Freud's alloy of gold and copper) is preserved. From one point of view, theorists in this area must take the social, economic, and political factors into account in shaping their clinical approach and methodology. From another point of view, therapists may have to enter the political area in some manner to secure the right to treatment for all patients. The risk in all this is that authentic and effective psychoanalytic psychotherapy may become a resource of the few. And the many, contrary to Freud's supposition, will be once again deprived of effective treatment.

REFERENCES

Dickes, R. (1975). Technical considerations of the therapeutic and working alliances. *International Journal of Psychoanalytic Psychotherapy* 4:1-24.
Freud, S. (1919). Lines of advance in psycho-analytic therapy. *Standard Edition* 17:157-168. London: Hogarth, 1955.
Kanzer, M. (1975). The therapeutic and working alliances. *International Journal of Psychoanalytic Psychotherapy* 4:48-68.

Langs, R. J. (1975). The therapeutic relationship and deviations in technique. *International Journal of Psycho-analytic Psychotherapy* 4:106-141.

Zetzel, E. R. (1956). Current concepts of transference. *International Journal of Psycho-Analysis* 37:369-376.

_____, and Meissner, W. W. (1973). *Basic Concepts in Psychoanalytic Psychiatry.* New York: Basic Books.

W. W. MEISSNER, M.D.

Assistant Clinical Professor of Psychiatry, Harvard Medical School Staff Psychiatrist, Massachusetts Mental Health Center, Boston and Cambridge City Hospital Chairman of Faculty, Boston Psychoanalytic Society and Institute, Inc.

Contents of Volumes 1-4

Volume I

Volume II

Volume III

Volume IV

Author Index

Subject Index